ADOLF ™
A Tale of the Twentieth Century

CADENCE BOOKS GRAPHIC NOVEL

ADOLF ™

A Tale of the Twentieth Century

STORY & ART BY

OSAMU TEZUKA

STORY & ART BY
OSAMU TEZUKA

Translation/Yuji Oniki

Touch-Up Art & Lettering/Yoshiyuki Higuchi
Cover Design/Viz Graphics
Editor/Annette Roman

Senior Editor/Trish Ledoux
Managing Editor/Satoru Fujii
Executive Editor/Seiji Horibuchi
Publisher/Keizo Inoue

Printed in Canada

Published by Cadence Books, Inc.
P.O. Box 77010 • San Francisco, CA 94107

10 9 8 7 6 5 4 3 2 1
First printing, November 1995

CONTENTS

INTRODUCTION

OSAMU TEZUKA AND *ADOLF*
By Frederik L. Schodt

It's about time. That was my reaction when I first heard that Osamu Tezuka's *Adolf* would be published in English. Japanese comics and animation are "hot" in the English-speaking world today, with translated versions of both appearing regularly. Among fans, the Japanese words *manga* (comics) and *anime* (animation) have even become a part of their everyday vocabulary. But there is one Japanese manga (and anime) artist who has never received the attention due him. And that is Osamu Tezuka, otherwise known in Japan as the *Manga no Kamisama*, or "God of Comics."

Many readers of *Adolf* are probably most familiar with American-style "comic books," a misnomer, if ever there was one, for what are usually slim and colorful magazines often starring superheroes or amusing cartoon characters. Indeed, for many readers, *Adolf* may be the first example of comics in a book format, with a narrative structure like that of a novel. These qualities are, however, a hallmark of Osamu Tezuka's work, for perhaps more than anyone else, he continually tried to make comics a full-fledged medium of creative expression on a par with films and novels.

Born in 1928 and raised in the cosmopolitan town of Takarazuka, Tezuka began drawing cartoons as a small child. He had an abiding interest in theater and film, especially animation. His love of early American Disney and Max Fleischer animated cartoons, in particular, would later show up in his rounded, "cute" drawing style. In another day and time, Tezuka most certainly would have become a film or animation director, but the economic and social constraints of the prewar period steered him instead into medical school, where he struggled valiantly to acquire a respectable career. Yet cartoons and comics remained the way he expressed himself, and he was unable to stop drawing them.

Right after the end of World War II, while still in medical school, Tezuka made his official debut as a cartoonis, with a short four-panel comic strip entitled *Ma-chan no Nikki* (Ma-chan's Diary), which was published in a local newspaper. It wasn't a particularly unusual strip, and it adhered to the conventions of the time, but shortly thereafter Tezuka began creating increasingly longer works with a strong narrative element, such as (with Shichima Sakai in 1947) *Shintakarajima* (New Treasure Island). In paperback compilations, many of these works ran hundreds of pages in length, and some, such as *Lost World* and *Next World*, had science fiction themes with exotic-sounding English titles on their covers.

Unlike other Japanese children's comics at the time, which tended to be slow-paced and static with many panels drawn from the same perspective, Tezuka incorporated more and more ideas from film and animation in his work. Rather than use a great deal of words, he tried to tell stories visually. In fact, to the pretelevision, entertainment-starved readers of Tezuka's early manga published during the postwar period, it often seemed as though they were watching a film with closeups, pans, and wide-angle shots. Although such sales were unheard of at the time, some of Tezuka's early manga "books" reportedly sold nearly 400,000 copies, without the benefit of publicity.

Tezuka triggered a revolution in Japanese comics. He inspired an entire generation of young people and artists to think of them in a different way, and he continually experimented with their potential. He obtained his physician's license, but he never practiced medicine. Instead, he moved to Tokyo to pursue a full-time career as an artist, drawing both comics and, later, creating animation. Because he had a keen intellect and a fundamentally inquisitive nature, comics and animation also became a vehicle for him to personally explore whatever struck his fancy, including literature, history, and the basic meaning of life. Although he began drawing for children (and continued to do so throughout his lifetime), Tezuka also helped popularize what came to be known in Japan as "story manga," or long, narrative comics, for adult men and women.

A productive powerhouse and a one-man dream factory, by the time Tezuka died prematurely of cancer in 1989 he is said to have drawn over 150,000 pages of comics, a total of over 500 titles. His stories include a 1953 version of Dostoyevsky's *Crime and Punishment* (the only other work by Tezuka previously translated and published in English), three different adaptations of Goethe's *Faust* (1949, 1971, and 1988), and a life story of the Buddha (1973-83). Some of his works—such as *Phoenix*, a tale of reincarnation and the cosmos, which he called his "life's work"—are thousands of pages long, and their creation spanned decades. When compiled into paperback and deluxe hardcover editions, many comprise over a dozen volumes.

Tezuka was not the only "story manga" artist in Japan, but his importance cannot be overestimated. The audience for Japanese manga is no longer limited to children; manga are enjoyed by nearly all age groups and both genders. In fact, nearly 40 percent of all published books and magazines in Japan today are said to take the form of comics, making Japan the first nation in the world to accord the medium such stature.

When Tezuka died on February 10, 1989, his passing was given nearly as much media attention in Japan as that of the emperor, who preceded him by only a few weeks. In an editorial the day after Tezuka's death, the prestigious *Asahi* newspaper noted that foreign visitors to Japan are often shocked to see so many adults reading comics. The writer observed that one reason comics are so popular in Japan is that "Japan had Osamu Tezuka, whereas other nations did not."

Why has Tezuka remained so unknown outside of Japan for so long? In North America, comics were stigmatized and trivialized in the 1950s, and the industry found itself in a competitive rather than symbiotic relationship with television; the main comics publishers today cater to a very small market of readers who are overwhelmingly young males still interested primarily in superheroes drawn in a standardized fashion. Tezuka's novelistic stories were too long for American comics, too complex in theme, and rendered in too "different" a style. In addition, making his work even more problematic, Tezuka often drew serious stories in a "cartoony" style instead of a highly "realistic" style, and inserted gags that only long-time Japanese fans (with whom he had a unique dialogue) could appreciate.

Tezuka's name may have little recognition outside of Japan, but his influence has nonetheless been great. In the early 1960s, he animated *Tetsuwan Atom*, or "Mighty Atom," the tale of a little boy robot, as well as his popular story of lions in Africa, *Jungle Taitei*, or "Jungle Emperor." Both of these works were exported to the United States, where they were widely shown on television under the titles *Astro Boy* and *Kimba, The White Lion* respectively. An entire generation of young Americans watched them, but because they were so skillfully dubbed into English, few ever realized they were watching Japanese animation, let alone something by Osamu Tezuka.

Subsequently, there have been legal and quasi legal comic book versions of *Astro Boy* published in the United States that were drawn by American artists and based on the animation rather than on Tezuka's original story, and which also give Tezuka little credit. Similarly, in 1994, despite official denials to the contrary, Disney's enormously popular *The Lion King* animation clearly relied on Tezuka's *Kimba* series for certain character designs and situations, leading to angry charges of plagiarism from Japan and the manga- and anime- fan community in the United States.

From 1983 to 1985, *Adolf* was serialized in the prestigious *Shukan Bunshun* magazine in Japan. The series targeted not children but adults and was drawn in a relatively realistic (for Tezuka) style. When it appeared, *Adolf* attracted great attention. In addition to being one of the first manga books to be published in a deluxe hardcover format and sold not in the manga corners of stores but in the literature section, it won the Kodansha Manga Award in 1986. It is widely regarded as one of Tezuka's finest works.

Although *Adolf* is a work of fiction, it incorporates a great deal of well-known and not so well-known aspects of actual history. To many non-Japanese readers, in fact, *Adolf* provides a perspective on World War II that is new, unusual, and provocative. It is not only a Japanese view of what was truly a global war, but it is Osamu Tezuka's.

In Japan, Tezuka is often called a "humanist." He had an ability to look beyond people's superficial actions and view them in their totality, to consider them in the context of their environment, history, and even (occasionally) their karma. As a result, one characteristic of Tezuka's characters—even those in stories for children—is their complexity. Evil characters occasionally display flashes of good. Similarly, essentially "good" characters sometimes err and display qualities of "evil." There is no codified binary-style "us vs. them" or "black-or-white" logic in most of Tezuka's stories.

Tezuka was, nonetheless, adamantly opposed to war in any form. Although he grew up with the nationalistic propaganda of prewar Japan, he became a convinced internationalist. Too young to be drafted, Tezuka and other students his age were mobilized to work in factories to support the war effort. But Tezuka was eminently unsuited to this militaristic environment and the Spartan discipline required in this endeavor. Worse yet, his job exposed him directly to some of the worst firebombing of World War II, in which the city of Osaka (and much of its population) was torched by American bombers. The result was a permanent loathing of militarism, whether in Japan or elsewhere, and of what Tezuka called the "ego of the State." Being struck by an inebriated U.S. soldier on one occasion during the Occupation only reinforced his beliefs.

To those unfamiliar with Japanese history, one of the central constructs of Tezuka's *Adolf* story—that before World War II a Jewish boy and a half-Japanese, half-German boy live near each other in the city of Kobe and become friends— may seem forced. But this scenario is entirely possible, and it is easy to imagine how Tezuka might have conceived of it. As a youth, Tezuka lived only a short distance from the port city of Kobe, which has long hosted a diverse population of foreign residents. During World War II, although Japan was one of the Axis powers, it never adopted the anti-Semitic ideology of its Nazi German ally. In fact, Japan sheltered a large number of Jewish refugees. As a result, at the time, there really were both Germans and Jews living in the Kobe area.

Now, thanks to the pioneering efforts of the publisher Viz Communications and the skills of the very talented translator, Yuji Oniki, we can finally enjoy one of Osamu Tezuka's most fascinating stories in English. *It's about time.*

Frederik L. Schodt is the author of Manga! Manga! The World of Japanese Comics *and other books on Japan. His book* Dreamland Japan: Writings on Modern Manga *is scheduled to be published in 1996. He often served as a translator and interpreter for Osamu Tezuka.*

CHAPTER
ONE

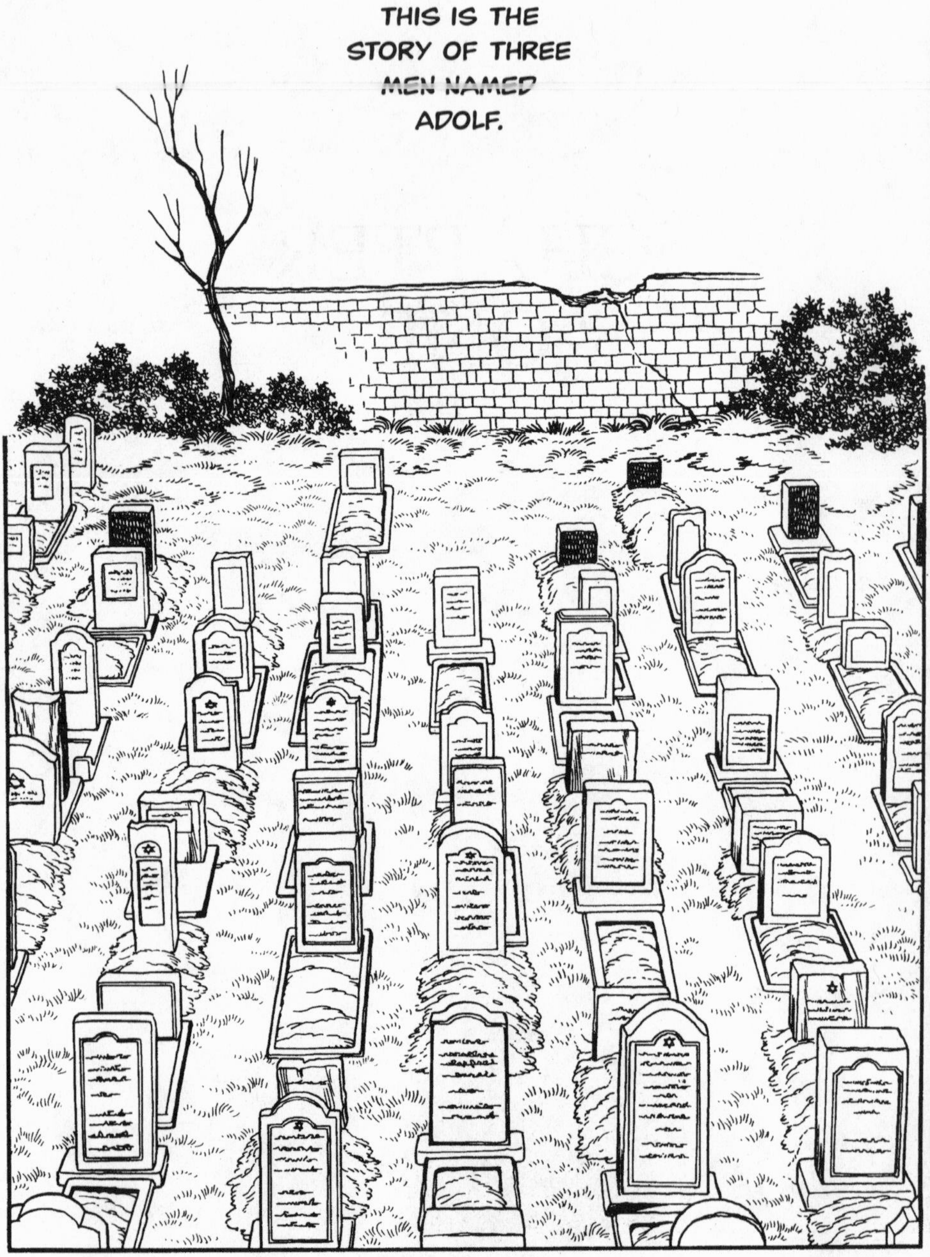
THIS IS THE STORY OF THREE MEN NAMED ADOLF.

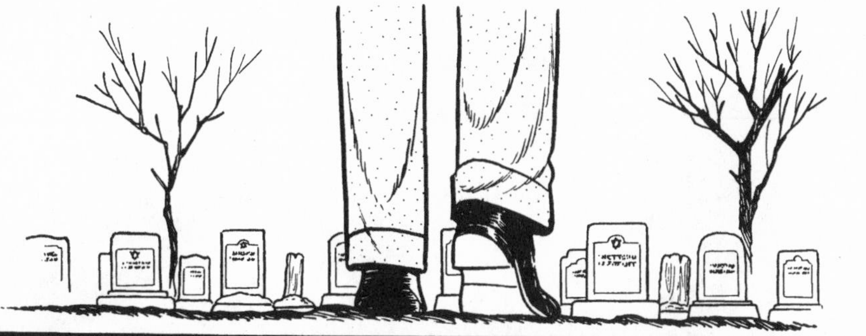

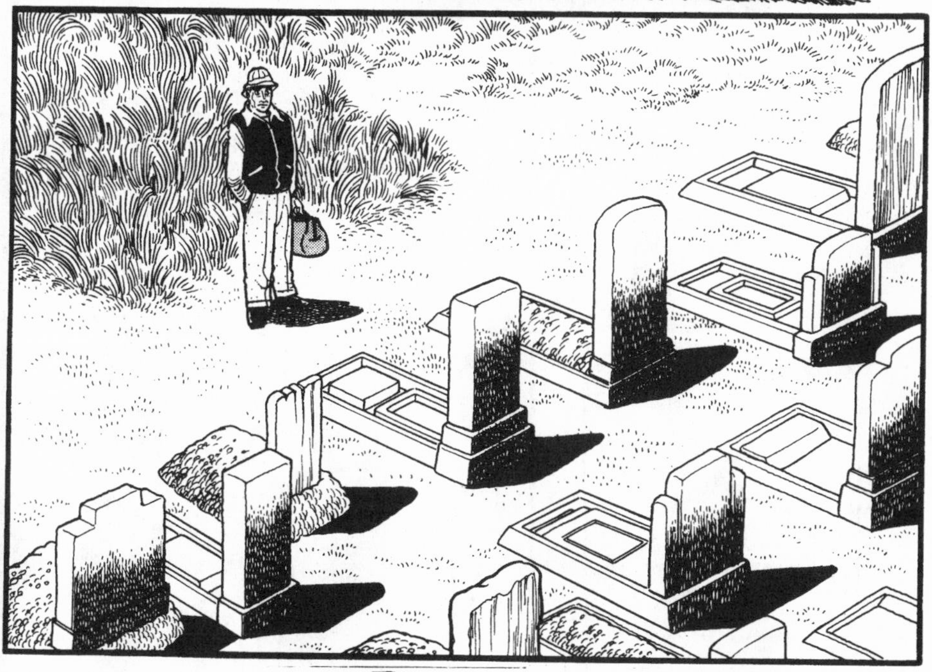

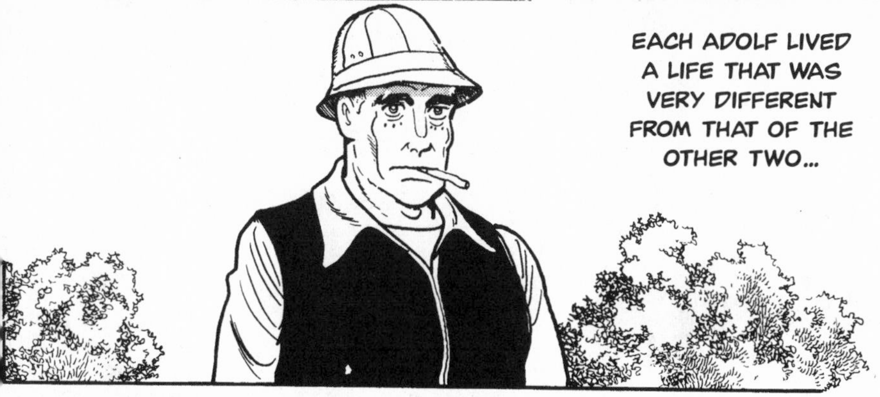
EACH ADOLF LIVED A LIFE THAT WAS VERY DIFFERENT FROM THAT OF THE OTHER TWO...

Adolf

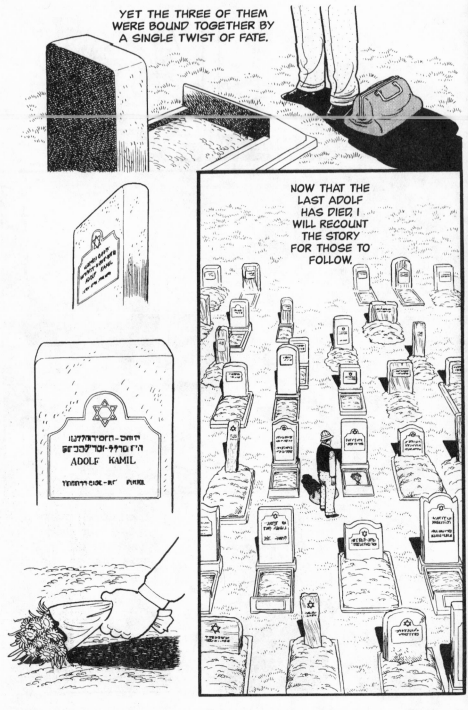

YET THE THREE OF THEM WERE BOUND TOGETHER BY A SINGLE TWIST OF FATE.

ADOLF KAMIL

NOW THAT THE LAST ADOLF HAS DIED, I WILL RECOUNT THE STORY FOR THOSE TO FOLLOW.

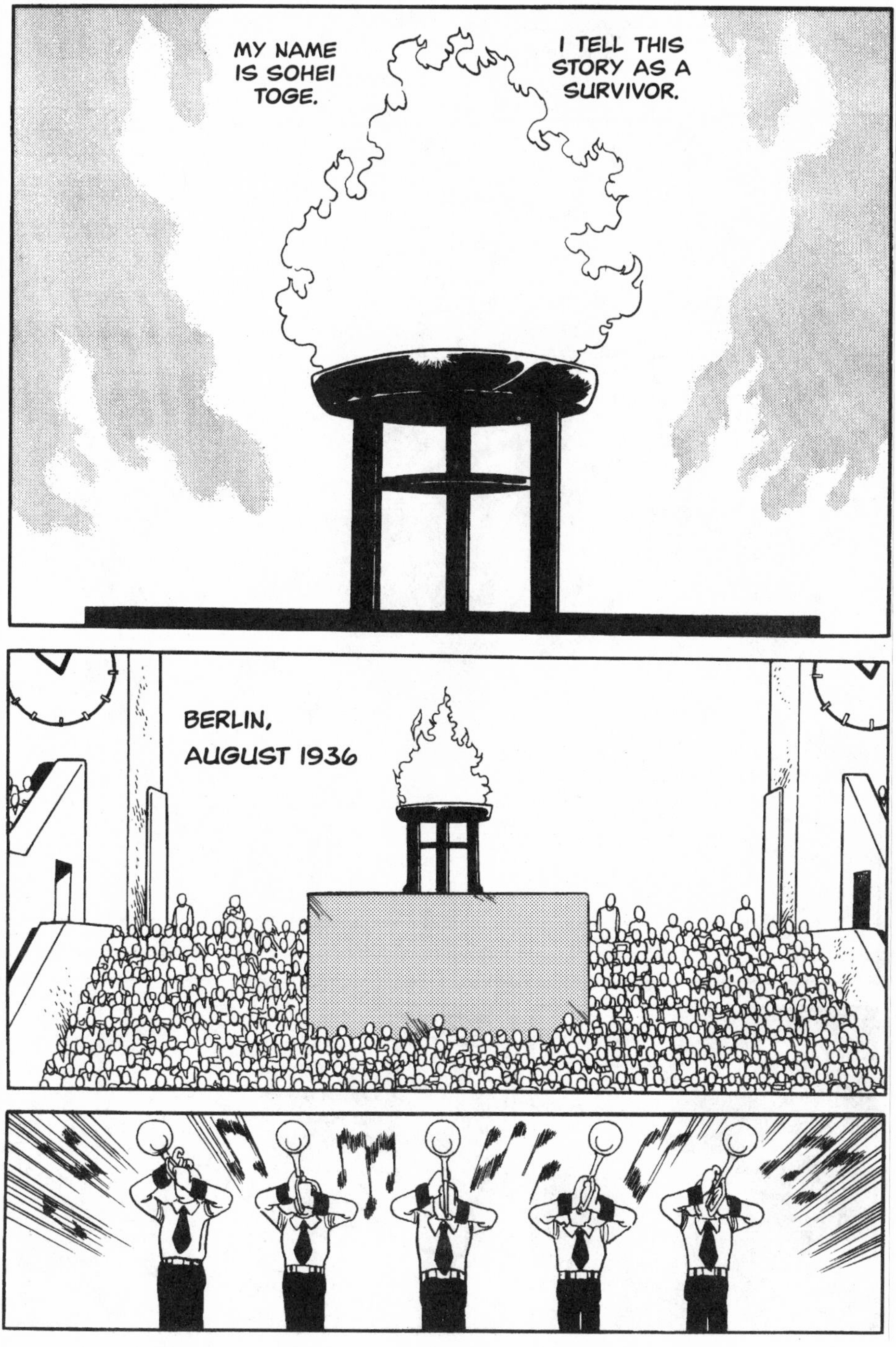
MY NAME IS SOHEI TOGE.
I TELL THIS STORY AS A SURVIVOR.
BERLIN, AUGUST 1936

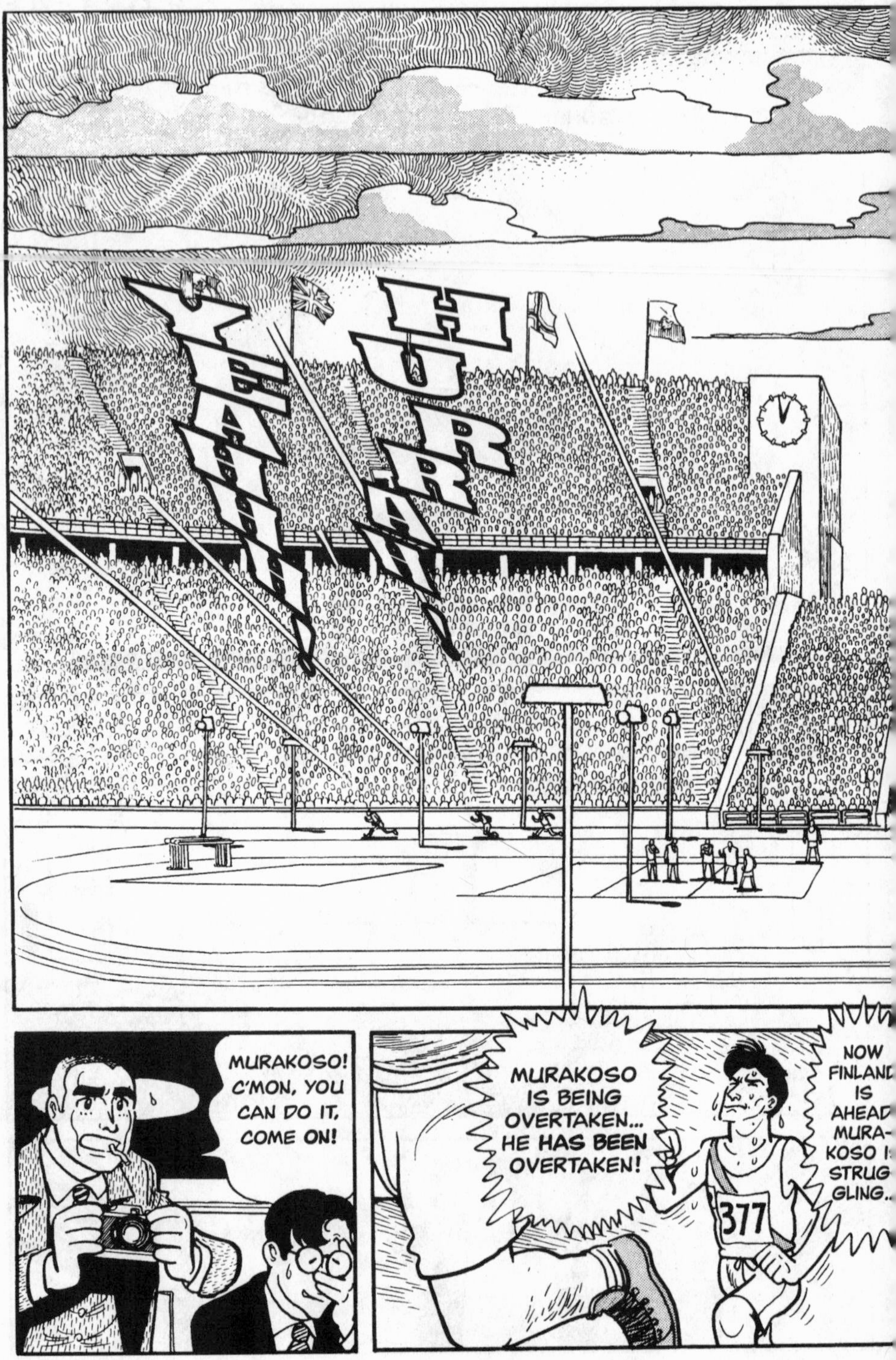
YEAHHHH!
HURRAH!
MURAKOSO! C'MON, YOU CAN DO IT, COME ON!
MURAKOSO IS BEING OVERTAKEN... HE HAS BEEN OVERTAKEN!
NOW FINLAND IS AHEAD MURAKOSO IS STRUGGLING...
377

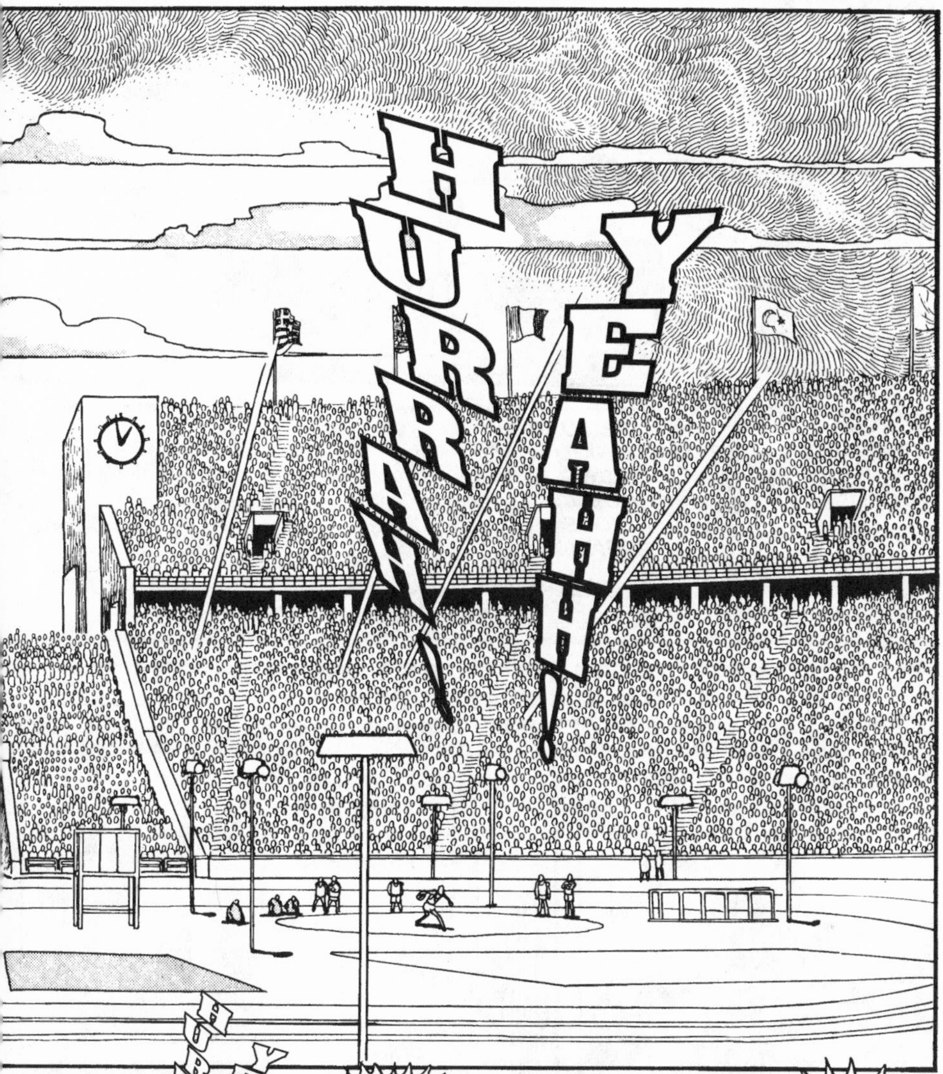
HURRAH!
YEAH!

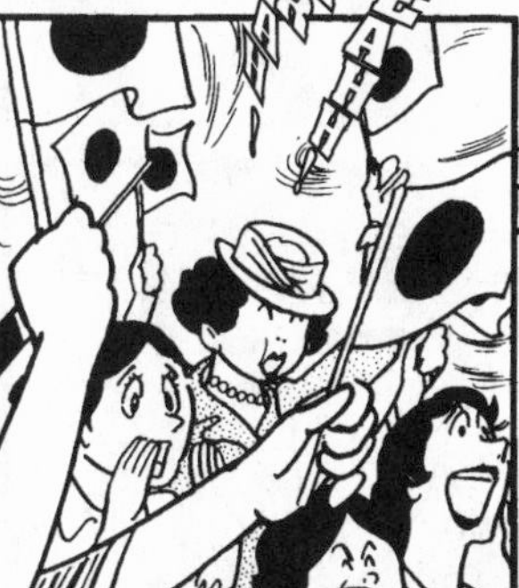

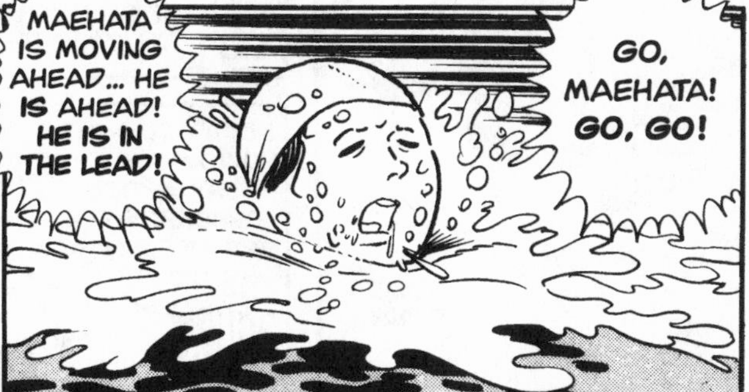
MAEHATA IS MOVING AHEAD... HE IS AHEAD! HE IS IN THE LEAD!
GO, MAEHATA! GO, GO!

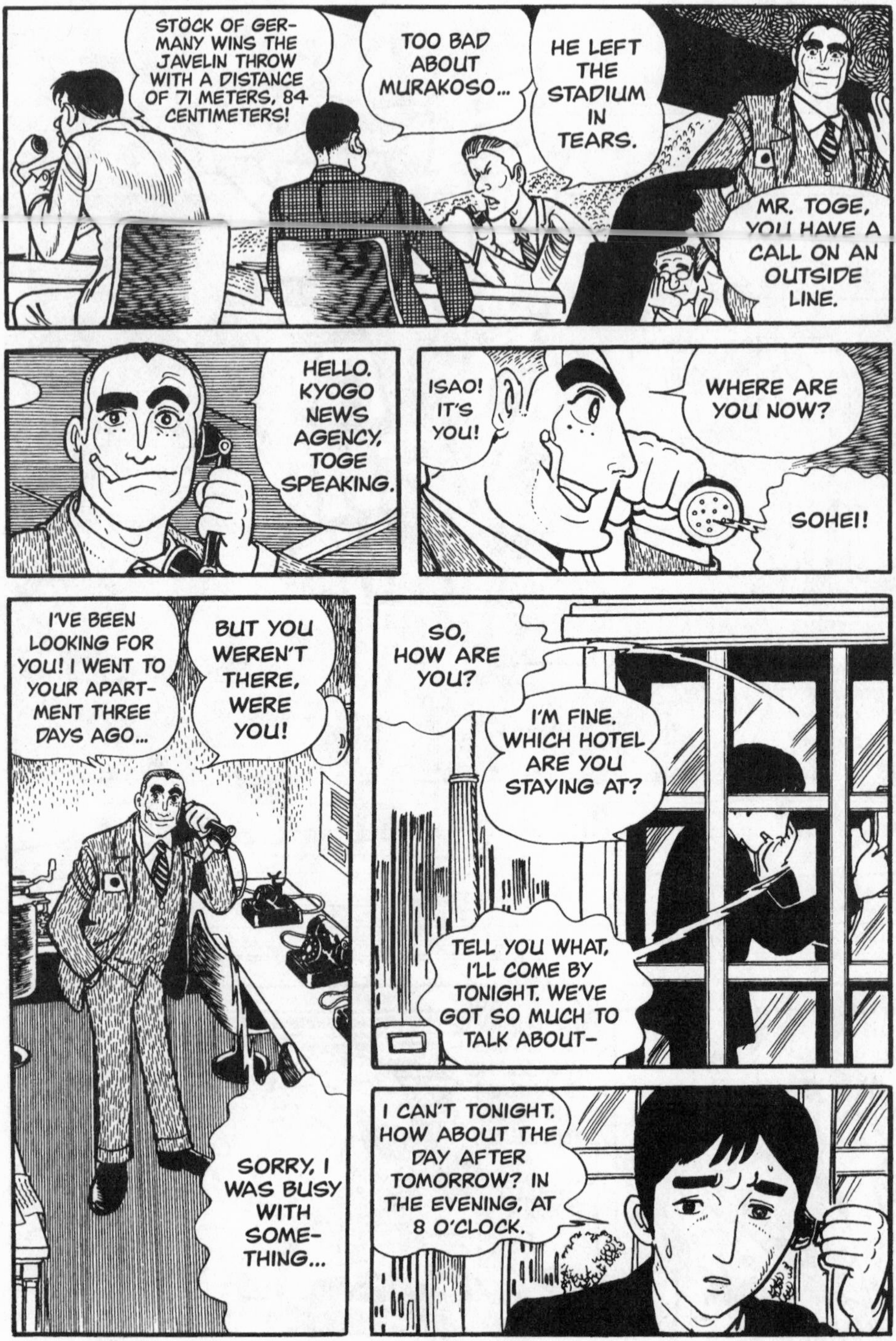
STOCK OF GERMANY WINS THE JAVELIN THROW WITH A DISTANCE OF 71 METERS, 84 CENTIMETERS!
TOO BAD ABOUT MURAKOSO...
HE LEFT THE STADIUM IN TEARS.
MR. TOGE, YOU HAVE A CALL ON AN OUTSIDE LINE.
HELLO. KYOGO NEWS AGENCY, TOGE SPEAKING.
ISAO! IT'S YOU!
WHERE ARE YOU NOW?
SOHEI!
I'VE BEEN LOOKING FOR YOU! I WENT TO YOUR APARTMENT THREE DAYS AGO...
BUT YOU WEREN'T THERE, WERE YOU!
SORRY, I WAS BUSY WITH SOMETHING...
SO, HOW ARE YOU?
I'M FINE. WHICH HOTEL ARE YOU STAYING AT?
TELL YOU WHAT, I'LL COME BY TONIGHT. WE'VE GOT SO MUCH TO TALK ABOUT-
I CAN'T TONIGHT. HOW ABOUT THE DAY AFTER TOMORROW? IN THE EVENING, AT 8 O'CLOCK.

I HAVE SOMETHING IMPORTANT TO TELL YOU...

WHAT? SOMETHING ABOUT YOUR NEW FRAU? HEH, HEH.

NO, I'M SERIOUS. THIS IS VITAL. I HAVE SOMETHING TO GIVE YOU...

YOU'LL BE STUNNED!

WHEN THE PUBLIC HEARS ABOUT THIS, HITLER'S GOING TO FALL! THIS WILL THROW THE NAZI PARTY INTO UTTER CHAOS!

WHAT'S THAT? IT'S SO LOUD IN HERE! I CAN'T HEAR YOU VERY WELL!

WHAT'S GOIN' ON?

OH, THE GERMANS HAVE PROBABLY JUST WON ANOTHER ONE...

HURRAH!

YEAHH!

YEAHH!

GERMANY'S HEINE WINS THE GOLD IN THE HAMMER THROW WITH A DISTANCE OF 56 METERS, 49 CENTIMETERS! GERMANY ALSO WINS THE SILVER, WITH BRASK!

KLAP KLAP KLAP

KLAP

KLAP

KLAP

19

Adolf

KLAP KLAP KLAP KLAP KLAP KLAP

OKAY, SOHEI? THE DAY AFTER TOMORROW, 8 O'CLOCK, AT MY PLACE. DON'T BE LATE! ANY DELAY AND IT MIGHT BE TOO LATE...

WHAT'RE YOU GETTING SO WORKED UP ABOUT?

ALL RIGHT, ALL RIGHT, I PROMISE.

ANOTHER GOLD FOR GERMANY. GREAT PUBLICITY FOR THE NAZIS!

LOOK HOW PLEASED THE FÜHRER IS.

AUGUST 7, THE DATE OF THEIR MEETING...

THE EVENT OF THE DAY WAS THE POLE VAULT. THE COMPETITION FINALLY BOILED DOWN TO A FIERCE STRUGGLE BETWEEN THE UNITED STATES AND JAPAN.

HURRA! YEAH! HOORAY! HURRA!

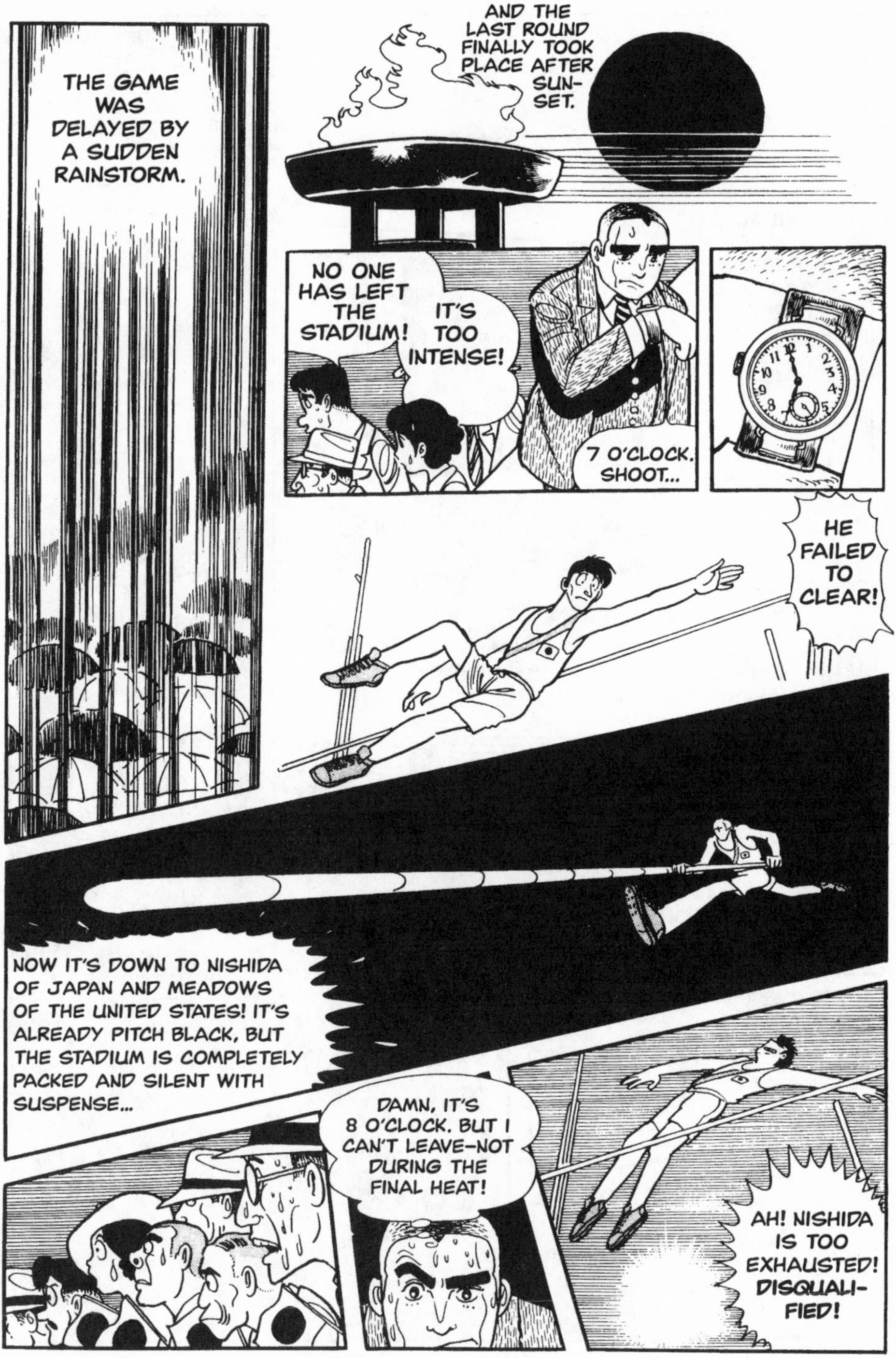
THE GAME WAS DELAYED BY A SUDDEN RAINSTORM.
AND THE LAST ROUND FINALLY TOOK PLACE AFTER SUN-SET.
NO ONE HAS LEFT THE STADIUM!
IT'S TOO INTENSE!
7 O'CLOCK. SHOOT...
HE FAILED TO CLEAR!
NOW IT'S DOWN TO NISHIDA OF JAPAN AND MEADOWS OF THE UNITED STATES! IT'S ALREADY PITCH BLACK, BUT THE STADIUM IS COMPLETELY PACKED AND SILENT WITH SUSPENSE...
DAMN, IT'S 8 O'CLOCK. BUT I CAN'T LEAVE–NOT DURING THE FINAL HEAT!
AH! NISHIDA IS TOO EXHAUSTED! DISQUALI-FIED!

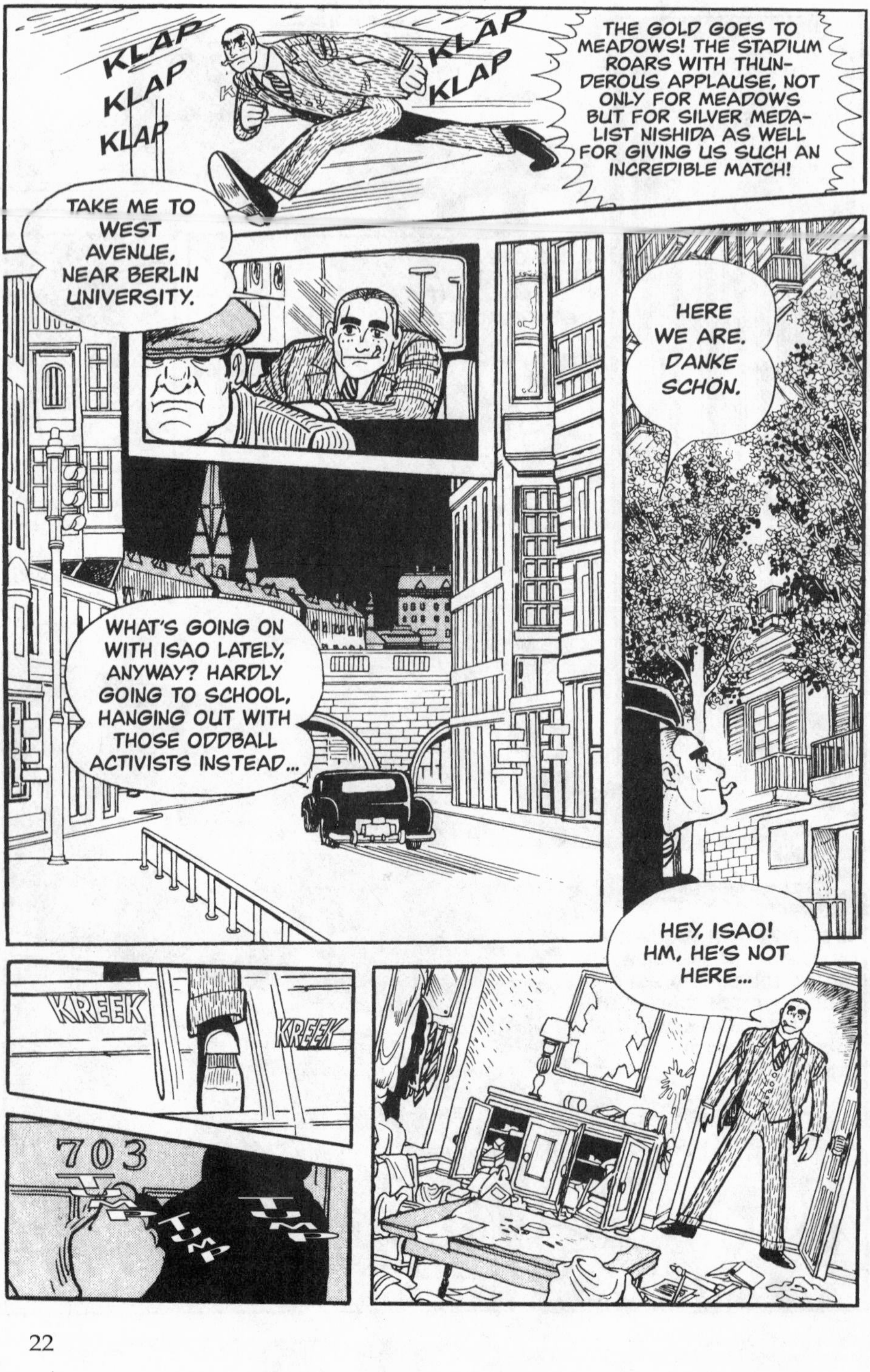
KLAP
KLAP
KLAP
KLAP
KLAP
THE GOLD GOES TO MEADOWS! THE STADIUM ROARS WITH THUNDEROUS APPLAUSE, NOT ONLY FOR MEADOWS BUT FOR SILVER MEDALIST NISHIDA AS WELL FOR GIVING US SUCH AN INCREDIBLE MATCH!
TAKE ME TO WEST AVENUE, NEAR BERLIN UNIVERSITY.
WHAT'S GOING ON WITH ISAO LATELY, ANYWAY? HARDLY GOING TO SCHOOL, HANGING OUT WITH THOSE ODDBALL ACTIVISTS INSTEAD...
HERE WE ARE. DANKE SCHÖN.
KREEK
KREEK
703
TUMP
TUMP
HEY, ISAO! HM, HE'S NOT HERE...

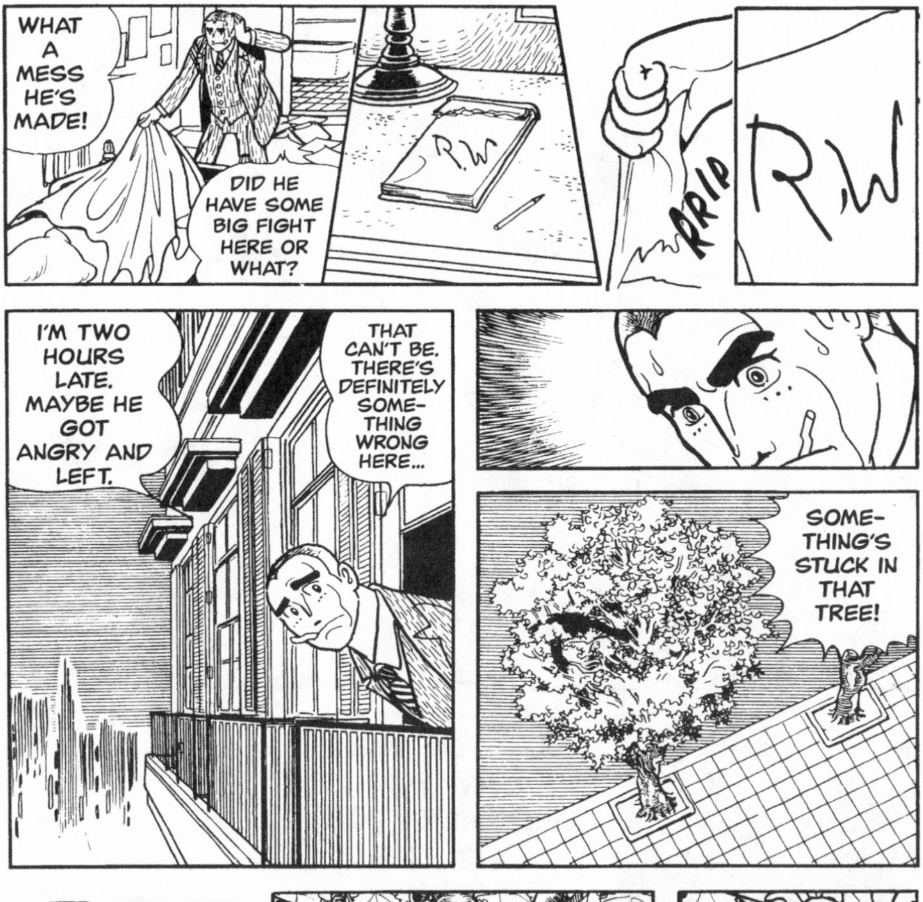
WHAT A MESS HE'S MADE!
DID HE HAVE SOME BIG FIGHT HERE OR WHAT?
R.W
RRIP
R.W
I'M TWO HOURS LATE. MAYBE HE GOT ANGRY AND LEFT.
THAT CAN'T BE. THERE'S DEFINITELY SOME-THING WRONG HERE...
SOME-THING'S STUCK IN THAT TREE!
ISAO!

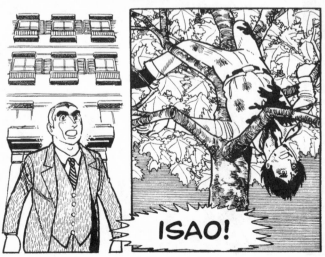

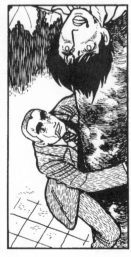

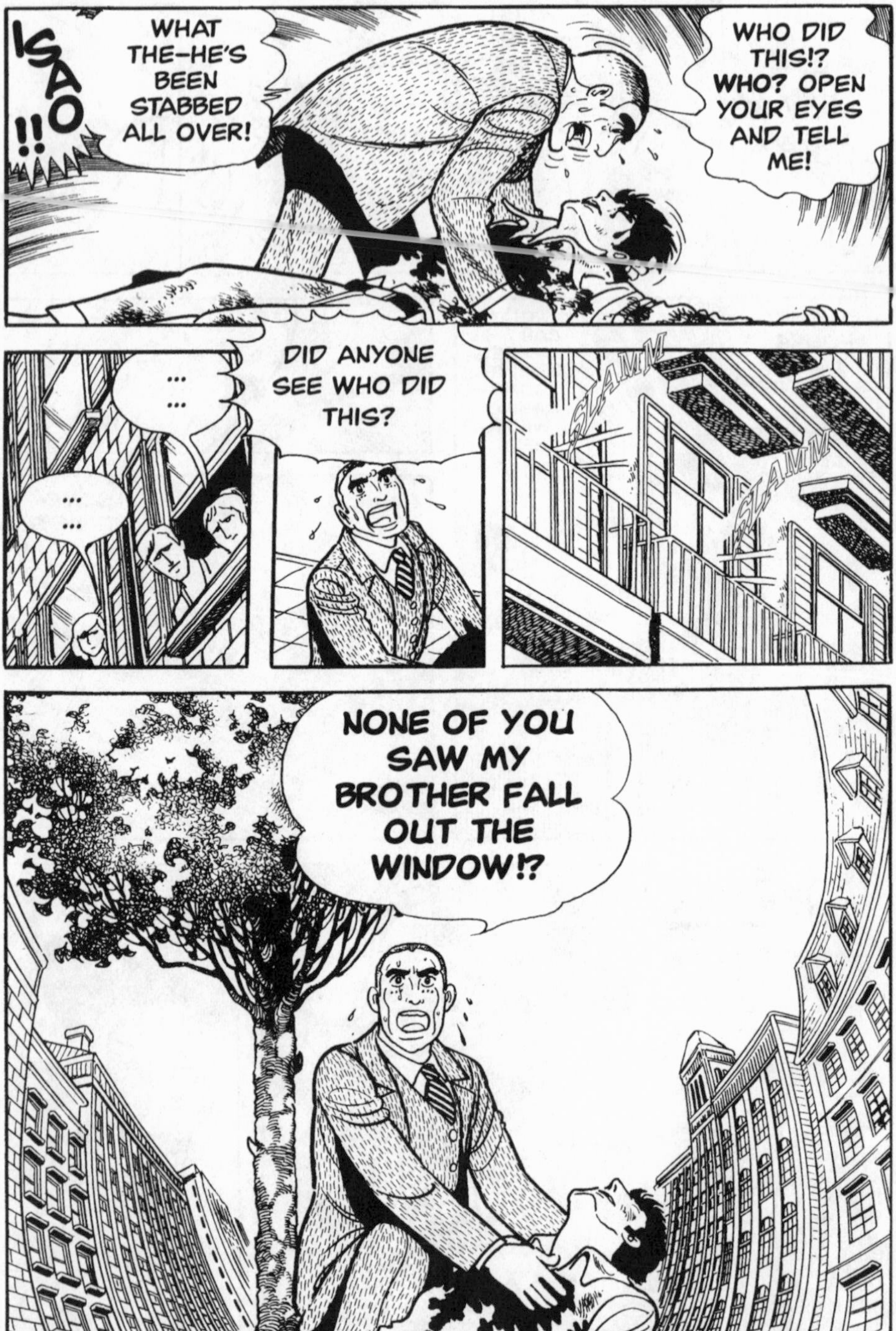
ISAO!!
WHAT THE–HE'S BEEN STABBED ALL OVER!
WHO DID THIS!? WHO? OPEN YOUR EYES AND TELL ME!
...
...
...
...
DID ANYONE SEE WHO DID THIS?
SLAMM
SLAMM
NONE OF YOU SAW MY BROTHER FALL OUT THE WINDOW!?

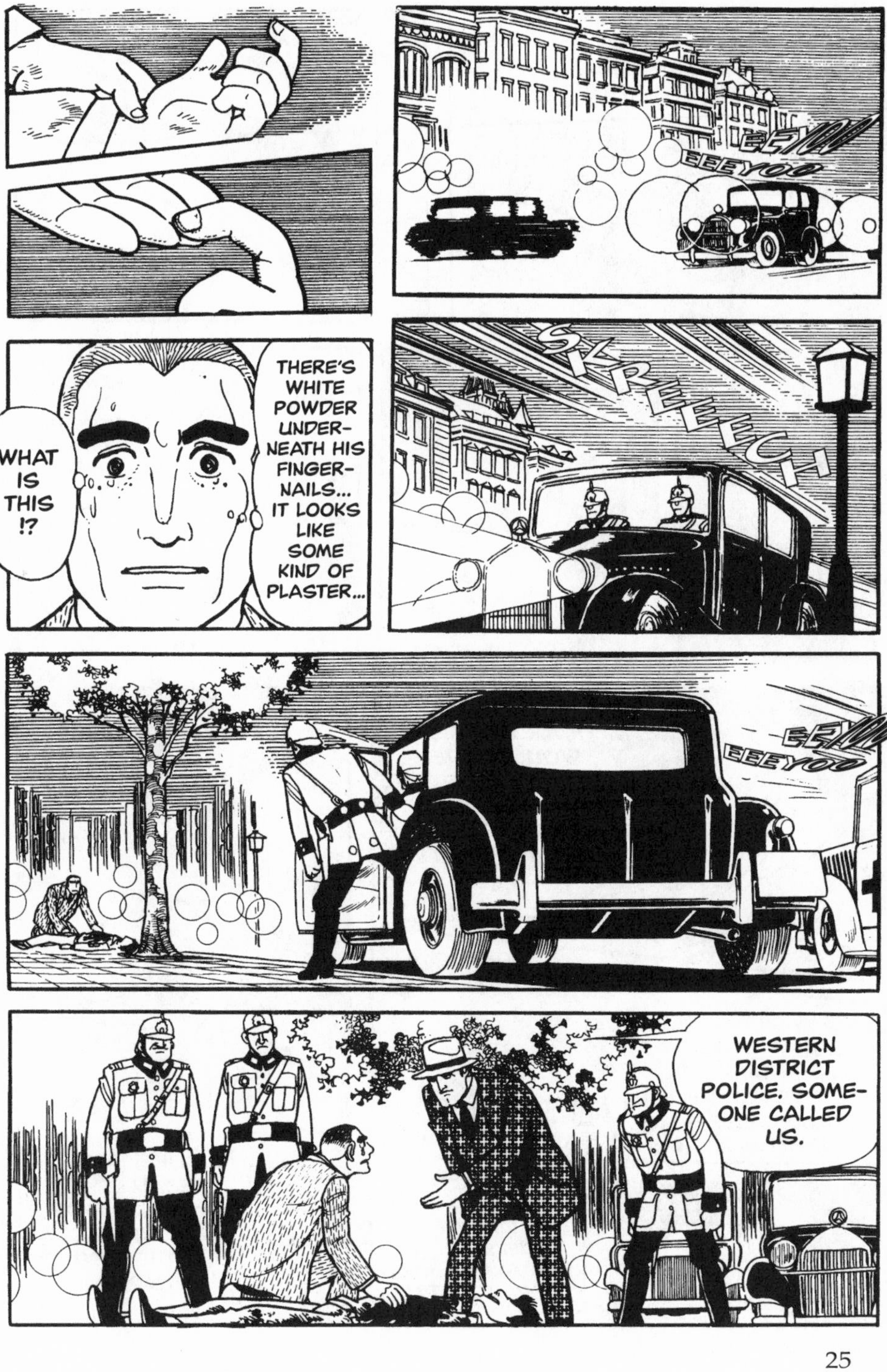
EEEYOO
EEEYOO
SKREEEECH
THERE'S WHITE POWDER UNDERNEATH HIS FINGERNAILS... IT LOOKS LIKE SOME KIND OF PLASTER...
WHAT IS THIS !?
EEEYOO
EEEYOO
WESTERN DISTRICT POLICE. SOMEONE CALLED US.

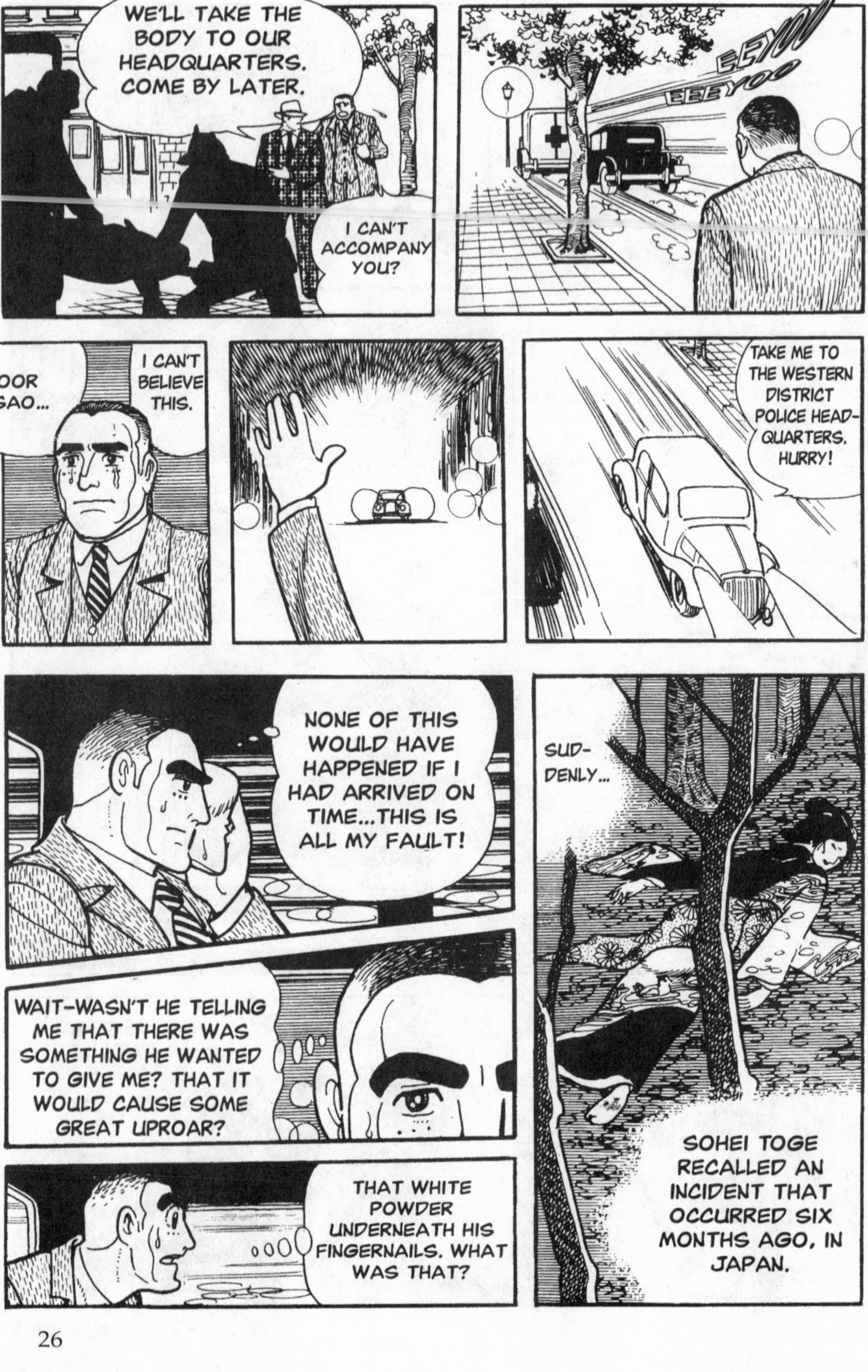
WE'LL TAKE THE BODY TO OUR HEADQUARTERS. COME BY LATER.
I CAN'T ACCOMPANY YOU?
EEYOO
EEEYOO
POOR ISAO...
I CAN'T BELIEVE THIS.
TAKE ME TO THE WESTERN DISTRICT POLICE HEAD-QUARTERS. HURRY!
NONE OF THIS WOULD HAVE HAPPENED IF I HAD ARRIVED ON TIME...THIS IS ALL MY FAULT!
WAIT–WASN'T HE TELLING ME THAT THERE WAS SOMETHING HE WANTED TO GIVE ME? THAT IT WOULD CAUSE SOME GREAT UPROAR?
THAT WHITE POWDER UNDERNEATH HIS FINGERNAILS. WHAT WAS THAT?
SUD-DENLY...
SOHEI TOGE RECALLED AN INCIDENT THAT OCCURRED SIX MONTHS AGO, IN JAPAN.

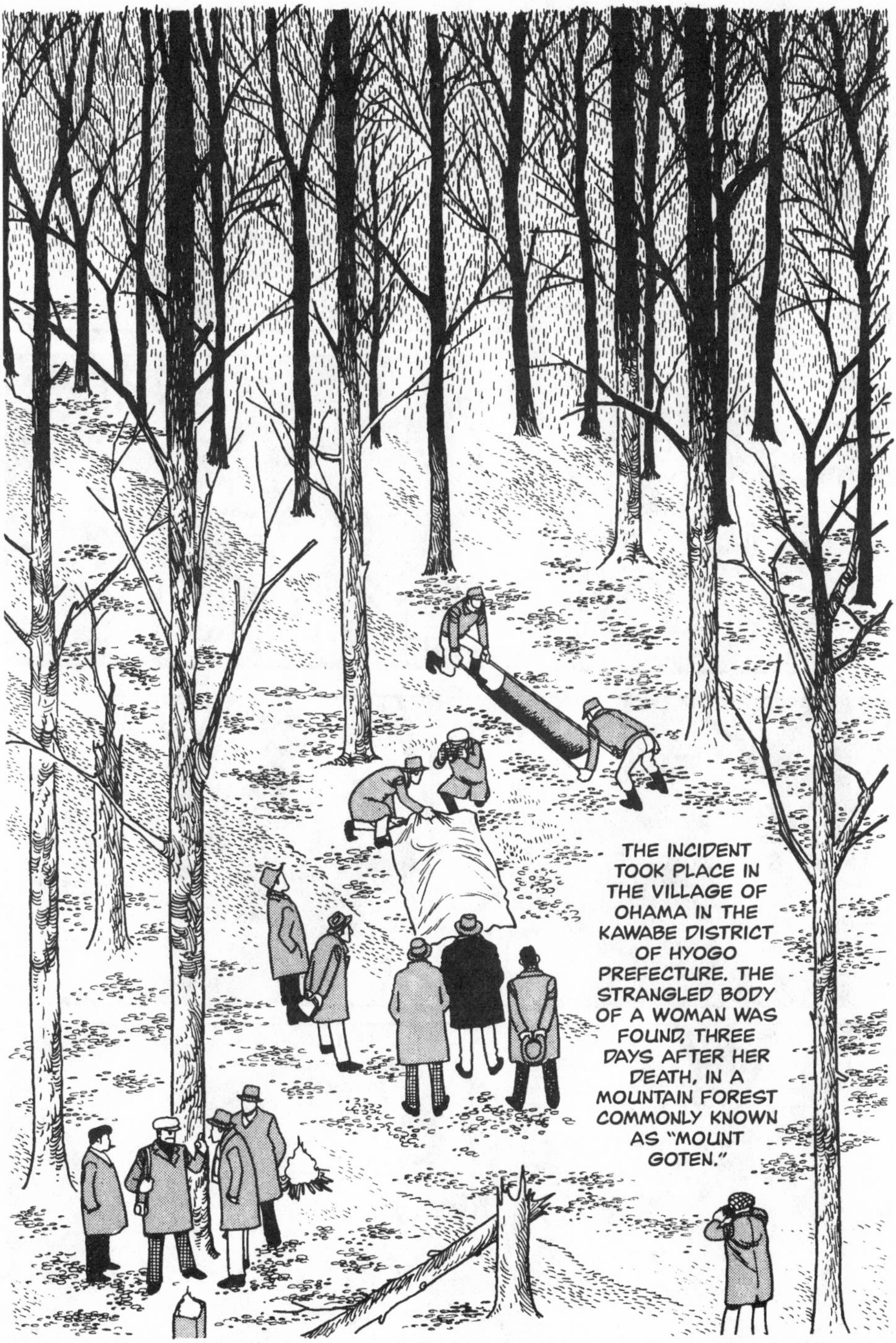
THE INCIDENT TOOK PLACE IN THE VILLAGE OF OHAMA IN THE KAWABE DISTRICT OF HYOGO PREFECTURE. THE STRANGLED BODY OF A WOMAN WAS FOUND, THREE DAYS AFTER HER DEATH, IN A MOUNTAIN FOREST COMMONLY KNOWN AS "MOUNT GOTEN."

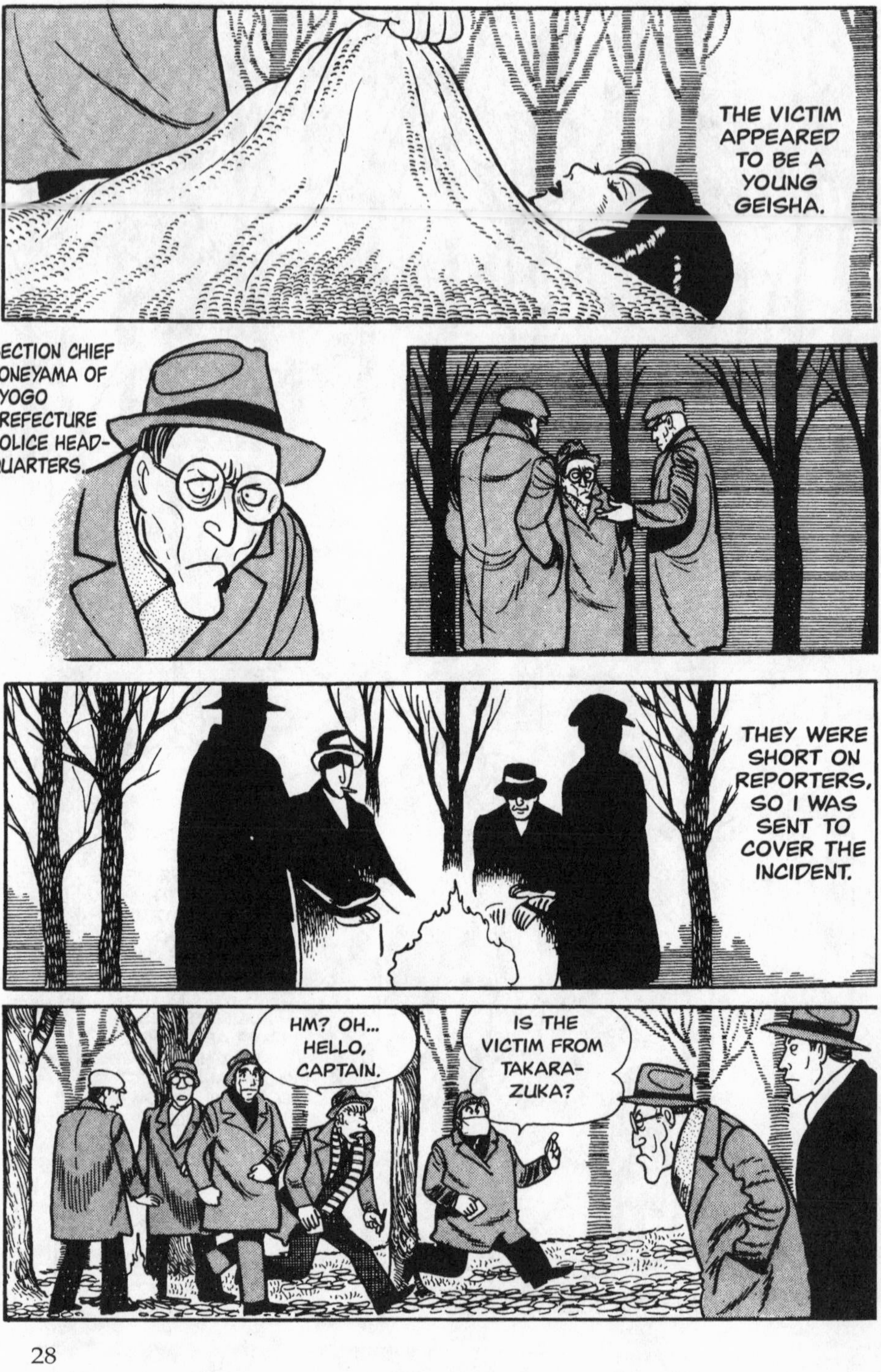
THE VICTIM APPEARED TO BE A YOUNG GEISHA.
SECTION CHIEF YONEYAMA OF HYOGO PREFECTURE POLICE HEAD-QUARTERS.
THEY WERE SHORT ON REPORTERS, SO I WAS SENT TO COVER THE INCIDENT.
HM? OH... HELLO, CAPTAIN.
IS THE VICTIM FROM TAKARA-ZUKA?

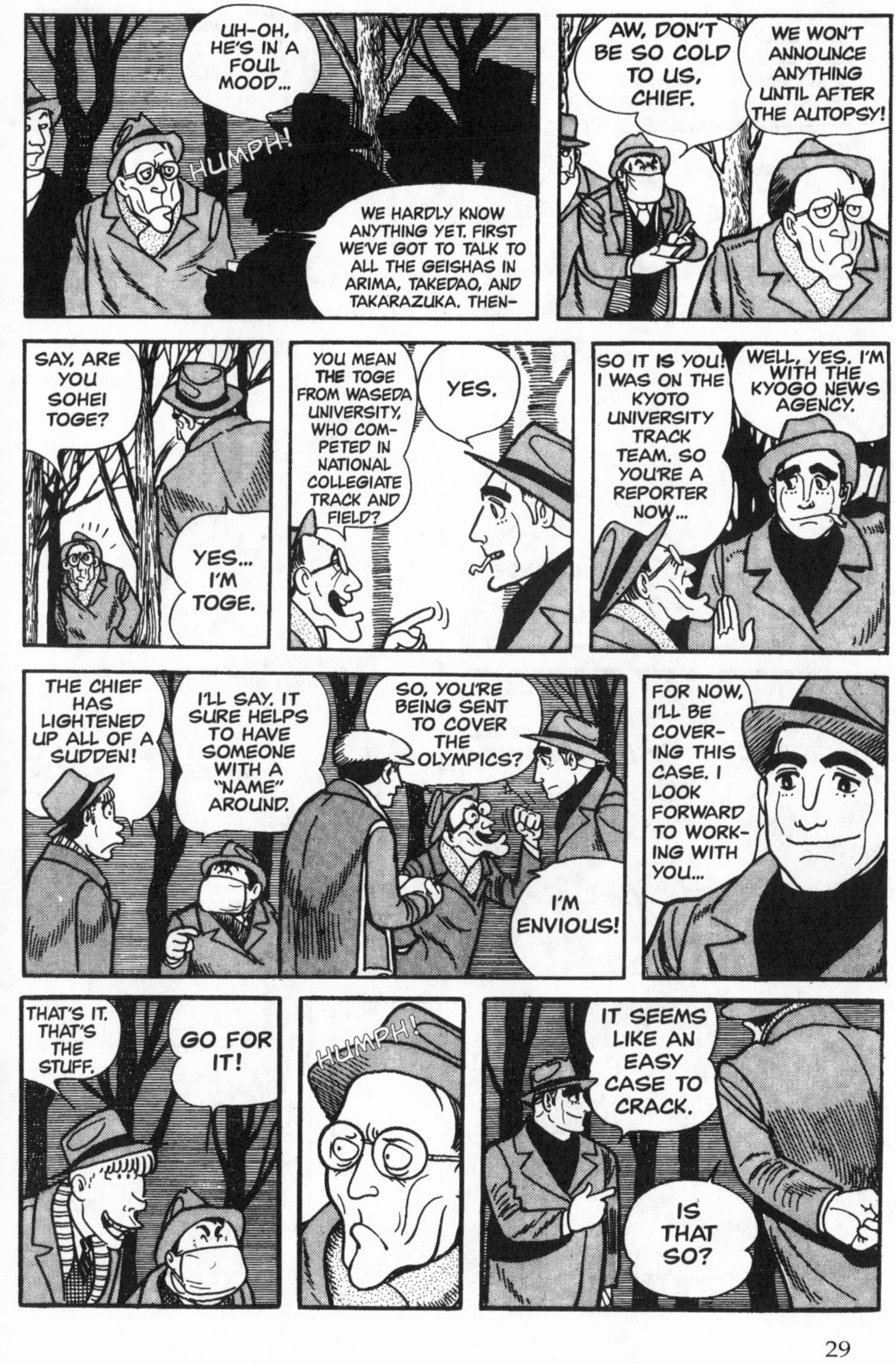
UH-OH, HE'S IN A FOUL MOOD...
HUMPH!
WE HARDLY KNOW ANYTHING YET. FIRST WE'VE GOT TO TALK TO ALL THE GEISHAS IN ARIMA, TAKEDAO, AND TAKARAZUKA. THEN-
AW, DON'T BE SO COLD TO US, CHIEF.
WE WON'T ANNOUNCE ANYTHING UNTIL AFTER THE AUTOPSY!
SAY, ARE YOU SOHEI TOGE?
YES... I'M TOGE.
YOU MEAN THE TOGE FROM WASEDA UNIVERSITY, WHO COMPETED IN NATIONAL COLLEGIATE TRACK AND FIELD?
YES.
SO IT IS YOU! I WAS ON THE KYOTO UNIVERSITY TRACK TEAM. SO YOU'RE A REPORTER NOW...
WELL, YES. I'M WITH THE KYOGO NEWS AGENCY.
THE CHIEF HAS LIGHTENED UP ALL OF A SUDDEN!
I'LL SAY. IT SURE HELPS TO HAVE SOMEONE WITH A "NAME" AROUND.
SO, YOU'RE BEING SENT TO COVER THE OLYMPICS?
I'M ENVIOUS!
FOR NOW, I'LL BE COVERING THIS CASE. I LOOK FORWARD TO WORKING WITH YOU...
THAT'S IT. THAT'S THE STUFF.
GO FOR IT!
HUMPH!
IT SEEMS LIKE AN EASY CASE TO CRACK.
IS THAT SO?

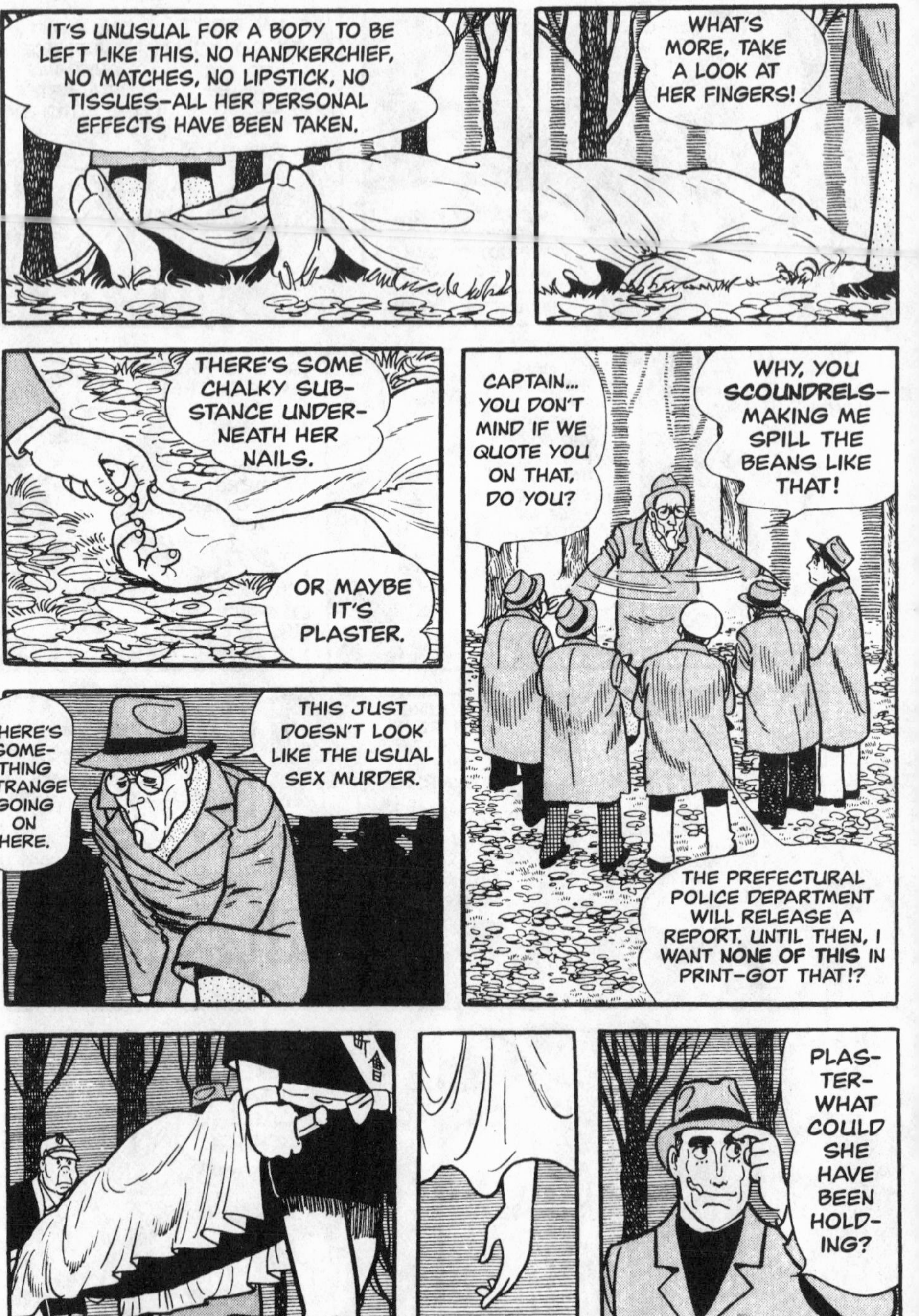
IT'S UNUSUAL FOR A BODY TO BE LEFT LIKE THIS. NO HANDKERCHIEF, NO MATCHES, NO LIPSTICK, NO TISSUES–ALL HER PERSONAL EFFECTS HAVE BEEN TAKEN.
WHAT'S MORE, TAKE A LOOK AT HER FINGERS!
THERE'S SOME CHALKY SUBSTANCE UNDERNEATH HER NAILS.
OR MAYBE IT'S PLASTER.
CAPTAIN... YOU DON'T MIND IF WE QUOTE YOU ON THAT, DO YOU?
WHY, YOU **SCOUNDRELS**–MAKING ME SPILL THE BEANS LIKE THAT!
THE PREFECTURAL POLICE DEPARTMENT WILL RELEASE A REPORT. UNTIL THEN, I WANT **NONE OF THIS** IN PRINT–GOT THAT!?
THERE'S SOMETHING STRANGE GOING ON HERE.
THIS JUST DOESN'T LOOK LIKE THE USUAL SEX MURDER.
PLASTER–WHAT COULD SHE HAVE BEEN HOLDING?

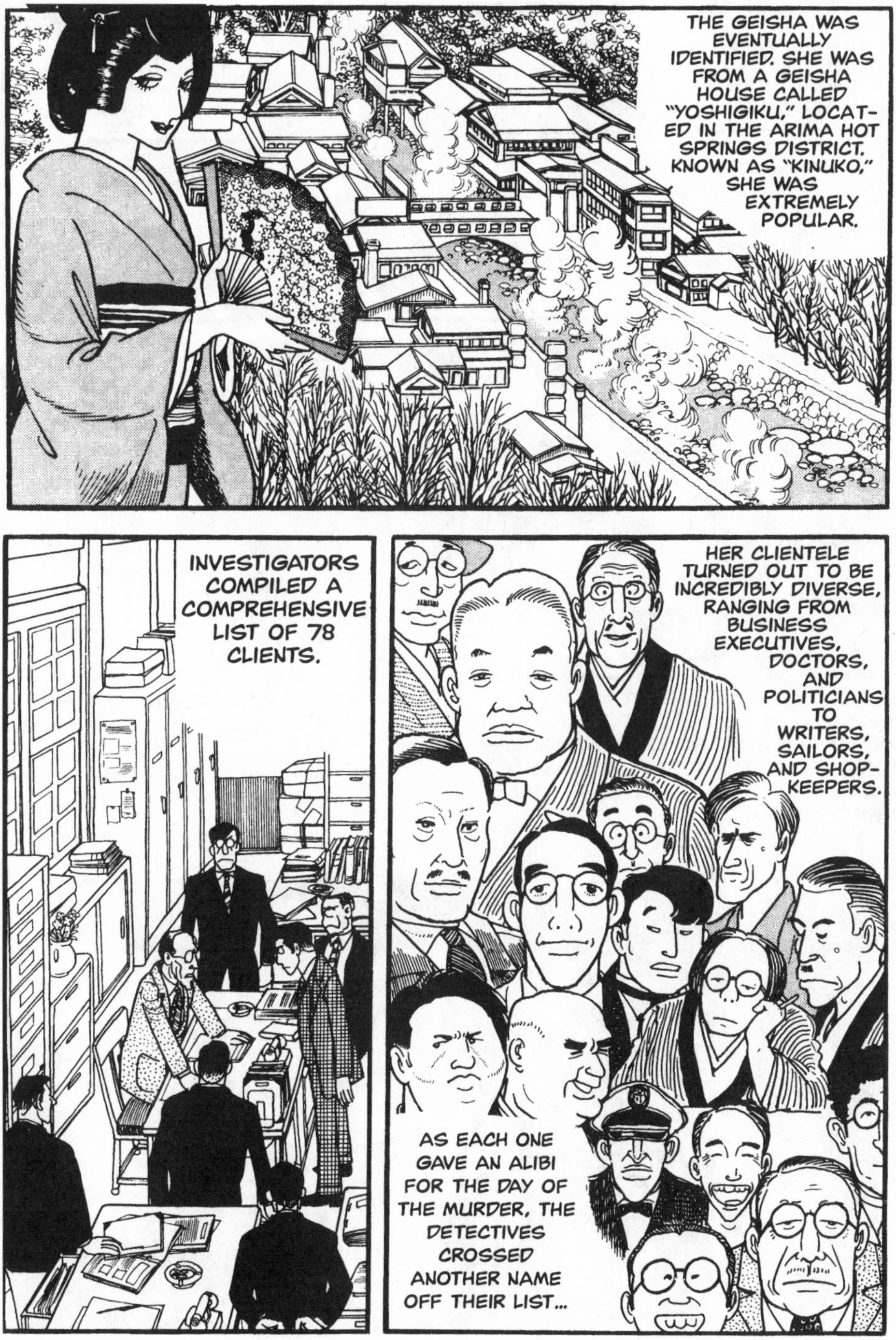
THE GEISHA WAS EVENTUALLY IDENTIFIED. SHE WAS FROM A GEISHA HOUSE CALLED "YOSHIGIKU," LOCATED IN THE ARIMA HOT SPRINGS DISTRICT. KNOWN AS "KINUKO," SHE WAS EXTREMELY POPULAR.
INVESTIGATORS COMPILED A COMPREHENSIVE LIST OF 78 CLIENTS.
HER CLIENTELE TURNED OUT TO BE INCREDIBLY DIVERSE, RANGING FROM BUSINESS EXECUTIVES, DOCTORS, AND POLITICIANS TO WRITERS, SAILORS, AND SHOPKEEPERS.
AS EACH ONE GAVE AN ALIBI FOR THE DAY OF THE MURDER, THE DETECTIVES CROSSED ANOTHER NAME OFF THEIR LIST...

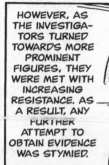

HOWEVER, AS THE INVESTIGATORS TURNED TOWARDS MORE PROMINENT FIGURES, THEY WERE MET WITH INCREASING RESISTANCE. AS A RESULT, ANY FURTHER ATTEMPT TO OBTAIN EVIDENCE WAS STYMIED.

ONE OF THEIR SUSPECTS WAS A FORMIDABLE FIGURE, THE PRESIDENT OF A LARGE COMPANY. THREE WITNESSES CLAIMED TO HAVE SEEN THE VICTIM WALKING WITH THIS MAN ON THE DAY OF THE MURDER.

HOWEVER, THE SUSPECT LEFT FOR AMERICA ON BUSINESS DIRECTLY AFTER THE INCIDENT. THE INVESTIGATORS AWAITED HIS RETURN, ONLY TO LEARN THAT HE HAD SUDDENLY DIED WHILE ABROAD...

BY AUGUST, THE MURDER REMAINED UNSOLVED, AND I WAS CALLED BACK AND ASSIGNED TO BERLIN. SO HERE I AM.

.....
.....

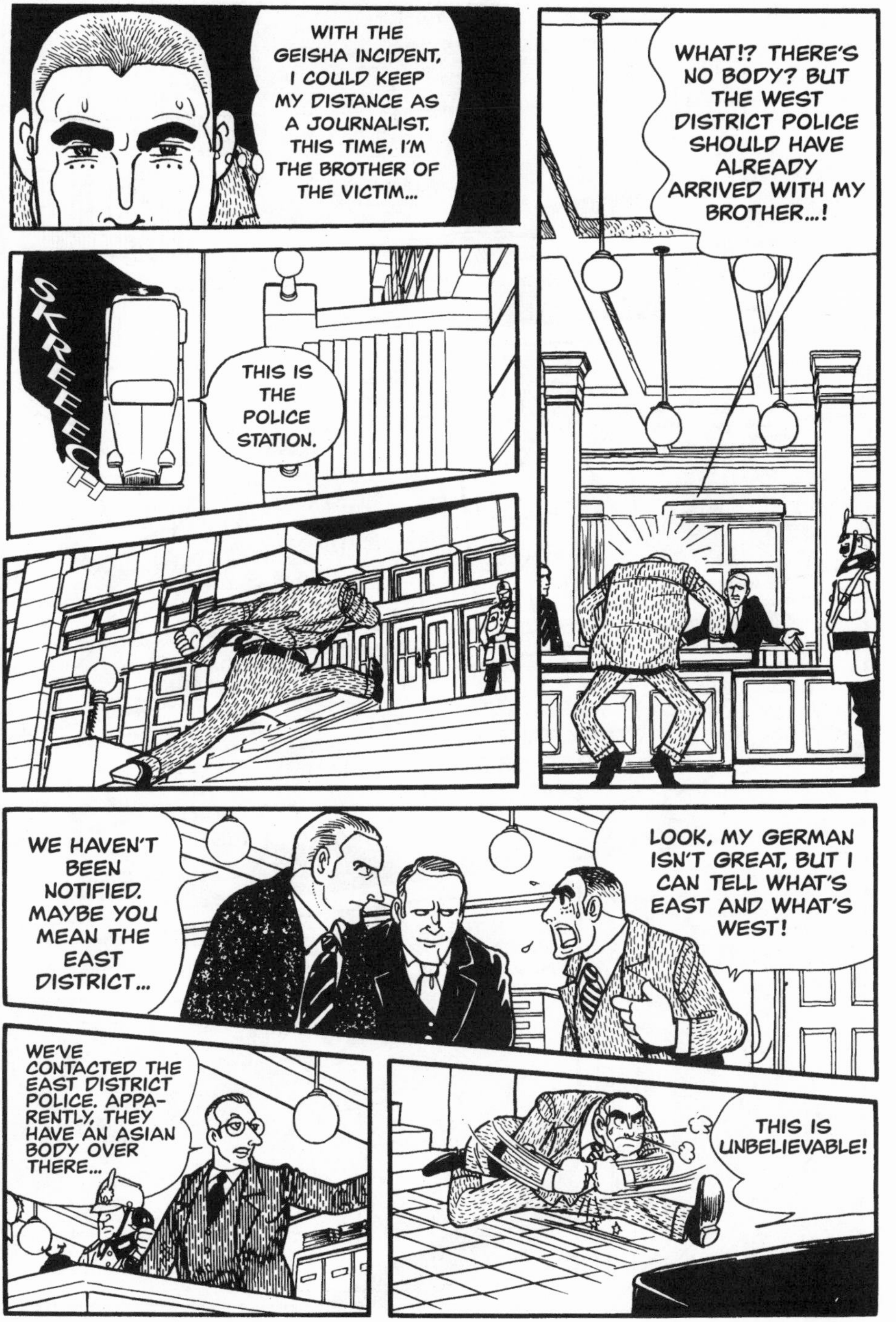
WITH THE GEISHA INCIDENT, I COULD KEEP MY DISTANCE AS A JOURNALIST. THIS TIME, I'M THE BROTHER OF THE VICTIM...
SKREEECH
THIS IS THE POLICE STATION.
WHAT!? THERE'S NO BODY? BUT THE WEST DISTRICT POLICE SHOULD HAVE ALREADY ARRIVED WITH MY BROTHER...!
WE HAVEN'T BEEN NOTIFIED. MAYBE YOU MEAN THE EAST DISTRICT...
LOOK, MY GERMAN ISN'T GREAT, BUT I CAN TELL WHAT'S EAST AND WHAT'S WEST!
WE'VE CONTACTED THE EAST DISTRICT POLICE. APPARENTLY, THEY HAVE AN ASIAN BODY OVER THERE...
THIS IS UNBELIEVABLE!

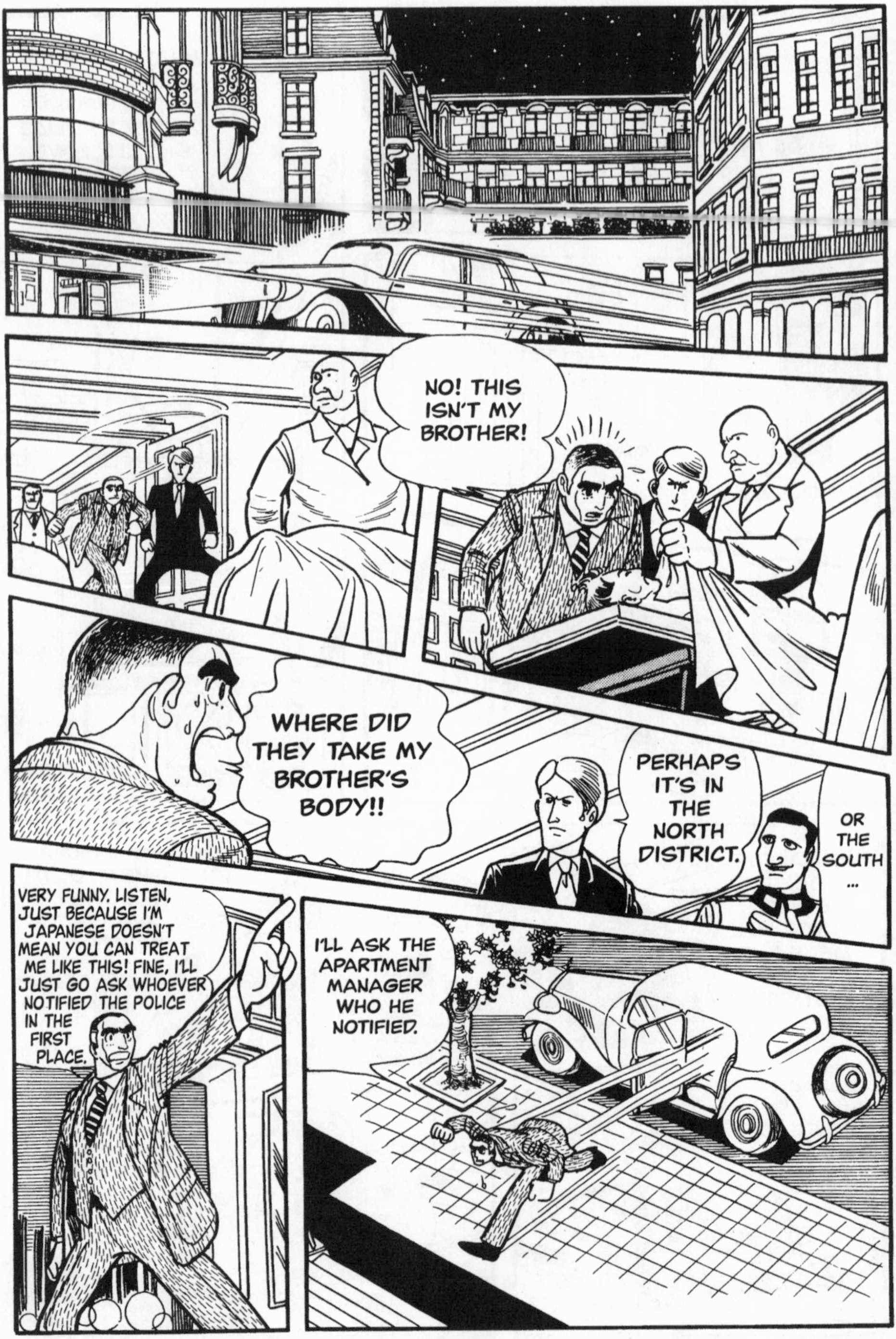
NO! THIS ISN'T MY BROTHER!
WHERE DID THEY TAKE MY BROTHER'S BODY!!
PERHAPS IT'S IN THE NORTH DISTRICT.
OR THE SOUTH ...
VERY FUNNY. LISTEN, JUST BECAUSE I'M JAPANESE DOESN'T MEAN YOU CAN TREAT ME LIKE THIS! FINE, I'LL JUST GO ASK WHOEVER NOTIFIED THE POLICE IN THE FIRST PLACE.
I'LL ASK THE APARTMENT MANAGER WHO HE NOTIFIED.

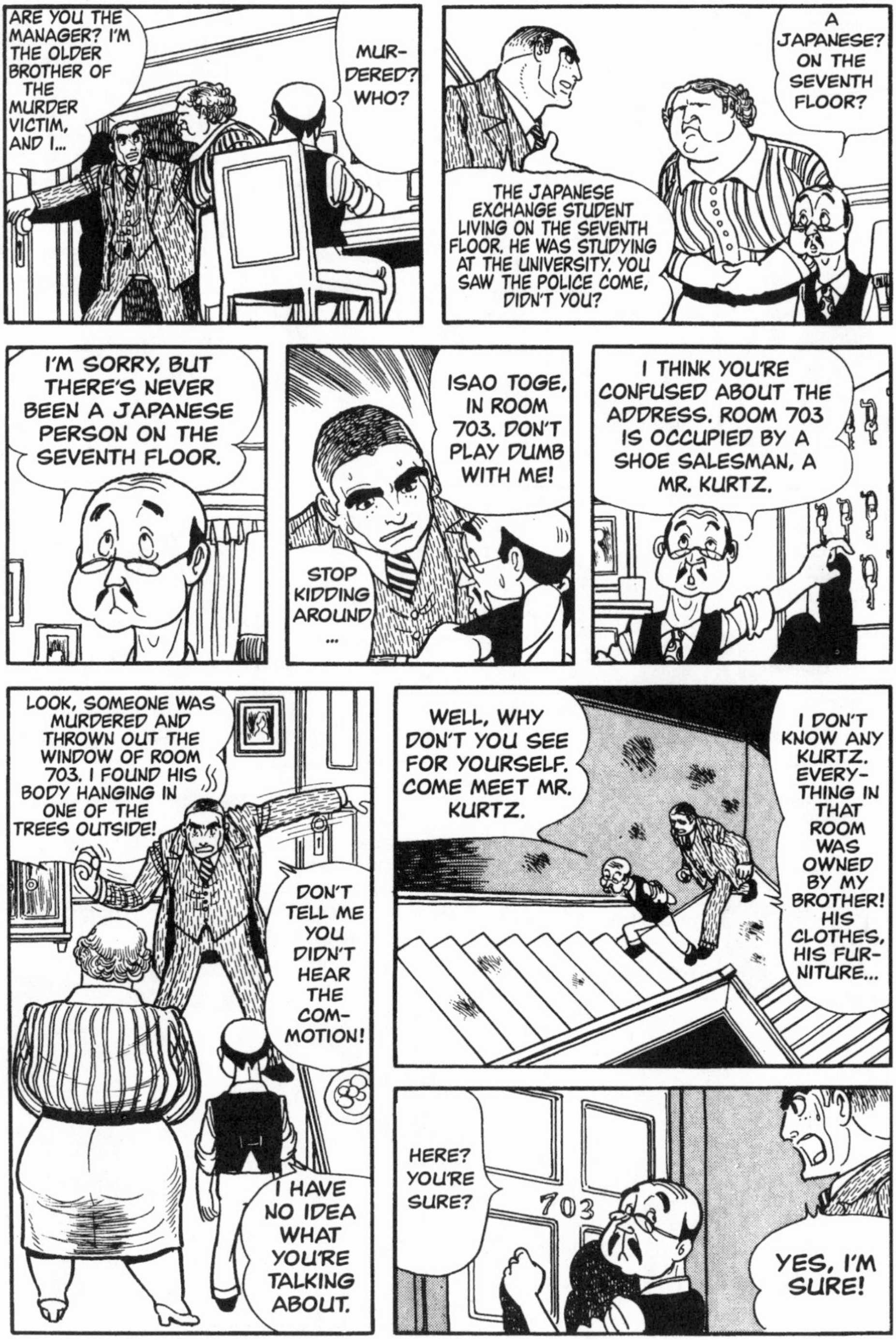
ARE YOU THE MANAGER? I'M THE OLDER BROTHER OF THE MURDER VICTIM, AND I...
MUR-DERED? WHO?
THE JAPANESE EXCHANGE STUDENT LIVING ON THE SEVENTH FLOOR. HE WAS STUDYING AT THE UNIVERSITY. YOU SAW THE POLICE COME, DIDN'T YOU?
A JAPANESE? ON THE SEVENTH FLOOR?
I'M SORRY, BUT THERE'S NEVER BEEN A JAPANESE PERSON ON THE SEVENTH FLOOR.
ISAO TOGE, IN ROOM 703. DON'T PLAY DUMB WITH ME!
STOP KIDDING AROUND ...
I THINK YOU'RE CONFUSED ABOUT THE ADDRESS. ROOM 703 IS OCCUPIED BY A SHOE SALESMAN, A MR. KURTZ.
LOOK, SOMEONE WAS MURDERED AND THROWN OUT THE WINDOW OF ROOM 703. I FOUND HIS BODY HANGING IN ONE OF THE TREES OUTSIDE!
DON'T TELL ME YOU DIDN'T HEAR THE COM-MOTION!
I HAVE NO IDEA WHAT YOU'RE TALKING ABOUT.
WELL, WHY DON'T YOU SEE FOR YOURSELF. COME MEET MR. KURTZ.
I DON'T KNOW ANY KURTZ. EVERY-THING IN THAT ROOM WAS OWNED BY MY BROTHER! HIS CLOTHES, HIS FUR-NITURE...
HERE? YOU'RE SURE?
703
YES, I'M SURE!

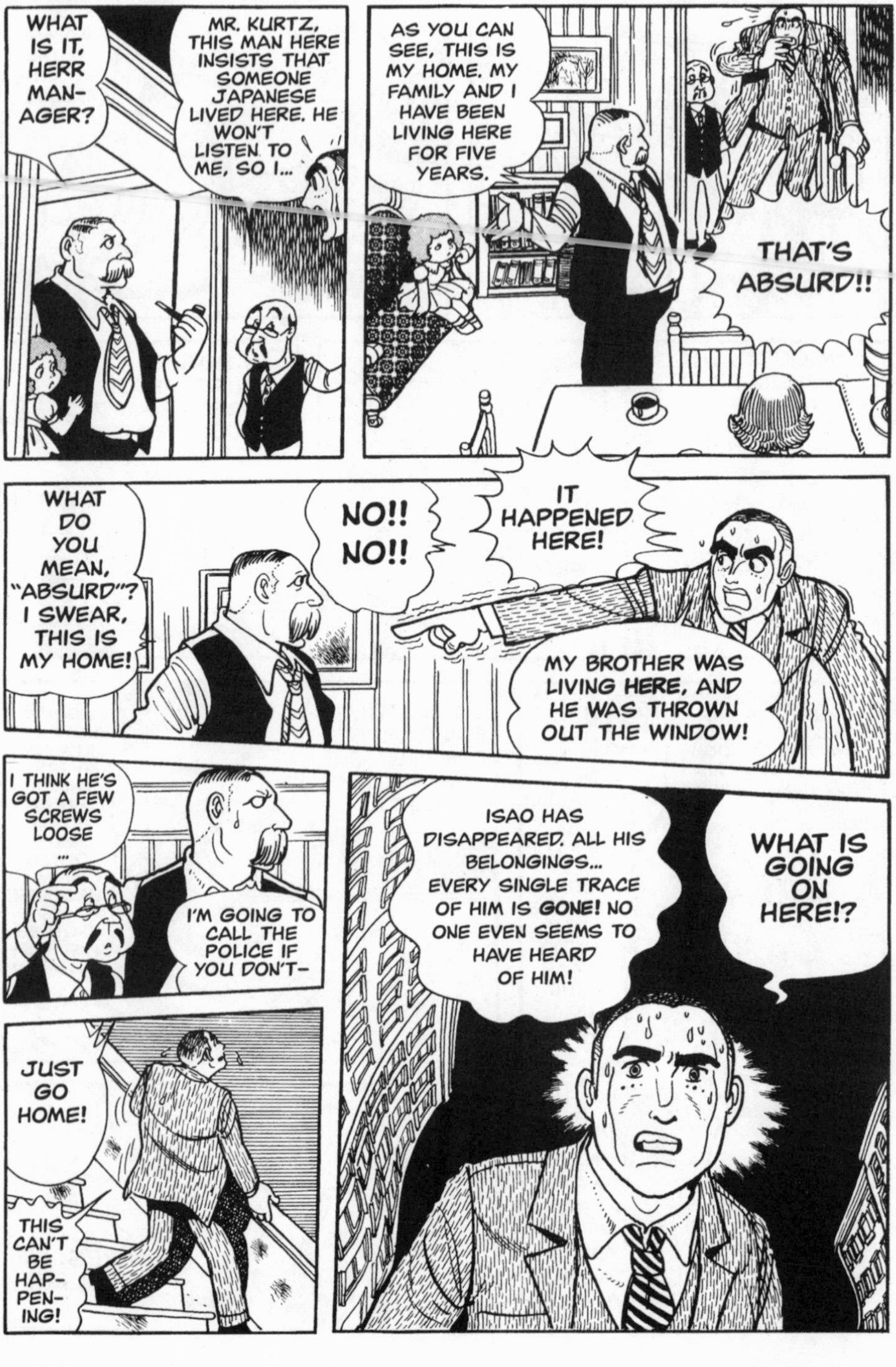
WHAT IS IT, HERR MANAGER?
MR. KURTZ, THIS MAN HERE INSISTS THAT SOMEONE JAPANESE LIVED HERE. HE WON'T LISTEN TO ME, SO I...
AS YOU CAN SEE, THIS IS MY HOME. MY FAMILY AND I HAVE BEEN LIVING HERE FOR FIVE YEARS.
THAT'S ABSURD!!
WHAT DO YOU MEAN, "ABSURD"? I SWEAR, THIS IS MY HOME!
NO!! NO!!
IT HAPPENED HERE!
MY BROTHER WAS LIVING HERE, AND HE WAS THROWN OUT THE WINDOW!
I THINK HE'S GOT A FEW SCREWS LOOSE ...
I'M GOING TO CALL THE POLICE IF YOU DON'T-
JUST GO HOME!
THIS CAN'T BE HAPPENING!
ISAO HAS DISAPPEARED. ALL HIS BELONGINGS... EVERY SINGLE TRACE OF HIM IS GONE! NO ONE EVEN SEEMS TO HAVE HEARD OF HIM!
WHAT IS GOING ON HERE!?

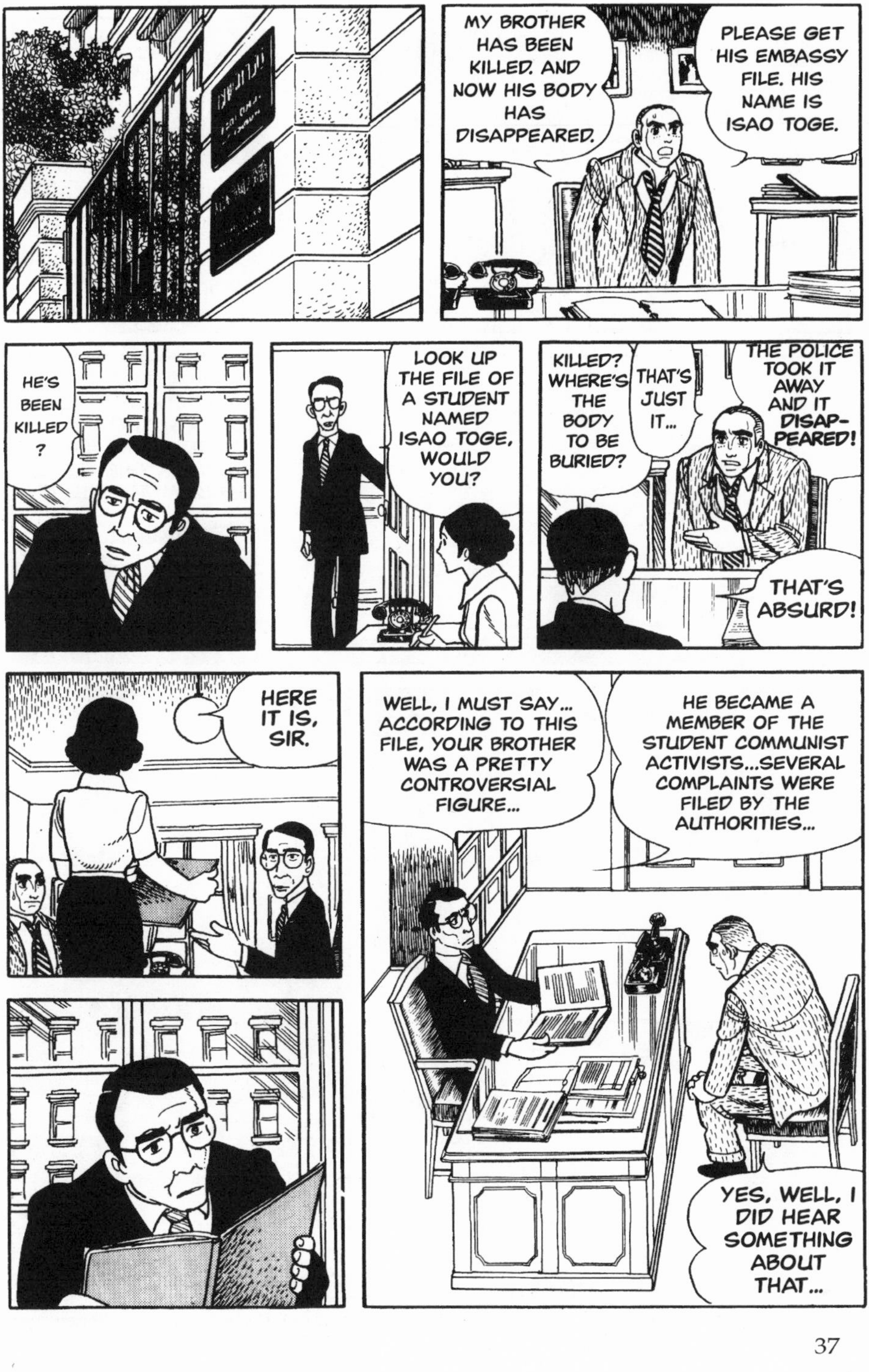
MY BROTHER HAS BEEN KILLED. AND NOW HIS BODY HAS DISAPPEARED.
PLEASE GET HIS EMBASSY FILE. HIS NAME IS ISAO TOGE.
HE'S BEEN KILLED?
LOOK UP THE FILE OF A STUDENT NAMED ISAO TOGE, WOULD YOU?
KILLED? WHERE'S THE BODY TO BE BURIED?
THAT'S JUST IT...
THE POLICE TOOK IT AWAY AND IT DISAPPEARED!
THAT'S ABSURD!
HERE IT IS, SIR.
WELL, I MUST SAY... ACCORDING TO THIS FILE, YOUR BROTHER WAS A PRETTY CONTROVERSIAL FIGURE...
HE BECAME A MEMBER OF THE STUDENT COMMUNIST ACTIVISTS...SEVERAL COMPLAINTS WERE FILED BY THE AUTHORITIES...
YES, WELL, I DID HEAR SOMETHING ABOUT THAT...

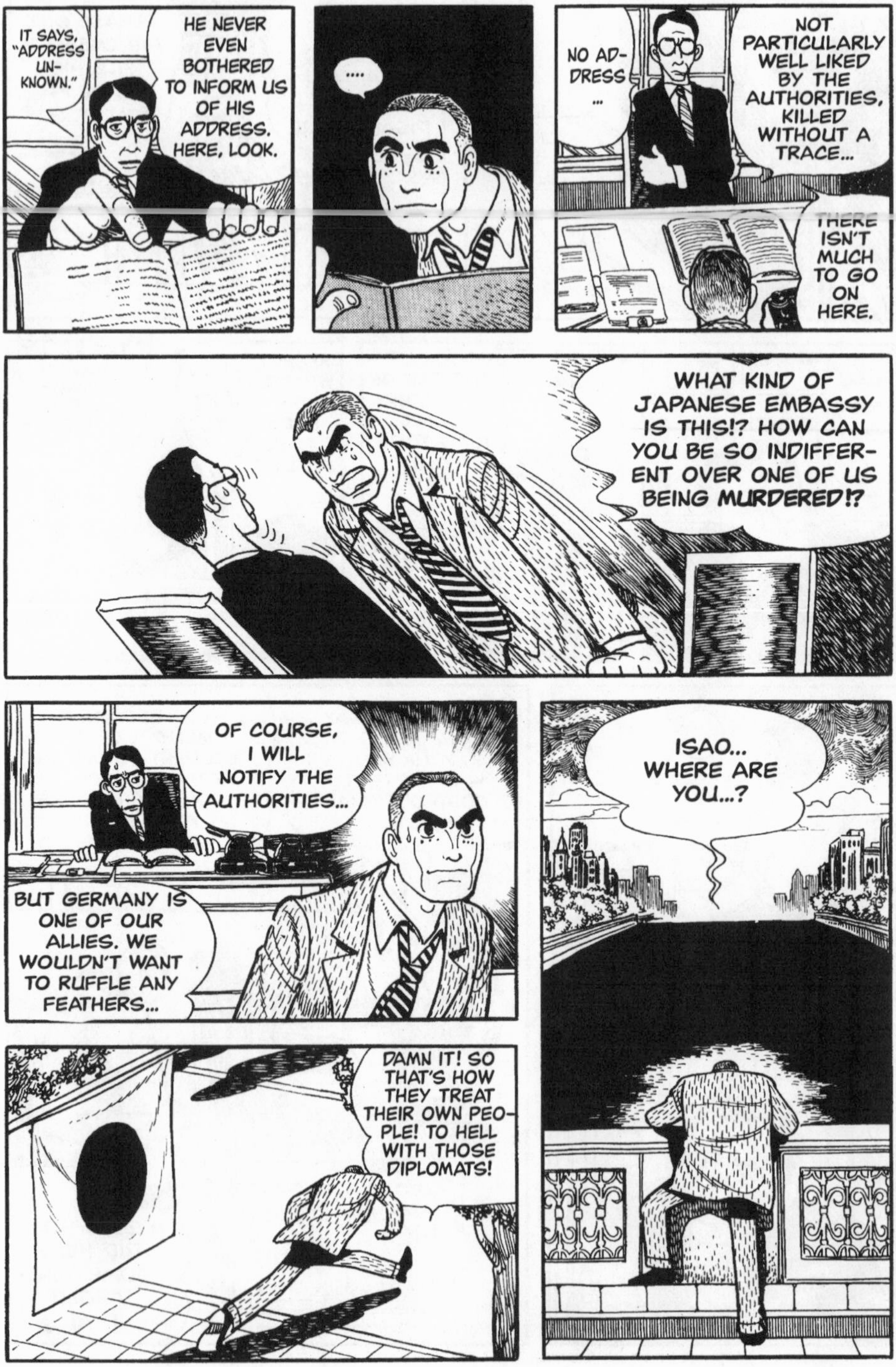
IT SAYS, "ADDRESS UN-KNOWN."
HE NEVER EVEN BOTHERED TO INFORM US OF HIS ADDRESS. HERE, LOOK.
....
NO AD-DRESS ...
NOT PARTICULARLY WELL LIKED BY THE AUTHORITIES, KILLED WITHOUT A TRACE...
THERE ISN'T MUCH TO GO ON HERE.
WHAT KIND OF JAPANESE EMBASSY IS THIS!? HOW CAN YOU BE SO INDIFFER-ENT OVER ONE OF US BEING MURDERED!?
OF COURSE, I WILL NOTIFY THE AUTHORITIES...
BUT GERMANY IS ONE OF OUR ALLIES. WE WOULDN'T WANT TO RUFFLE ANY FEATHERS...
ISAO... WHERE ARE YOU...?
DAMN IT! SO THAT'S HOW THEY TREAT THEIR OWN PEO-PLE! TO HELL WITH THOSE DIPLOMATS!

I'LL FIND YOU, EVEN IF I HAVE TO DO IT ALL BY MYSELF!

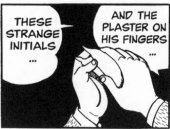

THESE STRANGE INITIALS ...

AND THE PLASTER ON HIS FINGERS ...

THOSE ARE THE ONLY TWO CLUES I HAVE.

THE CLOSING CEREMONY OF THE BERLIN OLYMPICS OCCURRED SEVERAL DAYS LATER. HITLER DELIVERED A LONG SPEECH TO SPECTATORS FROM AROUND THE WORLD, DECLARING THE EVENT A GREAT SUCCESS.

IN FACT, THE NAZIS HAD EXPLOITED THE OLYMPICS AS A MASSIVE PROMOTIONAL CAMPAIGN TO DEMONSTRATE THEIR POWER TO THE REST OF THE WORLD.

MEANWHILE, THE NAZIS WERE LENDING SUPPORT TO THE TREACHEROUS REBEL FORCES IN SPAIN, LED BY GENERAL FRANCO.

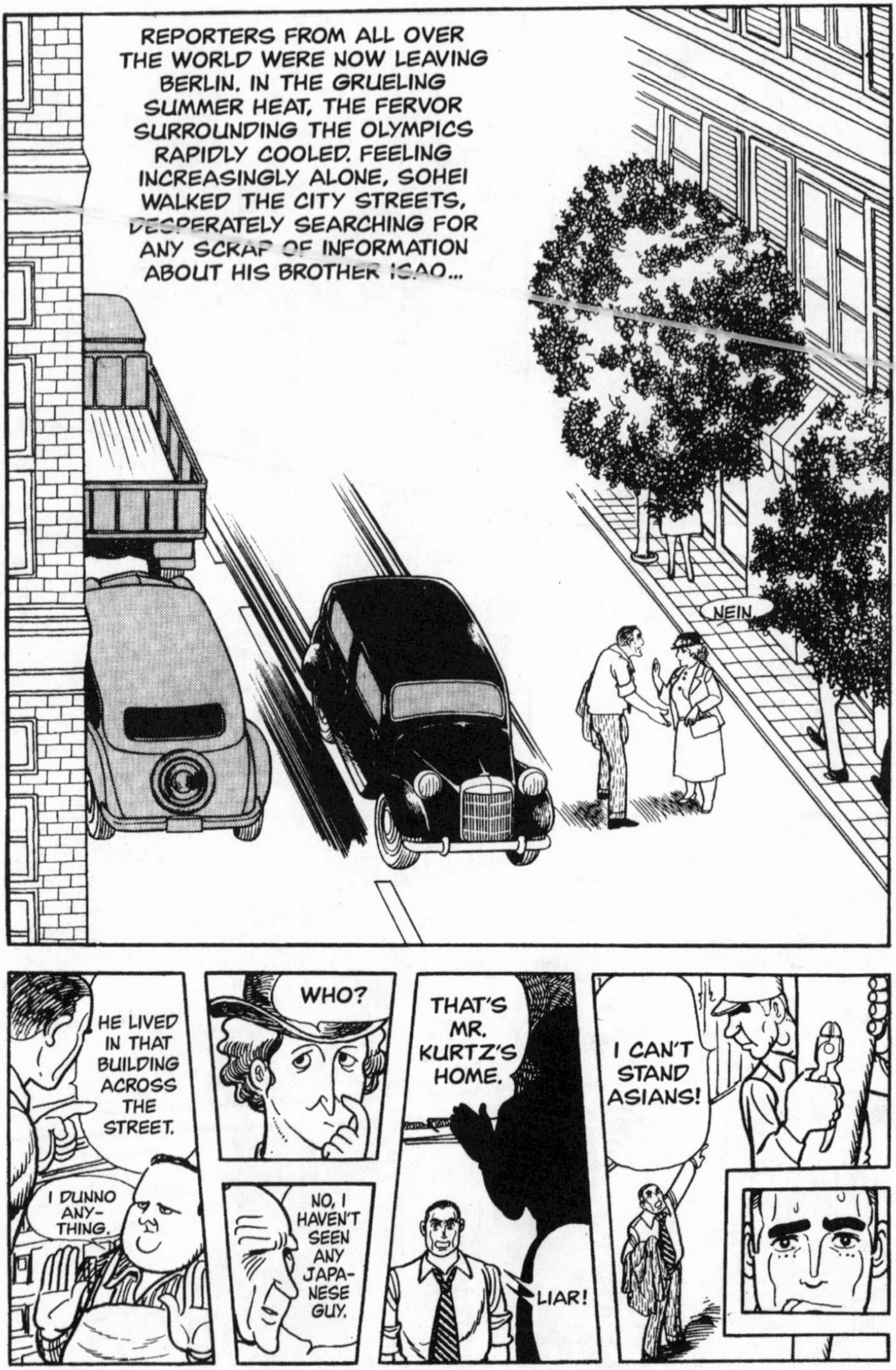
REPORTERS FROM ALL OVER THE WORLD WERE NOW LEAVING BERLIN. IN THE GRUELING SUMMER HEAT, THE FERVOR SURROUNDING THE OLYMPICS RAPIDLY COOLED. FEELING INCREASINGLY ALONE, SOHEI WALKED THE CITY STREETS, DESPERATELY SEARCHING FOR ANY SCRAP OF INFORMATION ABOUT HIS BROTHER ISAO...
NEIN.
HE LIVED IN THAT BUILDING ACROSS THE STREET.
I DUNNO ANYTHING.
WHO?
NO, I HAVEN'T SEEN ANY JAPANESE GUY.
THAT'S MR. KURTZ'S HOME.
LIAR!
I CAN'T STAND ASIANS!

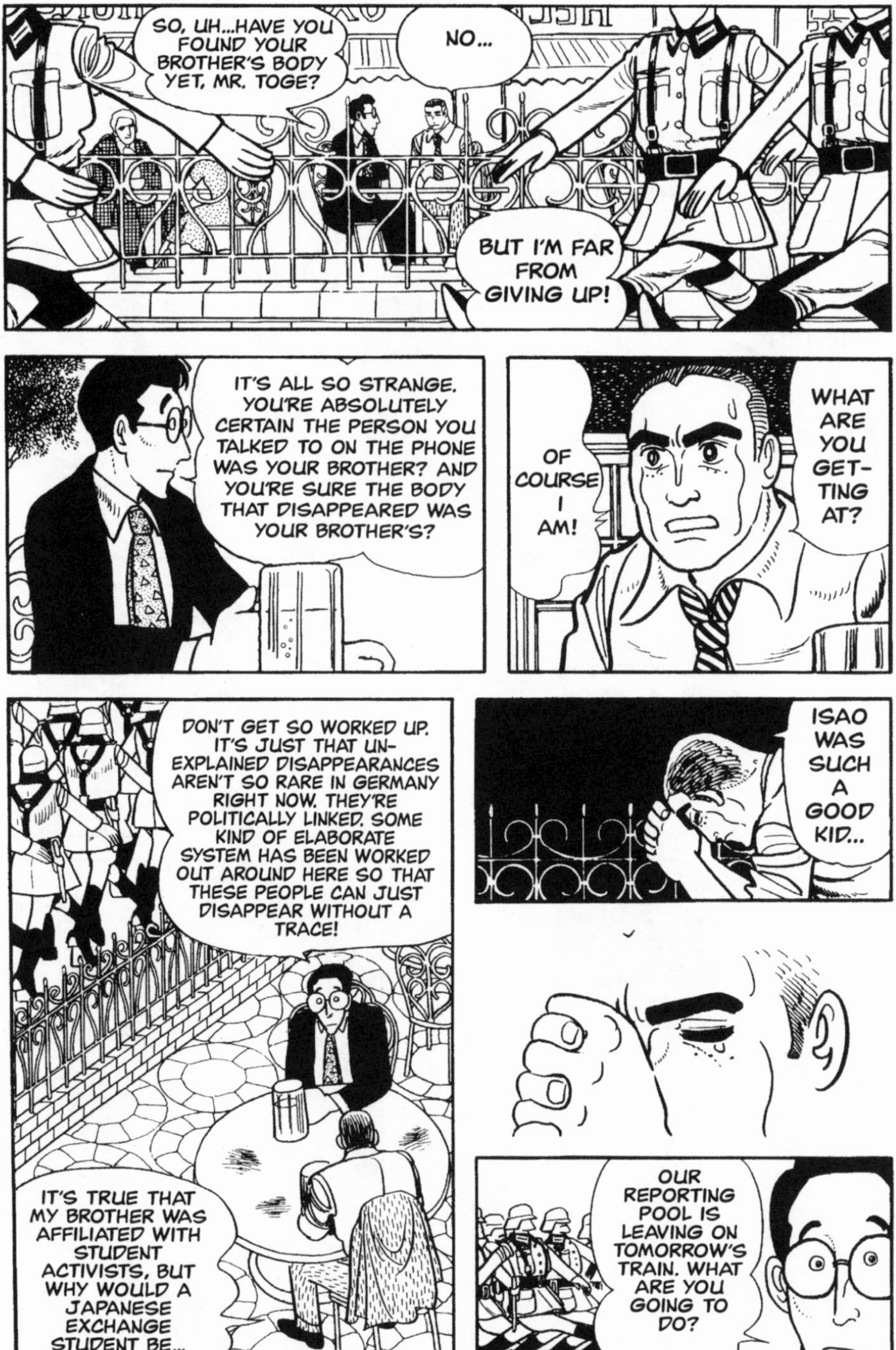
SO, UH...HAVE YOU FOUND YOUR BROTHER'S BODY YET, MR. TOGE?
NO...
BUT I'M FAR FROM GIVING UP!
IT'S ALL SO STRANGE. YOU'RE ABSOLUTELY CERTAIN THE PERSON YOU TALKED TO ON THE PHONE WAS YOUR BROTHER? AND YOU'RE SURE THE BODY THAT DISAPPEARED WAS YOUR BROTHER'S?
OF COURSE I AM!
WHAT ARE YOU GET-TING AT?
DON'T GET SO WORKED UP. IT'S JUST THAT UN-EXPLAINED DISAPPEARANCES AREN'T SO RARE IN GERMANY RIGHT NOW. THEY'RE POLITICALLY LINKED. SOME KIND OF ELABORATE SYSTEM HAS BEEN WORKED OUT AROUND HERE SO THAT THESE PEOPLE CAN JUST DISAPPEAR WITHOUT A TRACE!
IT'S TRUE THAT MY BROTHER WAS AFFILIATED WITH STUDENT ACTIVISTS, BUT WHY WOULD A JAPANESE EXCHANGE STUDENT BE...
ISAO WAS SUCH A GOOD KID...
OUR REPORTING POOL IS LEAVING ON TOMORROW'S TRAIN. WHAT ARE YOU GOING TO DO?

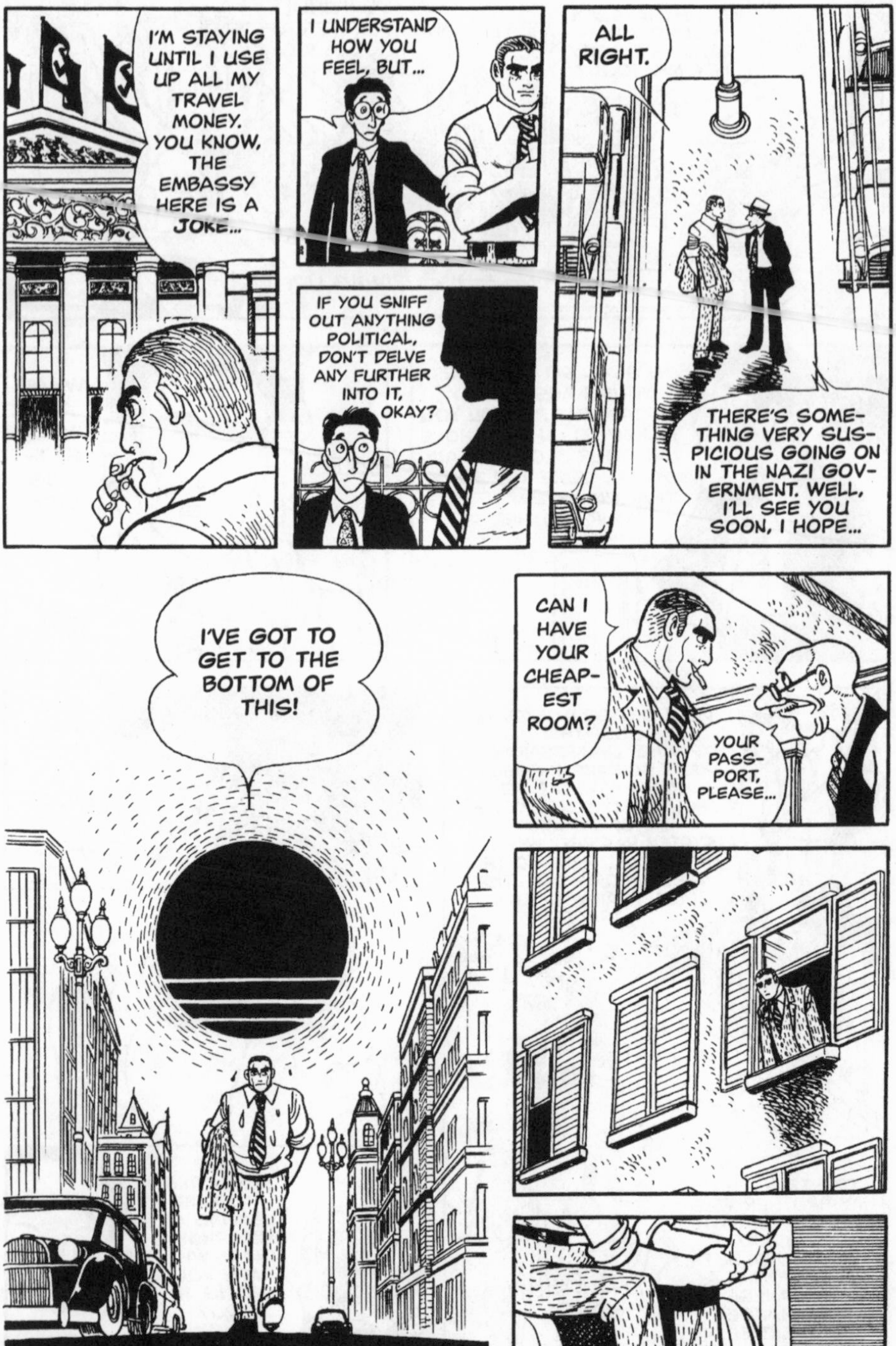
I'M STAYING UNTIL I USE UP ALL MY TRAVEL MONEY. YOU KNOW, THE EMBASSY HERE IS A JOKE...
I UNDERSTAND HOW YOU FEEL, BUT...
IF YOU SNIFF OUT ANYTHING POLITICAL, DON'T DELVE ANY FURTHER INTO IT, OKAY?
ALL RIGHT.
THERE'S SOMETHING VERY SUSPICIOUS GOING ON IN THE NAZI GOVERNMENT. WELL, I'LL SEE YOU SOON, I HOPE...
I'VE GOT TO GET TO THE BOTTOM OF THIS!
CAN I HAVE YOUR CHEAPEST ROOM?
YOUR PASSPORT, PLEASE...

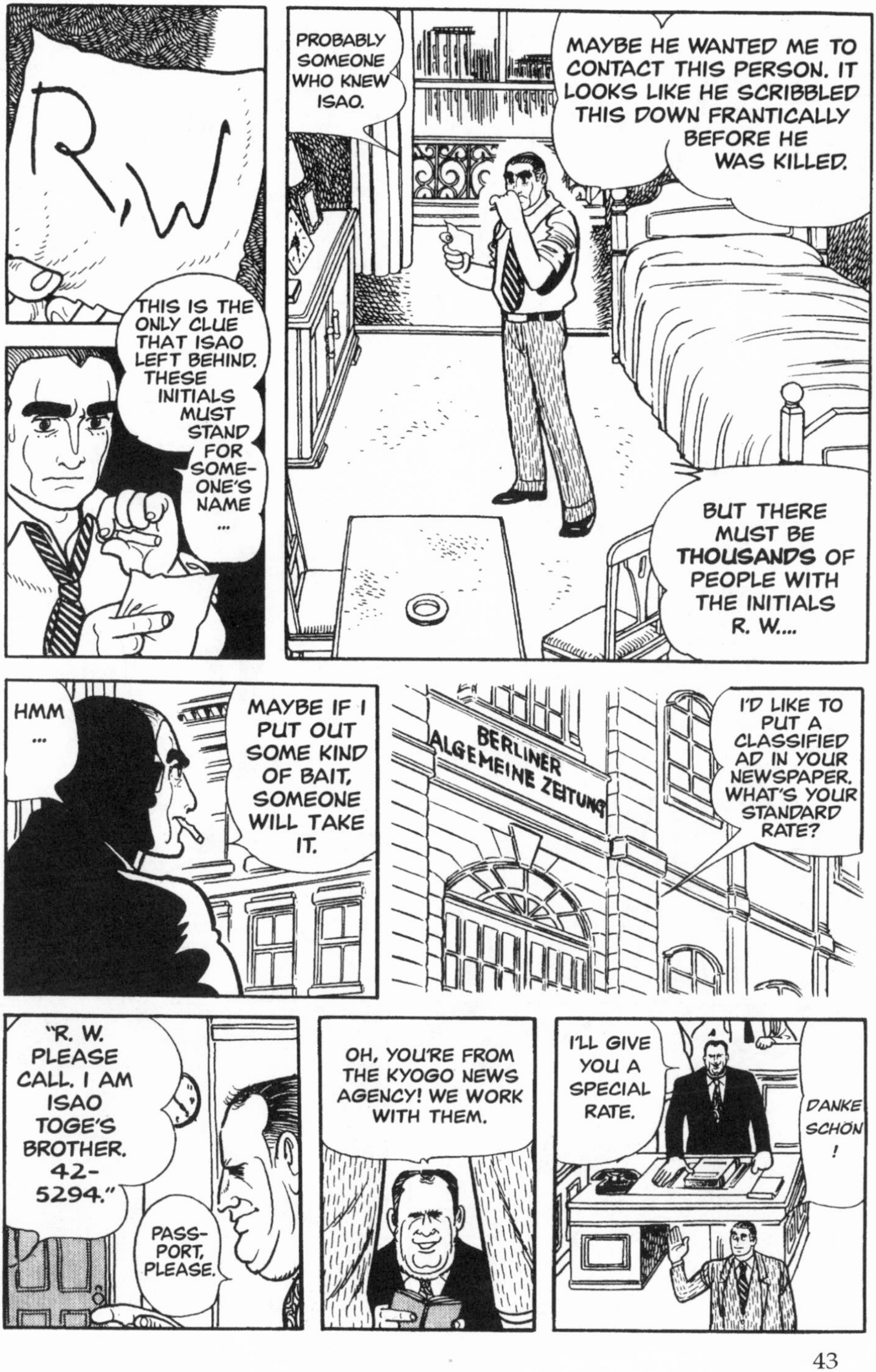
R, W
THIS IS THE ONLY CLUE THAT ISAO LEFT BEHIND. THESE INITIALS MUST STAND FOR SOMEONE'S NAME ...
PROBABLY SOMEONE WHO KNEW ISAO.
MAYBE HE WANTED ME TO CONTACT THIS PERSON. IT LOOKS LIKE HE SCRIBBLED THIS DOWN FRANTICALLY BEFORE HE WAS KILLED.
BUT THERE MUST BE **THOUSANDS** OF PEOPLE WITH THE INITIALS R. W....
HMM ...
MAYBE IF I PUT OUT SOME KIND OF BAIT, SOMEONE WILL TAKE IT.
BERLINER ALGEMEINE ZEITUNG
I'D LIKE TO PUT A CLASSIFIED AD IN YOUR NEWSPAPER. WHAT'S YOUR STANDARD RATE?
"R. W. PLEASE CALL. I AM ISAO TOGE'S BROTHER. 42-5294."
PASSPORT, PLEASE.
OH, YOU'RE FROM THE KYOGO NEWS AGENCY! WE WORK WITH THEM.
I'LL GIVE YOU A SPECIAL RATE.
DANKE SCHÖN !

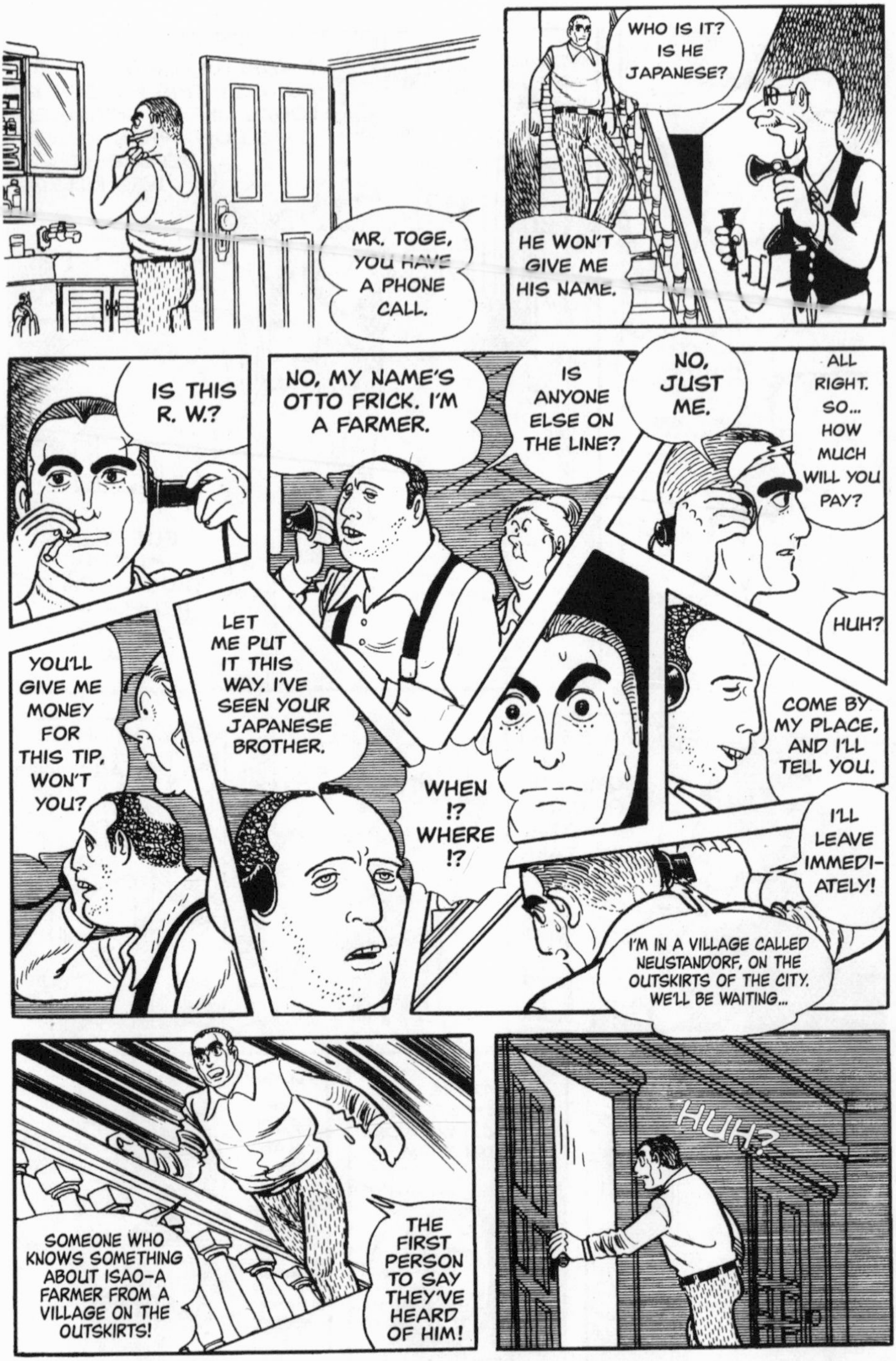
MR. TOGE, YOU HAVE A PHONE CALL.
WHO IS IT? IS HE JAPANESE?
HE WON'T GIVE ME HIS NAME.
IS THIS R. W.?
NO, MY NAME'S OTTO FRICK. I'M A FARMER.
IS ANYONE ELSE ON THE LINE?
NO, JUST ME.
ALL RIGHT. SO... HOW MUCH WILL YOU PAY?
HUH?
YOU'LL GIVE ME MONEY FOR THIS TIP, WON'T YOU?
LET ME PUT IT THIS WAY. I'VE SEEN YOUR JAPANESE BROTHER.
WHEN!? WHERE!?
COME BY MY PLACE, AND I'LL TELL YOU.
I'LL LEAVE IMMEDIATELY!
I'M IN A VILLAGE CALLED NEUSTANDORF, ON THE OUTSKIRTS OF THE CITY. WE'LL BE WAITING...
SOMEONE WHO KNOWS SOMETHING ABOUT ISAO–A FARMER FROM A VILLAGE ON THE OUTSKIRTS!
THE FIRST PERSON TO SAY THEY'VE HEARD OF HIM!
HUH?

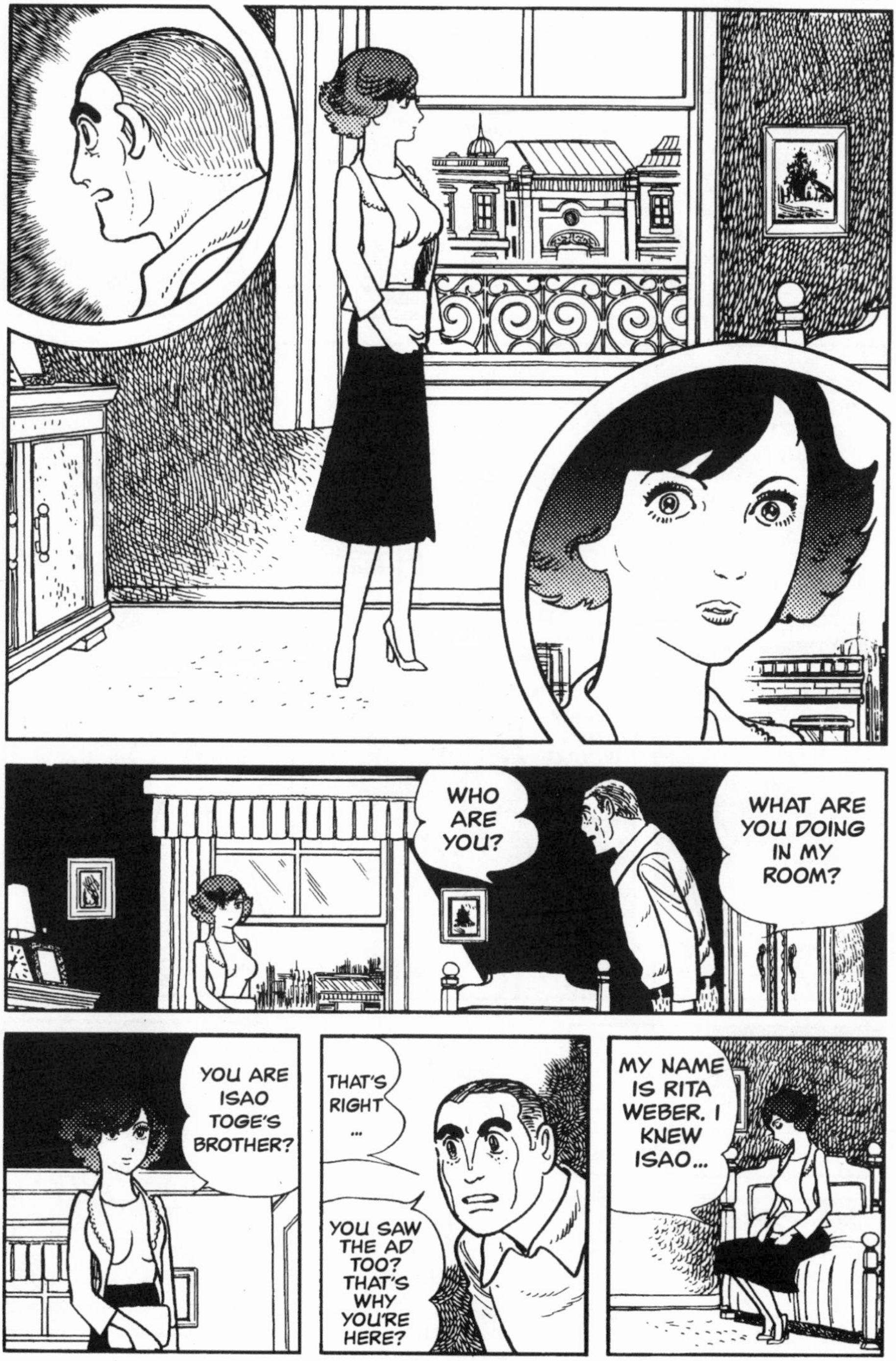
WHO ARE YOU?
WHAT ARE YOU DOING IN MY ROOM?
YOU ARE ISAO TOGE'S BROTHER?
THAT'S RIGHT ...
YOU SAW THE AD TOO? THAT'S WHY YOU'RE HERE?
MY NAME IS RITA WEBER. I KNEW ISAO...

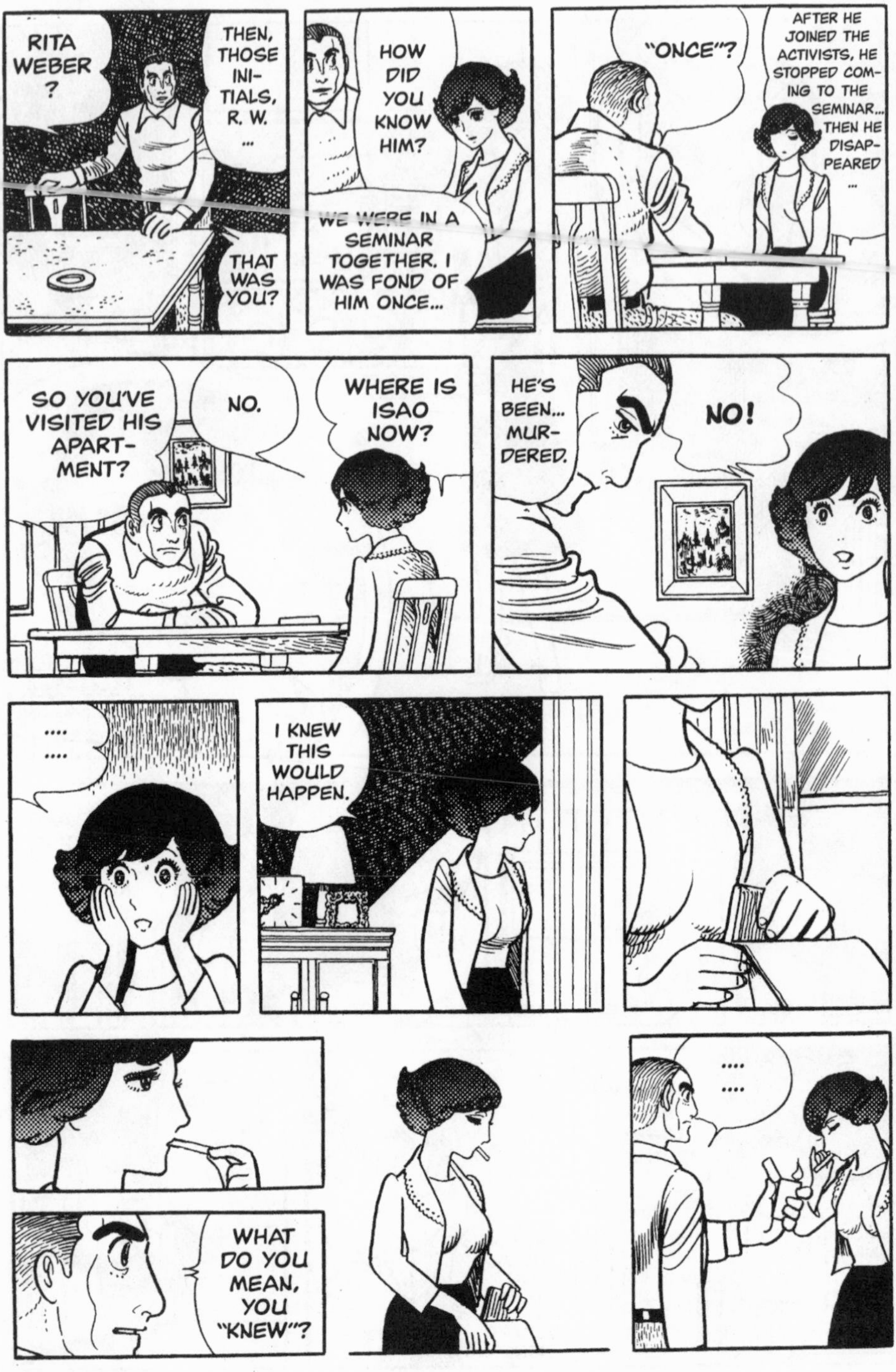
RITA WEBER ?
THEN, THOSE INITIALS, R. W. ...
THAT WAS YOU?
HOW DID YOU KNOW HIM?
WE WERE IN A SEMINAR TOGETHER. I WAS FOND OF HIM ONCE...
"ONCE"?
AFTER HE JOINED THE ACTIVISTS, HE STOPPED COMING TO THE SEMINAR... THEN HE DISAPPEARED ...
SO YOU'VE VISITED HIS APARTMENT?
NO.
WHERE IS ISAO NOW?
HE'S BEEN... MURDERED.
NO!
....
I KNEW THIS WOULD HAPPEN.
WHAT DO YOU MEAN, YOU "KNEW"?
....

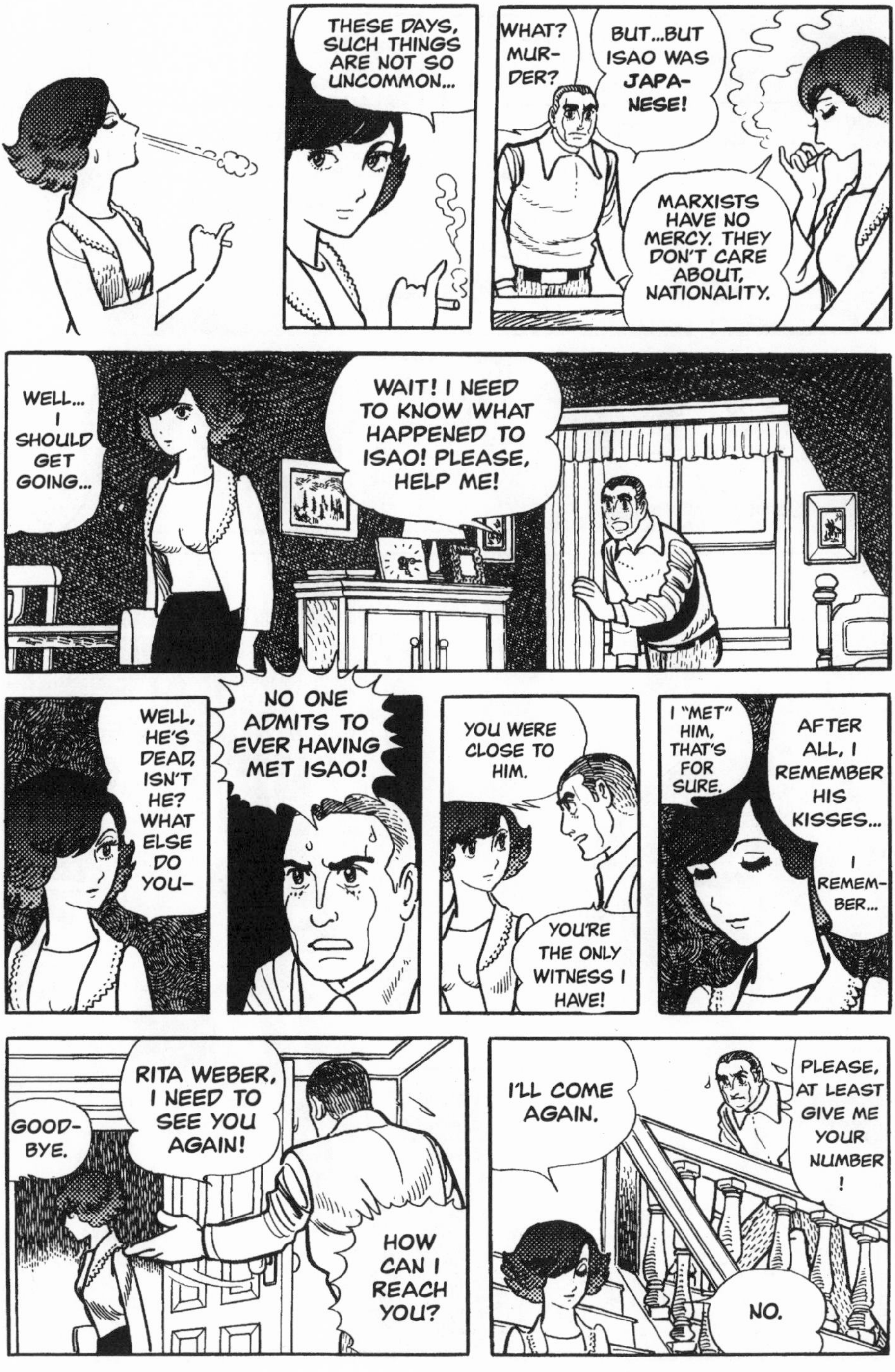
THESE DAYS, SUCH THINGS ARE NOT SO UNCOMMON...
WHAT? MUR-DER?
BUT...BUT ISAO WAS JAPA-NESE!
MARXISTS HAVE NO MERCY. THEY DON'T CARE ABOUT, NATIONALITY.
WELL... I SHOULD GET GOING...
WAIT! I NEED TO KNOW WHAT HAPPENED TO ISAO! PLEASE, HELP ME!
WELL, HE'S DEAD, ISN'T HE? WHAT ELSE DO YOU-
NO ONE ADMITS TO EVER HAVING MET ISAO!
YOU WERE CLOSE TO HIM.
YOU'RE THE ONLY WITNESS I HAVE!
I "MET" HIM, THAT'S FOR SURE.
AFTER ALL, I REMEMBER HIS KISSES...
I REMEM-BER...
GOOD-BYE.
RITA WEBER, I NEED TO SEE YOU AGAIN!
HOW CAN I REACH YOU?
I'LL COME AGAIN.
PLEASE, AT LEAST GIVE ME YOUR NUMBER!
NO.

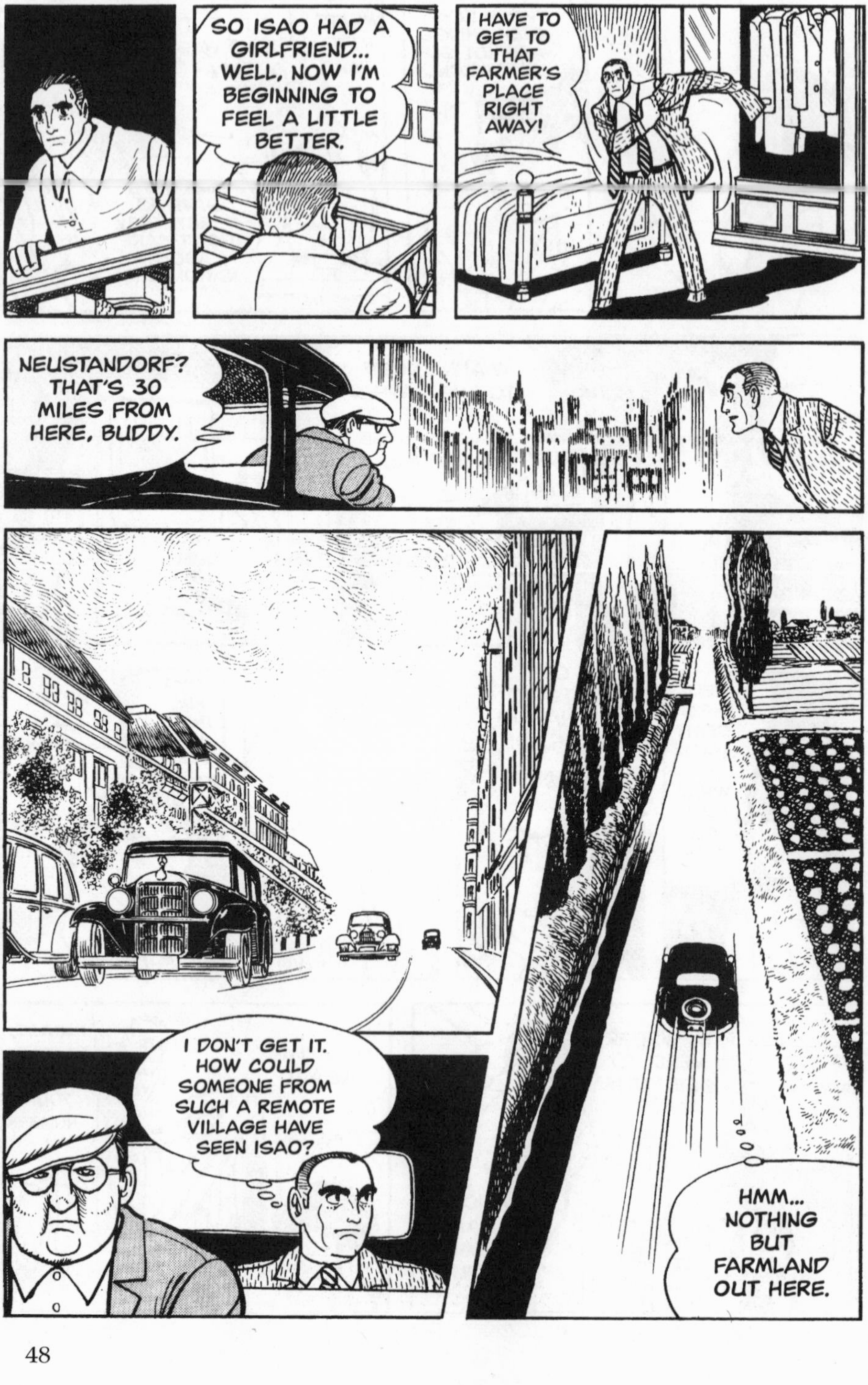
SO ISAO HAD A GIRLFRIEND... WELL, NOW I'M BEGINNING TO FEEL A LITTLE BETTER.
I HAVE TO GET TO THAT FARMER'S PLACE RIGHT AWAY!
NEUSTANDORF? THAT'S 30 MILES FROM HERE, BUDDY.
I DON'T GET IT. HOW COULD SOMEONE FROM SUCH A REMOTE VILLAGE HAVE SEEN ISAO?
HMM... NOTHING BUT FARMLAND OUT HERE.

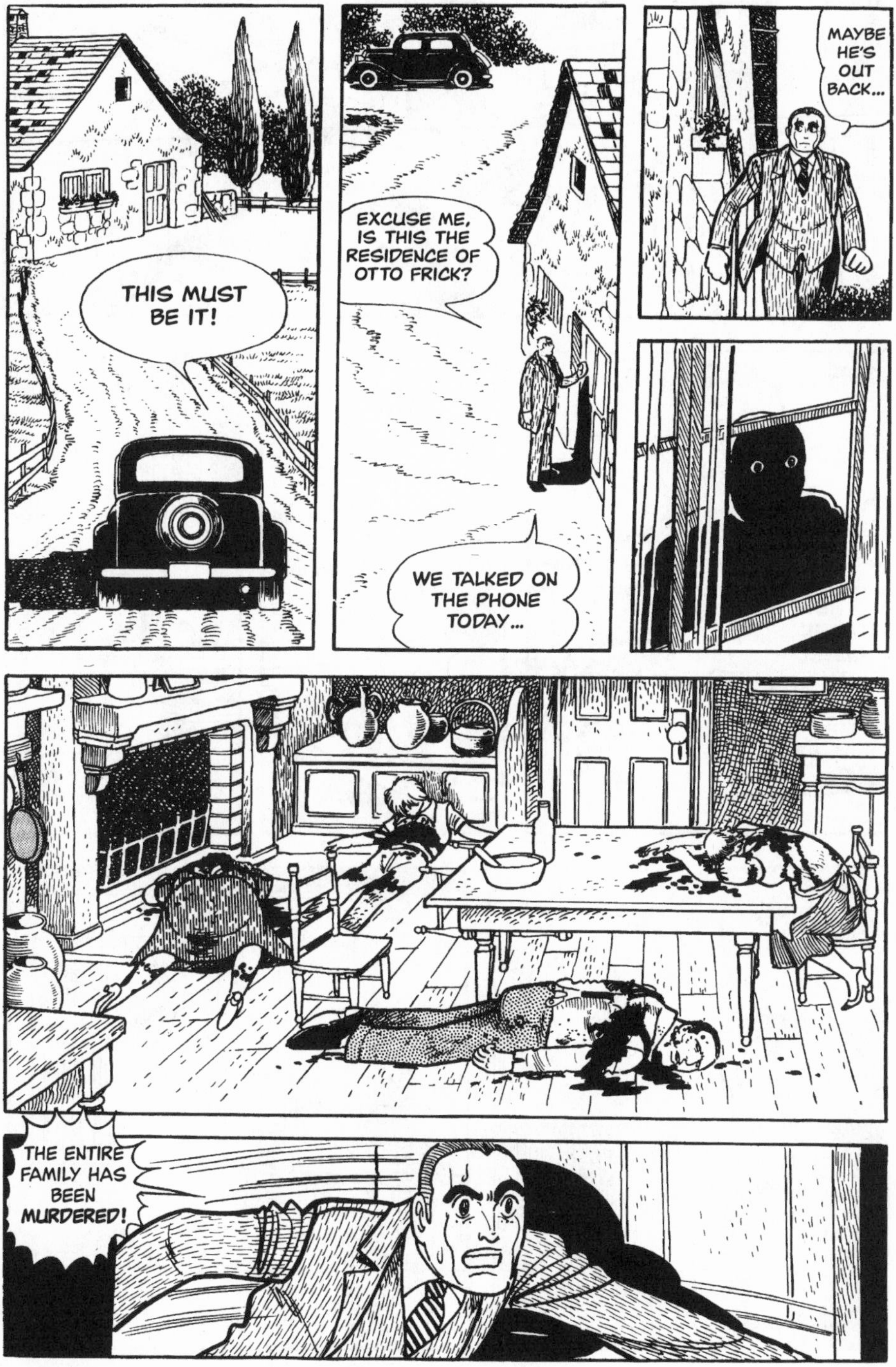
THIS MUST BE IT!
EXCUSE ME, IS THIS THE RESIDENCE OF OTTO FRICK?
WE TALKED ON THE PHONE TODAY...
MAYBE HE'S OUT BACK...
THE ENTIRE FAMILY HAS BEEN MURDERED!

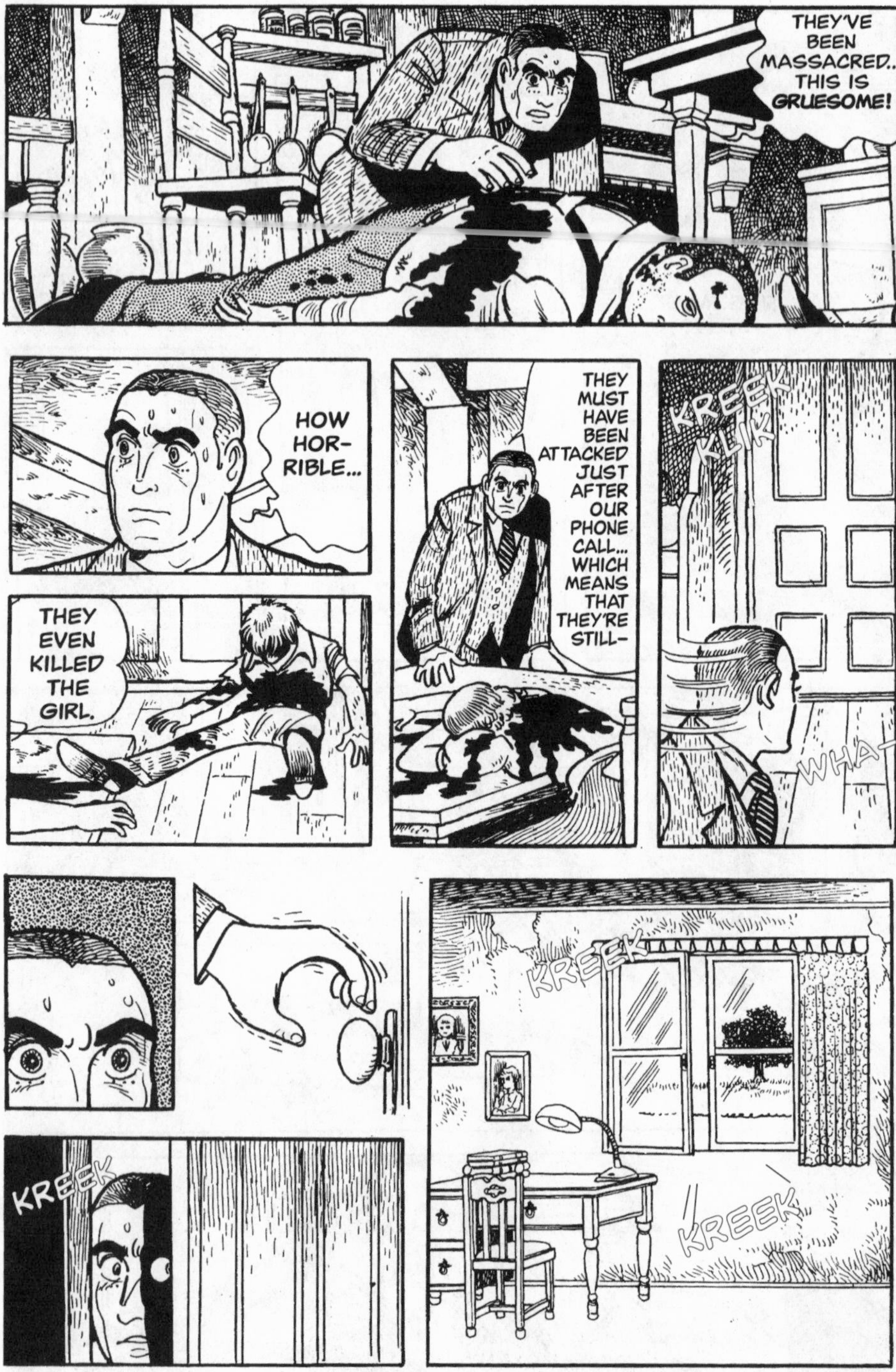
THEY'VE BEEN MASSACRED.. THIS IS GRUESOME!
HOW HOR-RIBLE...
THEY EVEN KILLED THE GIRL.
THEY MUST HAVE BEEN ATTACKED JUST AFTER OUR PHONE CALL... WHICH MEANS THAT THEY'RE STILL-
KREEK
KLIK
WHA-!?
KREEK
KREEK
KREEK

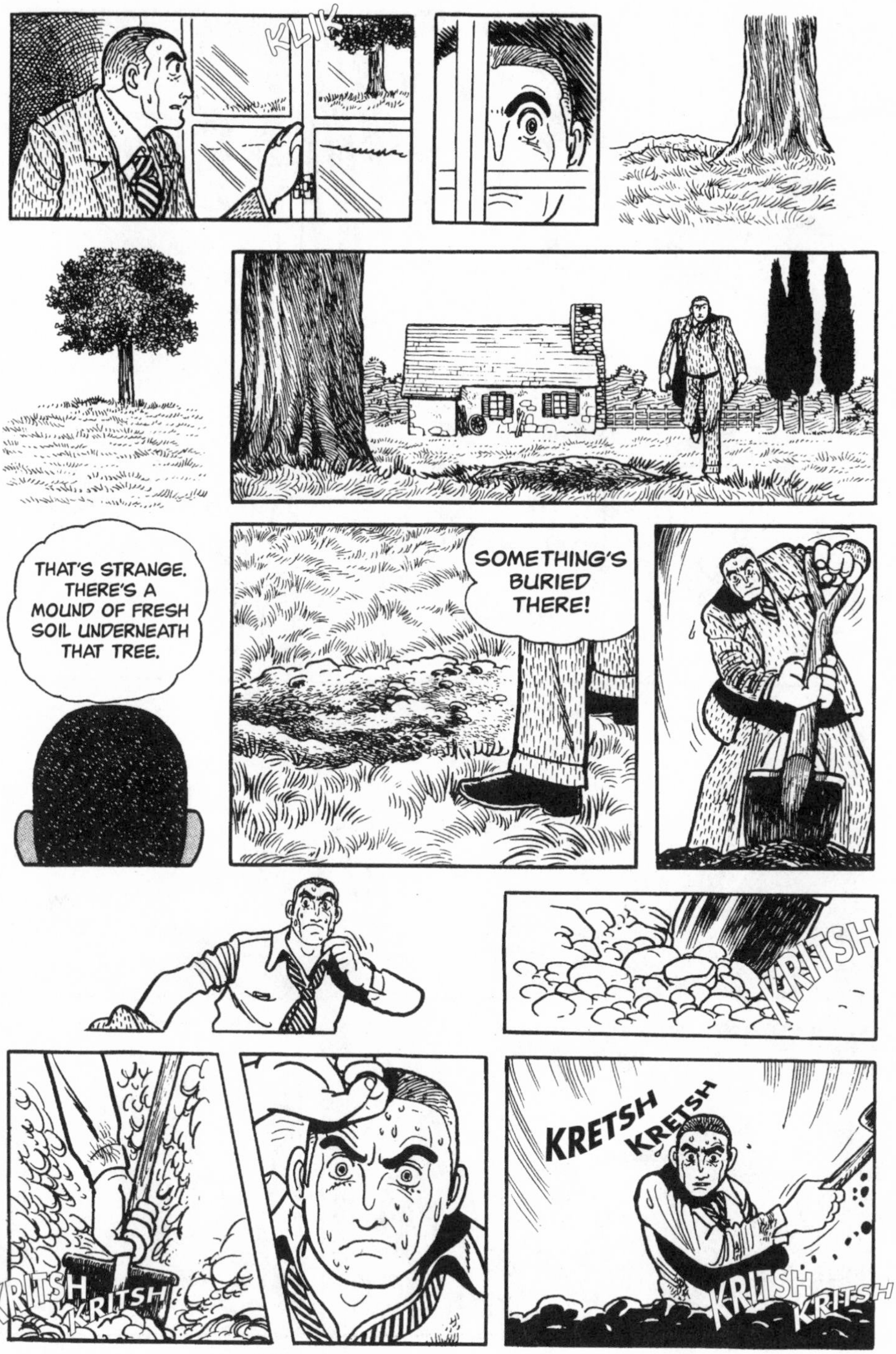
KLIK
THAT'S STRANGE. THERE'S A MOUND OF FRESH SOIL UNDERNEATH THAT TREE.
SOMETHING'S BURIED THERE!
KRITSH
KRITSH KRITSH
KRETSH KRETSH
KRITSH KRITSH

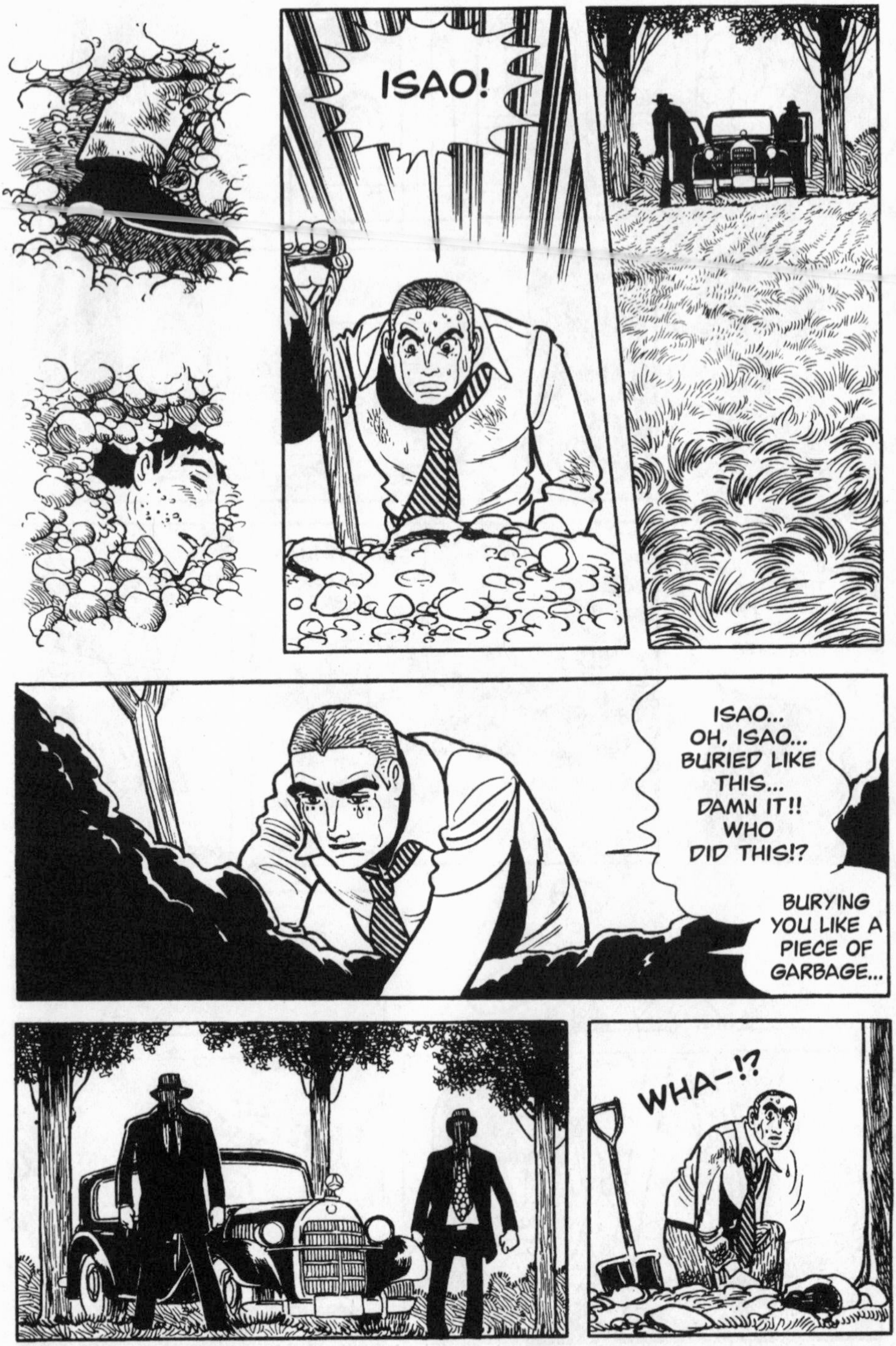
ISAO!
ISAO... OH, ISAO... BURIED LIKE THIS... DAMN IT!! WHO DID THIS!?
BURYING YOU LIKE A PIECE OF GARBAGE...
WHA-!?

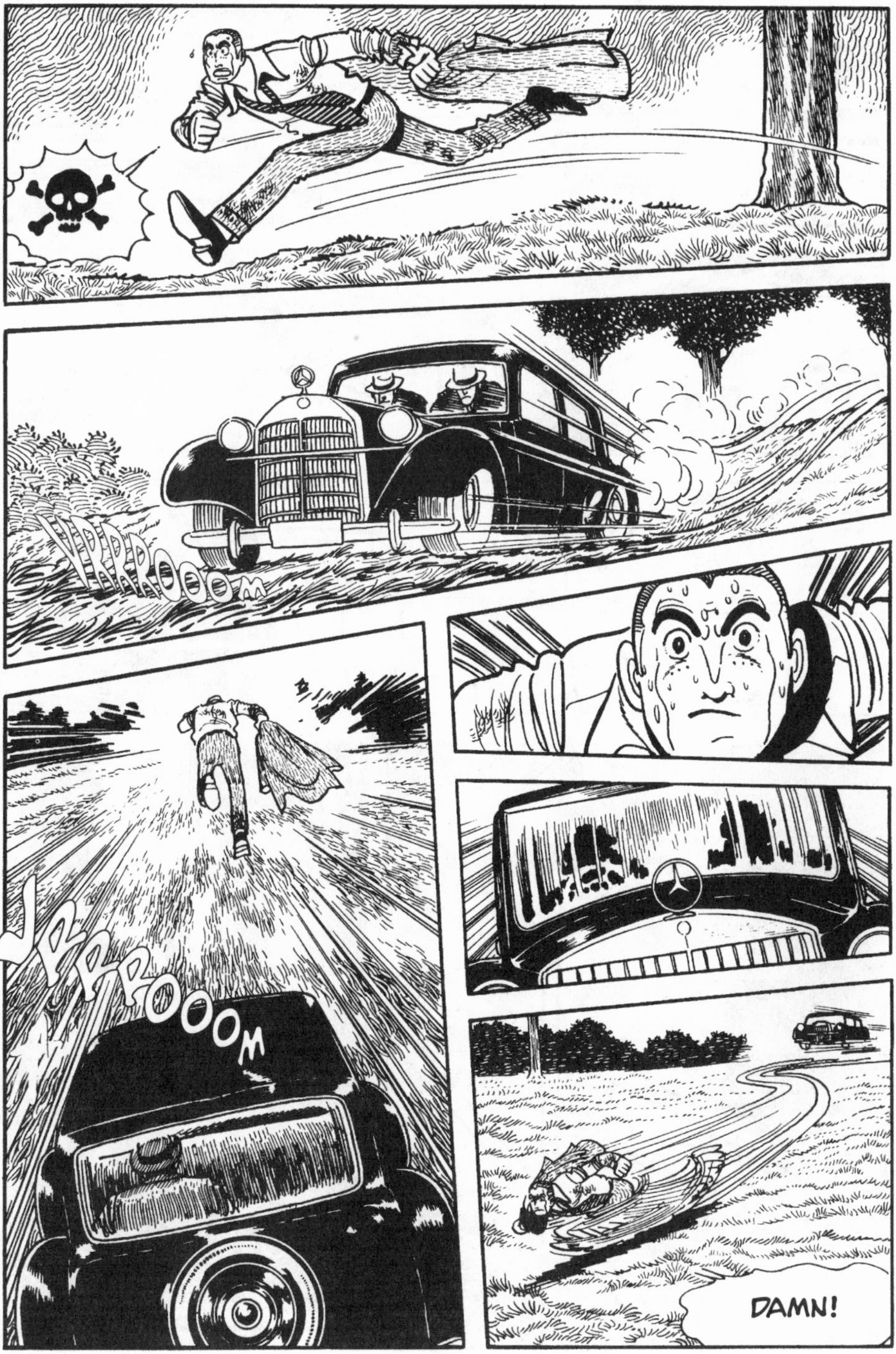
VRRRROOOOM
VRRROOOM
DAMN!

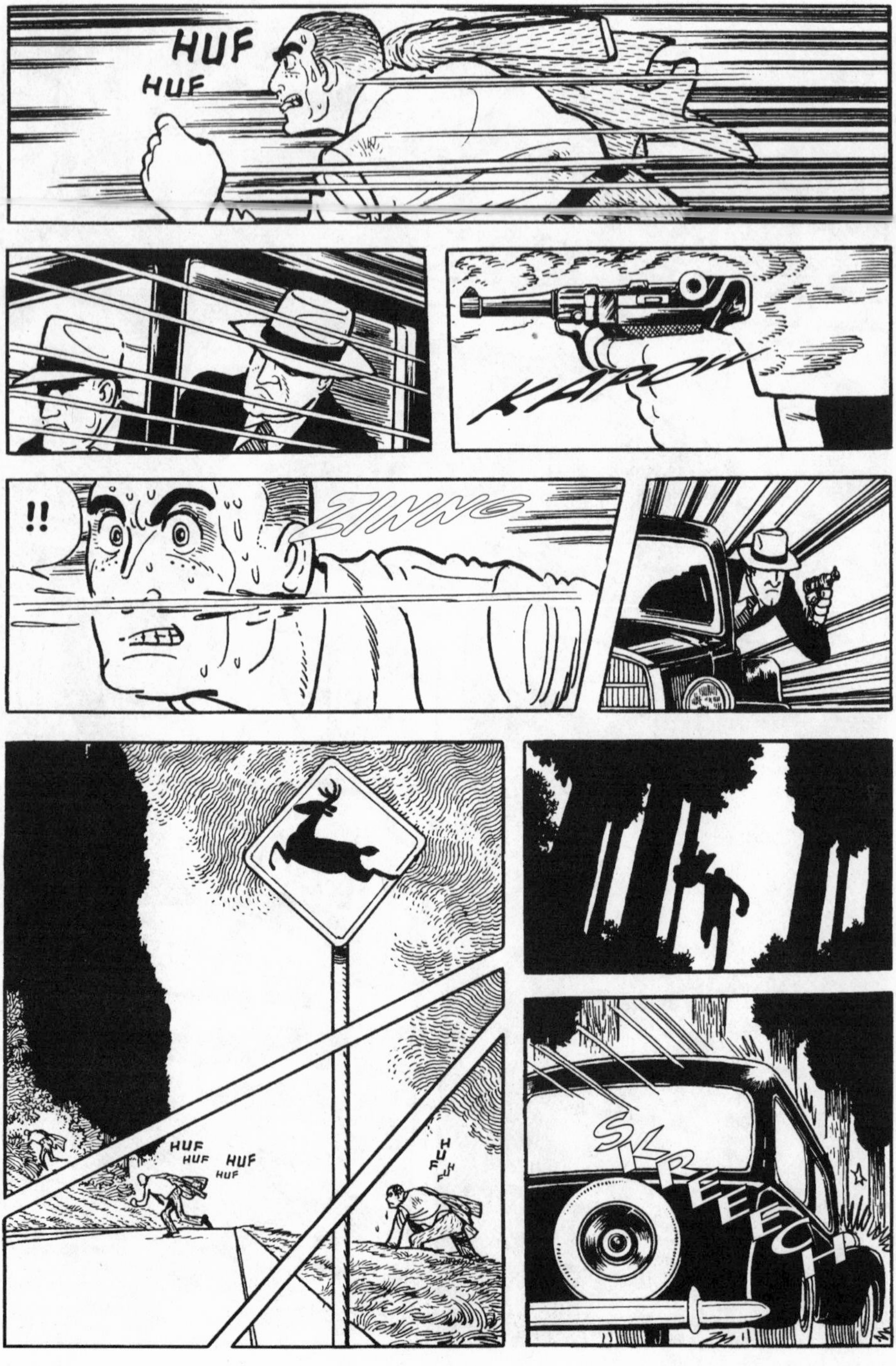
HUF
HUF
KAPOW
!!
ZINNG
HUF
HUF
HUF
HUF
SKREEECH

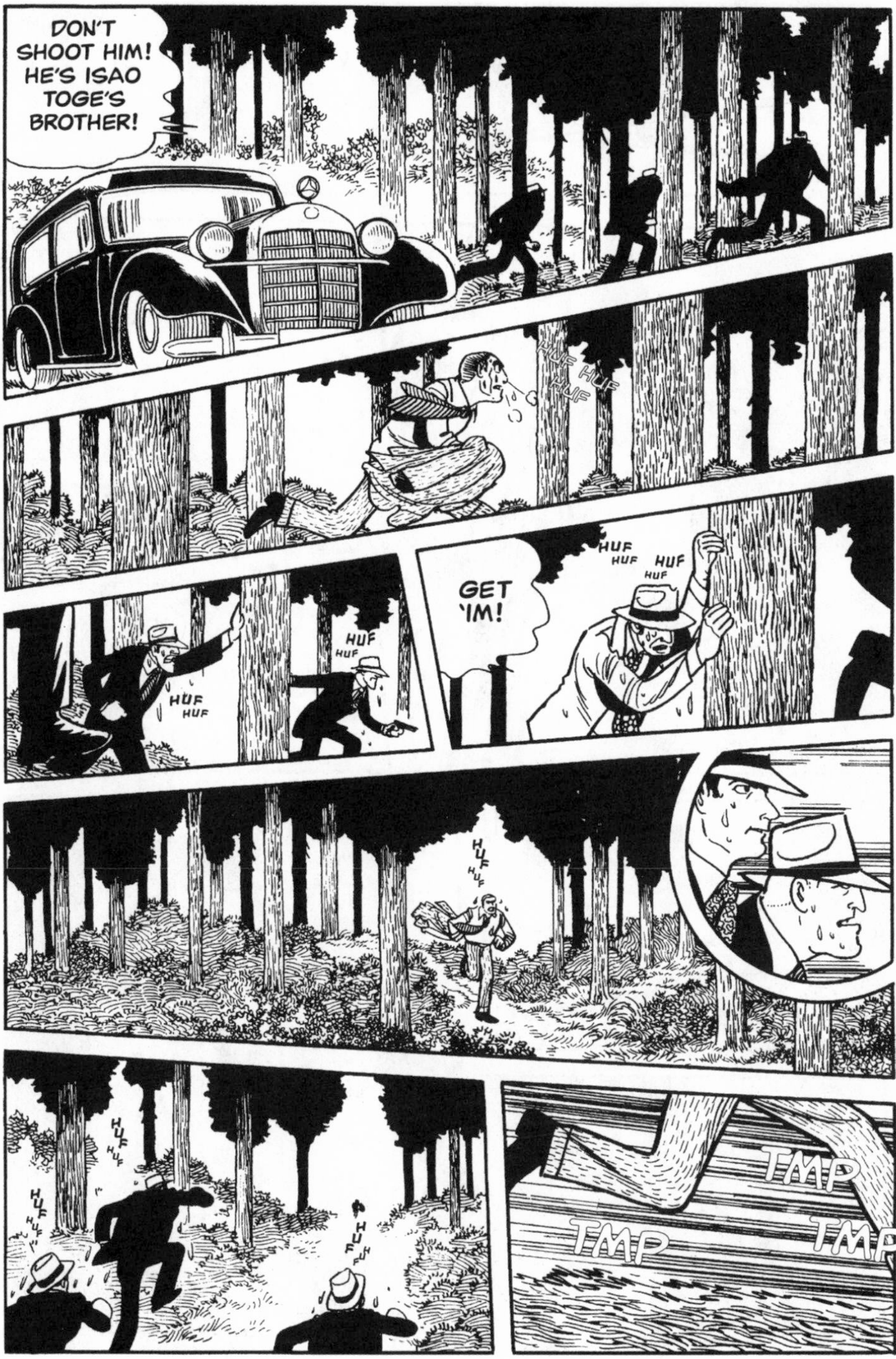
DON'T SHOOT HIM! HE'S ISAO TOGE'S BROTHER!
HUF HUF HUF
HUF HUF
HUF HUF
HUF HUF HUF HUF
GET 'IM!
HUF HUF
HUF HUF
HUF HUF
HUFUH
TMP
TMP
TMP

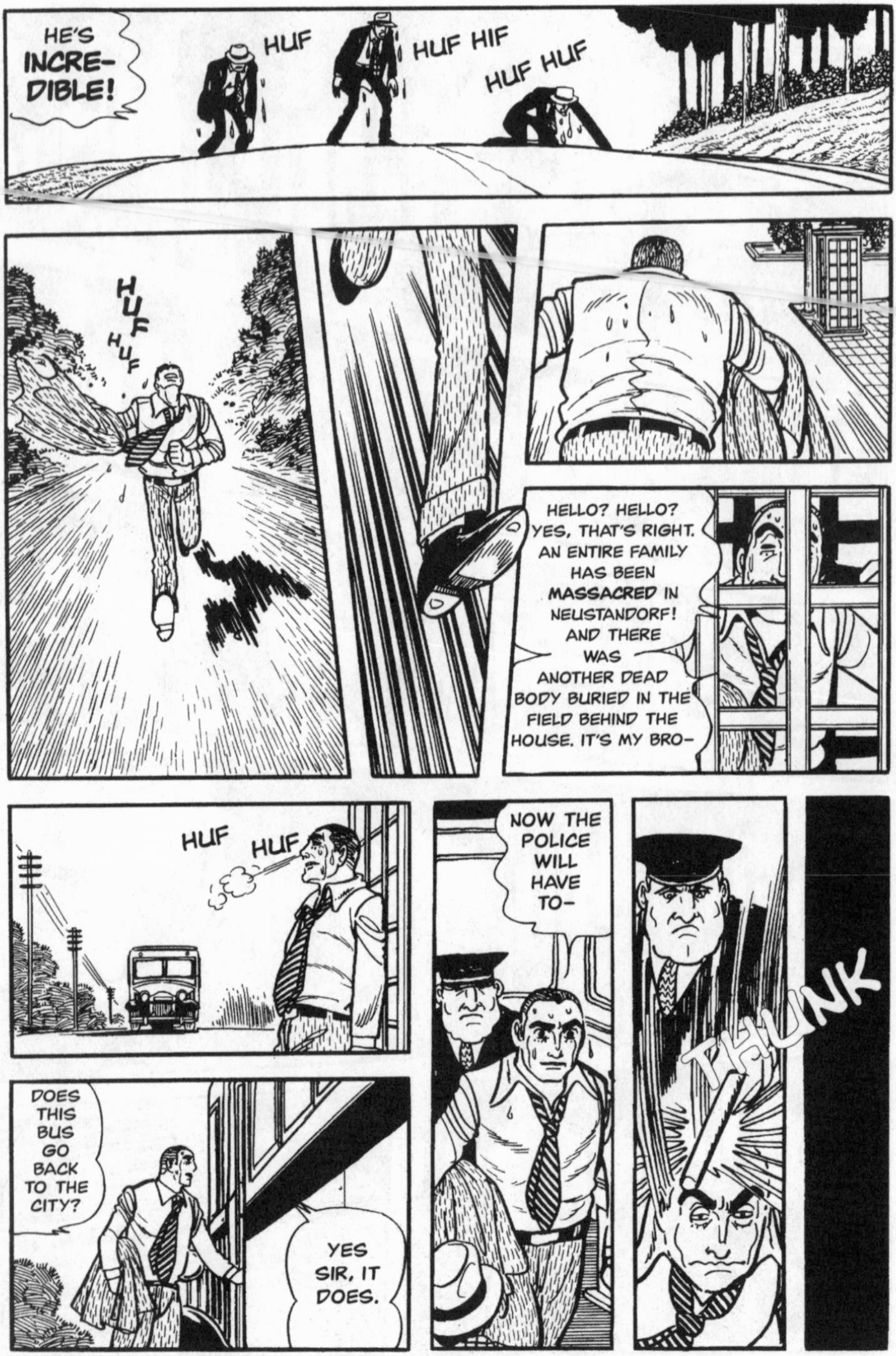
HE'S INCREDIBLE!
HUF
HUF HIF
HUF HUF
HUF HUF
HELLO? HELLO? YES, THAT'S RIGHT. AN ENTIRE FAMILY HAS BEEN MASSACRED IN NEUSTANDORF! AND THERE WAS ANOTHER DEAD BODY BURIED IN THE FIELD BEHIND THE HOUSE. IT'S MY BRO-
HUF
HUF
DOES THIS BUS GO BACK TO THE CITY?
YES SIR, IT DOES.
NOW THE POLICE WILL HAVE TO-
THUNK

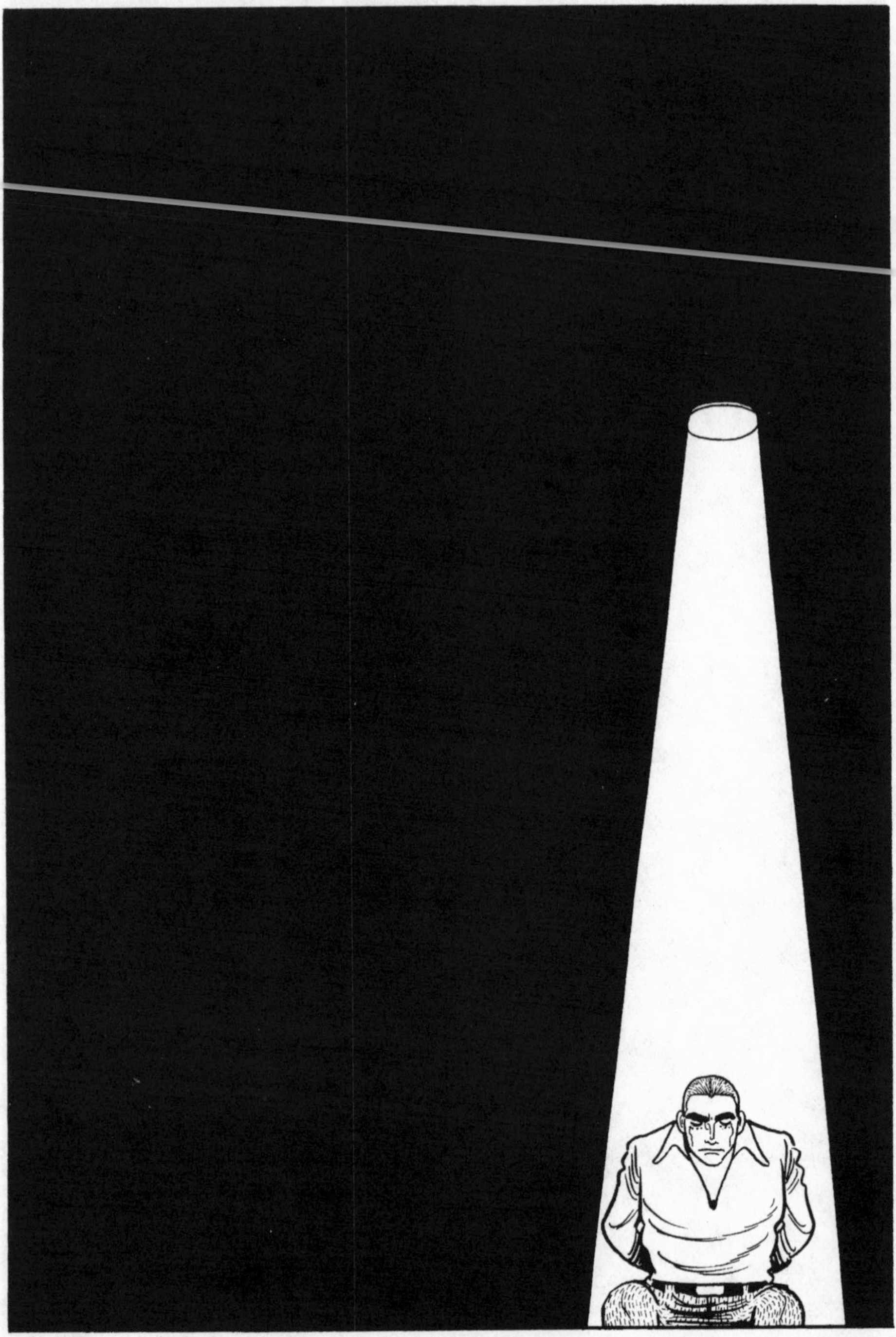

CHAPTER
TWO

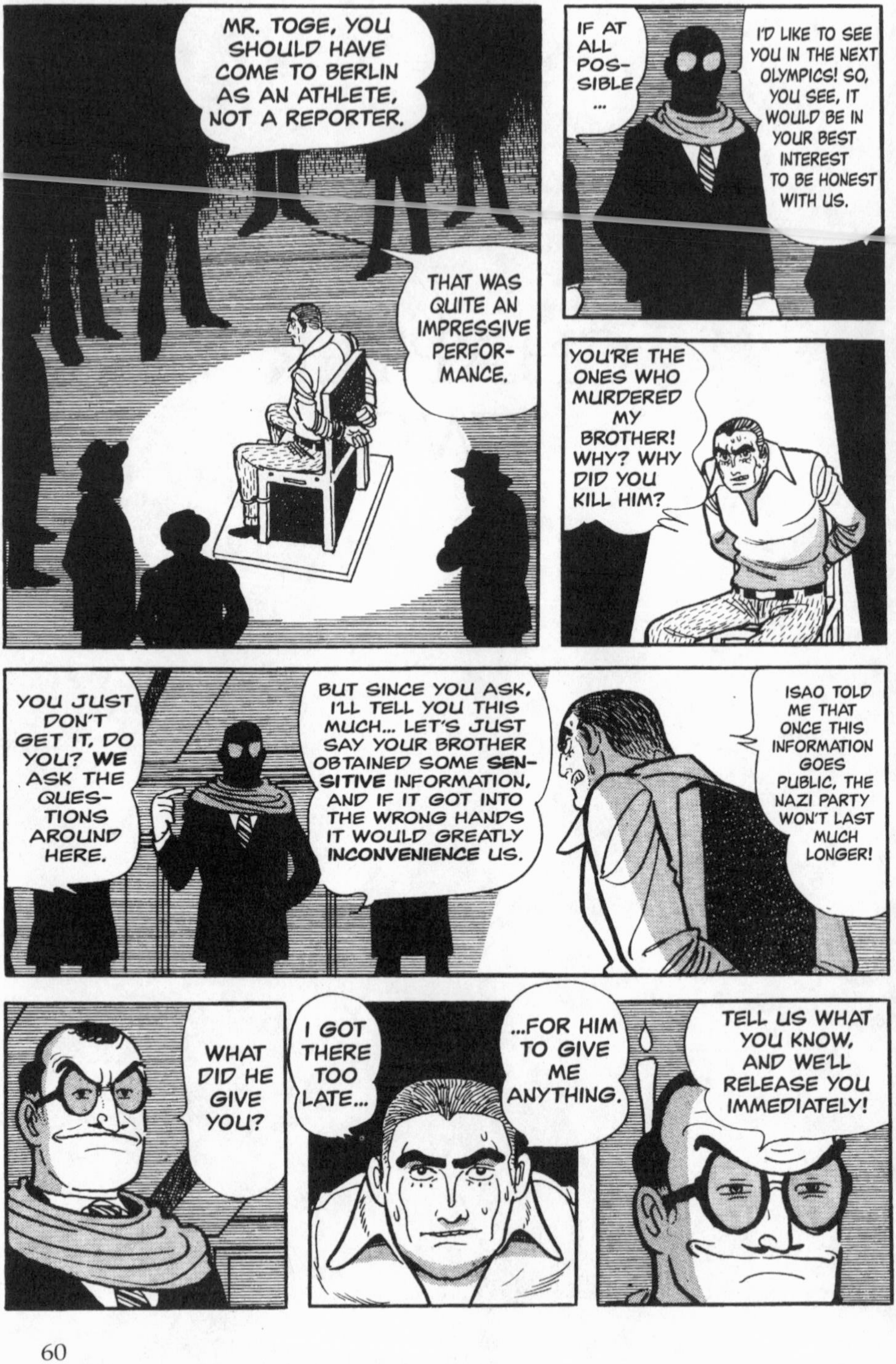
MR. TOGE, YOU SHOULD HAVE COME TO BERLIN AS AN ATHLETE, NOT A REPORTER.
THAT WAS QUITE AN IMPRESSIVE PERFOR-MANCE.
IF AT ALL POS-SIBLE ...
I'D LIKE TO SEE YOU IN THE NEXT OLYMPICS! SO, YOU SEE, IT WOULD BE IN YOUR BEST INTEREST TO BE HONEST WITH US.
YOU'RE THE ONES WHO MURDERED MY BROTHER! WHY? WHY DID YOU KILL HIM?
YOU JUST DON'T GET IT, DO YOU? WE ASK THE QUES-TIONS AROUND HERE.
BUT SINCE YOU ASK, I'LL TELL YOU THIS MUCH... LET'S JUST SAY YOUR BROTHER OBTAINED SOME SEN-SITIVE INFORMATION, AND IF IT GOT INTO THE WRONG HANDS IT WOULD GREATLY INCONVENIENCE US.
ISAO TOLD ME THAT ONCE THIS INFORMATION GOES PUBLIC, THE NAZI PARTY WON'T LAST MUCH LONGER!
WHAT DID HE GIVE YOU?
I GOT THERE TOO LATE...
...FOR HIM TO GIVE ME ANYTHING.
TELL US WHAT YOU KNOW, AND WE'LL RELEASE YOU IMMEDIATELY!

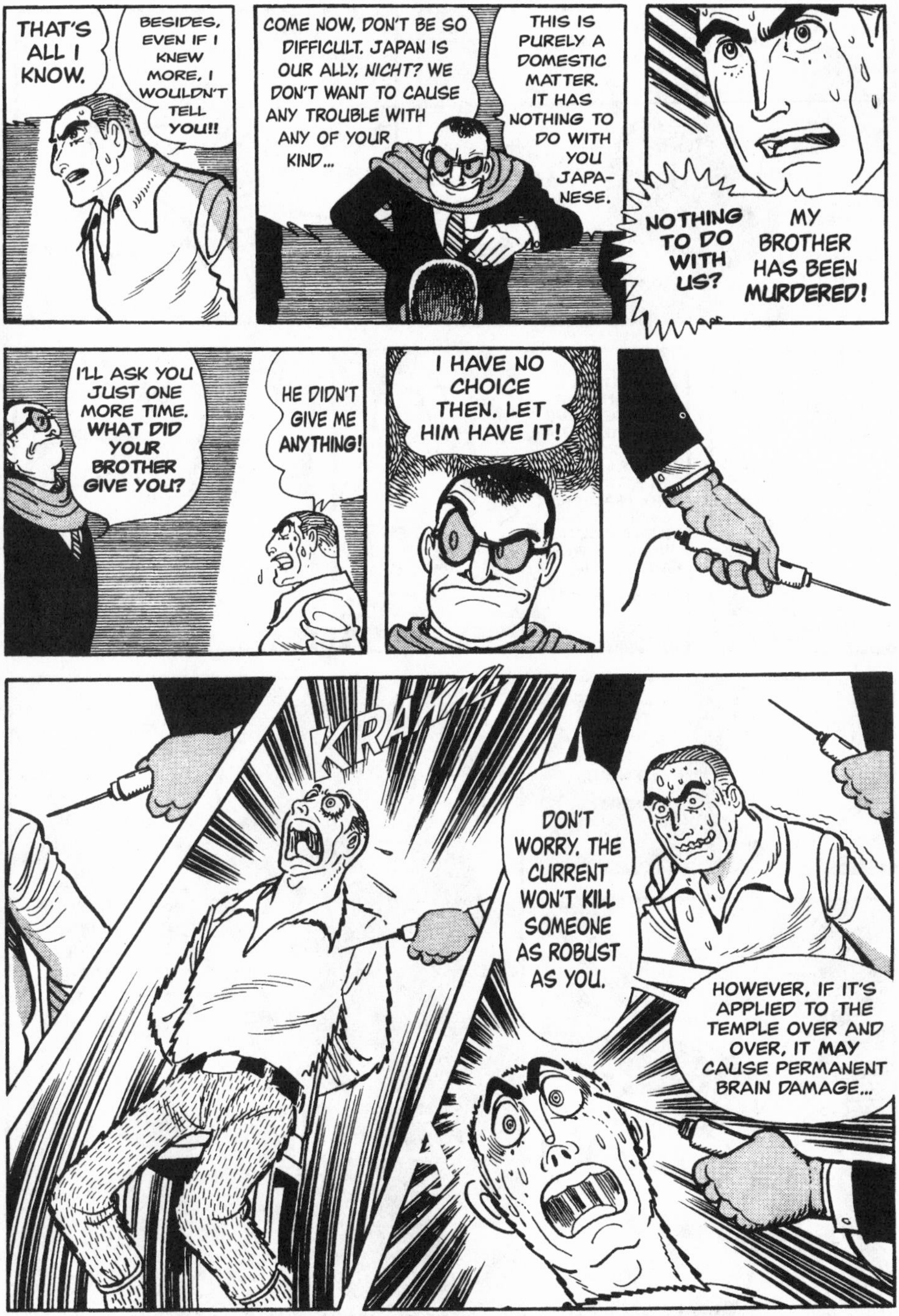
THAT'S ALL I KNOW.
BESIDES, EVEN IF I KNEW MORE, I WOULDN'T TELL YOU!!
COME NOW, DON'T BE SO DIFFICULT. JAPAN IS OUR ALLY, NICHT? WE DON'T WANT TO CAUSE ANY TROUBLE WITH ANY OF YOUR KIND...
THIS IS PURELY A DOMESTIC MATTER. IT HAS NOTHING TO DO WITH YOU JAPANESE.
NOTHING TO DO WITH US?
MY BROTHER HAS BEEN MURDERED!
I'LL ASK YOU JUST ONE MORE TIME. WHAT DID YOUR BROTHER GIVE YOU?
HE DIDN'T GIVE ME ANYTHING!
I HAVE NO CHOICE THEN. LET HIM HAVE IT!
KRAKKK
DON'T WORRY. THE CURRENT WON'T KILL SOMEONE AS ROBUST AS YOU.
HOWEVER, IF IT'S APPLIED TO THE TEMPLE OVER AND OVER, IT MAY CAUSE PERMANENT BRAIN DAMAGE...

Adolf

YOU'RE A GOOD MAN.

NOW BE GOOD TO YOURSELF AND YOU'LL GO BACK TO JAPAN!

TELL ME... WHAT DID YOU GET FROM YOUR BROTHER!?

...
...

OUCH.

WASS?

AT FIRST IT'S QUITE A "SHOCK"... BUT... YOU SEE... I'VE ALWAYS HAD A STRONG TOLERANCE TO ELECTRICITY... WHY, ISAO AND I USED TO PLAY "ELECTROCUTION" WHEN WE WERE KIDS. HA, HA, HA.

ALL RIGHT, THEN. DOUBLE THE CURRENT.

AAARGH!

STUBBORN BASTARD. WE'VE BEEN AT THIS FOR HALF AN HOUR AND HE STILL WON'T ...

HE'S SINGING SOME ODD SONG!

...FROM THE CAPITAL... DUE NORTH... IN THE FOREST OF WASEDA...

DOUBLE THE CURRENT AGAIN!

THAT WOULD BE TOO DANGEROUS.

IF WE DESTROY HIS CEREBRUM, HE WON'T BE ABLE TO TELL US ANYTHING.

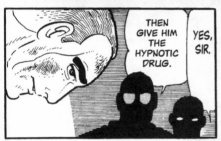

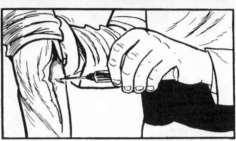

THEN GIVE HIM THE HYPNOTIC DRUG.

YES, SIR.

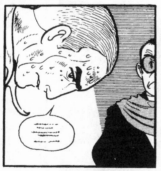

I CAN'T HEAR HIM.

HIS HEARTBEAT IS FAINT AND IRREGULAR. IF WE DON'T LET HIM REST, THERE'S A GOOD CHANCE HE'LL DIE.

IT'S NO WONDER—SHOOTING ALL THAT SCOPOLAMINE INTO HIM AFTER THIS SHOCK TREATMENT!

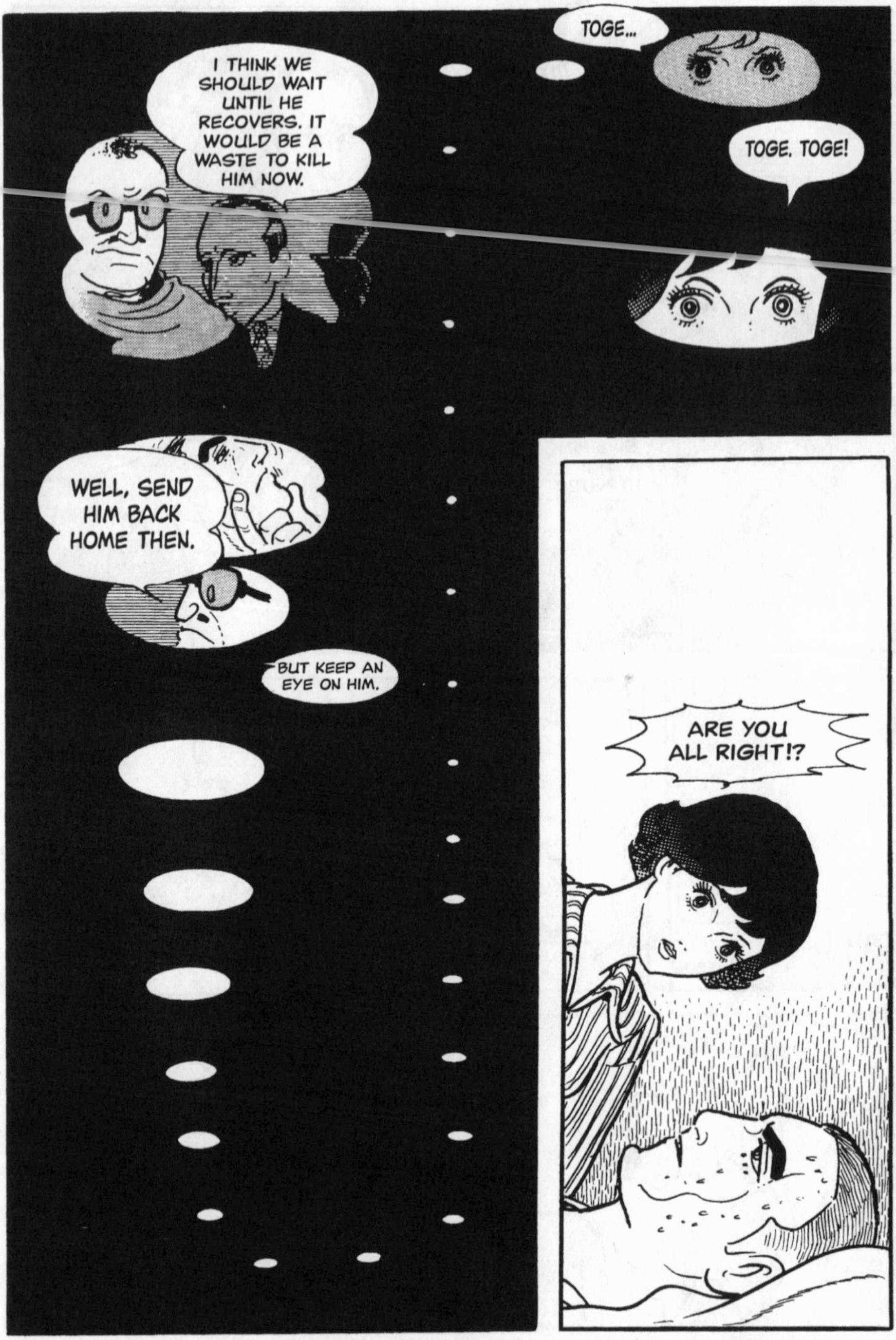
I THINK WE SHOULD WAIT UNTIL HE RECOVERS. IT WOULD BE A WASTE TO KILL HIM NOW.
TOGE...
TOGE. TOGE!
WELL, SEND HIM BACK HOME THEN.
BUT KEEP AN EYE ON HIM.
ARE YOU ALL RIGHT!?

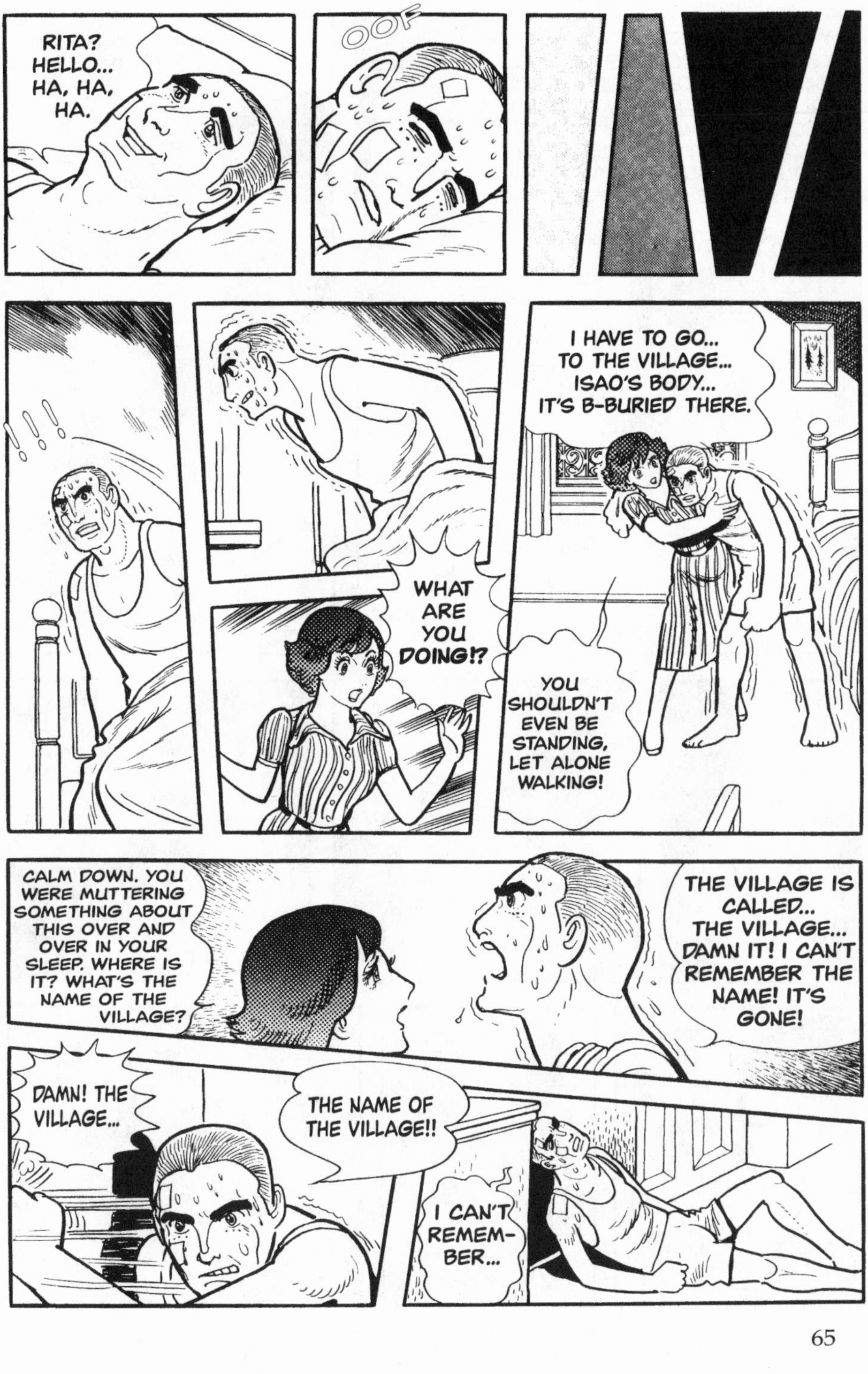
RITA? HELLO... HA, HA, HA.
OOF
!!!
I HAVE TO GO... TO THE VILLAGE... ISAO'S BODY... IT'S B-BURIED THERE.
WHAT ARE YOU DOING!?
YOU SHOULDN'T EVEN BE STANDING, LET ALONE WALKING!
CALM DOWN. YOU WERE MUTTERING SOMETHING ABOUT THIS OVER AND OVER IN YOUR SLEEP. WHERE IS IT? WHAT'S THE NAME OF THE VILLAGE?
THE VILLAGE IS CALLED... THE VILLAGE... DAMN IT! I CAN'T REMEMBER THE NAME! IT'S GONE!
DAMN! THE VILLAGE...
THE NAME OF THE VILLAGE!!
I CAN'T REMEM-BER...

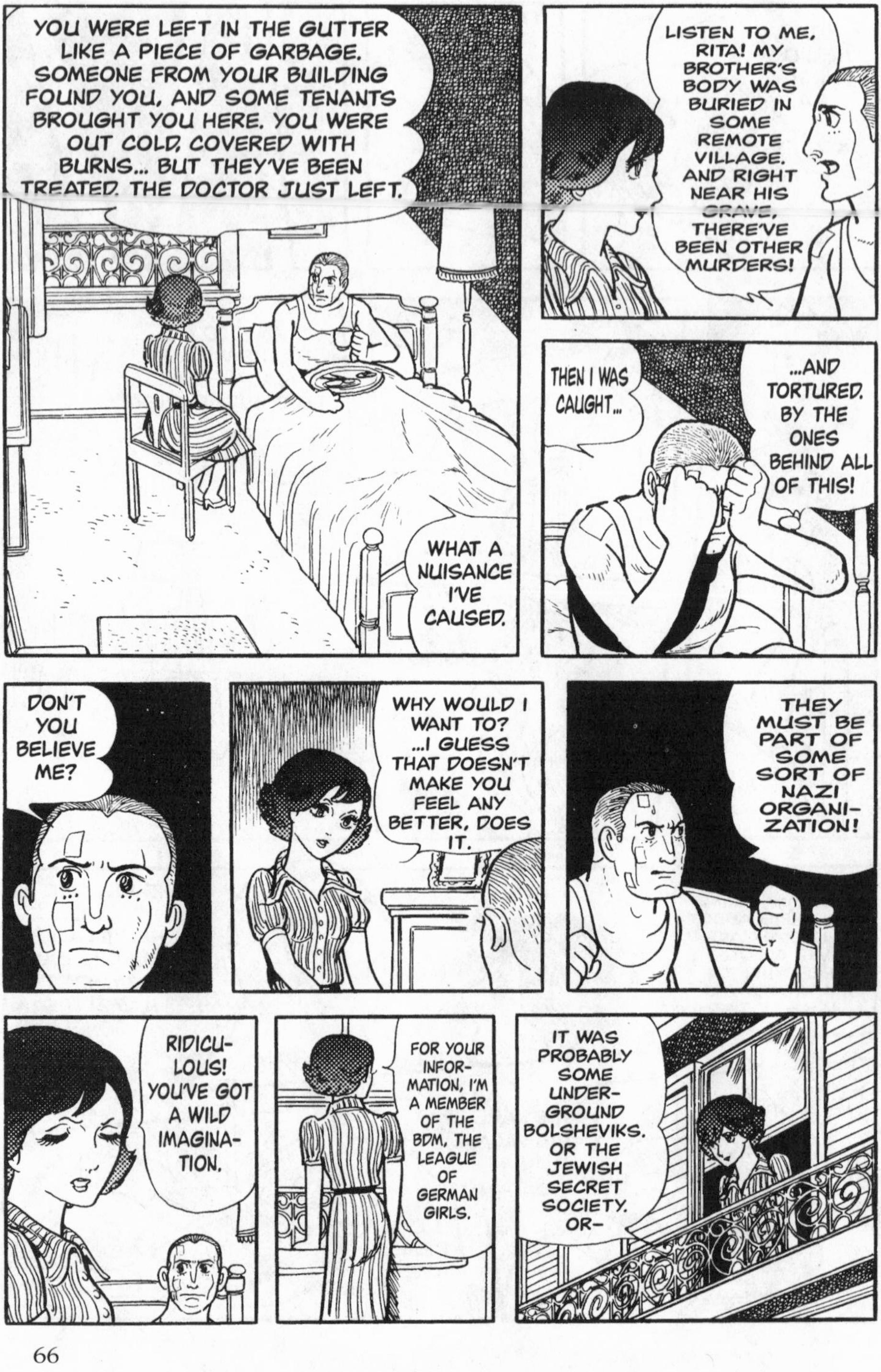
YOU WERE LEFT IN THE GUTTER LIKE A PIECE OF GARBAGE. SOMEONE FROM YOUR BUILDING FOUND YOU, AND SOME TENANTS BROUGHT YOU HERE. YOU WERE OUT COLD, COVERED WITH BURNS... BUT THEY'VE BEEN TREATED. THE DOCTOR JUST LEFT.
WHAT A NUISANCE I'VE CAUSED.
LISTEN TO ME, RITA! MY BROTHER'S BODY WAS BURIED IN SOME REMOTE VILLAGE. AND RIGHT NEAR HIS GRAVE, THERE'VE BEEN OTHER MURDERS!
THEN I WAS CAUGHT...
...AND TORTURED. BY THE ONES BEHIND ALL OF THIS!
DON'T YOU BELIEVE ME?
WHY WOULD I WANT TO? ...I GUESS THAT DOESN'T MAKE YOU FEEL ANY BETTER, DOES IT.
THEY MUST BE PART OF SOME SORT OF NAZI ORGANI-ZATION!
RIDICU-LOUS! YOU'VE GOT A WILD IMAGINA-TION.
FOR YOUR INFOR-MATION, I'M A MEMBER OF THE BDM, THE LEAGUE OF GERMAN GIRLS.
IT WAS PROBABLY SOME UNDER-GROUND BOLSHEVIKS. OR THE JEWISH SECRET SOCIETY. OR-

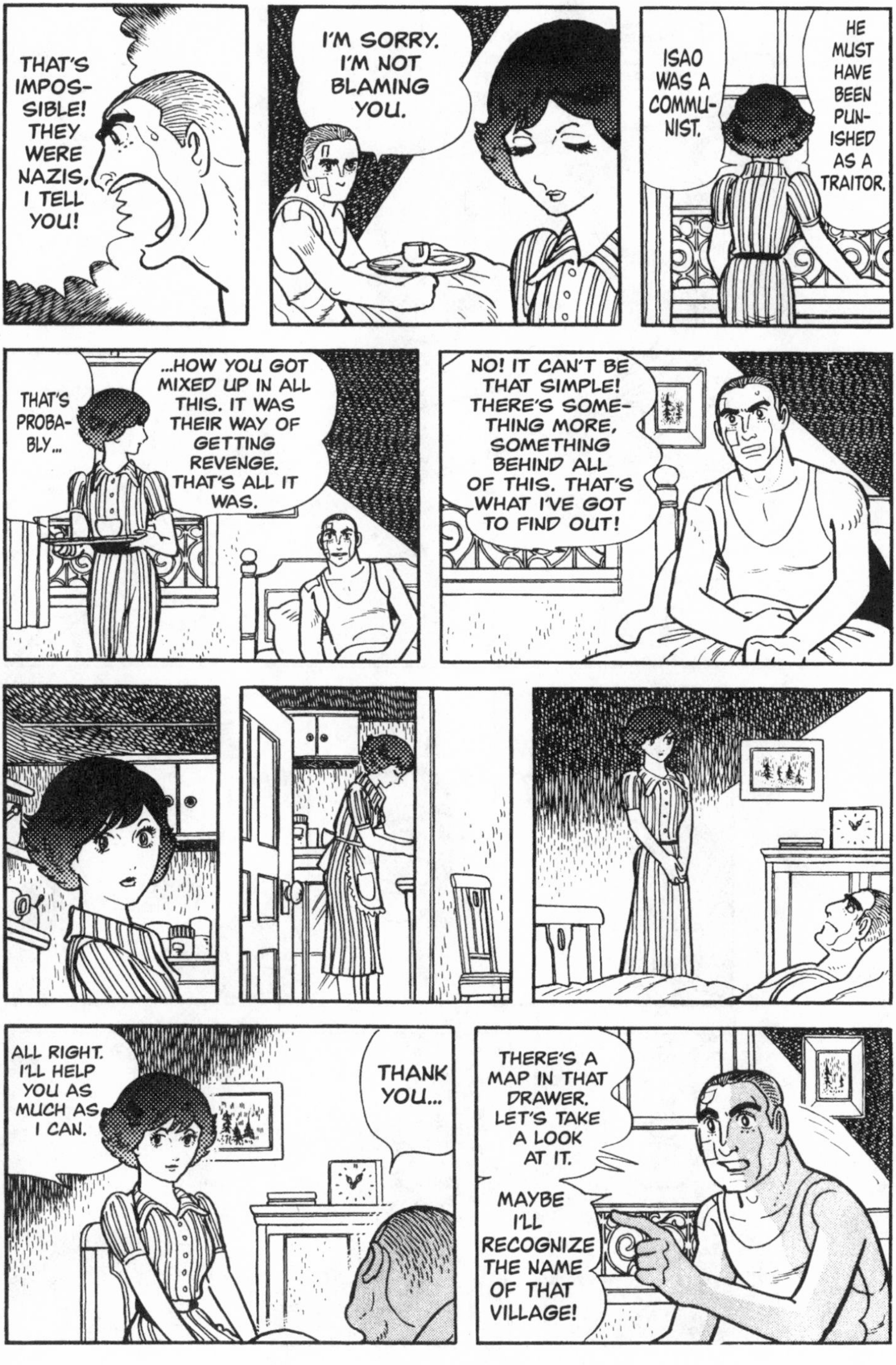
THAT'S IMPOS-SIBLE! THEY WERE NAZIS, I TELL YOU!
I'M SORRY. I'M NOT BLAMING YOU.
ISAO WAS A COMMU-NIST.
HE MUST HAVE BEEN PUN-ISHED AS A TRAITOR.
THAT'S PROBA-BLY...
...HOW YOU GOT MIXED UP IN ALL THIS. IT WAS THEIR WAY OF GETTING REVENGE. THAT'S ALL IT WAS.
NO! IT CAN'T BE THAT SIMPLE! THERE'S SOME-THING MORE, SOMETHING BEHIND ALL OF THIS. THAT'S WHAT I'VE GOT TO FIND OUT!
ALL RIGHT. I'LL HELP YOU AS MUCH AS I CAN.
THANK YOU...
THERE'S A MAP IN THAT DRAWER. LET'S TAKE A LOOK AT IT.
MAYBE I'LL RECOGNIZE THE NAME OF THAT VILLAGE!

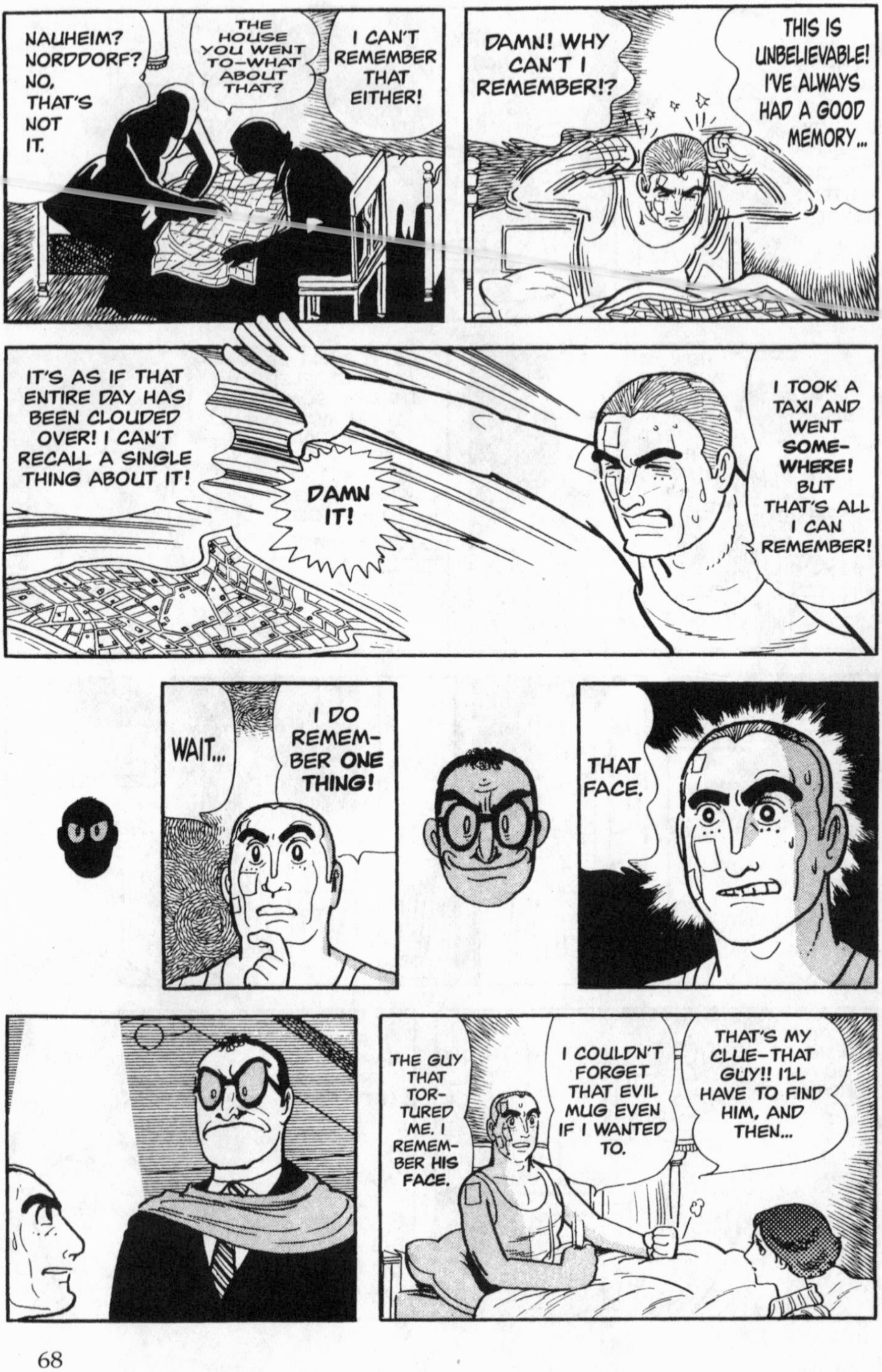
NAUHEIM? NORDDORF? NO, THAT'S NOT IT.
THE HOUSE YOU WENT TO—WHAT ABOUT THAT?
I CAN'T REMEMBER THAT EITHER!
DAMN! WHY CAN'T I REMEMBER!?
THIS IS UNBELIEVABLE! I'VE ALWAYS HAD A GOOD MEMORY...
IT'S AS IF THAT ENTIRE DAY HAS BEEN CLOUDED OVER! I CAN'T RECALL A SINGLE THING ABOUT IT!
DAMN IT!
I TOOK A TAXI AND WENT SOME-WHERE! BUT THAT'S ALL I CAN REMEMBER!
WAIT...
I DO REMEM-BER ONE THING!
THAT FACE.
THE GUY THAT TOR-TURED ME. I REMEM-BER HIS FACE.
I COULDN'T FORGET THAT EVIL MUG EVEN IF I WANTED TO.
THAT'S MY CLUE—THAT GUY!! I'LL HAVE TO FIND HIM, AND THEN...

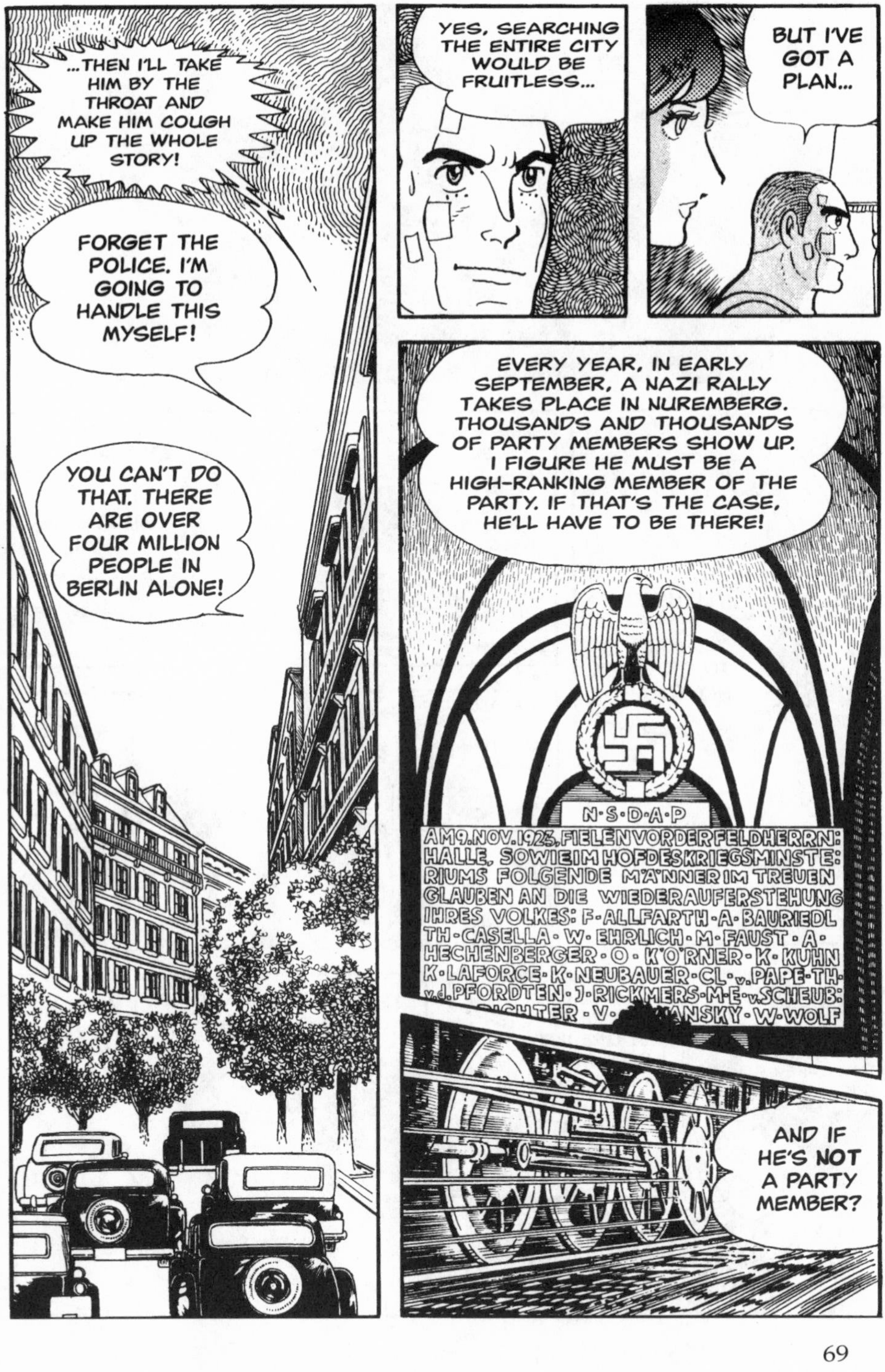
...THEN I'LL TAKE HIM BY THE THROAT AND MAKE HIM COUGH UP THE WHOLE STORY!
FORGET THE POLICE. I'M GOING TO HANDLE THIS MYSELF!
YOU CAN'T DO THAT. THERE ARE OVER FOUR MILLION PEOPLE IN BERLIN ALONE!
YES, SEARCHING THE ENTIRE CITY WOULD BE FRUITLESS...
BUT I'VE GOT A PLAN...
EVERY YEAR, IN EARLY SEPTEMBER, A NAZI RALLY TAKES PLACE IN NUREMBERG. THOUSANDS AND THOUSANDS OF PARTY MEMBERS SHOW UP. I FIGURE HE MUST BE A HIGH-RANKING MEMBER OF THE PARTY. IF THAT'S THE CASE, HE'LL HAVE TO BE THERE!
N·S·D·A·P
AM 9. NOV. 1923, FIELEN VOR DER FELDHERRN: HALLE, SOWIE IM HOF DES KRIEGSMINSTE: RIUMS FOLGENDE MÄNNER IM TREUEN GLAUBEN AN DIE WIEDERAUFERSTEHUNG IHRES VOLKES: F·ALLFARTH·A·BAURIEDL TH·CASELLA·W·EHRLICH·M·FAUST·A· HECHENBERGER·O·KÖRNER·K·KUHN K·LAFORCE·K·NEUBAUER·CL·v.PAPE·TH· v.d.PFORDTEN·J·RICKMERS·M·E·v.SCHEUB:
AND IF HE'S NOT A PARTY MEMBER?

Adolf

THEN...

KLAKKETA KLAKKETA

I'LL USE MYSELF AS BAIT TO DRAW HIM OUT!

THAT'S TOO DANGEROUS. YOU KNOW WHAT THEY'LL DO TO YOU...

EITHER THEY GET ME, OR I GET THEM. IT'S AS SIMPLE AS THAT.

IT'S ALL SO... SO RUTHLESS.

YOU'RE SURPRISED?

NO, BUT...

I JUST WONDER IF... IF ALL ASIANS ARE LIKE THIS.

IF I WERE YOU, I WOULD HAVE THE AUTHORITIES TAKE CARE OF THIS.

THAT'S BECAUSE YOU'RE NOT PERSONALLY INVOLVED.

THAT'S NOT TRUE!

I WAS IN LOVE WITH ISAO!!

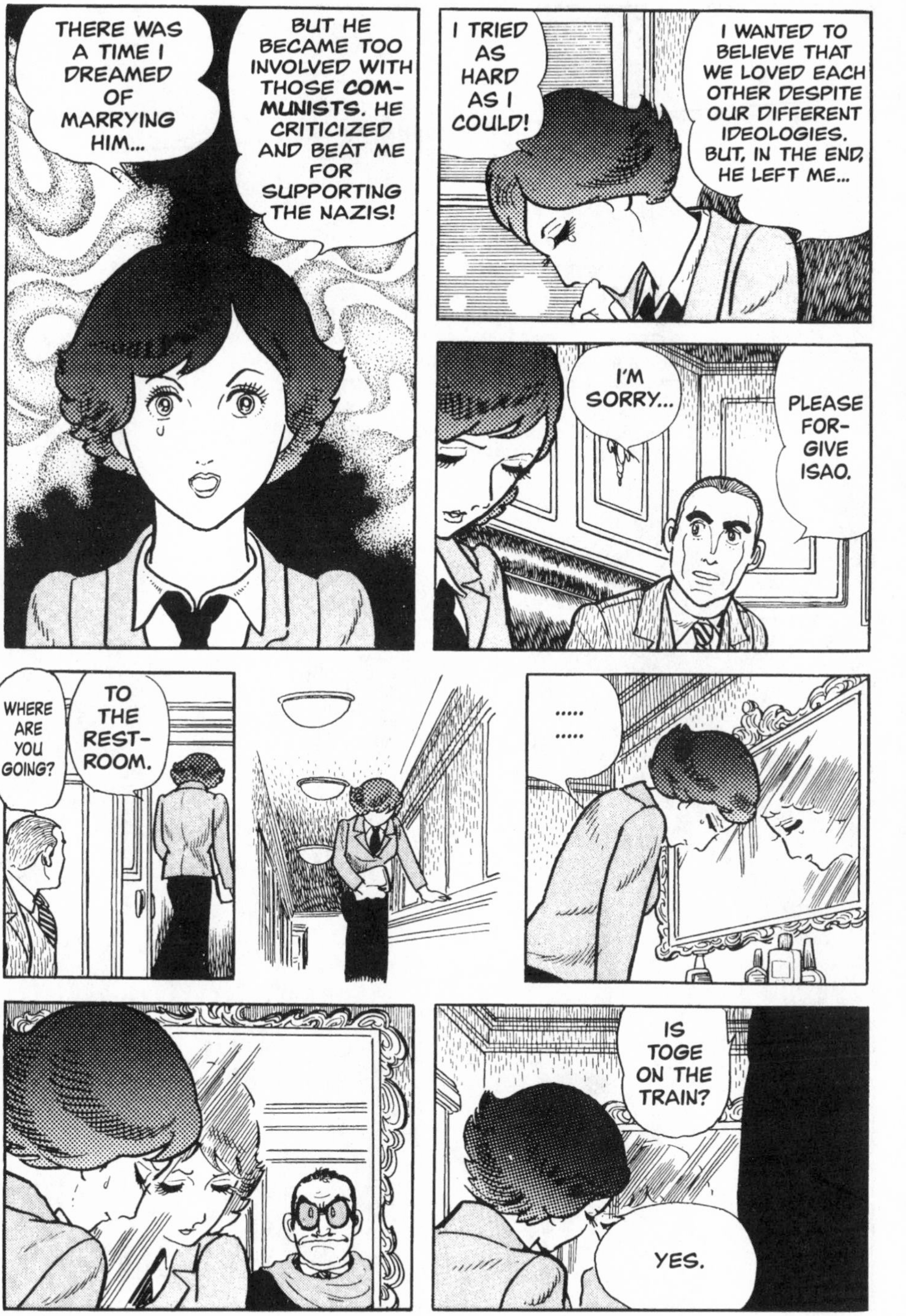
THERE WAS A TIME I DREAMED OF MARRYING HIM...
BUT HE BECAME TOO INVOLVED WITH THOSE COMMUNISTS. HE CRITICIZED AND BEAT ME FOR SUPPORTING THE NAZIS!
I TRIED AS HARD AS I COULD!
I WANTED TO BELIEVE THAT WE LOVED EACH OTHER DESPITE OUR DIFFERENT IDEOLOGIES. BUT, IN THE END, HE LEFT ME...
I'M SORRY...
PLEASE FORGIVE ISAO.
WHERE ARE YOU GOING?
TO THE RESTROOM.
....
IS TOGE ON THE TRAIN?
YES.

Adolf

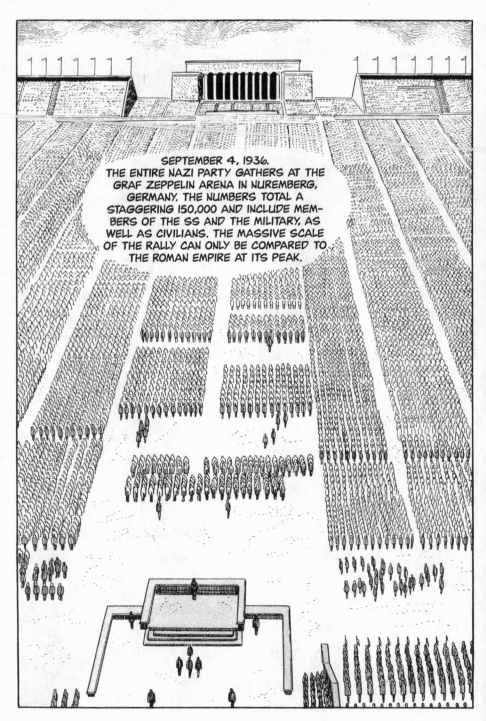

SEPTEMBER 4, 1936.
THE ENTIRE NAZI PARTY GATHERS AT THE
GRAF ZEPPELIN ARENA IN NUREMBERG,
GERMANY. THE NUMBERS TOTAL A
STAGGERING 150,000 AND INCLUDE MEM-
BERS OF THE SS AND THE MILITARY, AS
WELL AS CIVILIANS. THE MASSIVE SCALE
OF THE RALLY CAN ONLY BE COMPARED TO
THE ROMAN EMPIRE AT ITS PEAK.

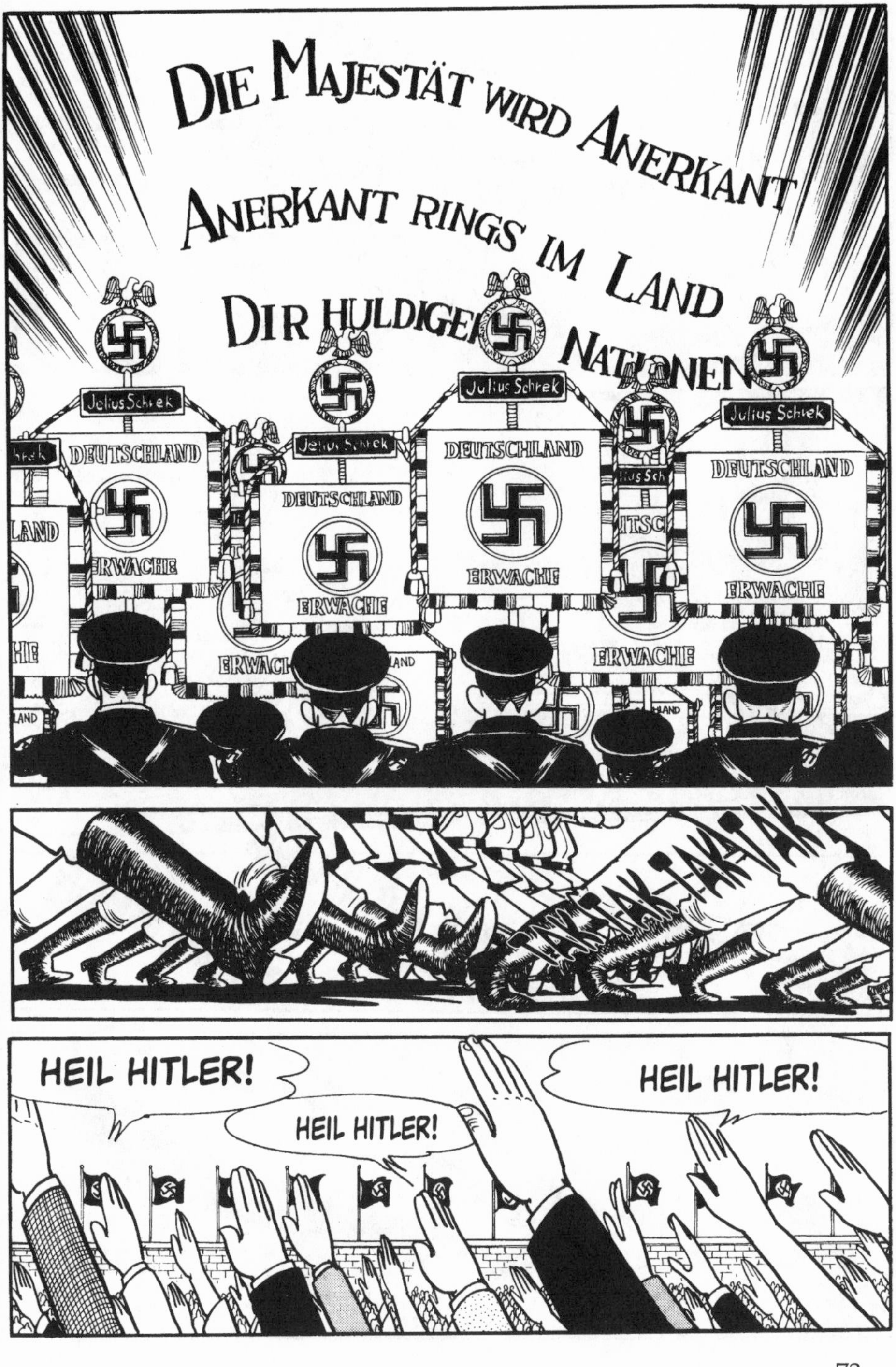
DIE MAJESTÄT WIRD ANERKANT
ANERKANT RINGS IM LAND
DIR HULDIGE NATIONEN
Julius Schrek
DEUTSCHLAND
ERWACHE
TAK-TAK-TAK-TAK
HEIL HITLER!
HEIL HITLER!
HEIL HITLER!

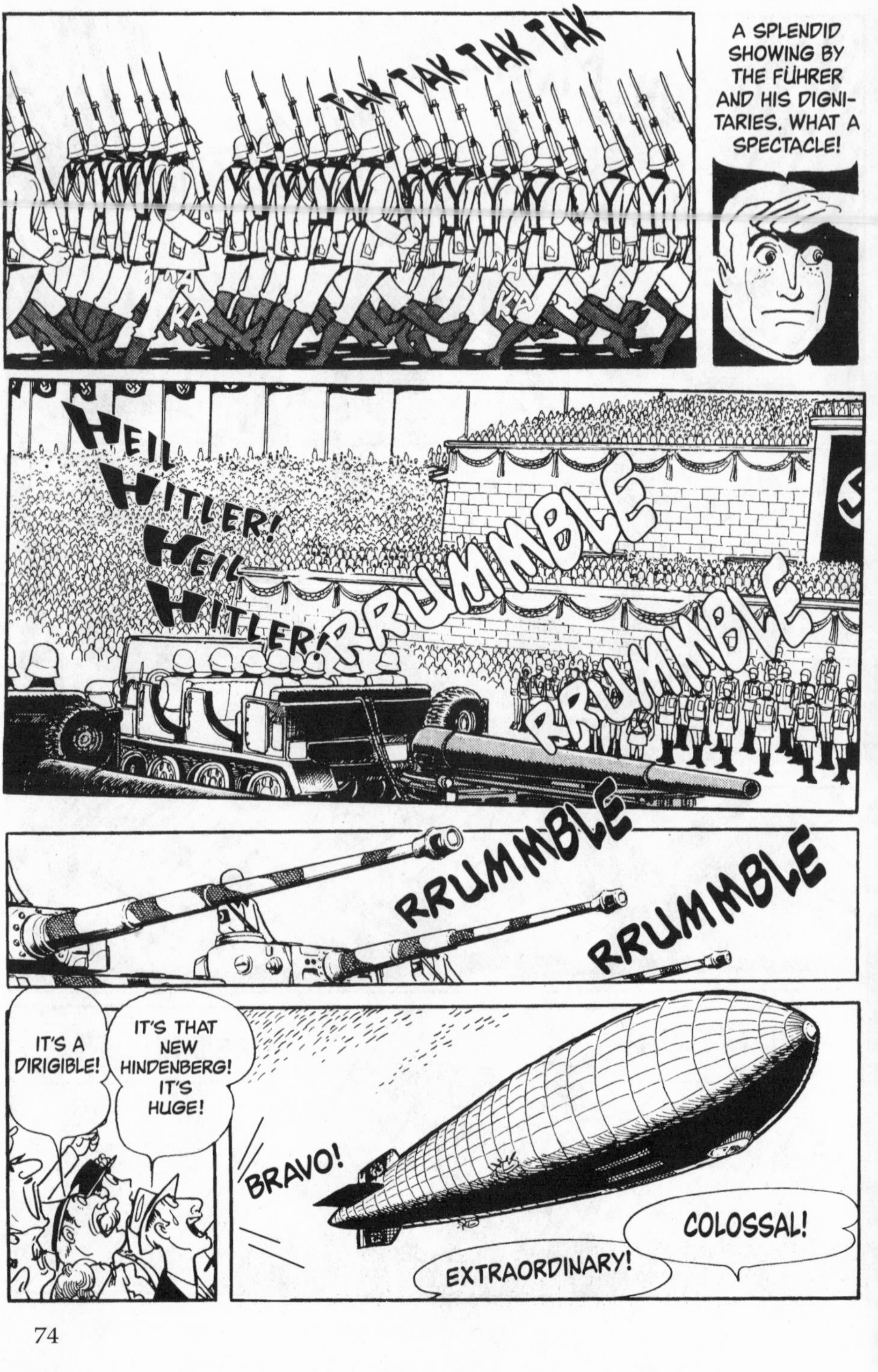
TAK TAK TAK TAK
A SPLENDID SHOWING BY THE FÜHRER AND HIS DIGNITARIES. WHAT A SPECTACLE!
HEIL HITLER! HEIL HITLER!
RRUMMBLE
RRUMMBLE
RRUMMBLE
RRUMMBLE
IT'S A DIRIGIBLE!
IT'S THAT NEW HINDENBERG! IT'S HUGE!
BRAVO!
COLOSSAL!
EXTRAORDINARY!

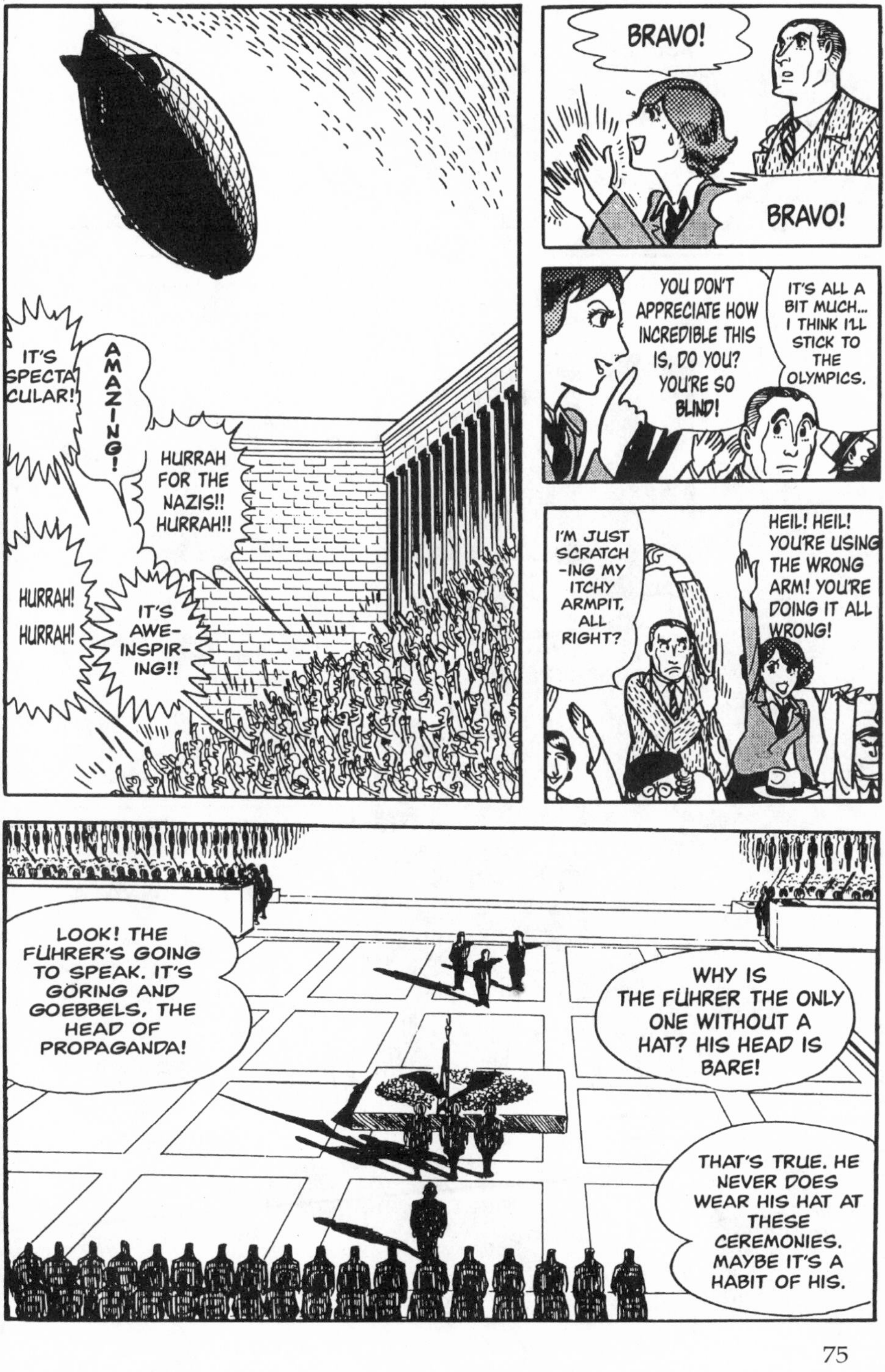
IT'S SPECTACULAR!
AMAZING!
HURRAH FOR THE NAZIS!! HURRAH!!
HURRAH! HURRAH!
IT'S AWE-INSPIRING!!
BRAVO!
BRAVO!
YOU DON'T APPRECIATE HOW INCREDIBLE THIS IS, DO YOU? YOU'RE SO BLIND!
IT'S ALL A BIT MUCH... I THINK I'LL STICK TO THE OLYMPICS.
I'M JUST SCRATCH-ING MY ITCHY ARMPIT, ALL RIGHT?
HEIL! HEIL! YOU'RE USING THE WRONG ARM! YOU'RE DOING IT ALL WRONG!
LOOK! THE FÜHRER'S GOING TO SPEAK. IT'S GÖRING AND GOEBBELS, THE HEAD OF PROPAGANDA!
WHY IS THE FÜHRER THE ONLY ONE WITHOUT A HAT? HIS HEAD IS BARE!
THAT'S TRUE. HE NEVER DOES WEAR HIS HAT AT THESE CEREMONIES. MAYBE IT'S A HABIT OF HIS.

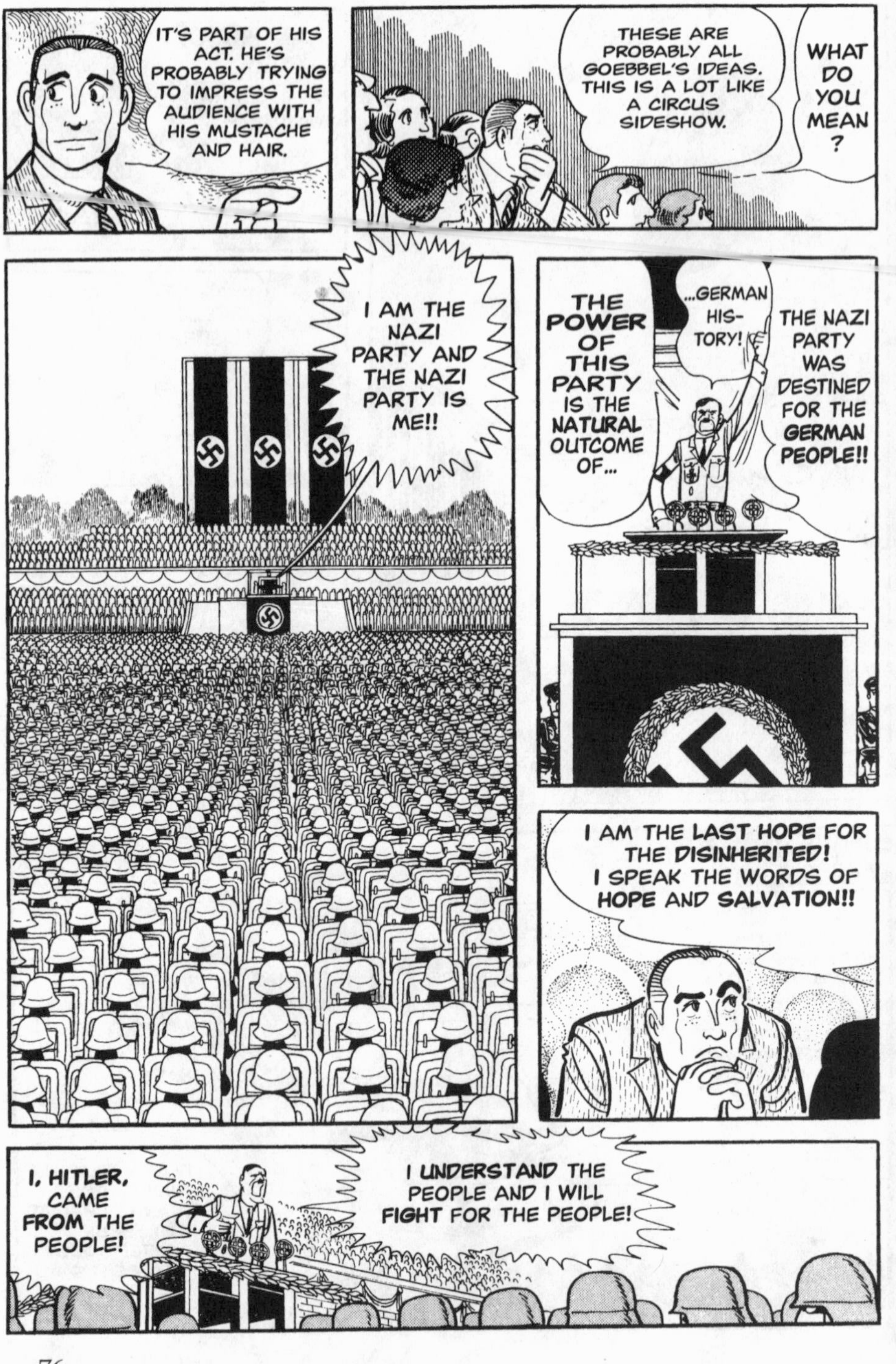
IT'S PART OF HIS ACT. HE'S PROBABLY TRYING TO IMPRESS THE AUDIENCE WITH HIS MUSTACHE AND HAIR.
THESE ARE PROBABLY ALL GOEBBEL'S IDEAS. THIS IS A LOT LIKE A CIRCUS SIDESHOW.
WHAT DO YOU MEAN ?
I AM THE NAZI PARTY AND THE NAZI PARTY IS ME!!
THE POWER OF THIS PARTY IS THE NATURAL OUTCOME OF...
...GERMAN HIS-TORY!
THE NAZI PARTY WAS DESTINED FOR THE GERMAN PEOPLE!!
I AM THE LAST HOPE FOR THE DISINHERITED! I SPEAK THE WORDS OF HOPE AND SALVATION!!
I, HITLER, CAME FROM THE PEOPLE!
I UNDERSTAND THE PEOPLE AND I WILL FIGHT FOR THE PEOPLE!

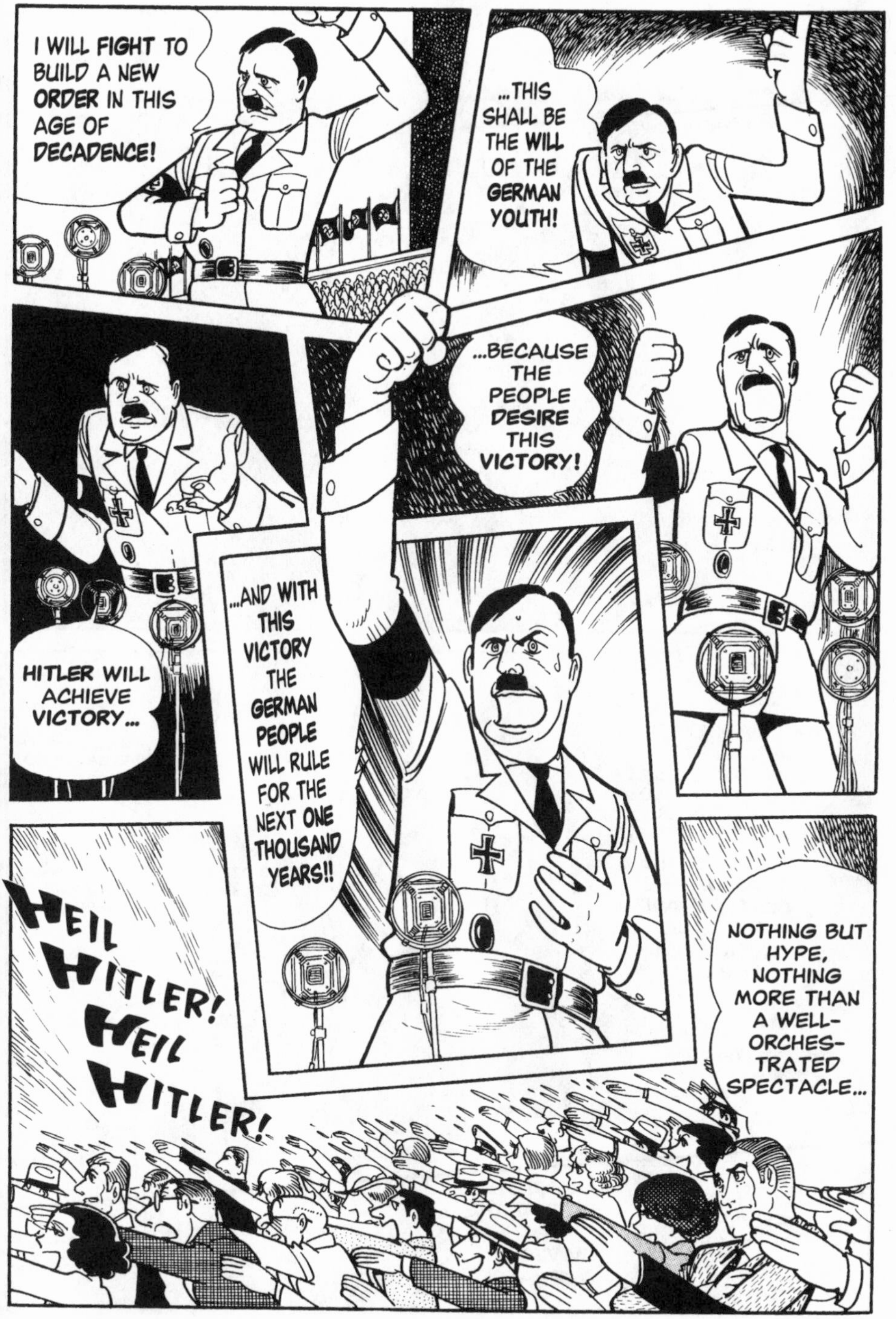
I WILL FIGHT TO BUILD A NEW ORDER IN THIS AGE OF DECADENCE!
...THIS SHALL BE THE WILL OF THE GERMAN YOUTH!
HITLER WILL ACHIEVE VICTORY...
...BECAUSE THE PEOPLE DESIRE THIS VICTORY!
...AND WITH THIS VICTORY THE GERMAN PEOPLE WILL RULE FOR THE NEXT ONE THOUSAND YEARS!!
HEIL HITLER! HEIL HITLER!
NOTHING BUT HYPE, NOTHING MORE THAN A WELL-ORCHES-TRATED SPECTACLE...

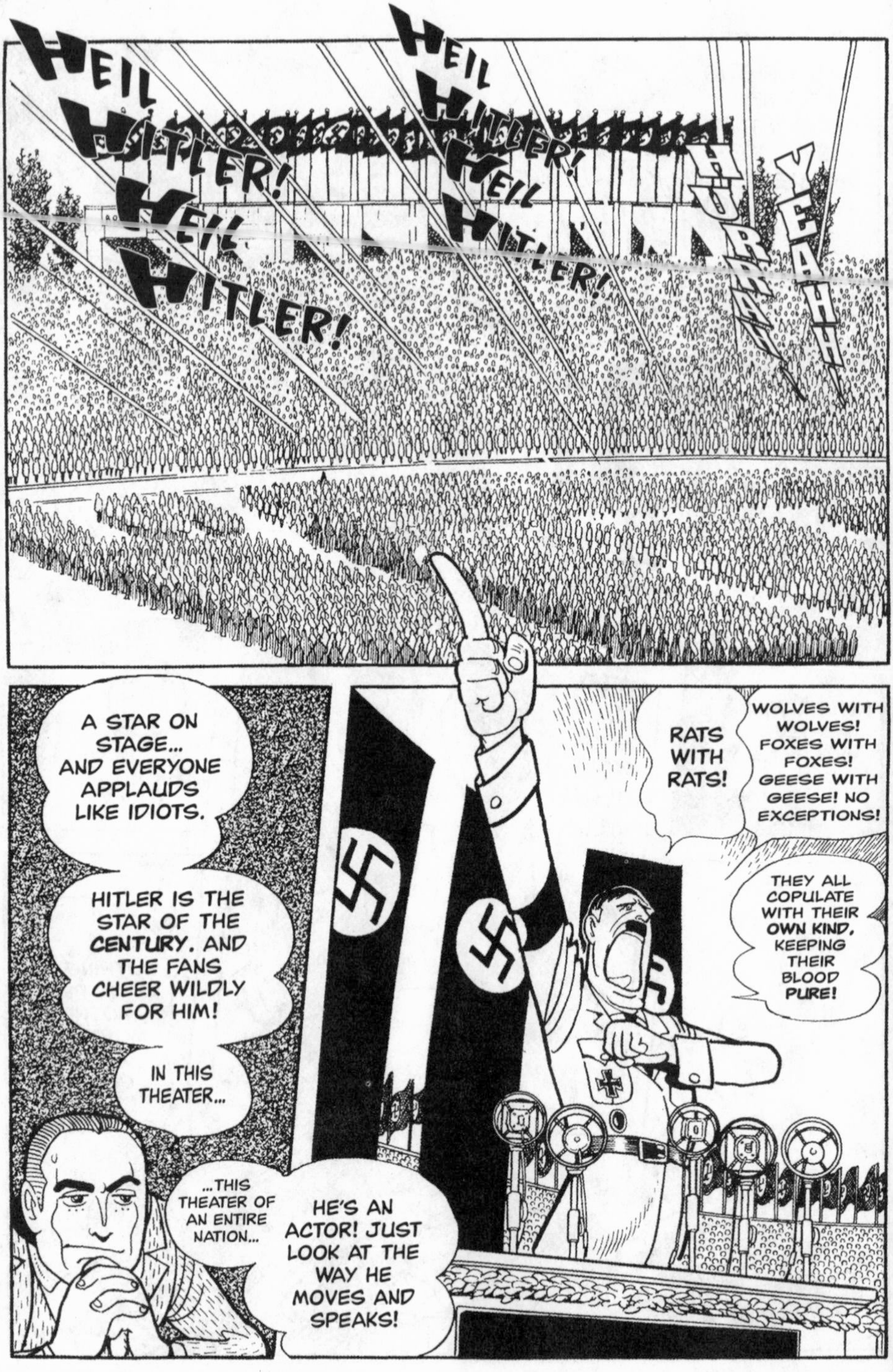
HEIL HITLER! HEIL HITLER!
HEIL HITLER! HEIL HITLER!
HURRAH
YEAHH
A STAR ON STAGE... AND EVERYONE APPLAUDS LIKE IDIOTS.
HITLER IS THE STAR OF THE CENTURY. AND THE FANS CHEER WILDLY FOR HIM!
IN THIS THEATER...
...THIS THEATER OF AN ENTIRE NATION...
HE'S AN ACTOR! JUST LOOK AT THE WAY HE MOVES AND SPEAKS!
RATS WITH RATS!
WOLVES WITH WOLVES! FOXES WITH FOXES! GEESE WITH GEESE! NO EXCEPTIONS!
THEY ALL COPULATE WITH THEIR OWN KIND, KEEPING THEIR BLOOD PURE!

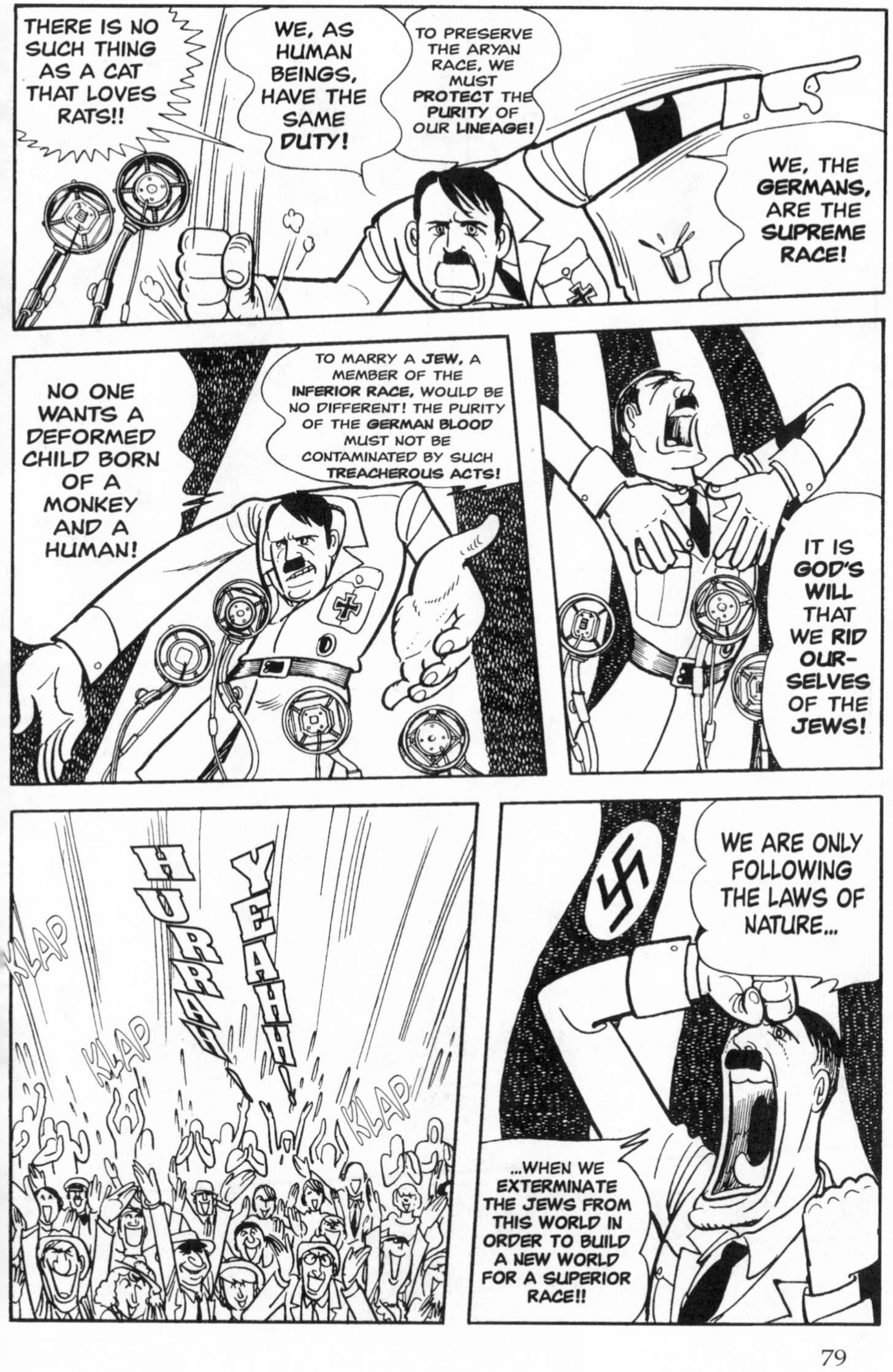
THERE IS NO SUCH THING AS A CAT THAT LOVES RATS!!
WE, AS HUMAN BEINGS, HAVE THE SAME DUTY!
TO PRESERVE THE ARYAN RACE, WE MUST PROTECT THE PURITY OF OUR LINEAGE!
WE, THE GERMANS, ARE THE SUPREME RACE!
NO ONE WANTS A DEFORMED CHILD BORN OF A MONKEY AND A HUMAN!
TO MARRY A JEW, A MEMBER OF THE INFERIOR RACE, WOULD BE NO DIFFERENT! THE PURITY OF THE GERMAN BLOOD MUST NOT BE CONTAMINATED BY SUCH TREACHEROUS ACTS!
IT IS GOD'S WILL THAT WE RID OUR-SELVES OF THE JEWS!
KLAP
KLAP
KLAP
WE ARE ONLY FOLLOWING THE LAWS OF NATURE...
...WHEN WE EXTERMINATE THE JEWS FROM THIS WORLD IN ORDER TO BUILD A NEW WORLD FOR A SUPERIOR RACE!!

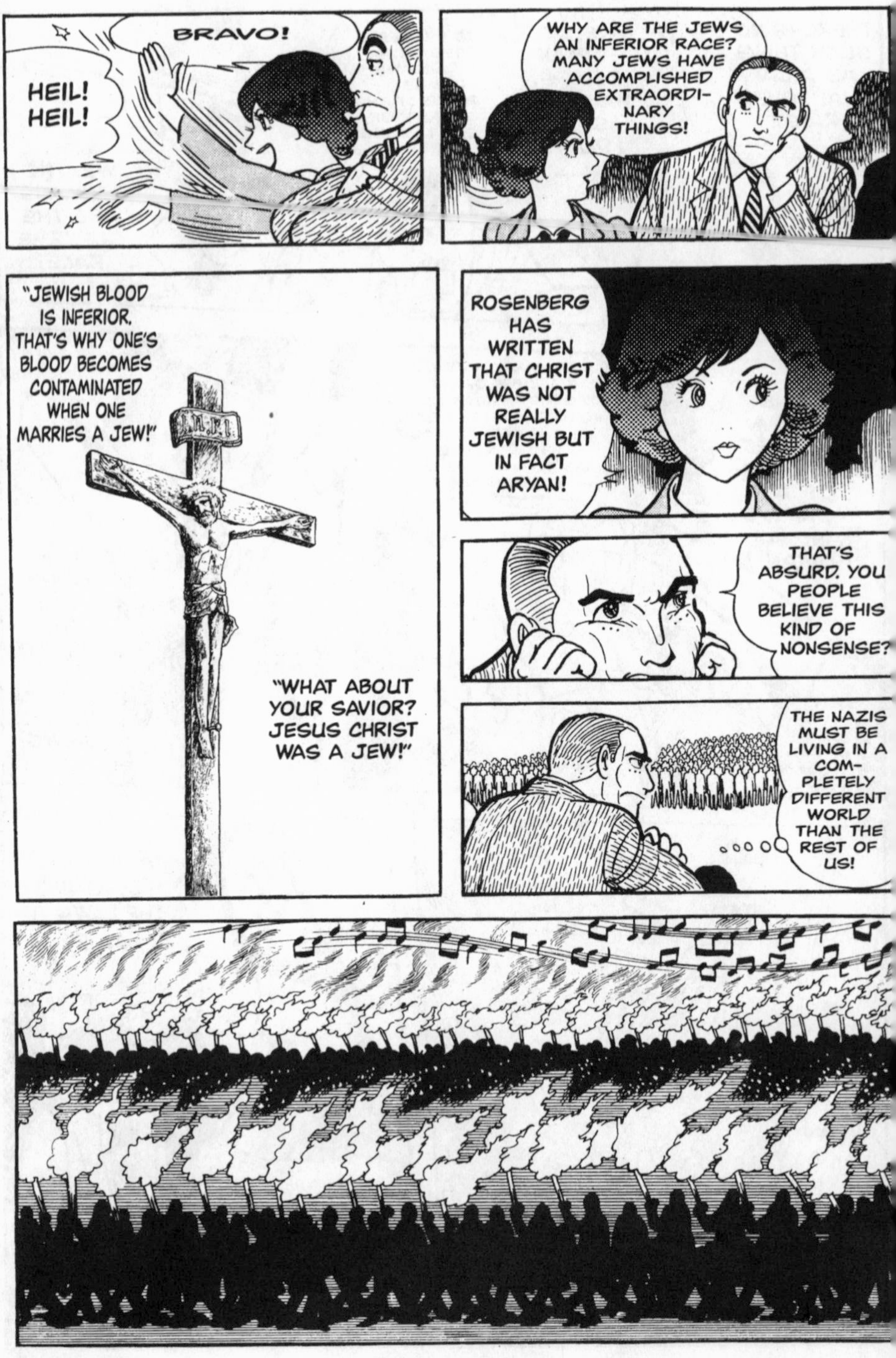
HEIL! HEIL!
BRAVO!
WHY ARE THE JEWS AN INFERIOR RACE? MANY JEWS HAVE ACCOMPLISHED EXTRAORDINARY THINGS!
"JEWISH BLOOD IS INFERIOR. THAT'S WHY ONE'S BLOOD BECOMES CONTAMINATED WHEN ONE MARRIES A JEW!"
"WHAT ABOUT YOUR SAVIOR? JESUS CHRIST WAS A JEW!"
ROSENBERG HAS WRITTEN THAT CHRIST WAS NOT REALLY JEWISH BUT IN FACT ARYAN!
THAT'S ABSURD. YOU PEOPLE BELIEVE THIS KIND OF NONSENSE?
THE NAZIS MUST BE LIVING IN A COMPLETELY DIFFERENT WORLD THAN THE REST OF US!

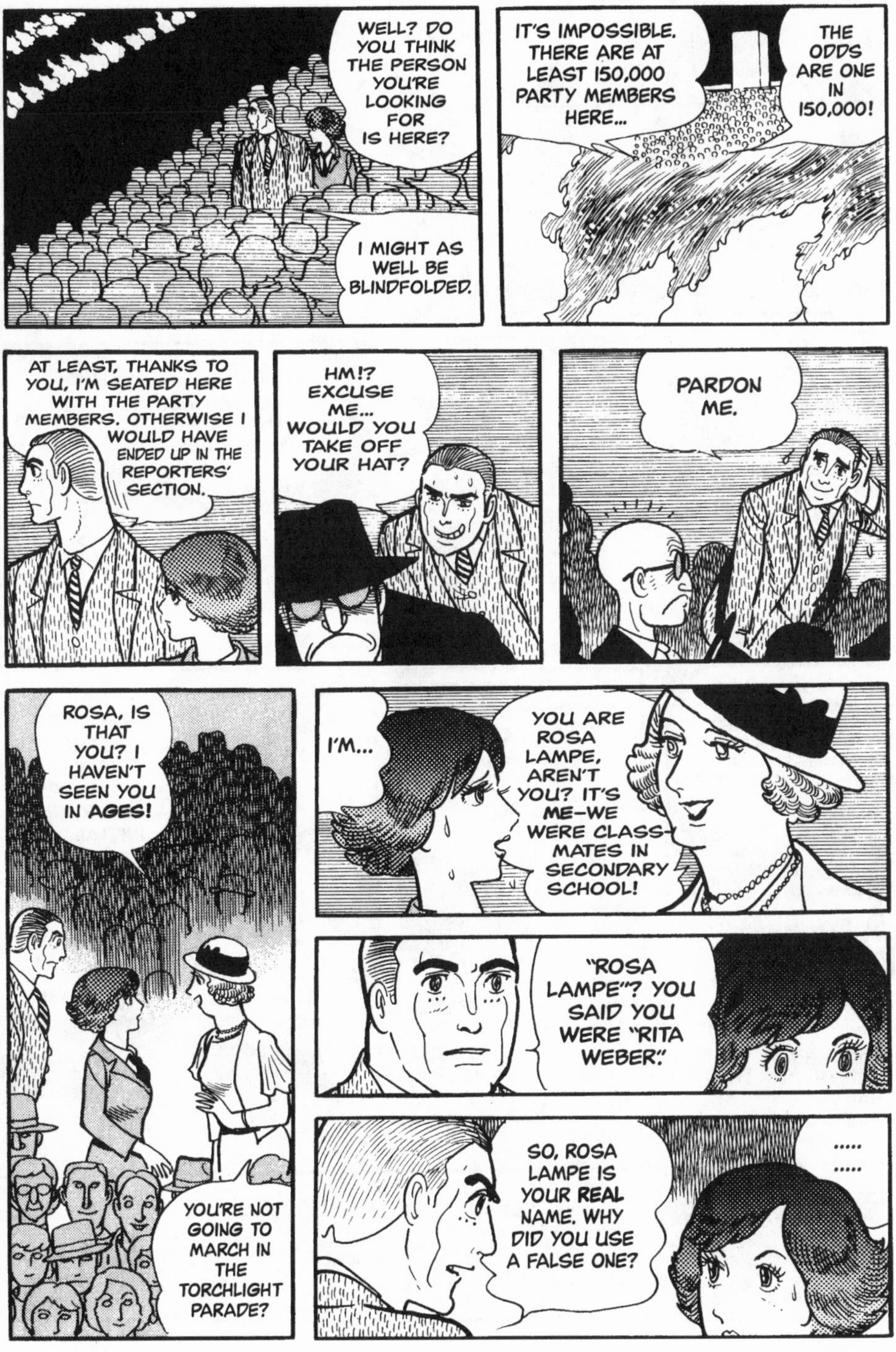
WELL? DO YOU THINK THE PERSON YOU'RE LOOKING FOR IS HERE?
I MIGHT AS WELL BE BLINDFOLDED.
IT'S IMPOSSIBLE. THERE ARE AT LEAST 150,000 PARTY MEMBERS HERE...
THE ODDS ARE ONE IN 150,000!
AT LEAST, THANKS TO YOU, I'M SEATED HERE WITH THE PARTY MEMBERS. OTHERWISE I WOULD HAVE ENDED UP IN THE REPORTERS' SECTION.
HM!? EXCUSE ME... WOULD YOU TAKE OFF YOUR HAT?
PARDON ME.
ROSA, IS THAT YOU? I HAVEN'T SEEN YOU IN AGES!
YOU'RE NOT GOING TO MARCH IN THE TORCHLIGHT PARADE?
I'M...
YOU ARE ROSA LAMPE, AREN'T YOU? IT'S ME—WE WERE CLASSMATES IN SECONDARY SCHOOL!
"ROSA LAMPE"? YOU SAID YOU WERE "RITA WEBER."
SO, ROSA LAMPE IS YOUR REAL NAME. WHY DID YOU USE A FALSE ONE?
....

Adolf

NO...

DID YOU LIE TO MY BROTHER TOO?

I DON'T UNDERSTAND. WHAT IS IT WITH YOU?

THOSE INITIALS MY BROTHER LEFT BEHIND... "R. W." WHAT DO THEY MEAN?

NOW I'M RIGHT BACK WHERE I STARTED.

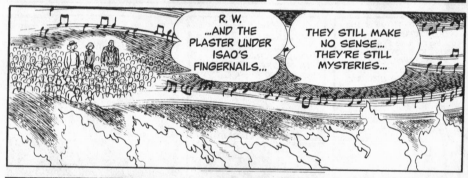

R. W. ...AND THE PLASTER UNDER ISAO'S FINGERNAILS...

THEY STILL MAKE NO SENSE... THEY'RE STILL MYSTERIES...

I'M SORRY FOR USING A FALSE NAME. IT'S JUST THAT I COULDN'T TRUST YOU WHEN WE FIRST MET.

ISAO USED TO PLAY THIS MARCH ON THE PHONOGRAPH IN JAPAN

SUDDENLY, SOHEI TOGE WAS STRUCK BY THE NAME "RICHARD WAGNER." HIS INITIALS WERE R. W!

IT'S THE "TANN-HÄUSER MARCH."

HM? WHO WROTE IT?

RICHARD WAGNER, OF COURSE. IT'S THE FÜHRER'S FAVORITE SONG!

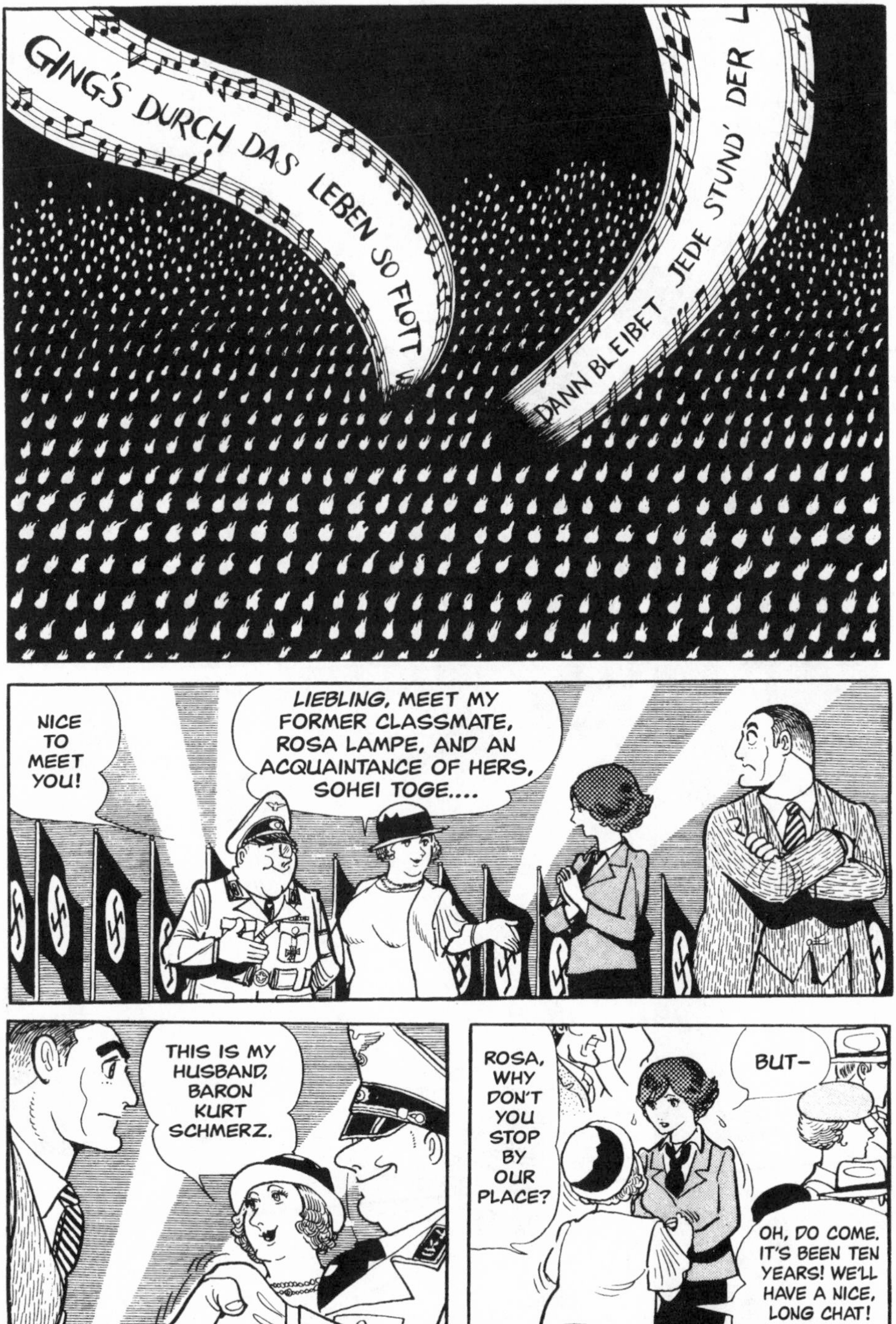
GING'S DURCH DAS LEBEN SO FLOTT
DANN BLEIBET JEDE STUND' DER
NICE TO MEET YOU!
LIEBLING, MEET MY FORMER CLASSMATE, ROSA LAMPE, AND AN ACQUAINTANCE OF HERS, SOHEI TOGE....
THIS IS MY HUSBAND, BARON KURT SCHMERZ.
ROSA, WHY DON'T YOU STOP BY OUR PLACE?
BUT–
OH, DO COME. IT'S BEEN TEN YEARS! WE'LL HAVE A NICE, LONG CHAT!

Adolf

BUT... I'M HELPING HIM LOOK FOR SOMEONE.

THE CEREMONY WILL LAST ANOTHER COUPLE OF DAYS. WHY DON'T YOU TAKE IT EASY TONIGHT?

WHY DON'T YOU COME ALONG AS WELL? WE WELCOME THE JAPANESE. I'M QUITE FOND OF YOUR COUNTRY, ACTUALLY.

BESIDES, WE LIVE IN A BEAUTIFUL OLD MANSION. YOU MUST COME AND SEE IT.

THE PARTY RALLY HAS BEEN HELD ANNUALLY IN NUREMBERG SINCE 1925.

1925 IS THE YEAR THE NAZI PARTY WAS RESURRECTED, YOU KNOW.

AS WELL AS THE YEAR **OUR** BOOK, MEIN KAMPF, WAS PUBLISHED.

I'VE NEVER BEEN IN SUCH A LUXURIOUS MANSION. IT'S LIKE THE NATIONAL DIET BUILDING IN TOKYO!

WILL-KOMMEN, YOU WILL FIND THE LIVING ROOM BEYOND THIS HALL.

WHAT? THERE'S YET ANOTHER ROOM?

ARE YOU SURE YOU'RE NOT JUST MAKING ME GO AROUND IN CIRCLES?

YES, SIR.

...AND THIS PAINTING? WERE SCHMERZ'S ANCESTORS SHOEMAKERS?

HUH?

AND THIS IS TRISTAN UND ISOLDE.

HERR SCHMERZ COM-MISSIONED A FAMOUS PAINTER IN BERLIN TO PAINT THESE WORKS!

YOU MUST BE JOKING! THIS IS NATÜRLICH A SCENE FROM DIE MEISTERSINGER VON NÜRBERG.

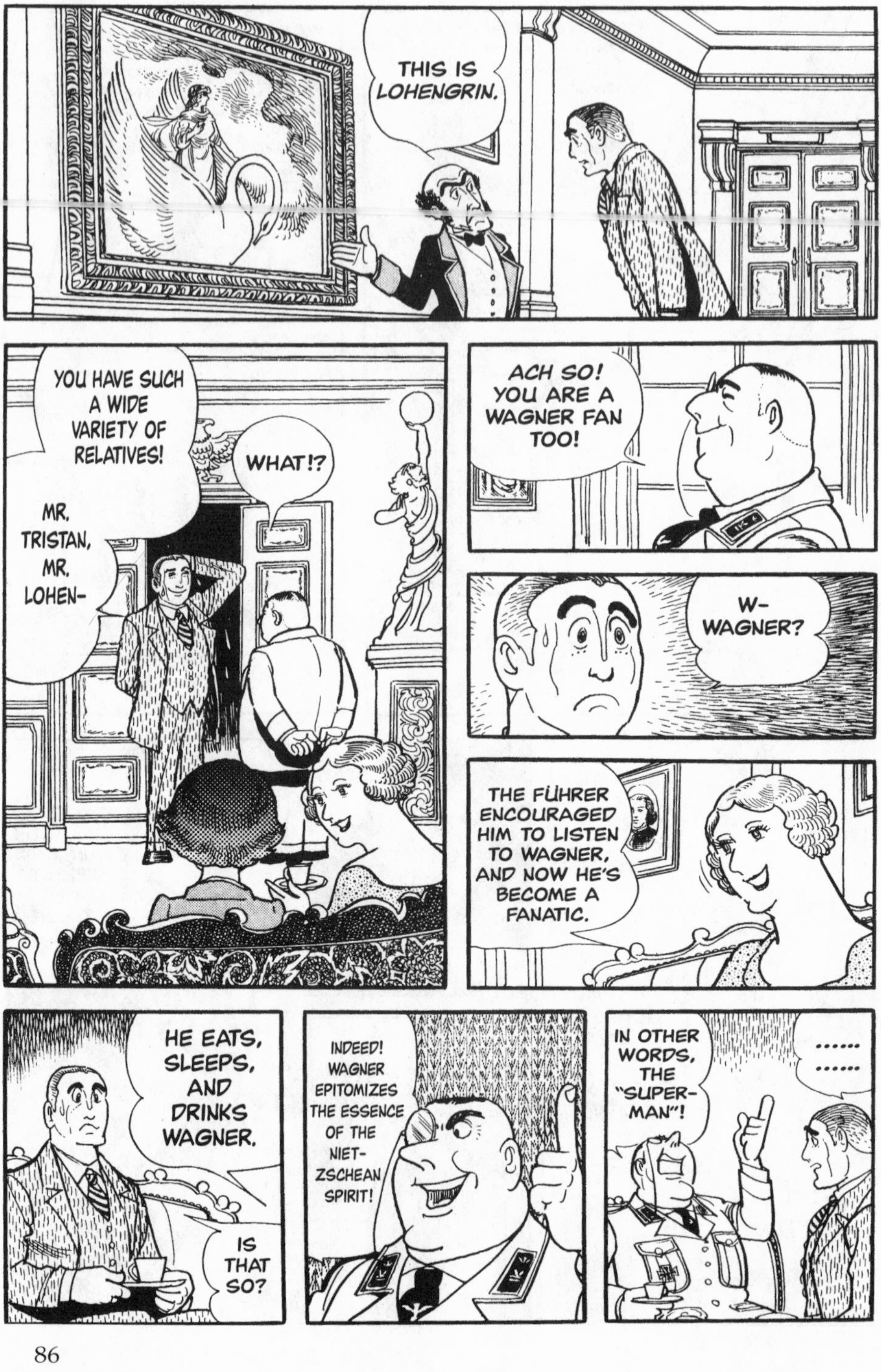
THIS IS LOHENGRIN.
YOU HAVE SUCH A WIDE VARIETY OF RELATIVES!
MR. TRISTAN, MR. LOHEN-
WHAT!?
ACH SO! YOU ARE A WAGNER FAN TOO!
W- WAGNER?
THE FÜHRER ENCOURAGED HIM TO LISTEN TO WAGNER, AND NOW HE'S BECOME A FANATIC.
HE EATS, SLEEPS, AND DRINKS WAGNER.
IS THAT SO?
INDEED! WAGNER EPITOMIZES THE ESSENCE OF THE NIETZSCHEAN SPIRIT!
IN OTHER WORDS, THE "SUPERMAN"!
......
......

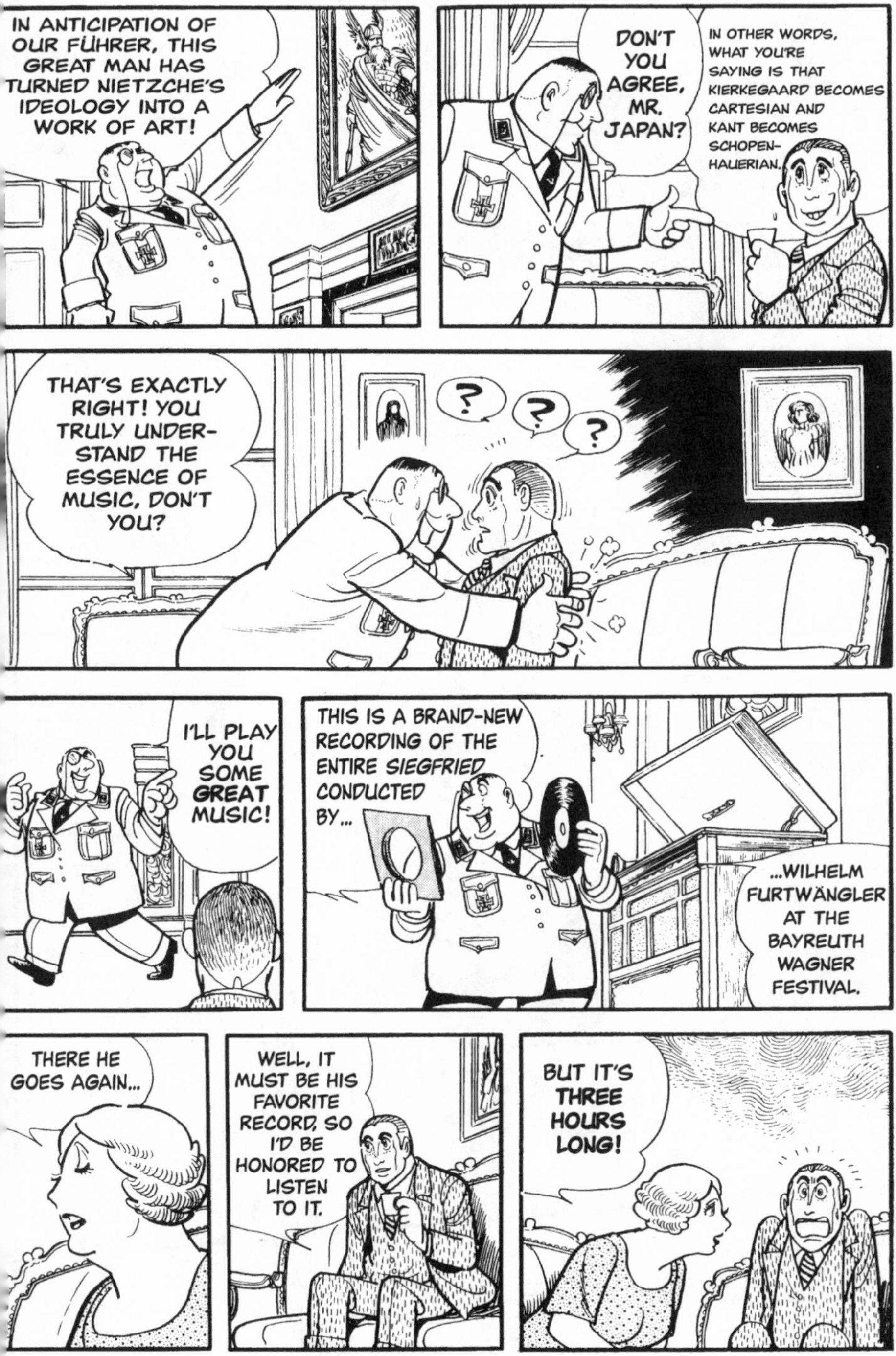
IN ANTICIPATION OF OUR FÜHRER, THIS GREAT MAN HAS TURNED NIETZCHE'S IDEOLOGY INTO A WORK OF ART!
DON'T YOU AGREE, MR. JAPAN?
IN OTHER WORDS, WHAT YOU'RE SAYING IS THAT KIERKEGAARD BECOMES CARTESIAN AND KANT BECOMES SCHOPEN-HAUERIAN.
THAT'S EXACTLY RIGHT! YOU TRULY UNDER-STAND THE ESSENCE OF MUSIC, DON'T YOU?
?
?
?
I'LL PLAY YOU SOME GREAT MUSIC!
THIS IS A BRAND-NEW RECORDING OF THE ENTIRE SIEGFRIED CONDUCTED BY...
...WILHELM FURTWÄNGLER AT THE BAYREUTH WAGNER FESTIVAL.
THERE HE GOES AGAIN...
WELL, IT MUST BE HIS FAVORITE RECORD, SO I'D BE HONORED TO LISTEN TO IT.
BUT IT'S THREE HOURS LONG!

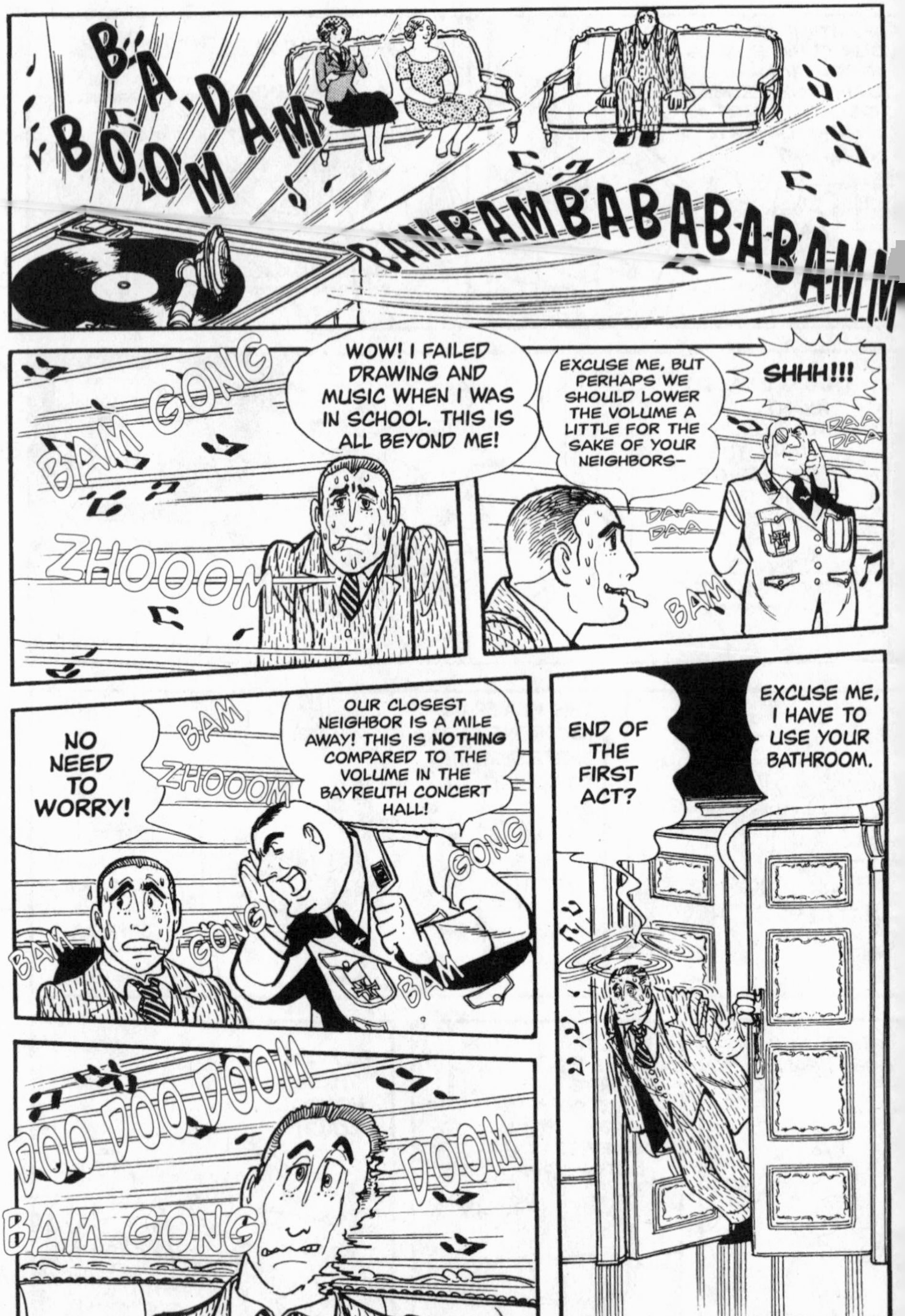
BADA BOOM AM
BAMBAMBABABABAMM
BAM GONG
ZHOOOM
WOW! I FAILED DRAWING AND MUSIC WHEN I WAS IN SCHOOL. THIS IS ALL BEYOND ME!
EXCUSE ME, BUT PERHAPS WE SHOULD LOWER THE VOLUME A LITTLE FOR THE SAKE OF YOUR NEIGHBORS—
SHHH!!!
DAA DAA
DAA DAA
BAM
NO NEED TO WORRY!
BAM
ZHOOOM
OUR CLOSEST NEIGHBOR IS A MILE AWAY! THIS IS NOTHING COMPARED TO THE VOLUME IN THE BAYREUTH CONCERT HALL!
GONG
BAM
GONG
BAM
DOO DOO DOOM
DOOM
BAM GONG
END OF THE FIRST ACT?
EXCUSE ME, I HAVE TO USE YOUR BATHROOM.

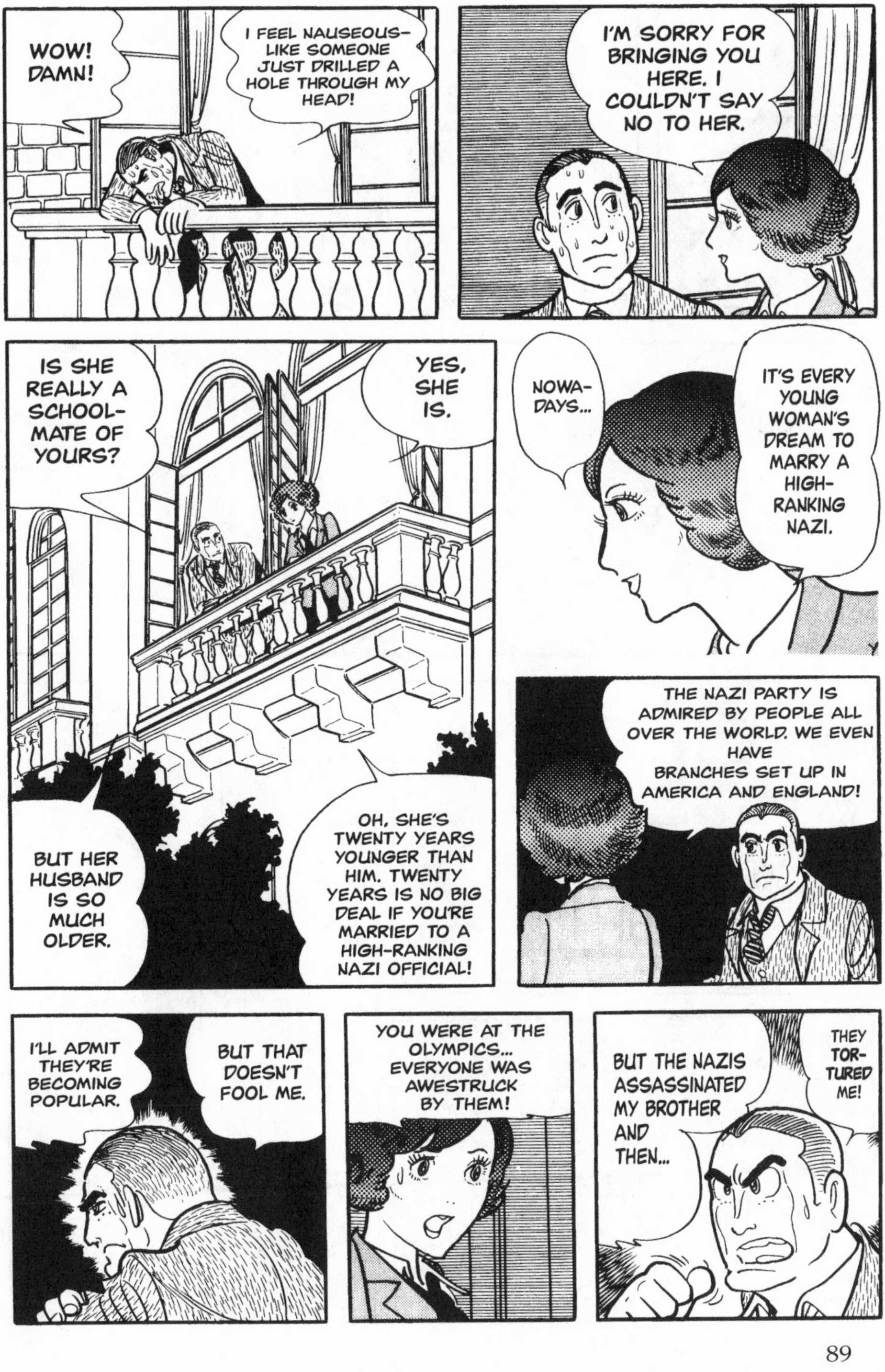
WOW! DAMN!
I FEEL NAUSEOUS-LIKE SOMEONE JUST DRILLED A HOLE THROUGH MY HEAD!
I'M SORRY FOR BRINGING YOU HERE. I COULDN'T SAY NO TO HER.
IS SHE REALLY A SCHOOL-MATE OF YOURS?
YES, SHE IS.
BUT HER HUSBAND IS SO MUCH OLDER.
OH, SHE'S TWENTY YEARS YOUNGER THAN HIM. TWENTY YEARS IS NO BIG DEAL IF YOU'RE MARRIED TO A HIGH-RANKING NAZI OFFICIAL!
NOWA-DAYS...
IT'S EVERY YOUNG WOMAN'S DREAM TO MARRY A HIGH-RANKING NAZI.
THE NAZI PARTY IS ADMIRED BY PEOPLE ALL OVER THE WORLD. WE EVEN HAVE BRANCHES SET UP IN AMERICA AND ENGLAND!
I'LL ADMIT THEY'RE BECOMING POPULAR.
BUT THAT DOESN'T FOOL ME.
YOU WERE AT THE OLYMPICS... EVERYONE WAS AWESTRUCK BY THEM!
BUT THE NAZIS ASSASSINATED MY BROTHER AND THEN...
THEY TOR-TURED ME!

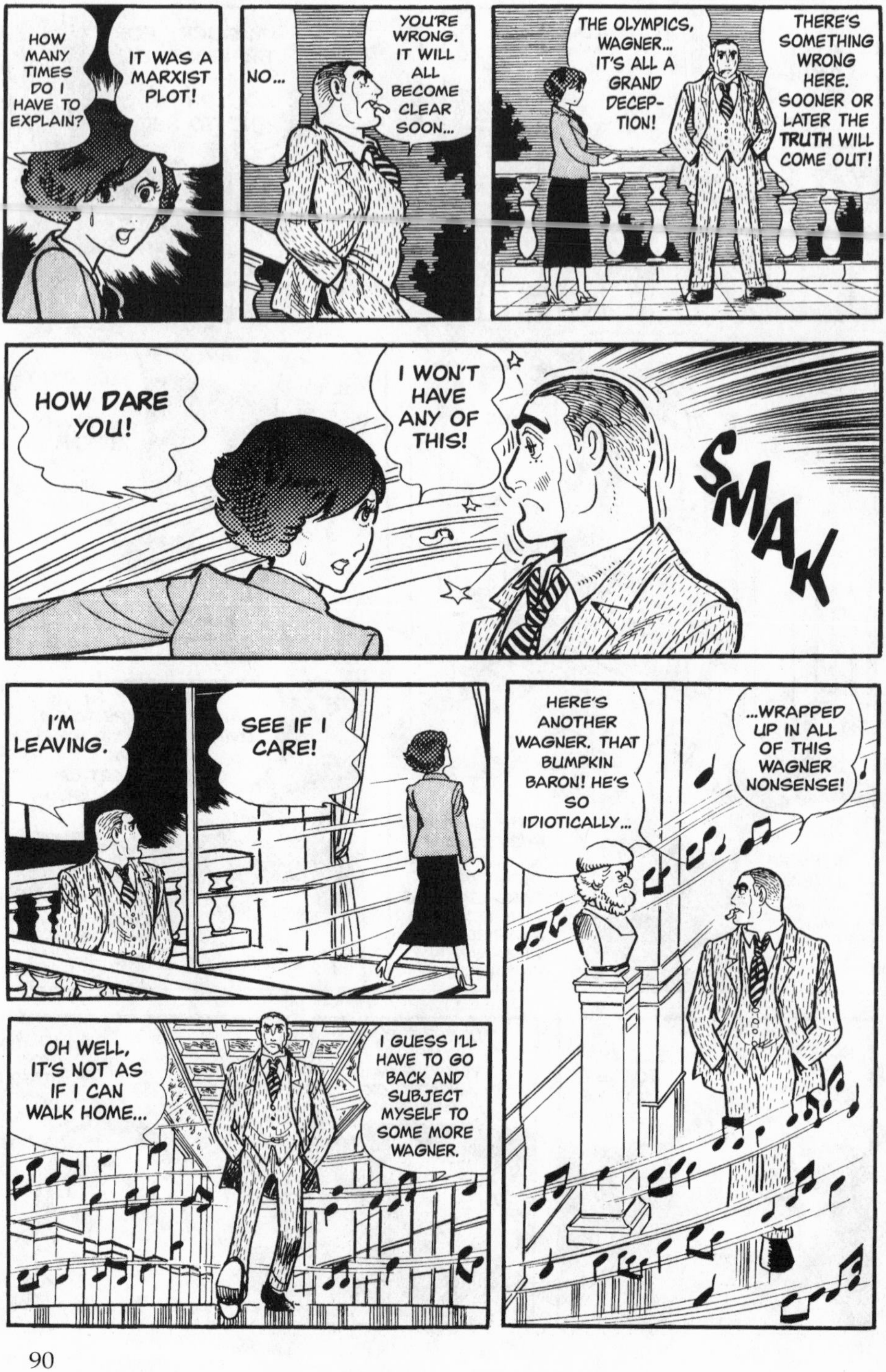
HOW MANY TIMES DO I HAVE TO EXPLAIN?
IT WAS A MARXIST PLOT!
NO...
YOU'RE WRONG. IT WILL ALL BECOME CLEAR SOON...
THE OLYMPICS, WAGNER... IT'S ALL A GRAND DECEP-TION!
THERE'S SOMETHING WRONG HERE. SOONER OR LATER THE TRUTH WILL COME OUT!
HOW DARE YOU!
I WON'T HAVE ANY OF THIS!
SMAK
I'M LEAVING.
SEE IF I CARE!
OH WELL, IT'S NOT AS IF I CAN WALK HOME...
I GUESS I'LL HAVE TO GO BACK AND SUBJECT MYSELF TO SOME MORE WAGNER.
HERE'S ANOTHER WAGNER. THAT BUMPKIN BARON! HE'S SO IDIOTICALLY...
...WRAPPED UP IN ALL OF THIS WAGNER NONSENSE!

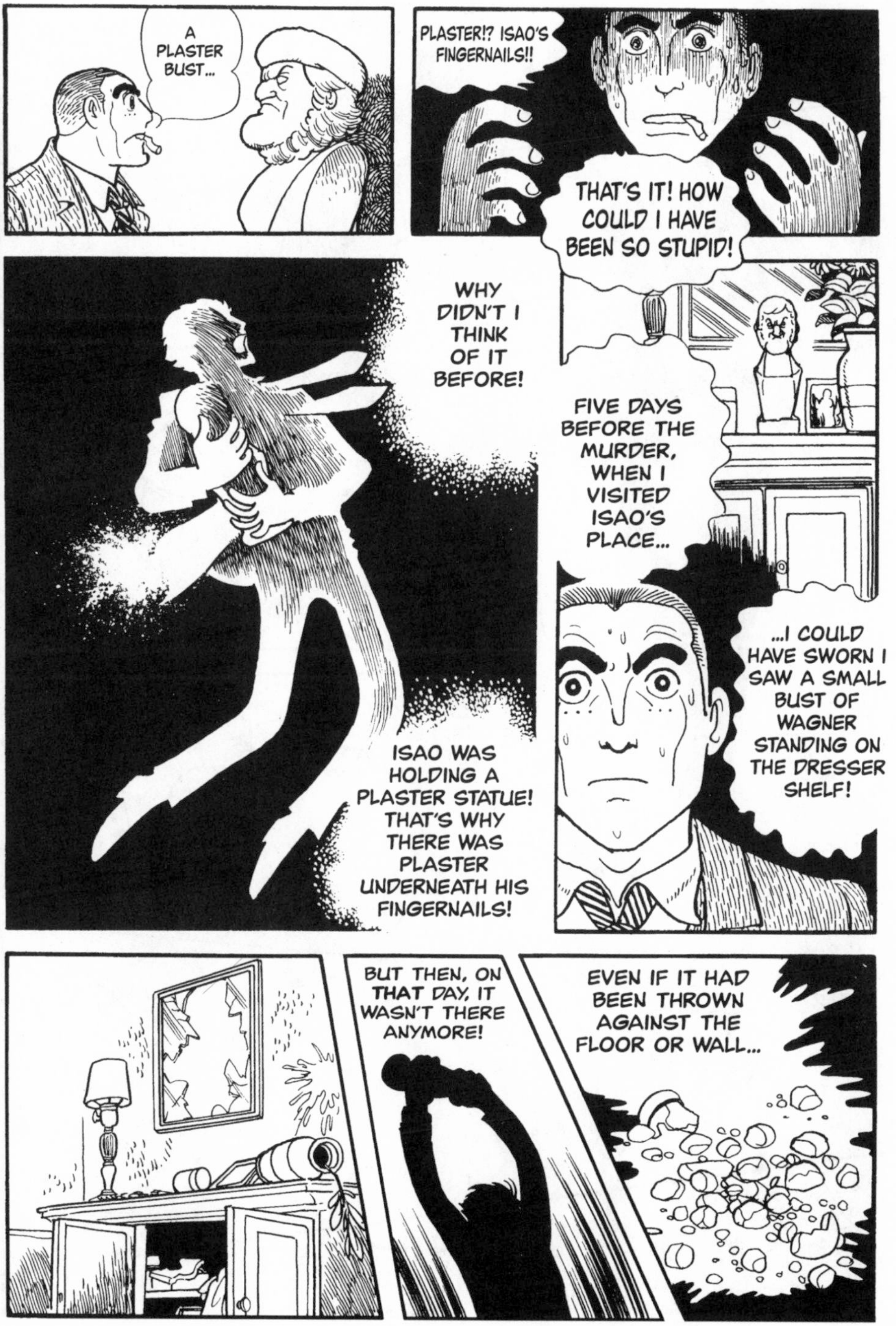
A PLASTER BUST...
PLASTER!? ISAO'S FINGERNAILS!!
THAT'S IT! HOW COULD I HAVE BEEN SO STUPID!
WHY DIDN'T I THINK OF IT BEFORE!
ISAO WAS HOLDING A PLASTER STATUE! THAT'S WHY THERE WAS PLASTER UNDERNEATH HIS FINGERNAILS!
FIVE DAYS BEFORE THE MURDER, WHEN I VISITED ISAO'S PLACE...
...I COULD HAVE SWORN I SAW A SMALL BUST OF WAGNER STANDING ON THE DRESSER SHELF!
BUT THEN, ON THAT DAY, IT WASN'T THERE ANYMORE!
EVEN IF IT HAD BEEN THROWN AGAINST THE FLOOR OR WALL...

THERE WOULD HAVE BEEN SOME REMNANT OF THE PLASTER LEFT IN THE ROOM OR UNDERNEATH THE WINDOW—BUT THERE WASN'T A SINGLE TRACE!

THAT BUST OF WAGNER WAS TAKEN AWAY BY SOMEBODY...

IT WAS SO IMPORTANT, SOMEONE KILLED ISAO TO GET IT!

WHAT COULD BE SO IMPORTANT ABOUT A BUST? WHAT WOULD BE THE POINT...

COME NOW, WHAT ARE YOU STANDING HERE FOR?

AH, YOU WERE PAYING YOUR RESPECTS TO WAGNER, *NICHT?* YOU MUST HAVE BEEN MOVED BY THE MUSIC. A TRUE WAGNERIAN!

PLEASE CALL ME A TAXI. I HAVE TO GO TO THE STATION, IMMEDIATELY...

THESE JAPANESE, THEY'RE SO UNFATHOMABLE!

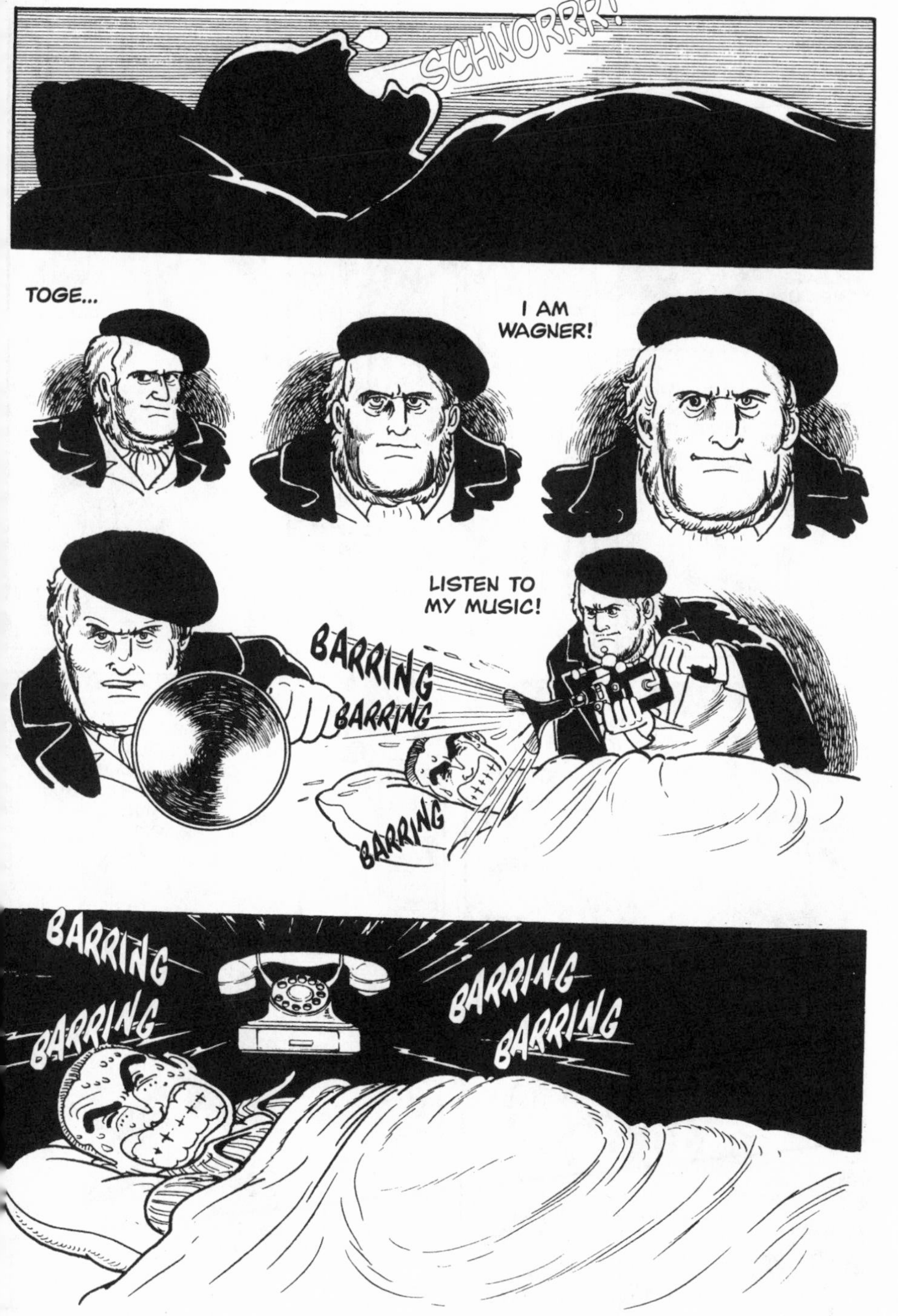
SCHNORRR!
TOGE...
I AM WAGNER!
LISTEN TO MY MUSIC!
BARRING
BARRING
BARRING
BARRING
BARRING
BARRING
BARRING

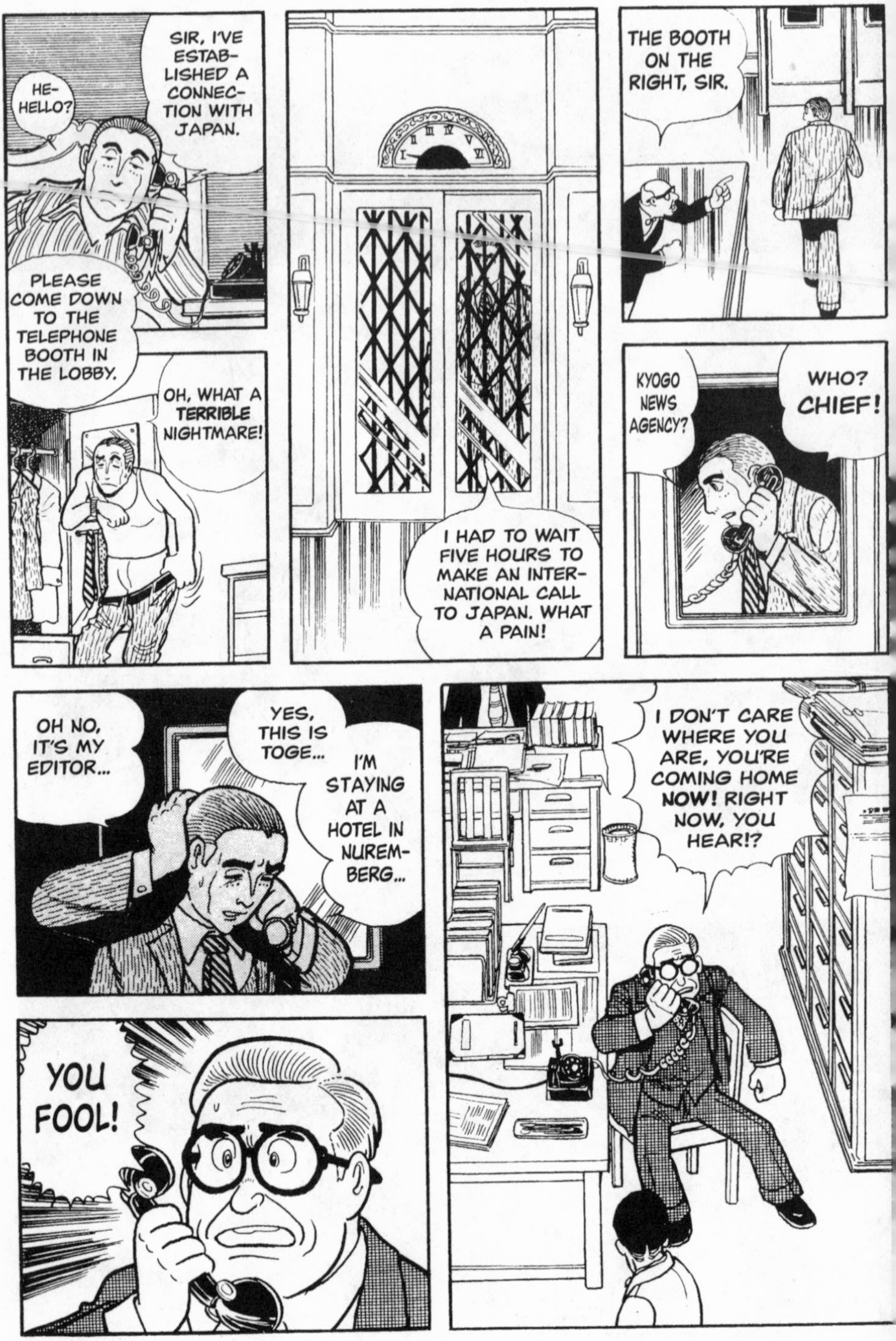
HE-HELLO?
SIR, I'VE ESTABLISHED A CONNECTION WITH JAPAN.
PLEASE COME DOWN TO THE TELEPHONE BOOTH IN THE LOBBY.
OH, WHAT A **TERRIBLE** NIGHTMARE!
I HAD TO WAIT FIVE HOURS TO MAKE AN INTERNATIONAL CALL TO JAPAN. WHAT A PAIN!
THE BOOTH ON THE RIGHT, SIR.
KYOGO NEWS AGENCY?
WHO? **CHIEF!**
OH NO, IT'S MY EDITOR...
YES, THIS IS TOGE...
I'M STAYING AT A HOTEL IN NUREMBERG...
YOU FOOL!
I DON'T CARE WHERE YOU ARE, YOU'RE COMING HOME **NOW!** RIGHT NOW, YOU HEAR!?

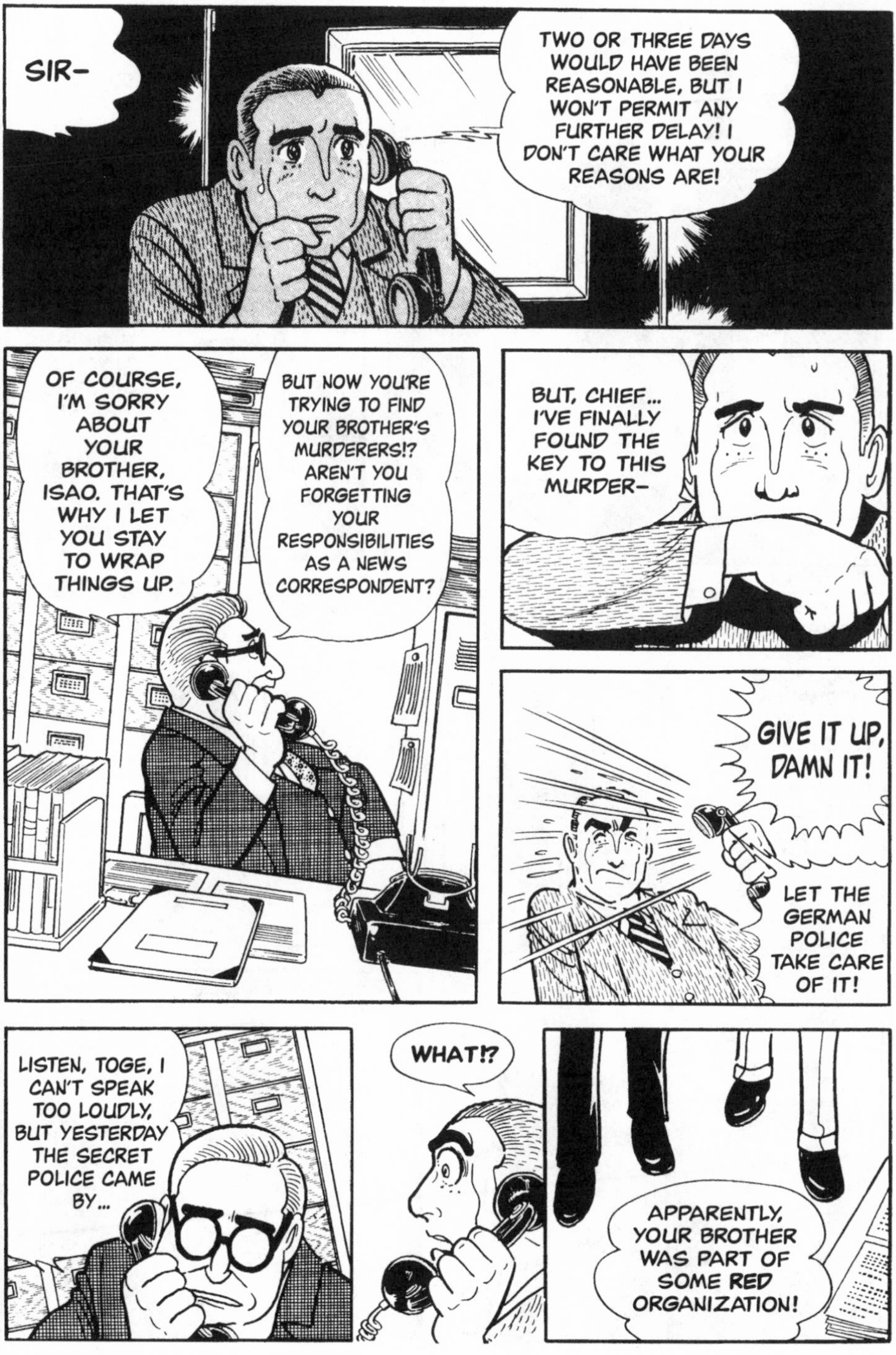
SIR-
TWO OR THREE DAYS WOULD HAVE BEEN REASONABLE, BUT I WON'T PERMIT ANY FURTHER DELAY! I DON'T CARE WHAT YOUR REASONS ARE!
OF COURSE, I'M SORRY ABOUT YOUR BROTHER, ISAO. THAT'S WHY I LET YOU STAY TO WRAP THINGS UP.
BUT NOW YOU'RE TRYING TO FIND YOUR BROTHER'S MURDERERS!? AREN'T YOU FORGETTING YOUR RESPONSIBILITIES AS A NEWS CORRESPONDENT?
BUT, CHIEF... I'VE FINALLY FOUND THE KEY TO THIS MURDER-
GIVE IT UP, DAMN IT!
LET THE GERMAN POLICE TAKE CARE OF IT!
LISTEN, TOGE, I CAN'T SPEAK TOO LOUDLY, BUT YESTERDAY THE SECRET POLICE CAME BY...
WHAT!?
APPARENTLY, YOUR BROTHER WAS PART OF SOME RED ORGANIZATION!

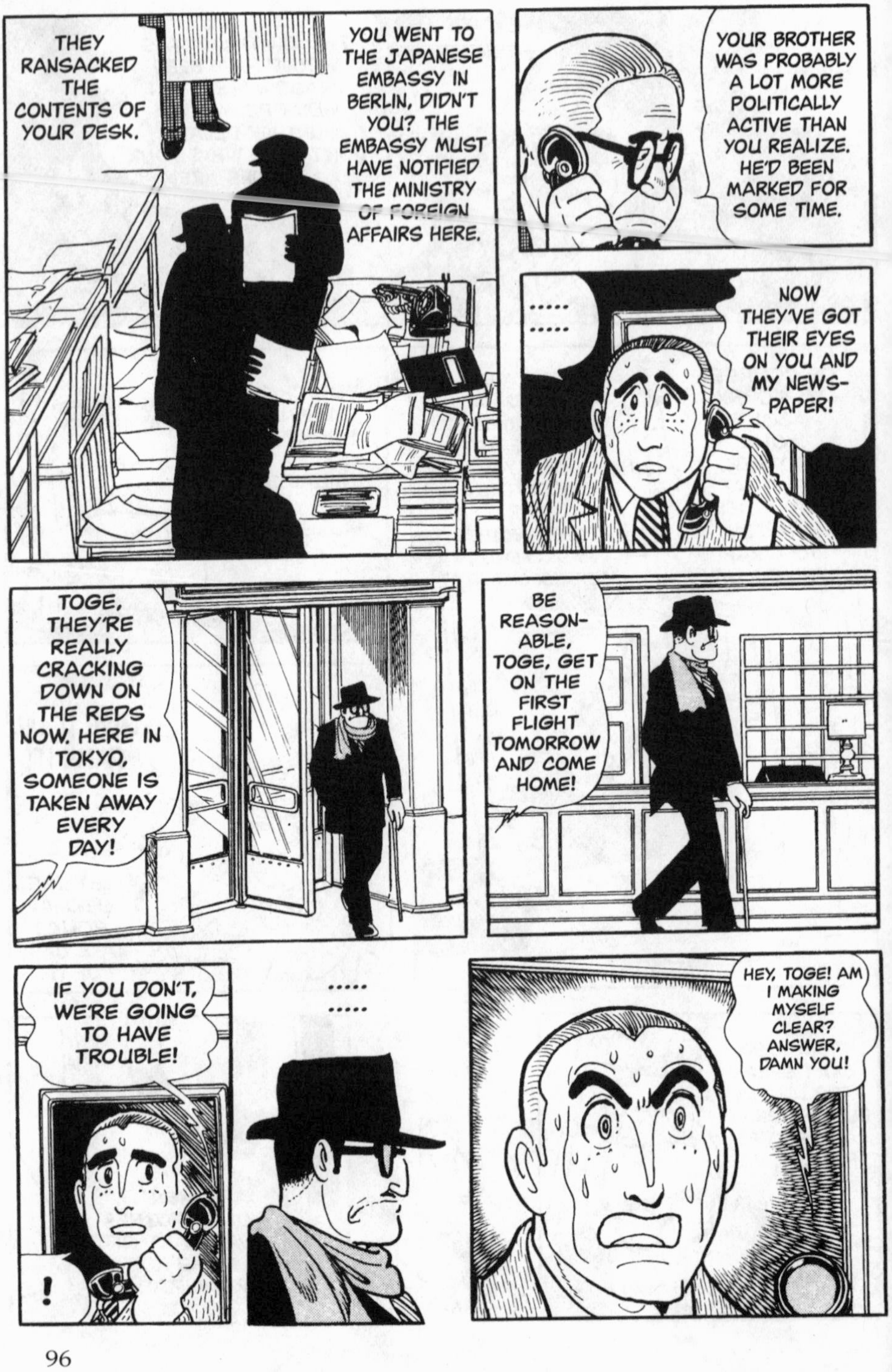
THEY RANSACKED THE CONTENTS OF YOUR DESK.
YOU WENT TO THE JAPANESE EMBASSY IN BERLIN, DIDN'T YOU? THE EMBASSY MUST HAVE NOTIFIED THE MINISTRY OF FOREIGN AFFAIRS HERE.
YOUR BROTHER WAS PROBABLY A LOT MORE POLITICALLY ACTIVE THAN YOU REALIZE. HE'D BEEN MARKED FOR SOME TIME.
....
NOW THEY'VE GOT THEIR EYES ON YOU AND MY NEWS-PAPER!
TOGE, THEY'RE REALLY CRACKING DOWN ON THE REDS NOW. HERE IN TOKYO, SOMEONE IS TAKEN AWAY EVERY DAY!
BE REASON-ABLE, TOGE, GET ON THE FIRST FLIGHT TOMORROW AND COME HOME!
IF YOU DON'T, WE'RE GOING TO HAVE TROUBLE!
!
....
HEY, TOGE! AM I MAKING MYSELF CLEAR? ANSWER, DAMN YOU!

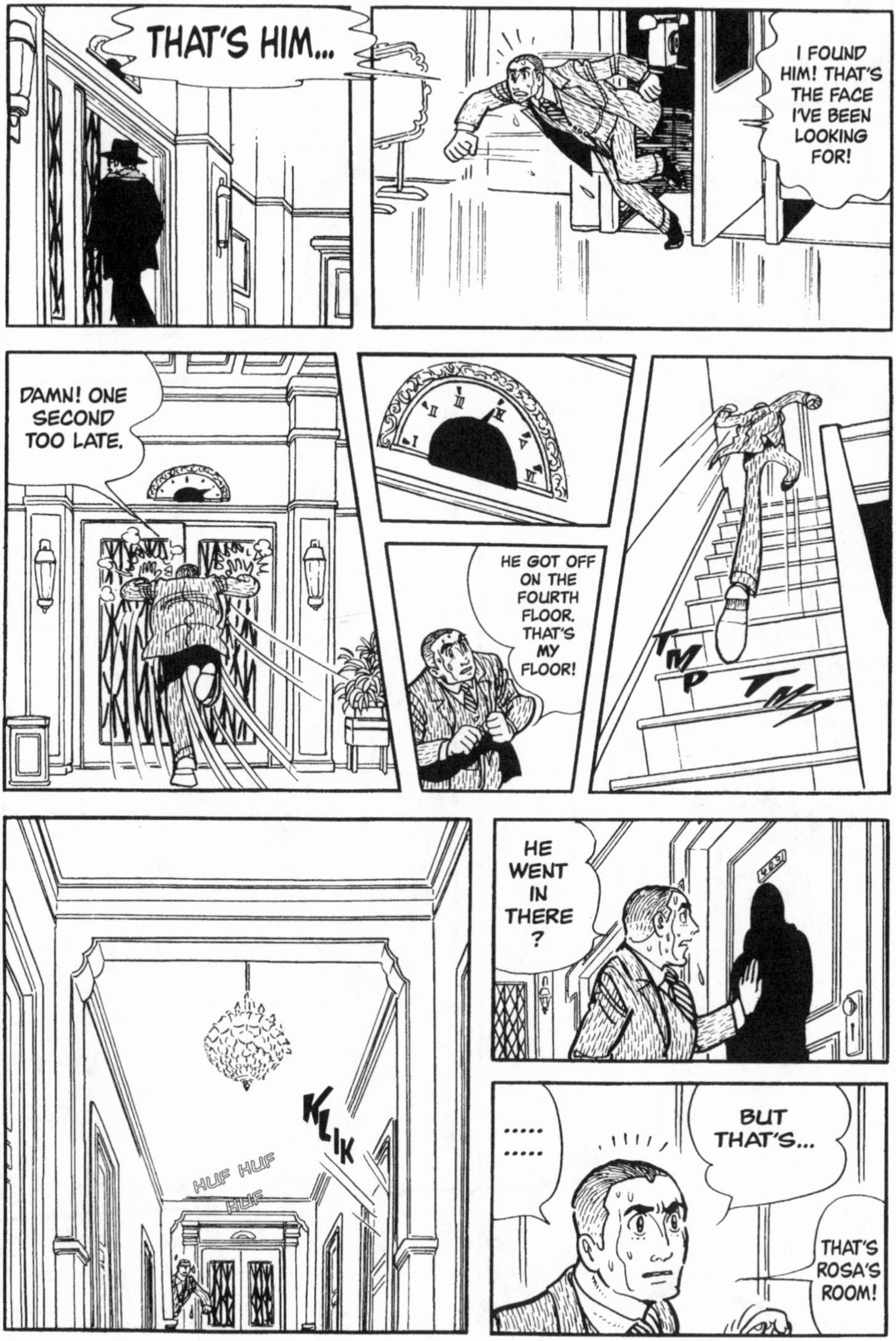
THAT'S HIM...
I FOUND HIM! THAT'S THE FACE I'VE BEEN LOOKING FOR!
DAMN! ONE SECOND TOO LATE.
HE GOT OFF ON THE FOURTH FLOOR. THAT'S MY FLOOR!
TMP TMP
KLIK
HUF HUF HUF
HE WENT IN THERE?
.....
.....
BUT THAT'S...
THAT'S ROSA'S ROOM!

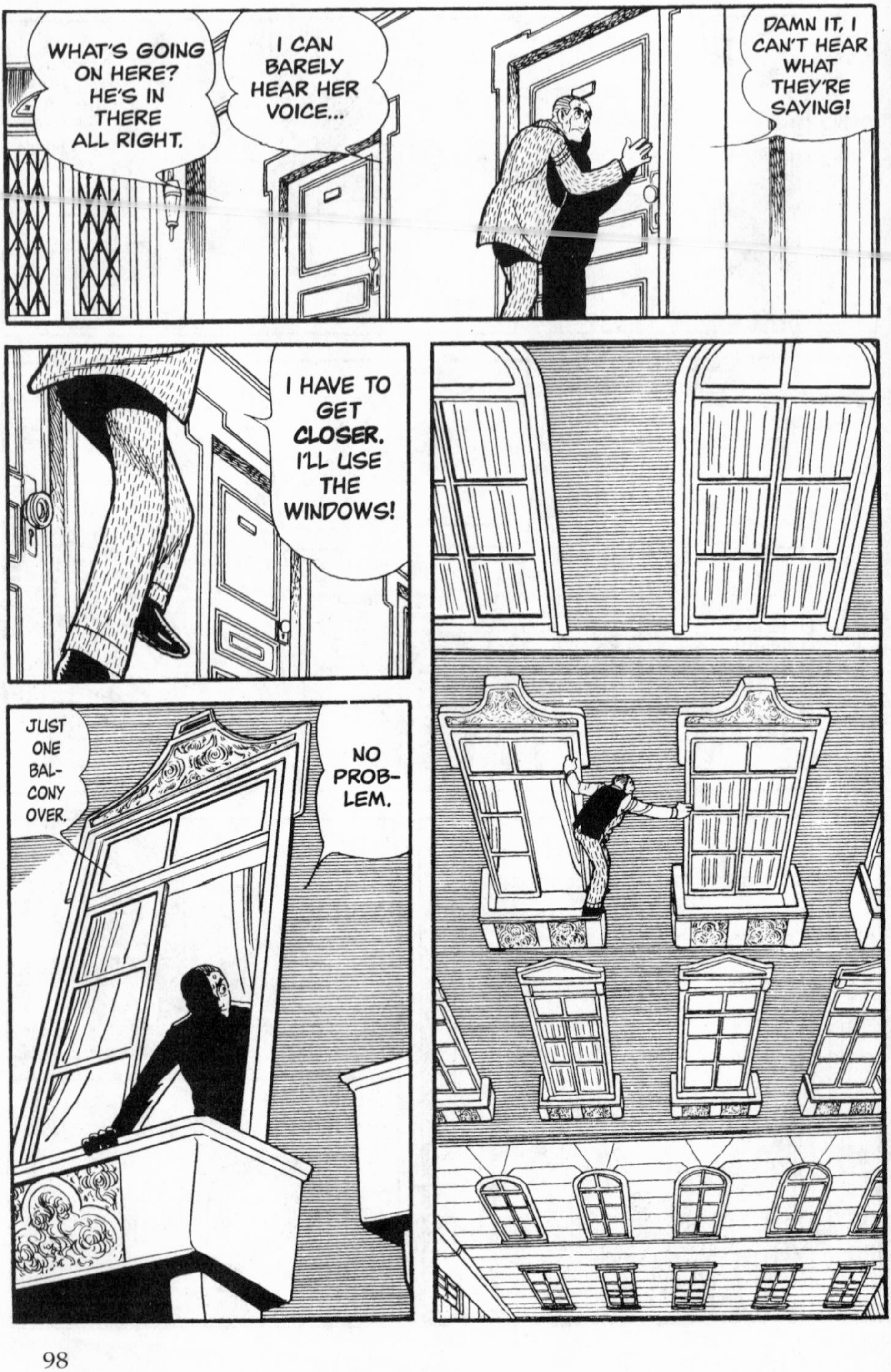
WHAT'S GOING ON HERE? HE'S IN THERE ALL RIGHT.
I CAN BARELY HEAR HER VOICE...
DAMN IT, I CAN'T HEAR WHAT THEY'RE SAYING!
I HAVE TO GET CLOSER. I'LL USE THE WINDOWS!
JUST ONE BAL-CONY OVER.
NO PROB-LEM.

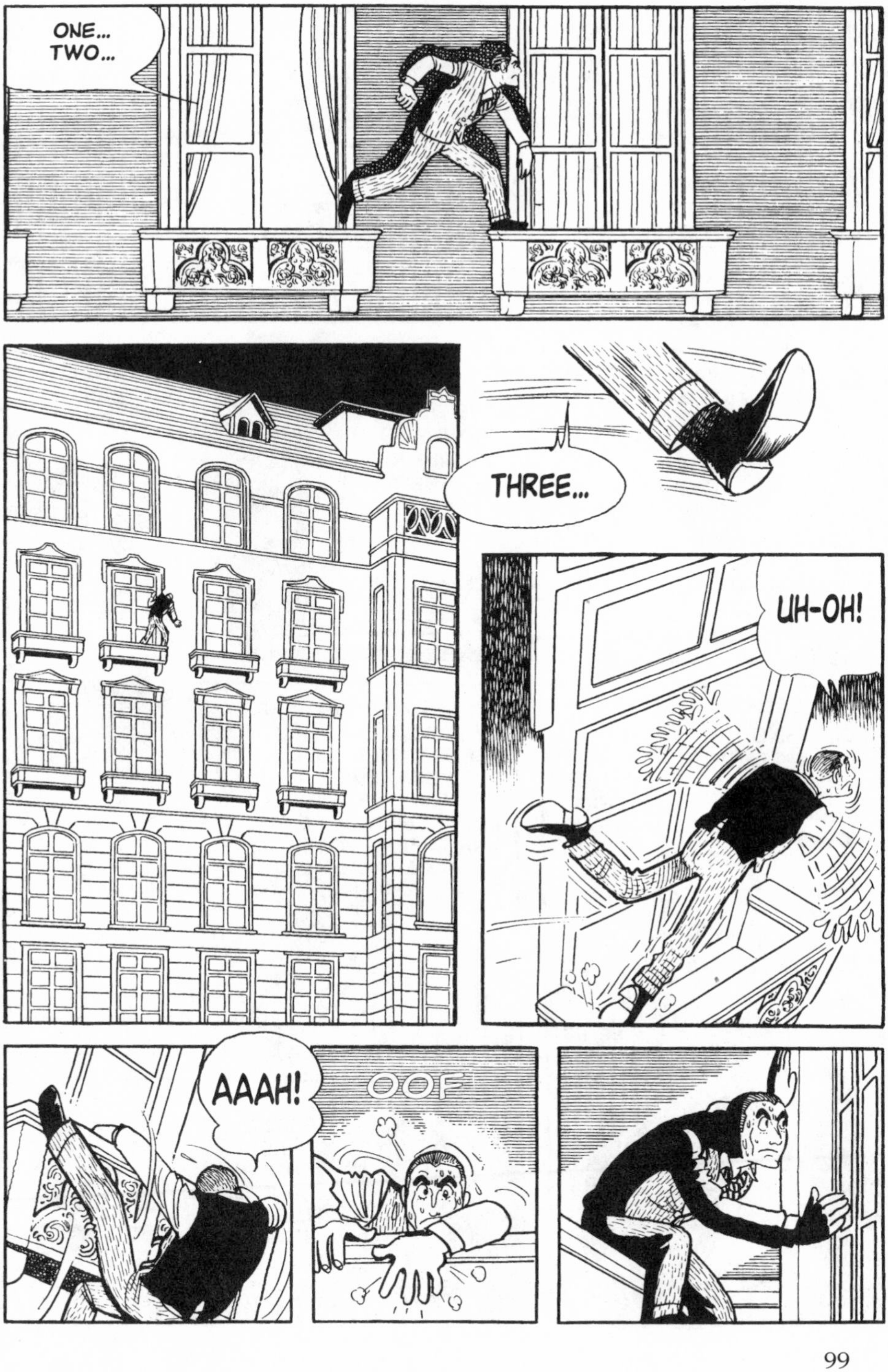
ONE... TWO...
THREE...
UH-OH!
AAAH!
OOF

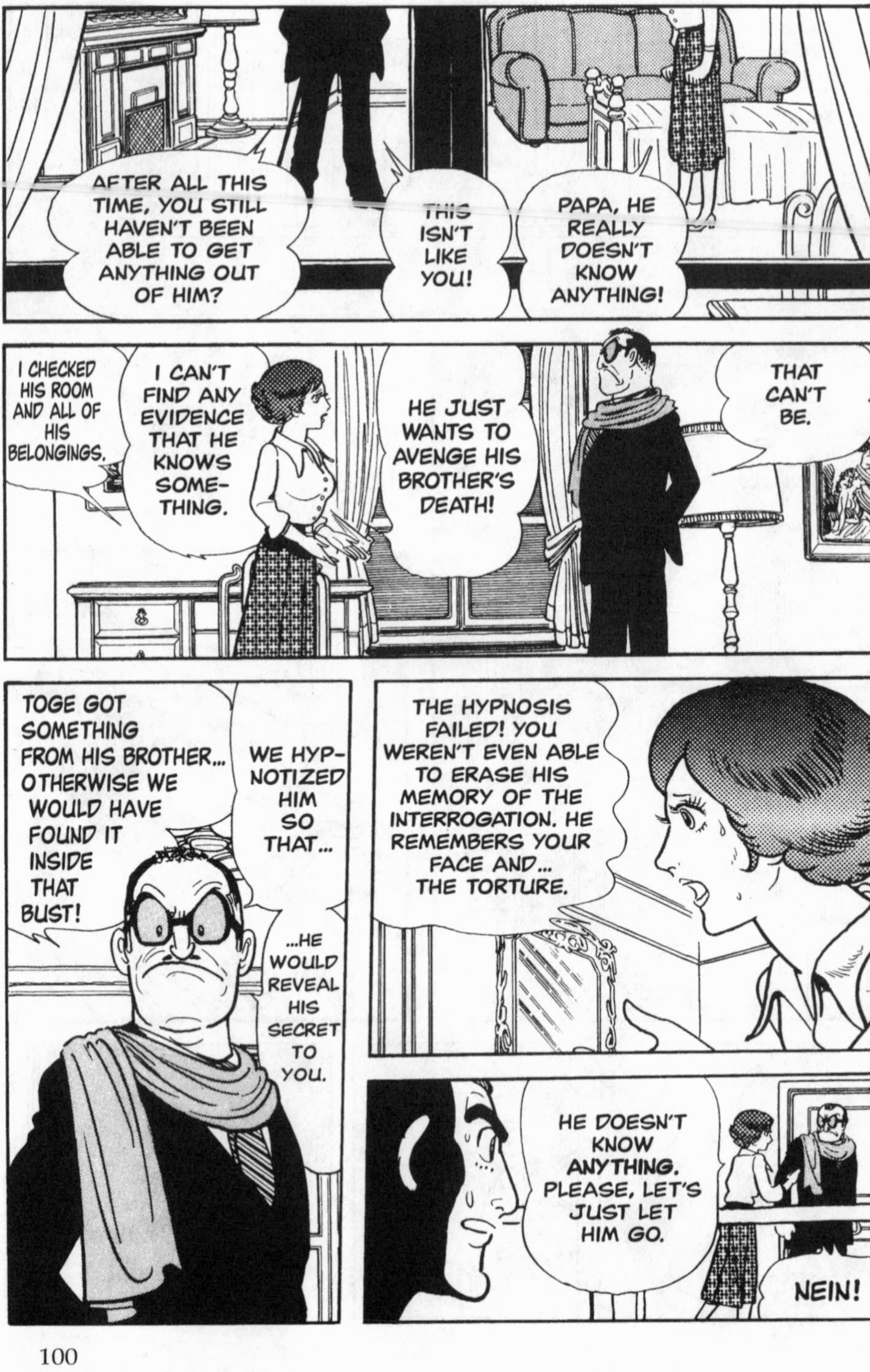
AFTER ALL THIS TIME, YOU STILL HAVEN'T BEEN ABLE TO GET ANYTHING OUT OF HIM?
THIS ISN'T LIKE YOU!
PAPA, HE REALLY DOESN'T KNOW ANYTHING!
I CHECKED HIS ROOM AND ALL OF HIS BELONGINGS.
I CAN'T FIND ANY EVIDENCE THAT HE KNOWS SOME-THING.
HE JUST WANTS TO AVENGE HIS BROTHER'S DEATH!
THAT CAN'T BE.
TOGE GOT SOMETHING FROM HIS BROTHER... OTHERWISE WE WOULD HAVE FOUND IT INSIDE THAT BUST!
WE HYP-NOTIZED HIM SO THAT...
...HE WOULD REVEAL HIS SECRET TO YOU.
THE HYPNOSIS FAILED! YOU WEREN'T EVEN ABLE TO ERASE HIS MEMORY OF THE INTERROGATION. HE REMEMBERS YOUR FACE AND... THE TORTURE.
HE DOESN'T KNOW ANYTHING. PLEASE, LET'S JUST LET HIM GO.
NEIN!

PAPA, I'M SICK OF THIS...

HE'S NOT A BAD PERSON!

ROSA...

THIS JOB MAY BE DIFFICULT, BUT AS A PARTY INFORMANT YOU MUST DO WHAT IS NECESSARY!

BUT I ALREADY HAVE!

I... I EVEN INFORMED ON ISAO... ...TO THE SS.

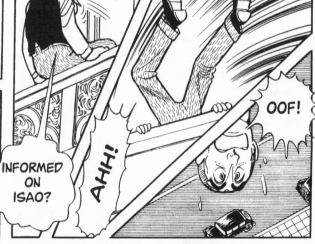

WH- WHAT?

INFORMED ON ISAO?

AHH!

OOF!

SHE BETRAYED ISAO!?

ROSA, LIEBLING, THIS IS YOUR DUTY TO YOUR COUNTRY!

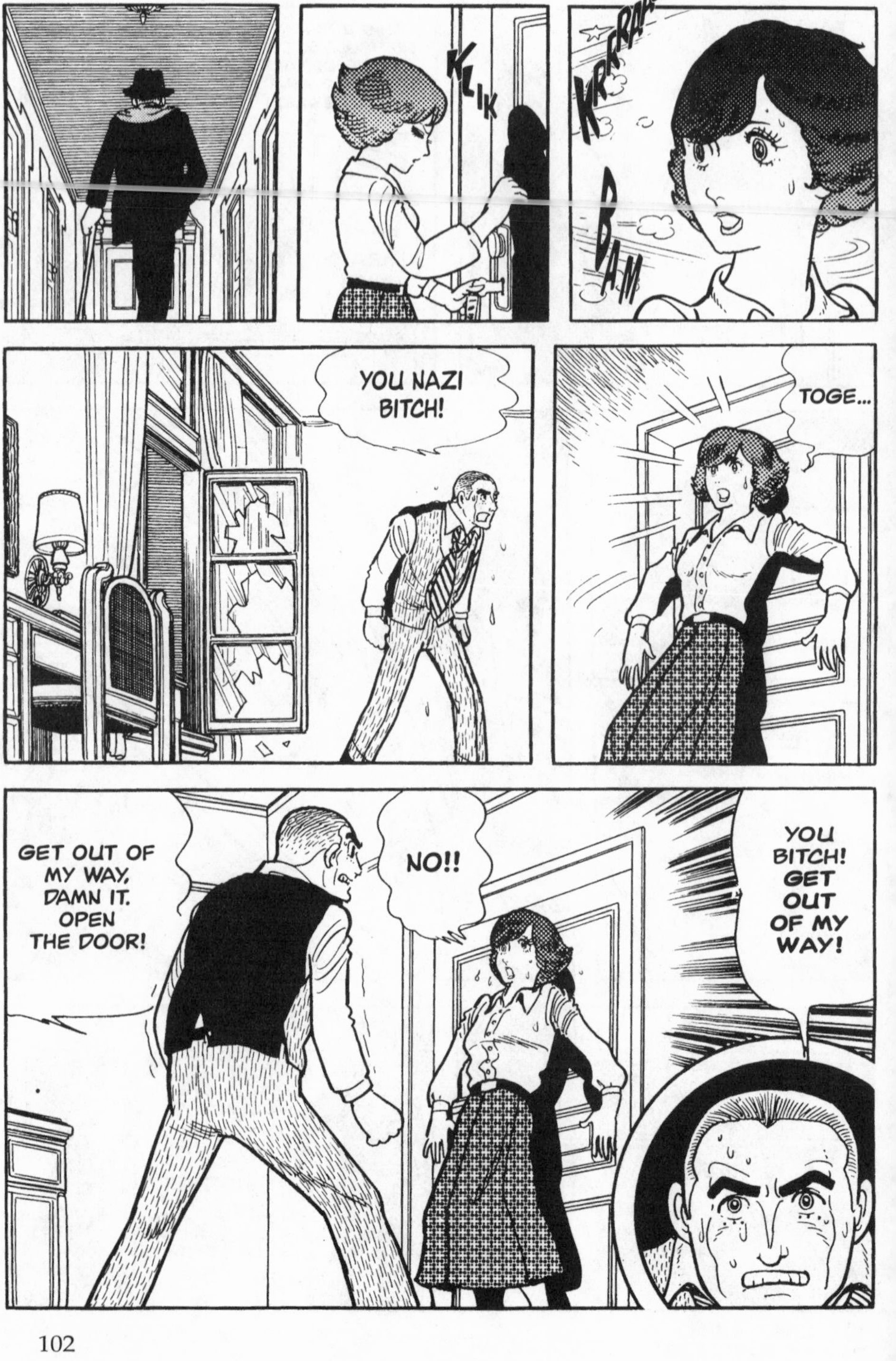
KLIK
KRRRAASH
BAM
YOU NAZI BITCH!
TOGE...
GET OUT OF MY WAY, DAMN IT. OPEN THE DOOR!
NO!!
YOU BITCH! GET OUT OF MY WAY!

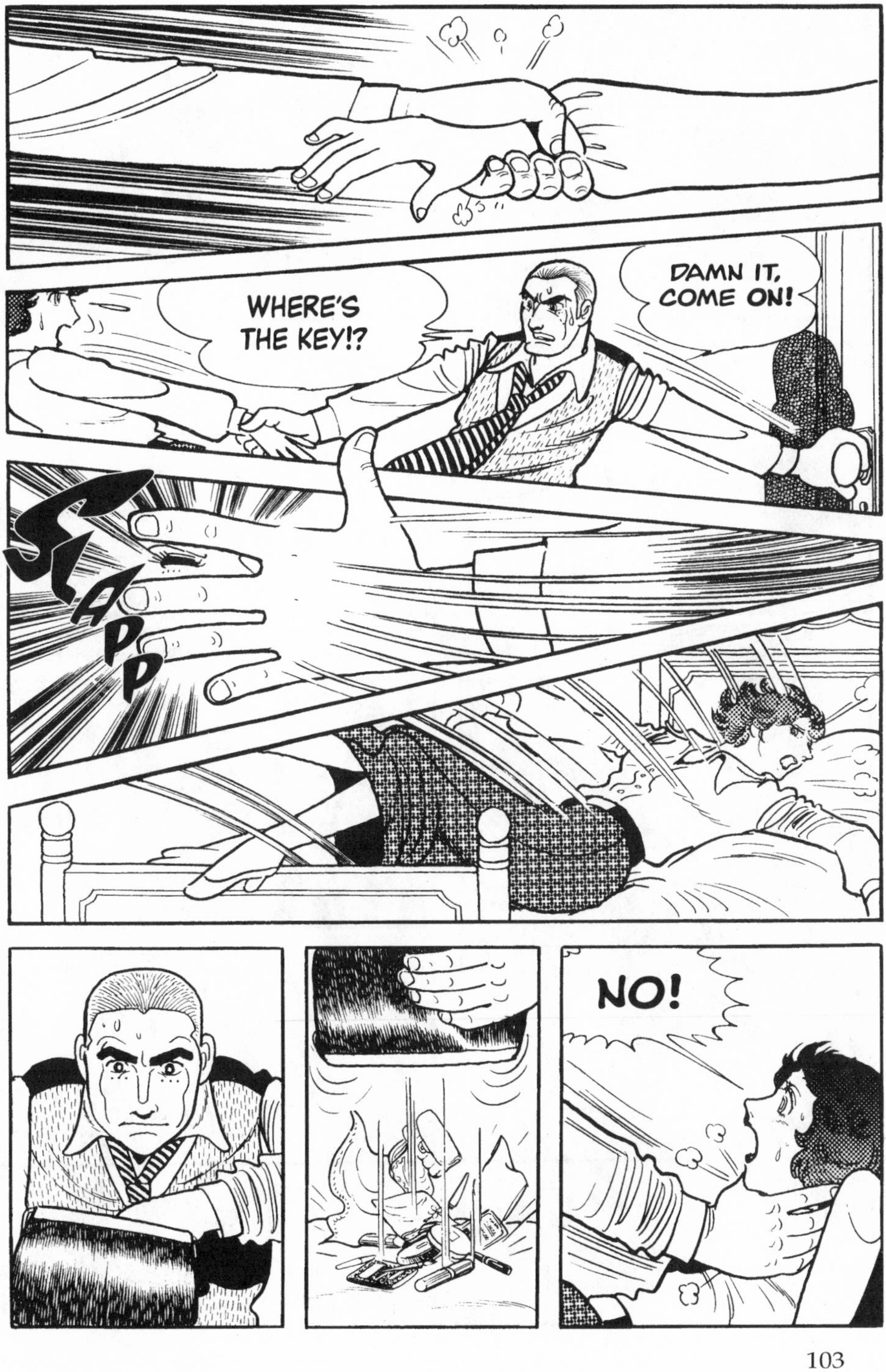
WHERE'S THE KEY!?
DAMN IT, COME ON!
SLAPP
NO!

Adolf

WHERE'S
THE
KEY!?

RRRIP

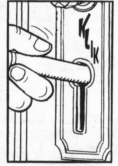

KLIK

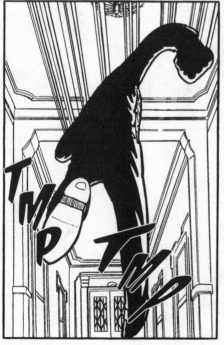

TMP TMP

COME
ON!

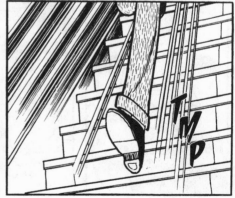

TMP

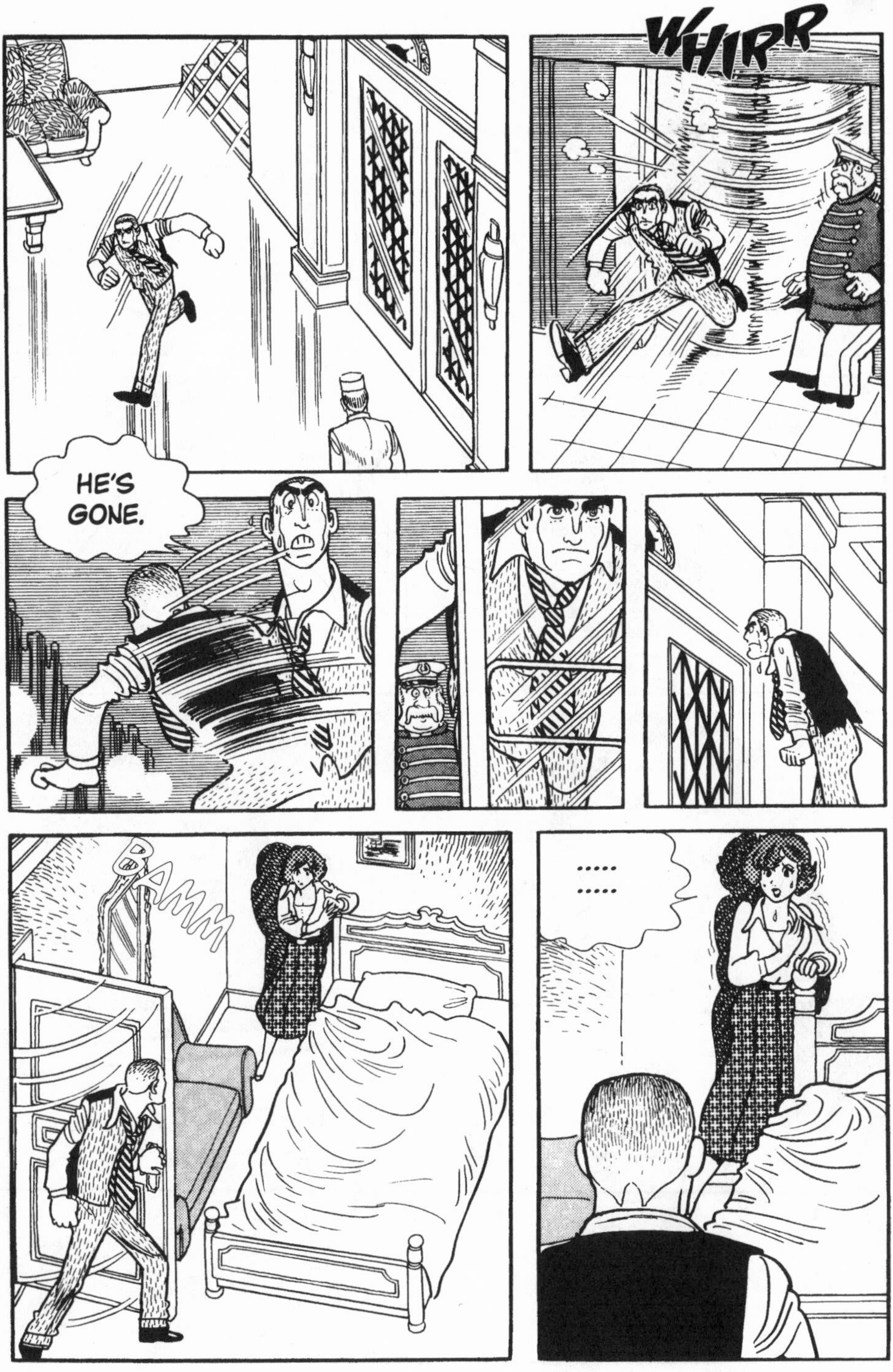
WHIRR
HE'S GONE.
BAMM
.....
.....

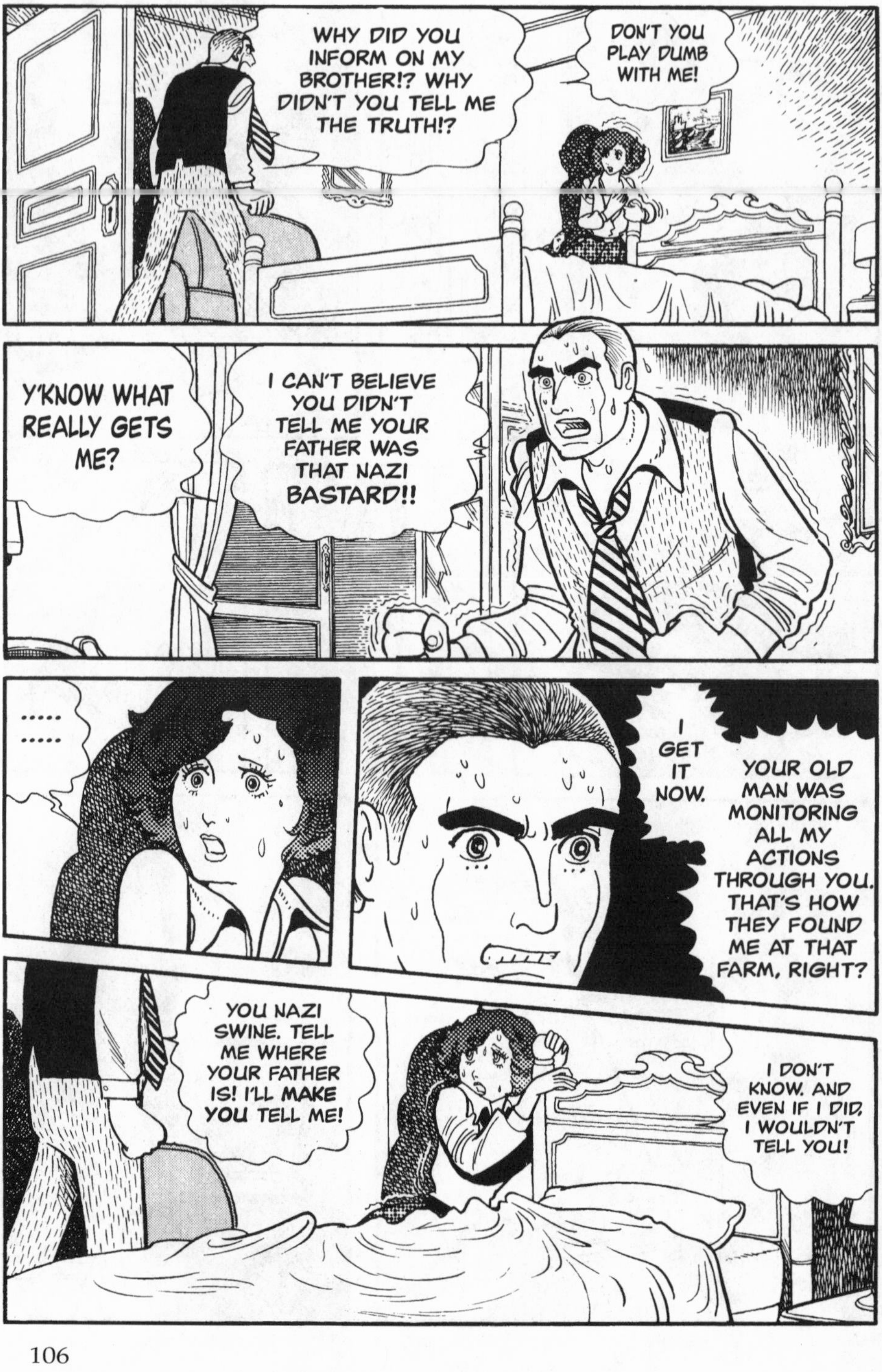
WHY DID YOU INFORM ON MY BROTHER!? WHY DIDN'T YOU TELL ME THE TRUTH!?
DON'T YOU PLAY DUMB WITH ME!
Y'KNOW WHAT REALLY GETS ME?
I CAN'T BELIEVE YOU DIDN'T TELL ME YOUR FATHER WAS THAT NAZI BASTARD!!
....
I GET IT NOW.
YOUR OLD MAN WAS MONITORING ALL MY ACTIONS THROUGH YOU. THAT'S HOW THEY FOUND ME AT THAT FARM, RIGHT?
YOU NAZI SWINE. TELL ME WHERE YOUR FATHER IS! I'LL MAKE YOU TELL ME!
I DON'T KNOW. AND EVEN IF I DID, I WOULDN'T TELL YOU!

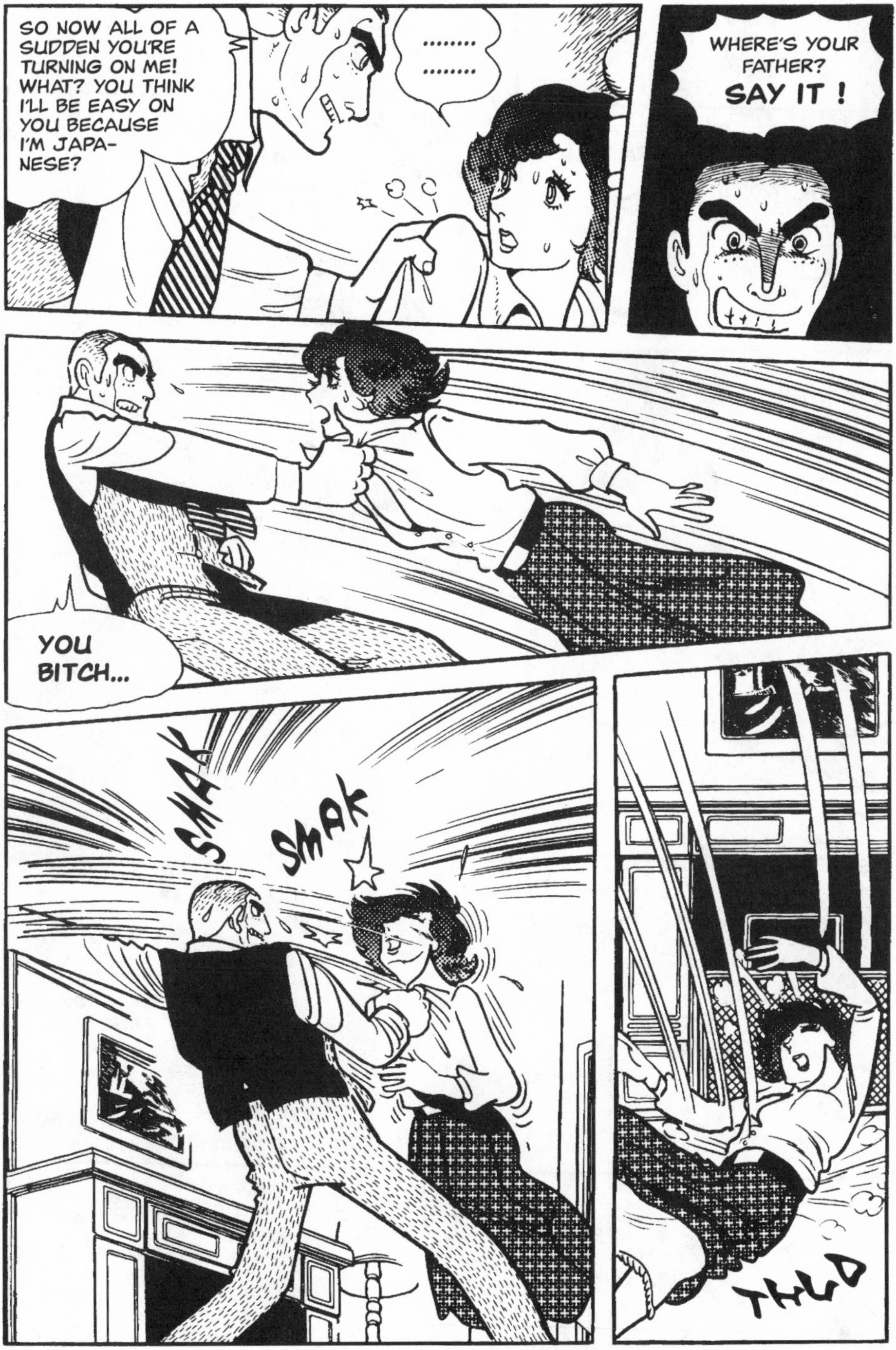
SO NOW ALL OF A SUDDEN YOU'RE TURNING ON ME! WHAT? YOU THINK I'LL BE EASY ON YOU BECAUSE I'M JAPA-NESE?
....
....
WHERE'S YOUR FATHER? SAY IT !
YOU BITCH...
SMAK
SMAK
THUD

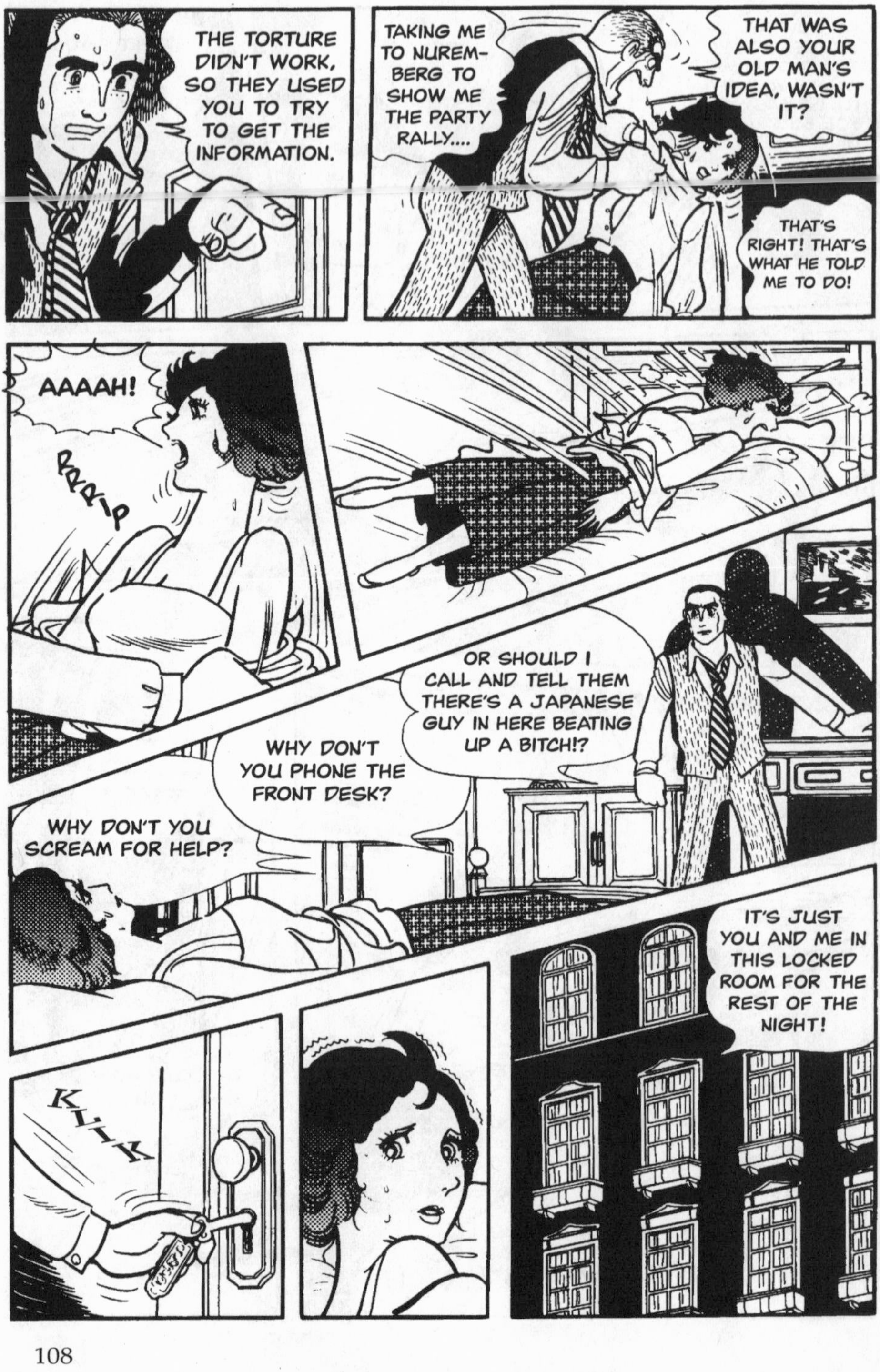
THE TORTURE DIDN'T WORK, SO THEY USED YOU TO TRY TO GET THE INFORMATION.
TAKING ME TO NUREMBERG TO SHOW ME THE PARTY RALLY....
THAT WAS ALSO YOUR OLD MAN'S IDEA, WASN'T IT?
THAT'S RIGHT! THAT'S WHAT HE TOLD ME TO DO!
AAAAH!
RRRIP
WHY DON'T YOU SCREAM FOR HELP?
WHY DON'T YOU PHONE THE FRONT DESK?
OR SHOULD I CALL AND TELL THEM THERE'S A JAPANESE GUY IN HERE BEATING UP A BITCH!?
KLIK
IT'S JUST YOU AND ME IN THIS LOCKED ROOM FOR THE REST OF THE NIGHT!

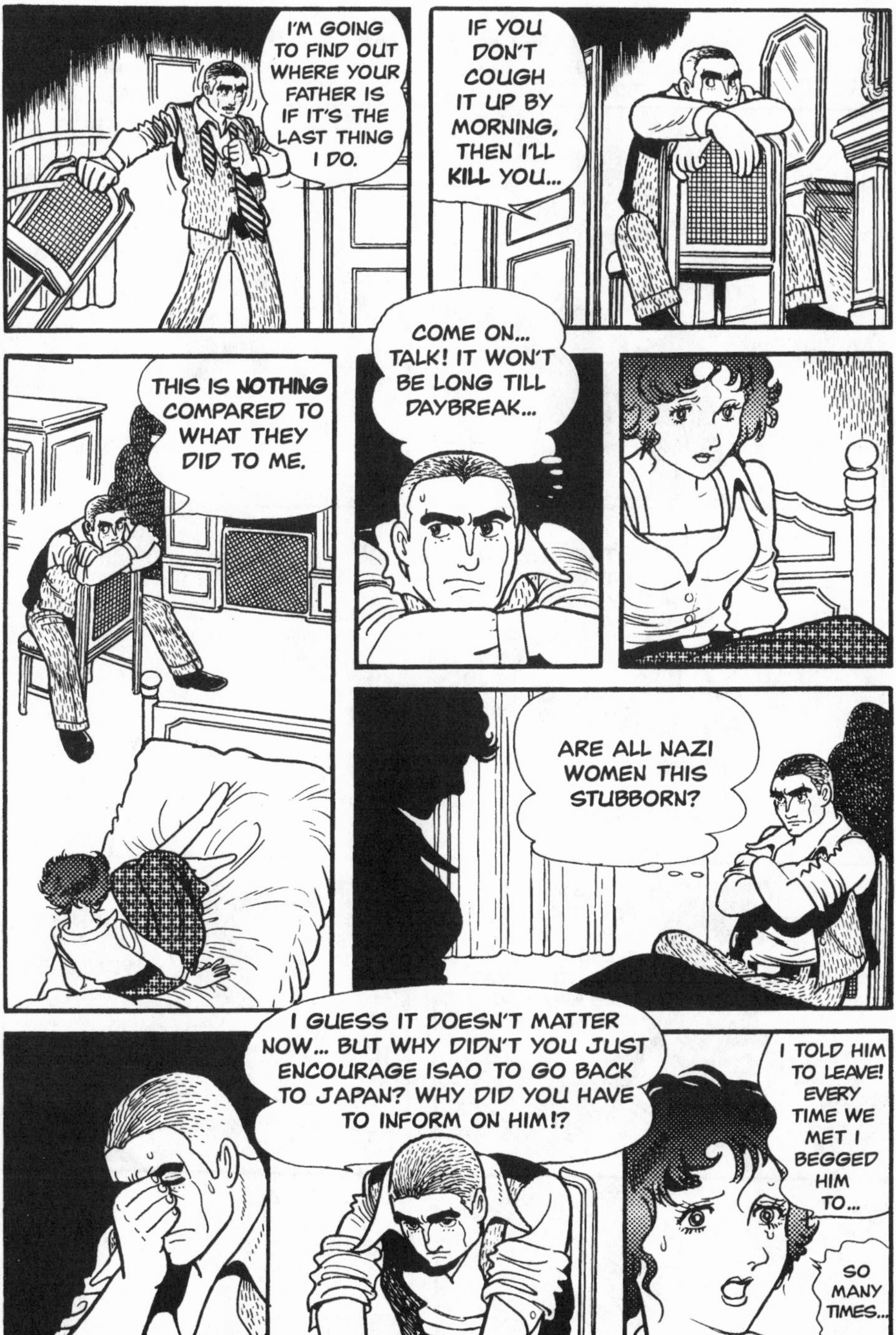
I'M GOING TO FIND OUT WHERE YOUR FATHER IS IF IT'S THE LAST THING I DO.
IF YOU DON'T COUGH IT UP BY MORNING, THEN I'LL KILL YOU...
THIS IS NOTHING COMPARED TO WHAT THEY DID TO ME.
COME ON... TALK! IT WON'T BE LONG TILL DAYBREAK...
ARE ALL NAZI WOMEN THIS STUBBORN?
I GUESS IT DOESN'T MATTER NOW... BUT WHY DIDN'T YOU JUST ENCOURAGE ISAO TO GO BACK TO JAPAN? WHY DID YOU HAVE TO INFORM ON HIM!?
I TOLD HIM TO LEAVE! EVERY TIME WE MET I BEGGED HIM TO...
SO MANY TIMES...

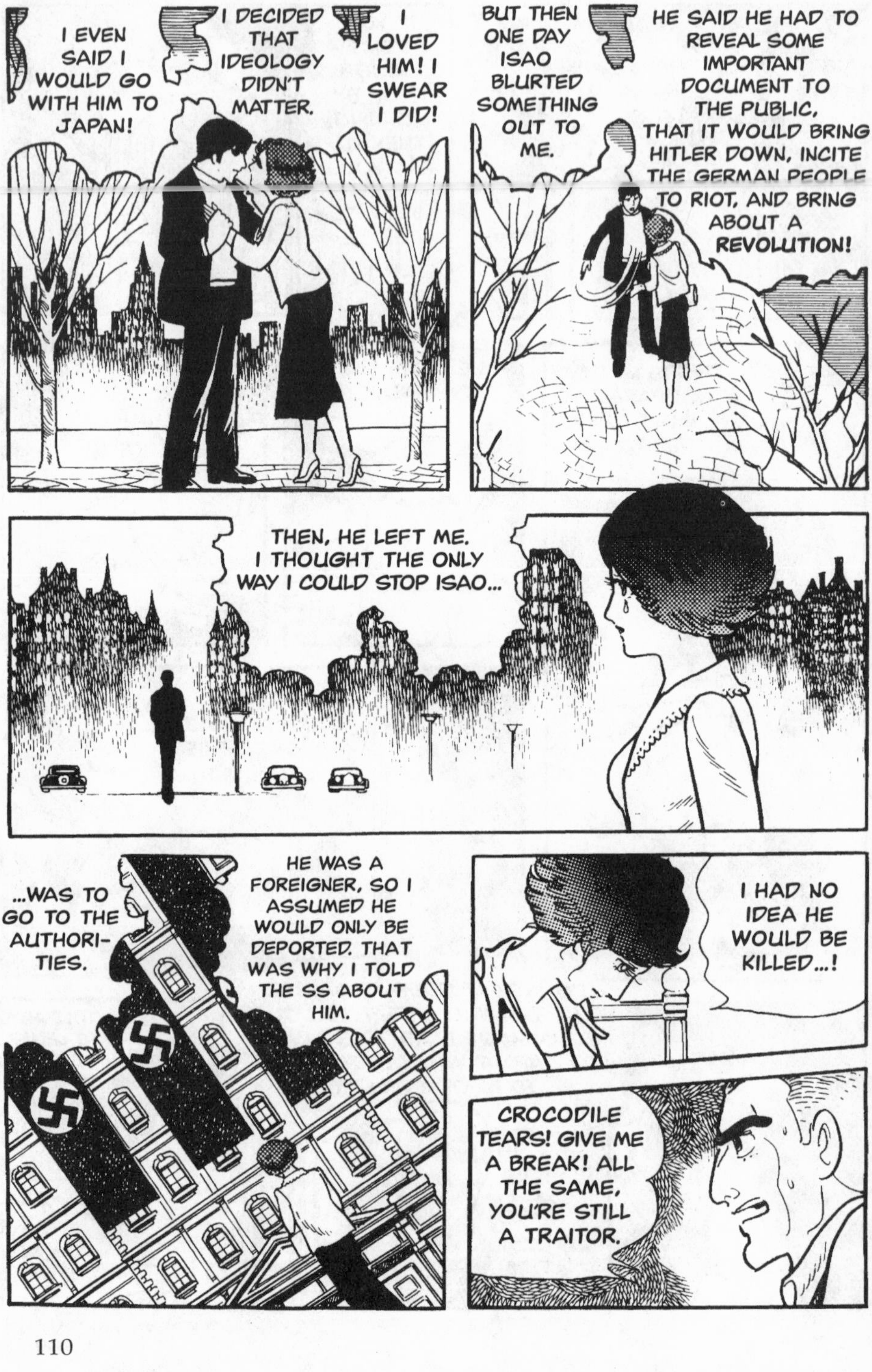
I EVEN SAID I WOULD GO WITH HIM TO JAPAN!
I DECIDED THAT IDEOLOGY DIDN'T MATTER.
I LOVED HIM! I SWEAR I DID!
BUT THEN ONE DAY ISAO BLURTED SOMETHING OUT TO ME.
HE SAID HE HAD TO REVEAL SOME IMPORTANT DOCUMENT TO THE PUBLIC, THAT IT WOULD BRING HITLER DOWN, INCITE THE GERMAN PEOPLE TO RIOT, AND BRING ABOUT A REVOLUTION!
THEN, HE LEFT ME. I THOUGHT THE ONLY WAY I COULD STOP ISAO...
...WAS TO GO TO THE AUTHORITIES.
HE WAS A FOREIGNER, SO I ASSUMED HE WOULD ONLY BE DEPORTED. THAT WAS WHY I TOLD THE SS ABOUT HIM.
I HAD NO IDEA HE WOULD BE KILLED...!
CROCODILE TEARS! GIVE ME A BREAK! ALL THE SAME, YOU'RE STILL A TRAITOR.

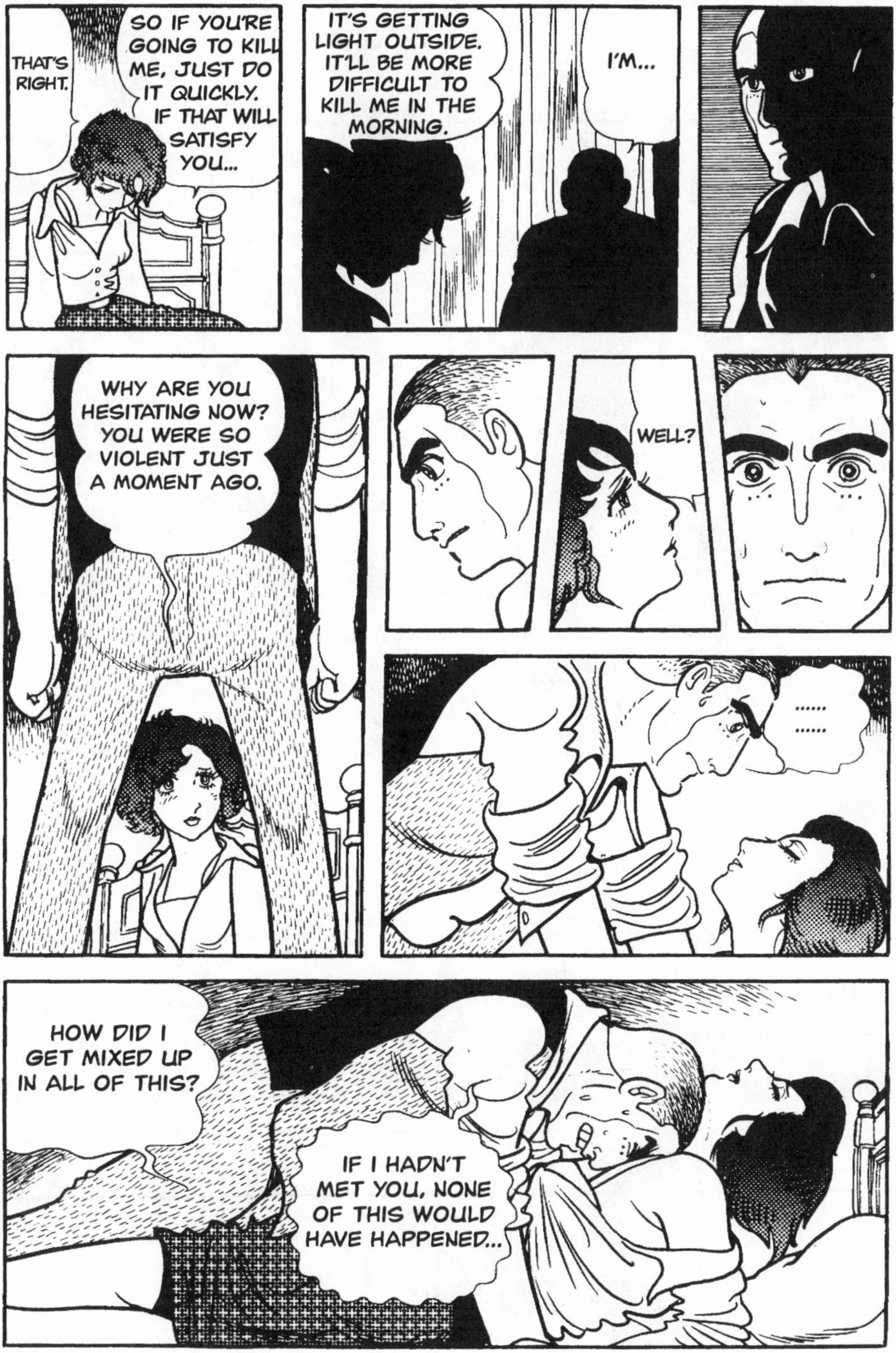
THAT'S RIGHT.
SO IF YOU'RE GOING TO KILL ME, JUST DO IT QUICKLY. IF THAT WILL SATISFY YOU...
IT'S GETTING LIGHT OUTSIDE. IT'LL BE MORE DIFFICULT TO KILL ME IN THE MORNING.
I'M...
WHY ARE YOU HESITATING NOW? YOU WERE SO VIOLENT JUST A MOMENT AGO.
WELL?
......
......
HOW DID I GET MIXED UP IN ALL OF THIS?
IF I HADN'T MET YOU, NONE OF THIS WOULD HAVE HAPPENED...

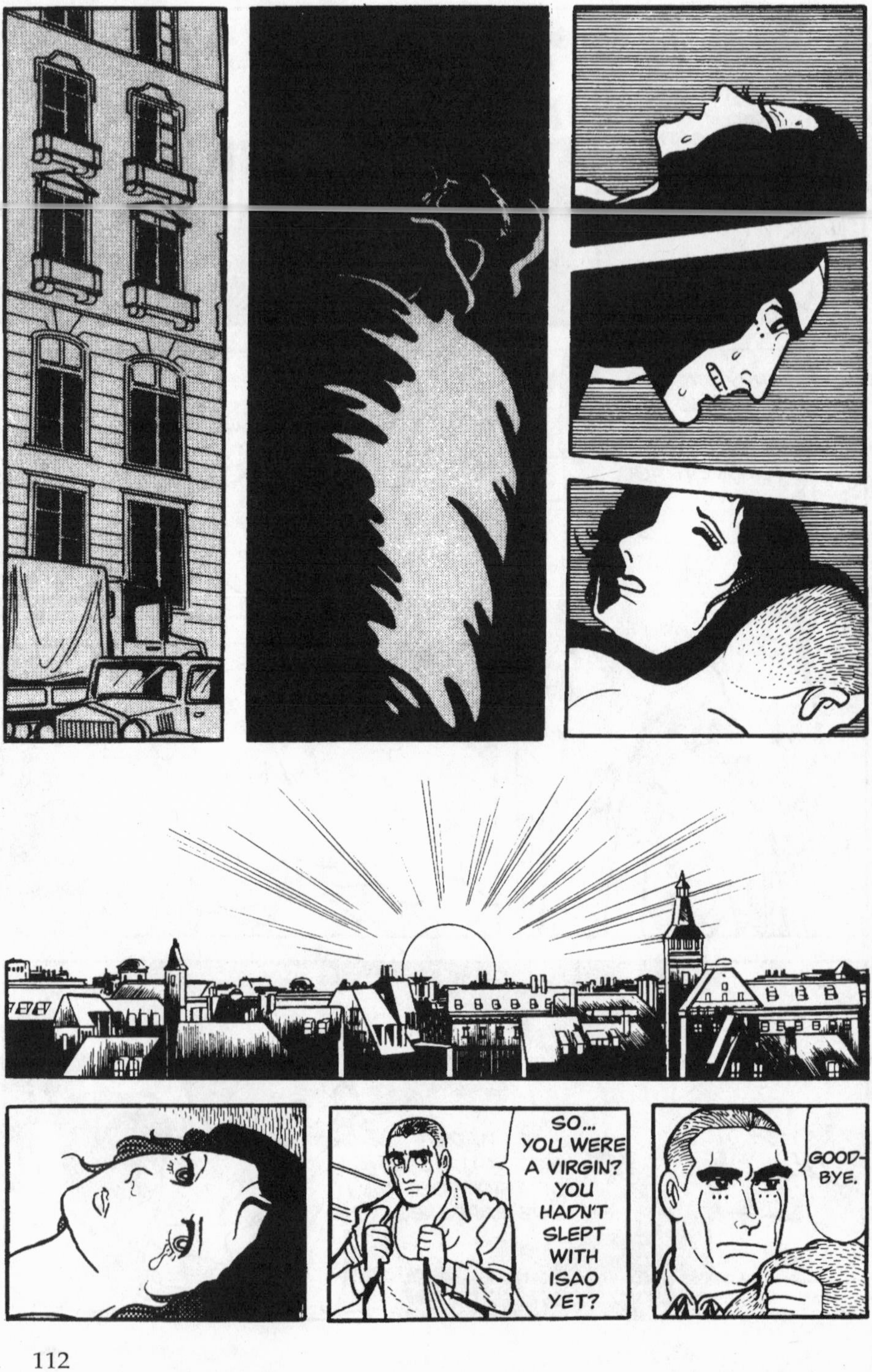
SO... YOU WERE A VIRGIN? YOU HADN'T SLEPT WITH ISAO YET?
GOOD-BYE.

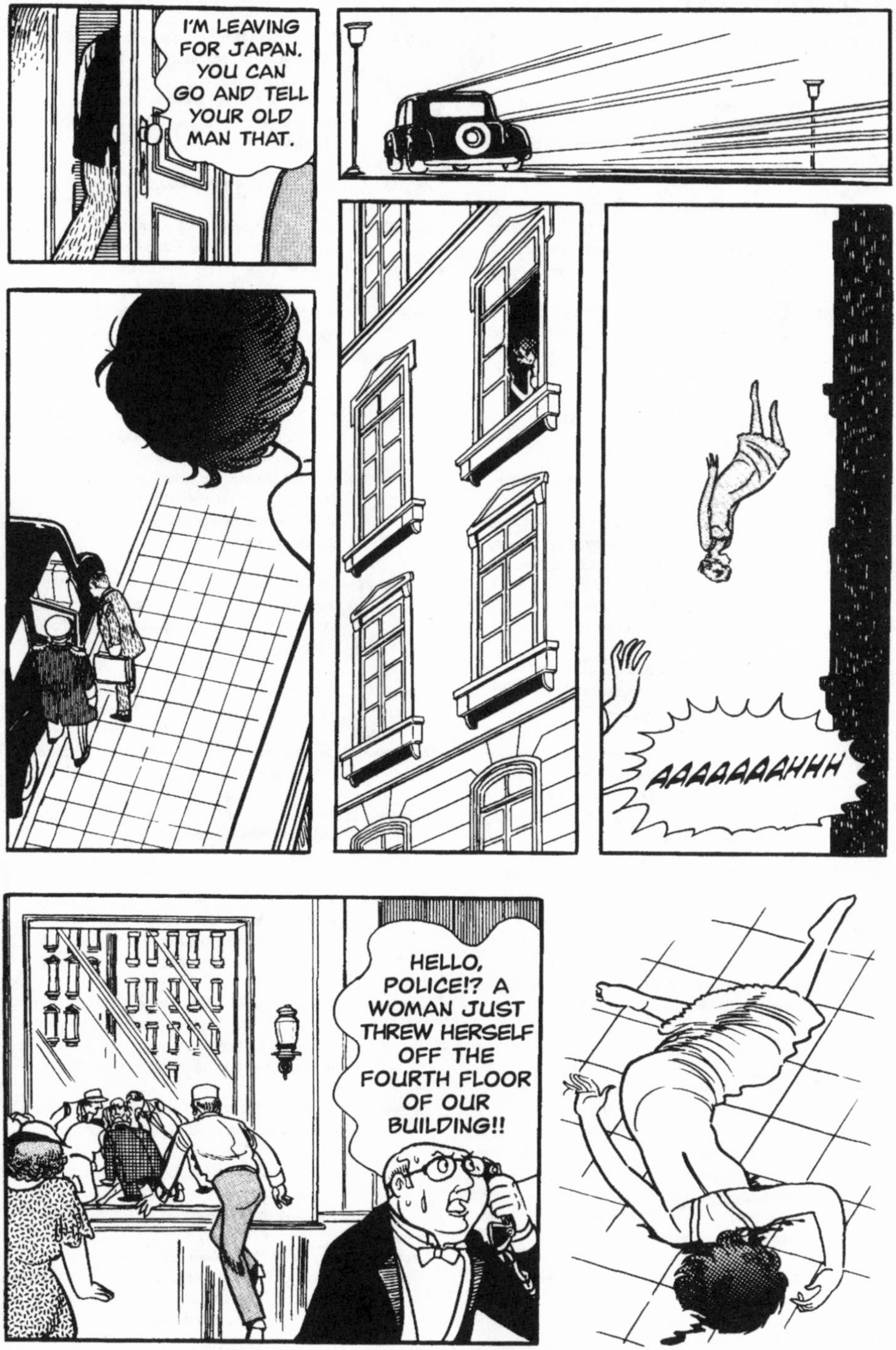
I'M LEAVING FOR JAPAN. YOU CAN GO AND TELL YOUR OLD MAN THAT.
AAAAAAAHHH
HELLO, POLICE!? A WOMAN JUST THREW HERSELF OFF THE FOURTH FLOOR OF OUR BUILDING!!

1936 TIMELINE

January 13 Japan sets up an autonomous government in North China.

January 15 Japan withdraws from the London Naval Disarmament Conference, an agreement between the major powers to maintain a balance of naval power, and begins producing vast numbers of munitions.

January 17 In a speech given in Berlin, German Propaganda Chief Joseph Goebbels declares, "We can do without butter, but, despite all our love of peace, not without arms. One cannot shoot with butter but with guns."

February 10 A German law is enacted making the Gestapo a Supreme Reich Agency, thus giving Heinrich Himmler, chief of the SS and the Gestapo, absolute control over German internal security.

February 19 The Leftist Popular Front, a Communist organization, establishes a ruling cabinet in Spain.

February 26 Seeking a military-socialist dictatorship under the emperor and an end to moderate's pressure to curb military involvement in politics, Japanese Army extremists attempt to force radical government reforms by assassinating the minister of finance, the director-general of military education, and a former prime minister, Makoto Saito. Most military units remain loyal, and the outburst is readily contained.

March 7 Disregarding the Treaty of Versailles and the Locarno Treaties, Germany sends troops into the demilitarized left bank of the Rhineland.

March 9 Foreign Minister Koki Hirota is appointed Japanese prime minister, and the cabinet is restructured in order to allow the military greater power. Hirota himself favors expansion into China, and he is a prime force behind Japan's decision to become a member of the Axis Powers.

May 9 Italy designates Ethiopia, Eritria, and Somaliland as Italian East Africa.

May 12 Italy announces its intentions to withdraw from the League of Nations, which was created to peacefully negotiate disputes between nations.

May 18 The Japanese War Ministry is re-established.

June 2 Chinese military commanders in the southwest of China demand that the Nationalists resist the Japanese military buildup in North China rather than persist in participating in regional disputes between their own people. A growing number of Chinese have grown weary of internal bickering and the weak stand of the Nanking government as Japan furthers its military expansion throughout Asia.

June 30 The French government declares the Fascist Party of France illegal.

July 4 The Japanese Ministry of Education institutes a policy of eight years of compulsory schooling.

July 5 A Japanese military tribunal sentences seventeen persons to death for their involvement in the incident of February 26.

July 13 Tokyo is declared the location for the 1940 Olympics.

July 18 General Francisco Franco moves to oust the Spanish government and replace it with his own Fascist government, triggering the Spanish Civil War.

August 7 Japan's National Policy, calling for a military buildup against the Soviet Union and the United States, becomes official.

August 15 Japanese Premier Hirota—who has become increasingly receptive to the views of military extremists—outlines Japan's foreign policy goals to the emperor. They include expansion into the Dutch East Indies, Manchurian economic growth, independence for the Philippines, and the elimination of white rule in Asia—all while maintaining peaceful relations with the United States and Britain.

October 27 The Rome-Berlin Axis, an alliance between Italy and Germany, is forged. The pact is ostensibly created to carry out "the supreme obligation…to defend the great institutions of Europe."

November 1 Franklin D. Roosevelt is overwhelmingly elected to a second term as president of the United States.

November 18 Germany and Italy formally recognize the Franco government in Spain.

November 25 Japan and Germany, declaring their agreement to oppose Communism together, sign the Anti-Comintern Pact.

December 5 The Popular Front Movement, a Japanese political alliance which includes socialists, Communists, and other banned liberal activists, is suppressed. Over 1,000 members are arrested.

December 10 Edward VIII abdicates the throne of England to marry an American divorcée, Wallis Warfield Simpson. The two were considered Nazi sympathizers because they supported the Nazis' opposition to Communism.

December 12 In the Siam incident in China, Chiang Kaishek, leader of the Nationalists, is kidnapped by regional military leaders. Chou Enlai, a Communist leader, negotiates Chiang Kaishek's release, as well as an agreement that the Nationalists and Communists join forces to fight the Japanese under Chiang Kiashek's leadership.

December 31 The London Naval Disarmament Treaty, in effect since January 1, 1931, expires. The treaty was a meaningless formality anyway, since many of the signatory states had no intention of honoring it.

CHAPTER
THREE

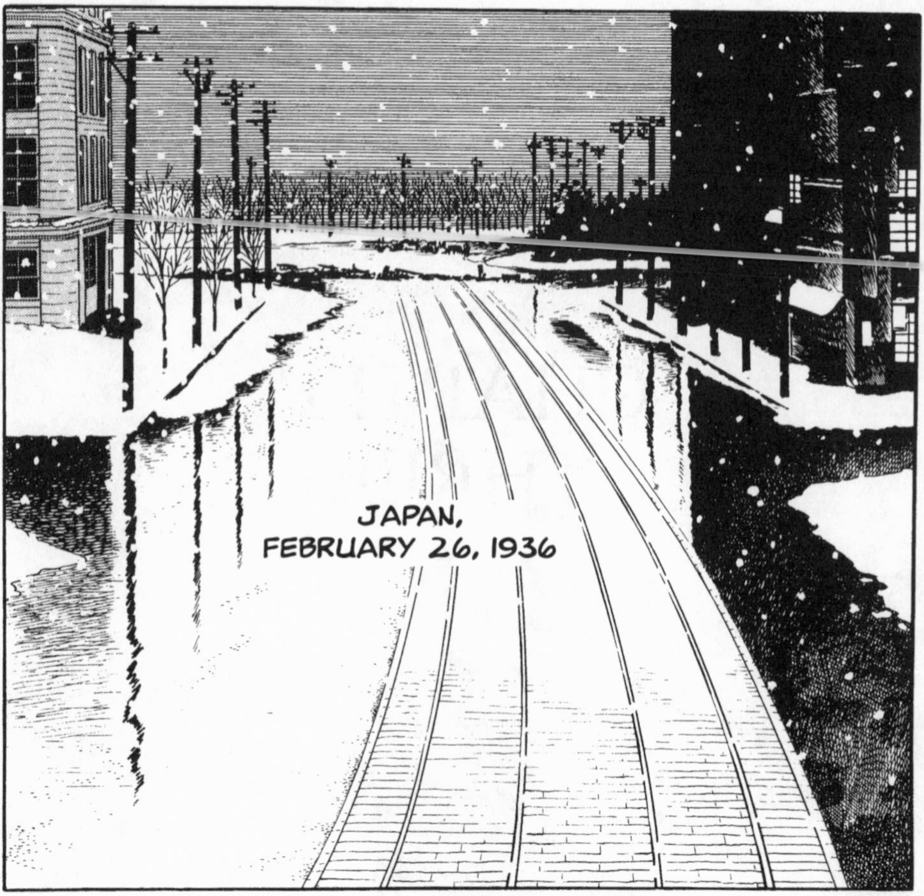
JAPAN,
FEBRUARY 26, 1936

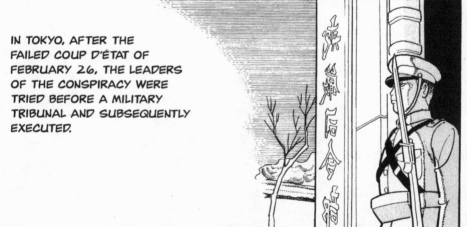

IN TOKYO, AFTER THE FAILED COUP D'ÉTAT OF FEBRUARY 26, THE LEADERS OF THE CONSPIRACY WERE TRIED BEFORE A MILITARY TRIBUNAL AND SUBSEQUENTLY EXECUTED.

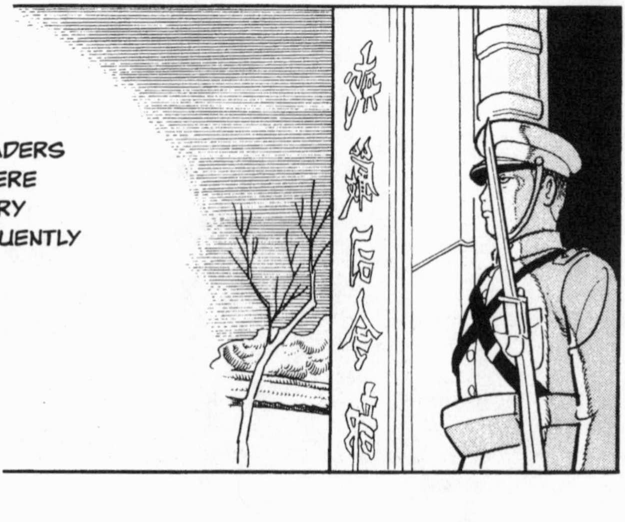

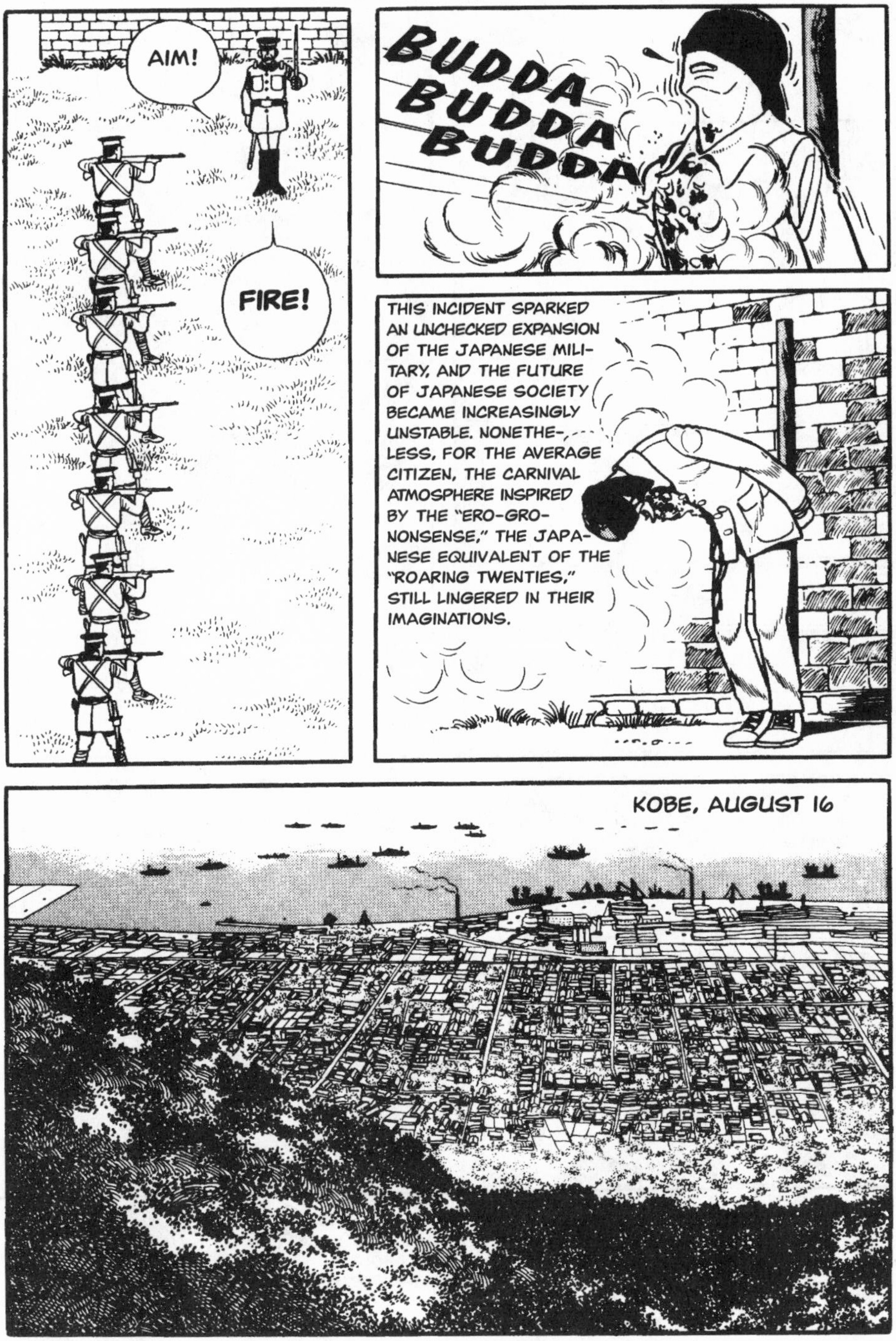
AIM!
FIRE!
BUDDA BUDDA BUDDA
THIS INCIDENT SPARKED AN UNCHECKED EXPANSION OF THE JAPANESE MILITARY, AND THE FUTURE OF JAPANESE SOCIETY BECAME INCREASINGLY UNSTABLE. NONETHELESS, FOR THE AVERAGE CITIZEN, THE CARNIVAL ATMOSPHERE INSPIRED BY THE "ERO-GRO-NONSENSE," THE JAPANESE EQUIVALENT OF THE "ROARING TWENTIES," STILL LINGERED IN THEIR IMAGINATIONS.
KOBE, AUGUST 16

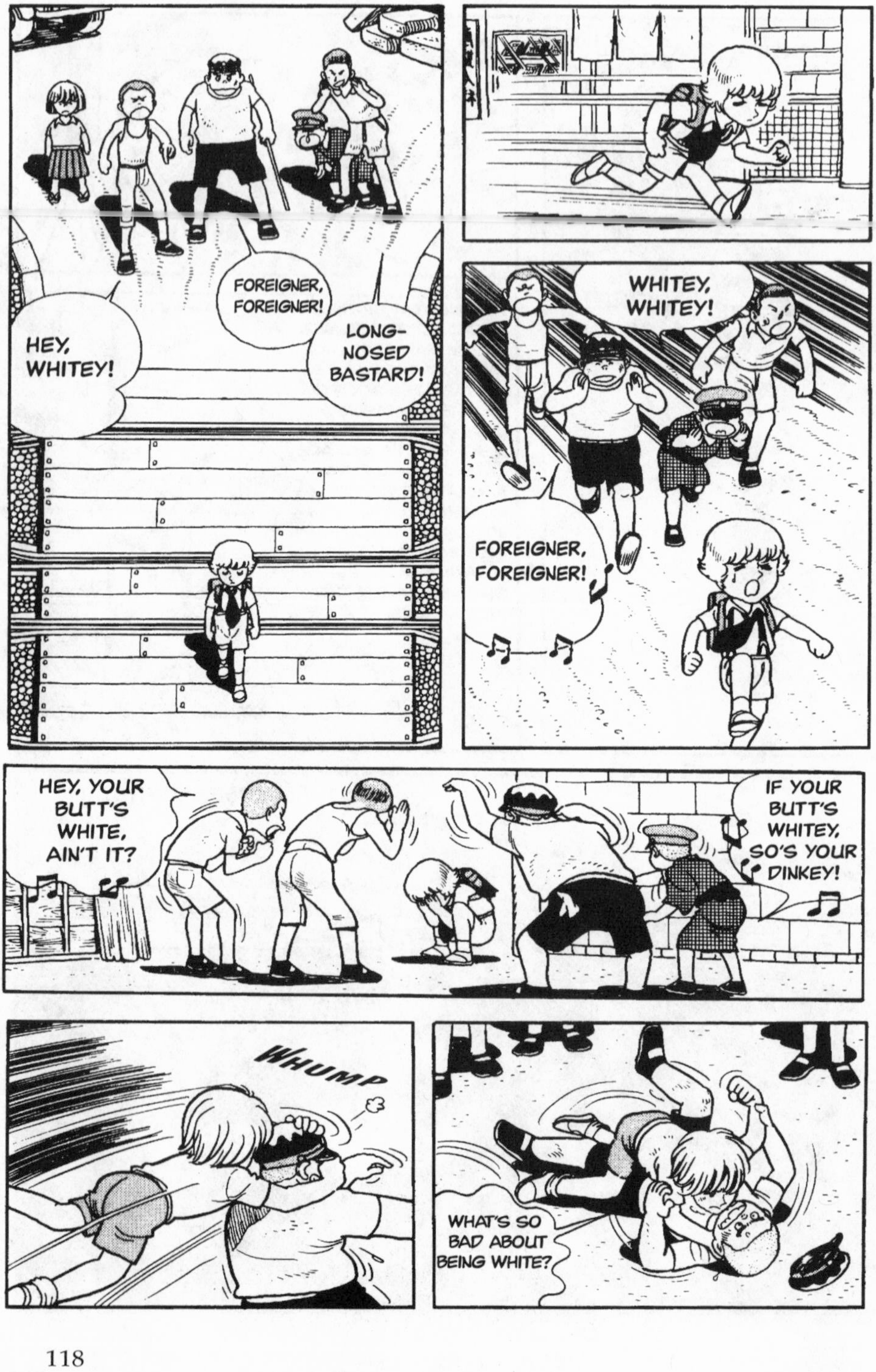
HEY, WHITEY!
FOREIGNER, FOREIGNER!
LONG-NOSED BASTARD!
WHITEY, WHITEY!
FOREIGNER, FOREIGNER!
HEY, YOUR BUTT'S WHITE, AIN'T IT?
IF YOUR BUTT'S WHITEY, SO'S YOUR DINKEY!
WHUMP
WHAT'S SO BAD ABOUT BEING WHITE?

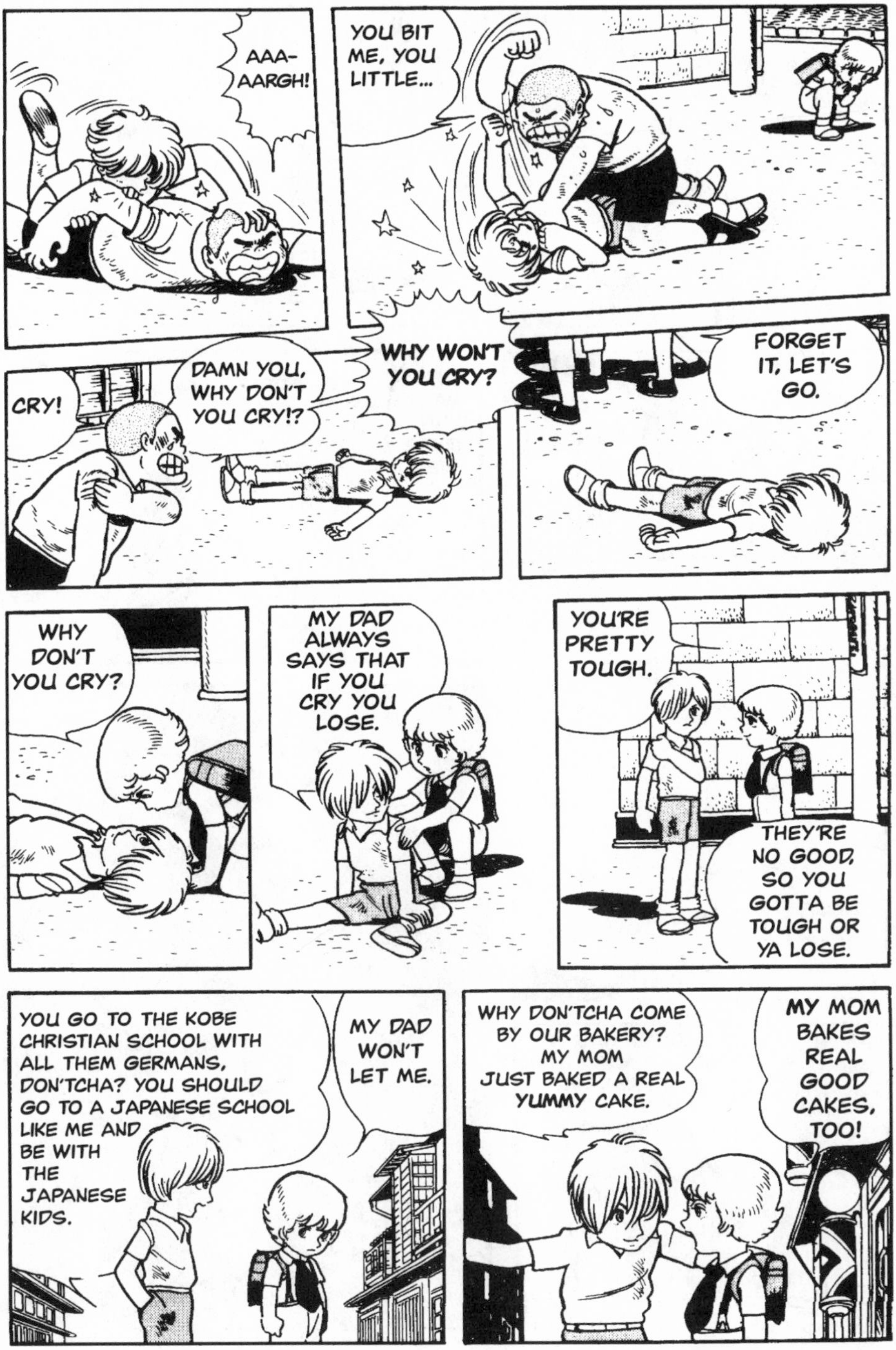
AAA-
AARGH!
YOU BIT ME, YOU LITTLE...
WHY WON'T YOU CRY?
CRY!
DAMN YOU, WHY DON'T YOU CRY!?
FORGET IT, LET'S GO.
WHY DON'T YOU CRY?
MY DAD ALWAYS SAYS THAT IF YOU CRY YOU LOSE.
YOU'RE PRETTY TOUGH.
THEY'RE NO GOOD, SO YOU GOTTA BE TOUGH OR YA LOSE.
YOU GO TO THE KOBE CHRISTIAN SCHOOL WITH ALL THEM GERMANS, DON'TCHA? YOU SHOULD GO TO A JAPANESE SCHOOL LIKE ME AND BE WITH THE JAPANESE KIDS.
MY DAD WON'T LET ME.
WHY DON'TCHA COME BY OUR BAKERY? MY MOM JUST BAKED A REAL YUMMY CAKE.
MY MOM BAKES REAL GOOD CAKES, TOO!

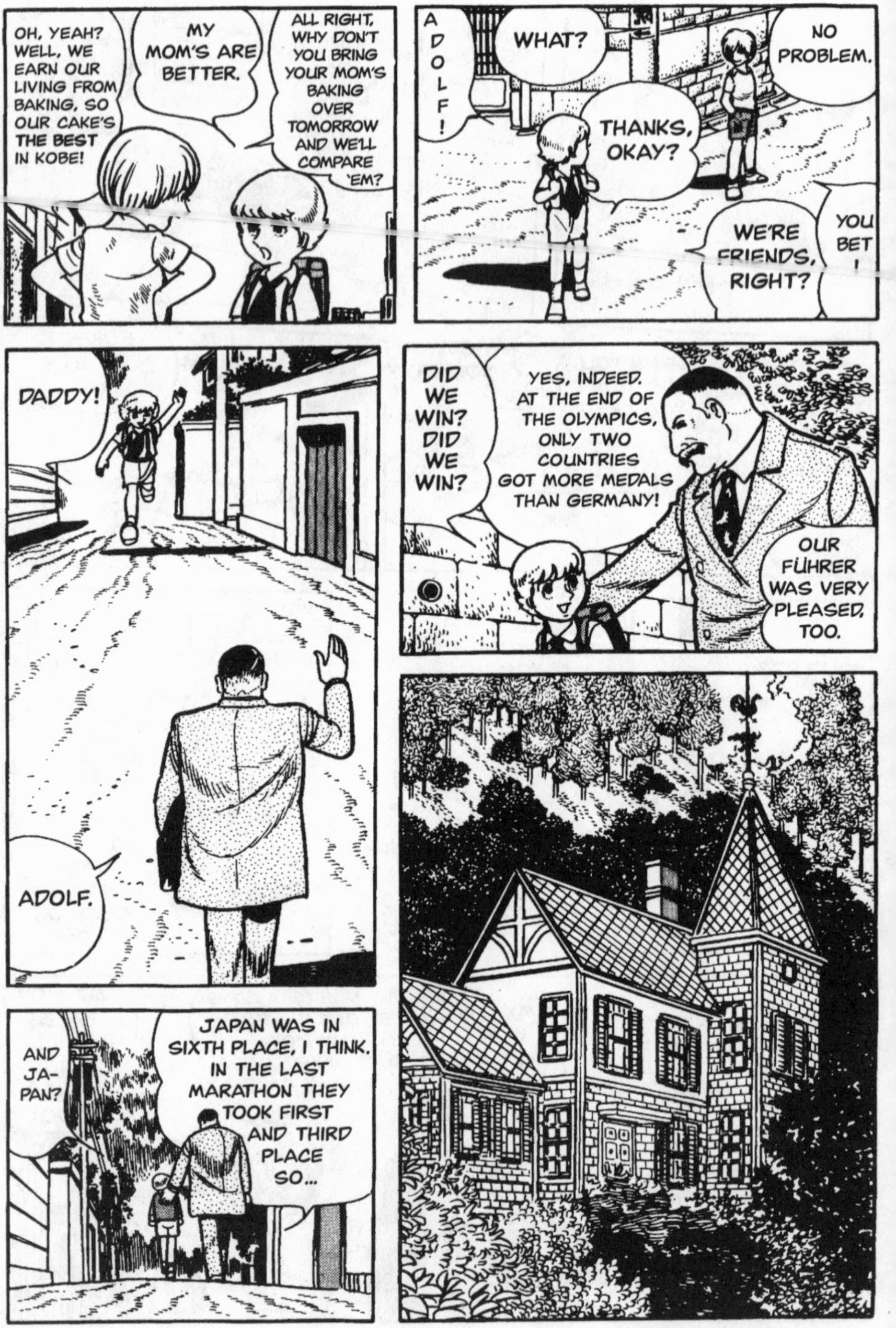
OH, YEAH? WELL, WE EARN OUR LIVING FROM BAKING, SO OUR CAKE'S THE BEST IN KOBE!
MY MOM'S ARE BETTER.
ALL RIGHT, WHY DON'T YOU BRING YOUR MOM'S BAKING OVER TOMORROW AND WE'LL COMPARE 'EM?
ADOLF!
WHAT?
NO PROBLEM.
THANKS, OKAY?
WE'RE FRIENDS, RIGHT?
YOU BET!
DADDY!
ADOLF.
DID WE WIN? DID WE WIN?
YES, INDEED. AT THE END OF THE OLYMPICS, ONLY TWO COUNTRIES GOT MORE MEDALS THAN GERMANY!
OUR FÜHRER WAS VERY PLEASED, TOO.
AND JA-PAN?
JAPAN WAS IN SIXTH PLACE, I THINK. IN THE LAST MARATHON THEY TOOK FIRST AND THIRD PLACE SO...

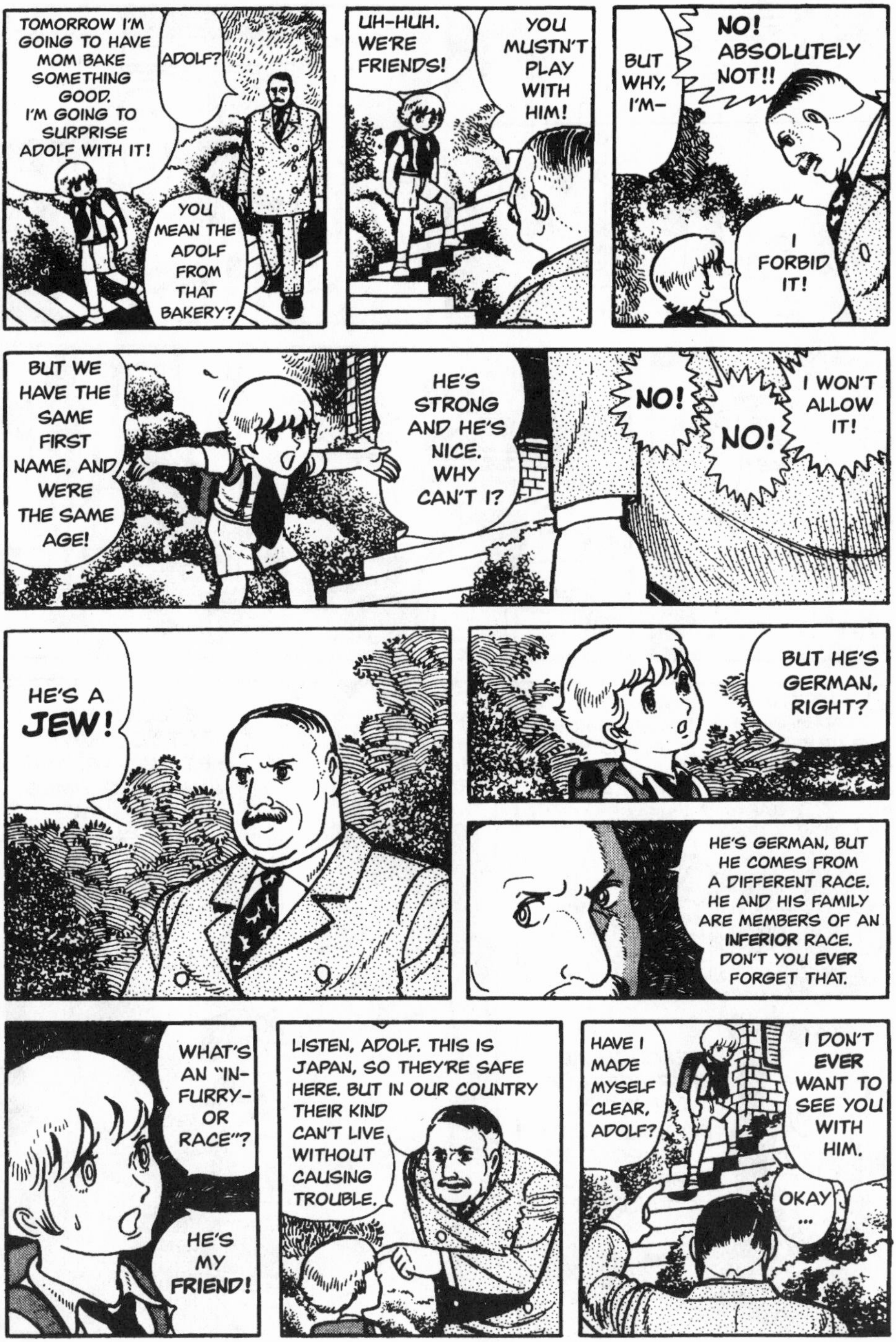
TOMORROW I'M GOING TO HAVE MOM BAKE SOMETHING GOOD. I'M GOING TO SURPRISE ADOLF WITH IT!
ADOLF?
YOU MEAN THE ADOLF FROM THAT BAKERY?
UH-HUH. WE'RE FRIENDS!
YOU MUSTN'T PLAY WITH HIM!
BUT WHY, I'M–
NO! ABSOLUTELY NOT!!
I FORBID IT!
BUT WE HAVE THE SAME FIRST NAME, AND WE'RE THE SAME AGE!
HE'S STRONG AND HE'S NICE. WHY CAN'T I?
NO!
NO!
I WON'T ALLOW IT!
HE'S A JEW!
BUT HE'S GERMAN, RIGHT?
HE'S GERMAN, BUT HE COMES FROM A DIFFERENT RACE. HE AND HIS FAMILY ARE MEMBERS OF AN INFERIOR RACE. DON'T YOU EVER FORGET THAT.
WHAT'S AN "IN-FURRY-OR RACE"?
HE'S MY FRIEND!
LISTEN, ADOLF. THIS IS JAPAN, SO THEY'RE SAFE HERE. BUT IN OUR COUNTRY THEIR KIND CAN'T LIVE WITHOUT CAUSING TROUBLE.
HAVE I MADE MYSELF CLEAR, ADOLF?
I DON'T EVER WANT TO SEE YOU WITH HIM.
OKAY ...

Adolf

DEAR, I—

HI, MOM!

DO WE HAVE COMPANY?

SOMEONE FROM THE POLICE.

WHAT? THE POLICE?

I'M SORRY TO DISTURB YOU. I'M YONEYAMA, HYOGO PREFECTURE'S CHIEF OF INVESTIGATIONS.

I MUST SAY, MR. KAUFMANN, I'M QUITE RELIEVED TO FIND THAT YOU CAN SPEAK JAPANESE.

WELL, I'VE BEEN IN KOBE FOR 15 YEARS, AND MY WIFE IS JAPANESE...

NO, I DON'T RECALL ANYONE BY THAT NAME. WHY DO YOU ASK?

EXCUSE ME, BUT YOU HAVE MET THIS WOMAN NUMEROUS TIMES. YOU KNOW THAT SHE WAS FOUND DEAD IN THE MOUNTAINS LAST JANUARY?

EXCUSE ME FOR BEING SO ABRUPT, BUT DO YOU RECALL SOMEONE BY THE NAME OF "KINUKO"?

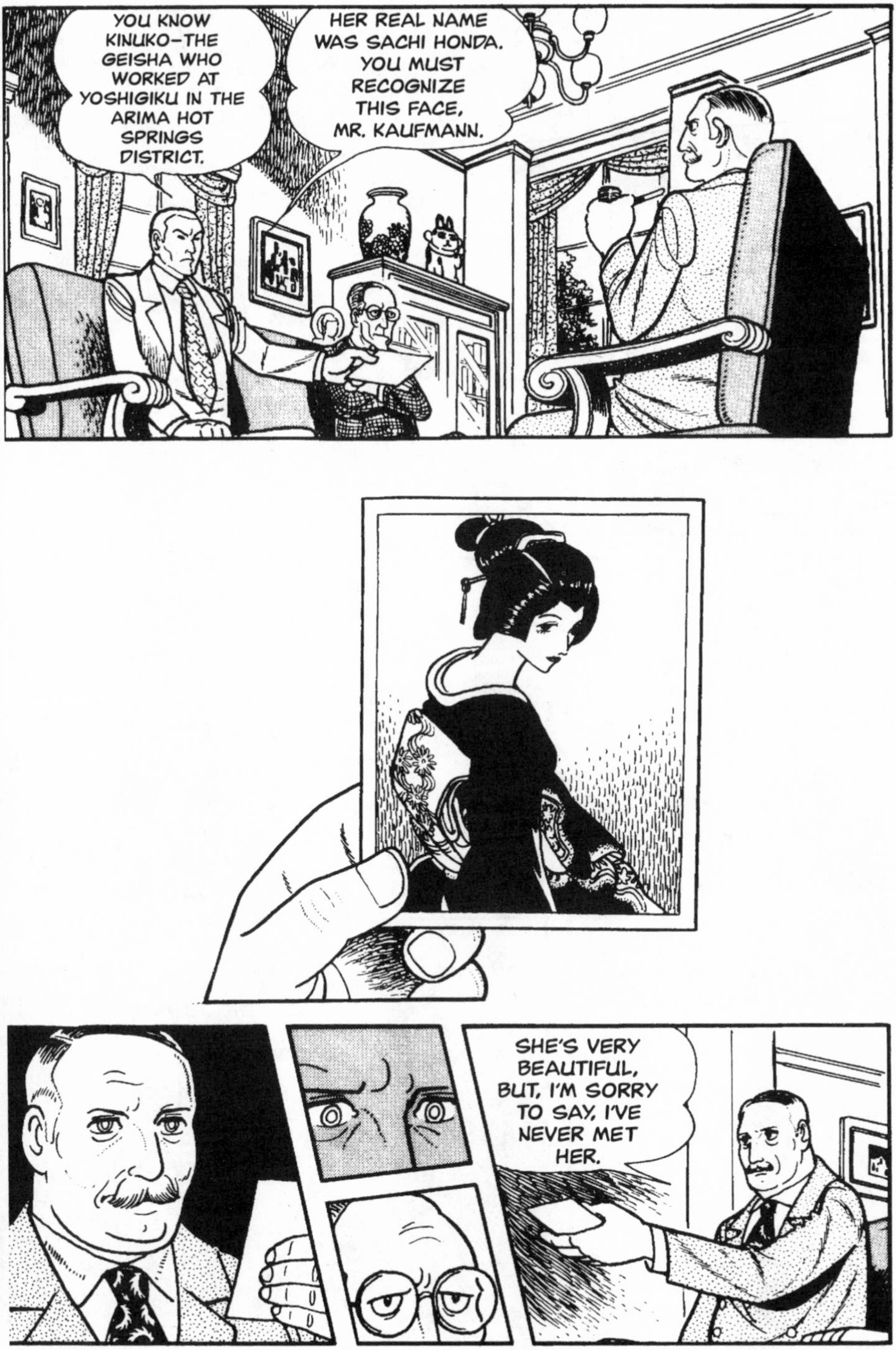
YOU KNOW KINUKO—THE GEISHA WHO WORKED AT YOSHIGIKU IN THE ARIMA HOT SPRINGS DISTRICT.
HER REAL NAME WAS SACHI HONDA. YOU MUST RECOGNIZE THIS FACE, MR. KAUFMANN.
SHE'S VERY BEAUTIFUL, BUT, I'M SORRY TO SAY, I'VE NEVER MET HER.

Adolf

ARE YOU SURE?

I SWEAR IT.

ACCORDING TO THIS LIST, OUT OF THE 12 TIMES YOU STAYED THERE LAST YEAR AND THIS YEAR, YOU REQUESTED KINUKO FROM YOSHIGIKU EIGHT TIMES.

I'VE HAD TO TAKE HIGH-RANKING OFFICIALS FROM MY HOMELAND TO ARIMA PLENTY OF TIMES. YOU CAN'T EXPECT ME TO REMEMBER WHICH GEISHA I CALLED ON FOR THOSE OCCASIONS.

THAT'S ODD, BECAUSE WE HAVE A LIST OF THE DAYS YOU SPENT AT ONE OF THE ARIMA INNS...

8/12
9/5 - 7
9/19
10/26 -28
11/4

INDEED. BUT THE OWNER OF YOSHIGIKU INSISTED THAT SHE SAW YOU ALONE WITH THE VICTIM ON AT LEAST FIVE OF THOSE EIGHT OCCASIONS.

THAT'S ABSURD!

I MUST SAY, I FIND THESE ACCUSA-TIONS APPALLING!

I WON'T ALLOW YOU TO SPEAK OF SUCH MATTERS IN MY HOUSE. PLEASE LEAVE!

I'M VERY SORRY, BUT THIS IS JUST A ROUTINE PART OF OUR INVESTIGA-TION.

PERMIT ME TO ASK YOU THIS... WHERE WERE YOU BETWEEN THE 28TH AND 31ST OF JANUARY?

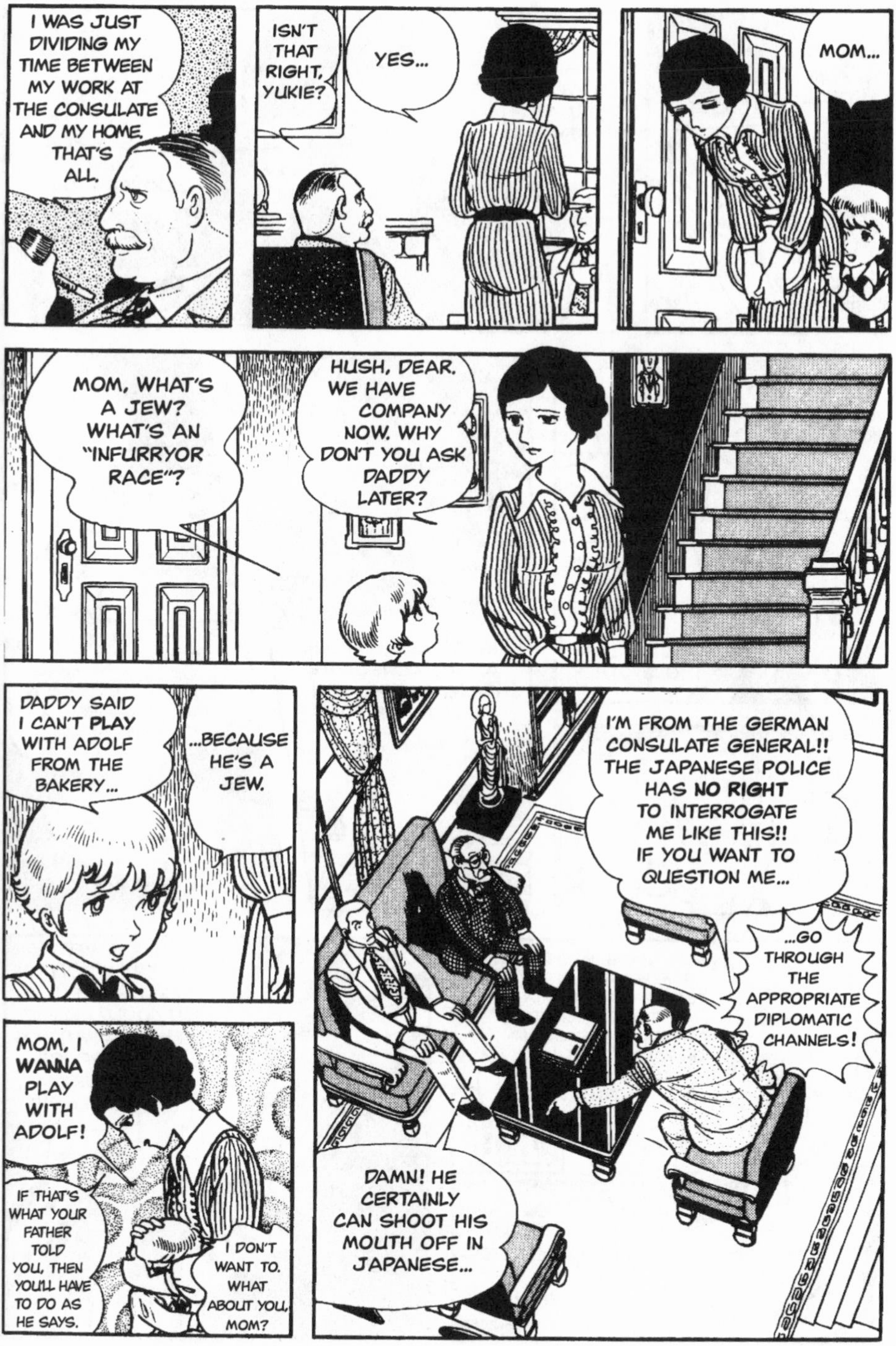
I WAS JUST DIVIDING MY TIME BETWEEN MY WORK AT THE CONSULATE AND MY HOME. THAT'S ALL.
ISN'T THAT RIGHT, YUKIE?
YES...
MOM...
MOM, WHAT'S A JEW? WHAT'S AN "INFURRYOR RACE"?
HUSH, DEAR. WE HAVE COMPANY NOW. WHY DON'T YOU ASK DADDY LATER?
DADDY SAID I CAN'T PLAY WITH ADOLF FROM THE BAKERY...
...BECAUSE HE'S A JEW.
MOM, I WANNA PLAY WITH ADOLF!
IF THAT'S WHAT YOUR FATHER TOLD YOU, THEN YOU'LL HAVE TO DO AS HE SAYS.
I DON'T WANT TO. WHAT ABOUT YOU, MOM?
I'M FROM THE GERMAN CONSULATE GENERAL!! THE JAPANESE POLICE HAS NO RIGHT TO INTERROGATE ME LIKE THIS!! IF YOU WANT TO QUESTION ME...
...GO THROUGH THE APPROPRIATE DIPLOMATIC CHANNELS!
DAMN! HE CERTAINLY CAN SHOOT HIS MOUTH OFF IN JAPANESE...

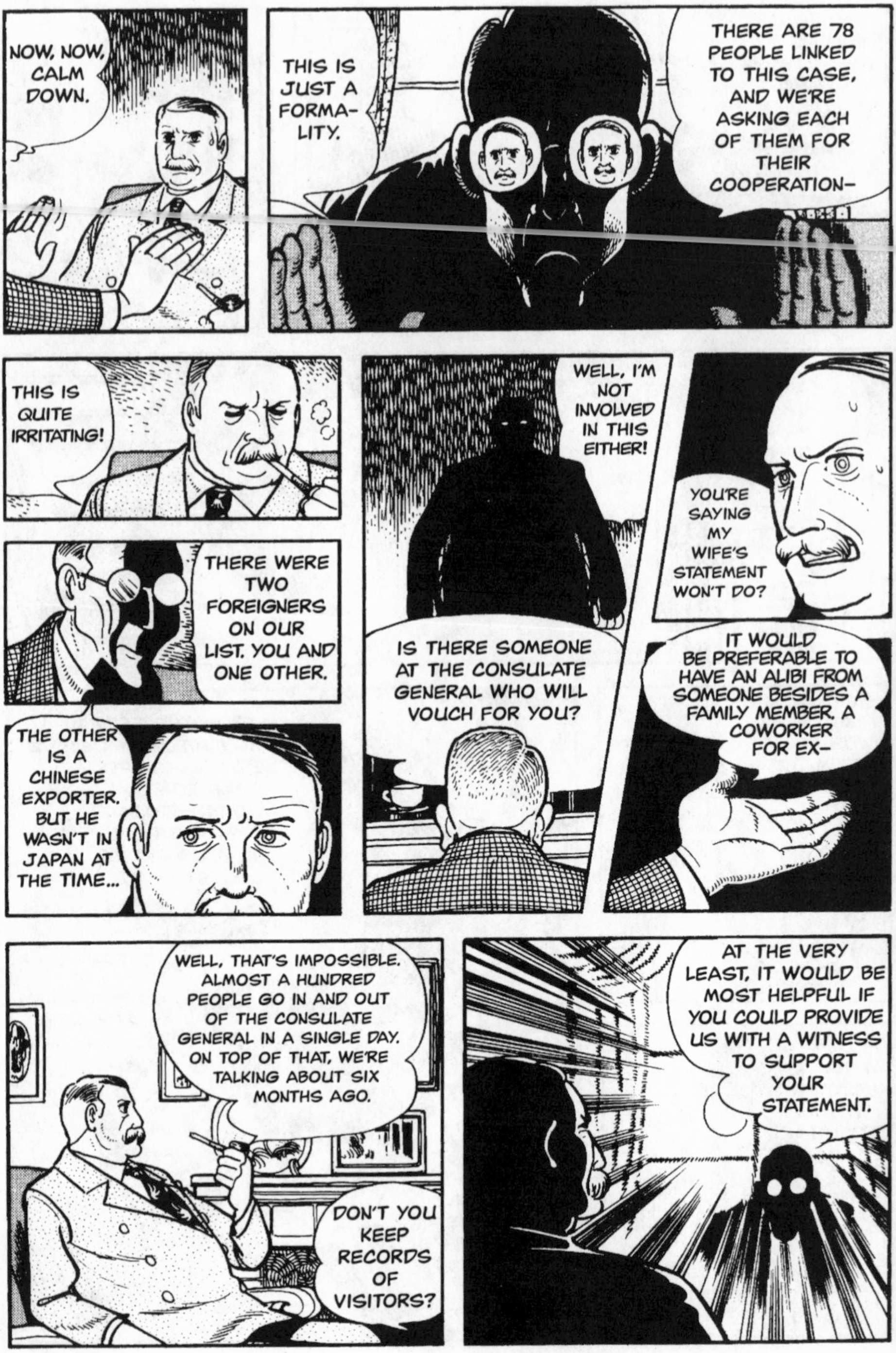
NOW, NOW, CALM DOWN.
THIS IS JUST A FORMA-LITY.
THERE ARE 78 PEOPLE LINKED TO THIS CASE, AND WE'RE ASKING EACH OF THEM FOR THEIR COOPERATION–
THIS IS QUITE IRRITATING!
THERE WERE TWO FOREIGNERS ON OUR LIST. YOU AND ONE OTHER.
THE OTHER IS A CHINESE EXPORTER. BUT HE WASN'T IN JAPAN AT THE TIME...
WELL, I'M NOT INVOLVED IN THIS EITHER!
IS THERE SOMEONE AT THE CONSULATE GENERAL WHO WILL VOUCH FOR YOU?
YOU'RE SAYING MY WIFE'S STATEMENT WON'T DO?
IT WOULD BE PREFERABLE TO HAVE AN ALIBI FROM SOMEONE BESIDES A FAMILY MEMBER. A COWORKER FOR EX–
WELL, THAT'S IMPOSSIBLE. ALMOST A HUNDRED PEOPLE GO IN AND OUT OF THE CONSULATE GENERAL IN A SINGLE DAY. ON TOP OF THAT, WE'RE TALKING ABOUT SIX MONTHS AGO.
DON'T YOU KEEP RECORDS OF VISITORS?
AT THE VERY LEAST, IT WOULD BE MOST HELPFUL IF YOU COULD PROVIDE US WITH A WITNESS TO SUPPORT YOUR STATEMENT.

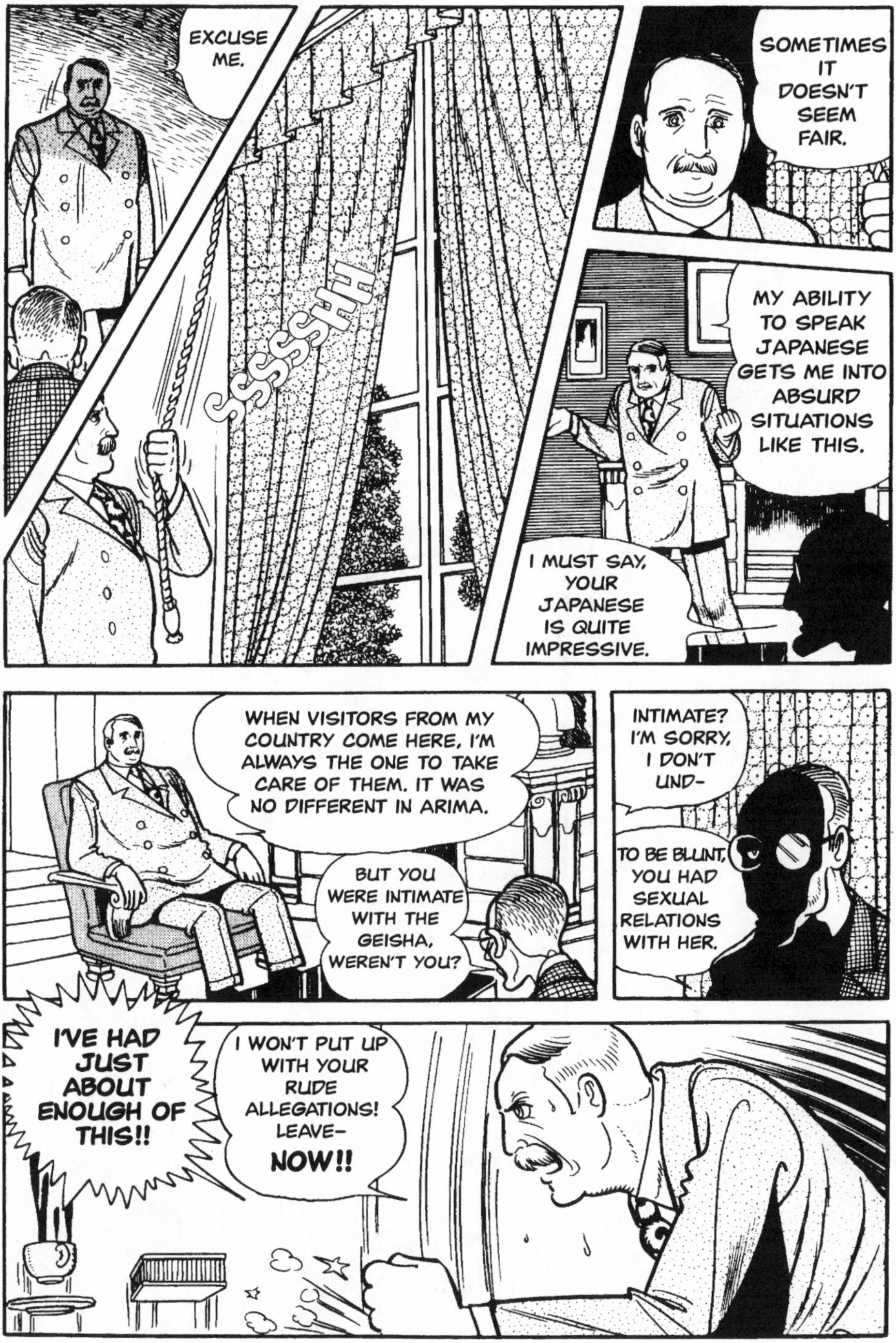
EXCUSE ME.
SSSSSHH
SOMETIMES IT DOESN'T SEEM FAIR.
MY ABILITY TO SPEAK JAPANESE GETS ME INTO ABSURD SITUATIONS LIKE THIS.
I MUST SAY, YOUR JAPANESE IS QUITE IMPRESSIVE.
WHEN VISITORS FROM MY COUNTRY COME HERE, I'M ALWAYS THE ONE TO TAKE CARE OF THEM. IT WAS NO DIFFERENT IN ARIMA.
BUT YOU WERE INTIMATE WITH THE GEISHA, WEREN'T YOU?
INTIMATE? I'M SORRY, I DON'T UND-
TO BE BLUNT, YOU HAD SEXUAL RELATIONS WITH HER.
I'VE HAD JUST ABOUT ENOUGH OF THIS!!
I WON'T PUT UP WITH YOUR RUDE ALLEGATIONS! LEAVE- NOW!!

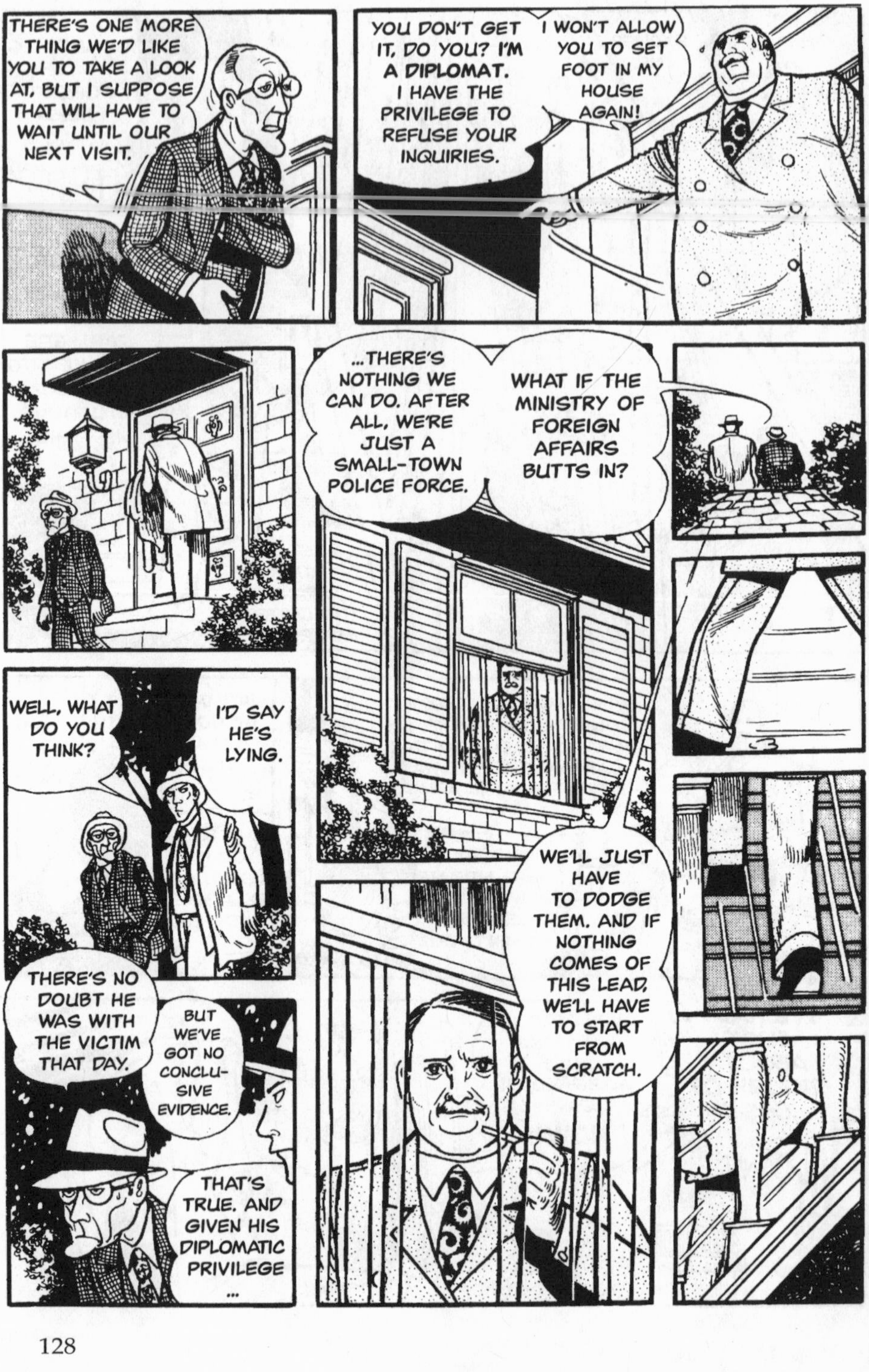
THERE'S ONE MORE THING WE'D LIKE YOU TO TAKE A LOOK AT, BUT I SUPPOSE THAT WILL HAVE TO WAIT UNTIL OUR NEXT VISIT.
YOU DON'T GET IT, DO YOU? I'M A DIPLOMAT. I HAVE THE PRIVILEGE TO REFUSE YOUR INQUIRIES.
I WON'T ALLOW YOU TO SET FOOT IN MY HOUSE AGAIN!
WELL, WHAT DO YOU THINK?
I'D SAY HE'S LYING.
THERE'S NO DOUBT HE WAS WITH THE VICTIM THAT DAY.
BUT WE'VE GOT NO CONCLUSIVE EVIDENCE.
THAT'S TRUE. AND GIVEN HIS DIPLOMATIC PRIVILEGE ...
...THERE'S NOTHING WE CAN DO. AFTER ALL, WE'RE JUST A SMALL-TOWN POLICE FORCE.
WHAT IF THE MINISTRY OF FOREIGN AFFAIRS BUTTS IN?
WE'LL JUST HAVE TO DODGE THEM. AND IF NOTHING COMES OF THIS LEAD, WE'LL HAVE TO START FROM SCRATCH.

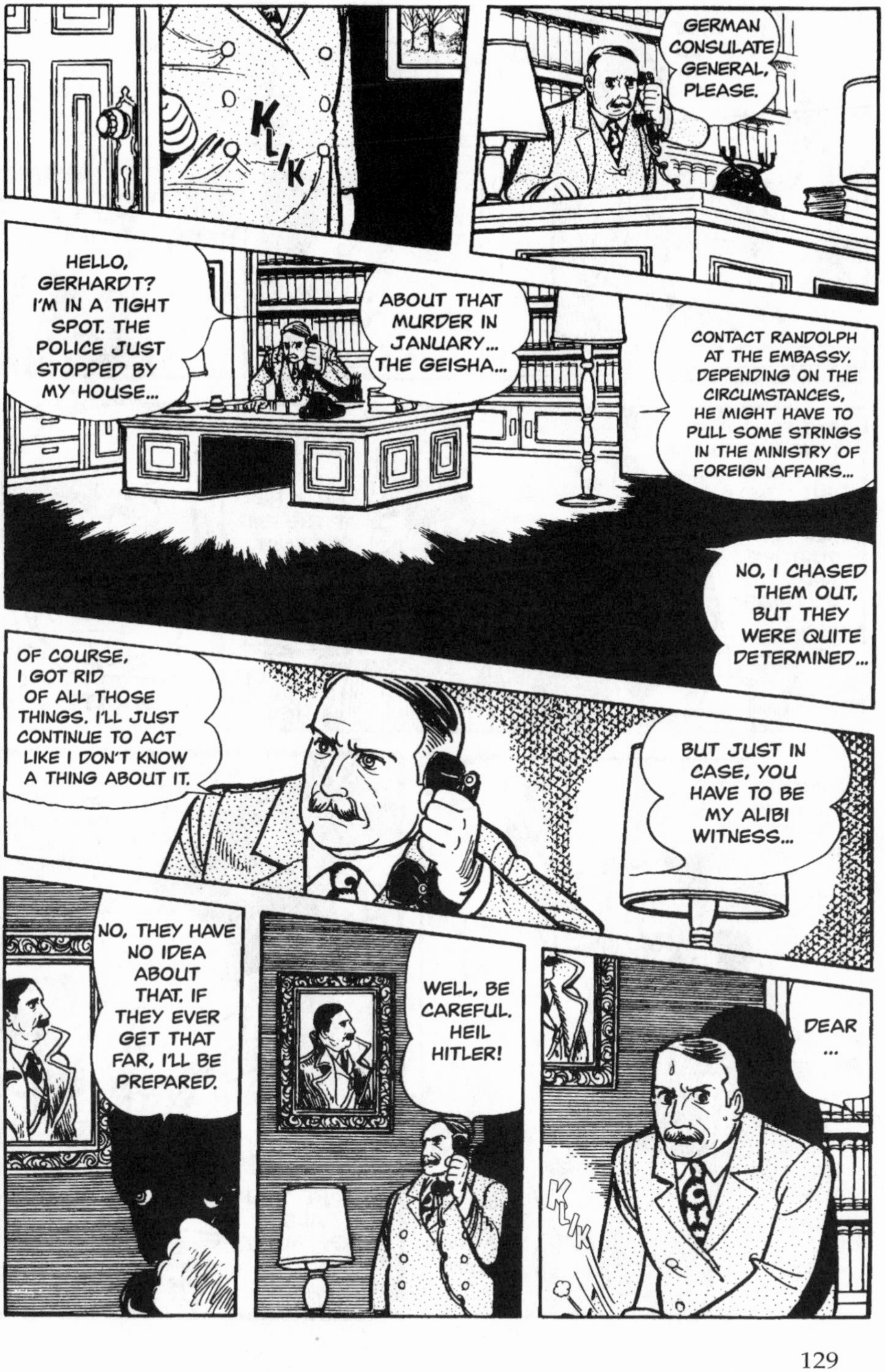
KLIK
GERMAN CONSULATE GENERAL, PLEASE.
HELLO, GERHARDT? I'M IN A TIGHT SPOT. THE POLICE JUST STOPPED BY MY HOUSE...
ABOUT THAT MURDER IN JANUARY... THE GEISHA...
CONTACT RANDOLPH AT THE EMBASSY. DEPENDING ON THE CIRCUMSTANCES, HE MIGHT HAVE TO PULL SOME STRINGS IN THE MINISTRY OF FOREIGN AFFAIRS...
NO, I CHASED THEM OUT, BUT THEY WERE QUITE DETERMINED...
OF COURSE, I GOT RID OF ALL THOSE THINGS. I'LL JUST CONTINUE TO ACT LIKE I DON'T KNOW A THING ABOUT IT.
BUT JUST IN CASE, YOU HAVE TO BE MY ALIBI WITNESS...
NO, THEY HAVE NO IDEA ABOUT THAT. IF THEY EVER GET THAT FAR, I'LL BE PREPARED.
WELL, BE CAREFUL. HEIL HITLER!
DEAR ...
KLIK

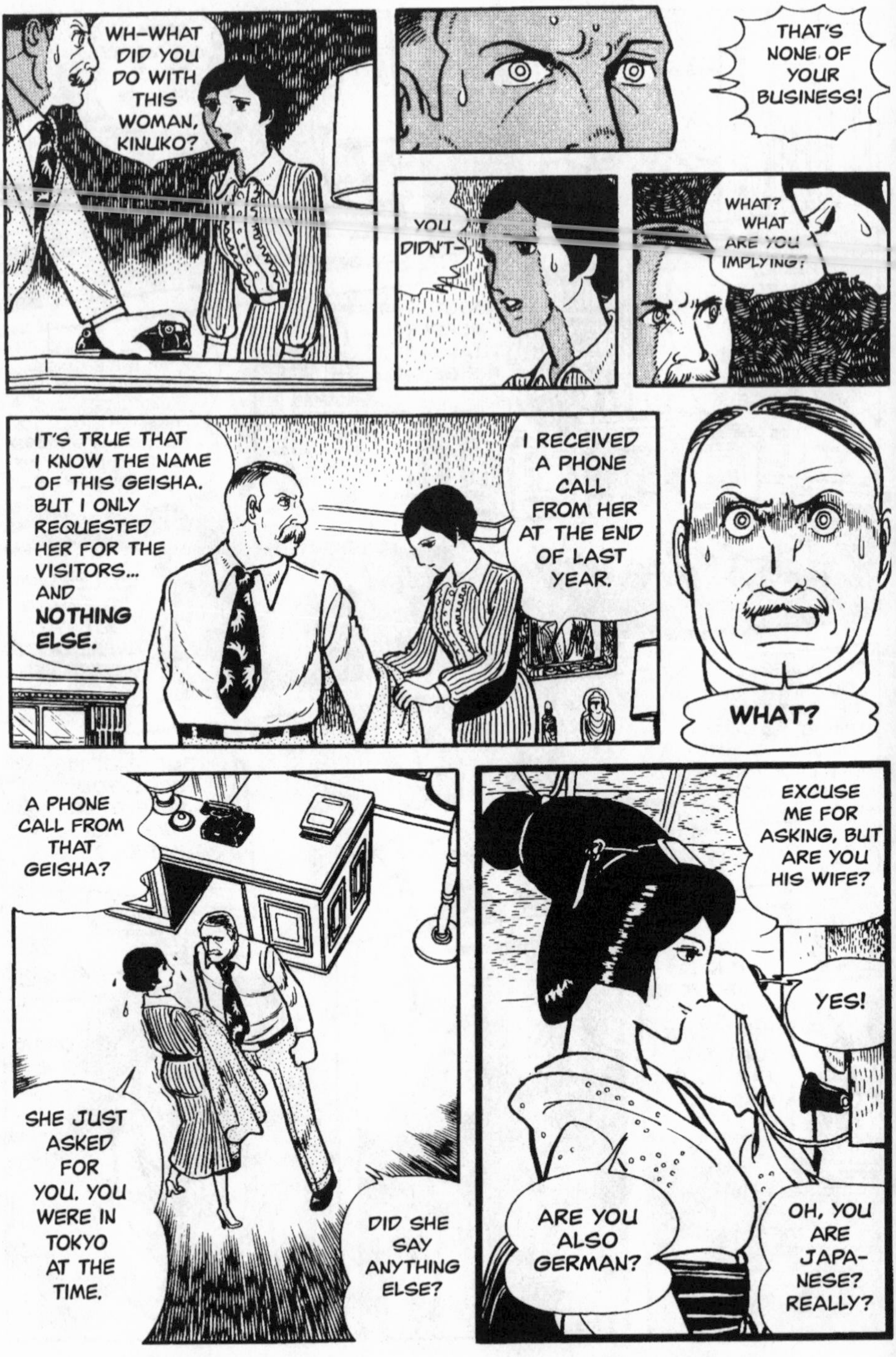
WH-WHAT DID YOU DO WITH THIS WOMAN, KINUKO?
THAT'S NONE OF YOUR BUSINESS!
YOU DIDN'T-
WHAT? WHAT ARE YOU IMPLYING?
IT'S TRUE THAT I KNOW THE NAME OF THIS GEISHA. BUT I ONLY REQUESTED HER FOR THE VISITORS... AND NOTHING ELSE.
I RECEIVED A PHONE CALL FROM HER AT THE END OF LAST YEAR.
WHAT?
A PHONE CALL FROM THAT GEISHA?
SHE JUST ASKED FOR YOU. YOU WERE IN TOKYO AT THE TIME.
DID SHE SAY ANYTHING ELSE?
EXCUSE ME FOR ASKING, BUT ARE YOU HIS WIFE?
YES!
ARE YOU ALSO GERMAN?
OH, YOU ARE JAPA-NESE? REALLY?

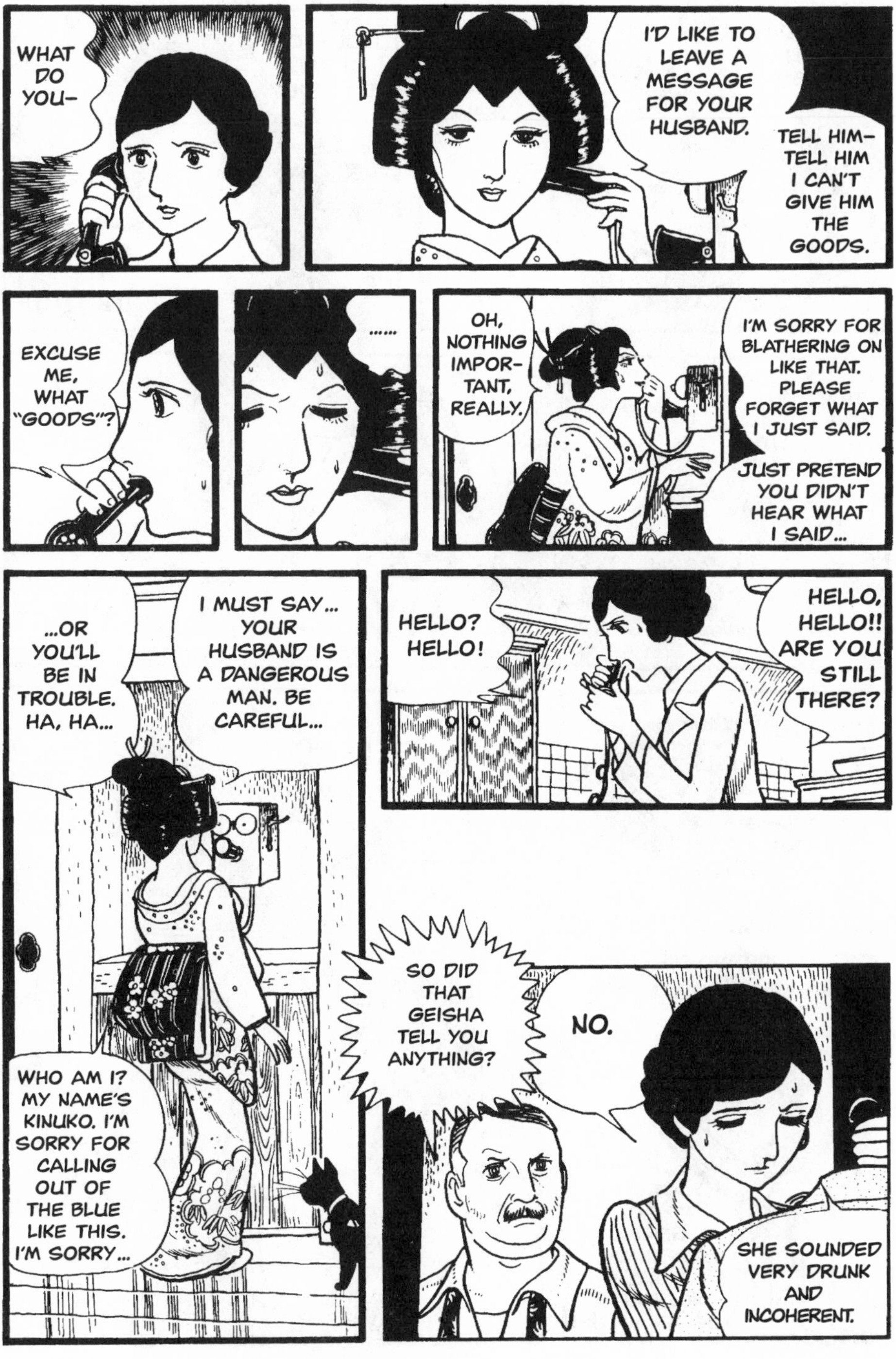
WHAT DO YOU-
I'D LIKE TO LEAVE A MESSAGE FOR YOUR HUSBAND.
TELL HIM- TELL HIM I CAN'T GIVE HIM THE GOODS.
EXCUSE ME, WHAT "GOODS"?
......
OH, NOTHING IMPOR- TANT, REALLY.
I'M SORRY FOR BLATHERING ON LIKE THAT. PLEASE FORGET WHAT I JUST SAID.
JUST PRETEND YOU DIDN'T HEAR WHAT I SAID...
...OR YOU'LL BE IN TROUBLE. HA, HA...
I MUST SAY... YOUR HUSBAND IS A DANGEROUS MAN. BE CAREFUL...
WHO AM I? MY NAME'S KINUKO. I'M SORRY FOR CALLING OUT OF THE BLUE LIKE THIS. I'M SORRY...
HELLO? HELLO!
HELLO, HELLO!! ARE YOU STILL THERE?
SO DID THAT GEISHA TELL YOU ANYTHING?
NO.
SHE SOUNDED VERY DRUNK AND INCOHERENT.

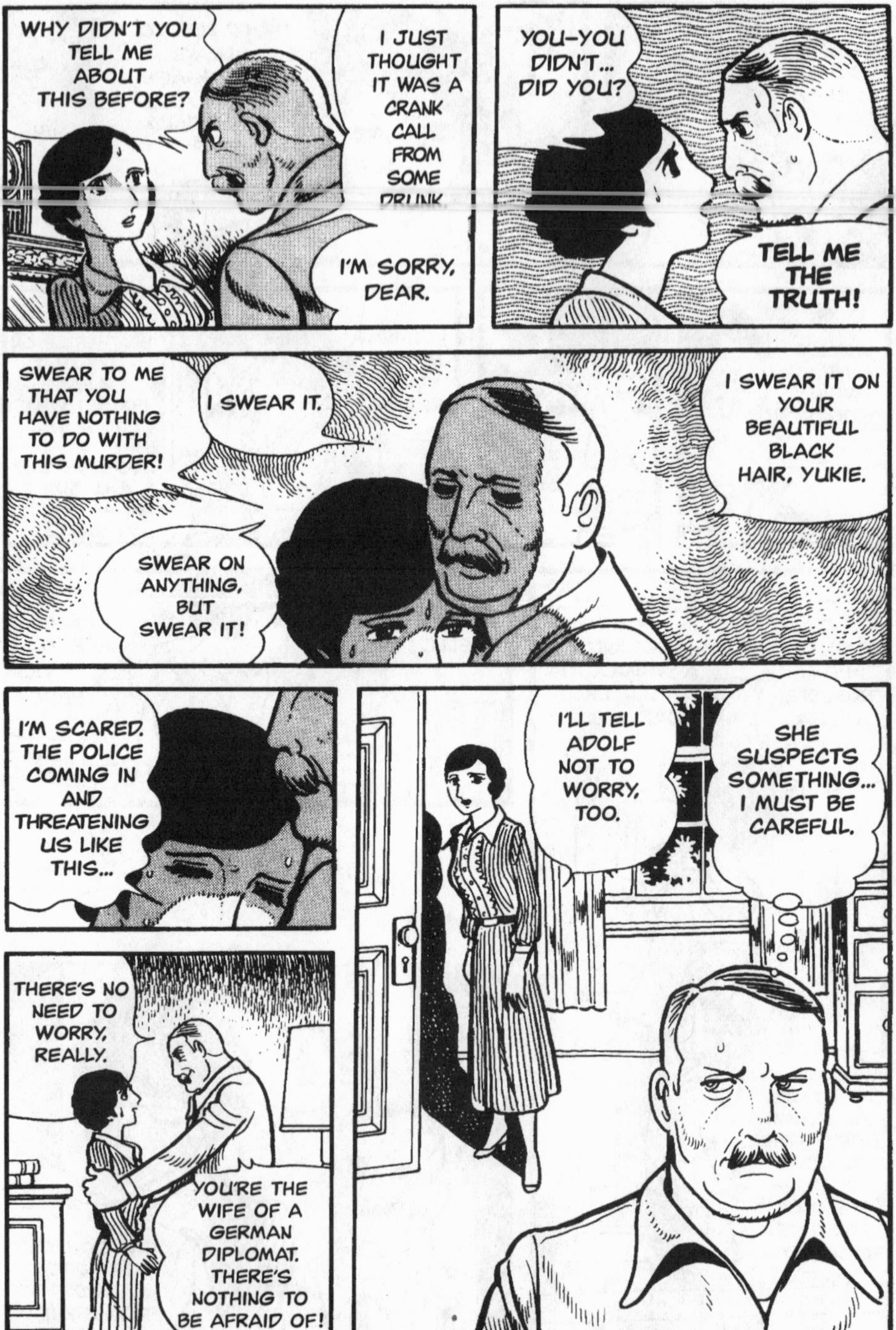
WHY DIDN'T YOU TELL ME ABOUT THIS BEFORE?
I JUST THOUGHT IT WAS A CRANK CALL FROM SOME DRUNK.
I'M SORRY, DEAR.
YOU-YOU DIDN'T... DID YOU?
TELL ME THE TRUTH!
SWEAR TO ME THAT YOU HAVE NOTHING TO DO WITH THIS MURDER!
I SWEAR IT.
SWEAR ON ANYTHING, BUT SWEAR IT!
I SWEAR IT ON YOUR BEAUTIFUL BLACK HAIR, YUKIE.
I'M SCARED. THE POLICE COMING IN AND THREATENING US LIKE THIS...
THERE'S NO NEED TO WORRY, REALLY.
YOU'RE THE WIFE OF A GERMAN DIPLOMAT. THERE'S NOTHING TO BE AFRAID OF!
I'LL TELL ADOLF NOT TO WORRY, TOO.
SHE SUSPECTS SOMETHING... I MUST BE CAREFUL.

I'M STAR-VED!

I BAKED SOME COOKIES.

SEE? THEY'RE DONE.

THEY'RE SWELL!

NOW, NOW. YOU SHOULD SAY "DELICIOUS."

BUT ADOLF FROM THE BAKERY SAYS "SWELL."

HE HAS NO MANNERS! YOU SHOULDN'T IMITATE THE WAY THAT BOY SPEAKS.

DARN. YOU DON'T LIKE HIM EITHER, DO YOU?

THAT'S NOT TRUE.

I LIKE HIS PERSONALITY.

133

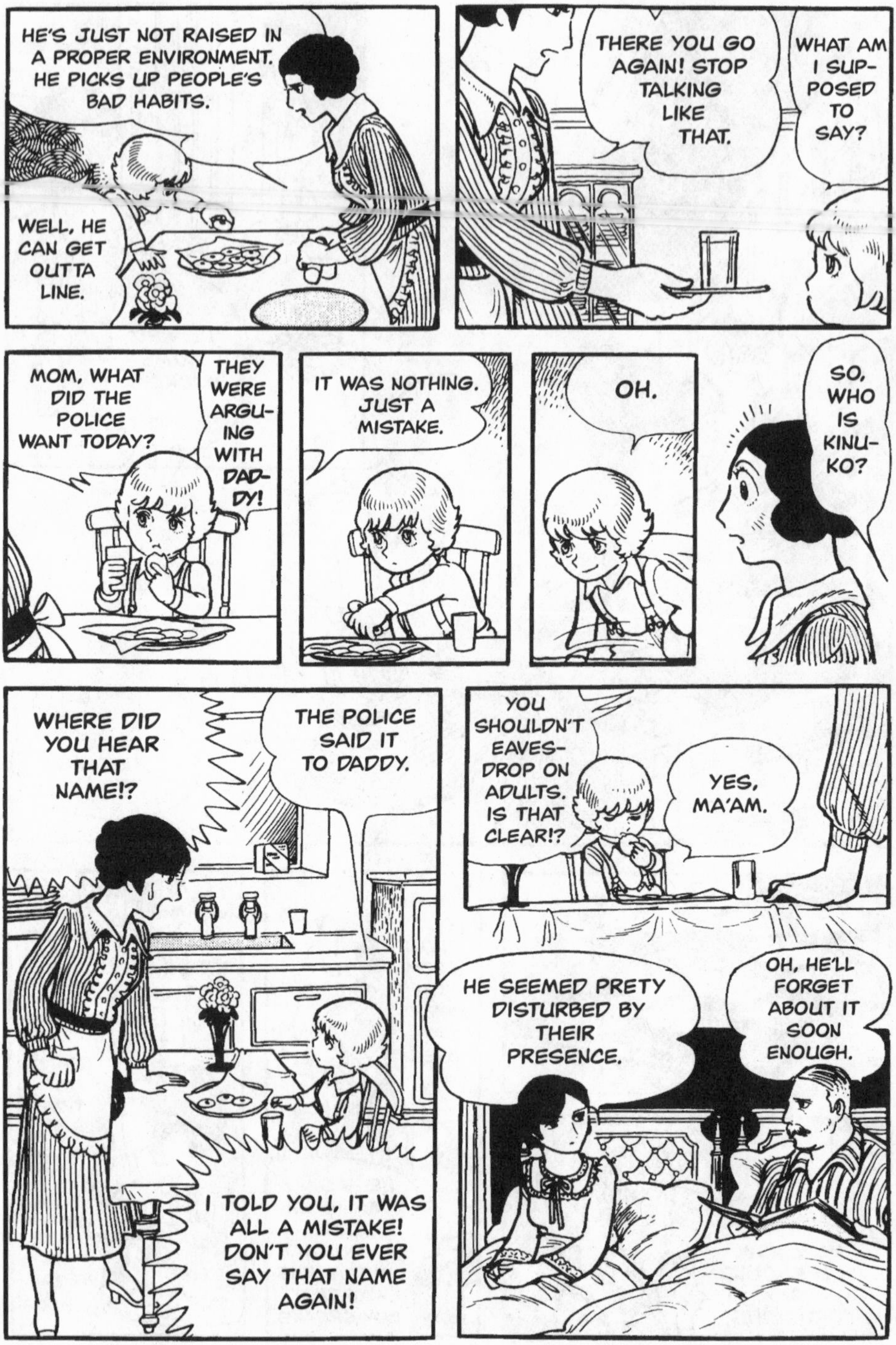
HE'S JUST NOT RAISED IN A PROPER ENVIRONMENT. HE PICKS UP PEOPLE'S BAD HABITS.
WELL, HE CAN GET OUTTA LINE.
THERE YOU GO AGAIN! STOP TALKING LIKE THAT.
WHAT AM I SUP-POSED TO SAY?
MOM, WHAT DID THE POLICE WANT TODAY?
THEY WERE ARGU-ING WITH DAD-DY!
IT WAS NOTHING. JUST A MISTAKE.
OH.
SO, WHO IS KINU-KO?
WHERE DID YOU HEAR THAT NAME!?
THE POLICE SAID IT TO DADDY.
I TOLD YOU, IT WAS ALL A MISTAKE! DON'T YOU EVER SAY THAT NAME AGAIN!
YOU SHOULDN'T EAVES-DROP ON ADULTS. IS THAT CLEAR!?
YES, MA'AM.
HE SEEMED PRETY DISTURBED BY THEIR PRESENCE.
OH, HE'LL FORGET ABOUT IT SOON ENOUGH.

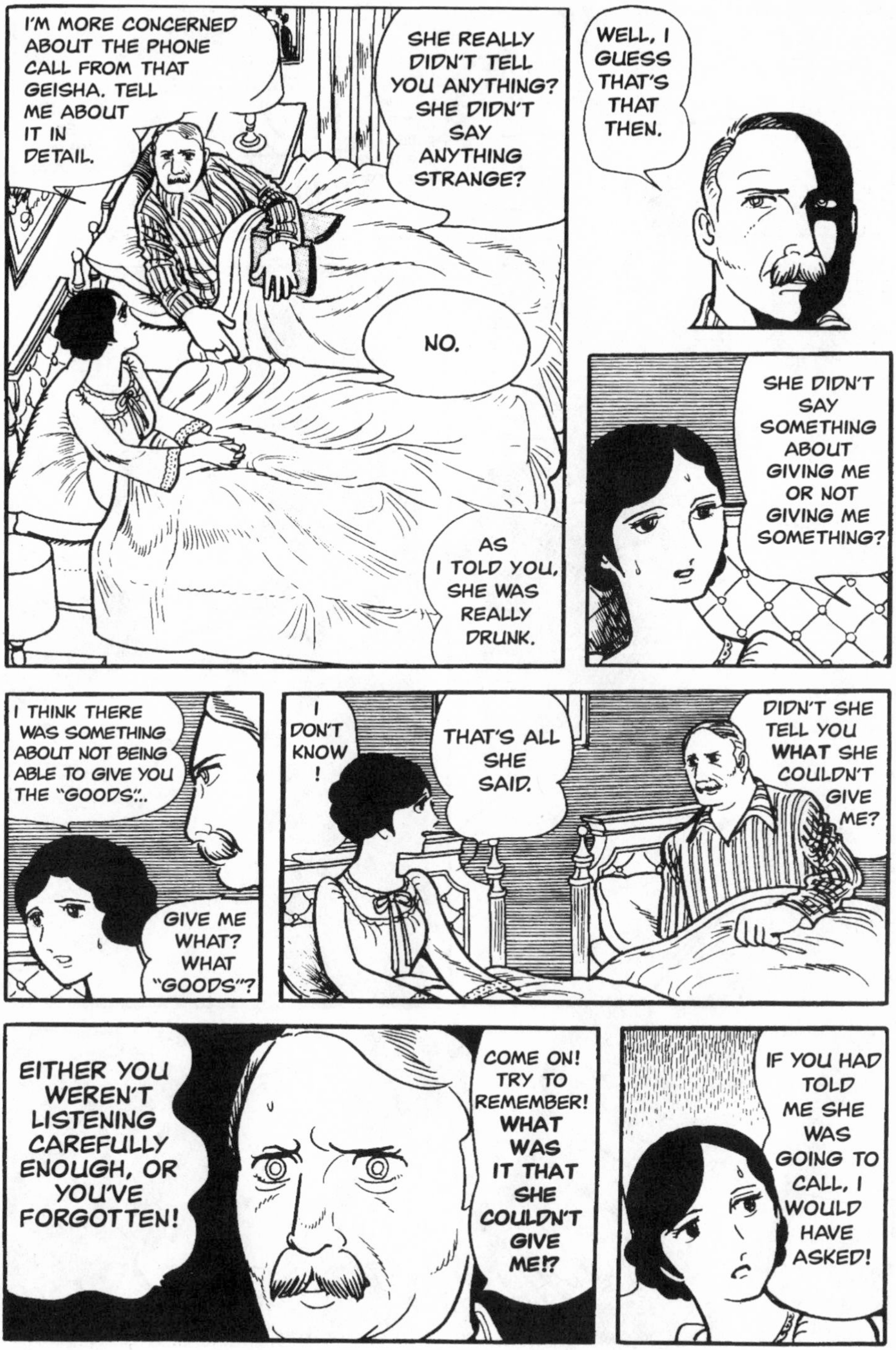
I'M MORE CONCERNED ABOUT THE PHONE CALL FROM THAT GEISHA. TELL ME ABOUT IT IN DETAIL.
SHE REALLY DIDN'T TELL YOU ANYTHING? SHE DIDN'T SAY ANYTHING STRANGE?
NO.
AS I TOLD YOU, SHE WAS REALLY DRUNK.
WELL, I GUESS THAT'S THAT THEN.
SHE DIDN'T SAY SOMETHING ABOUT GIVING ME OR NOT GIVING ME SOMETHING?
I THINK THERE WAS SOMETHING ABOUT NOT BEING ABLE TO GIVE YOU THE "GOODS"...
GIVE ME WHAT? WHAT "GOODS"?
I DON'T KNOW!
THAT'S ALL SHE SAID.
DIDN'T SHE TELL YOU **WHAT** SHE COULDN'T GIVE ME?
EITHER YOU WEREN'T LISTENING CAREFULLY ENOUGH, OR YOU'VE FORGOTTEN!
COME ON! TRY TO REMEMBER! **WHAT WAS IT THAT SHE COULDN'T GIVE ME!?**
IF YOU HAD TOLD ME SHE WAS GOING TO CALL, I WOULD HAVE ASKED!

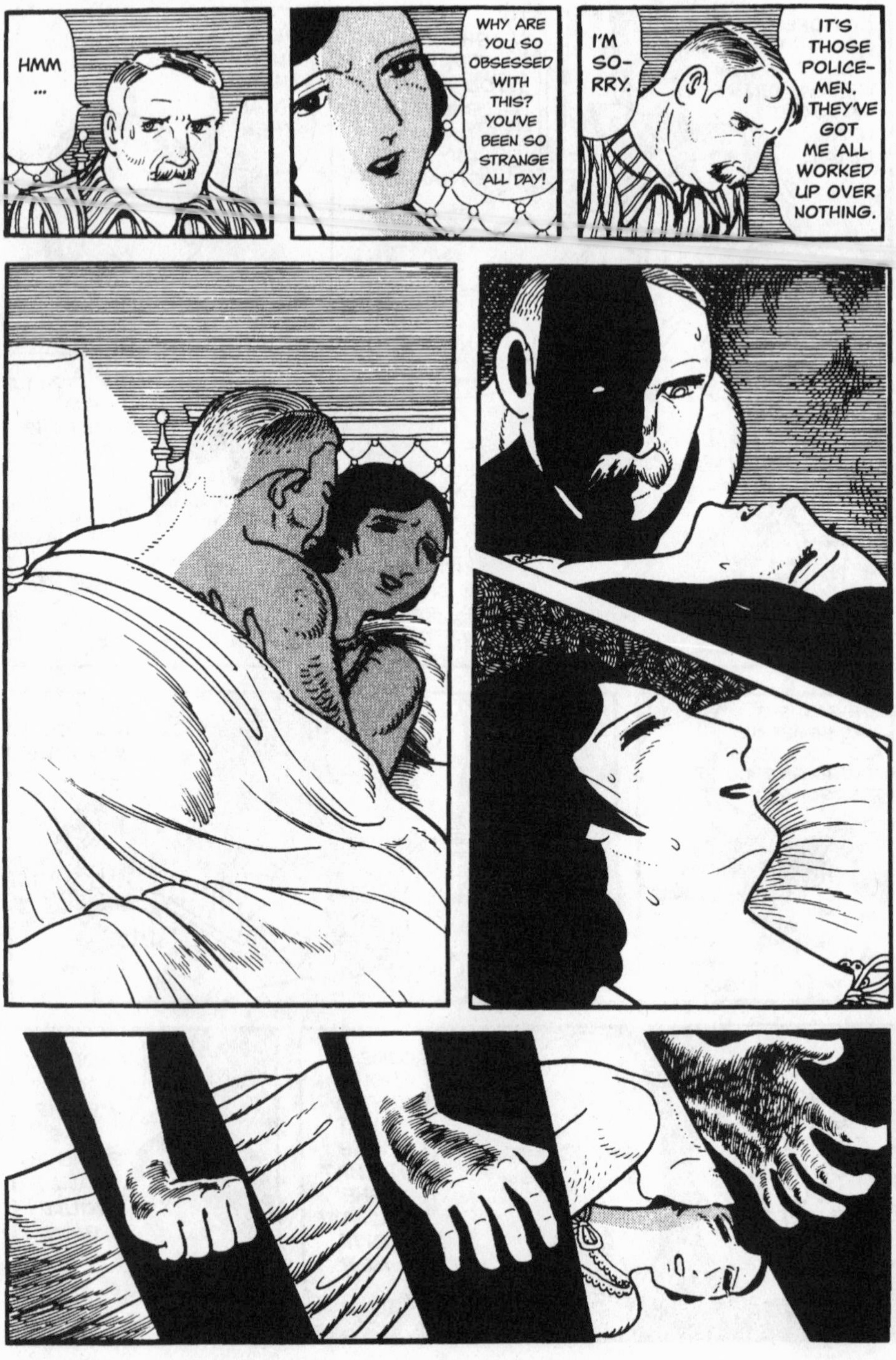
HMM ...
WHY ARE YOU SO OBSESSED WITH THIS? YOU'VE BEEN SO STRANGE ALL DAY!
I'M SO-RRY.
IT'S THOSE POLICE-MEN. THEY'VE GOT ME ALL WORKED UP OVER NOTHING.

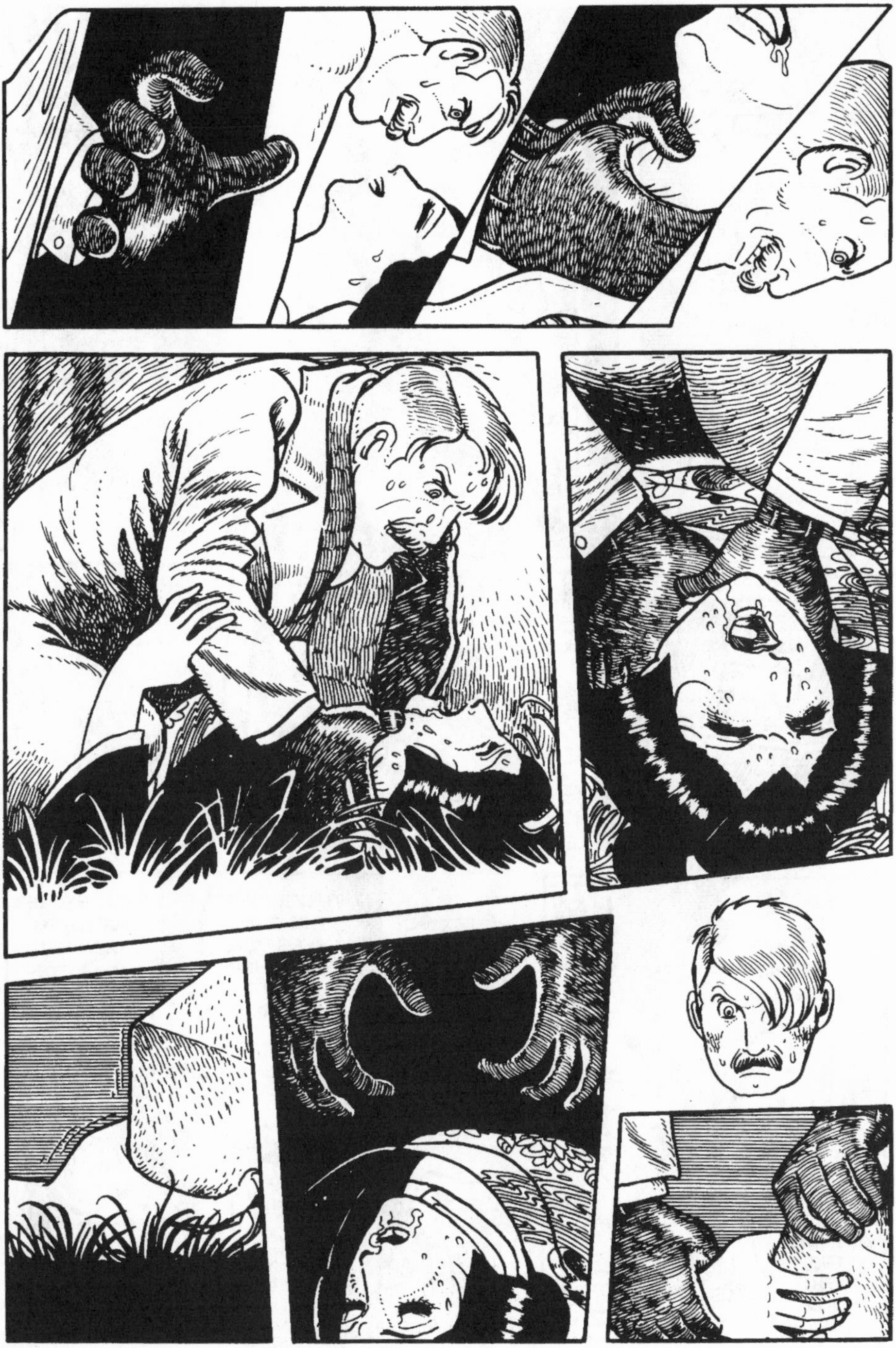

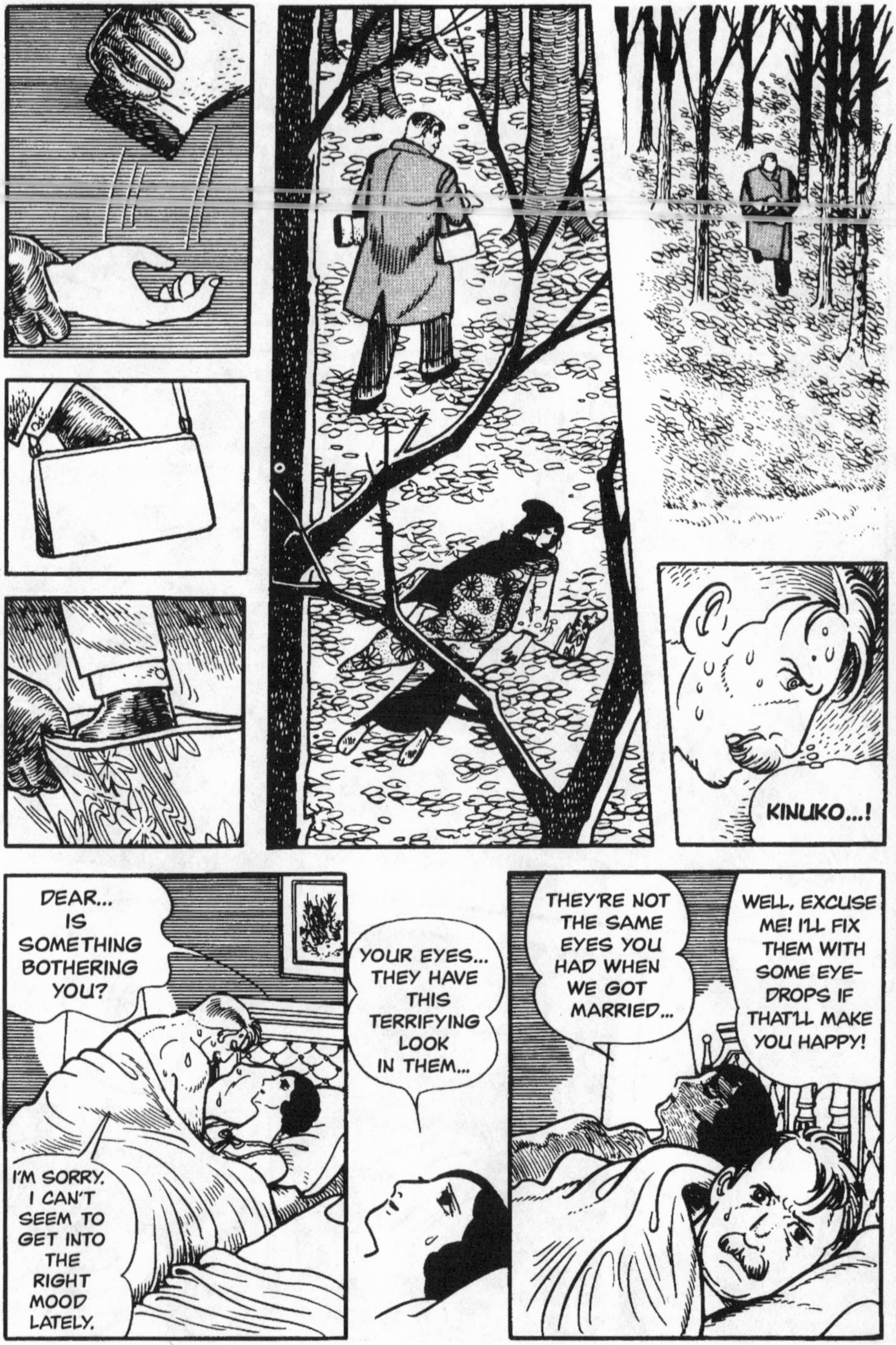
KINUKO...!
DEAR... IS SOMETHING BOTHERING YOU?
I'M SORRY. I CAN'T SEEM TO GET INTO THE RIGHT MOOD LATELY.
YOUR EYES... THEY HAVE THIS TERRIFYING LOOK IN THEM...
THEY'RE NOT THE SAME EYES YOU HAD WHEN WE GOT MARRIED...
WELL, EXCUSE ME! I'LL FIX THEM WITH SOME EYE-DROPS IF THAT'LL MAKE YOU HAPPY!

KLAKKETA KLAKKETA

CHRRRR CHRRRR

WELL? AREN'T **OUR** COOKIES **MUCH** BETTER!?

WELL?

HMM... MOM'S ARE GOOD— BUT MAYBE NOT AS GOOD AS YOURS.

YOUR FAMILY RUNS A BAKERY, SO IT'S ONLY NATURAL!

THAT'S RIGHT. WE'RE PROFESSIONALS AND YOU'RE AMATEURS.

THAT'S THE DIFFERENCE.

ALSO...

YOU'RE A JEW, SO YOU'RE DIFFERENT FROM GERMANS.

HEY, I'M GERMAN TOO, Y'KNOW.

BUT YOU REALLY AREN'T, ARE YOU? YOU'RE A JEW IN DISGUISE, RIGHT?

I'M NOT IN DISGUISE!

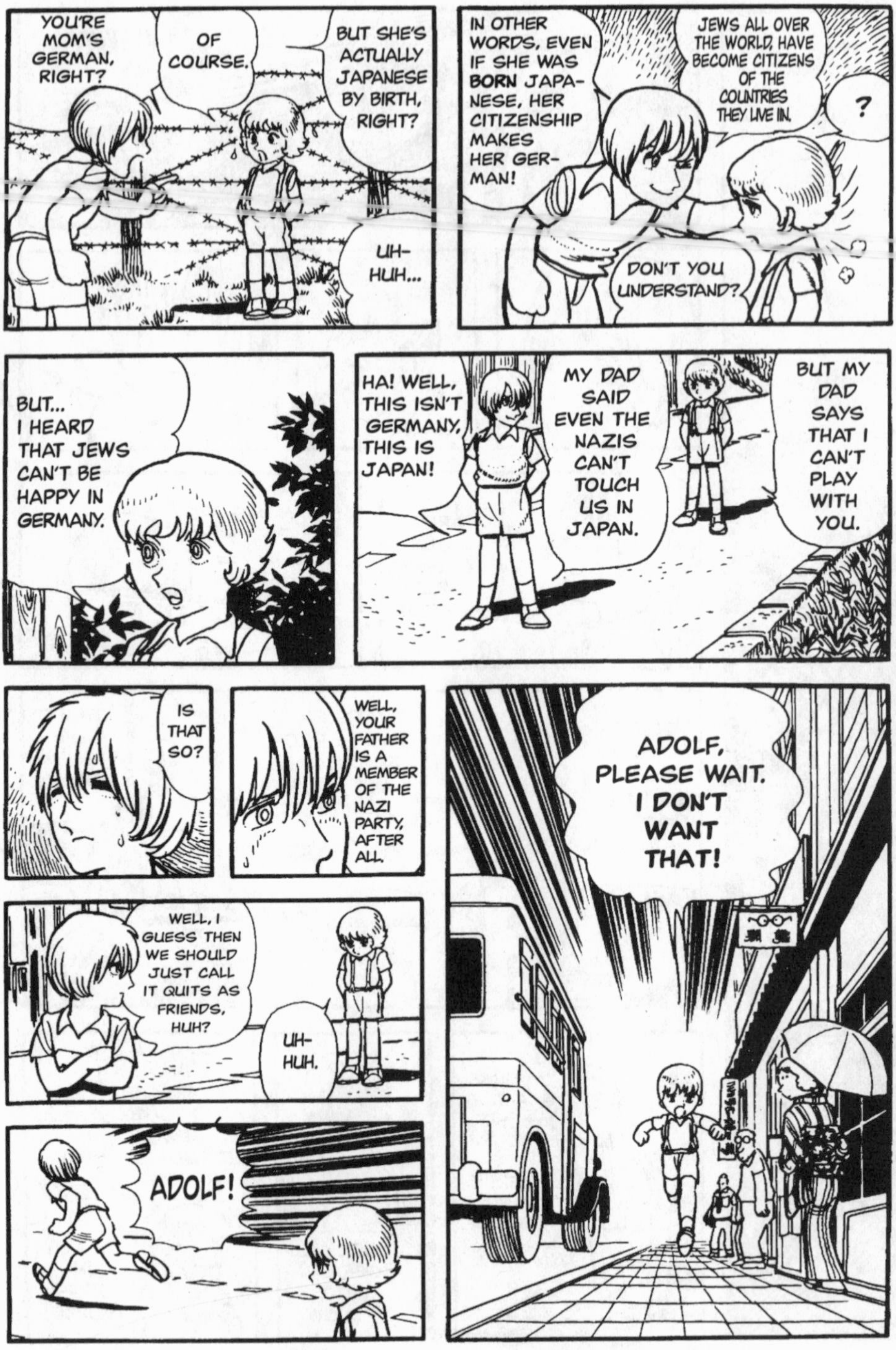
YOU'RE MOM'S GERMAN, RIGHT?
OF COURSE.
BUT SHE'S ACTUALLY JAPANESE BY BIRTH, RIGHT?
UH-HUH...
IN OTHER WORDS, EVEN IF SHE WAS BORN JAPANESE, HER CITIZENSHIP MAKES HER GERMAN!
JEWS ALL OVER THE WORLD, HAVE BECOME CITIZENS OF THE COUNTRIES THEY LIVE IN.
?
DON'T YOU UNDERSTAND?
BUT... I HEARD THAT JEWS CAN'T BE HAPPY IN GERMANY.
HA! WELL, THIS ISN'T GERMANY, THIS IS JAPAN!
MY DAD SAID EVEN THE NAZIS CAN'T TOUCH US IN JAPAN.
BUT MY DAD SAYS THAT I CAN'T PLAY WITH YOU.
IS THAT SO?
WELL, YOUR FATHER IS A MEMBER OF THE NAZI PARTY, AFTER ALL.
WELL, I GUESS THEN WE SHOULD JUST CALL IT QUITS AS FRIENDS, HUH?
UH-HUH.
ADOLF!
ADOLF, PLEASE WAIT. I DON'T WANT THAT!

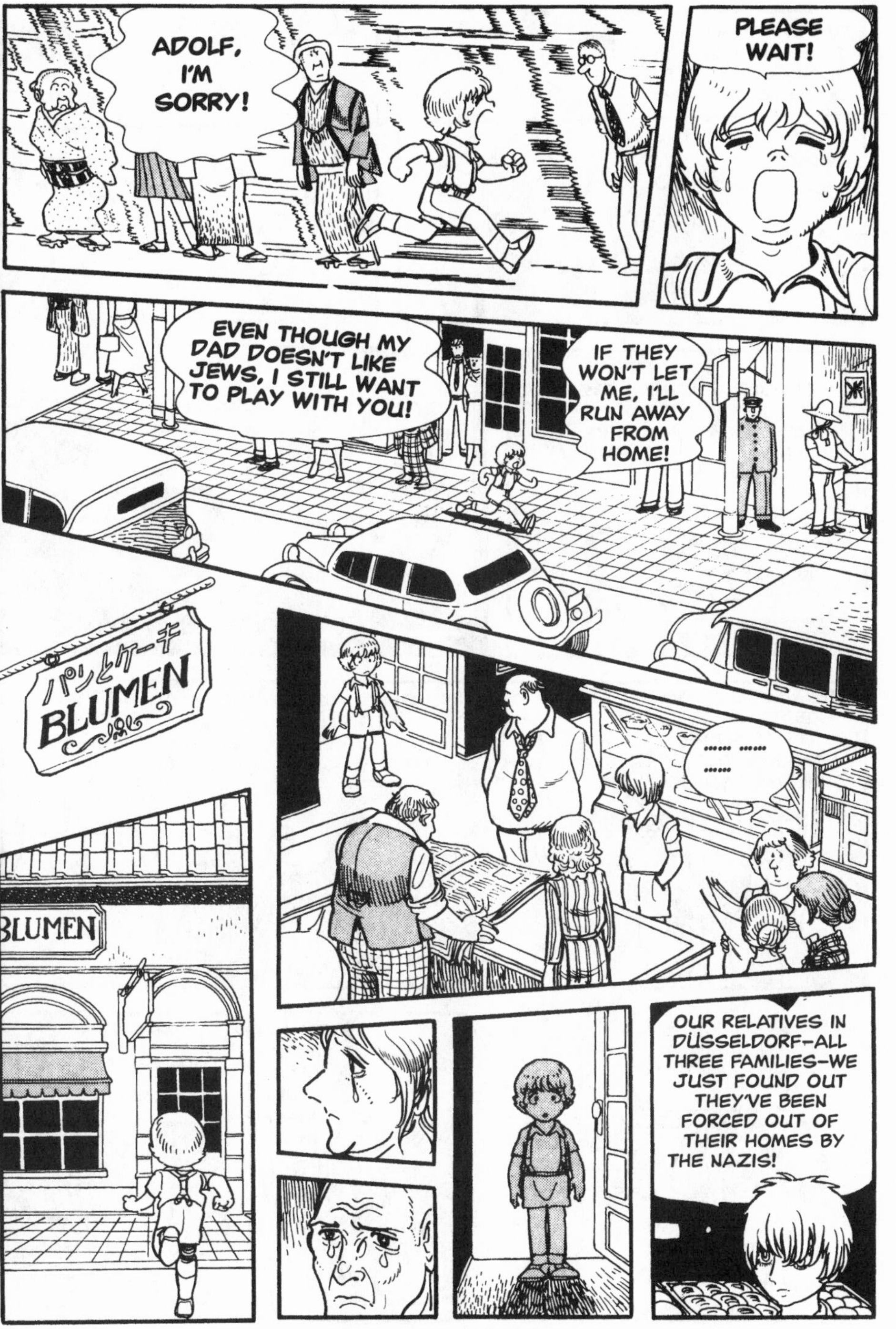
ADOLF, I'M SORRY!
PLEASE WAIT!
EVEN THOUGH MY DAD DOESN'T LIKE JEWS, I STILL WANT TO PLAY WITH YOU!
IF THEY WON'T LET ME, I'LL RUN AWAY FROM HOME!
パンとケーキ
BLUMEN
BLUMEN
....
......
OUR RELATIVES IN DÜSSELDORF—ALL THREE FAMILIES—WE JUST FOUND OUT THEY'VE BEEN FORCED OUT OF THEIR HOMES BY THE NAZIS!

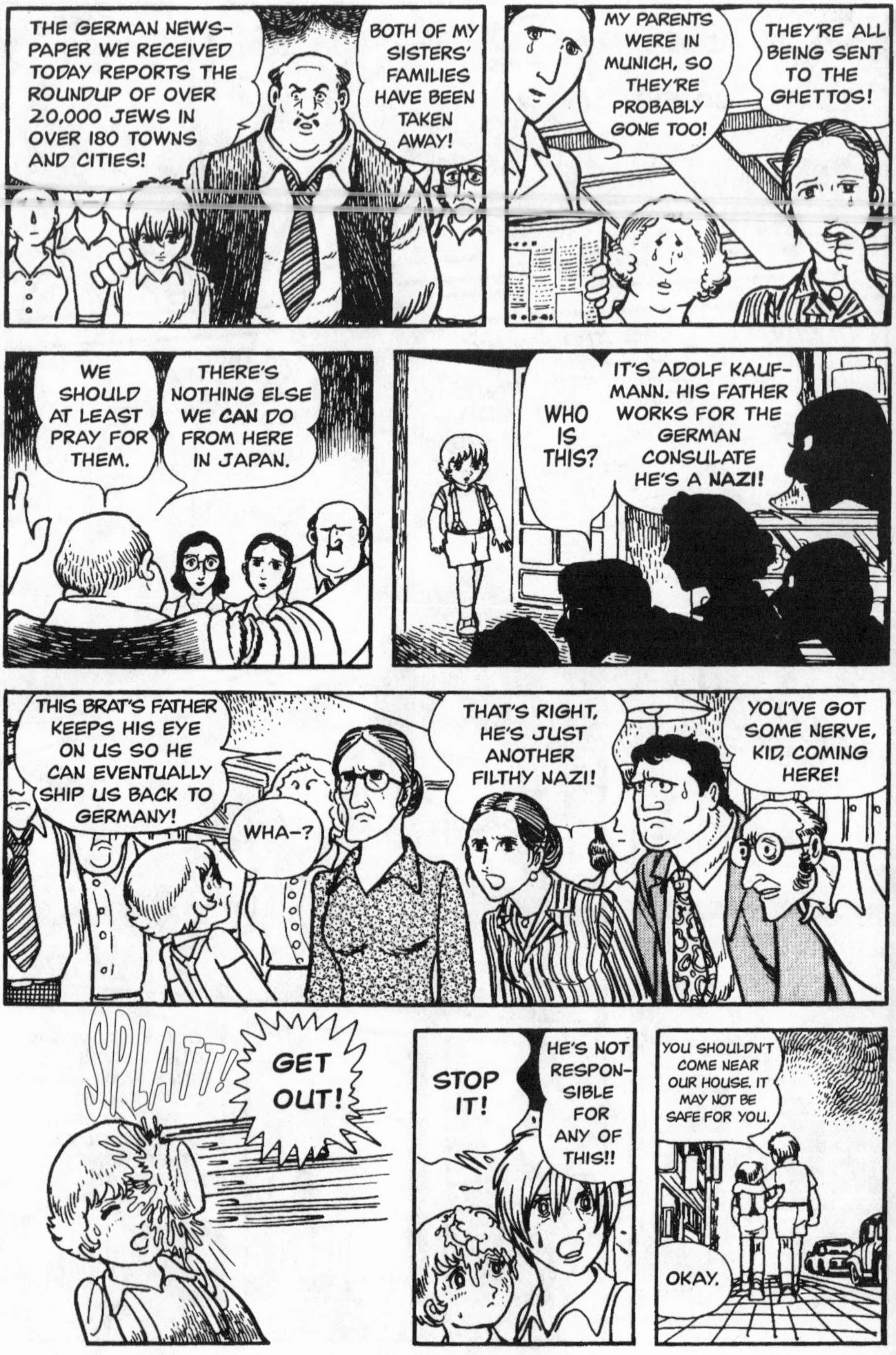
THE GERMAN NEWSPAPER WE RECEIVED TODAY REPORTS THE ROUNDUP OF OVER 20,000 JEWS IN OVER 180 TOWNS AND CITIES!
BOTH OF MY SISTERS' FAMILIES HAVE BEEN TAKEN AWAY!
MY PARENTS WERE IN MUNICH, SO THEY'RE PROBABLY GONE TOO!
THEY'RE ALL BEING SENT TO THE GHETTOS!
WE SHOULD AT LEAST PRAY FOR THEM.
THERE'S NOTHING ELSE WE CAN DO FROM HERE IN JAPAN.
WHO IS THIS?
IT'S ADOLF KAUFMANN. HIS FATHER WORKS FOR THE GERMAN CONSULATE HE'S A NAZI!
THIS BRAT'S FATHER KEEPS HIS EYE ON US SO HE CAN EVENTUALLY SHIP US BACK TO GERMANY!
WHA-?
THAT'S RIGHT, HE'S JUST ANOTHER FILTHY NAZI!
YOU'VE GOT SOME NERVE, KID, COMING HERE!
SPLATT!
GET OUT!
STOP IT!
HE'S NOT RESPONSIBLE FOR ANY OF THIS!!
YOU SHOULDN'T COME NEAR OUR HOUSE. IT MAY NOT BE SAFE FOR YOU.
OKAY.

CHAPTER
FOUR

THE LUGOUQIAO BRIDGE, ALSO KNOWN AS THE MARCO POLO BRIDGE, IS LOCATED WEST OF BEIJING.

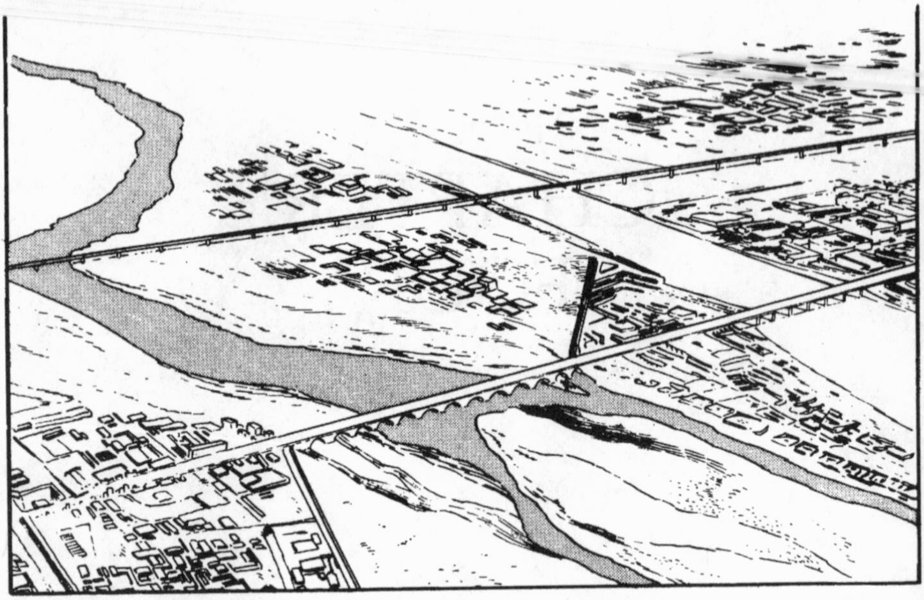

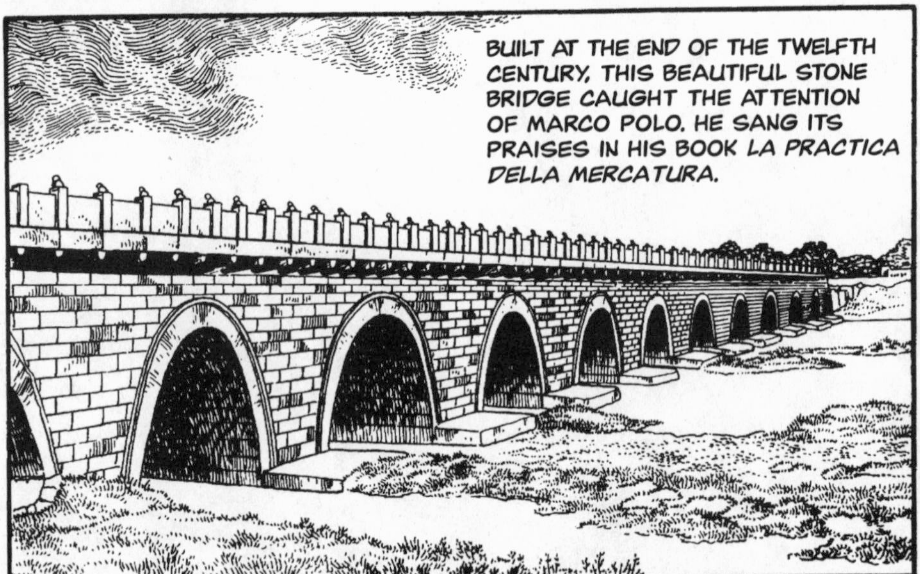
BUILT AT THE END OF THE TWELFTH CENTURY, THIS BEAUTIFUL STONE BRIDGE CAUGHT THE ATTENTION OF MARCO POLO. HE SANG ITS PRAISES IN HIS BOOK *LA PRACTICA DELLA MERCATURA.*

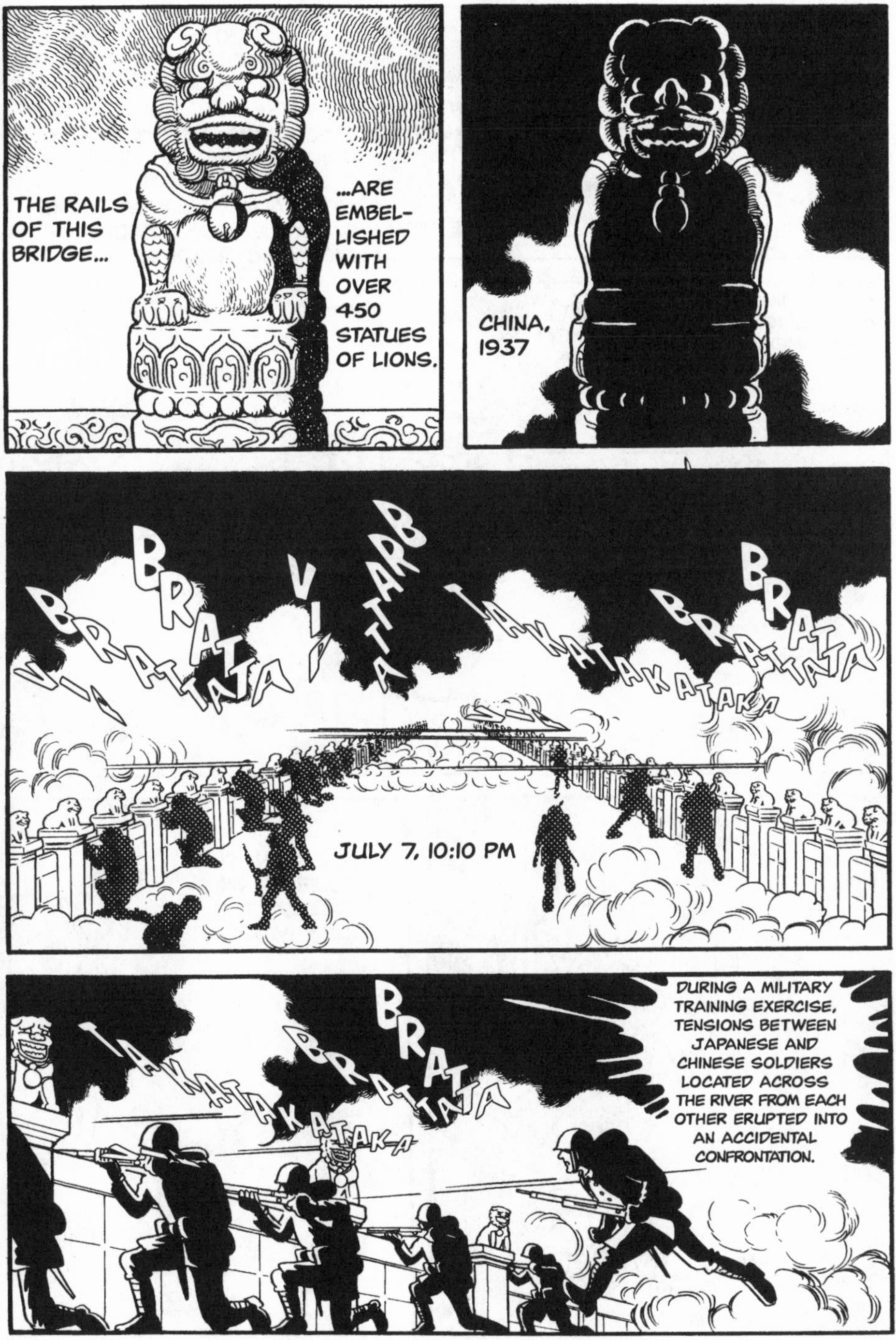
THE RAILS OF THIS BRIDGE...
...ARE EMBELLISHED WITH OVER 450 STATUES OF LIONS.
CHINA, 1937
BRATATATA
TAKATAKATAKA
BRATATATA
JULY 7, 10:10 PM
TAKATAKATAKA
BRATATATA
BRATATATA
DURING A MILITARY TRAINING EXERCISE, TENSIONS BETWEEN JAPANESE AND CHINESE SOLDIERS LOCATED ACROSS THE RIVER FROM EACH OTHER ERUPTED INTO AN ACCIDENTAL CONFRONTATION.

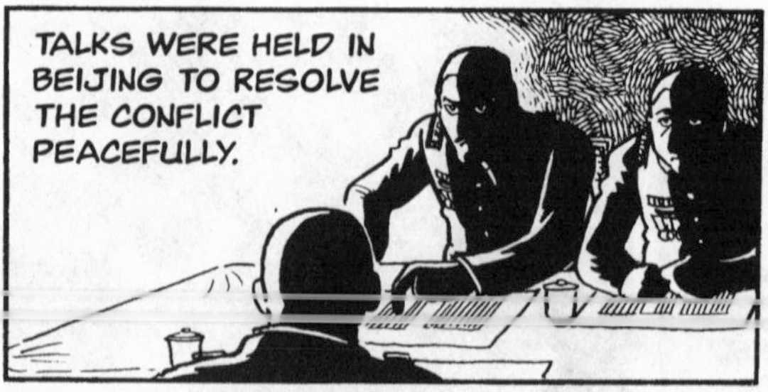
TALKS WERE HELD IN BEIJING TO RESOLVE THE CONFLICT PEACEFULLY.

JULY 10, 6:30 PM. THE JAPANESE GOVERNMENT ANNOUNCED THE DISPATCH OF TROOPS. THIS WAS HOW THE LOCAL WAR, OTHERWISE KNOWN AS THE "NORTH CHINA INCIDENT," BEGAN. ON AUGUST 24, JAPAN OFFICIALLY ANNOUNCED THE "NATIONAL MOBILIZATION OF PATRIOTIC TROOPS."

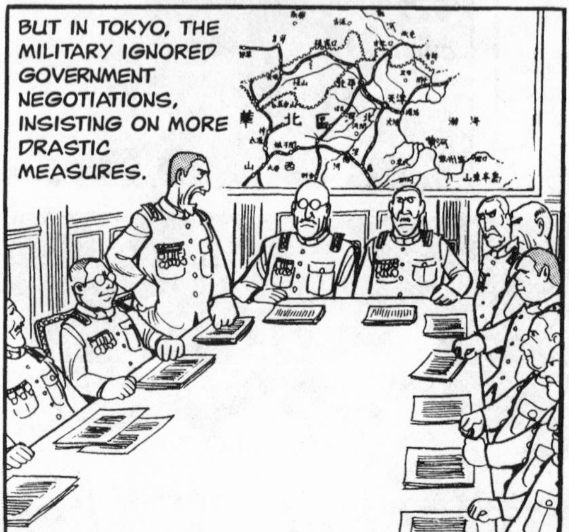
BUT IN TOKYO, THE MILITARY IGNORED GOVERNMENT NEGOTIATIONS, INSISTING ON MORE DRASTIC MEASURES.

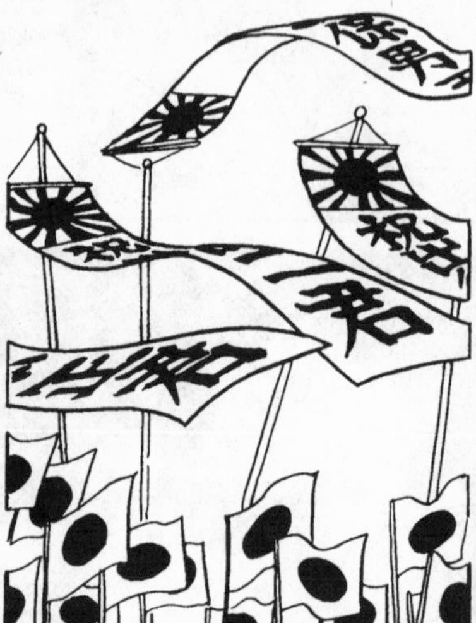

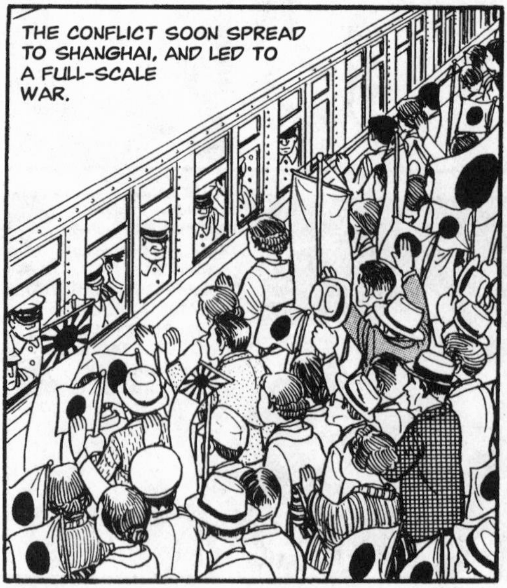
THE CONFLICT SOON SPREAD TO SHANGHAI, AND LED TO A FULL-SCALE WAR.

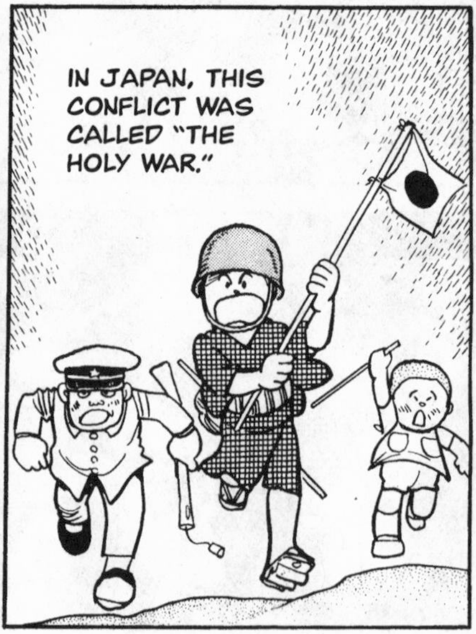
IN JAPAN, THIS CONFLICT WAS CALLED "THE HOLY WAR."

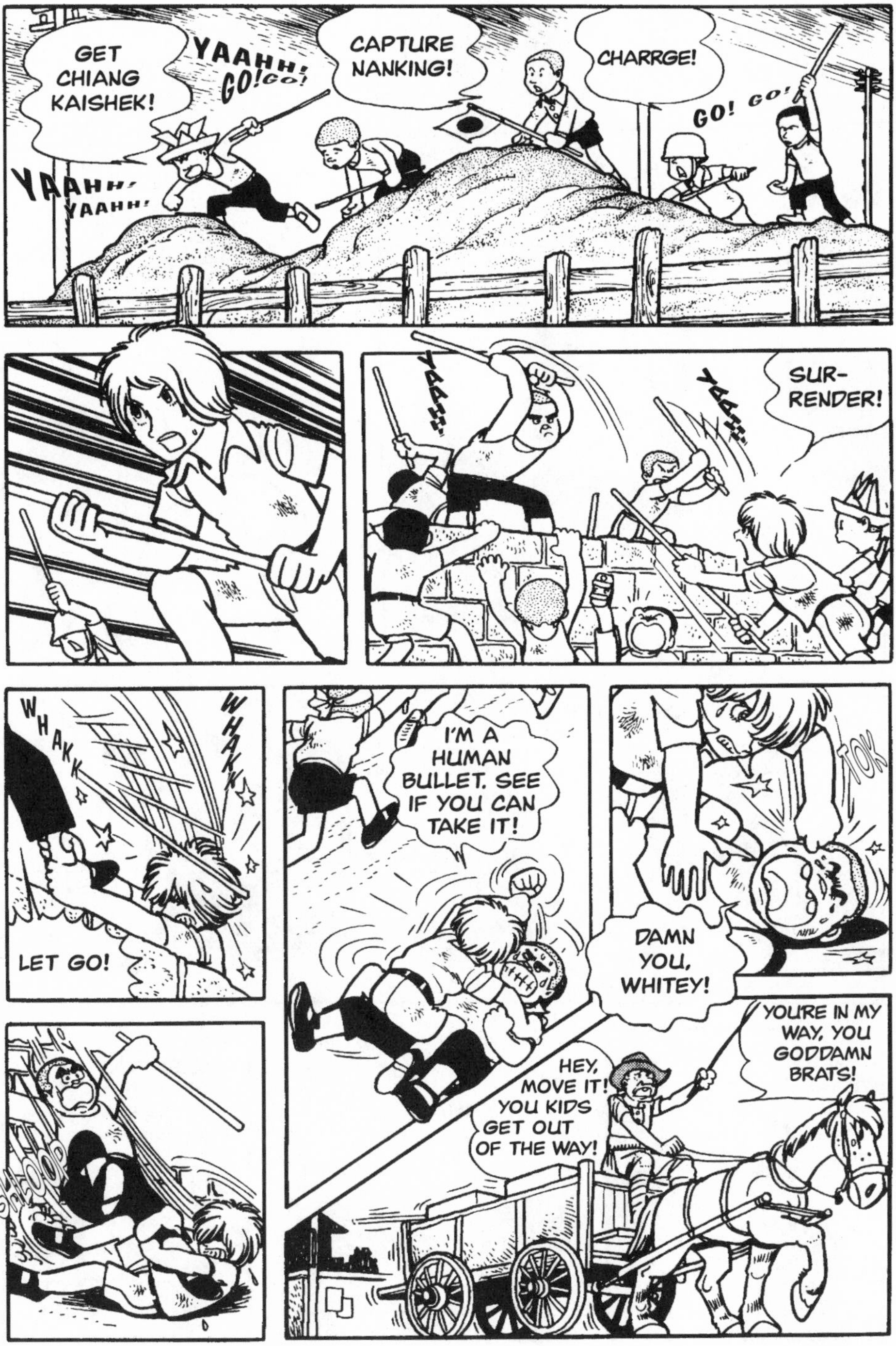
GET CHIANG KAISHEK!
YAAHH! GO! GO!
CAPTURE NANKING!
CHARRGE!
GO! GO!
YAAHH! YAAHH!
YAAHH!
YAAHH!
SUR-RENDER!
WHAKK
WHAKK
LET GO!
I'M A HUMAN BULLET. SEE IF YOU CAN TAKE IT!
TOK
DAMN YOU, WHITEY!
SHOOP
HEY, MOVE IT! YOU KIDS GET OUT OF THE WAY!
YOU'RE IN MY WAY, YOU GODDAMN BRATS!

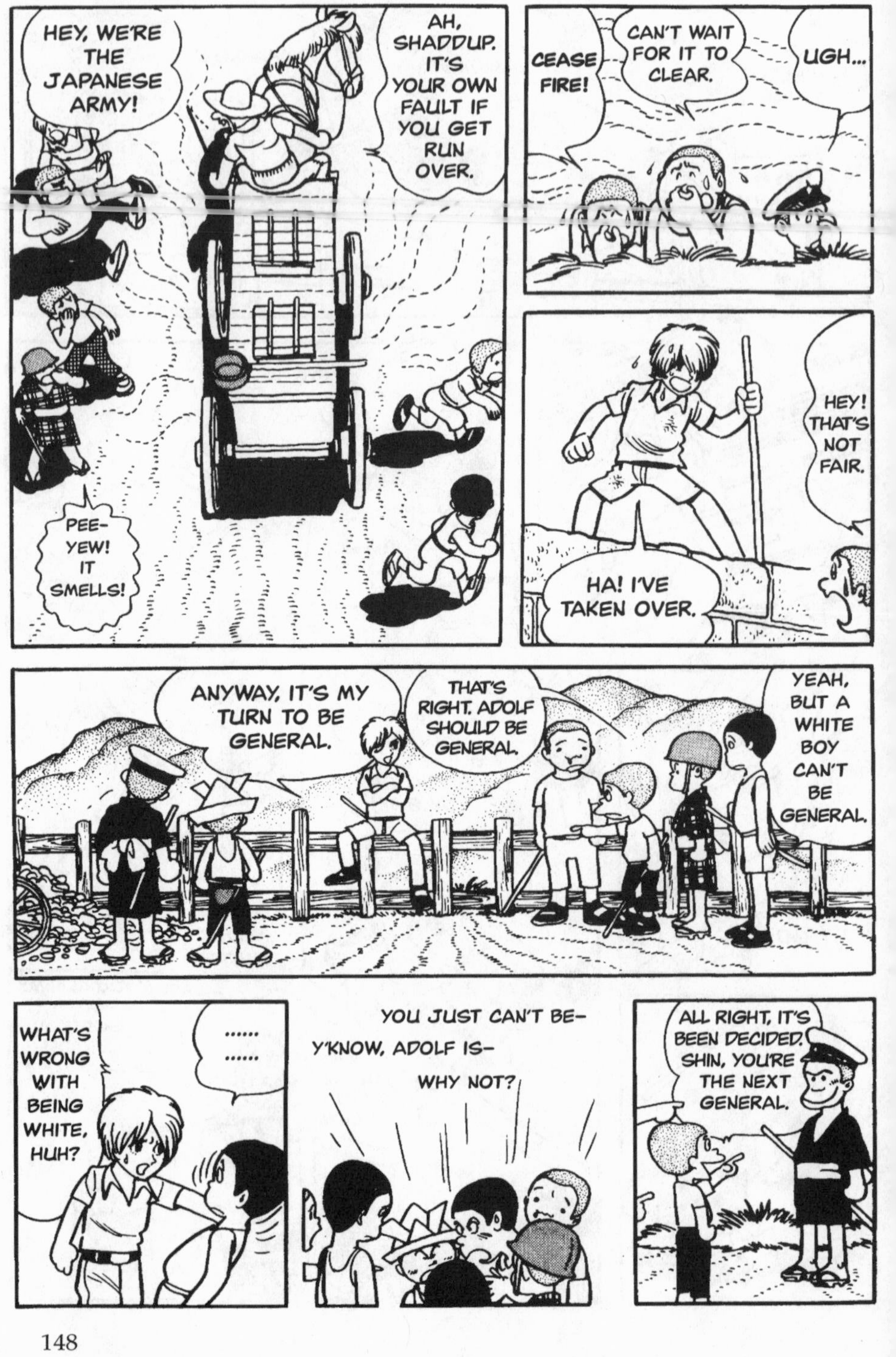
HEY, WE'RE THE JAPANESE ARMY!
AH, SHADDUP. IT'S YOUR OWN FAULT IF YOU GET RUN OVER.
PEE-YEW! IT SMELLS!
CEASE FIRE!
CAN'T WAIT FOR IT TO CLEAR.
UGH...
HEY! THAT'S NOT FAIR.
HA! I'VE TAKEN OVER.
ANYWAY, IT'S MY TURN TO BE GENERAL.
THAT'S RIGHT. ADOLF SHOULD BE GENERAL.
YEAH, BUT A WHITE BOY CAN'T BE GENERAL.
WHAT'S WRONG WITH BEING WHITE, HUH?
......
......
YOU JUST CAN'T BE-
Y'KNOW, ADOLF IS-
WHY NOT?
ALL RIGHT, IT'S BEEN DECIDED. SHIN, YOU'RE THE NEXT GENERAL.

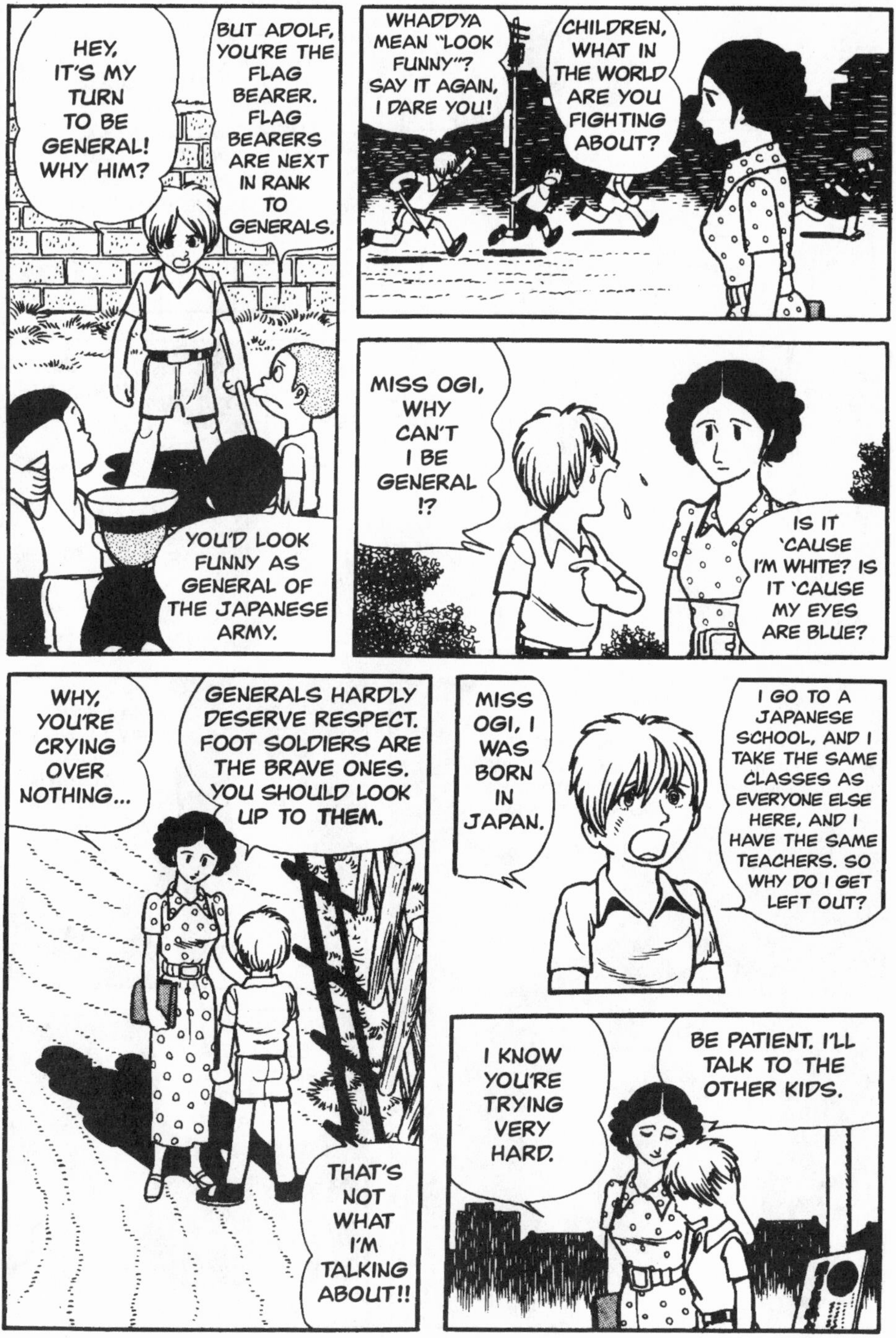
HEY, IT'S MY TURN TO BE GENERAL! WHY HIM?
BUT ADOLF, YOU'RE THE FLAG BEARER. FLAG BEARERS ARE NEXT IN RANK TO GENERALS.
YOU'D LOOK FUNNY AS GENERAL OF THE JAPANESE ARMY.
WHADDYA MEAN "LOOK FUNNY"? SAY IT AGAIN, I DARE YOU!
CHILDREN, WHAT IN THE WORLD ARE YOU FIGHTING ABOUT?
MISS OGI, WHY CAN'T I BE GENERAL !?
IS IT 'CAUSE I'M WHITE? IS IT 'CAUSE MY EYES ARE BLUE?
WHY, YOU'RE CRYING OVER NOTHING...
GENERALS HARDLY DESERVE RESPECT. FOOT SOLDIERS ARE THE BRAVE ONES. YOU SHOULD LOOK UP TO THEM.
THAT'S NOT WHAT I'M TALKING ABOUT!!
MISS OGI, I WAS BORN IN JAPAN.
I GO TO A JAPANESE SCHOOL, AND I TAKE THE SAME CLASSES AS EVERYONE ELSE HERE, AND I HAVE THE SAME TEACHERS. SO WHY DO I GET LEFT OUT?
I KNOW YOU'RE TRYING VERY HARD.
BE PATIENT. I'LL TALK TO THE OTHER KIDS.

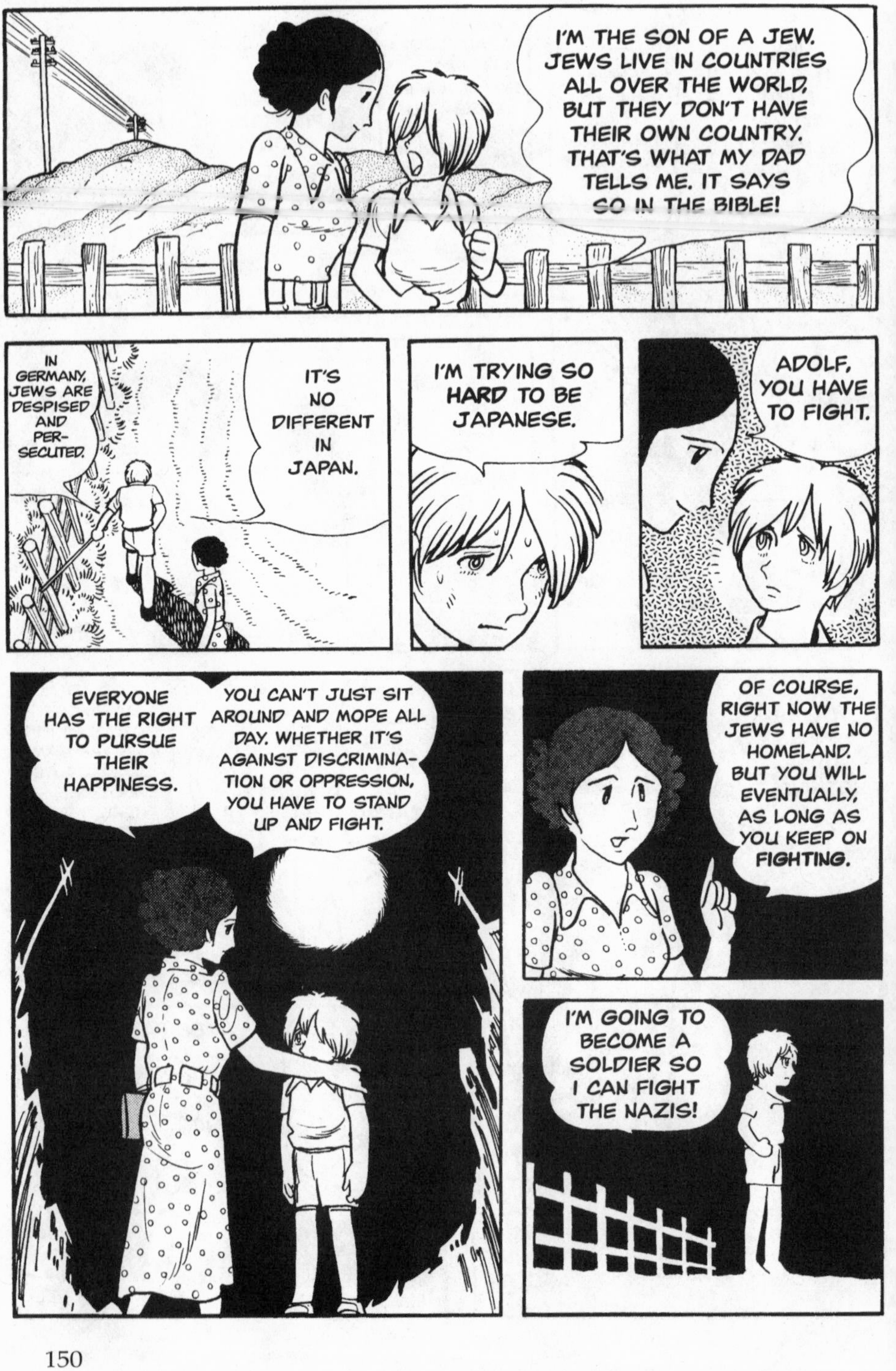
I'M THE SON OF A JEW. JEWS LIVE IN COUNTRIES ALL OVER THE WORLD, BUT THEY DON'T HAVE THEIR OWN COUNTRY. THAT'S WHAT MY DAD TELLS ME. IT SAYS SO IN THE BIBLE!
IN GERMANY, JEWS ARE DESPISED AND PERSECUTED.
IT'S NO DIFFERENT IN JAPAN.
I'M TRYING SO HARD TO BE JAPANESE.
ADOLF, YOU HAVE TO FIGHT.
EVERYONE HAS THE RIGHT TO PURSUE THEIR HAPPINESS.
YOU CAN'T JUST SIT AROUND AND MOPE ALL DAY. WHETHER IT'S AGAINST DISCRIMINATION OR OPPRESSION, YOU HAVE TO STAND UP AND FIGHT.
OF COURSE, RIGHT NOW THE JEWS HAVE NO HOMELAND. BUT YOU WILL EVENTUALLY, AS LONG AS YOU KEEP ON FIGHTING.
I'M GOING TO BECOME A SOLDIER SO I CAN FIGHT THE NAZIS!

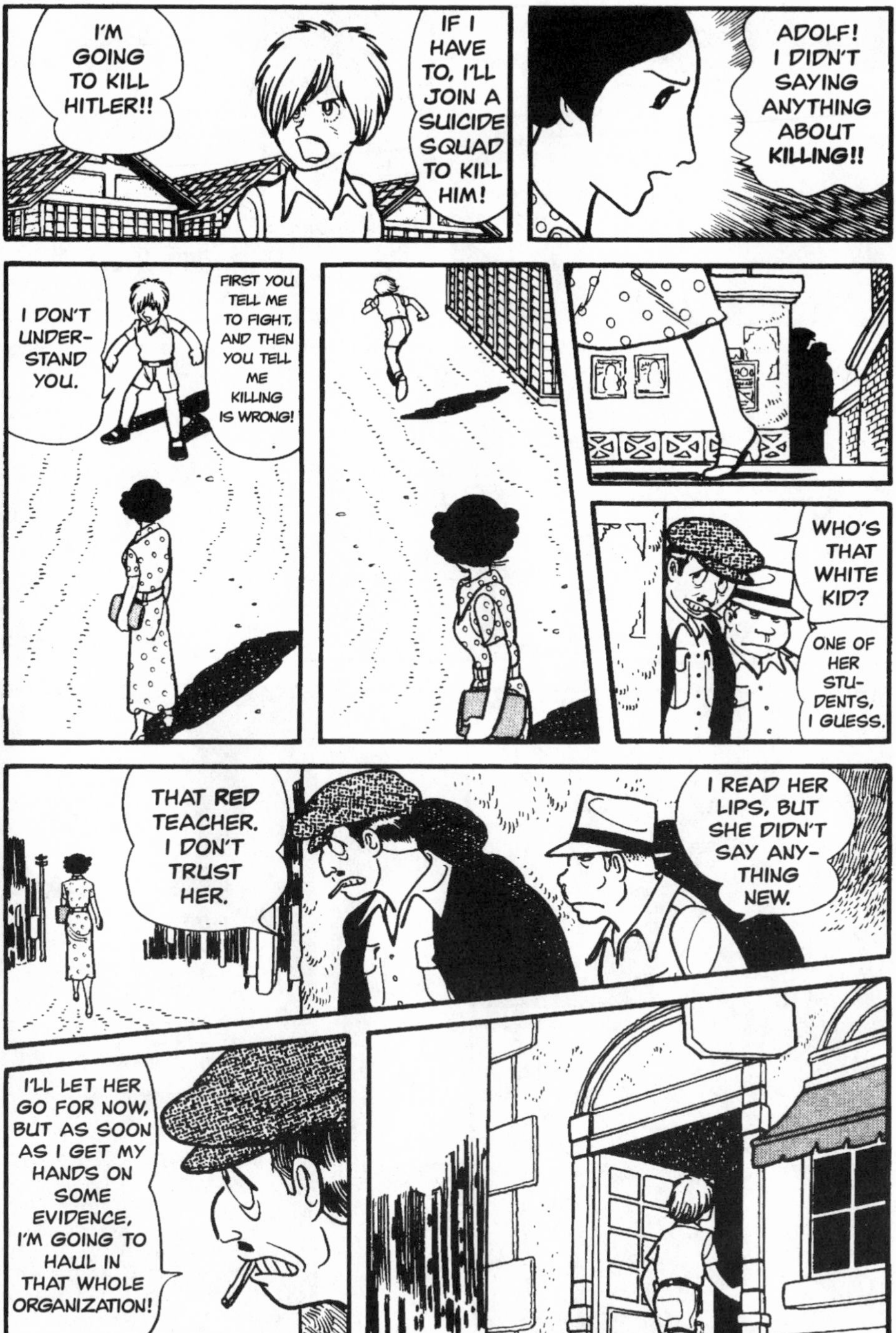
I'M GOING TO KILL HITLER!!
IF I HAVE TO, I'LL JOIN A SUICIDE SQUAD TO KILL HIM!
ADOLF! I DIDN'T SAYING ANYTHING ABOUT KILLING!!
I DON'T UNDER-STAND YOU.
FIRST YOU TELL ME TO FIGHT, AND THEN YOU TELL ME KILLING IS WRONG!
WHO'S THAT WHITE KID?
ONE OF HER STU-DENTS, I GUESS.
THAT RED TEACHER. I DON'T TRUST HER.
I READ HER LIPS, BUT SHE DIDN'T SAY ANY-THING NEW.
I'LL LET HER GO FOR NOW, BUT AS SOON AS I GET MY HANDS ON SOME EVIDENCE, I'M GOING TO HAUL IN THAT WHOLE ORGANIZATION!

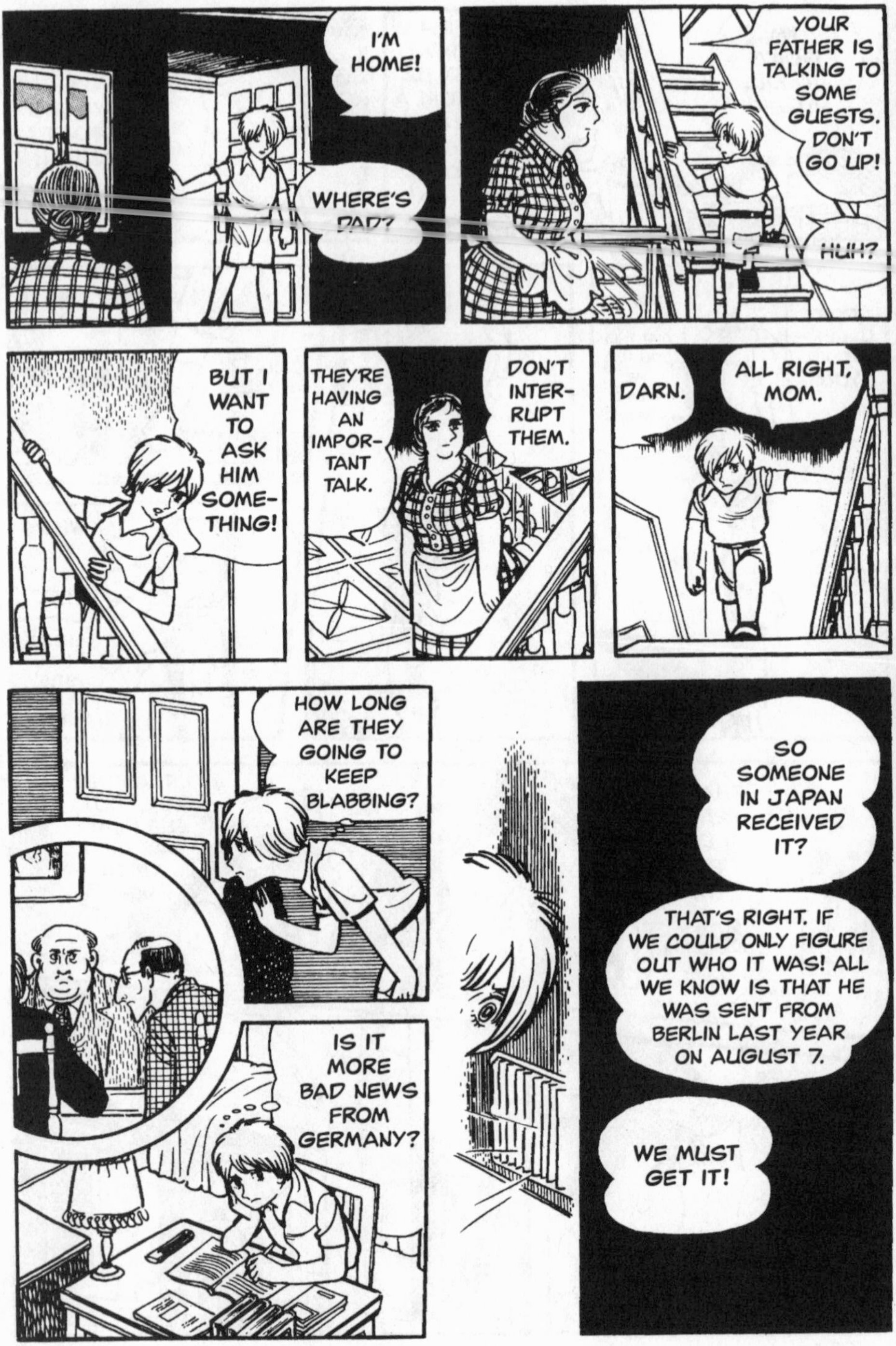
I'M HOME!
WHERE'S DAD?
YOUR FATHER IS TALKING TO SOME GUESTS. DON'T GO UP!
HUH?
BUT I WANT TO ASK HIM SOME-THING!
THEY'RE HAVING AN IMPOR-TANT TALK.
DON'T INTER-RUPT THEM.
DARN.
ALL RIGHT, MOM.
HOW LONG ARE THEY GOING TO KEEP BLABBING?
IS IT MORE BAD NEWS FROM GERMANY?
SO SOMEONE IN JAPAN RECEIVED IT?
THAT'S RIGHT. IF WE COULD ONLY FIGURE OUT WHO IT WAS! ALL WE KNOW IS THAT HE WAS SENT FROM BERLIN LAST YEAR ON AUGUST 7.
WE MUST GET IT!

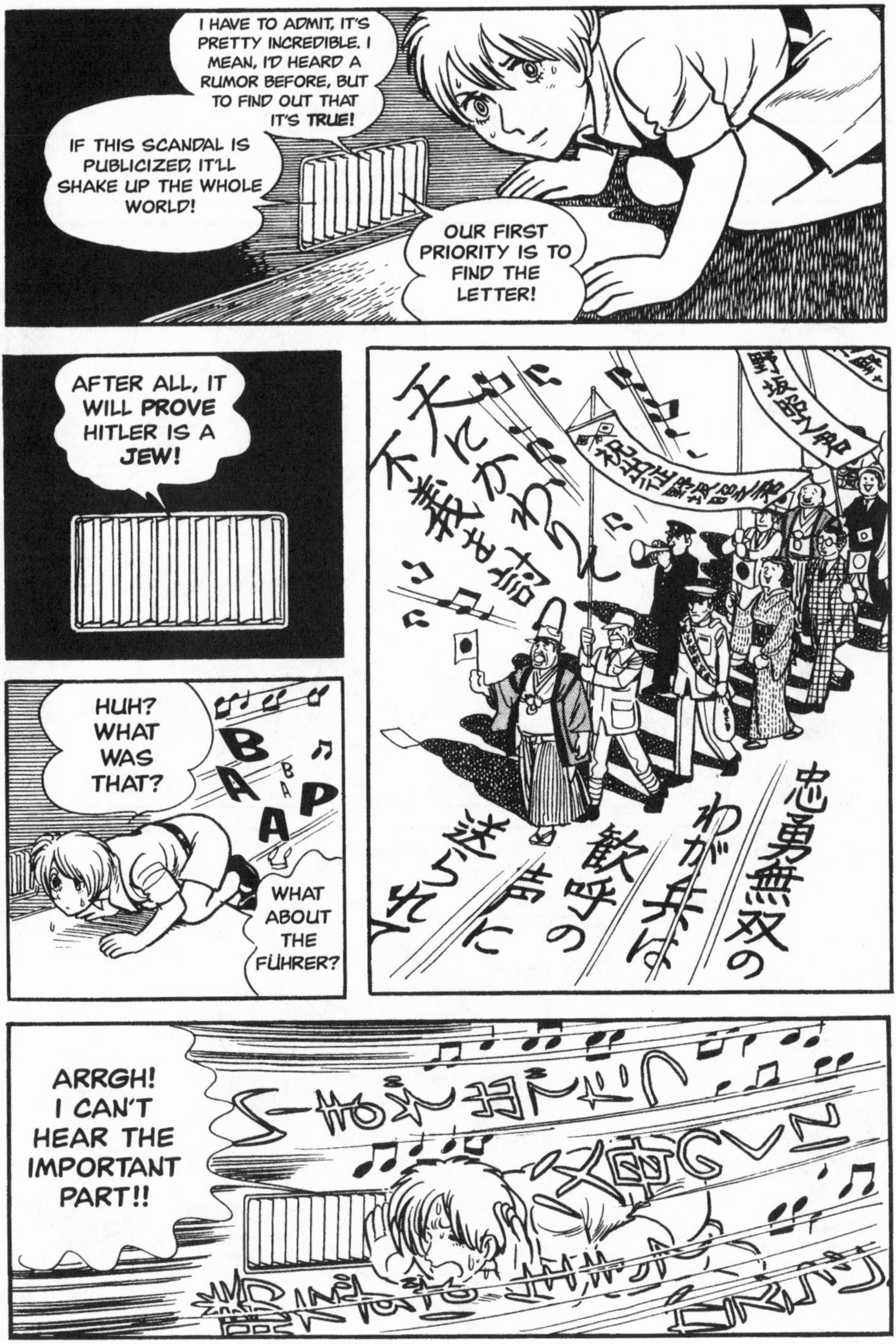
I HAVE TO ADMIT, IT'S PRETTY INCREDIBLE. I MEAN, I'D HEARD A RUMOR BEFORE, BUT TO FIND OUT THAT IT'S **TRUE**!
IF THIS SCANDAL IS PUBLICIZED, IT'LL SHAKE UP THE WHOLE WORLD!
OUR FIRST PRIORITY IS TO FIND THE LETTER!
AFTER ALL, IT WILL **PROVE** HITLER IS A **JEW**!
HUH? WHAT WAS THAT?
BAAP
BAAP
WHAT ABOUT THE FÜHRER?
天にかわりて
不義を討
忠勇無双の
わが兵は
歓呼の
声に
送られて
ARRGH! I CAN'T HEAR THE IMPORTANT PART!!

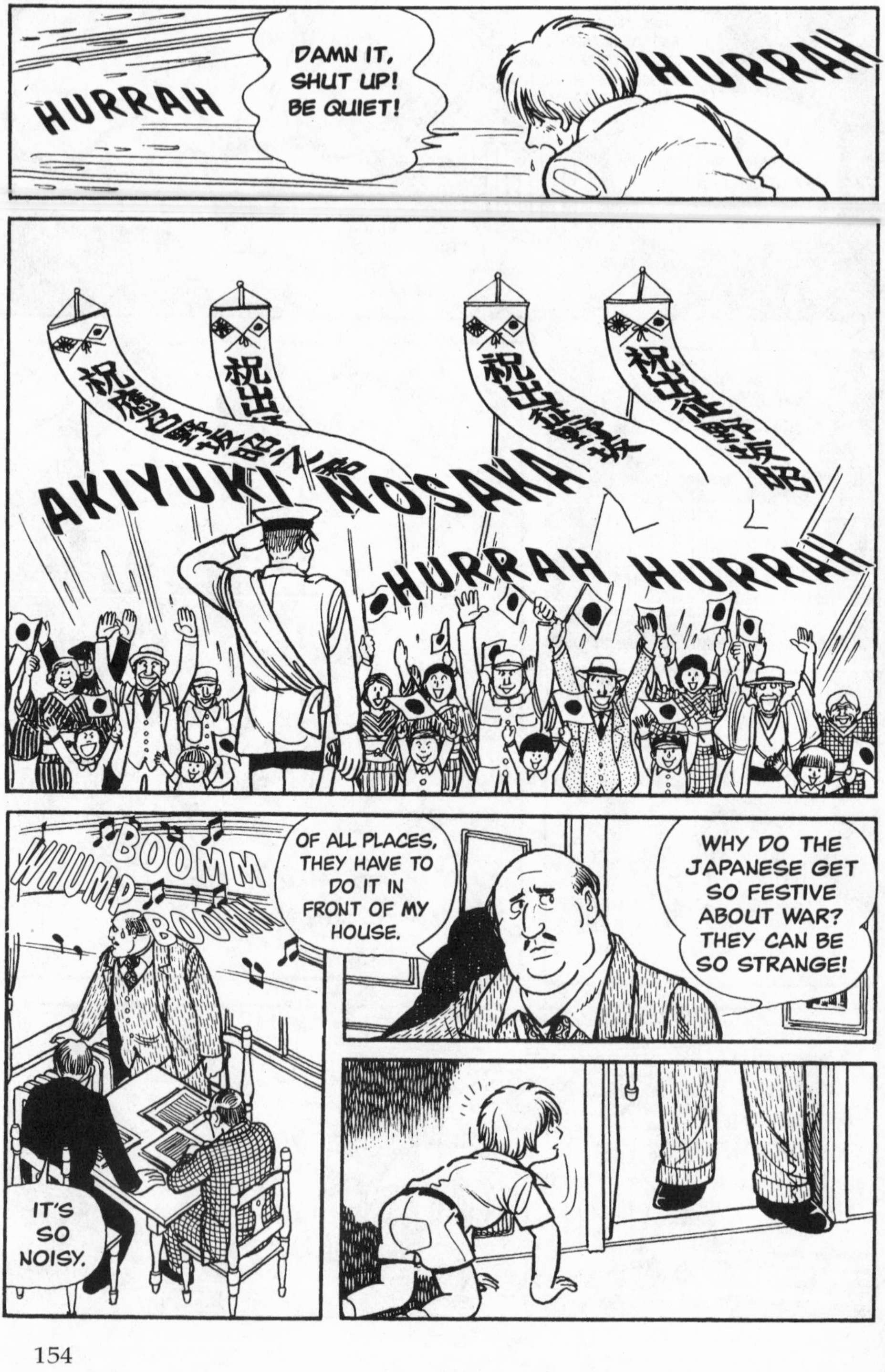
HURRAH
DAMN IT, SHUT UP! BE QUIET!
HURRAH
AKIYUKI NOSAKA
HURRAH HURRAH
WHUMP
BOOMM
BOOMM
IT'S SO NOISY.
OF ALL PLACES, THEY HAVE TO DO IT IN FRONT OF MY HOUSE.
WHY DO THE JAPANESE GET SO FESTIVE ABOUT WAR? THEY CAN BE SO STRANGE!

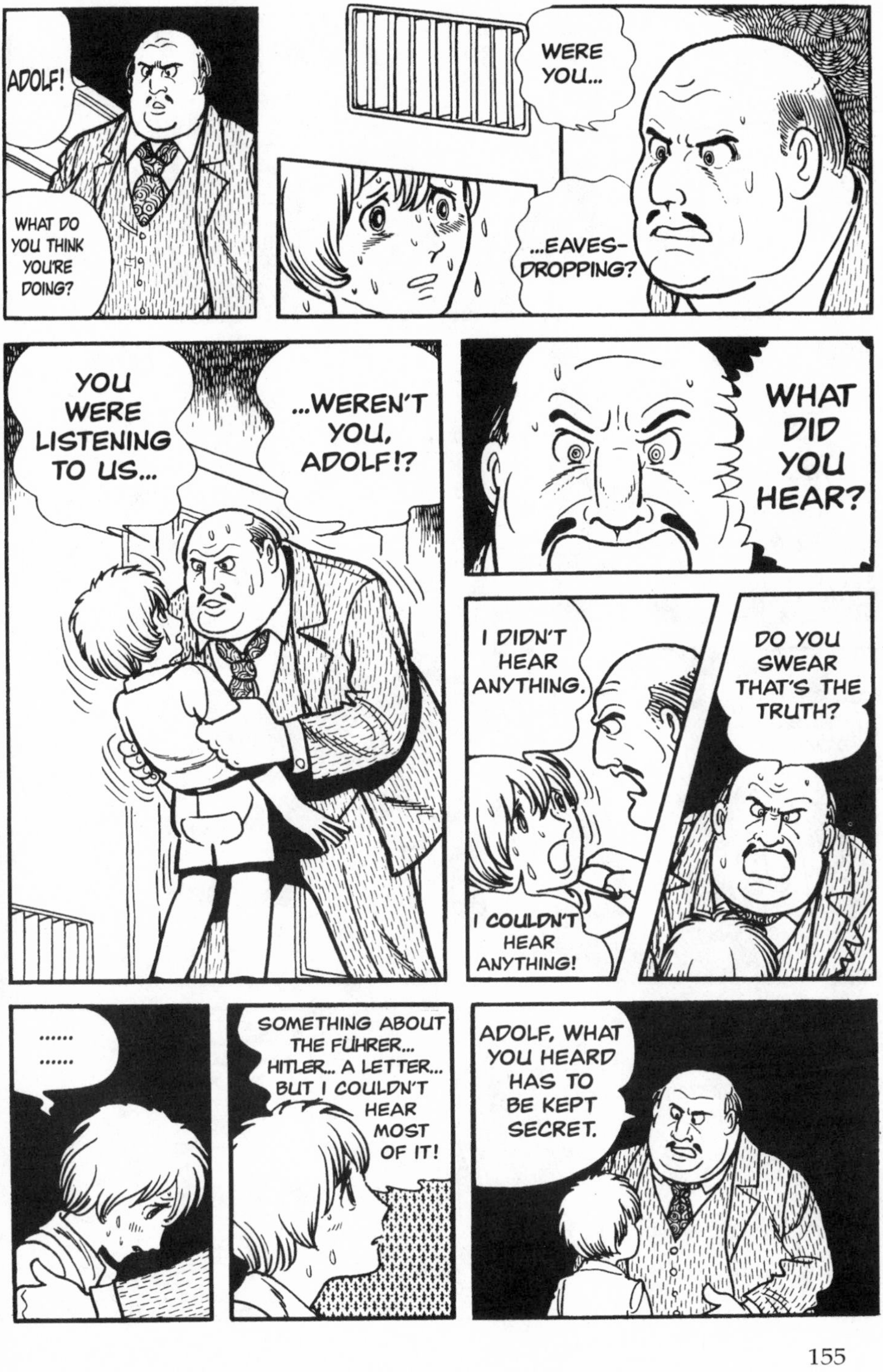
ADOLF!
WHAT DO YOU THINK YOU'RE DOING?
WERE YOU...
...EAVES-DROPPING?
YOU WERE LISTENING TO US...
...WEREN'T YOU, ADOLF!?
WHAT DID YOU HEAR?
I DIDN'T HEAR ANYTHING.
I COULDN'T HEAR ANYTHING!
DO YOU SWEAR THAT'S THE TRUTH?
......
......
SOMETHING ABOUT THE FÜHRER... HITLER... A LETTER... BUT I COULDN'T HEAR MOST OF IT!
ADOLF, WHAT YOU HEARD HAS TO BE KEPT SECRET.

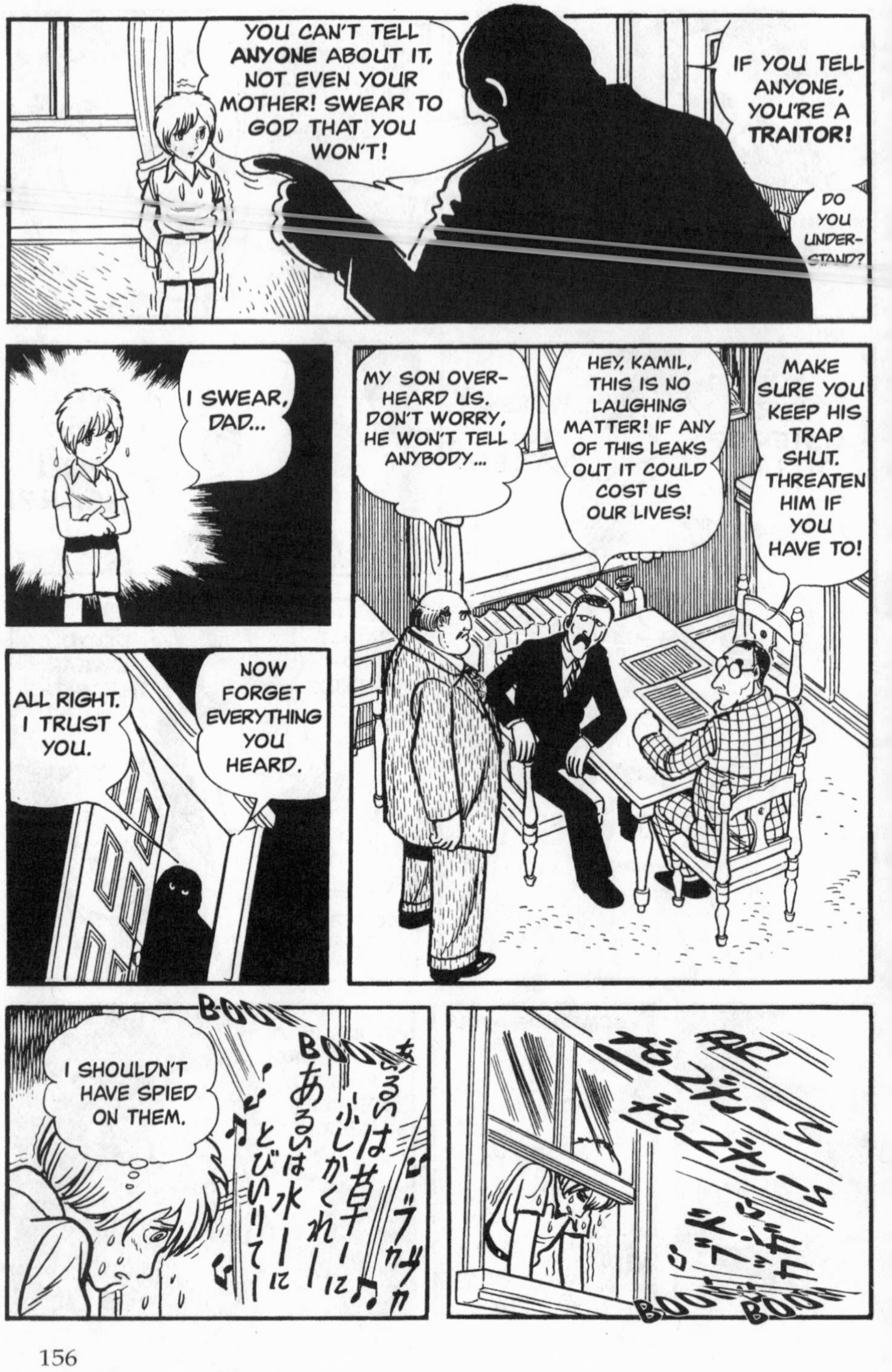
YOU CAN'T TELL ANYONE ABOUT IT, NOT EVEN YOUR MOTHER! SWEAR TO GOD THAT YOU WON'T!
IF YOU TELL ANYONE, YOU'RE A TRAITOR!
DO YOU UNDER-STAND?
I SWEAR, DAD...
ALL RIGHT. I TRUST YOU.
NOW FORGET EVERYTHING YOU HEARD.
MY SON OVER-HEARD US. DON'T WORRY, HE WON'T TELL ANYBODY...
HEY, KAMIL, THIS IS NO LAUGHING MATTER! IF ANY OF THIS LEAKS OUT IT COULD COST US OUR LIVES!
MAKE SURE YOU KEEP HIS TRAP SHUT. THREATEN HIM IF YOU HAVE TO!
I SHOULDN'T HAVE SPIED ON THEM.
あるいは草ーに
ふしかくれー
あるいは水ーに
とびいりてー

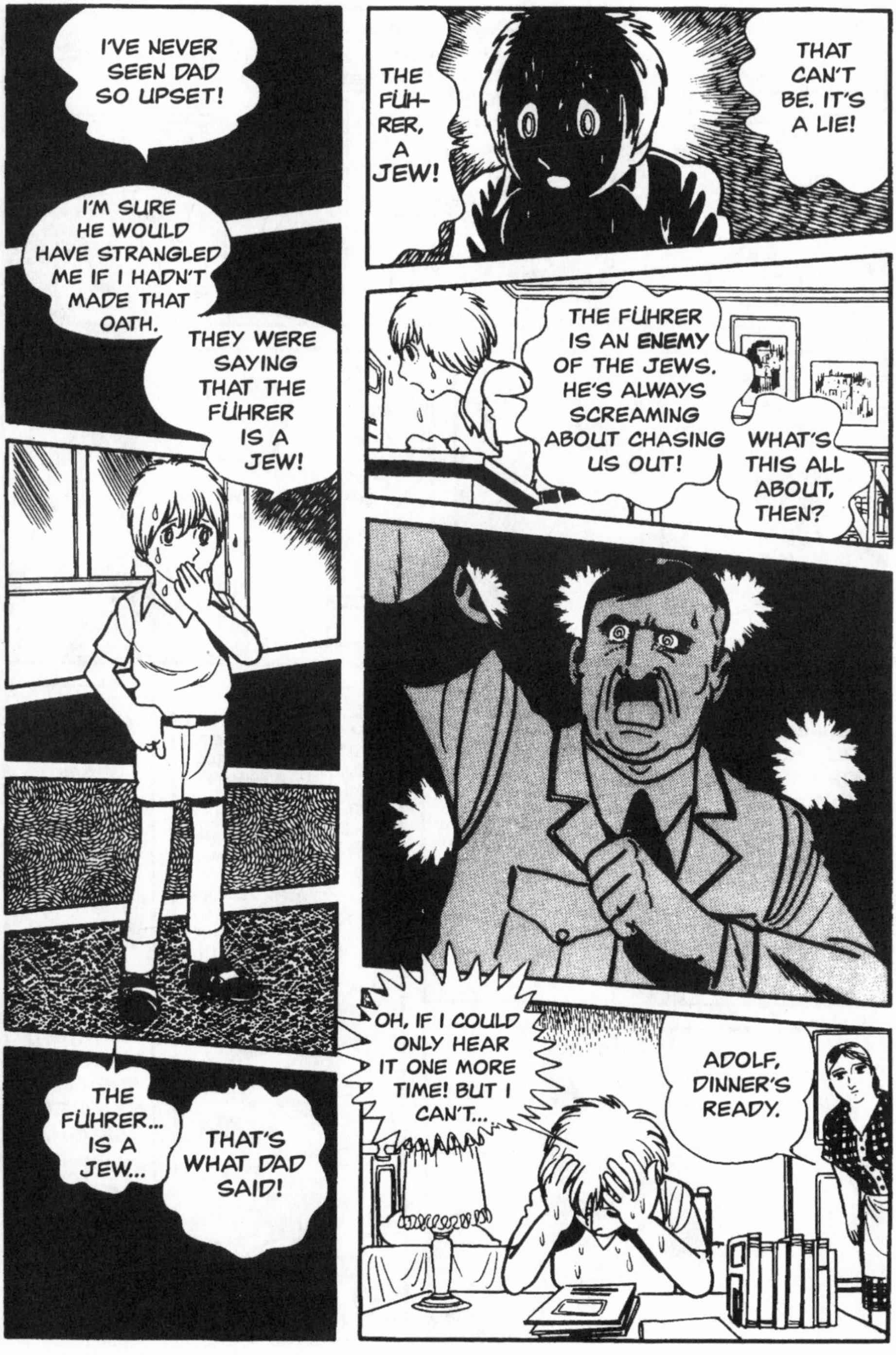
I'VE NEVER SEEN DAD SO UPSET!
I'M SURE HE WOULD HAVE STRANGLED ME IF I HADN'T MADE THAT OATH.
THEY WERE SAYING THAT THE FÜHRER IS A JEW!
THE FÜH-RER, A JEW!
THAT CAN'T BE. IT'S A LIE!
THE FÜHRER IS AN ENEMY OF THE JEWS. HE'S ALWAYS SCREAMING ABOUT CHASING US OUT!
WHAT'S THIS ALL ABOUT, THEN?
THE FÜHRER... IS A JEW...
THAT'S WHAT DAD SAID!
OH, IF I COULD ONLY HEAR IT ONE MORE TIME! BUT I CAN'T...
ADOLF, DINNER'S READY.

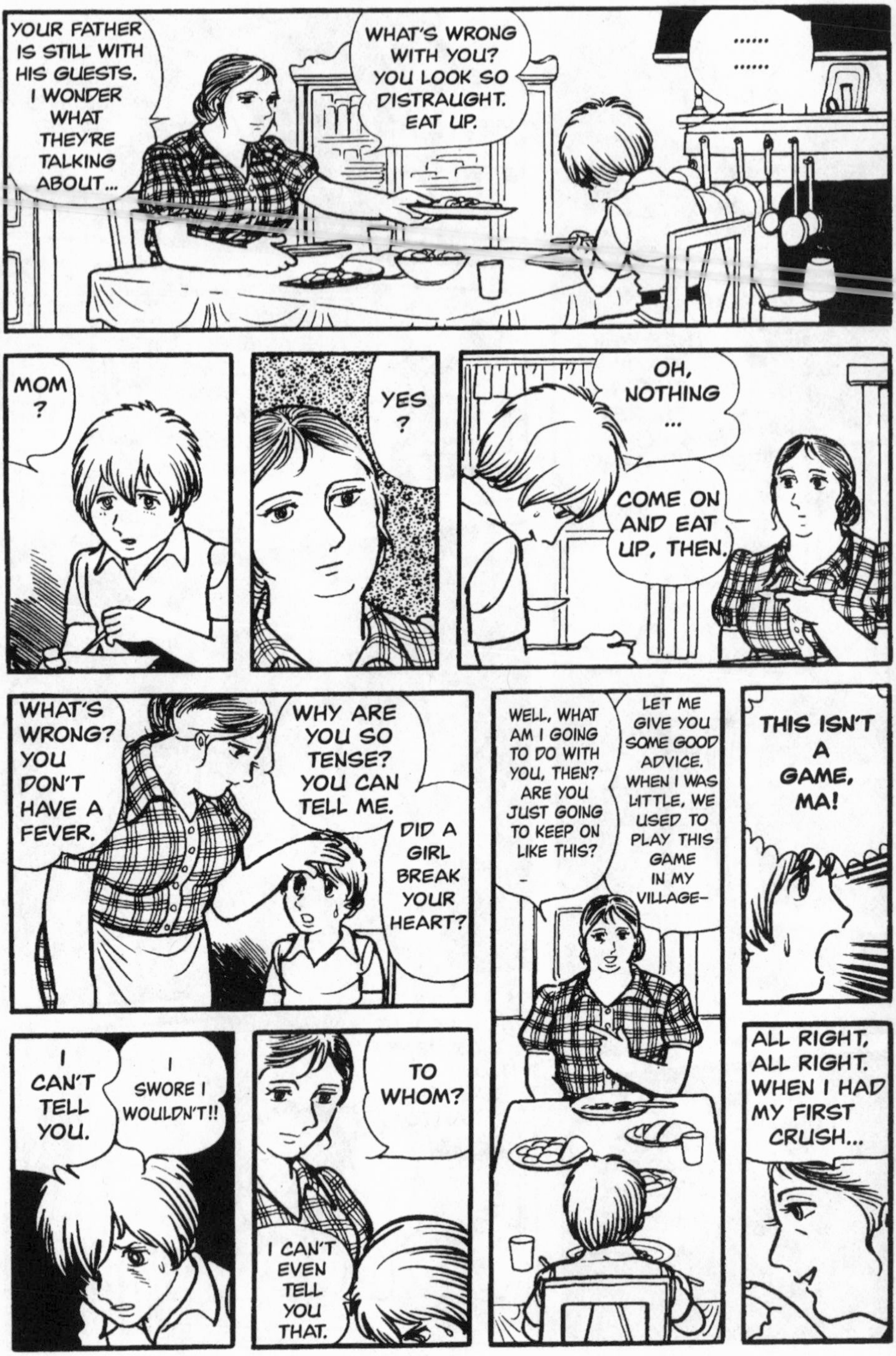
YOUR FATHER IS STILL WITH HIS GUESTS. I WONDER WHAT THEY'RE TALKING ABOUT...
WHAT'S WRONG WITH YOU? YOU LOOK SO DISTRAUGHT. EAT UP.
......
......
MOM ?
YES ?
OH, NOTHING ...
COME ON AND EAT UP, THEN.
WHAT'S WRONG? YOU DON'T HAVE A FEVER.
WHY ARE YOU SO TENSE? YOU CAN TELL ME.
DID A GIRL BREAK YOUR HEART?
WELL, WHAT AM I GOING TO DO WITH YOU, THEN? ARE YOU JUST GOING TO KEEP ON LIKE THIS?
LET ME GIVE YOU SOME GOOD ADVICE. WHEN I WAS LITTLE, WE USED TO PLAY THIS GAME IN MY VILLAGE-
THIS ISN'T A GAME, MA!
I CAN'T TELL YOU.
I SWORE I WOULDN'T!!
TO WHOM?
I CAN'T EVEN TELL YOU THAT.
ALL RIGHT, ALL RIGHT. WHEN I HAD MY FIRST CRUSH...

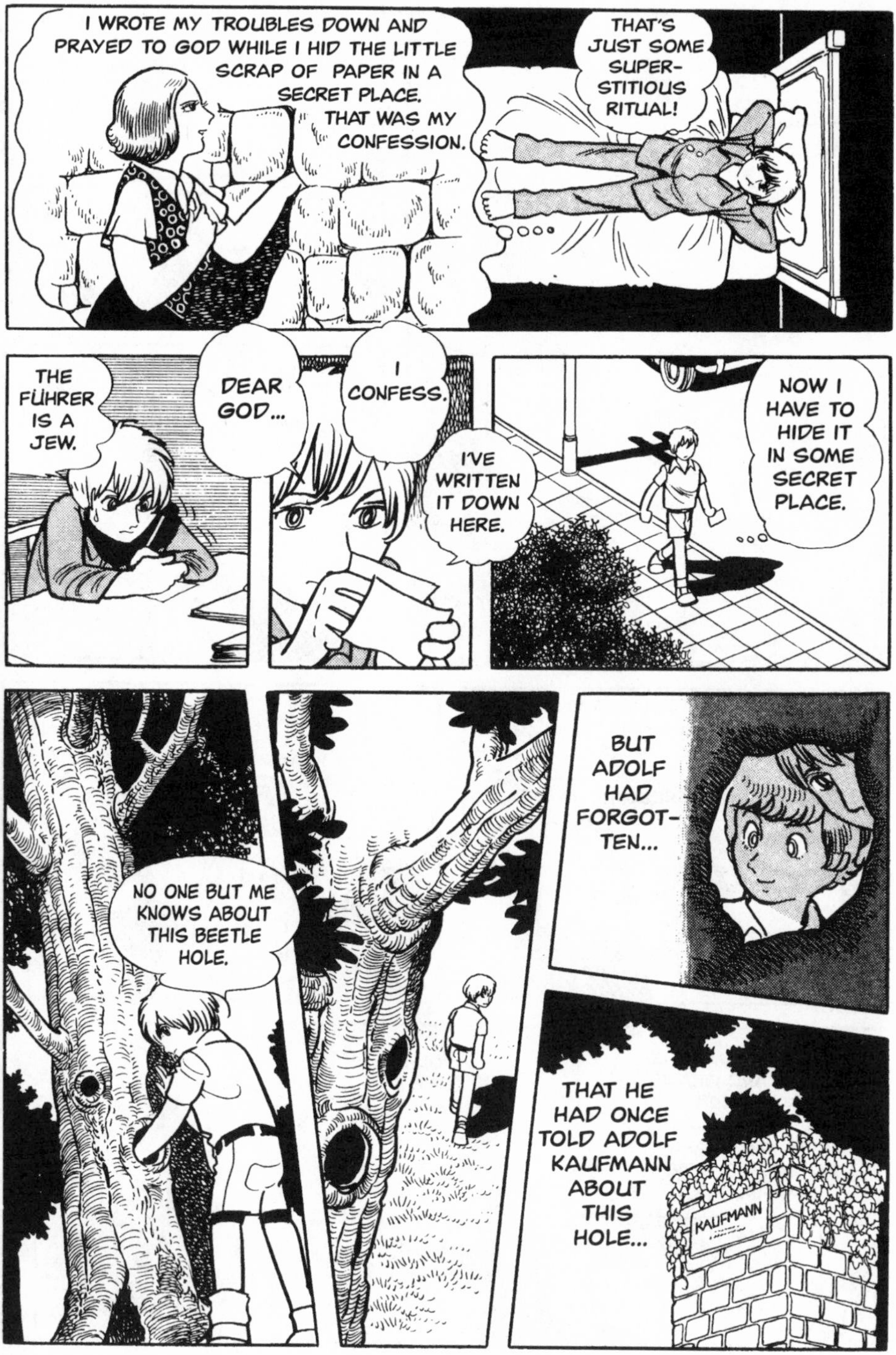
I WROTE MY TROUBLES DOWN AND PRAYED TO GOD WHILE I HID THE LITTLE SCRAP OF PAPER IN A SECRET PLACE.
THAT WAS MY CONFESSION.
THAT'S JUST SOME SUPER-STITIOUS RITUAL!
THE FÜHRER IS A JEW.
DEAR GOD...
I CONFESS.
I'VE WRITTEN IT DOWN HERE.
NOW I HAVE TO HIDE IT IN SOME SECRET PLACE.
NO ONE BUT ME KNOWS ABOUT THIS BEETLE HOLE.
BUT ADOLF HAD FORGOT-TEN...
THAT HE HAD ONCE TOLD ADOLF KAUFMANN ABOUT THIS HOLE...
KAUFMANN

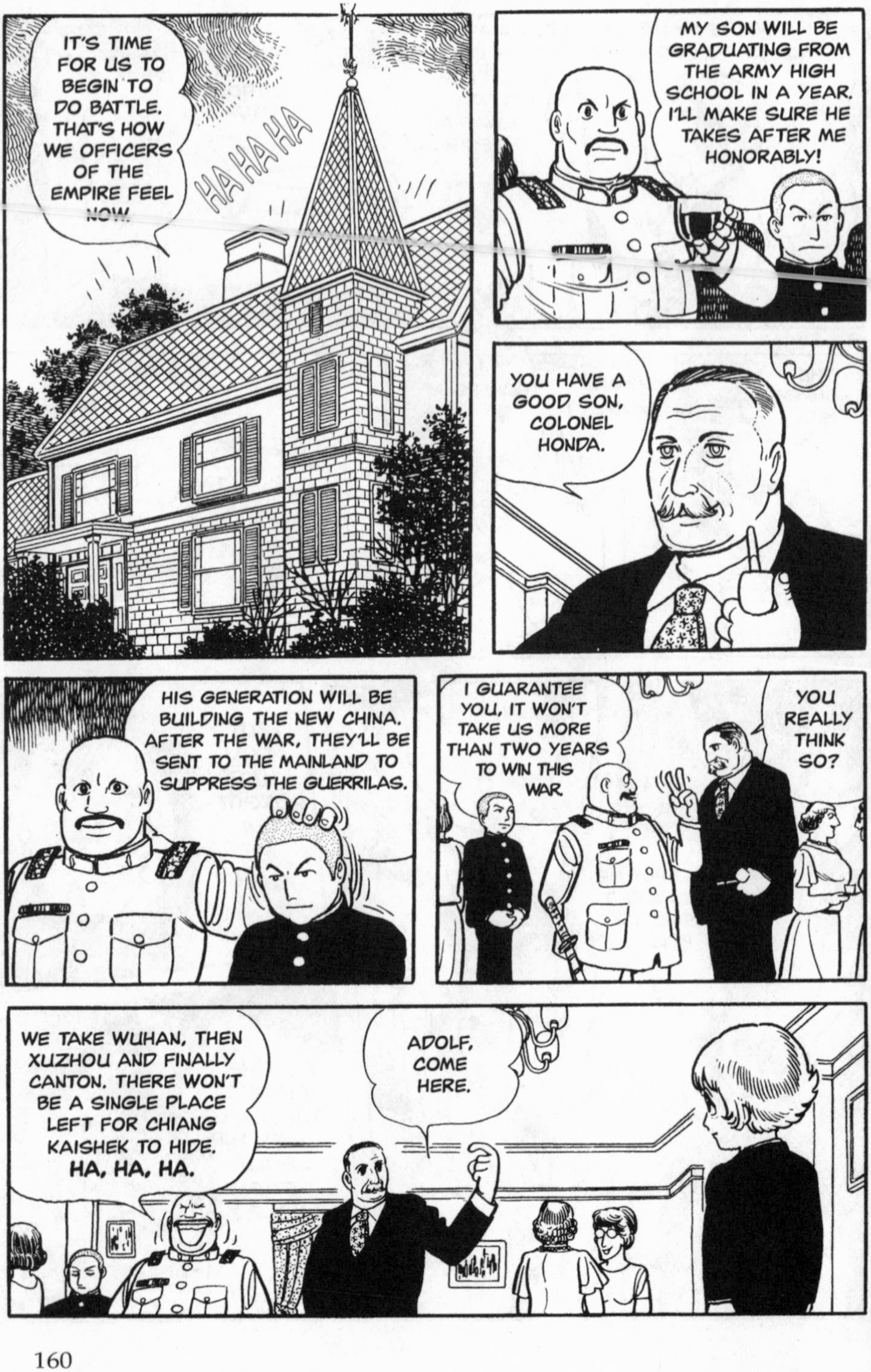
IT'S TIME FOR US TO BEGIN TO DO BATTLE. THAT'S HOW WE OFFICERS OF THE EMPIRE FEEL NOW.
HA HA HA
MY SON WILL BE GRADUATING FROM THE ARMY HIGH SCHOOL IN A YEAR. I'LL MAKE SURE HE TAKES AFTER ME HONORABLY!
YOU HAVE A GOOD SON, COLONEL HONDA.
HIS GENERATION WILL BE BUILDING THE NEW CHINA. AFTER THE WAR, THEY'LL BE SENT TO THE MAINLAND TO SUPPRESS THE GUERRILAS.
I GUARANTEE YOU, IT WON'T TAKE US MORE THAN TWO YEARS TO WIN THIS WAR.
YOU REALLY THINK SO?
WE TAKE WUHAN, THEN XUZHOU AND FINALLY CANTON. THERE WON'T BE A SINGLE PLACE LEFT FOR CHIANG KAISHEK TO HIDE. HA, HA, HA.
ADOLF, COME HERE.

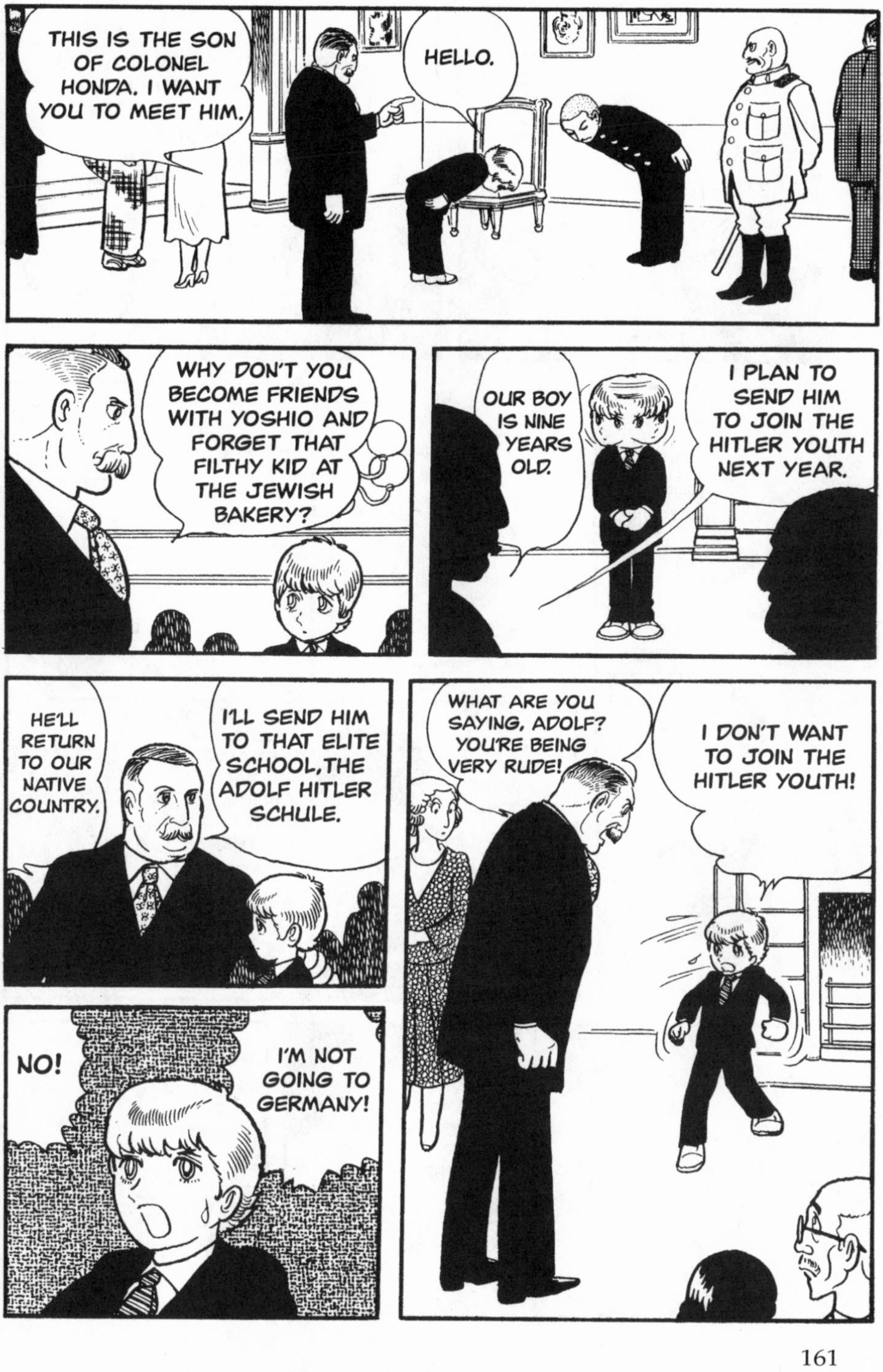
THIS IS THE SON OF COLONEL HONDA. I WANT YOU TO MEET HIM.
HELLO.
WHY DON'T YOU BECOME FRIENDS WITH YOSHIO AND FORGET THAT FILTHY KID AT THE JEWISH BAKERY?
OUR BOY IS NINE YEARS OLD.
I PLAN TO SEND HIM TO JOIN THE HITLER YOUTH NEXT YEAR.
HE'LL RETURN TO OUR NATIVE COUNTRY.
I'LL SEND HIM TO THAT ELITE SCHOOL, THE ADOLF HITLER SCHULE.
WHAT ARE YOU SAYING, ADOLF? YOU'RE BEING VERY RUDE!
I DON'T WANT TO JOIN THE HITLER YOUTH!
NO!
I'M NOT GOING TO GERMANY!

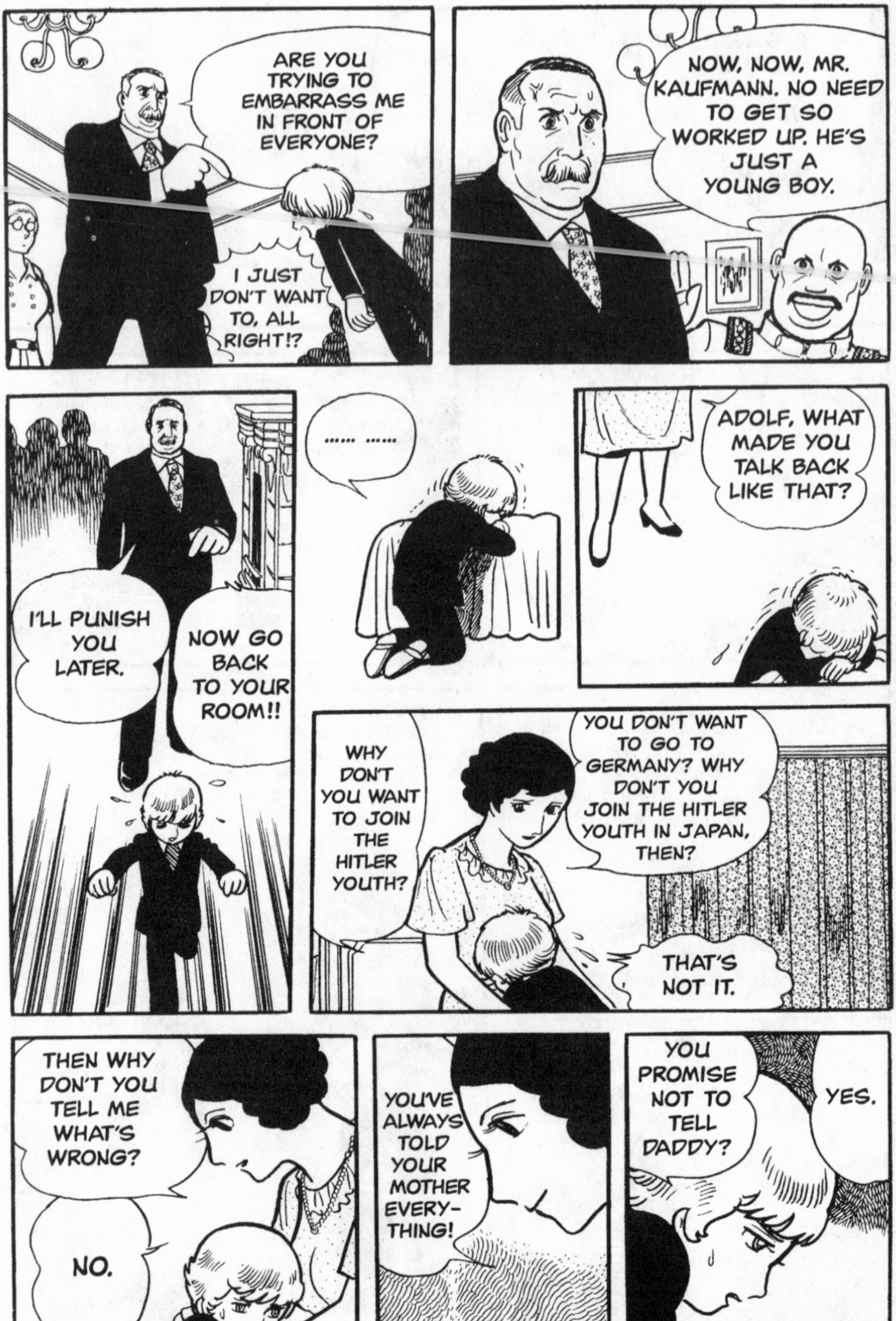
ARE YOU TRYING TO EMBARRASS ME IN FRONT OF EVERYONE?
I JUST DON'T WANT TO, ALL RIGHT!?
NOW, NOW, MR. KAUFMANN. NO NEED TO GET SO WORKED UP. HE'S JUST A YOUNG BOY.
I'LL PUNISH YOU LATER.
NOW GO BACK TO YOUR ROOM!!
....
ADOLF, WHAT MADE YOU TALK BACK LIKE THAT?
WHY DON'T YOU WANT TO JOIN THE HITLER YOUTH?
YOU DON'T WANT TO GO TO GERMANY? WHY DON'T YOU JOIN THE HITLER YOUTH IN JAPAN, THEN?
THAT'S NOT IT.
THEN WHY DON'T YOU TELL ME WHAT'S WRONG?
NO.
YOU'VE ALWAYS TOLD YOUR MOTHER EVERY-THING!
YOU PROMISE NOT TO TELL DADDY?
YES.

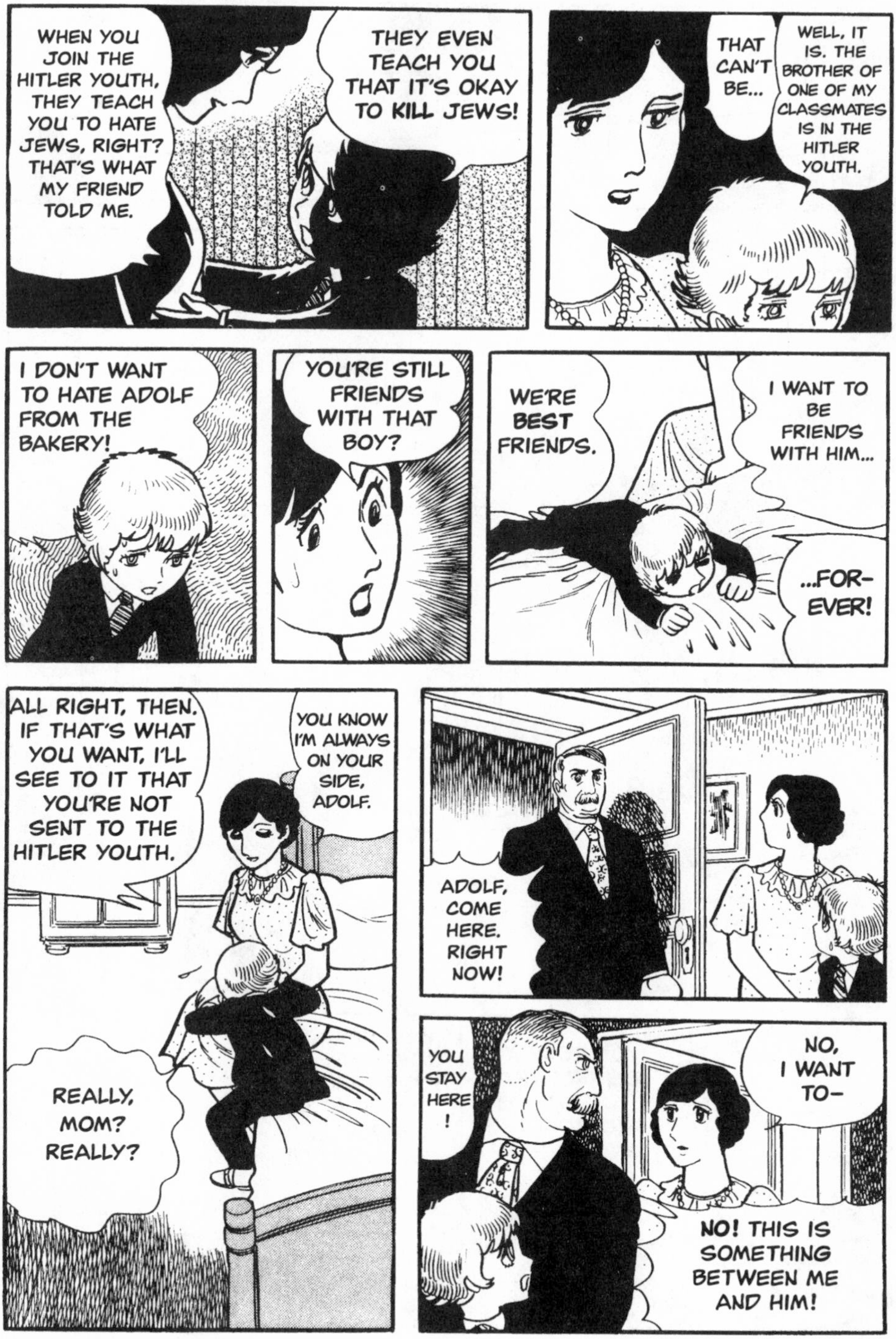
WHEN YOU JOIN THE HITLER YOUTH, THEY TEACH YOU TO HATE JEWS, RIGHT? THAT'S WHAT MY FRIEND TOLD ME.
THEY EVEN TEACH YOU THAT IT'S OKAY TO KILL JEWS!
THAT CAN'T BE...
WELL, IT IS. THE BROTHER OF ONE OF MY CLASSMATES IS IN THE HITLER YOUTH.
I DON'T WANT TO HATE ADOLF FROM THE BAKERY!
YOU'RE STILL FRIENDS WITH THAT BOY?
WE'RE BEST FRIENDS.
I WANT TO BE FRIENDS WITH HIM...
...FOR-EVER!
ALL RIGHT, THEN. IF THAT'S WHAT YOU WANT, I'LL SEE TO IT THAT YOU'RE NOT SENT TO THE HITLER YOUTH.
YOU KNOW I'M ALWAYS ON YOUR SIDE, ADOLF.
REALLY, MOM? REALLY?
ADOLF, COME HERE. RIGHT NOW!
YOU STAY HERE!
NO, I WANT TO–
NO! THIS IS SOMETHING BETWEEN ME AND HIM!

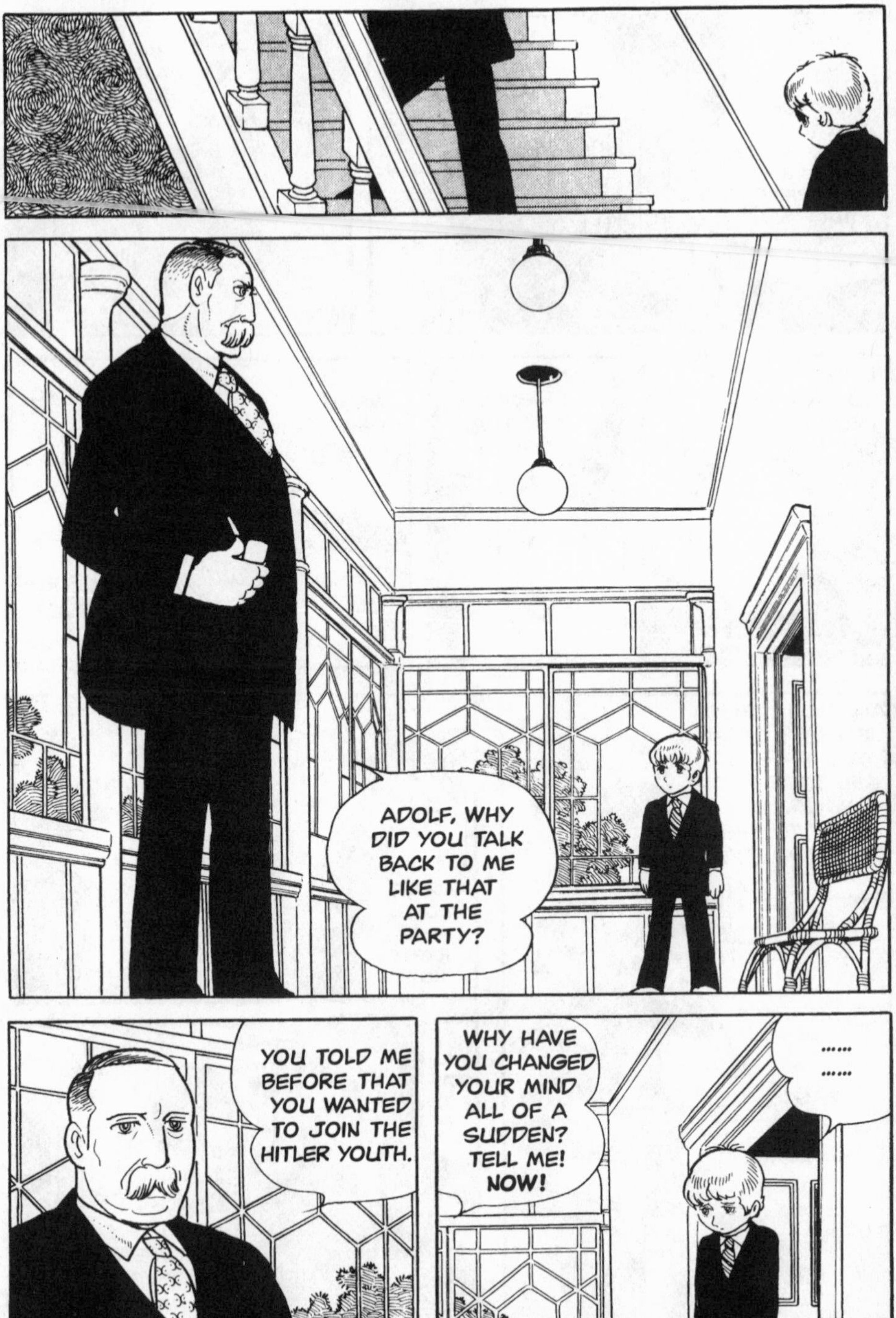
ADOLF, WHY DID YOU TALK BACK TO ME LIKE THAT AT THE PARTY?
YOU TOLD ME BEFORE THAT YOU WANTED TO JOIN THE HITLER YOUTH.
WHY HAVE YOU CHANGED YOUR MIND ALL OF A SUDDEN? TELL ME! NOW!
......
......

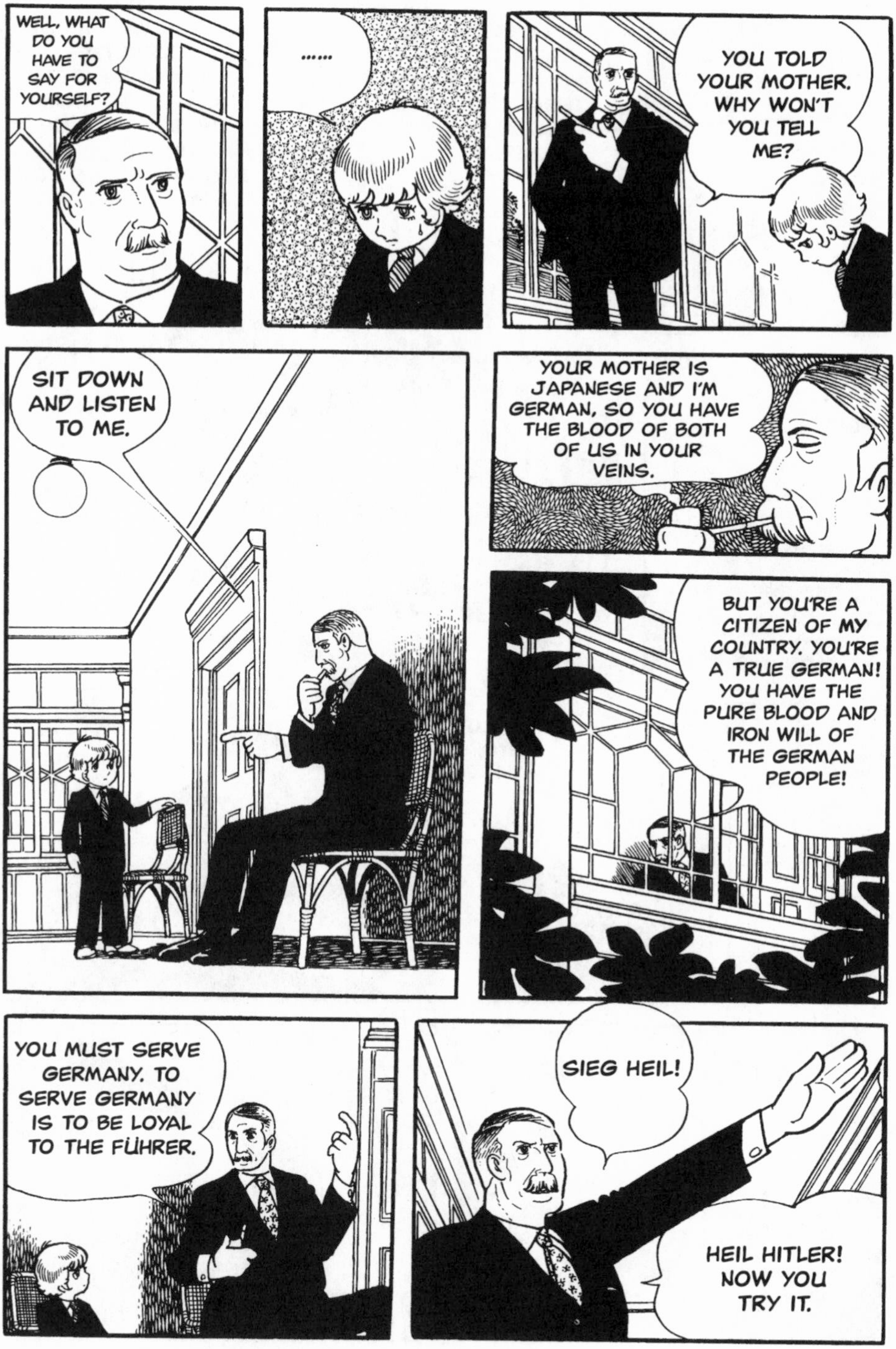
WELL, WHAT DO YOU HAVE TO SAY FOR YOURSELF?
......
YOU TOLD YOUR MOTHER. WHY WON'T YOU TELL ME?
SIT DOWN AND LISTEN TO ME.
YOUR MOTHER IS JAPANESE AND I'M GERMAN, SO YOU HAVE THE BLOOD OF BOTH OF US IN YOUR VEINS.
BUT YOU'RE A CITIZEN OF MY COUNTRY. YOU'RE A TRUE GERMAN! YOU HAVE THE PURE BLOOD AND IRON WILL OF THE GERMAN PEOPLE!
YOU MUST SERVE GERMANY. TO SERVE GERMANY IS TO BE LOYAL TO THE FÜHRER.
SIEG HEIL!
HEIL HITLER! NOW YOU TRY IT.

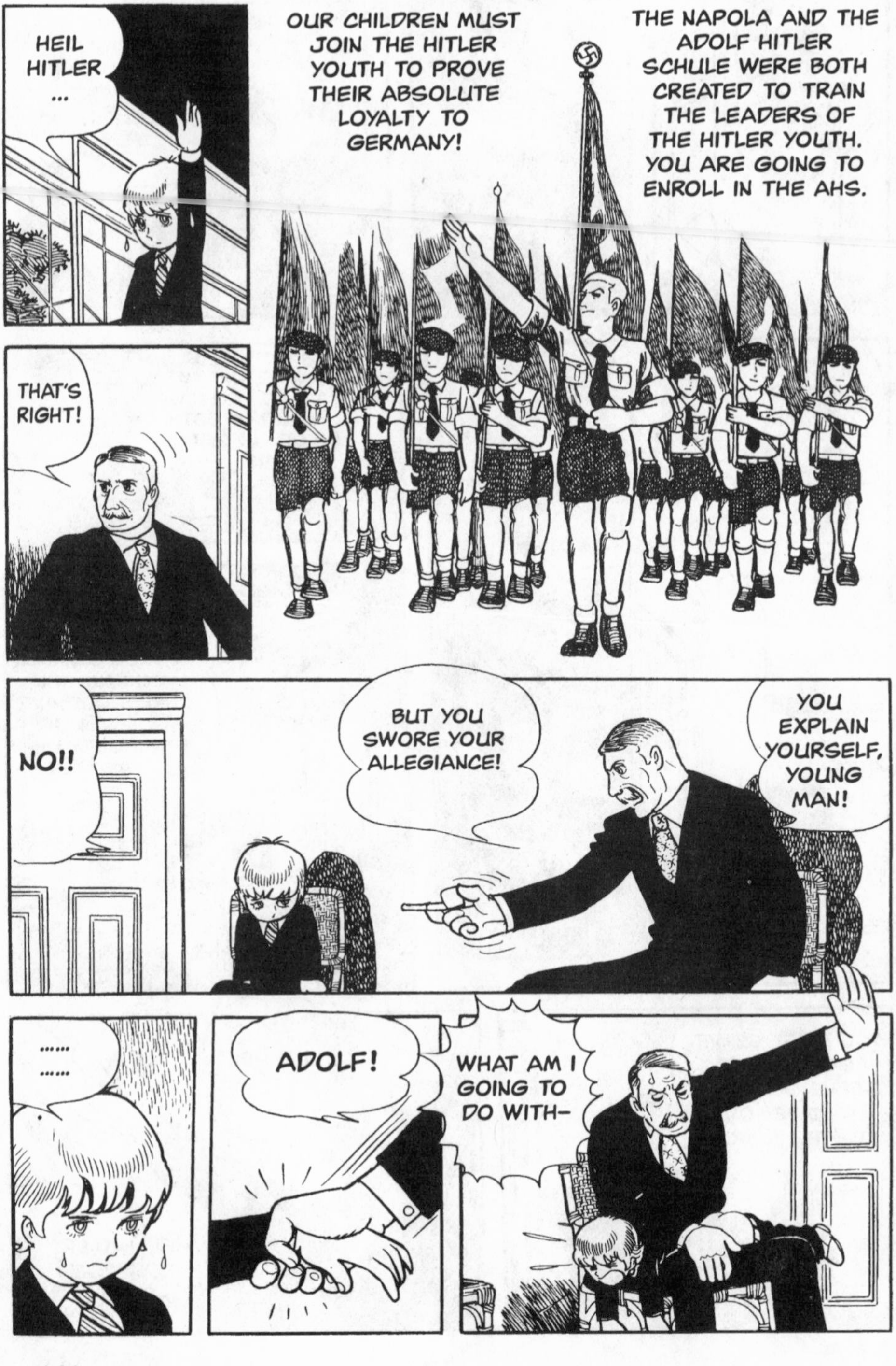
HEIL HITLER ...
OUR CHILDREN MUST JOIN THE HITLER YOUTH TO PROVE THEIR ABSOLUTE LOYALTY TO GERMANY!
THE NAPOLA AND THE ADOLF HITLER SCHULE WERE BOTH CREATED TO TRAIN THE LEADERS OF THE HITLER YOUTH. YOU ARE GOING TO ENROLL IN THE AHS.
THAT'S RIGHT!
NO!!
BUT YOU SWORE YOUR ALLEGIANCE!
YOU EXPLAIN YOURSELF, YOUNG MAN!
......
......
ADOLF!
WHAT AM I GOING TO DO WITH–

DEAR!

PLEASE STOP! ADOLF HASN'T DONE ANYTHING WRONG!!

HE'LL TELL YOU, BUT HE WON'T TELL ME!! THAT SPOILED BRAT!

YES, BECAUSE HE KNOWS THAT YOU'LL SCOLD HIM IF HE TELLS YOU. I PROMISED I WOULD KEEP IT A SECRET.

HE HAS HIS REASONS FOR NOT WANTING TO GO. AT THE VERY LEAST, HE SHOULD HAVE THE RIGHT TO CHOOSE HIS OWN SCHOOL.

ADOLF IS MY CHILD, AND I WILL CHOOSE HIS SCHOOL! WHAT'S WRONG WITH THAT?

BUT HALF OF HIM COMES FROM ME! HE COULD EVENTUALLY ATTEND A JAPANESE UNIVERSITY...

YUKIE!

DON'T JAPANESE WOMEN OBEY THEIR HUSBANDS WITH THE UTMOST FAITHFULNESS?

WHEN DID YOU LEARN TO BE SO STUBBORN?

ONE THING IS FOR CERTAIN...

I AM THE ONE WHO WILL DECIDE ADOLF'S FUTURE!

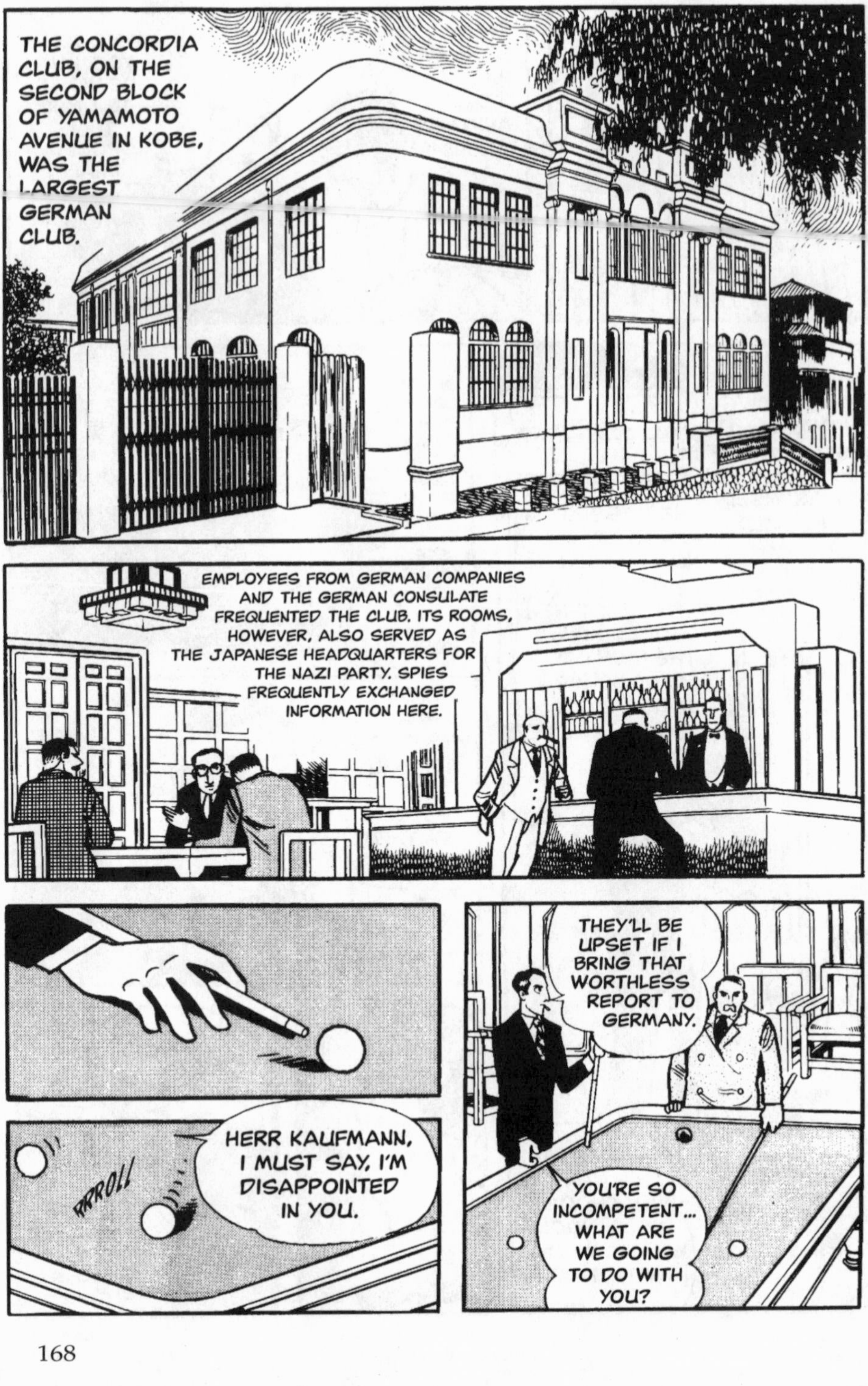
THE CONCORDIA CLUB, ON THE SECOND BLOCK OF YAMAMOTO AVENUE IN KOBE, WAS THE LARGEST GERMAN CLUB.
EMPLOYEES FROM GERMAN COMPANIES AND THE GERMAN CONSULATE FREQUENTED THE CLUB. ITS ROOMS, HOWEVER, ALSO SERVED AS THE JAPANESE HEADQUARTERS FOR THE NAZI PARTY. SPIES FREQUENTLY EXCHANGED INFORMATION HERE.
RRROLL
HERR KAUFMANN, I MUST SAY, I'M DISAPPOINTED IN YOU.
THEY'LL BE UPSET IF I BRING THAT WORTHLESS REPORT TO GERMANY.
YOU'RE SO INCOMPETENT... WHAT ARE WE GOING TO DO WITH YOU?

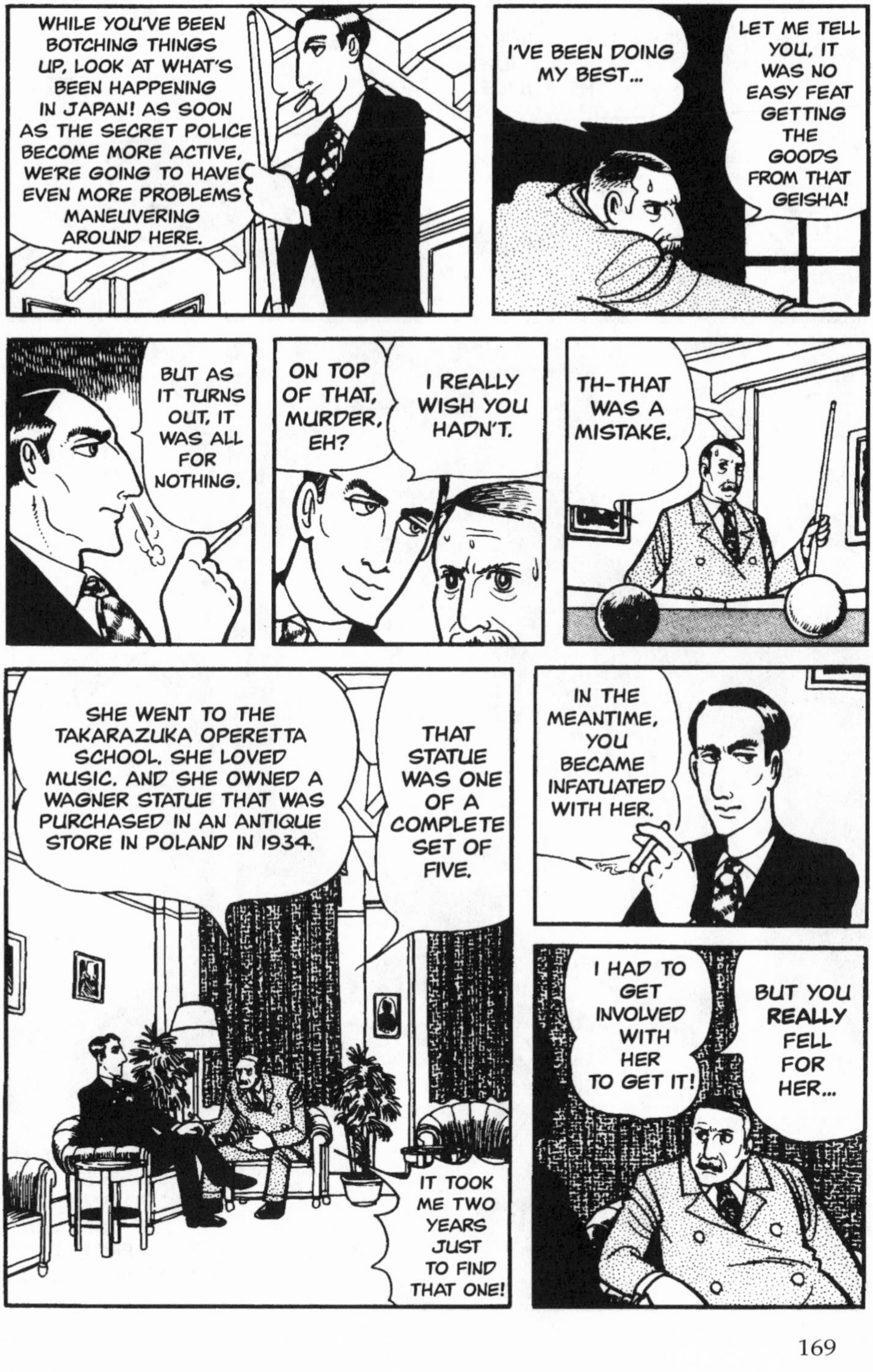
WHILE YOU'VE BEEN BOTCHING THINGS UP, LOOK AT WHAT'S BEEN HAPPENING IN JAPAN! AS SOON AS THE SECRET POLICE BECOME MORE ACTIVE, WE'RE GOING TO HAVE EVEN MORE PROBLEMS MANEUVERING AROUND HERE.
I'VE BEEN DOING MY BEST...
LET ME TELL YOU, IT WAS NO EASY FEAT GETTING THE GOODS FROM THAT GEISHA!
BUT AS IT TURNS OUT, IT WAS ALL FOR NOTHING.
ON TOP OF THAT, MURDER, EH?
I REALLY WISH YOU HADN'T.
TH-THAT WAS A MISTAKE.
SHE WENT TO THE TAKARAZUKA OPERETTA SCHOOL. SHE LOVED MUSIC. AND SHE OWNED A WAGNER STATUE THAT WAS PURCHASED IN AN ANTIQUE STORE IN POLAND IN 1934.
THAT STATUE WAS ONE OF A COMPLETE SET OF FIVE.
IT TOOK ME TWO YEARS JUST TO FIND THAT ONE!
IN THE MEANTIME, YOU BECAME INFATUATED WITH HER.
I HAD TO GET INVOLVED WITH HER TO GET IT!
BUT YOU REALLY FELL FOR HER...

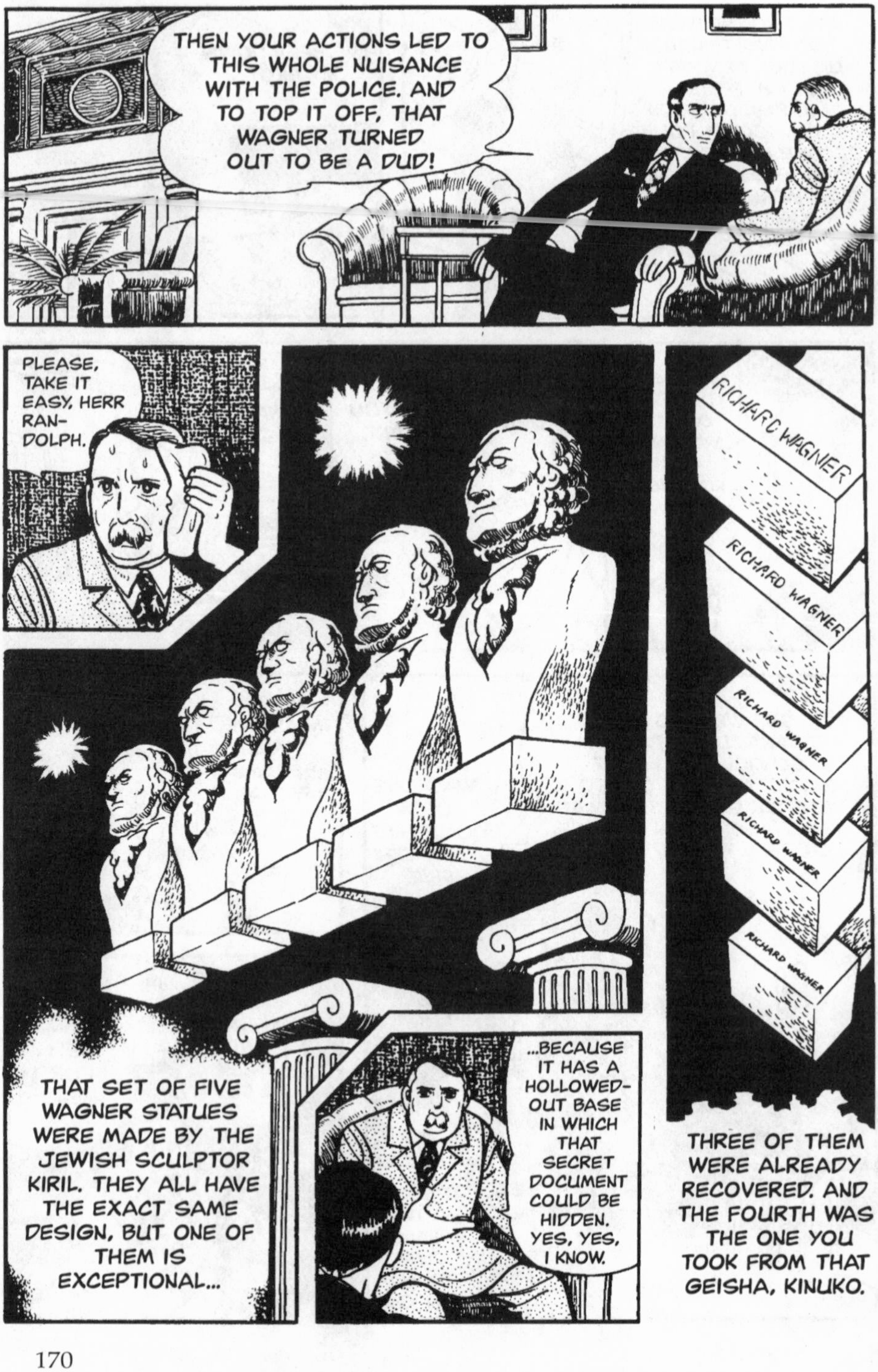
THEN YOUR ACTIONS LED TO THIS WHOLE NUISANCE WITH THE POLICE. AND TO TOP IT OFF, THAT WAGNER TURNED OUT TO BE A DUD!
PLEASE, TAKE IT EASY, HERR RAN-DOLPH.
THAT SET OF FIVE WAGNER STATUES WERE MADE BY THE JEWISH SCULPTOR KIRIL. THEY ALL HAVE THE EXACT SAME DESIGN, BUT ONE OF THEM IS EXCEPTIONAL...
...BECAUSE IT HAS A HOLLOWED-OUT BASE IN WHICH THAT SECRET DOCUMENT COULD BE HIDDEN. YES, YES, I KNOW.
RICHARD WAGNER
RICHARD WAGNER
RICHARD WAGNER
RICHARD WAGNER
RICHARD WAGNER
THREE OF THEM WERE ALREADY RECOVERED. AND THE FOURTH WAS THE ONE YOU TOOK FROM THAT GEISHA, KINUKO.

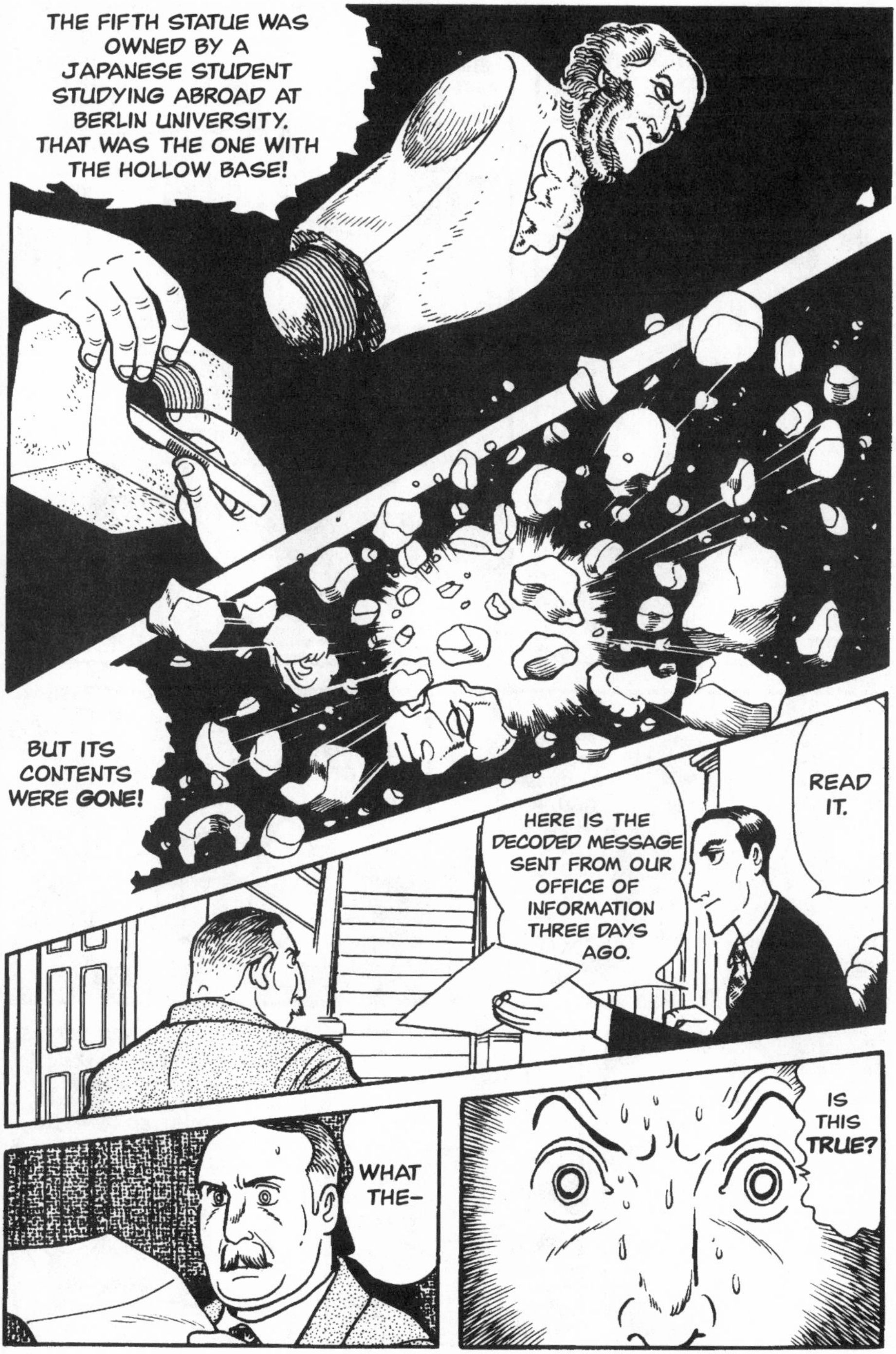
THE FIFTH STATUE WAS OWNED BY A JAPANESE STUDENT STUDYING ABROAD AT BERLIN UNIVERSITY. THAT WAS THE ONE WITH THE HOLLOW BASE!
BUT ITS CONTENTS WERE GONE!
HERE IS THE DECODED MESSAGE SENT FROM OUR OFFICE OF INFORMATION THREE DAYS AGO.
READ IT.
WHAT THE-
IS THIS TRUE?

Adolf

APPARENTLY THIS JAPANESE STUDENT ANTICIPATED THAT IT WOULD BE TAKEN AWAY FROM HIM, SO HE WENT TO THE POSTAL OFFICE OF UNTER DEN LINDEN AND SENT THE CONTENTS OFF TO JAPAN.

AND THE RECIPIENT?

WE ONLY KNOW THAT IT WAS ADDRESSED TO KOBE.

PERHAPS TO JEWS RESIDING IN JAPAN, PERHAPS TO THE RED BASTARDS AFFILIATED WITH THAT JAPANESE STUDENT. OR TO ANY OF HIS CLOSE RELATIVES...

WITH THOSE THREE POSSIBILITIES IN MIND, YOUR JOB IS TO...

...SEARCH ALL OF KOBE!

YOU'VE BEEN INCOMPETENT THROUGHOUT THIS MISSION, AND YOU'VE COMMITTED A TREMENDOUS BLUNDER.

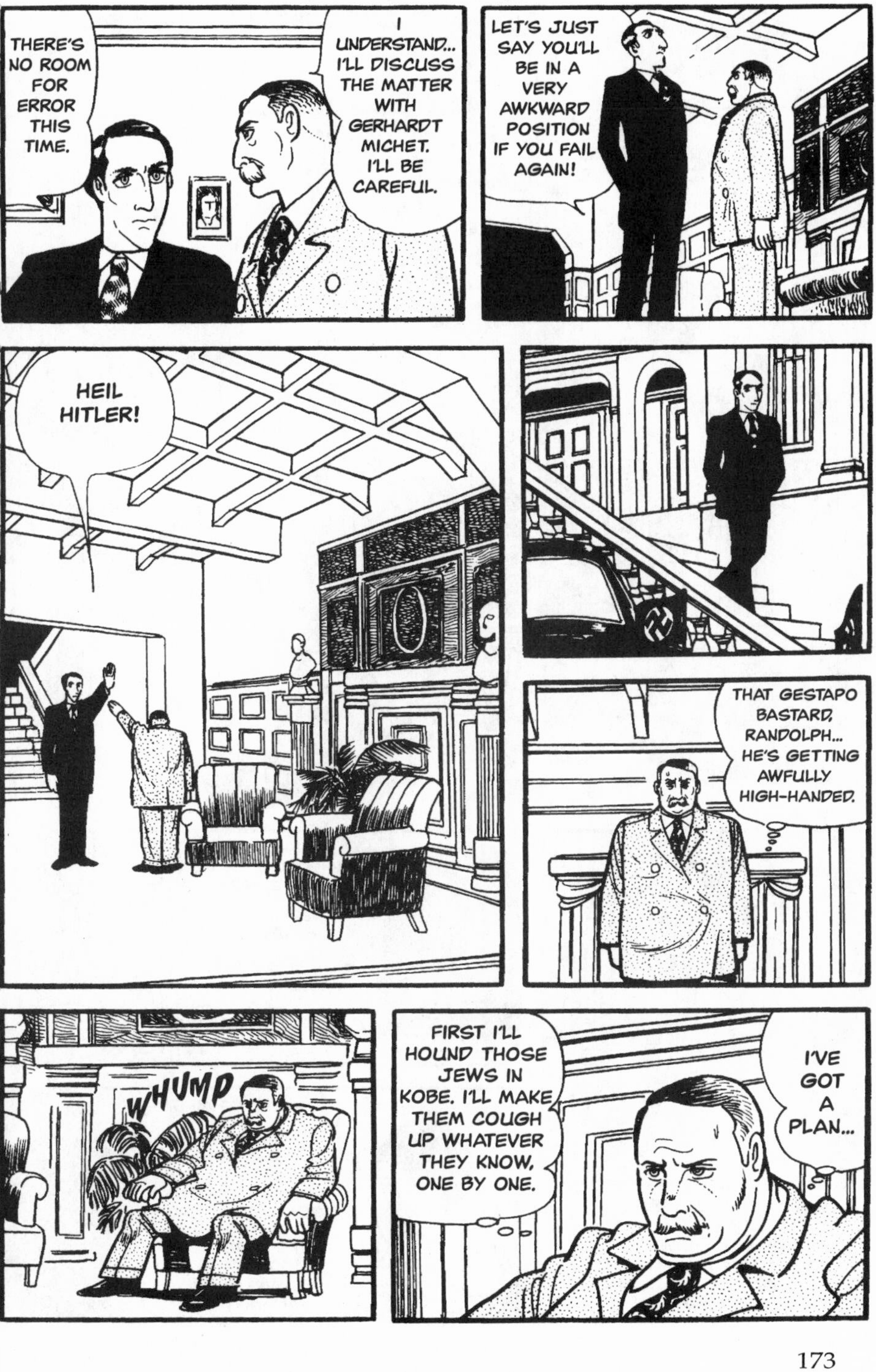
THERE'S NO ROOM FOR ERROR THIS TIME.
I UNDERSTAND... I'LL DISCUSS THE MATTER WITH GERHARDT MICHET. I'LL BE CAREFUL.
LET'S JUST SAY YOU'LL BE IN A VERY AWKWARD POSITION IF YOU FAIL AGAIN!
HEIL HITLER!
THAT GESTAPO BASTARD, RANDOLPH... HE'S GETTING AWFULLY HIGH-HANDED.
WHUMP
FIRST I'LL HOUND THOSE JEWS IN KOBE. I'LL MAKE THEM COUGH UP WHATEVER THEY KNOW, ONE BY ONE.
I'VE GOT A PLAN...

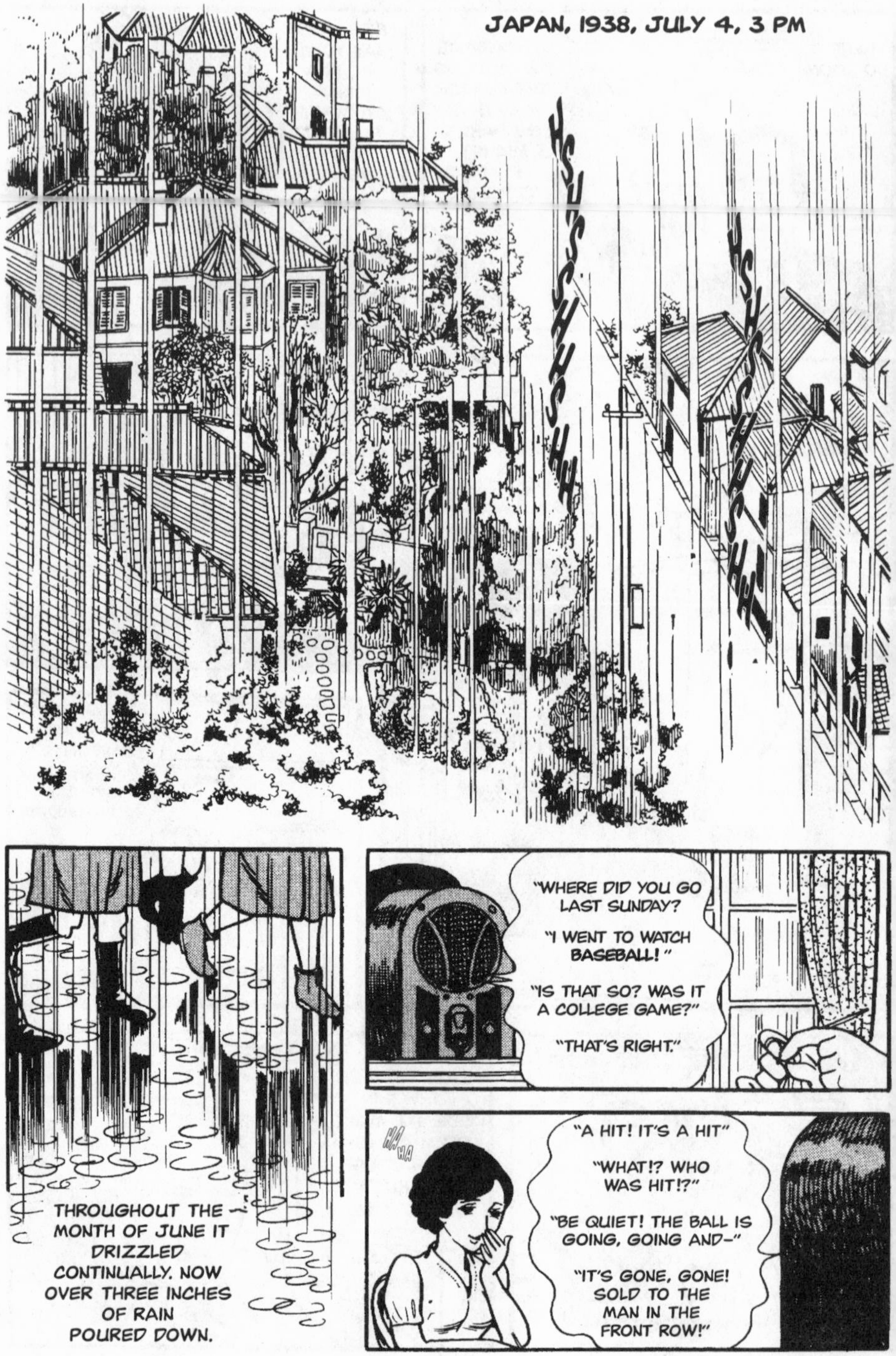
JAPAN, 1938, JULY 4, 3 PM
THROUGHOUT THE MONTH OF JUNE IT DRIZZLED CONTINUALLY. NOW OVER THREE INCHES OF RAIN POURED DOWN.
"WHERE DID YOU GO LAST SUNDAY?
"I WENT TO WATCH BASEBALL!"
"IS THAT SO? WAS IT A COLLEGE GAME?"
"THAT'S RIGHT."
HA HA
"A HIT! IT'S A HIT"
"WHAT!? WHO WAS HIT!?"
"BE QUIET! THE BALL IS GOING, GOING AND–"
"IT'S GONE, GONE! SOLD TO THE MAN IN THE FRONT ROW!"

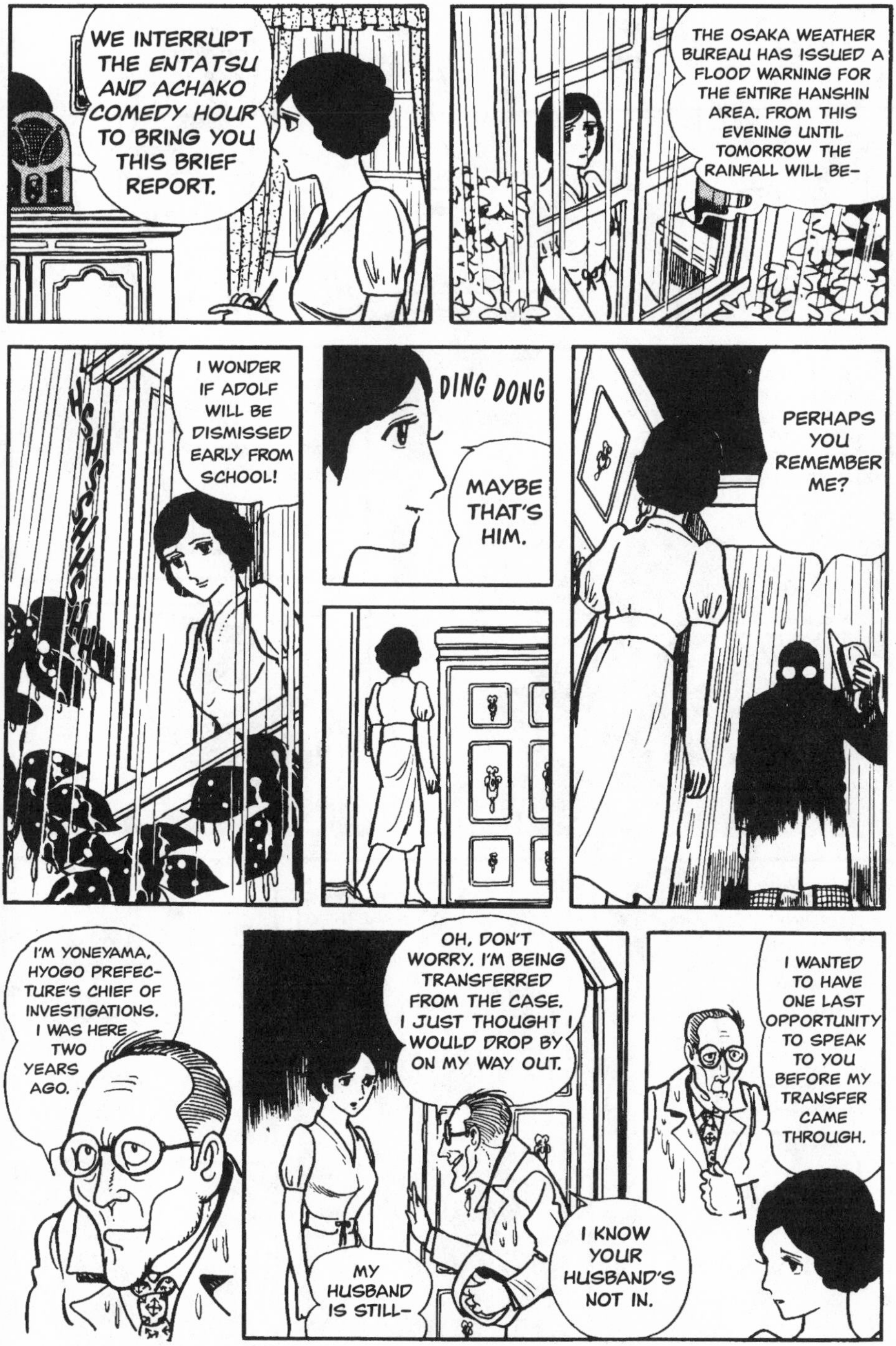
WE INTERRUPT THE ENTATSU AND ACHAKO COMEDY HOUR TO BRING YOU THIS BRIEF REPORT.
THE OSAKA WEATHER BUREAU HAS ISSUED A FLOOD WARNING FOR THE ENTIRE HANSHIN AREA. FROM THIS EVENING UNTIL TOMORROW THE RAINFALL WILL BE-
I WONDER IF ADOLF WILL BE DISMISSED EARLY FROM SCHOOL!
DING DONG
MAYBE THAT'S HIM.
PERHAPS YOU REMEMBER ME?
I'M YONEYAMA, HYOGO PREFECTURE'S CHIEF OF INVESTIGATIONS. I WAS HERE TWO YEARS AGO.
OH, DON'T WORRY. I'M BEING TRANSFERRED FROM THE CASE. I JUST THOUGHT I WOULD DROP BY ON MY WAY OUT.
MY HUSBAND IS STILL-
I KNOW YOUR HUSBAND'S NOT IN.
I WANTED TO HAVE ONE LAST OPPORTUNITY TO SPEAK TO YOU BEFORE MY TRANSFER CAME THROUGH.

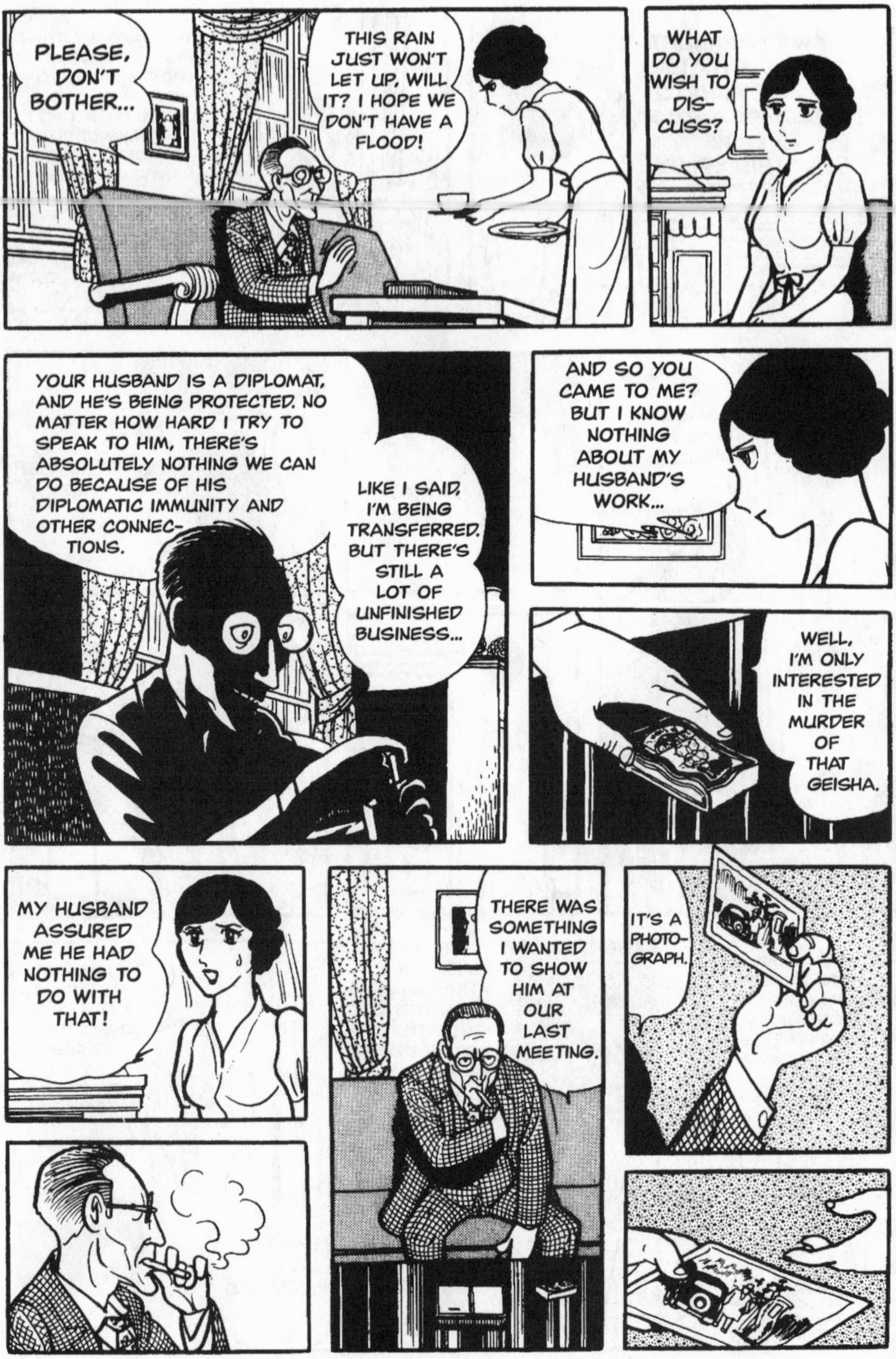
PLEASE, DON'T BOTHER...
THIS RAIN JUST WON'T LET UP, WILL IT? I HOPE WE DON'T HAVE A FLOOD!
WHAT DO YOU WISH TO DIS-CUSS?
YOUR HUSBAND IS A DIPLOMAT, AND HE'S BEING PROTECTED. NO MATTER HOW HARD I TRY TO SPEAK TO HIM, THERE'S ABSOLUTELY NOTHING WE CAN DO BECAUSE OF HIS DIPLOMATIC IMMUNITY AND OTHER CONNEC-TIONS.
LIKE I SAID, I'M BEING TRANSFERRED. BUT THERE'S STILL A LOT OF UNFINISHED BUSINESS...
AND SO YOU CAME TO ME? BUT I KNOW NOTHING ABOUT MY HUSBAND'S WORK...
WELL, I'M ONLY INTERESTED IN THE MURDER OF THAT GEISHA.
MY HUSBAND ASSURED ME HE HAD NOTHING TO DO WITH THAT!
THERE WAS SOMETHING I WANTED TO SHOW HIM AT OUR LAST MEETING.
IT'S A PHOTO-GRAPH.

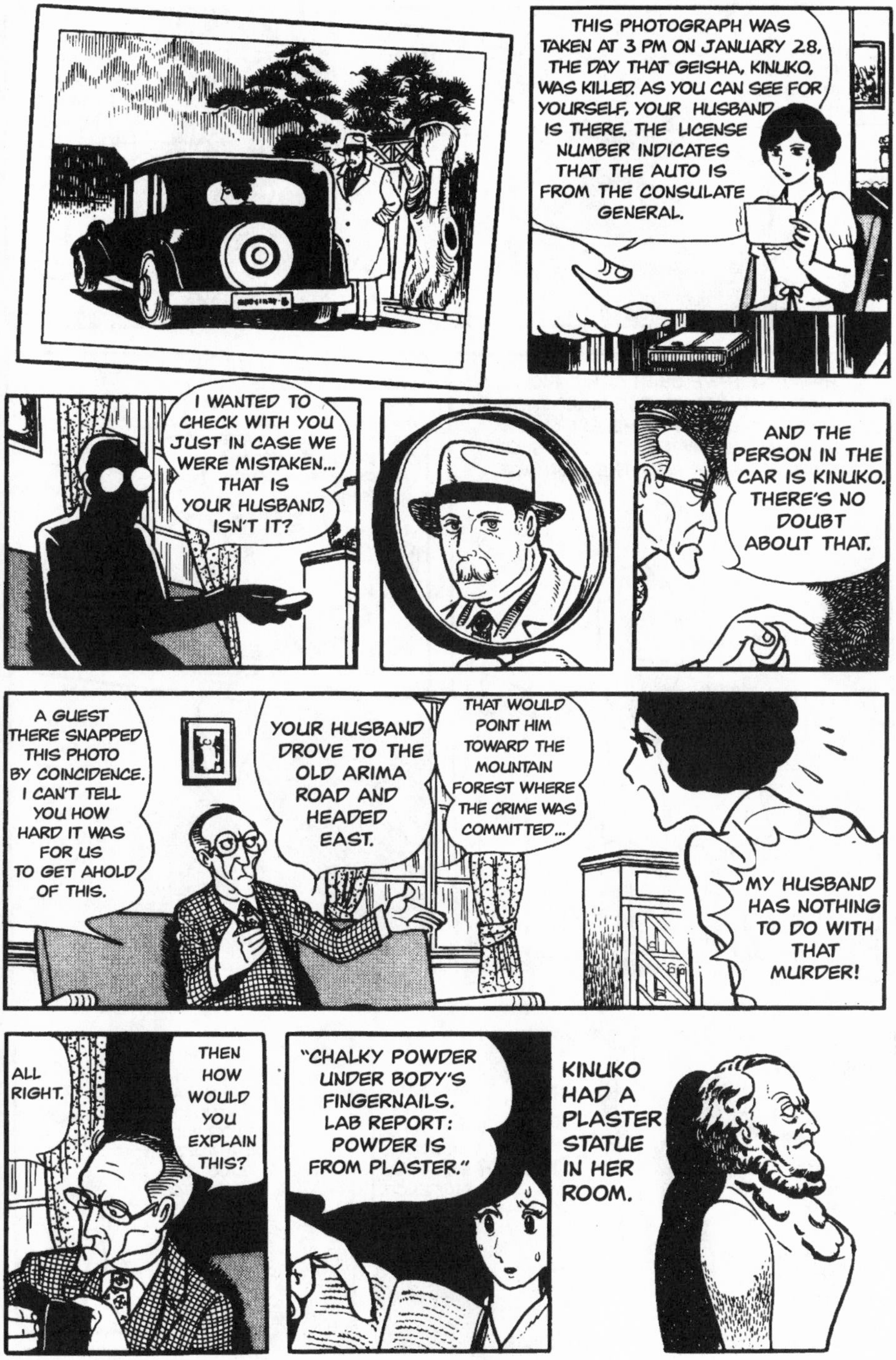
THIS PHOTOGRAPH WAS TAKEN AT 3 PM ON JANUARY 28, THE DAY THAT GEISHA, KINUKO, WAS KILLED. AS YOU CAN SEE FOR YOURSELF, YOUR HUSBAND IS THERE. THE LICENSE NUMBER INDICATES THAT THE AUTO IS FROM THE CONSULATE GENERAL.
I WANTED TO CHECK WITH YOU JUST IN CASE WE WERE MISTAKEN... THAT IS YOUR HUSBAND, ISN'T IT?
AND THE PERSON IN THE CAR IS KINUKO. THERE'S NO DOUBT ABOUT THAT.
A GUEST THERE SNAPPED THIS PHOTO BY COINCIDENCE. I CAN'T TELL YOU HOW HARD IT WAS FOR US TO GET AHOLD OF THIS.
YOUR HUSBAND DROVE TO THE OLD ARIMA ROAD AND HEADED EAST.
THAT WOULD POINT HIM TOWARD THE MOUNTAIN FOREST WHERE THE CRIME WAS COMMITTED...
MY HUSBAND HAS NOTHING TO DO WITH THAT MURDER!
ALL RIGHT.
THEN HOW WOULD YOU EXPLAIN THIS?
"CHALKY POWDER UNDER BODY'S FINGERNAILS. LAB REPORT: POWDER IS FROM PLASTER."
KINUKO HAD A PLASTER STATUE IN HER ROOM.

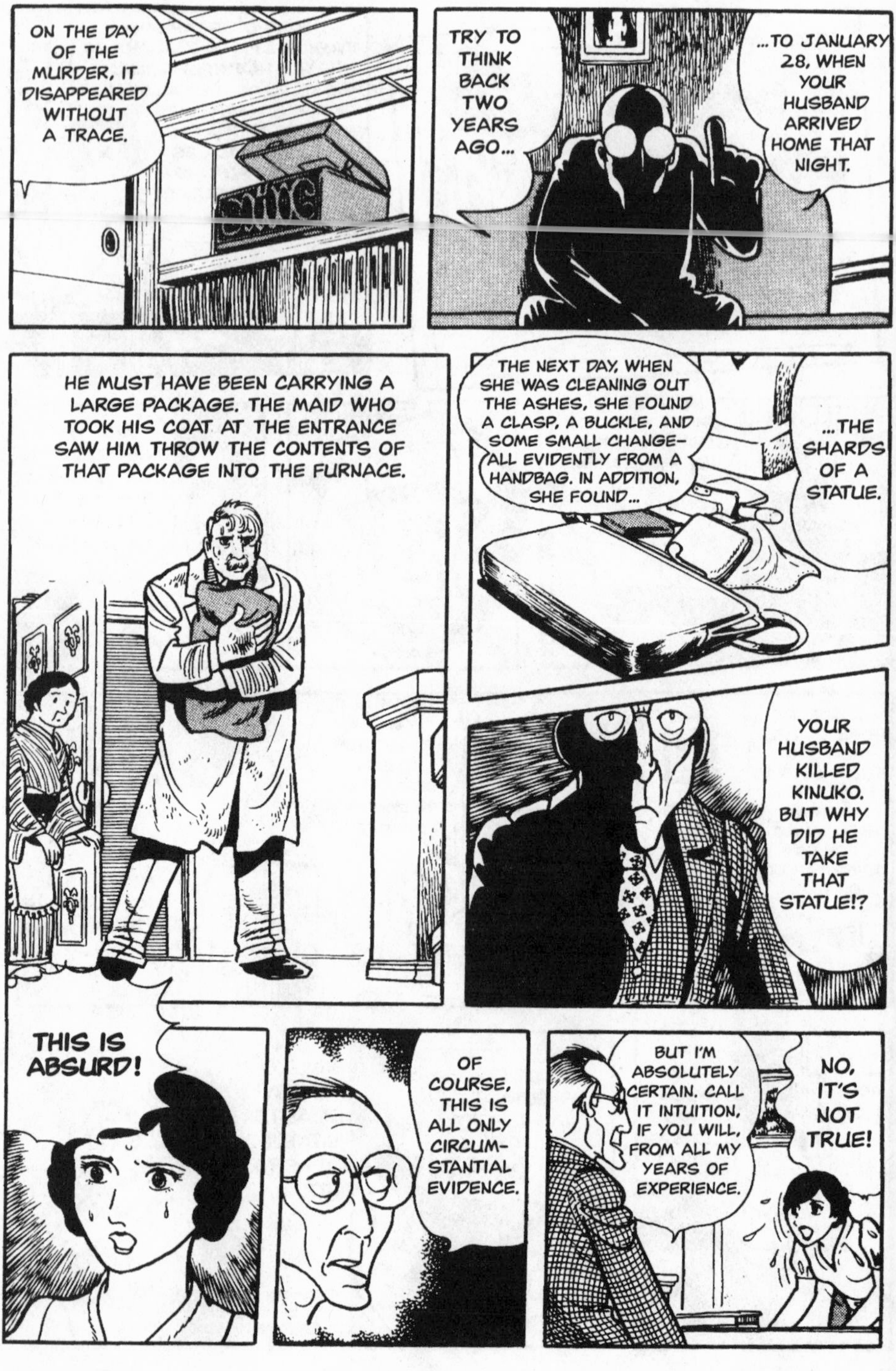
ON THE DAY OF THE MURDER, IT DISAPPEARED WITHOUT A TRACE.
TRY TO THINK BACK TWO YEARS AGO...
...TO JANUARY 28, WHEN YOUR HUSBAND ARRIVED HOME THAT NIGHT.
HE MUST HAVE BEEN CARRYING A LARGE PACKAGE. THE MAID WHO TOOK HIS COAT AT THE ENTRANCE SAW HIM THROW THE CONTENTS OF THAT PACKAGE INTO THE FURNACE.
THE NEXT DAY, WHEN SHE WAS CLEANING OUT THE ASHES, SHE FOUND A CLASP, A BUCKLE, AND SOME SMALL CHANGE-ALL EVIDENTLY FROM A HANDBAG. IN ADDITION, SHE FOUND...
...THE SHARDS OF A STATUE.
YOUR HUSBAND KILLED KINUKO. BUT WHY DID HE TAKE THAT STATUE!?
THIS IS ABSURD!
OF COURSE, THIS IS ALL ONLY CIRCUM-STANTIAL EVIDENCE.
BUT I'M ABSOLUTELY CERTAIN. CALL IT INTUITION, IF YOU WILL, FROM ALL MY YEARS OF EXPERIENCE.
NO, IT'S NOT TRUE!

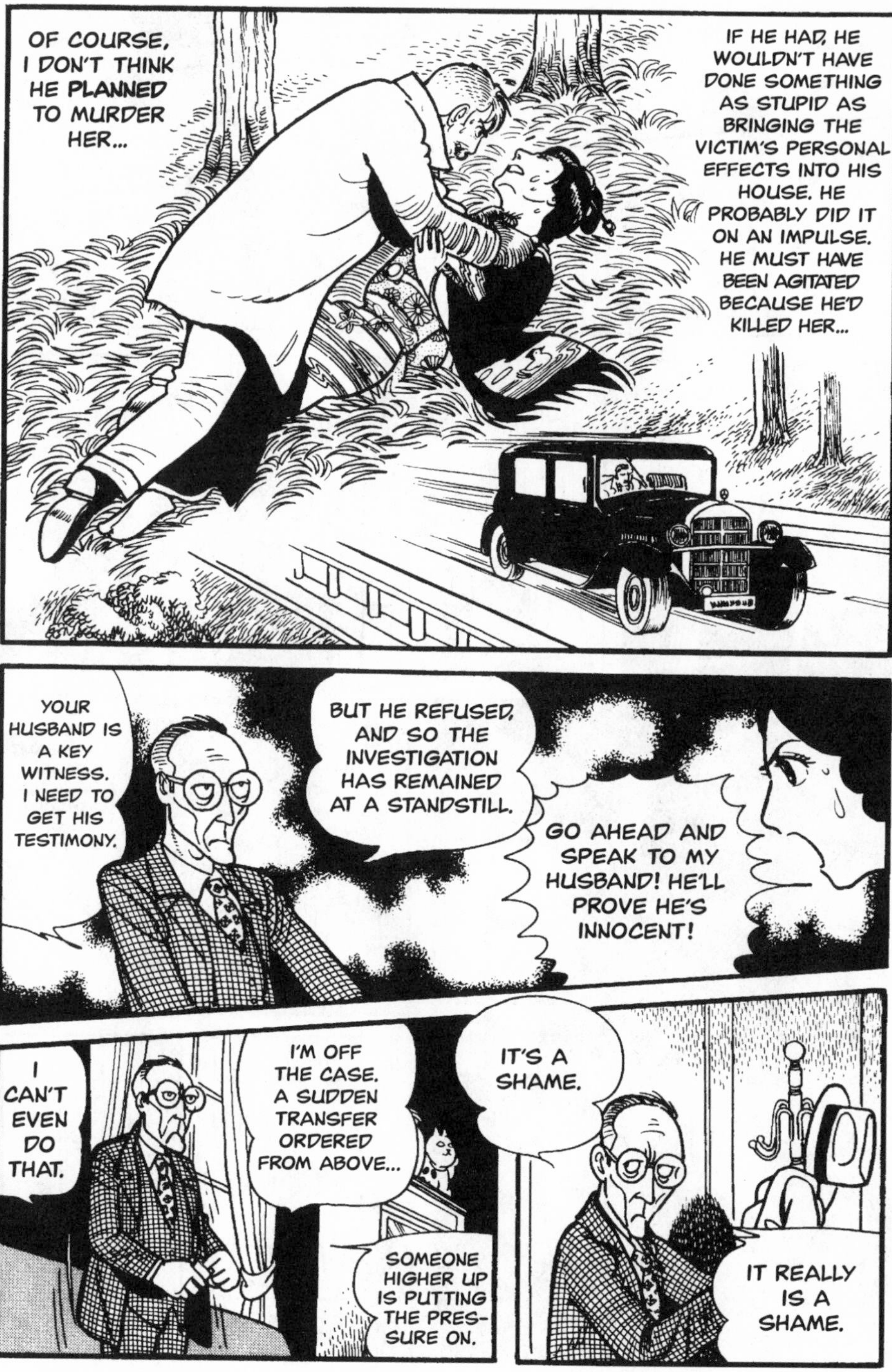
OF COURSE, I DON'T THINK HE PLANNED TO MURDER HER...
IF HE HAD, HE WOULDN'T HAVE DONE SOMETHING AS STUPID AS BRINGING THE VICTIM'S PERSONAL EFFECTS INTO HIS HOUSE. HE PROBABLY DID IT ON AN IMPULSE. HE MUST HAVE BEEN AGITATED BECAUSE HE'D KILLED HER...
YOUR HUSBAND IS A KEY WITNESS. I NEED TO GET HIS TESTIMONY.
BUT HE REFUSED, AND SO THE INVESTIGATION HAS REMAINED AT A STANDSTILL.
GO AHEAD AND SPEAK TO MY HUSBAND! HE'LL PROVE HE'S INNOCENT!
I CAN'T EVEN DO THAT.
I'M OFF THE CASE. A SUDDEN TRANSFER ORDERED FROM ABOVE...
SOMEONE HIGHER UP IS PUTTING THE PRESSURE ON.
IT'S A SHAME.
IT REALLY IS A SHAME.

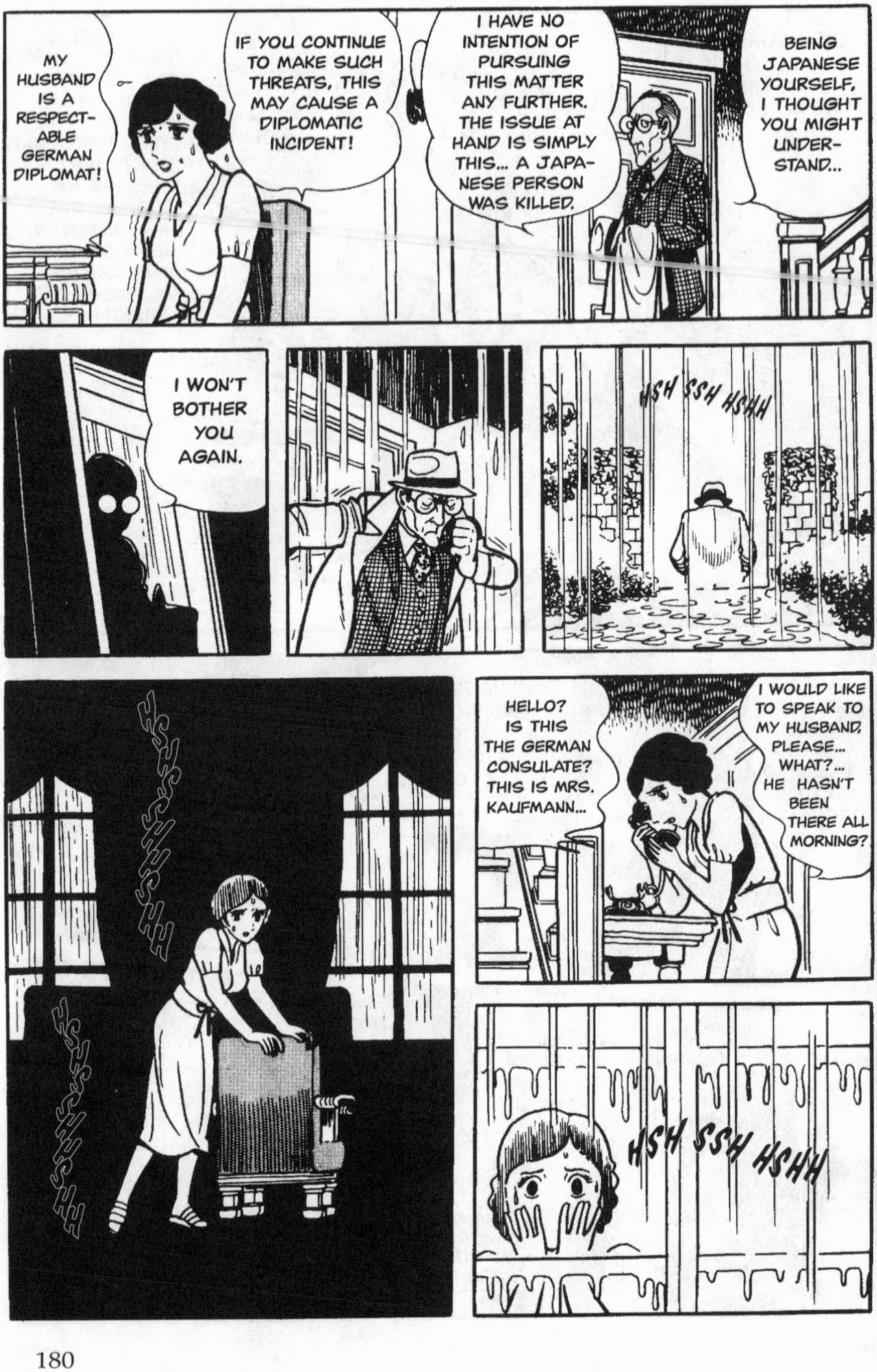
MY HUSBAND IS A RESPECTABLE GERMAN DIPLOMAT!
IF YOU CONTINUE TO MAKE SUCH THREATS, THIS MAY CAUSE A DIPLOMATIC INCIDENT!
I HAVE NO INTENTION OF PURSUING THIS MATTER ANY FURTHER. THE ISSUE AT HAND IS SIMPLY THIS... A JAPANESE PERSON WAS KILLED.
BEING JAPANESE YOURSELF, I THOUGHT YOU MIGHT UNDERSTAND...
I WON'T BOTHER YOU AGAIN.
HSH SSH HSHH
HSHHSHHSHH
HSHHSHHSHH
HELLO? IS THIS THE GERMAN CONSULATE? THIS IS MRS. KAUFMANN...
I WOULD LIKE TO SPEAK TO MY HUSBAND, PLEASE... WHAT?... HE HASN'T BEEN THERE ALL MORNING?
HSH SSH HSHH

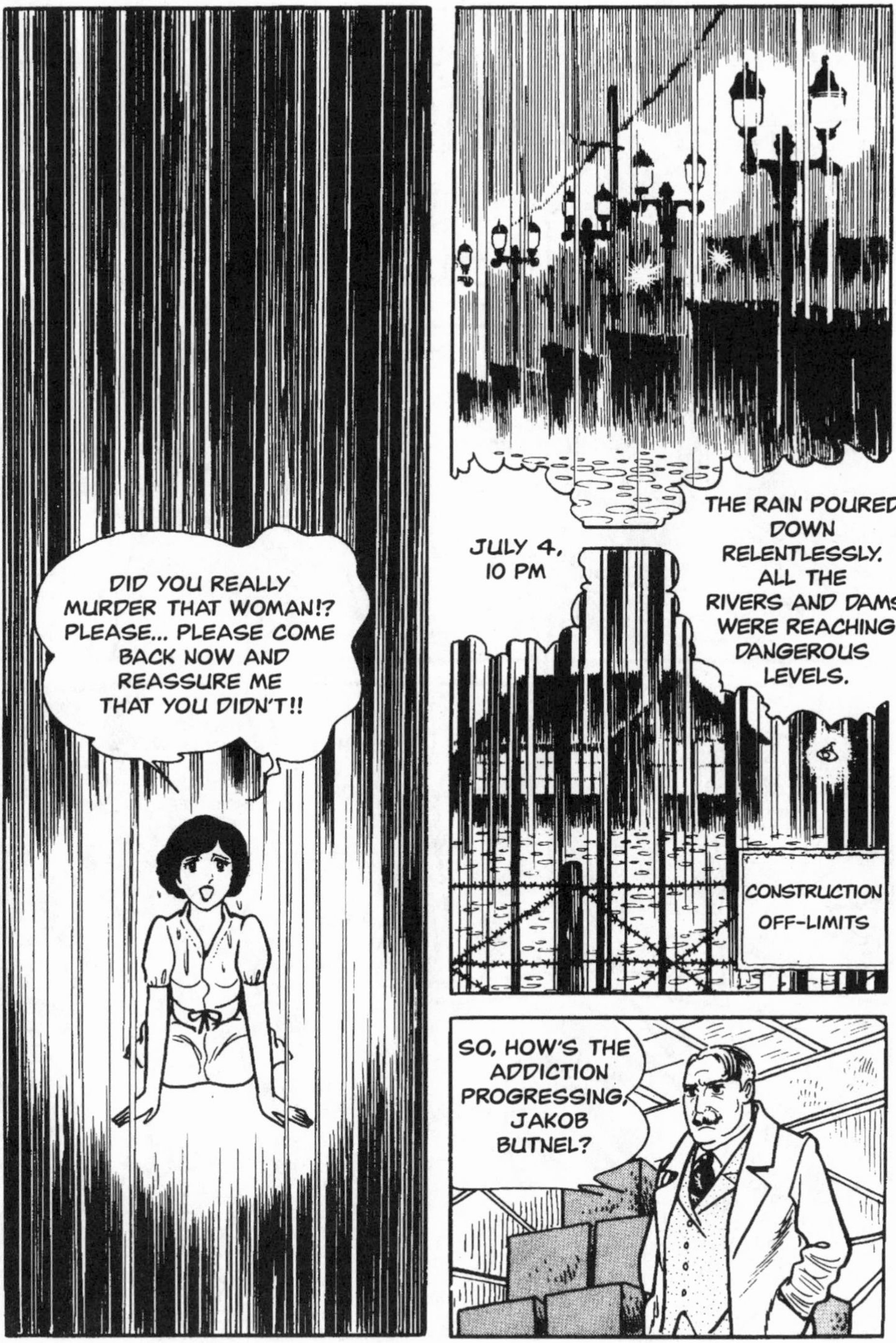
DID YOU REALLY MURDER THAT WOMAN!? PLEASE... PLEASE COME BACK NOW AND REASSURE ME THAT YOU DIDN'T!!
JULY 4, 10 PM
THE RAIN POURED DOWN RELENTLESSLY. ALL THE RIVERS AND DAMS WERE REACHING DANGEROUS LEVELS.
CONSTRUCTION OFF-LIMITS
SO, HOW'S THE ADDICTION PROGRESSING, JAKOB BUTNEL?

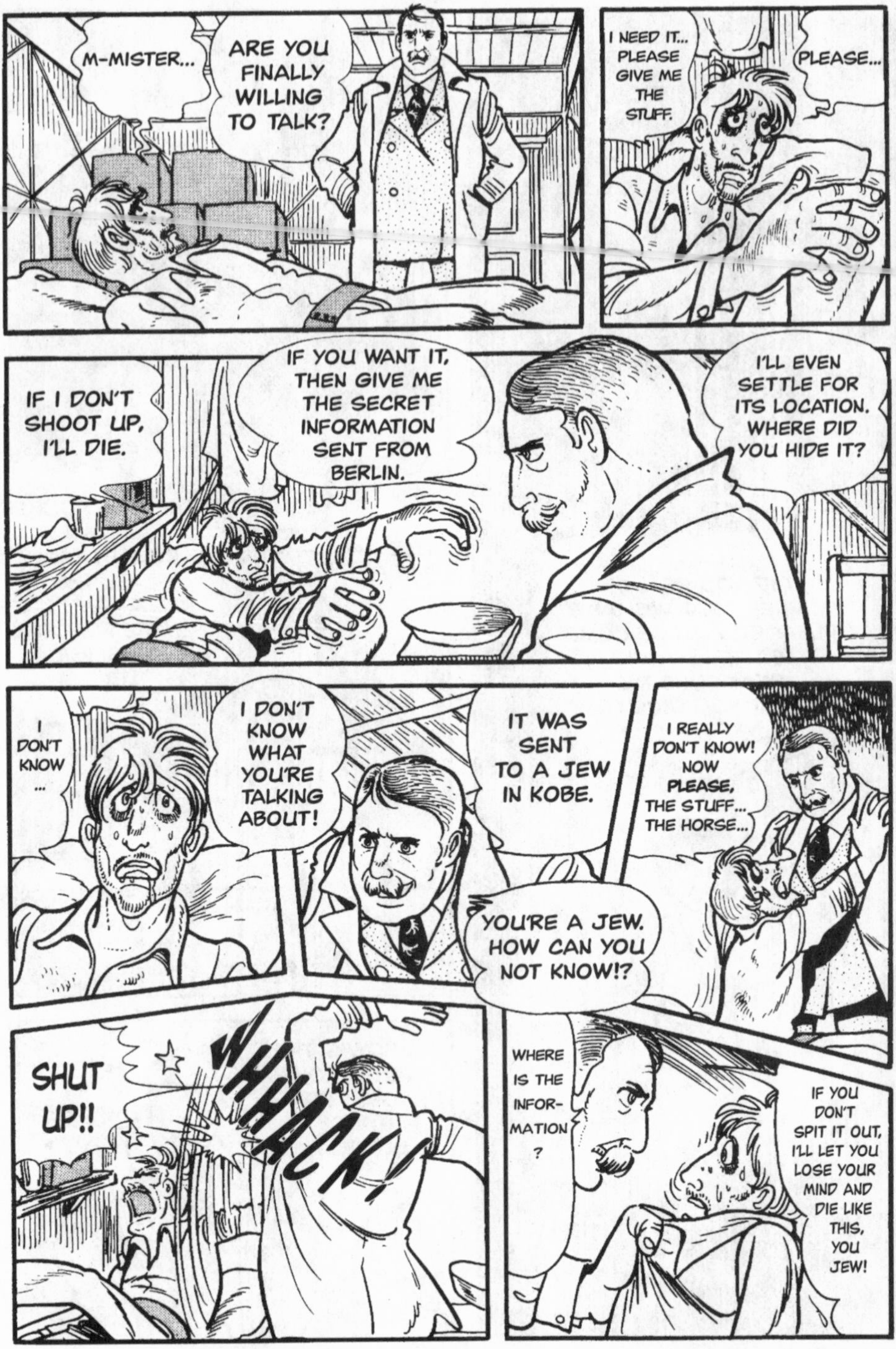
M-MISTER...
ARE YOU FINALLY WILLING TO TALK?
I NEED IT... PLEASE GIVE ME THE STUFF.
PLEASE...
IF I DON'T SHOOT UP, I'LL DIE.
IF YOU WANT IT, THEN GIVE ME THE SECRET INFORMATION SENT FROM BERLIN.
I'LL EVEN SETTLE FOR ITS LOCATION. WHERE DID YOU HIDE IT?
I DON'T KNOW ...
I DON'T KNOW WHAT YOU'RE TALKING ABOUT!
IT WAS SENT TO A JEW IN KOBE.
YOU'RE A JEW. HOW CAN YOU NOT KNOW!?
I REALLY DON'T KNOW! NOW PLEASE, THE STUFF... THE HORSE...
SHUT UP!!
WHHACK!
WHERE IS THE INFOR-MATION ?
IF YOU DON'T SPIT IT OUT, I'LL LET YOU LOSE YOUR MIND AND DIE LIKE THIS, YOU JEW!

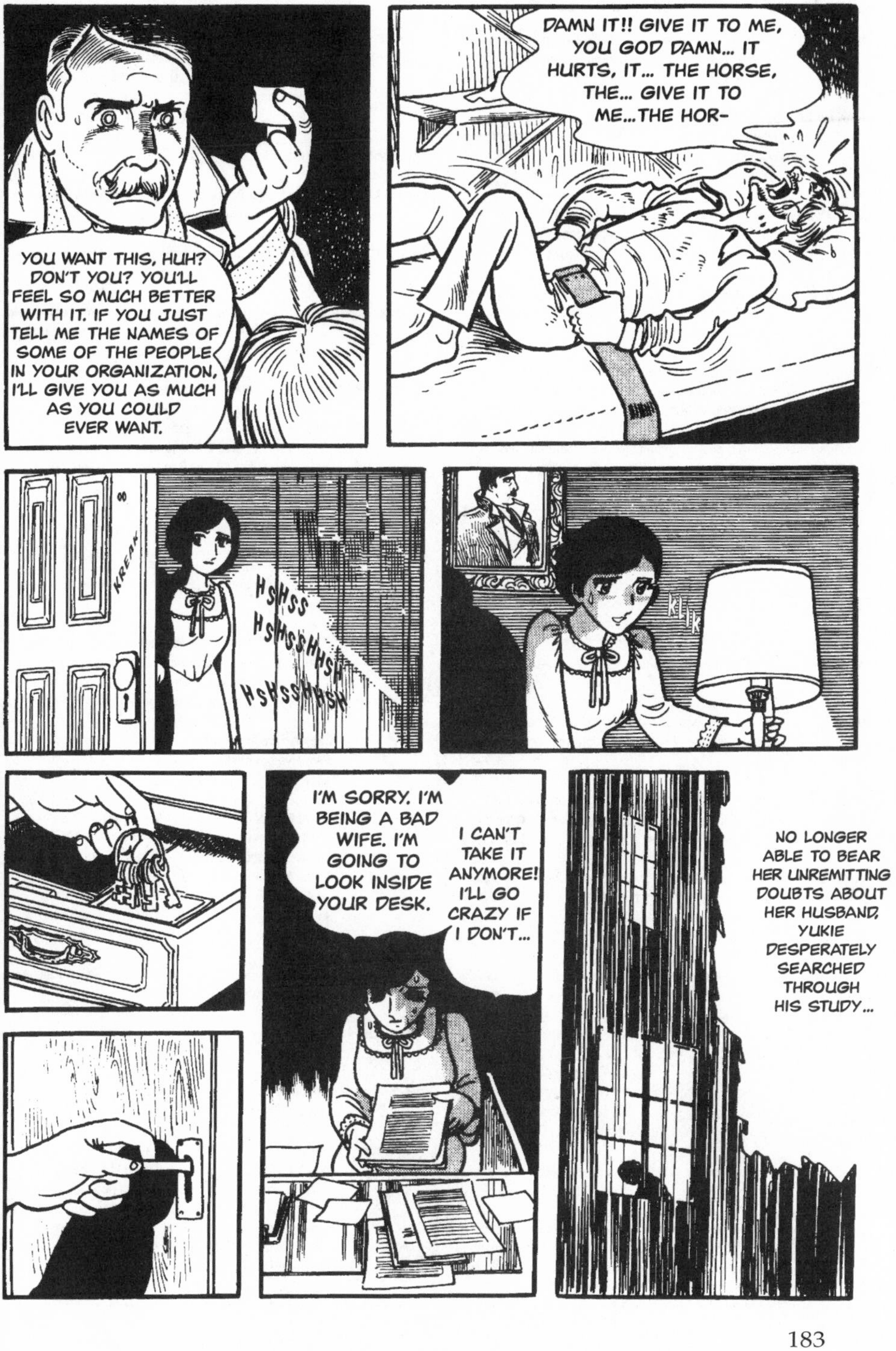
YOU WANT THIS, HUH? DON'T YOU? YOU'LL FEEL SO MUCH BETTER WITH IT. IF YOU JUST TELL ME THE NAMES OF SOME OF THE PEOPLE IN YOUR ORGANIZATION, I'LL GIVE YOU AS MUCH AS YOU COULD EVER WANT.
DAMN IT!! GIVE IT TO ME, YOU GOD DAMN... IT HURTS, IT... THE HORSE, THE... GIVE IT TO ME...THE HOR-
KREAK
HSHSS
HSHSSHHSH
HSHSSHHSH
KLIK
I'M SORRY. I'M BEING A BAD WIFE. I'M GOING TO LOOK INSIDE YOUR DESK.
I CAN'T TAKE IT ANYMORE! I'LL GO CRAZY IF I DON'T...
NO LONGER ABLE TO BEAR HER UNREMITTING DOUBTS ABOUT HER HUSBAND, YUKIE DESPERATELY SEARCHED THROUGH HIS STUDY...

1937 TIMELINE

January 23   In Japan, with the army bickering over policy and creating factions incapable of compromise, the Hirota Cabinet falls.

January 27   In China, the CCP (Communists) and KMT (Nationalists) agree to combine forces to defend China against the Japanese. Overall authority resides with Chiang Kaishek and the Nanking government.

January 30   Hitler demands that all former German colonies be returned to Germany, repudiates the clause of the Treaty of Versailles in which Germany accepted responsibility for instigating World War I, and stops reparation payments to countries it injured during that conflict. Simultaneously, Hitler declares that "peace is our greatest treasure."

February 4   General Senjuro Hayashi becomes Japan's premier, but the new government commands little more than token support from any influential groups.

February 22   Due to a boom in munitions manufacturing, the Tokyo Stock Market reaches an all-time trading high.

April 15   Helen Keller visits Japan.

April 16   Japan expands the territory of the pro-Japanese autonomous government in North China.

April 20   The Japanese vote out the Hayashi government, and the diet is dissolved.

April 26   The Spanish city of Guernica is devastated by German Air Force planes.

May 1   President Roosevelt signs the United States Neutrality Act to keep the U.S. out of the growing conflicts worldwide.

June 3   Prince Fumimaro Konoye is appointed premier of Japan. Hirota again takes over the foreign ministry. The new diet is named the Diet of National Union.

June 12   Soviet leader Joseph Stalin accuses the Soviet chief of army general staff, together with most of the Red Army's top generals, of treason. They are subsequently tried and executed.

July 7   The British government's study of Palestine recommends partitioning the mandated area: "While neither race [Arab nor Jewish] can justly rule all Palestine, we see no reason why, if it were practicable, each race should not rule part of it."

In China, the Japanese and Chinese military clash at the Marco Polo Bridge. This Marco Polo Bridge incident triggers the Sino-Japanese War.

July 17   Chiang Kaishek and Chou Enlai officially declare war against Japan.

Ignoring the Japanese government's declaration of a policy of nonescalation, the Japanese Army continues to escalate the war against China,

July 28   Berlin instructs its embassy in Tokyo to complain about Japanese broadcasts to Germany "in which they constantly represent the war against China as a struggle against Communism and force at least moral participation upon us. We do not welcome this propaganda."

August 8   Japan occupies Beijing.

August 15   The Japanese Air Force conducts the first transoceanic bombing of Nanking.

August 21   China and the Soviet Union sign a five-year pledge of nonaggression.

August 22   A Gallup poll shows 43 percent of the American public favor China in the Far East conflict, 2 percent favor Japan, and 55 percent favor neither side.

September 19   The Japanese Air Force launches a series of attacks on Nanking and Canton. China describes the raids as "wanton destruction and terrorization on the part of the Japanese forces, in utter disregard of all rules of international law." Air strikes continue through December 25.

October 23-24   The eastern German town of Danzig erupts in anti-Jewish rioting.

November 6   Italy joins Germany and Japan in the Anti-Comintern Pact.

November 30   France and Britain jointly take a position of neutrality in response to Germany's demands to regain lost territory.

December 1   Japan recognizes the Franco government in Spain.

French Foreign Minister Yvon Delbos launches an intensive but unsuccessful campaign to reinvigorate an alliance against Germany.

December 12   Germany announces it will never return to the League of Nations, noting that "at no period of its existence has it proved competent to make a useful contribution to the treatment of actual problems of world politics."

Japanese aircraft bomb and sink the Panay, a United States naval gunboat, on the Yangtze River, China.

Japanese-supported Chinese establish a provisional government in Beijing.

December 13   Japanese troops invade and occupy Nanking. This brutal attack came to be known as the Rape of Nanking.

December 14   The Japanese government begins cracking down on liberals. Police arrest 314 political opponents.

December 29   Berlin instructs its embassy in Tokyo on Germany's policy on the Sino-Japanese War: "The common interest of Germany and Japan directed against the Comintern requires that normal conditions in China be restored as soon as possible.... The lessons derived from the history of the Treaty of Versailles should be pondered by Japan."

CHAPTER
FIVE

Adolf

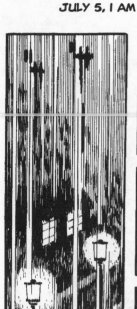

MOM... WHAT ARE YOU DOING?

ADOLF!

YOU SHOULD BE ASLEEP.

BUT THE RAIN'S SO NOISY... I CAN'T SLEEP.

WHY ARE YOU LOOKING THROUGH DADDY'S DESK?

NEVER MIND!

NOW GO BACK TO BED!

MOM, DADDY HASN'T BEEN COMING HOME AT NIGHT, HAS HE?

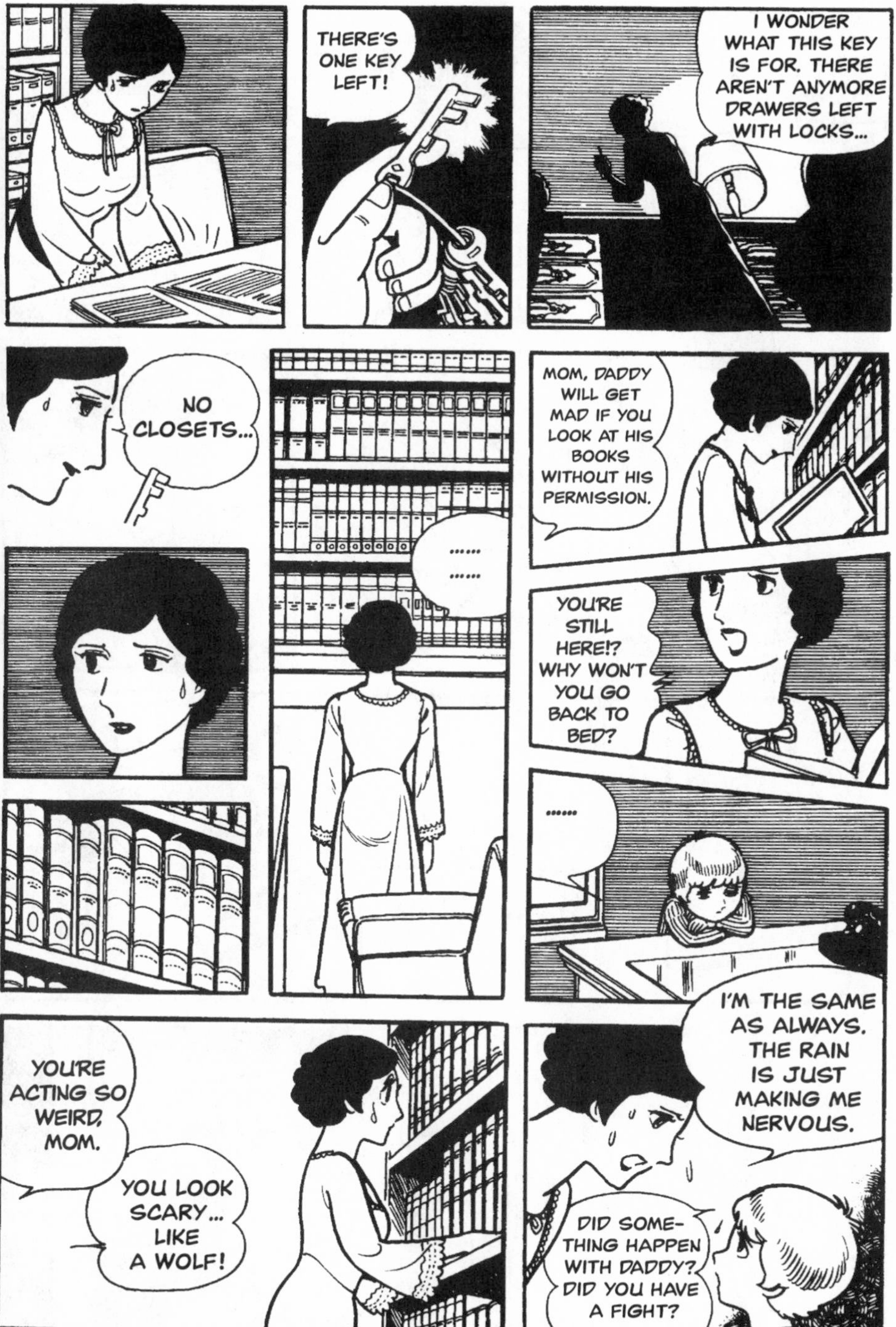
THERE'S ONE KEY LEFT!
I WONDER WHAT THIS KEY IS FOR. THERE AREN'T ANYMORE DRAWERS LEFT WITH LOCKS...
NO CLOSETS...
......
......
MOM, DADDY WILL GET MAD IF YOU LOOK AT HIS BOOKS WITHOUT HIS PERMISSION.
YOU'RE STILL HERE!? WHY WON'T YOU GO BACK TO BED?
......
YOU'RE ACTING SO WEIRD, MOM.
YOU LOOK SCARY... LIKE A WOLF!
I'M THE SAME AS ALWAYS. THE RAIN IS JUST MAKING ME NERVOUS.
DID SOMETHING HAPPEN WITH DADDY? DID YOU HAVE A FIGHT?

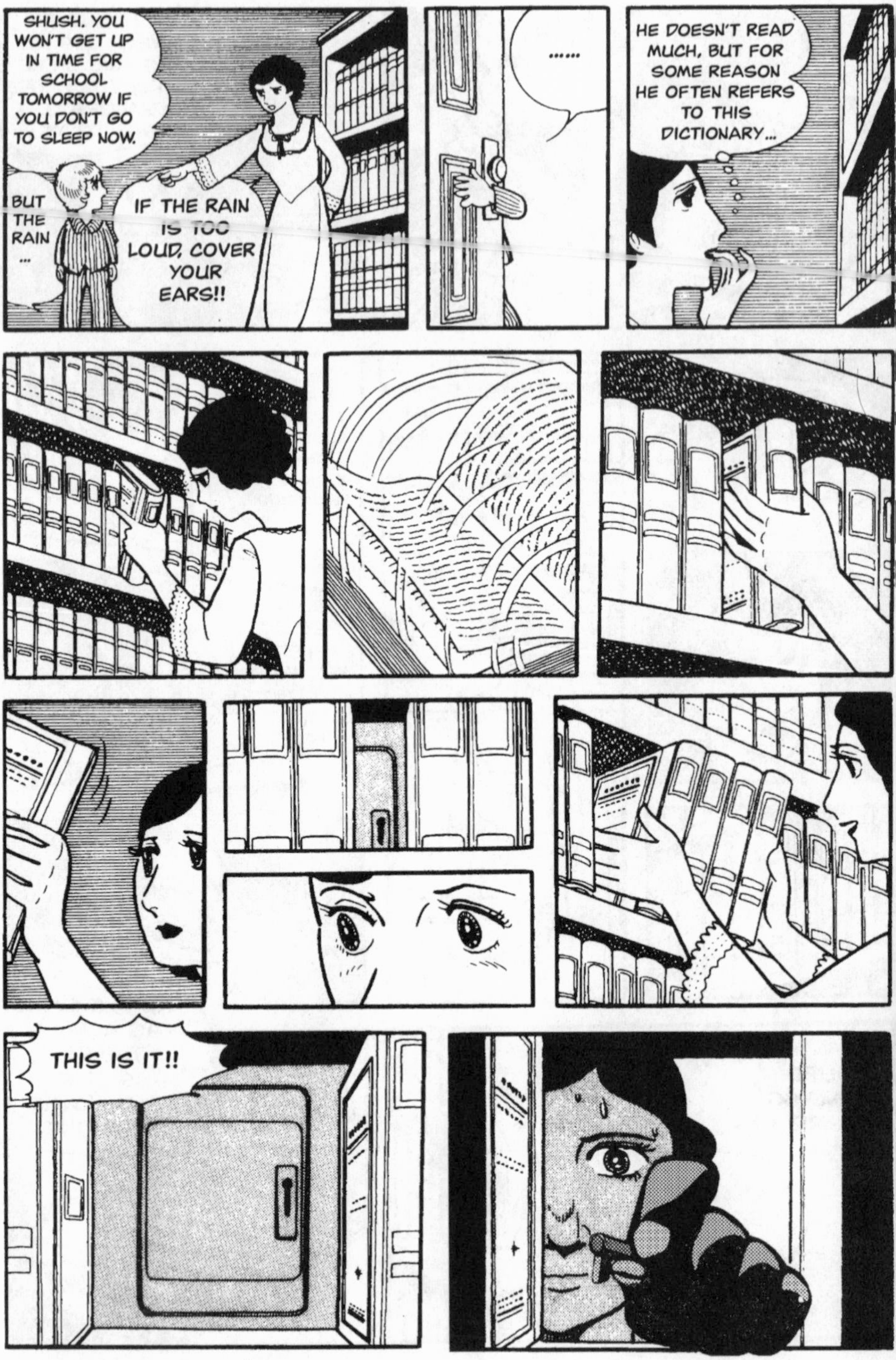
SHUSH. YOU WON'T GET UP IN TIME FOR SCHOOL TOMORROW IF YOU DON'T GO TO SLEEP NOW.
BUT THE RAIN ...
IF THE RAIN IS TOO LOUD, COVER YOUR EARS!!
......
HE DOESN'T READ MUCH, BUT FOR SOME REASON HE OFTEN REFERS TO THIS DICTIONARY...
THIS IS IT!!

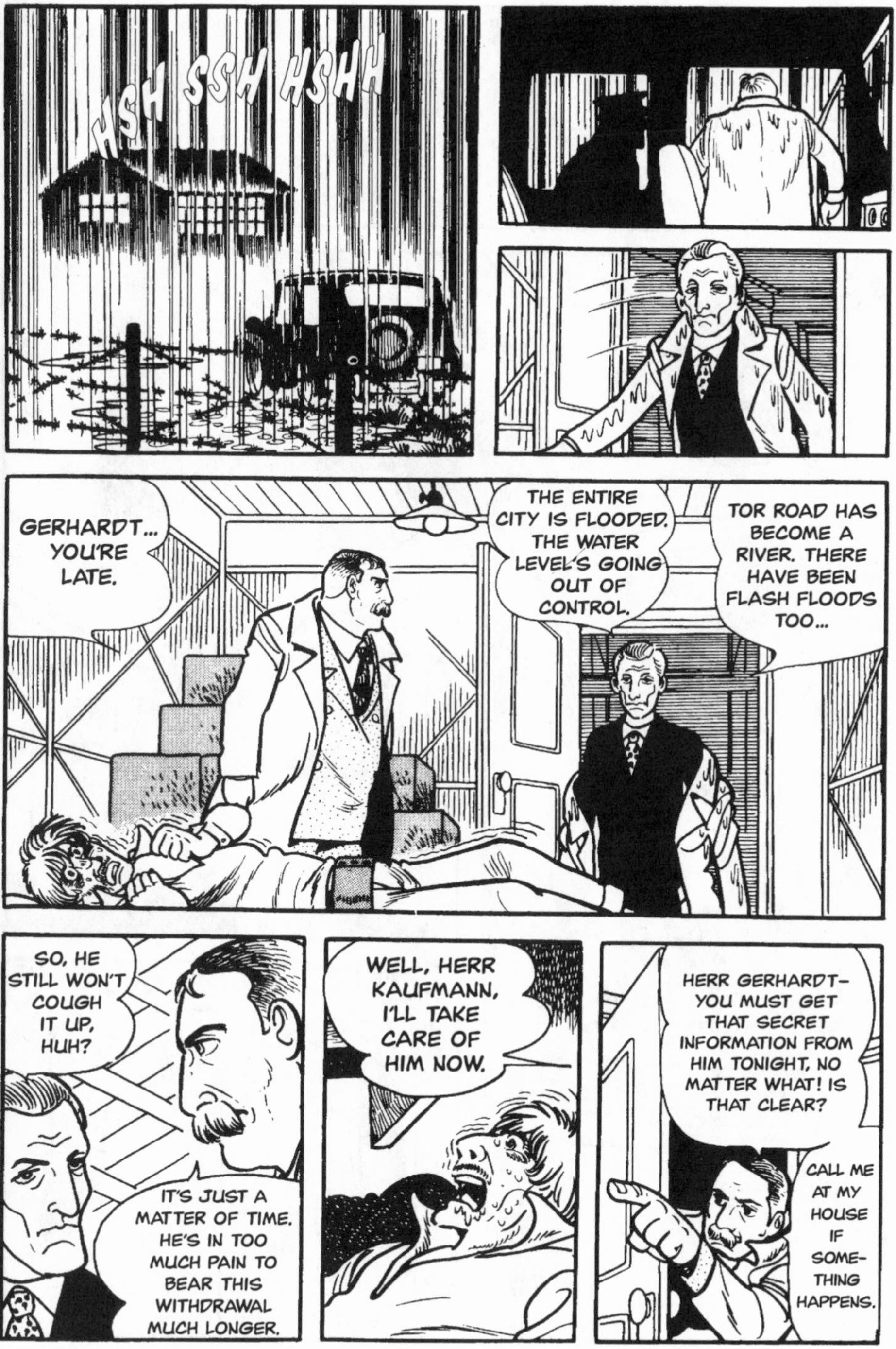
HSH SSH HSHH
GERHARDT... YOU'RE LATE.
THE ENTIRE CITY IS FLOODED. THE WATER LEVEL'S GOING OUT OF CONTROL.
TOR ROAD HAS BECOME A RIVER. THERE HAVE BEEN FLASH FLOODS TOO...
SO, HE STILL WON'T COUGH IT UP, HUH?
IT'S JUST A MATTER OF TIME. HE'S IN TOO MUCH PAIN TO BEAR THIS WITHDRAWAL MUCH LONGER.
WELL, HERR KAUFMANN, I'LL TAKE CARE OF HIM NOW.
HERR GERHARDT– YOU MUST GET THAT SECRET INFORMATION FROM HIM TONIGHT, NO MATTER WHAT! IS THAT CLEAR?
CALL ME AT MY HOUSE IF SOME-THING HAPPENS.

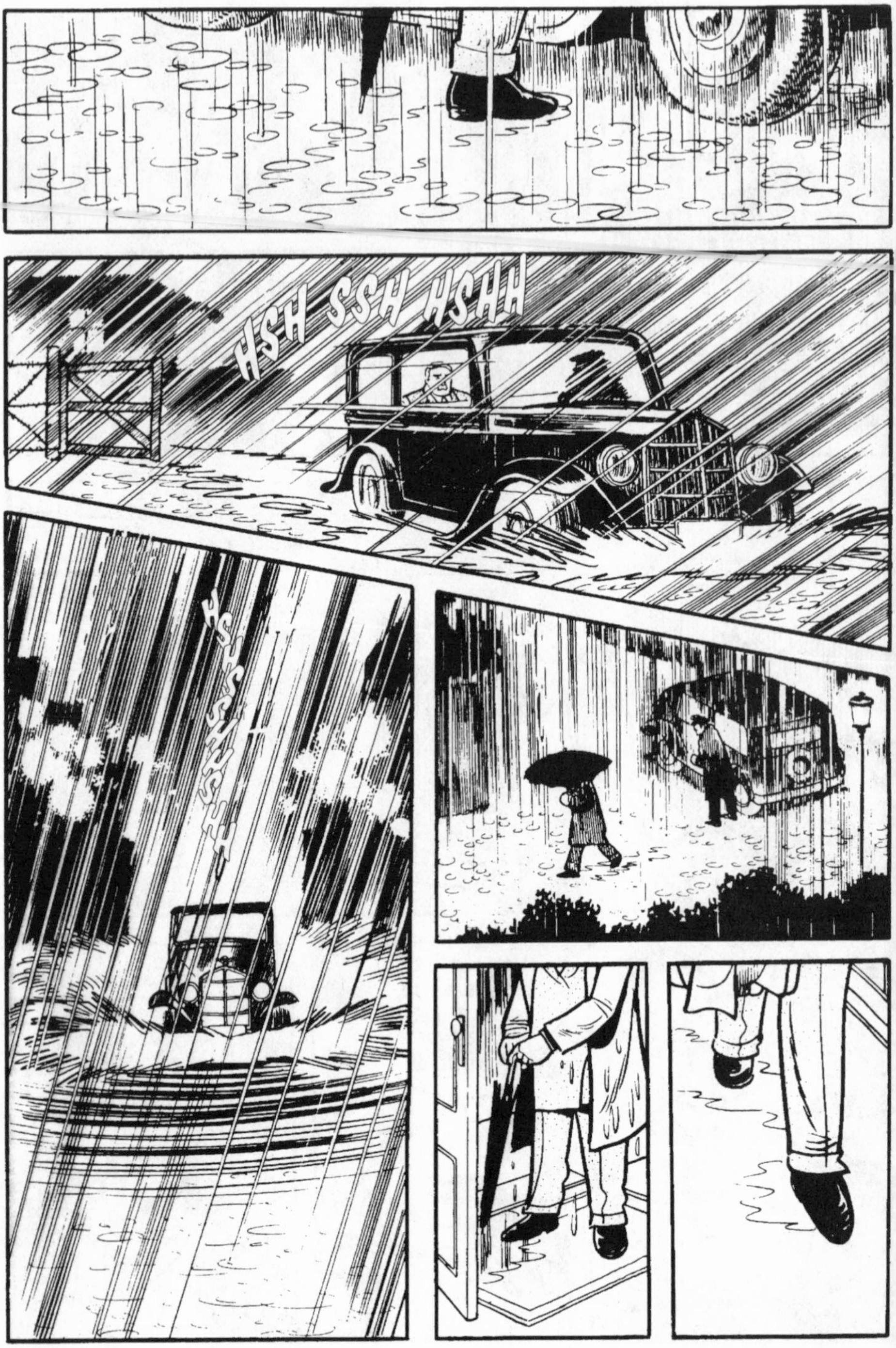
HSH SSH HSHH
HSHSHSHSHH

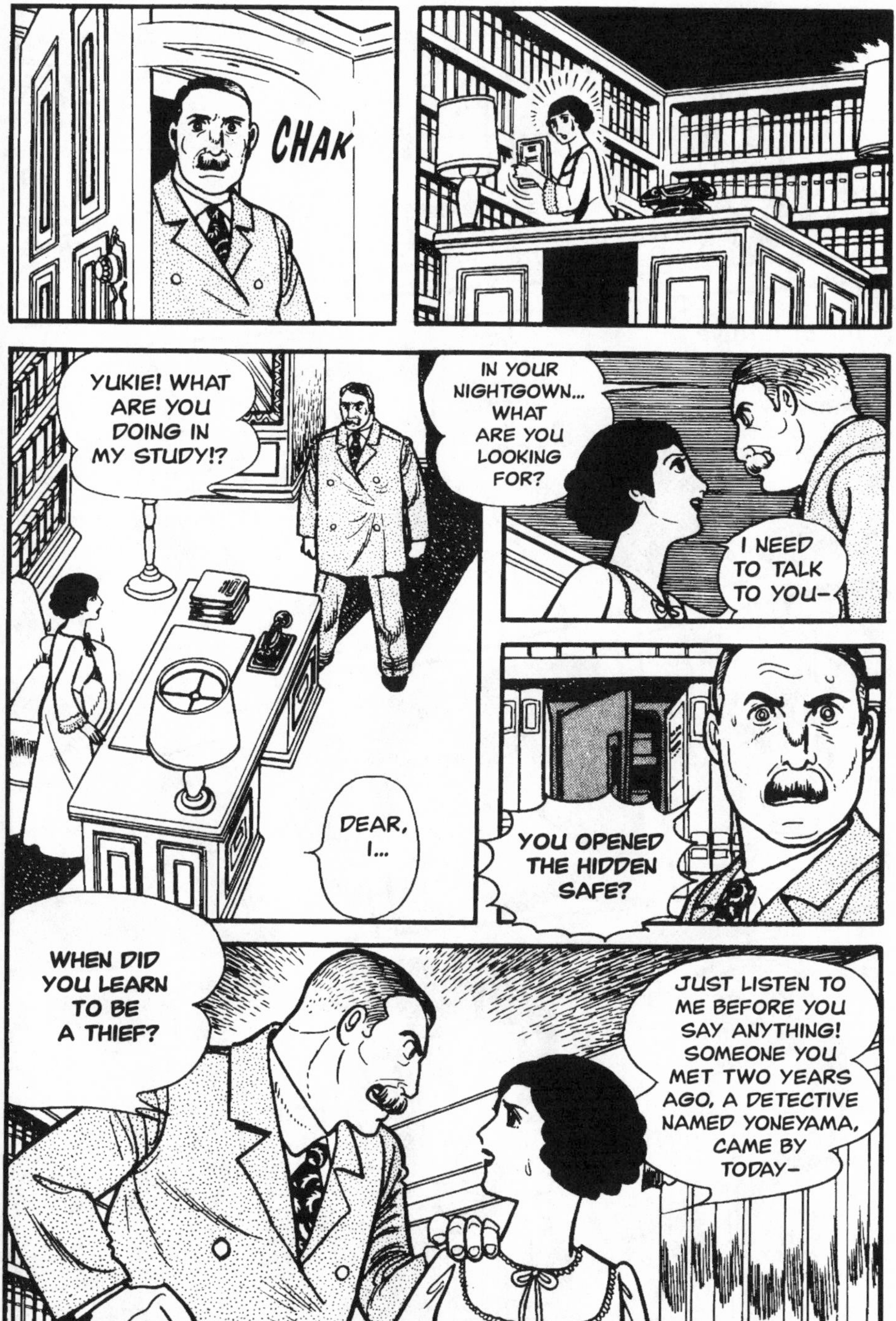
CHAK
YUKIE! WHAT ARE YOU DOING IN MY STUDY!?
DEAR, I...
IN YOUR NIGHTGOWN... WHAT ARE YOU LOOKING FOR?
I NEED TO TALK TO YOU-
YOU OPENED THE HIDDEN SAFE?
WHEN DID YOU LEARN TO BE A THIEF?
JUST LISTEN TO ME BEFORE YOU SAY ANYTHING! SOMEONE YOU MET TWO YEARS AGO, A DETECTIVE NAMED YONEYAMA, CAME BY TODAY-

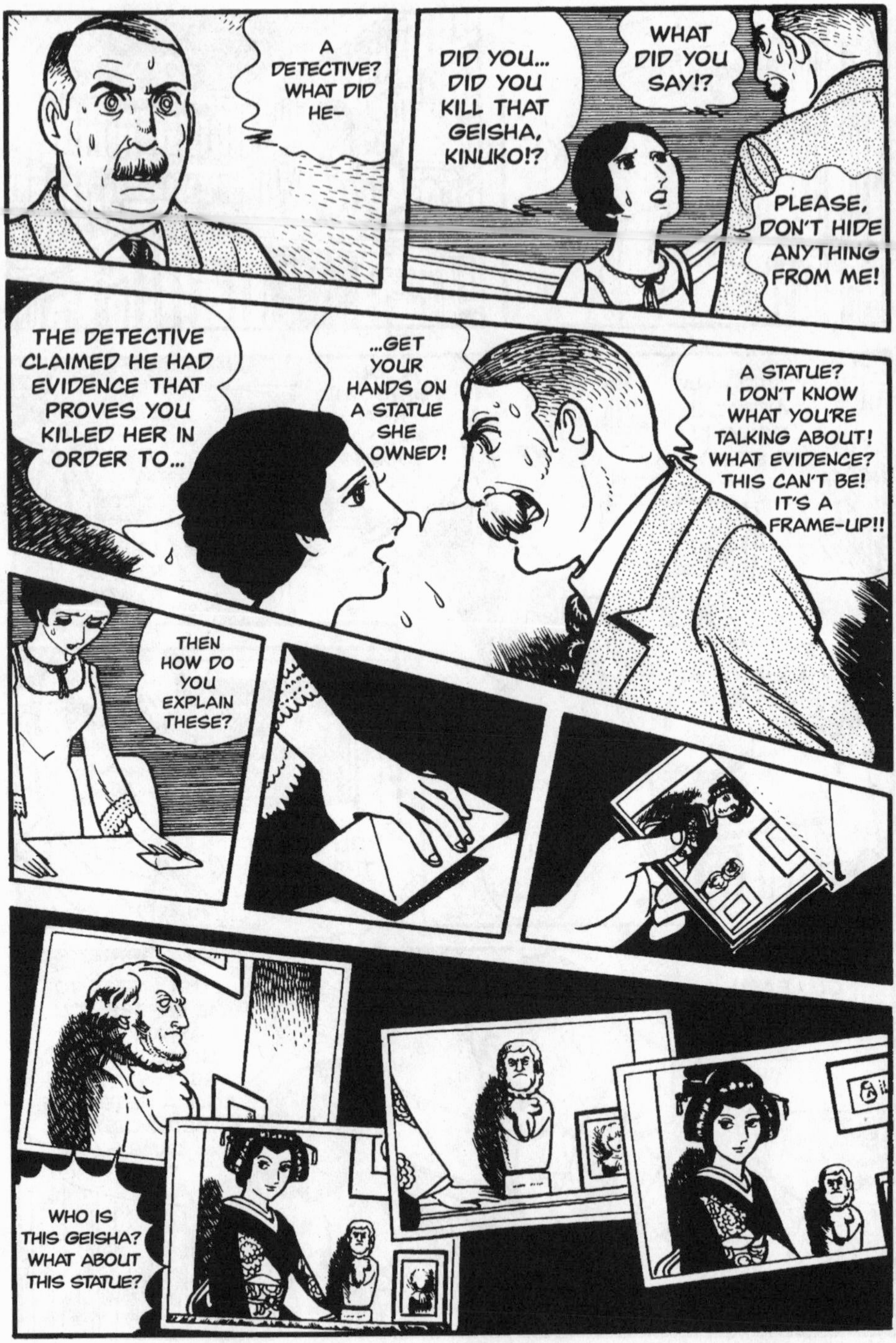
A DETECTIVE? WHAT DID HE–
DID YOU... DID YOU KILL THAT GEISHA, KINUKO!?
WHAT DID YOU SAY!?
PLEASE, DON'T HIDE ANYTHING FROM ME!
THE DETECTIVE CLAIMED HE HAD EVIDENCE THAT PROVES YOU KILLED HER IN ORDER TO...
...GET YOUR HANDS ON A STATUE SHE OWNED!
A STATUE? I DON'T KNOW WHAT YOU'RE TALKING ABOUT! WHAT EVIDENCE? THIS CAN'T BE! IT'S A FRAME-UP!!
THEN HOW DO YOU EXPLAIN THESE?
WHO IS THIS GEISHA? WHAT ABOUT THIS STATUE?

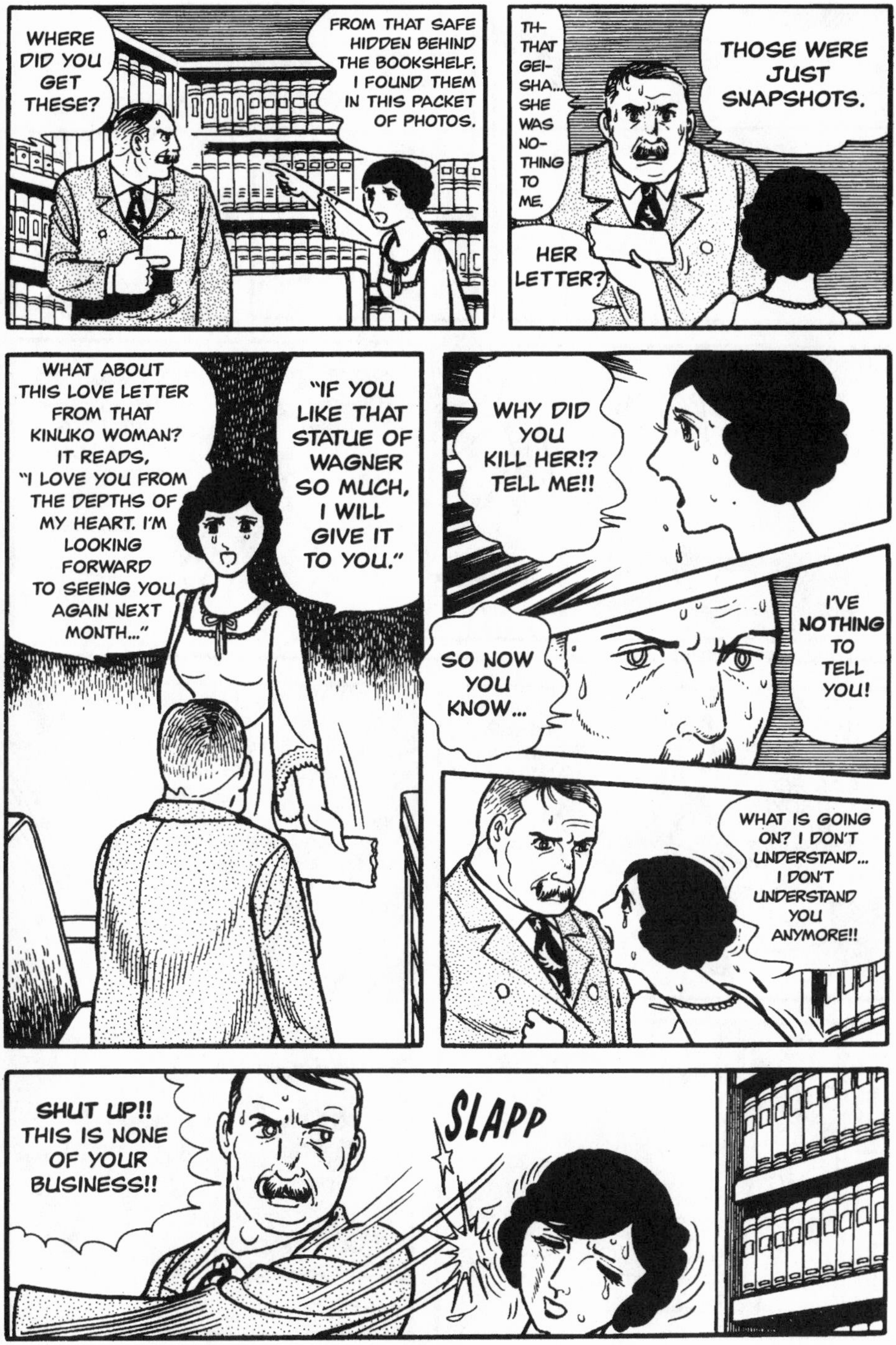
WHERE DID YOU GET THESE?
FROM THAT SAFE HIDDEN BEHIND THE BOOKSHELF. I FOUND THEM IN THIS PACKET OF PHOTOS.
TH-THAT GEI-SHA... SHE WAS NO-THING TO ME.
THOSE WERE JUST SNAPSHOTS.
HER LETTER?
WHAT ABOUT THIS LOVE LETTER FROM THAT KINUKO WOMAN? IT READS, "I LOVE YOU FROM THE DEPTHS OF MY HEART. I'M LOOKING FORWARD TO SEEING YOU AGAIN NEXT MONTH..."
"IF YOU LIKE THAT STATUE OF WAGNER SO MUCH, I WILL GIVE IT TO YOU."
WHY DID YOU KILL HER!? TELL ME!!
SO NOW YOU KNOW...
I'VE NOTHING TO TELL YOU!
WHAT IS GOING ON? I DON'T UNDERSTAND... I DON'T UNDERSTAND YOU ANYMORE!!
SHUT UP!! THIS IS NONE OF YOUR BUSINESS!!
SLAPP

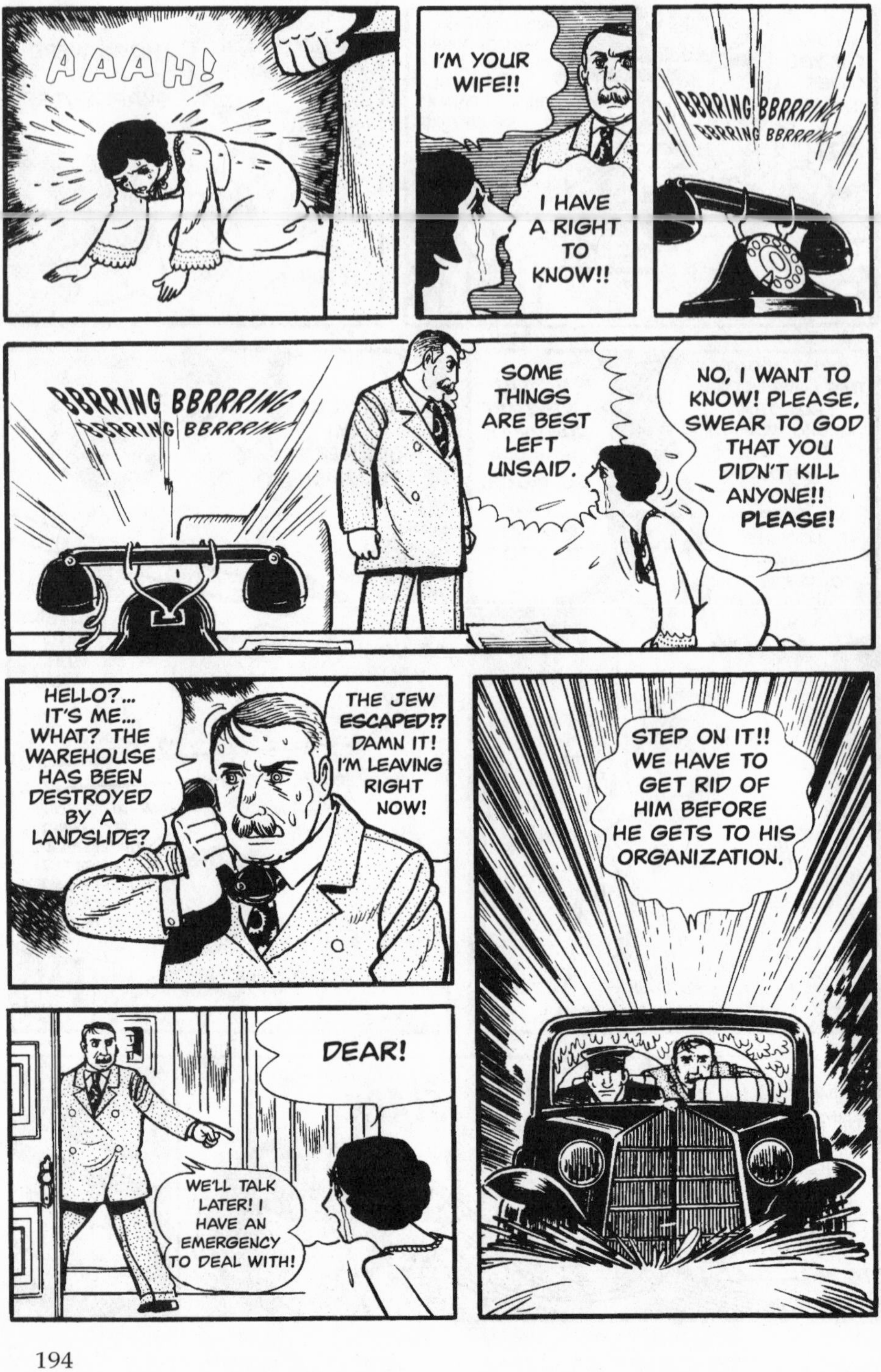
AAAH!
I'M YOUR WIFE!!
I HAVE A RIGHT TO KNOW!!
BBRRING BBRRRING
BBRRING BBRRRING
BBRRING BBRRRING
BBRRING BBRRRING
SOME THINGS ARE BEST LEFT UNSAID.
NO, I WANT TO KNOW! PLEASE, SWEAR TO GOD THAT YOU DIDN'T KILL ANYONE!! PLEASE!
HELLO?... IT'S ME... WHAT? THE WAREHOUSE HAS BEEN DESTROYED BY A LANDSLIDE?
THE JEW ESCAPED!? DAMN IT! I'M LEAVING RIGHT NOW!
DEAR!
WE'LL TALK LATER! I HAVE AN EMERGENCY TO DEAL WITH!
STEP ON IT!! WE HAVE TO GET RID OF HIM BEFORE HE GETS TO HIS ORGANIZATION.

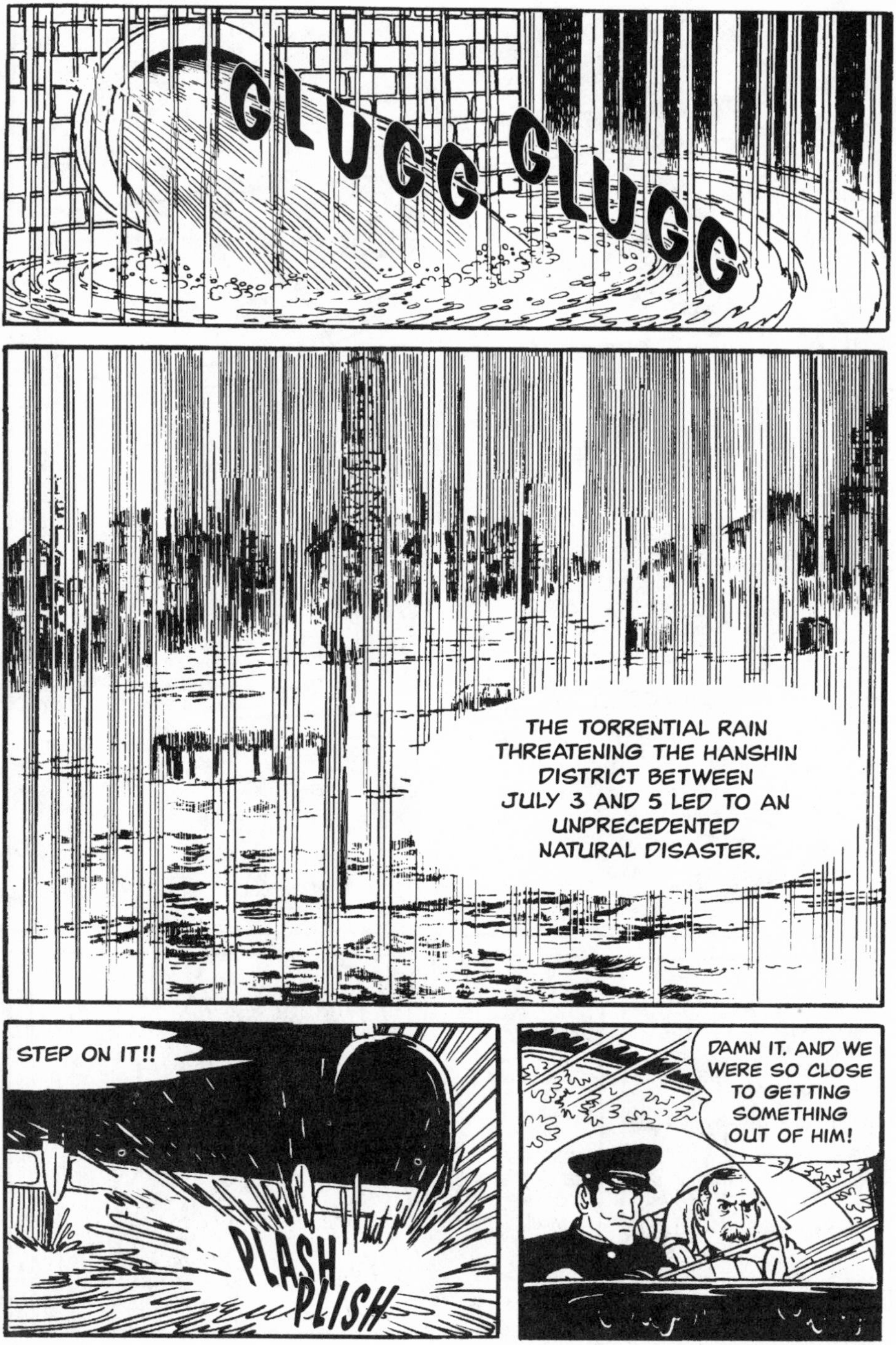
GLUGG GLUGG
THE TORRENTIAL RAIN THREATENING THE HANSHIN DISTRICT BETWEEN JULY 3 AND 5 LED TO AN UNPRECEDENTED NATURAL DISASTER.
STEP ON IT!!
PLASH
PLISH
DAMN IT. AND WE WERE SO CLOSE TO GETTING SOMETHING OUT OF HIM!

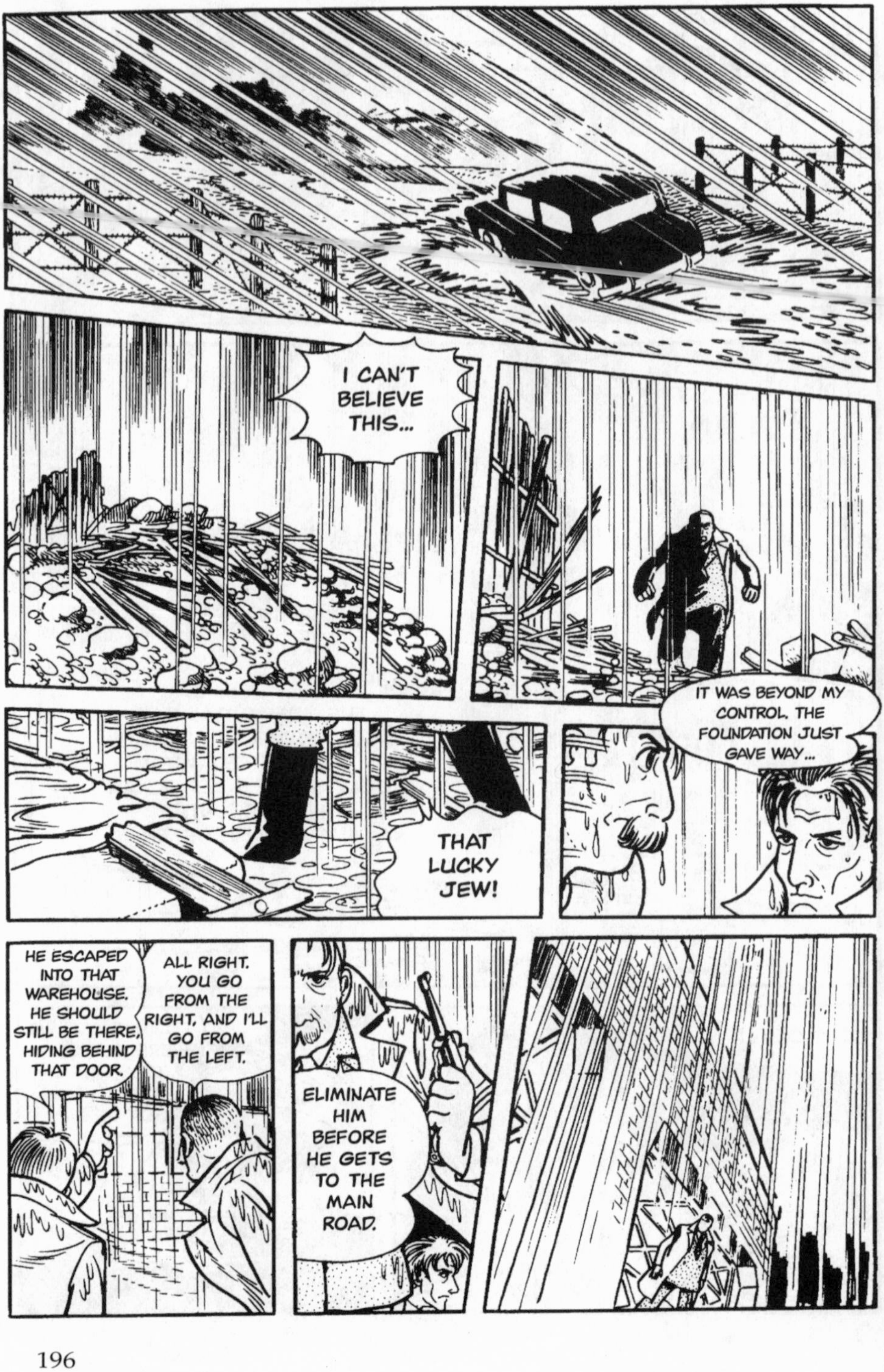
I CAN'T BELIEVE THIS...
THAT LUCKY JEW!
IT WAS BEYOND MY CONTROL. THE FOUNDATION JUST GAVE WAY...
HE ESCAPED INTO THAT WAREHOUSE. HE SHOULD STILL BE THERE, HIDING BEHIND THAT DOOR.
ALL RIGHT. YOU GO FROM THE RIGHT, AND I'LL GO FROM THE LEFT.
ELIMINATE HIM BEFORE HE GETS TO THE MAIN ROAD.

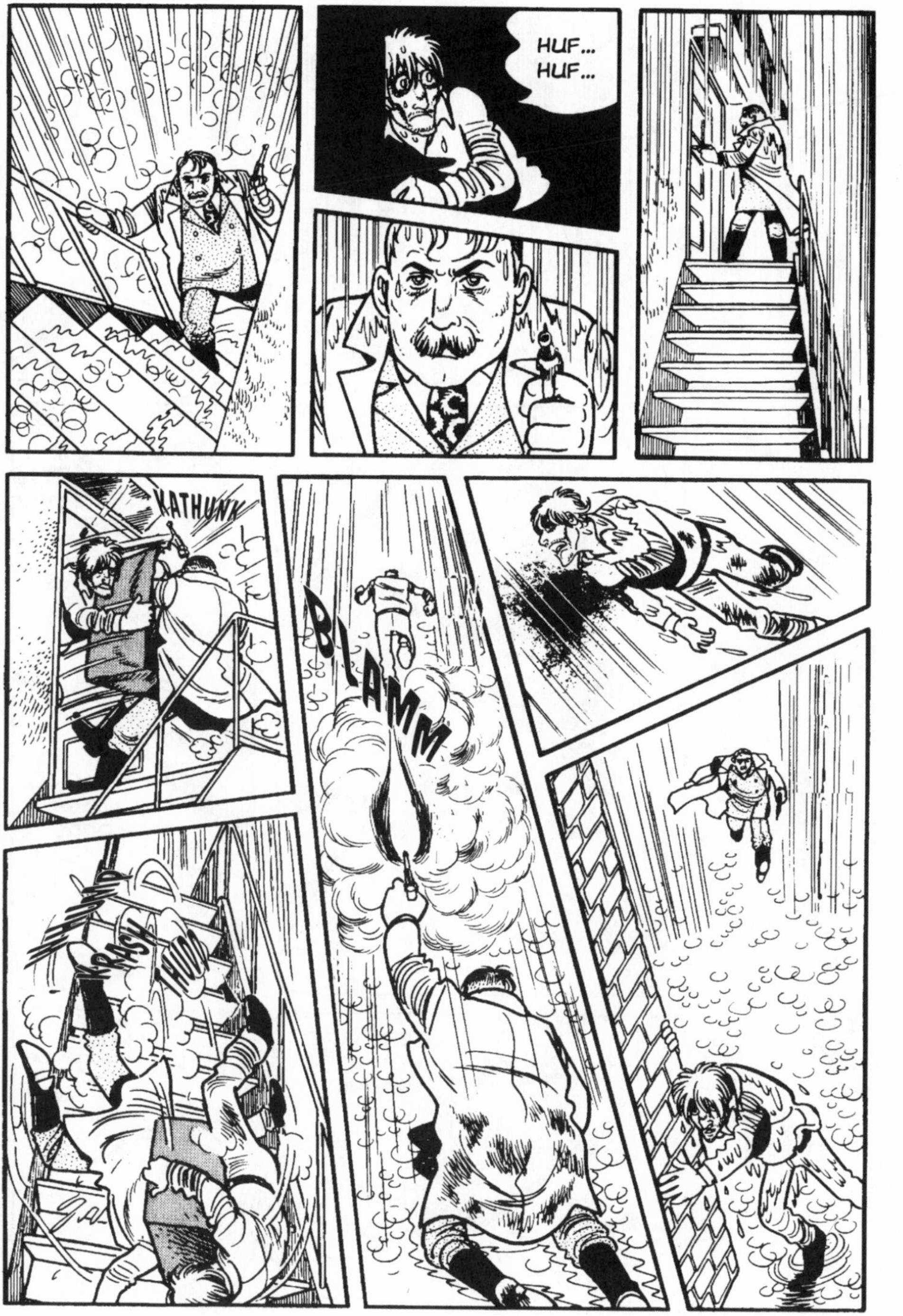
HUF...
HUF...
KATHUNK
BLAMM
THUMP
KRASH
THOD

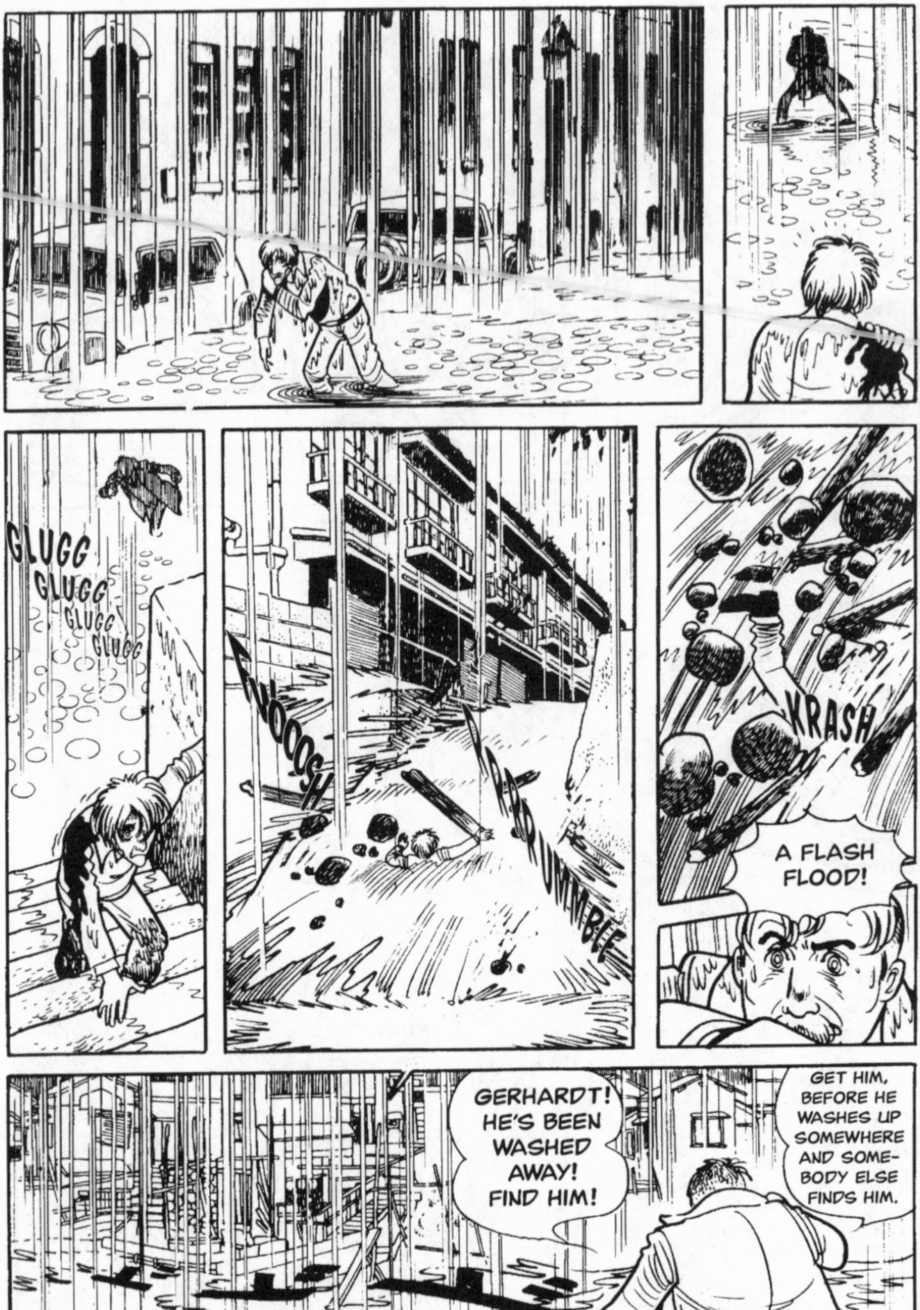
GLUGG
GLUGG
GLUGG
GLUGG
FWOOOSH
RRRRUMMBLE
KRASH
A FLASH FLOOD!
GERHARDT! HE'S BEEN WASHED AWAY! FIND HIM!
GET HIM, BEFORE HE WASHES UP SOMEWHERE AND SOME-BODY ELSE FINDS HIM.

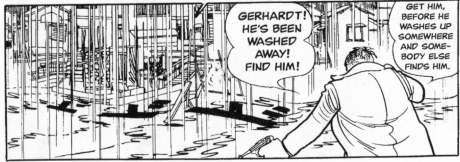

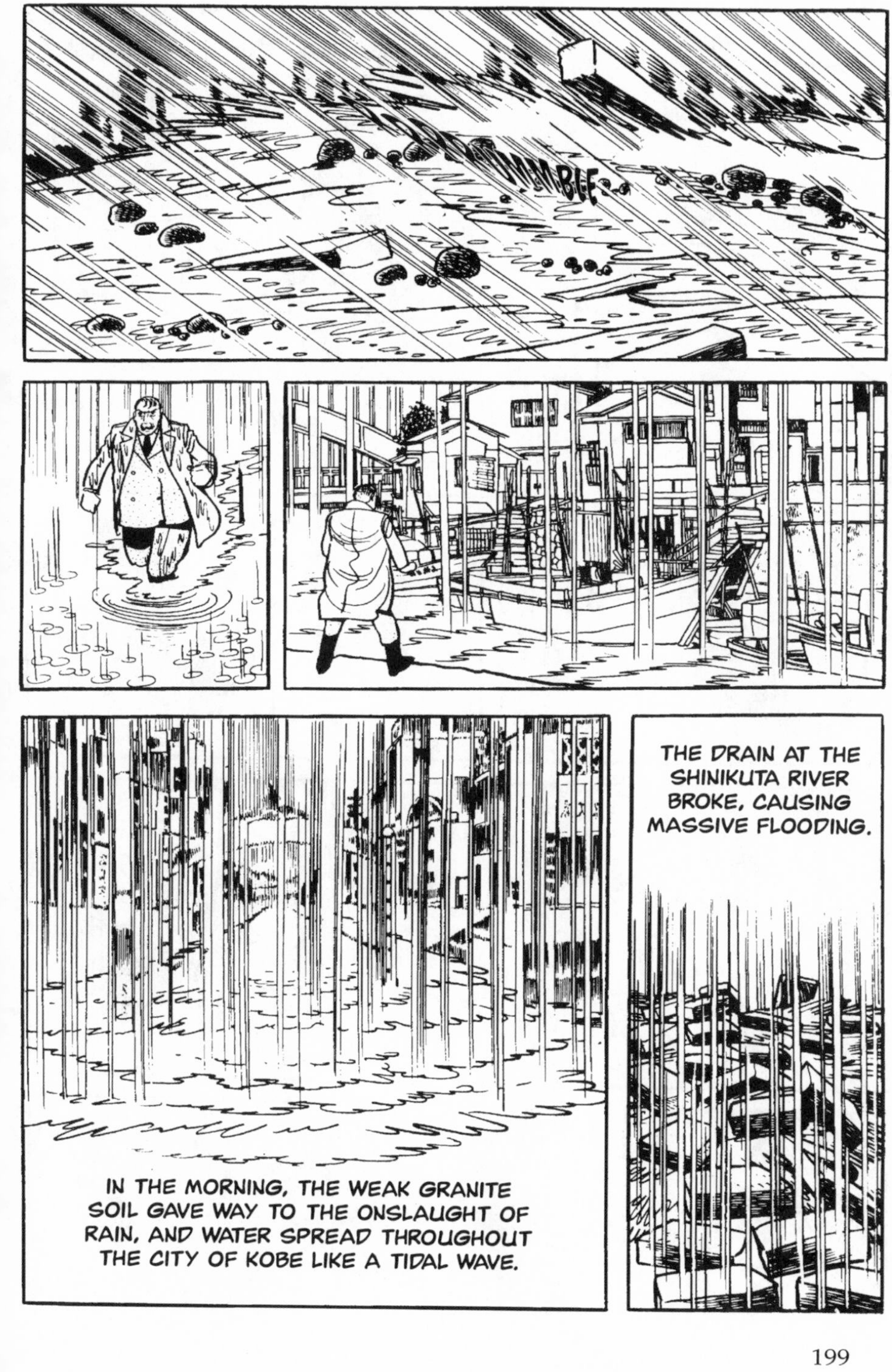
IN THE MORNING, THE WEAK GRANITE SOIL GAVE WAY TO THE ONSLAUGHT OF RAIN, AND WATER SPREAD THROUGHOUT THE CITY OF KOBE LIKE A TIDAL WAVE.
THE DRAIN AT THE SHINIKUTA RIVER BROKE, CAUSING MASSIVE FLOODING.

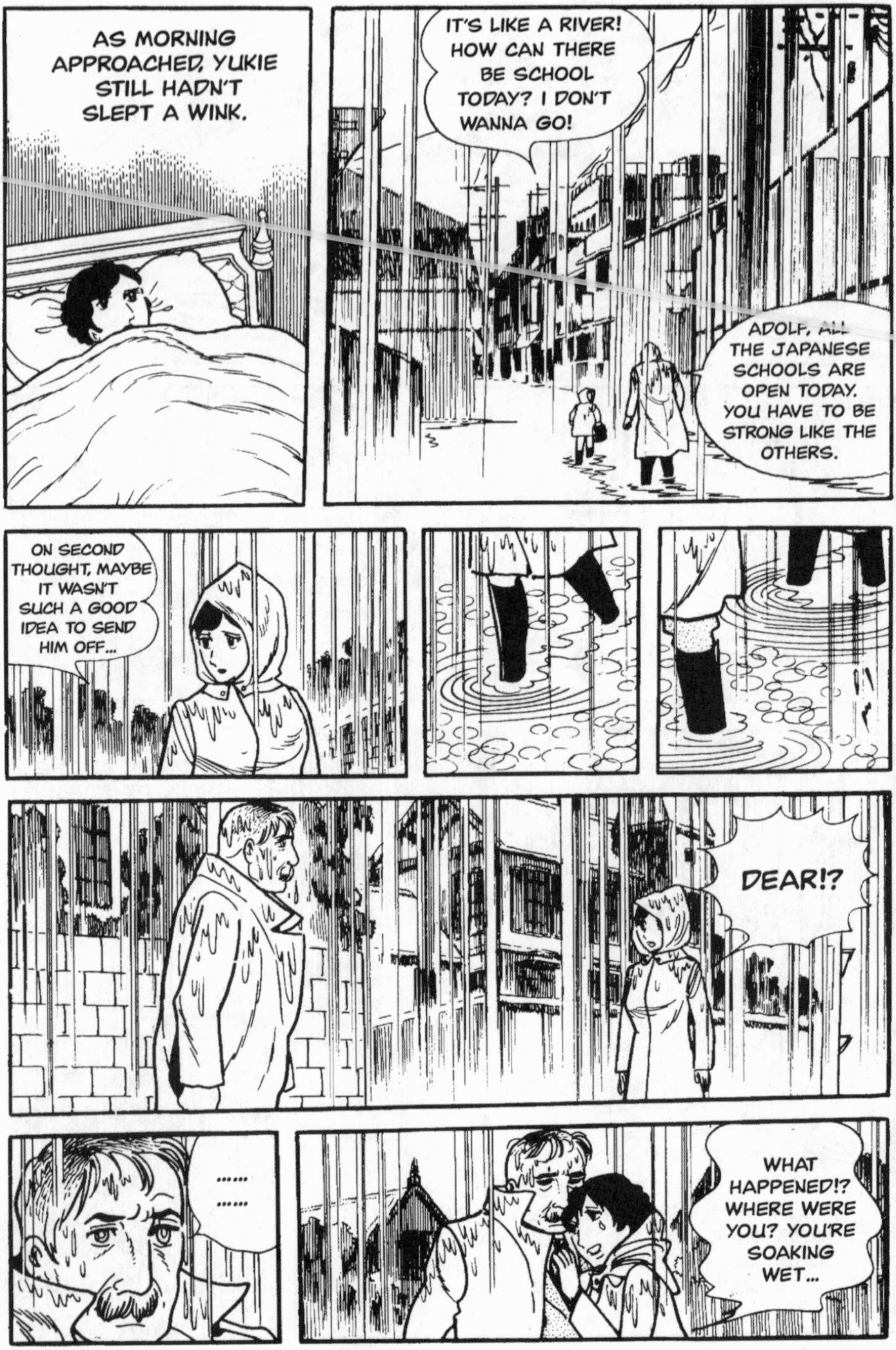
AS MORNING APPROACHED, YUKIE STILL HADN'T SLEPT A WINK.
IT'S LIKE A RIVER! HOW CAN THERE BE SCHOOL TODAY? I DON'T WANNA GO!
ADOLF, ALL THE JAPANESE SCHOOLS ARE OPEN TODAY. YOU HAVE TO BE STRONG LIKE THE OTHERS.
ON SECOND THOUGHT, MAYBE IT WASN'T SUCH A GOOD IDEA TO SEND HIM OFF...
DEAR!?
......
......
WHAT HAPPENED!? WHERE WERE YOU? YOU'RE SOAKING WET...

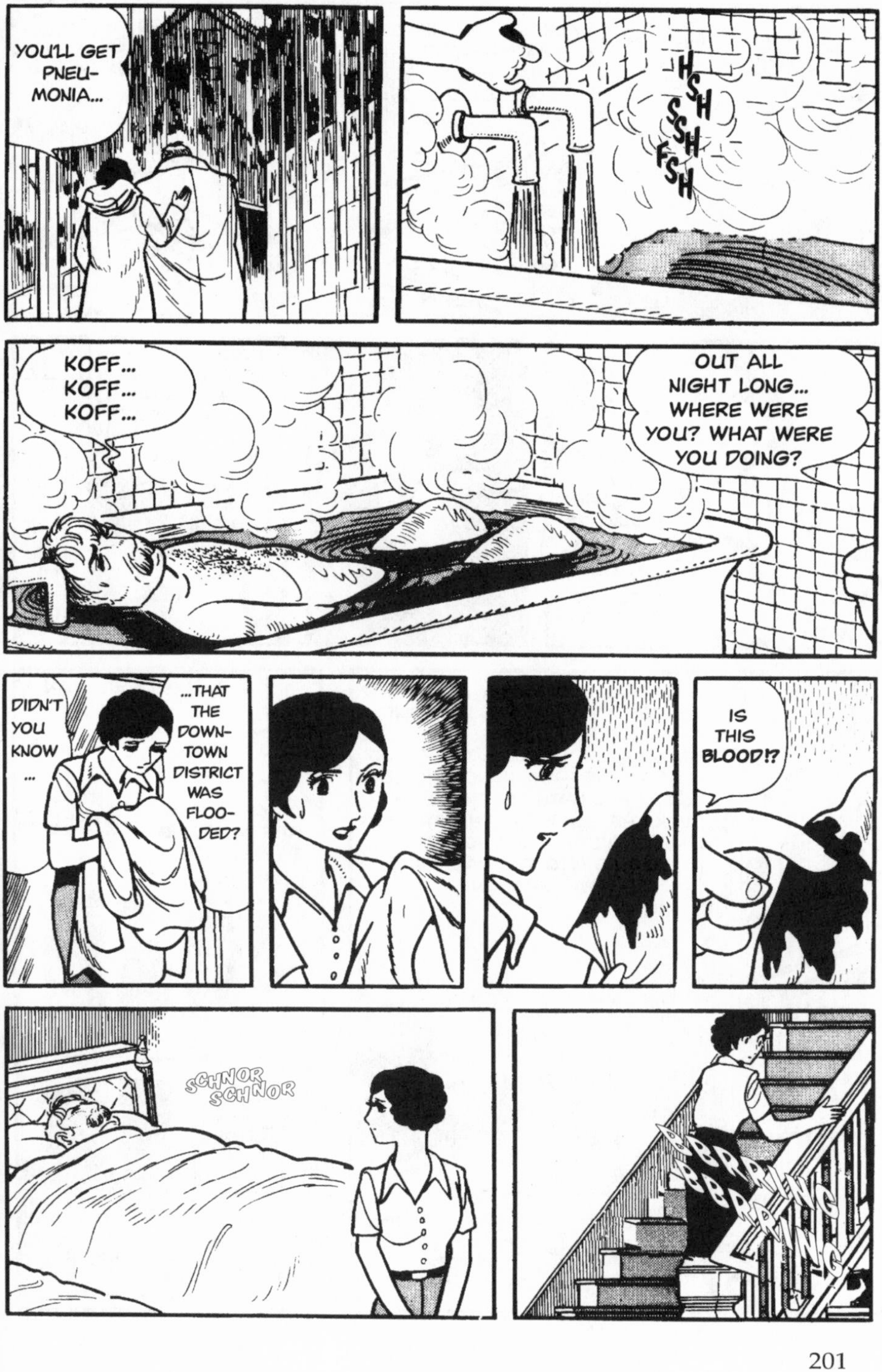
YOU'LL GET PNEU-MONIA...
HSH SSH FSH
KOFF... KOFF... KOFF...
OUT ALL NIGHT LONG... WHERE WERE YOU? WHAT WERE YOU DOING?
DIDN'T YOU KNOW ...
...THAT THE DOWN-TOWN DISTRICT WAS FLOO-DED?
IS THIS BLOOD!?
SCHNOR SCHNOR
BBBRRING BBBRRING

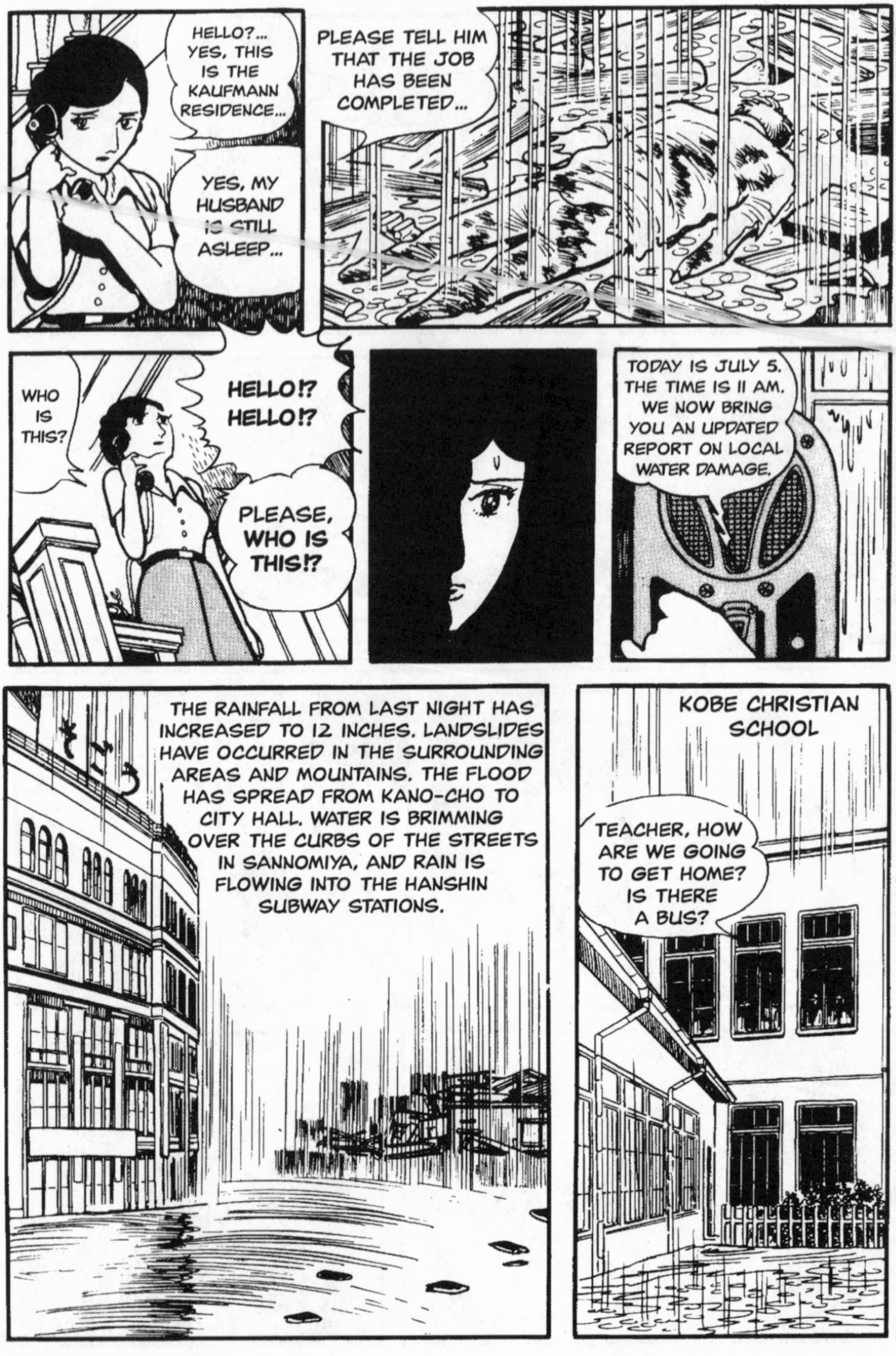
HELLO?... YES, THIS IS THE KAUFMANN RESIDENCE...
YES, MY HUSBAND IS STILL ASLEEP...
PLEASE TELL HIM THAT THE JOB HAS BEEN COMPLETED...
WHO IS THIS?
HELLO!? HELLO!?
PLEASE, WHO IS THIS!?
TODAY IS JULY 5. THE TIME IS 11 AM. WE NOW BRING YOU AN UPDATED REPORT ON LOCAL WATER DAMAGE.
THE RAINFALL FROM LAST NIGHT HAS INCREASED TO 12 INCHES. LANDSLIDES HAVE OCCURRED IN THE SURROUNDING AREAS AND MOUNTAINS. THE FLOOD HAS SPREAD FROM KANO-CHO TO CITY HALL. WATER IS BRIMMING OVER THE CURBS OF THE STREETS IN SANNOMIYA, AND RAIN IS FLOWING INTO THE HANSHIN SUBWAY STATIONS.
KOBE CHRISTIAN SCHOOL
TEACHER, HOW ARE WE GOING TO GET HOME? IS THERE A BUS?

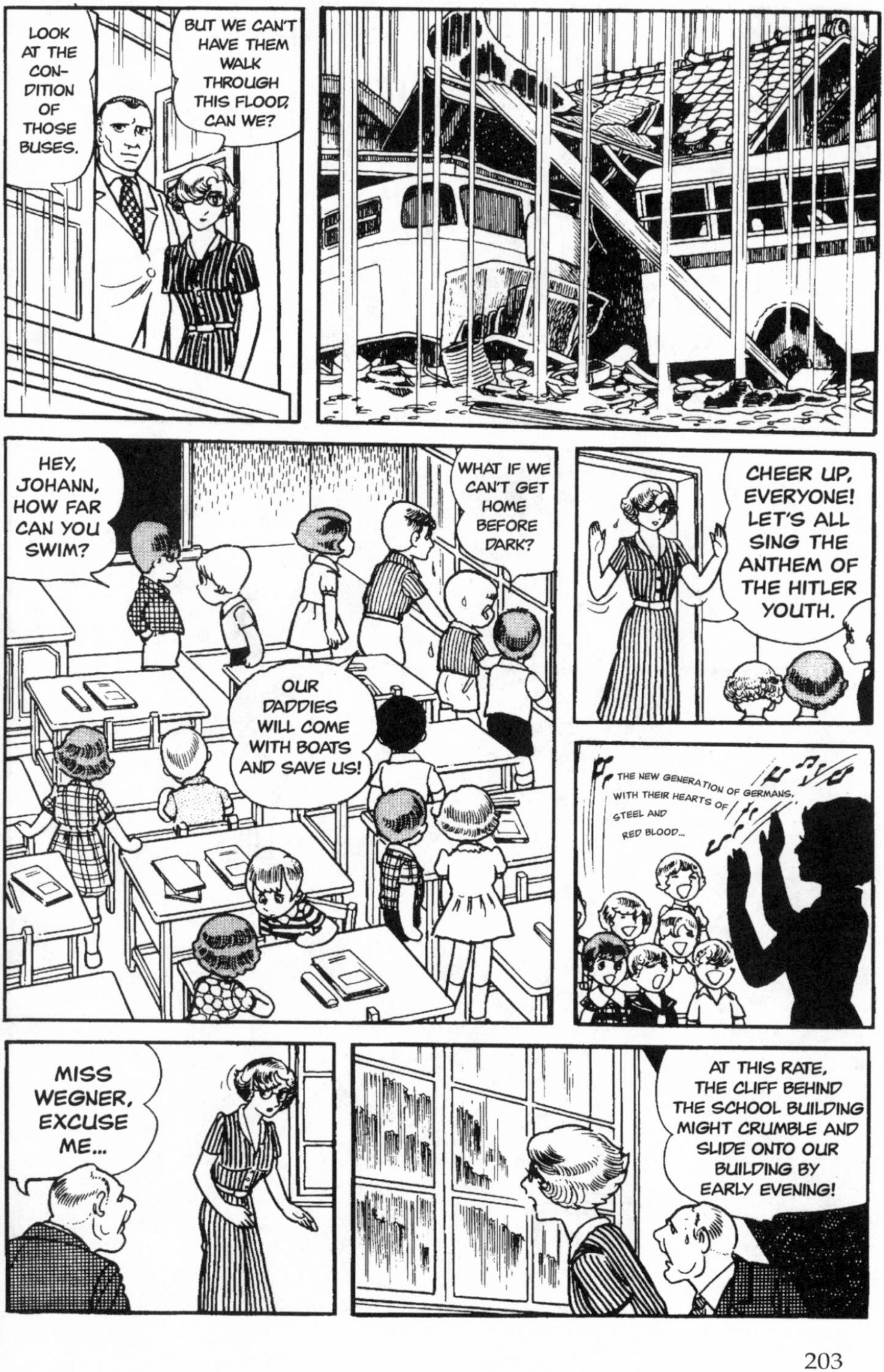
LOOK AT THE CON-DITION OF THOSE BUSES.
BUT WE CAN'T HAVE THEM WALK THROUGH THIS FLOOD, CAN WE?
HEY, JOHANN, HOW FAR CAN YOU SWIM?
WHAT IF WE CAN'T GET HOME BEFORE DARK?
OUR DADDIES WILL COME WITH BOATS AND SAVE US!
CHEER UP, EVERYONE! LET'S ALL SING THE ANTHEM OF THE HITLER YOUTH.
THE NEW GENERATION OF GERMANS, WITH THEIR HEARTS OF STEEL AND RED BLOOD...
MISS WEGNER, EXCUSE ME...
AT THIS RATE, THE CLIFF BEHIND THE SCHOOL BUILDING MIGHT CRUMBLE AND SLIDE ONTO OUR BUILDING BY EARLY EVENING!

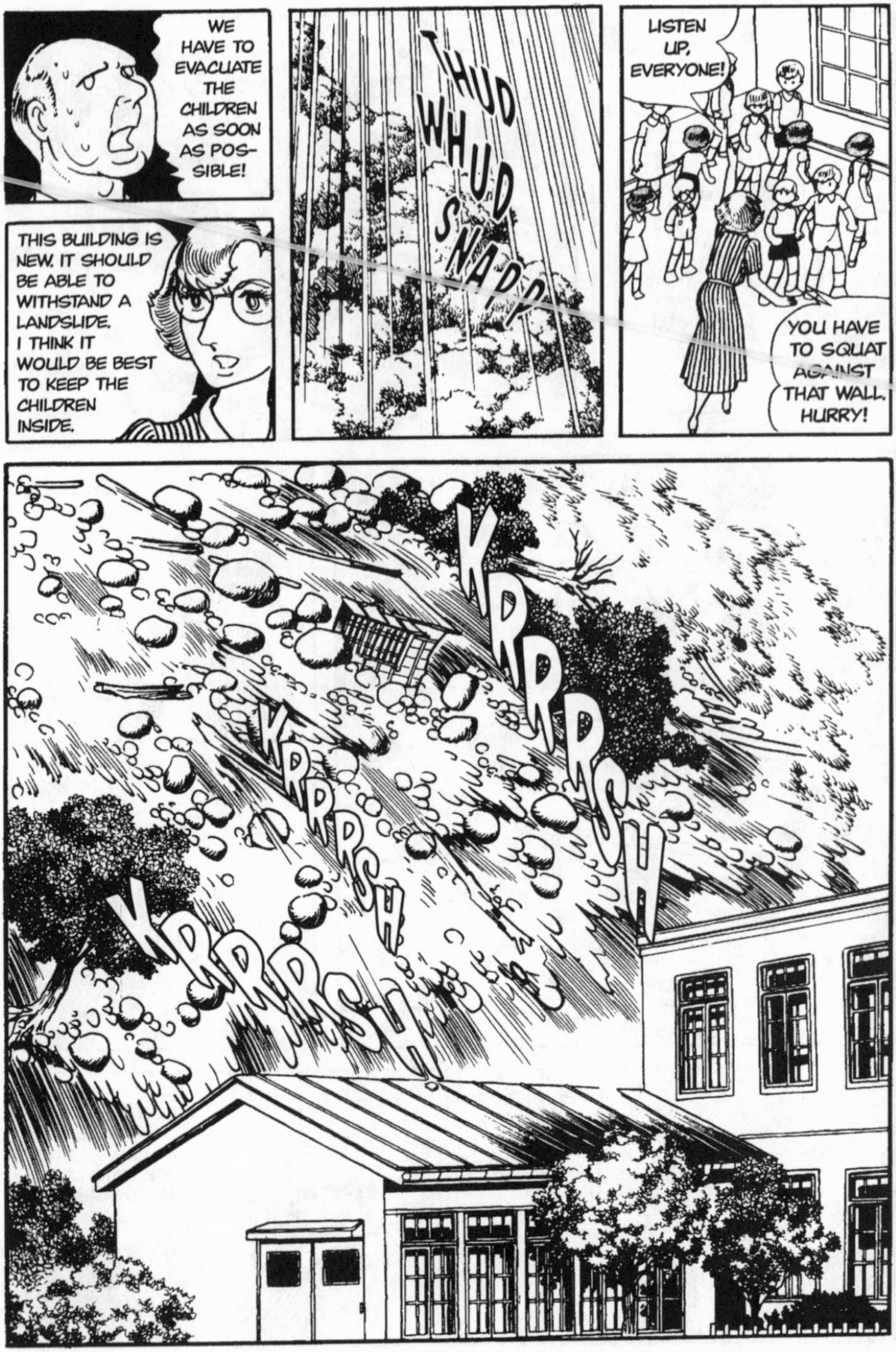
WE HAVE TO EVACUATE THE CHILDREN AS SOON AS POS-SIBLE!
THIS BUILDING IS NEW. IT SHOULD BE ABLE TO WITHSTAND A LANDSLIDE. I THINK IT WOULD BE BEST TO KEEP THE CHILDREN INSIDE.
THUD
WHUD
SNAPP
LISTEN UP, EVERYONE!
YOU HAVE TO SQUAT AGAINST THAT WALL. HURRY!
KRRRSH
KRRRSH
KRRRSH

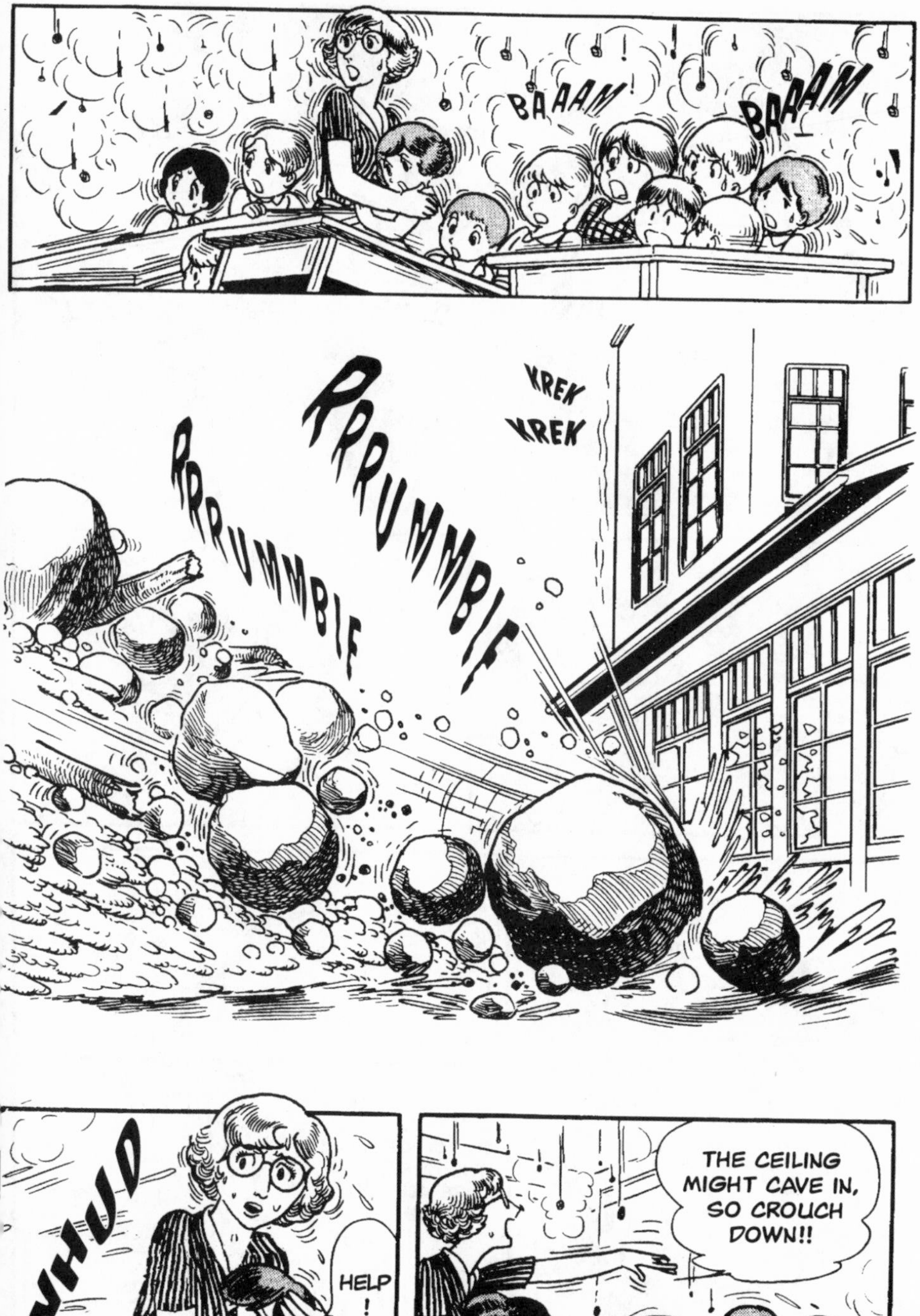
BAAAM
BAAAM
KREK
KREK
RRRUMMBLE
RRRUMMBLE
WHUD
HELP !
THE CEILING MIGHT CAVE IN, SO CROUCH DOWN!!

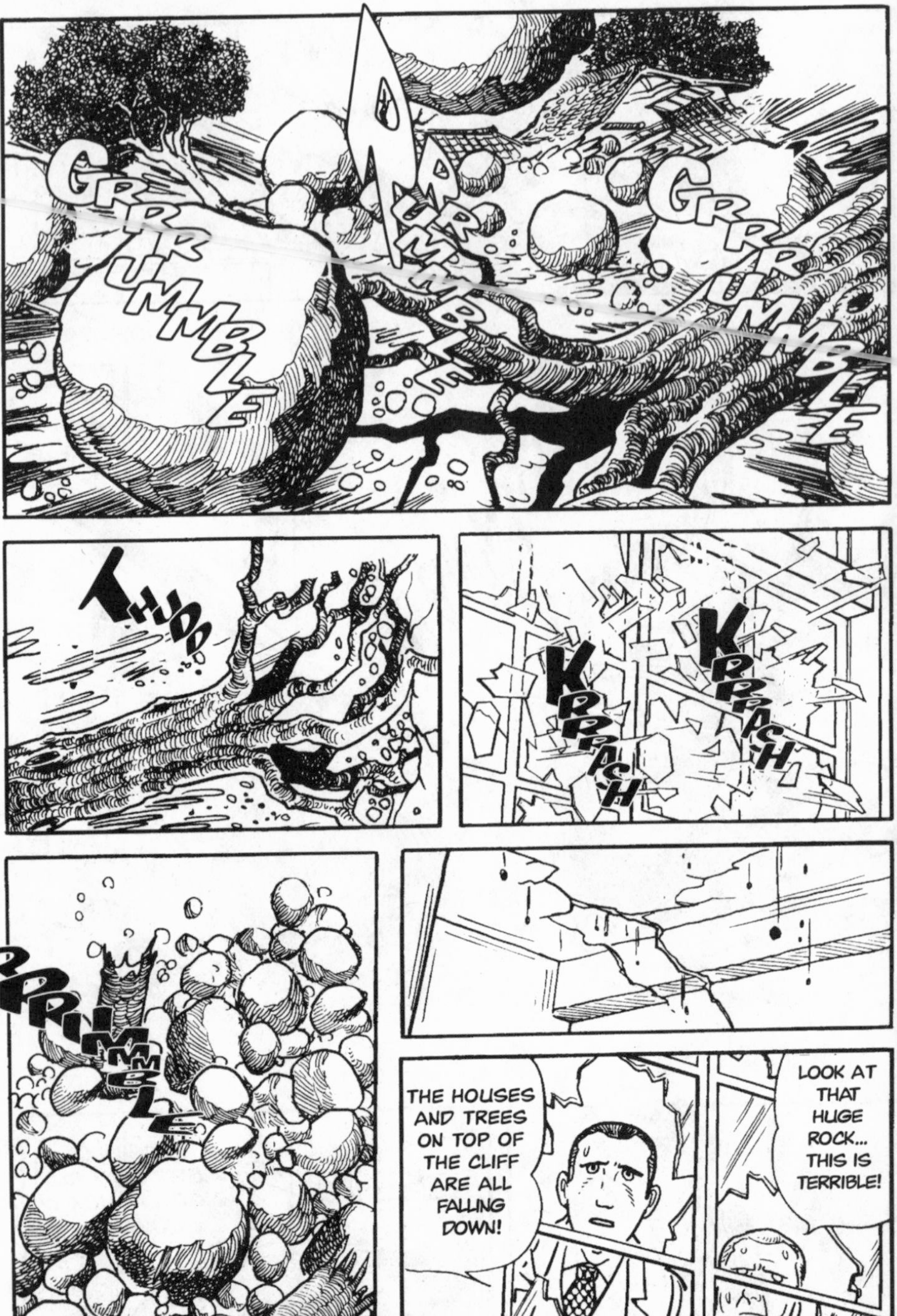
GRRRUMMBLE
GRRUMMBLE
GRRRUMMBLE
THUDD
KRRPCH
KRRPCH
RRRUMMBLE
THE HOUSES AND TREES ON TOP OF THE CLIFF ARE ALL FALLING DOWN!
LOOK AT THAT HUGE ROCK... THIS IS TERRIBLE!

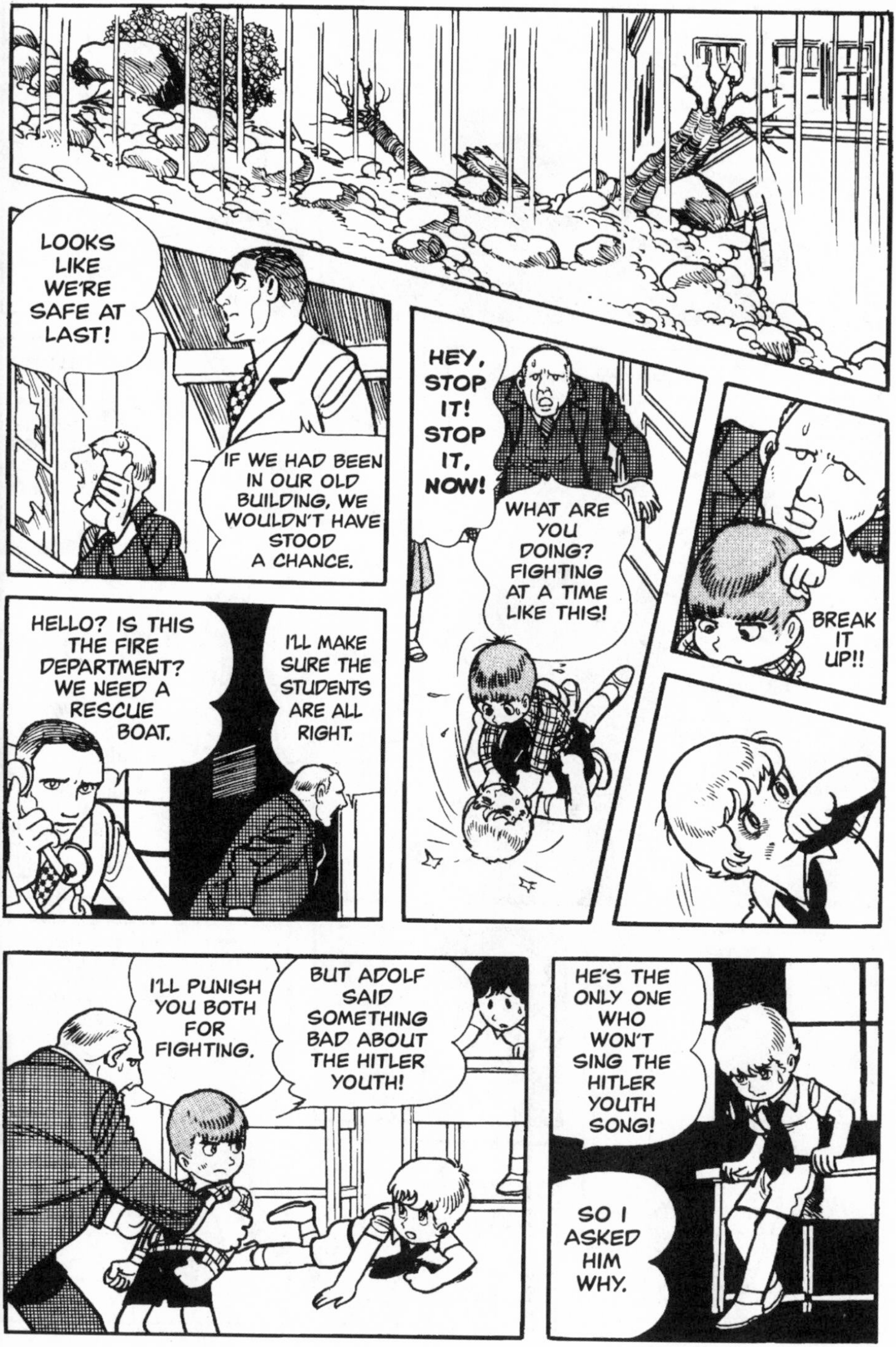
LOOKS LIKE WE'RE SAFE AT LAST!
IF WE HAD BEEN IN OUR OLD BUILDING, WE WOULDN'T HAVE STOOD A CHANCE.
HELLO? IS THIS THE FIRE DEPARTMENT? WE NEED A RESCUE BOAT.
I'LL MAKE SURE THE STUDENTS ARE ALL RIGHT.
HEY, STOP IT! STOP IT, NOW!
WHAT ARE YOU DOING? FIGHTING AT A TIME LIKE THIS!
BREAK IT UP!!
I'LL PUNISH YOU BOTH FOR FIGHTING.
BUT ADOLF SAID SOMETHING BAD ABOUT THE HITLER YOUTH!
HE'S THE ONLY ONE WHO WON'T SING THE HITLER YOUTH SONG!
SO I ASKED HIM WHY.

Adolf

 HE SAID HE CAN'T STAND THE HITLER YOUTH. THAT'S WHY HE WON'T SING.

 YOU REALLY SAID THAT, ADOLF?

 DON'T YOU CHERISH THE HITLER YOUTH?

YOU USED TO...

 NO. I CAN'T STAND THEM.

"THEM"? I CAN'T BELIEVE YOU'RE SAYING THIS...

 ...... TELL ME WHY. I'M THE PRINCIPAL. YOU CAN TELL ME ANYTHING.

 THE HITLER YOUTH... ...TEACHES US TO HATE JEWS.

 JEWS? WHAT ARE YOU SAYING?

I HAVE A JEWISH FRIEND.

 YOU MEAN THAT BAKER'S BOY, ADOLF? HE'S A PARASITE.

 HE IS NOT!

LISTEN, ADOLF. THE HITLER YOUTH EXPLAINS TO US THAT THE JEWS ARE GARBAGE SPREADING THEIR FILTH ALL OVER THE WORLD.

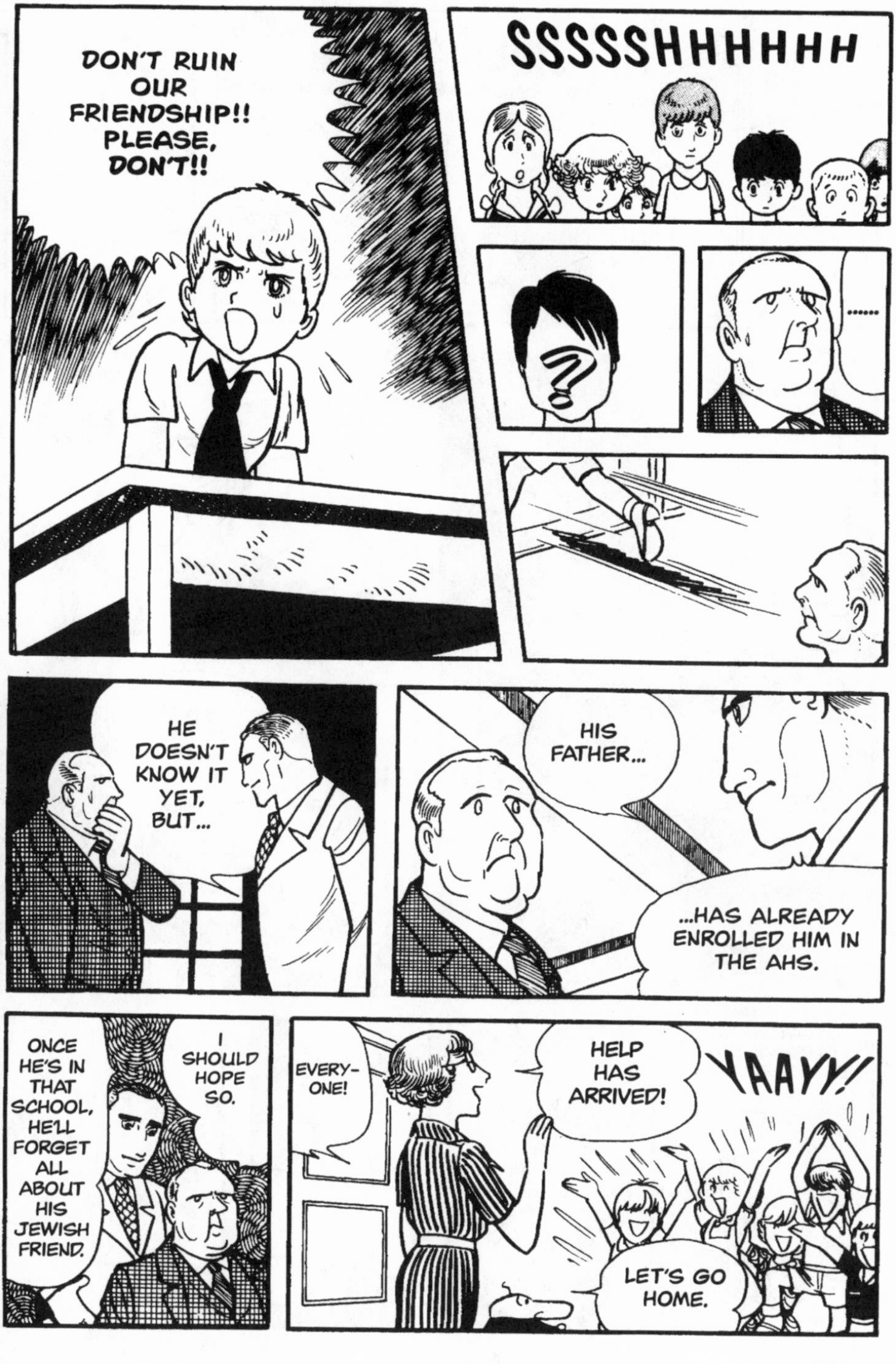
DON'T RUIN OUR FRIENDSHIP!! PLEASE, DON'T!!
SSSSSHHHHHH
......
HE DOESN'T KNOW IT YET, BUT...
HIS FATHER...
...HAS ALREADY ENROLLED HIM IN THE AHS.
ONCE HE'S IN THAT SCHOOL, HE'LL FORGET ALL ABOUT HIS JEWISH FRIEND.
I SHOULD HOPE SO.
EVERY-ONE!
HELP HAS ARRIVED!
YAAYY!
LET'S GO HOME.

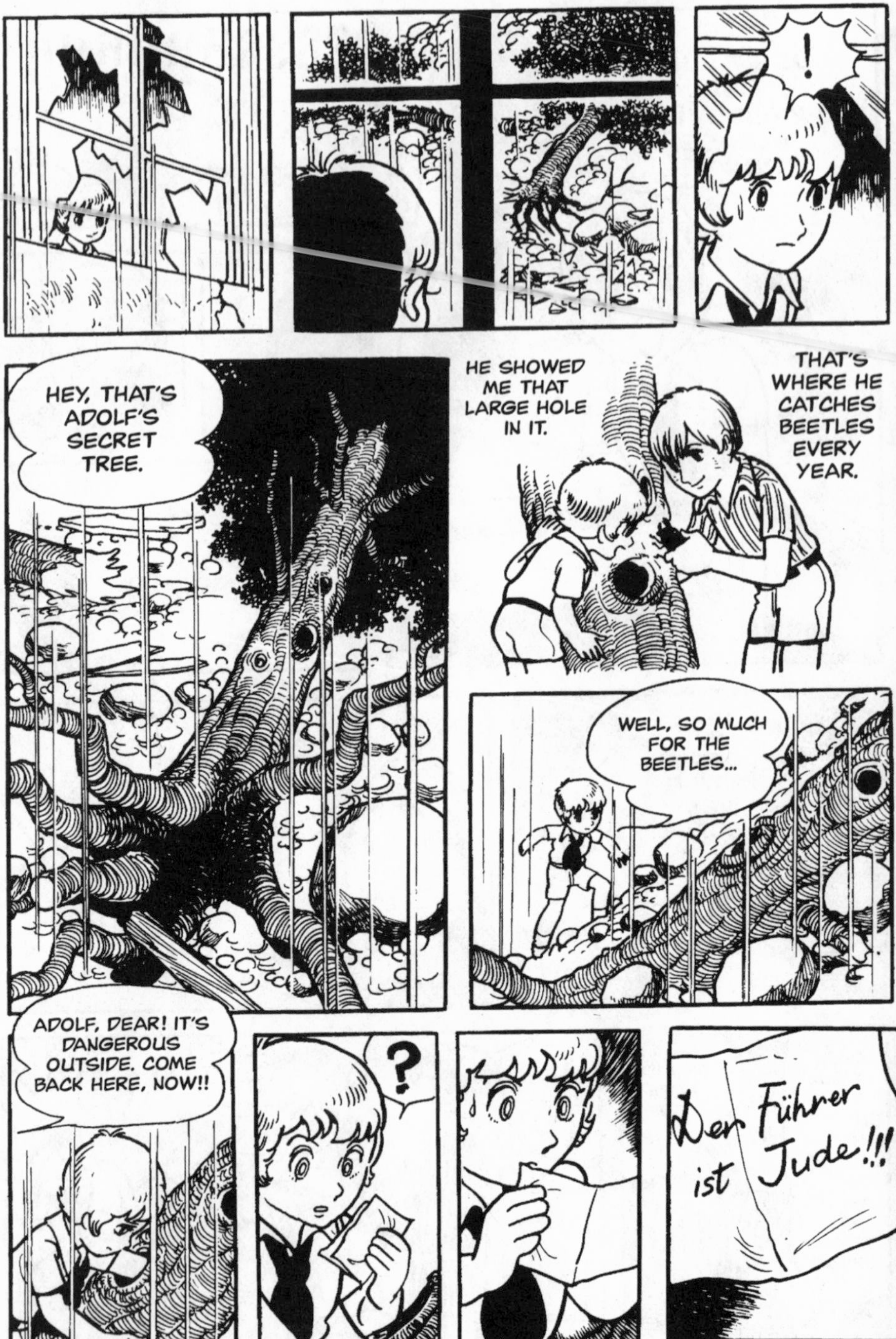
!
HEY, THAT'S ADOLF'S SECRET TREE.
HE SHOWED ME THAT LARGE HOLE IN IT.
THAT'S WHERE HE CATCHES BEETLES EVERY YEAR.
WELL, SO MUCH FOR THE BEETLES...
ADOLF, DEAR! IT'S DANGEROUS OUTSIDE. COME BACK HERE, NOW!!
?
Der Führer ist Jude!!!

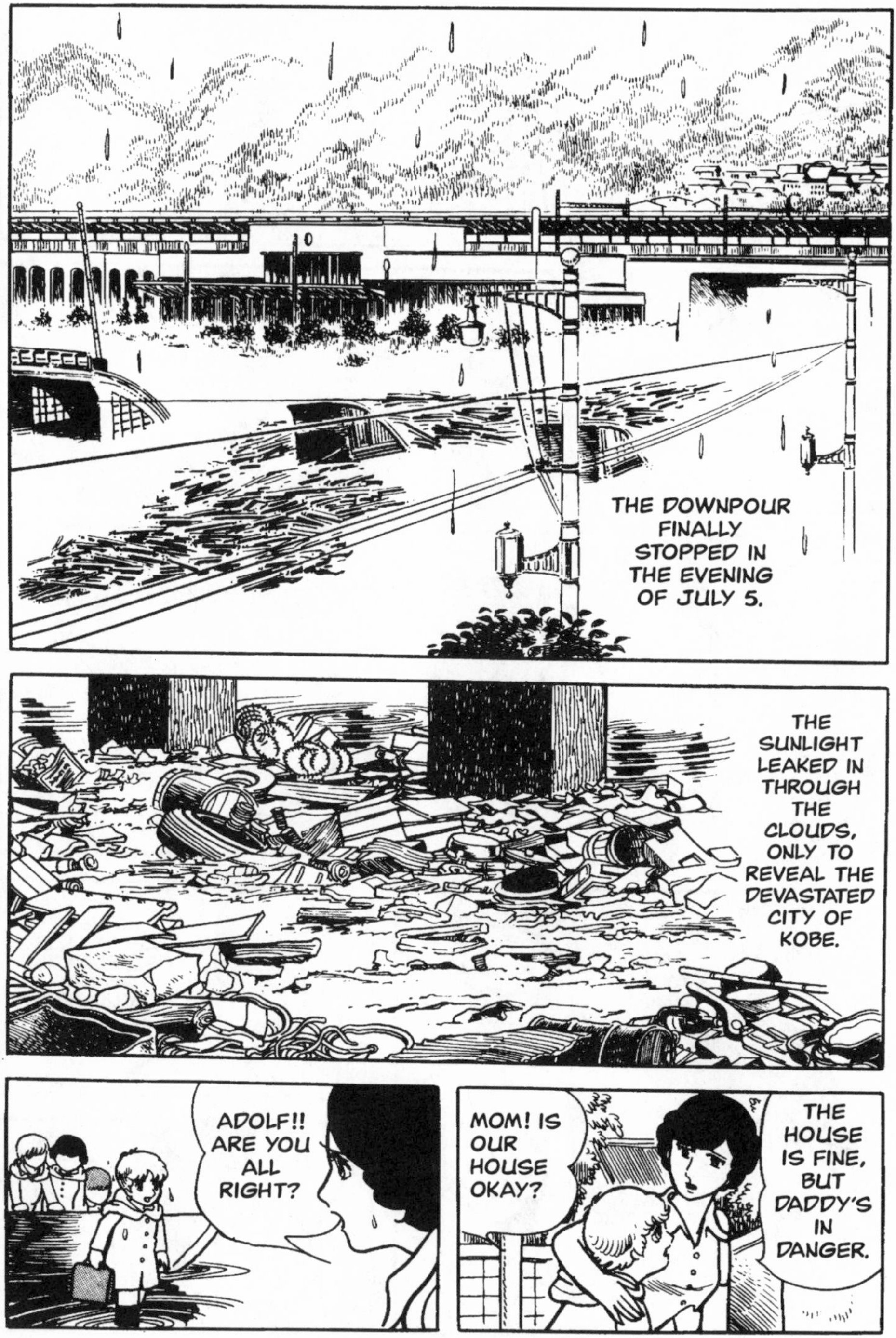
THE DOWNPOUR FINALLY STOPPED IN THE EVENING OF JULY 5.
THE SUNLIGHT LEAKED IN THROUGH THE CLOUDS, ONLY TO REVEAL THE DEVASTATED CITY OF KOBE.
ADOLF!! ARE YOU ALL RIGHT?
MOM! IS OUR HOUSE OKAY?
THE HOUSE IS FINE, BUT DADDY'S IN DANGER.

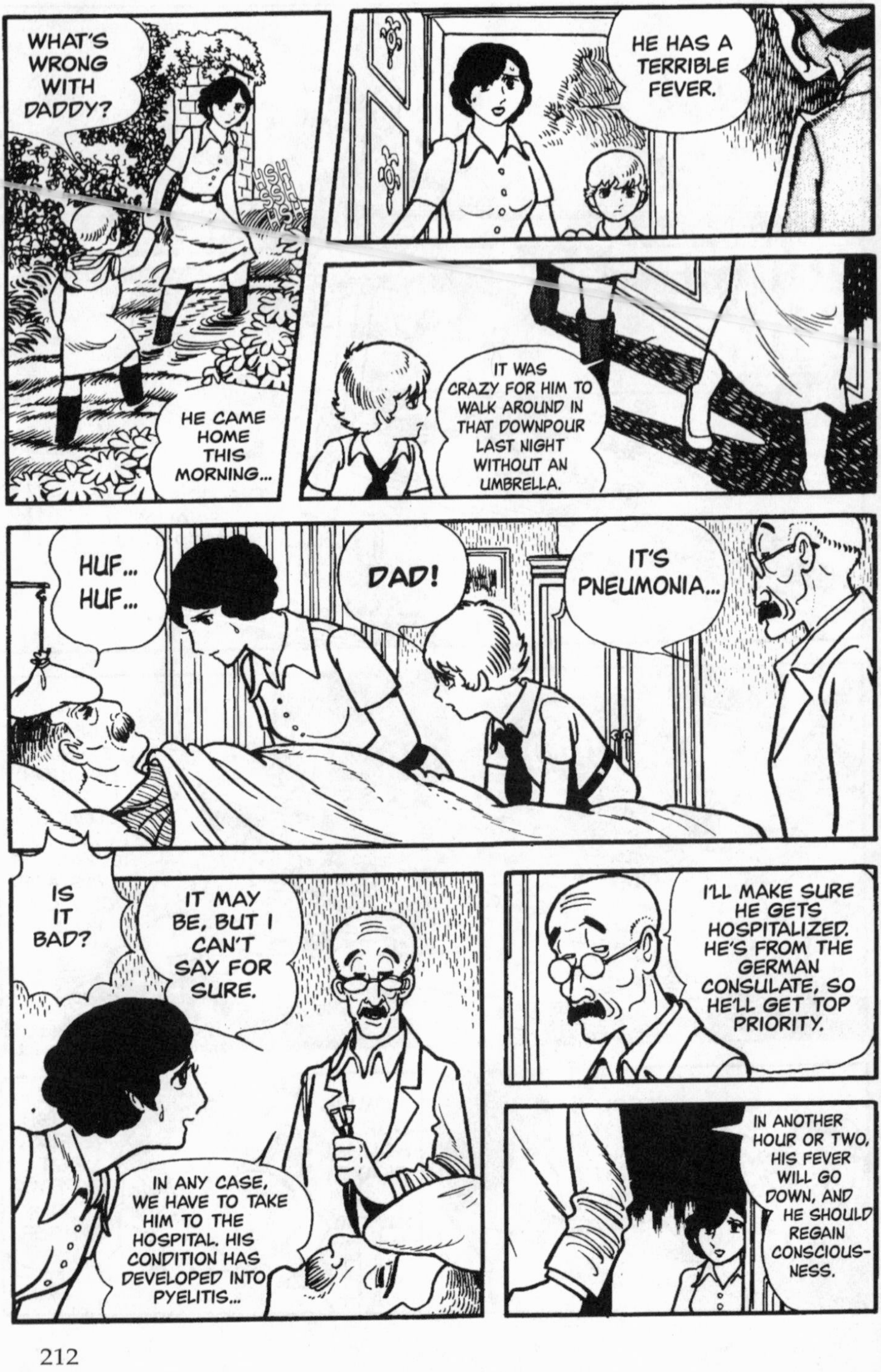
WHAT'S WRONG WITH DADDY?
HE CAME HOME THIS MORNING...
HE HAS A TERRIBLE FEVER.
IT WAS CRAZY FOR HIM TO WALK AROUND IN THAT DOWNPOUR LAST NIGHT WITHOUT AN UMBRELLA.
HUF... HUF...
DAD!
IT'S PNEUMONIA...
IS IT BAD?
IT MAY BE, BUT I CAN'T SAY FOR SURE.
IN ANY CASE, WE HAVE TO TAKE HIM TO THE HOSPITAL. HIS CONDITION HAS DEVELOPED INTO PYELITIS...
I'LL MAKE SURE HE GETS HOSPITALIZED. HE'S FROM THE GERMAN CONSULATE, SO HE'LL GET TOP PRIORITY.
IN ANOTHER HOUR OR TWO, HIS FEVER WILL GO DOWN, AND HE SHOULD REGAIN CONSCIOUS-NESS.

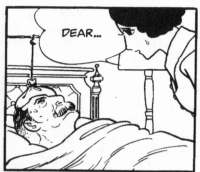

DEAR...

IS DADDY GOING TO BE OKAY?

UH. UH. UH. KINUKO...

KINUKO, DON'T COME HERE... DON'T!... I'M SORRY...

PLEASE, DEAR, PULL YOURSELF TOGETHER...

GERHARDT! DON'T LET HIM GET AWAY! FIND HIM...

KINUKO... PLEASE FORGIVE ME.

HE'S CALLING FOR KINUKO.

OH, HE'S JUST DELIRIOUS. HE'S IMAGINING THINGS.

WH-WHO'S THAT...?

IS THAT YOU, YUKIE?

HE'S BACK...

DAD, DO YOU RECOGNIZE ME?

ADOLF... DID THE SCHOOL... DID THE WATER GET YOU?

NO, NOTHING HAPPENED TO ME.

213

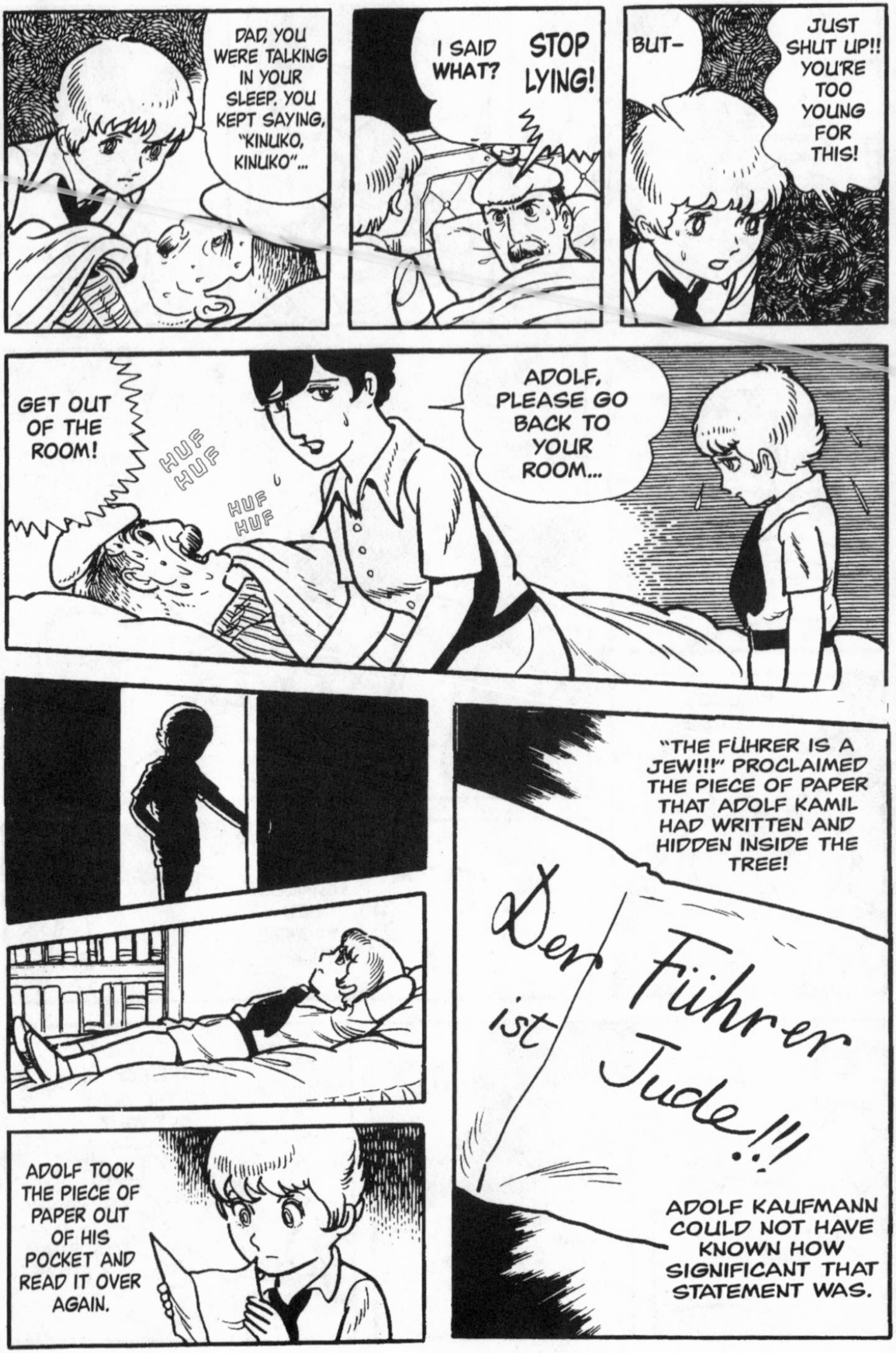
DAD, YOU WERE TALKING IN YOUR SLEEP. YOU KEPT SAYING, "KINUKO, KINUKO"...
I SAID WHAT?
STOP LYING!
BUT-
JUST SHUT UP!! YOU'RE TOO YOUNG FOR THIS!
GET OUT OF THE ROOM!
HUF HUF
HUF HUF
ADOLF, PLEASE GO BACK TO YOUR ROOM...
ADOLF TOOK THE PIECE OF PAPER OUT OF HIS POCKET AND READ IT OVER AGAIN.
"THE FÜHRER IS A JEW!!!" PROCLAIMED THE PIECE OF PAPER THAT ADOLF KAMIL HAD WRITTEN AND HIDDEN INSIDE THE TREE!
Der Führer ist Jude!!!
ADOLF KAUFMANN COULD NOT HAVE KNOWN HOW SIGNIFICANT THAT STATEMENT WAS.

HAS IT REALLY BEEN FIFTEEN YEARS SINCE I FELL OFF MY HORSE AT THE JAPAN UNIVERSITY RIDING EVENT? YOU WERE MY MENTOR'S DAUGHTER, AND YOU TOOK SUCH GOOD CARE OF ME...

YES, AND THAT ACCIDENT LED TO OUR MARRIAGE.

THAT'S RIGHT... BEING WITH YOU HERE LIKE THIS NOW MAKES THAT TIME SEEM LIKE A BEAUTIFUL DREAM...

I NEVER IMAGINED I WOULD MARRY A GERMAN. MY PARENTS WERE AGAINST IT, TOO...

BUT I LOVED YOU...

DO YOU REGRET MARRYING A GERMAN?

NO!

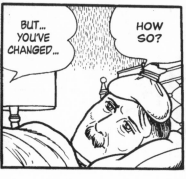

BUT... YOU'VE CHANGED...

HOW SO?

EVER SINCE YOU JOINED THE NAZI PARTY...

YOU HAVEN'T BEEN THE SAME.

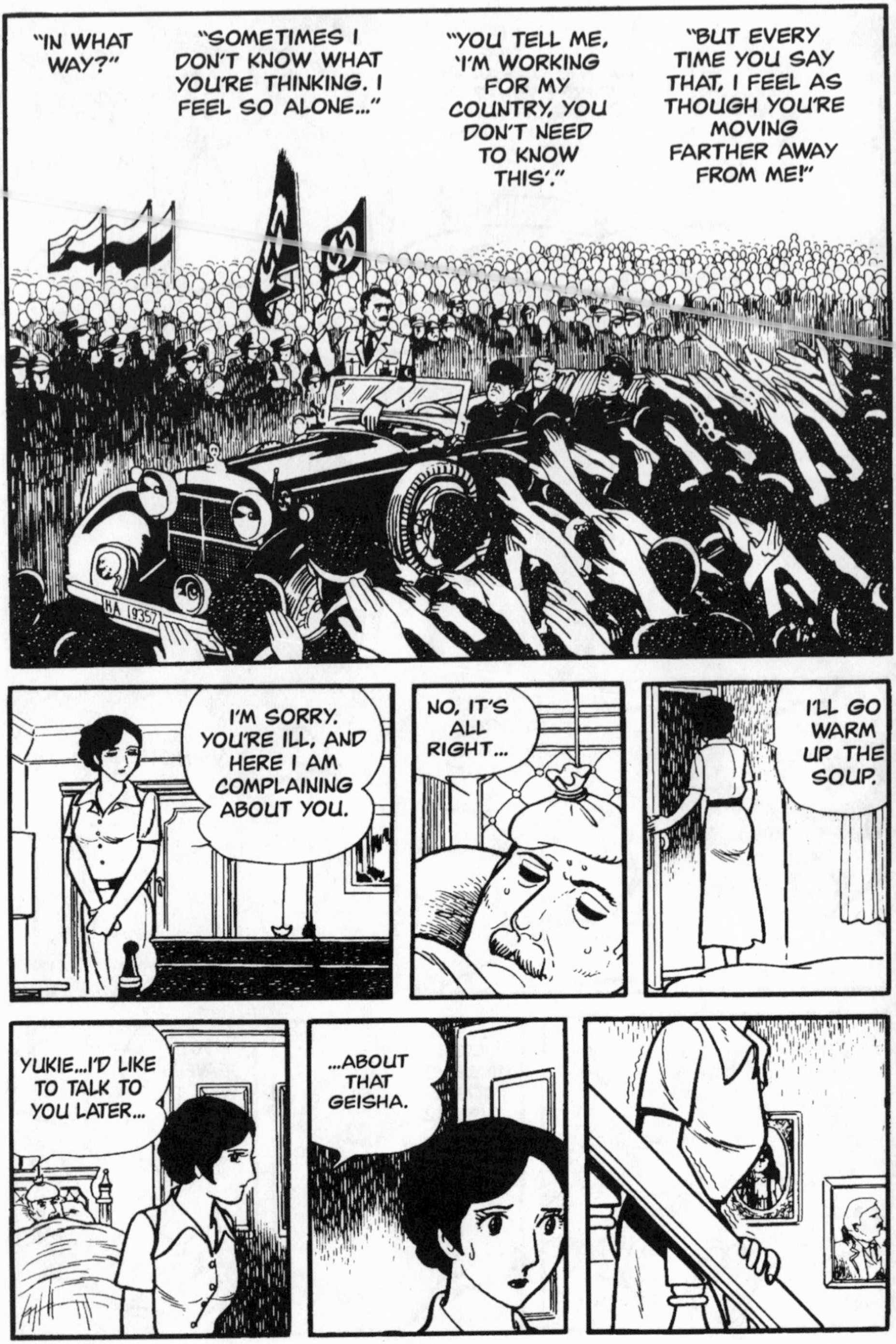
"IN WHAT WAY?"
"SOMETIMES I DON'T KNOW WHAT YOU'RE THINKING. I FEEL SO ALONE..."
"YOU TELL ME, 'I'M WORKING FOR MY COUNTRY, YOU DON'T NEED TO KNOW THIS'."
"BUT EVERY TIME YOU SAY THAT, I FEEL AS THOUGH YOU'RE MOVING FARTHER AWAY FROM ME!"
HA 19357
I'M SORRY. YOU'RE ILL, AND HERE I AM COMPLAINING ABOUT YOU.
NO, IT'S ALL RIGHT...
I'LL GO WARM UP THE SOUP.
YUKIE...I'D LIKE TO TALK TO YOU LATER...
...ABOUT THAT GEISHA.

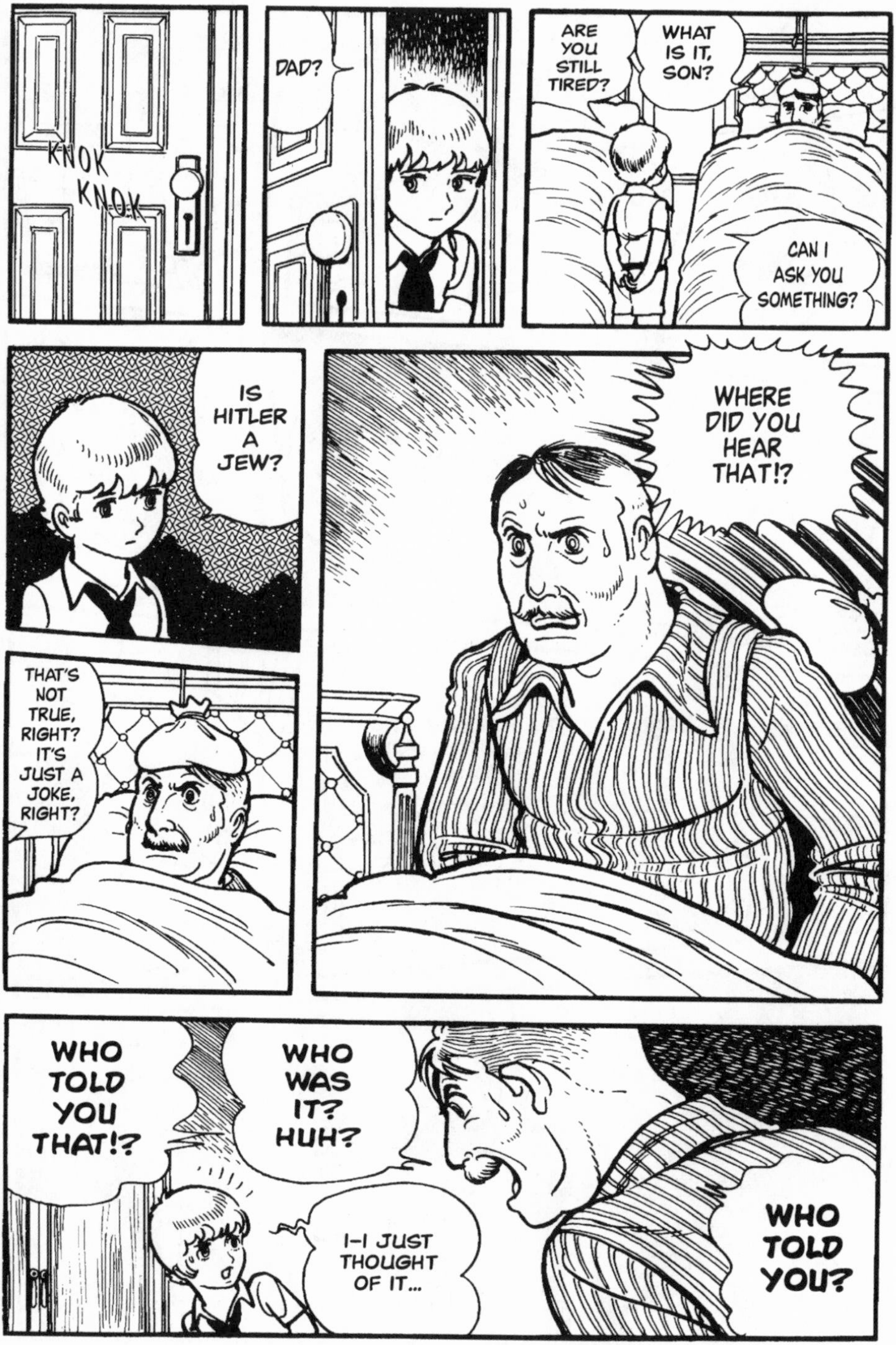
KNOK
KNOK
DAD?
ARE YOU STILL TIRED?
WHAT IS IT, SON?
CAN I ASK YOU SOMETHING?
IS HITLER A JEW?
THAT'S NOT TRUE, RIGHT? IT'S JUST A JOKE, RIGHT?
WHERE DID YOU HEAR THAT!?
WHO TOLD YOU THAT!?
WHO WAS IT? HUH?
I-I JUST THOUGHT OF IT...
WHO TOLD YOU?

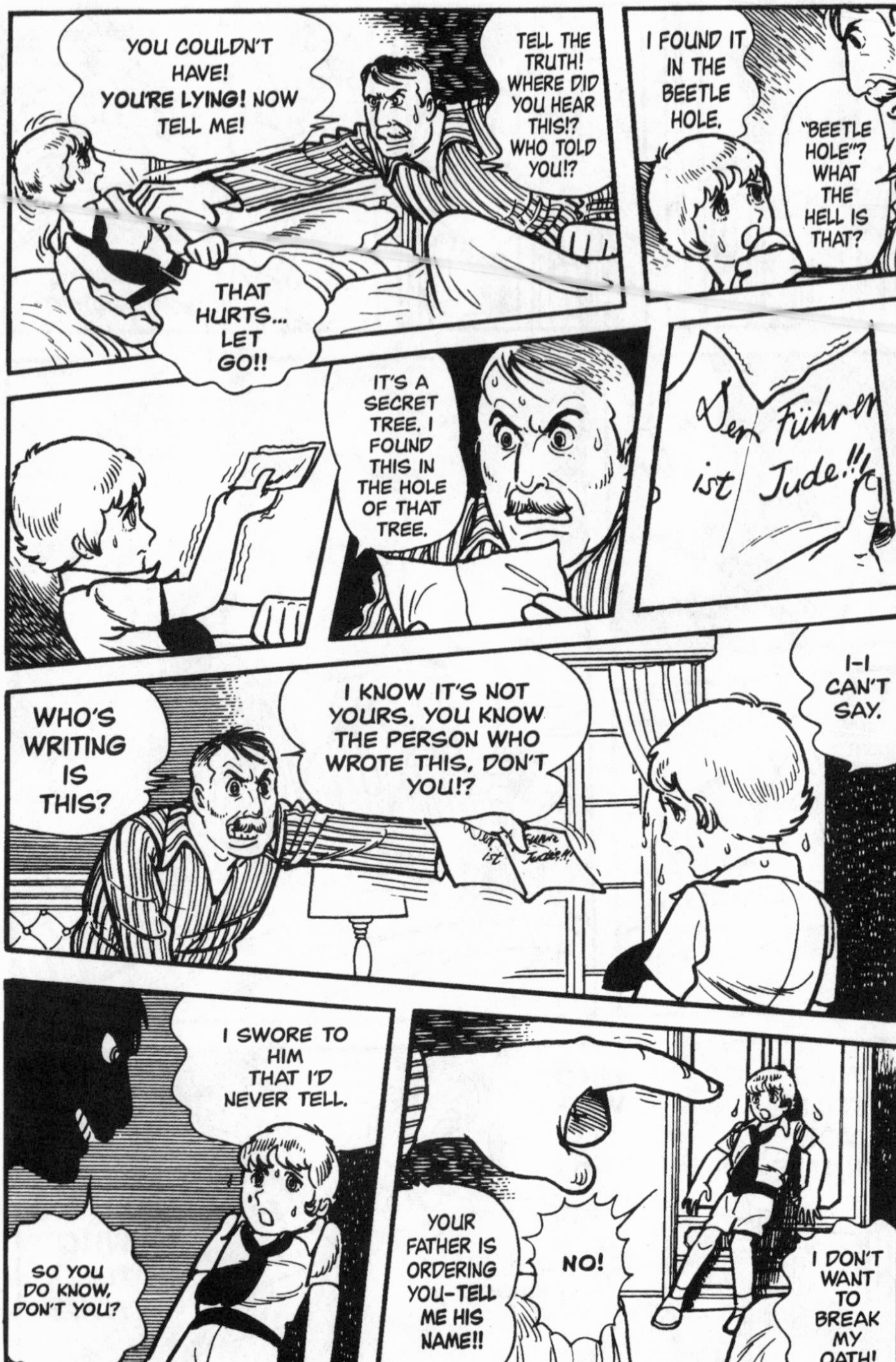
YOU COULDN'T HAVE! YOU'RE LYING! NOW TELL ME!
TELL THE TRUTH! WHERE DID YOU HEAR THIS!? WHO TOLD YOU!?
THAT HURTS... LET GO!!
I FOUND IT IN THE BEETLE HOLE.
"BEETLE HOLE"? WHAT THE HELL IS THAT?
IT'S A SECRET TREE. I FOUND THIS IN THE HOLE OF THAT TREE.
Der Führer ist Jude!!
WHO'S WRITING IS THIS?
I KNOW IT'S NOT YOURS. YOU KNOW THE PERSON WHO WROTE THIS, DON'T YOU!?
I-I CAN'T SAY.
I SWORE TO HIM THAT I'D NEVER TELL.
SO YOU DO KNOW, DON'T YOU?
YOUR FATHER IS ORDERING YOU-TELL ME HIS NAME!!
NO!
I DON'T WANT TO BREAK MY OATH!

ARE YOU GOING TO DISOBEY YOUR FATHER? IF YOU DON'T TELL ME, I'LL HURT YOU!!
NO!! I'D RATHER DIE!!
SMAKK
SMAKK
HUNH... KOFF...
KOFF... KOFF... KOFF...
KOFF
DAD!
KOFF KOFF KOFF KOFF
DEAR!!

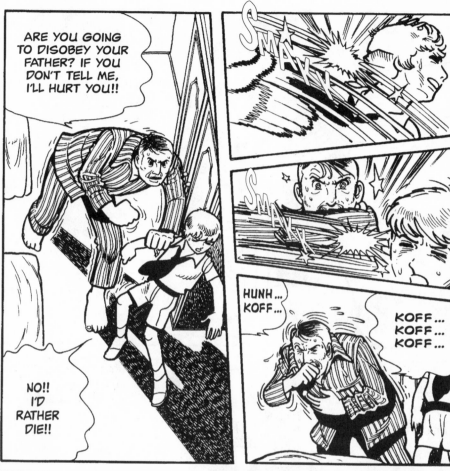

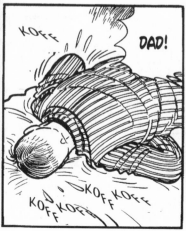

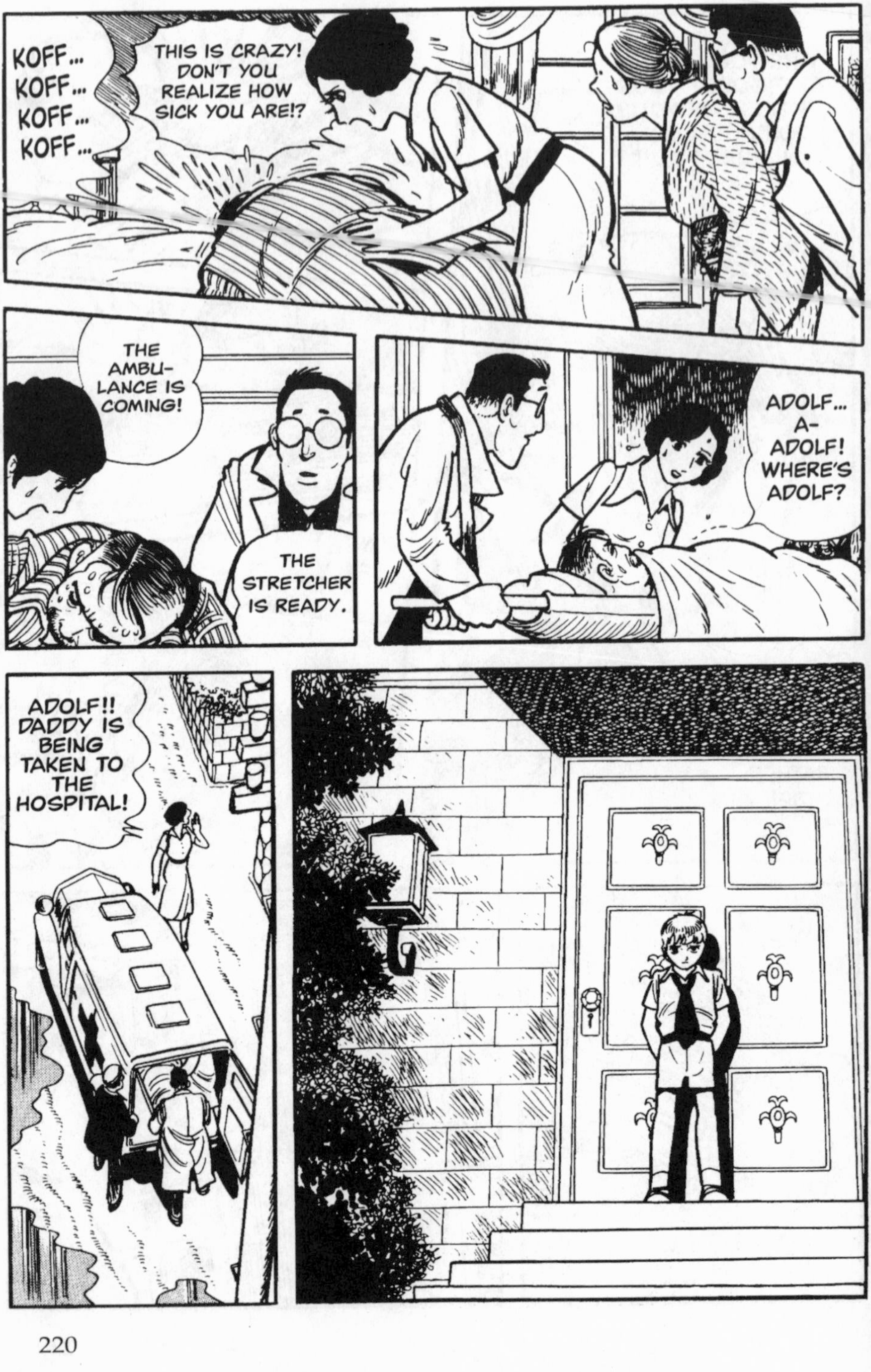
KOFF... KOFF... KOFF... KOFF...
THIS IS CRAZY! DON'T YOU REALIZE HOW SICK YOU ARE!?
THE AMBU-LANCE IS COMING!
THE STRETCHER IS READY.
ADOLF... A-ADOLF! WHERE'S ADOLF?
ADOLF!! DADDY IS BEING TAKEN TO THE HOSPITAL!

Adolf

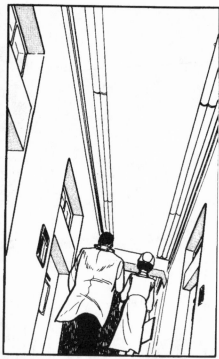

DRRIP

DRRIP
DRRIP

TO BE HONEST... HE'S IN CRITICAL CONDITION.

IT WILL ALL DEPEND ON HOW HE DOES TONIGHT... PERHAPS YOU SHOULD CONTACT HIS RELATIVES.

WHATEVER TRAUMA HE WENT THROUGH BEFORE COMING HERE HAS MADE HIS CONDITION MUCH WORSE.

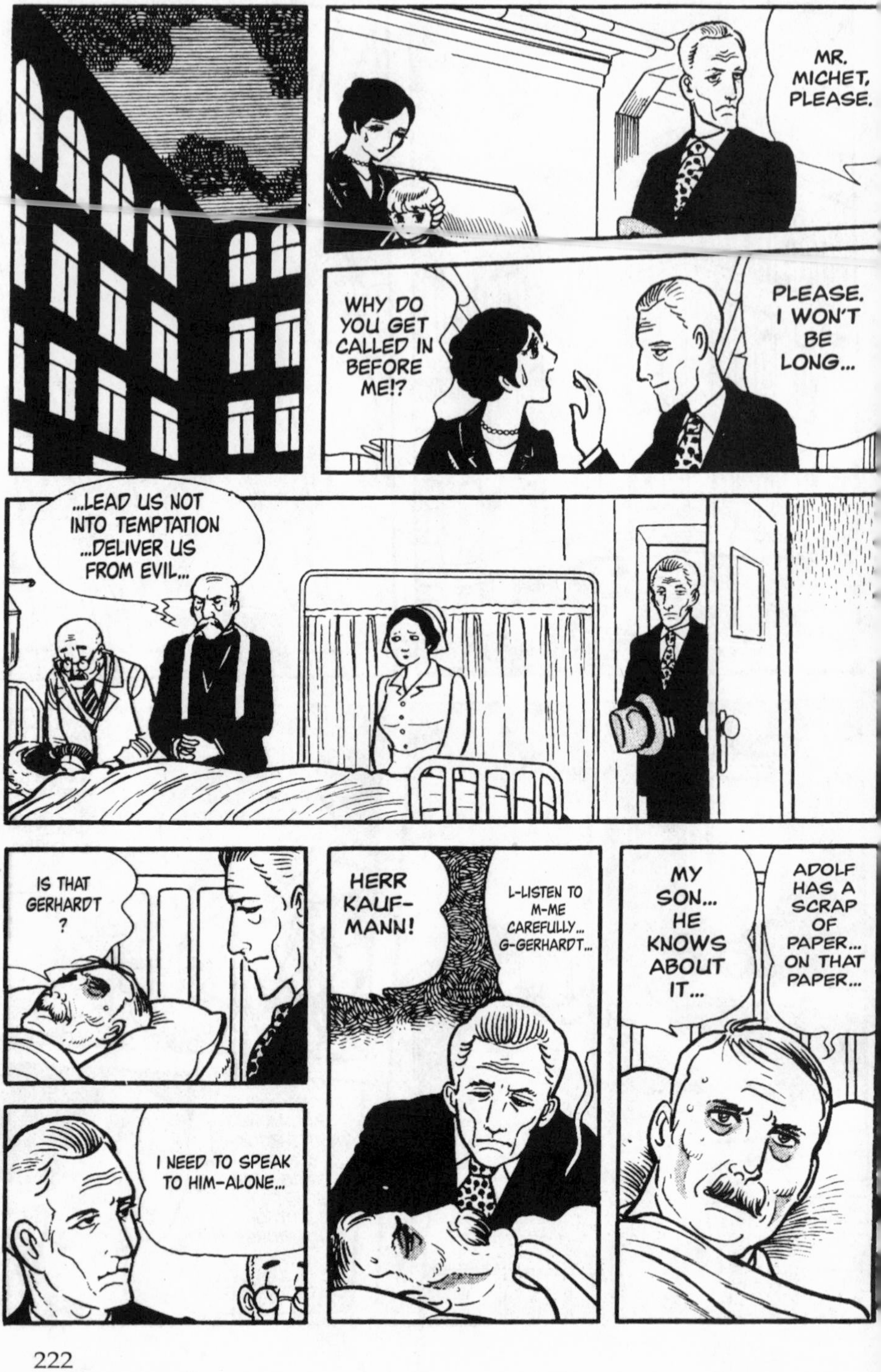
MR. MICHET, PLEASE.
WHY DO YOU GET CALLED IN BEFORE ME!?
PLEASE. I WON'T BE LONG...
...LEAD US NOT INTO TEMPTATION ...DELIVER US FROM EVIL...
IS THAT GERHARDT ?
I NEED TO SPEAK TO HIM–ALONE...
HERR KAUF-MANN!
L-LISTEN TO M-ME CAREFULLY... G-GERHARDT...
MY SON... HE KNOWS ABOUT IT...
ADOLF HAS A SCRAP OF PAPER... ON THAT PAPER...

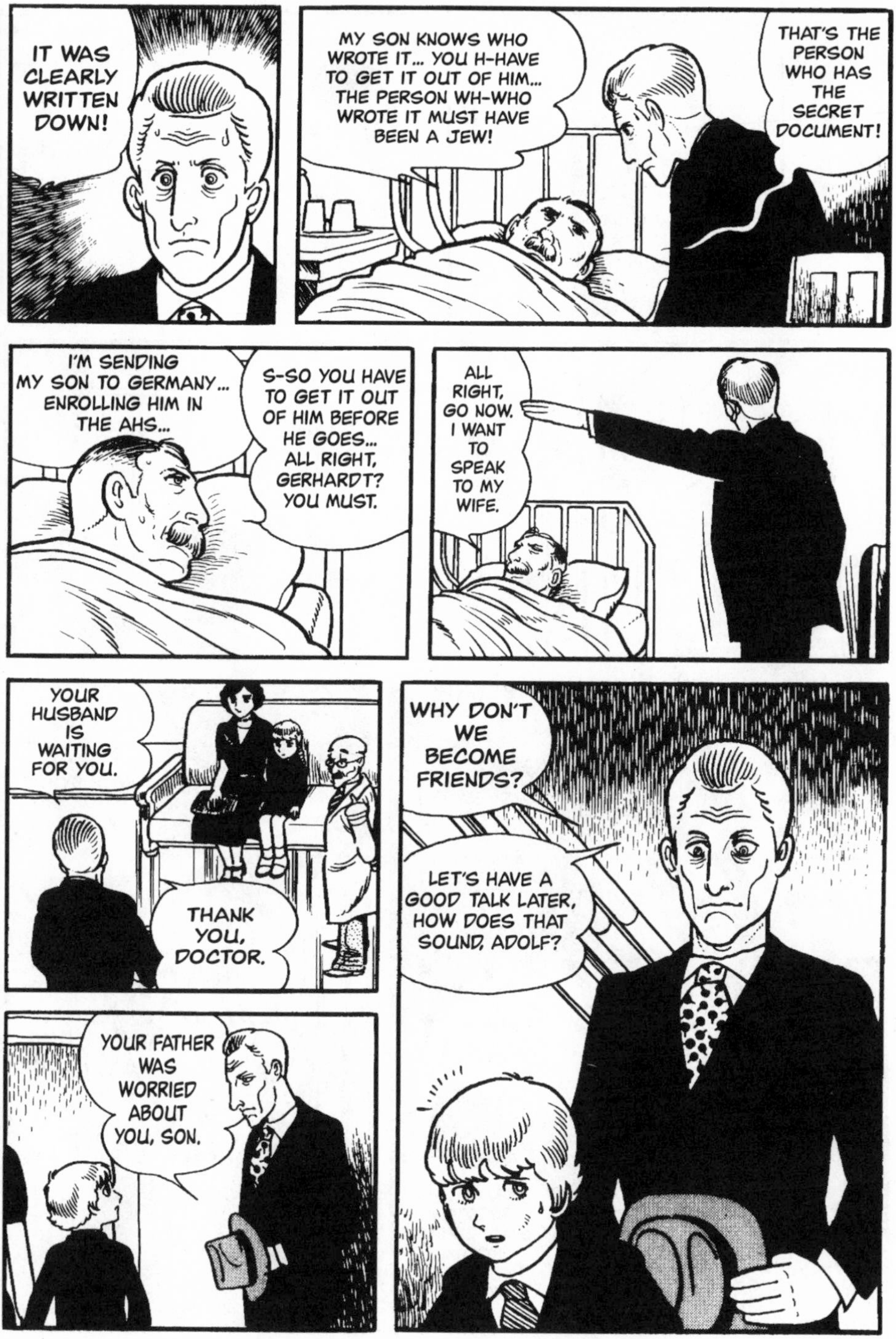
IT WAS CLEARLY WRITTEN DOWN!
MY SON KNOWS WHO WROTE IT... YOU H-HAVE TO GET IT OUT OF HIM... THE PERSON WH-WHO WROTE IT MUST HAVE BEEN A JEW!
THAT'S THE PERSON WHO HAS THE SECRET DOCUMENT!
I'M SENDING MY SON TO GERMANY... ENROLLING HIM IN THE AHS...
S-SO YOU HAVE TO GET IT OUT OF HIM BEFORE HE GOES... ALL RIGHT, GERHARDT? YOU MUST.
ALL RIGHT, GO NOW. I WANT TO SPEAK TO MY WIFE.
YOUR HUSBAND IS WAITING FOR YOU.
THANK YOU, DOCTOR.
YOUR FATHER WAS WORRIED ABOUT YOU, SON.
WHY DON'T WE BECOME FRIENDS?
LET'S HAVE A GOOD TALK LATER, HOW DOES THAT SOUND, ADOLF?

Adolf

COME IN PLEASE, MRS. KAUFMANN.

YOU WEREN'T ALLOWED VISITORS, SO I THOUGHT WE MIGHT NEVER GET TO SEE EACH OTHER AGAIN...

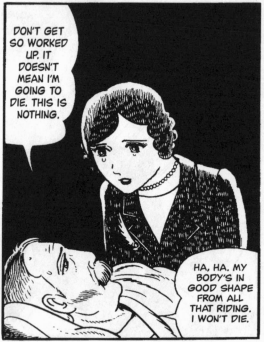

DON'T GET SO WORKED UP. IT DOESN'T MEAN I'M GOING TO DIE. THIS IS NOTHING.

HA, HA. MY BODY'S IN GOOD SHAPE FROM ALL THAT RIDING. I WON'T DIE.

ADOLF, DON'T LOOK SO SOMBER. WHY DON'T WE MAKE UP, HUH?

COME HERE.

COME AND HOLD YOUR FATHER'S HAND.

ADOLF WAS TERRIFIED OF HIS FATHER.

EVEN NOW, AS HE HELD HIS HAND...

HE COULDN'T HELP BUT WONDER WHETHER HIS FATHER WOULD STRIKE HIM WITH THE OTHER.... HE ONLY WANTED TO RUN AWAY FROM HIM.

ADOLF... BECOME A PROUD MAN... PROMISE ME THAT MUCH.

YOU'RE A GER-MAN!

GERMANS HAVE A PROUD GERMAN SOUL. DON'T YOU FORGET THAT.

I MAY LOOK TERRIFYING TO YOU...

BUT THAT'S BECAUSE I HAD TO SACRIFICE MYSELF FOR MY COUNTRY. THAT'S HOW LOYALTY WORKS...

.....
.....

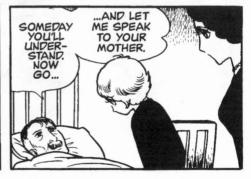

SOMEDAY YOU'LL UNDER-STAND. NOW GO...

...AND LET ME SPEAK TO YOUR MOTHER.

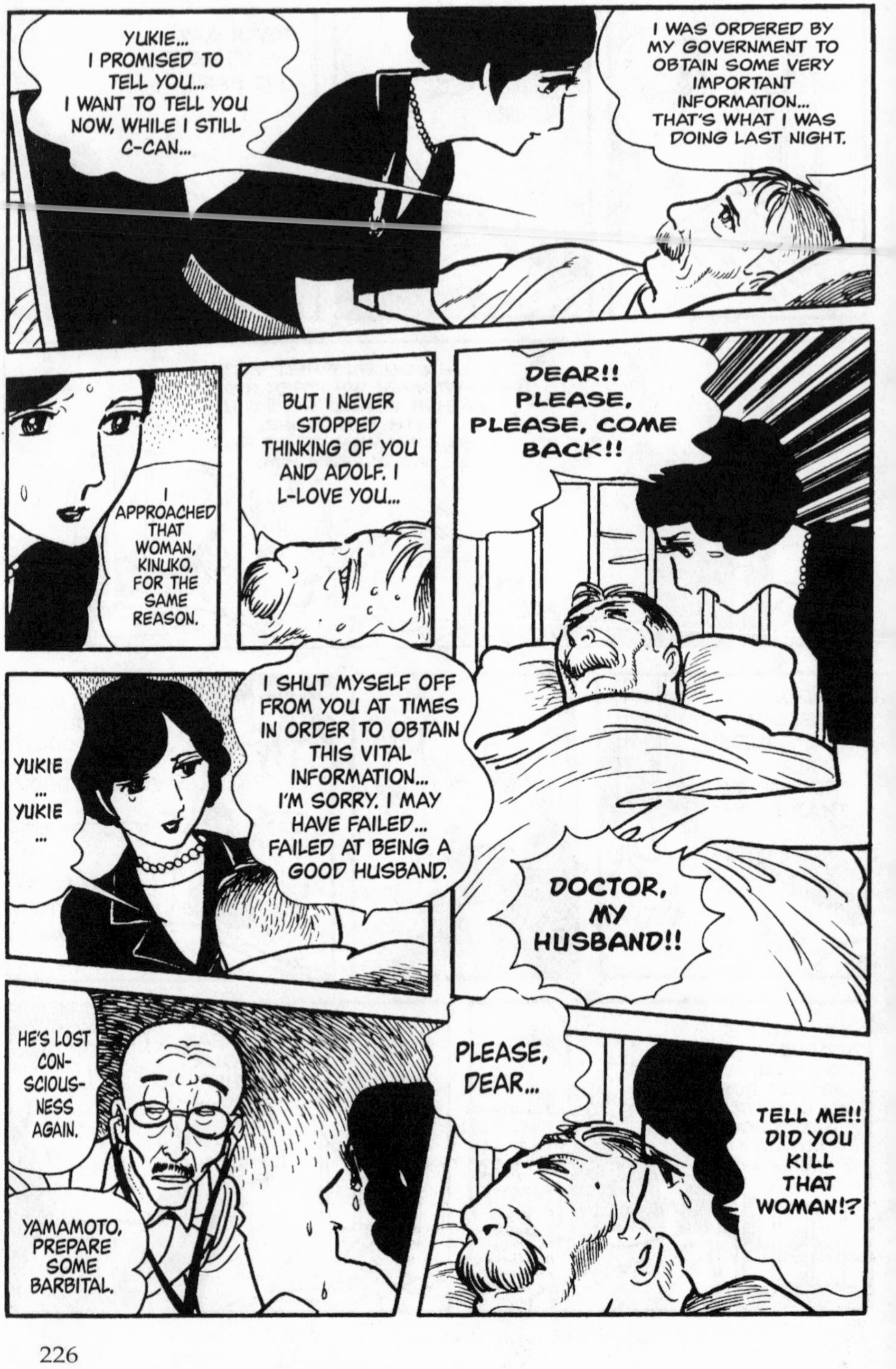
YUKIE... I PROMISED TO TELL YOU... I WANT TO TELL YOU NOW, WHILE I STILL C-CAN...
I WAS ORDERED BY MY GOVERNMENT TO OBTAIN SOME VERY IMPORTANT INFORMATION... THAT'S WHAT I WAS DOING LAST NIGHT.
I APPROACHED THAT WOMAN, KINUKO, FOR THE SAME REASON.
BUT I NEVER STOPPED THINKING OF YOU AND ADOLF. I L-LOVE YOU...
YUKIE ... YUKIE ...
I SHUT MYSELF OFF FROM YOU AT TIMES IN ORDER TO OBTAIN THIS VITAL INFORMATION... I'M SORRY. I MAY HAVE FAILED... FAILED AT BEING A GOOD HUSBAND.
DEAR!! PLEASE, PLEASE, COME BACK!!
DOCTOR, MY HUSBAND!!
HE'S LOST CONSCIOUSNESS AGAIN.
YAMAMOTO, PREPARE SOME BARBITAL.
PLEASE, DEAR...
TELL ME!! DID YOU KILL THAT WOMAN!?

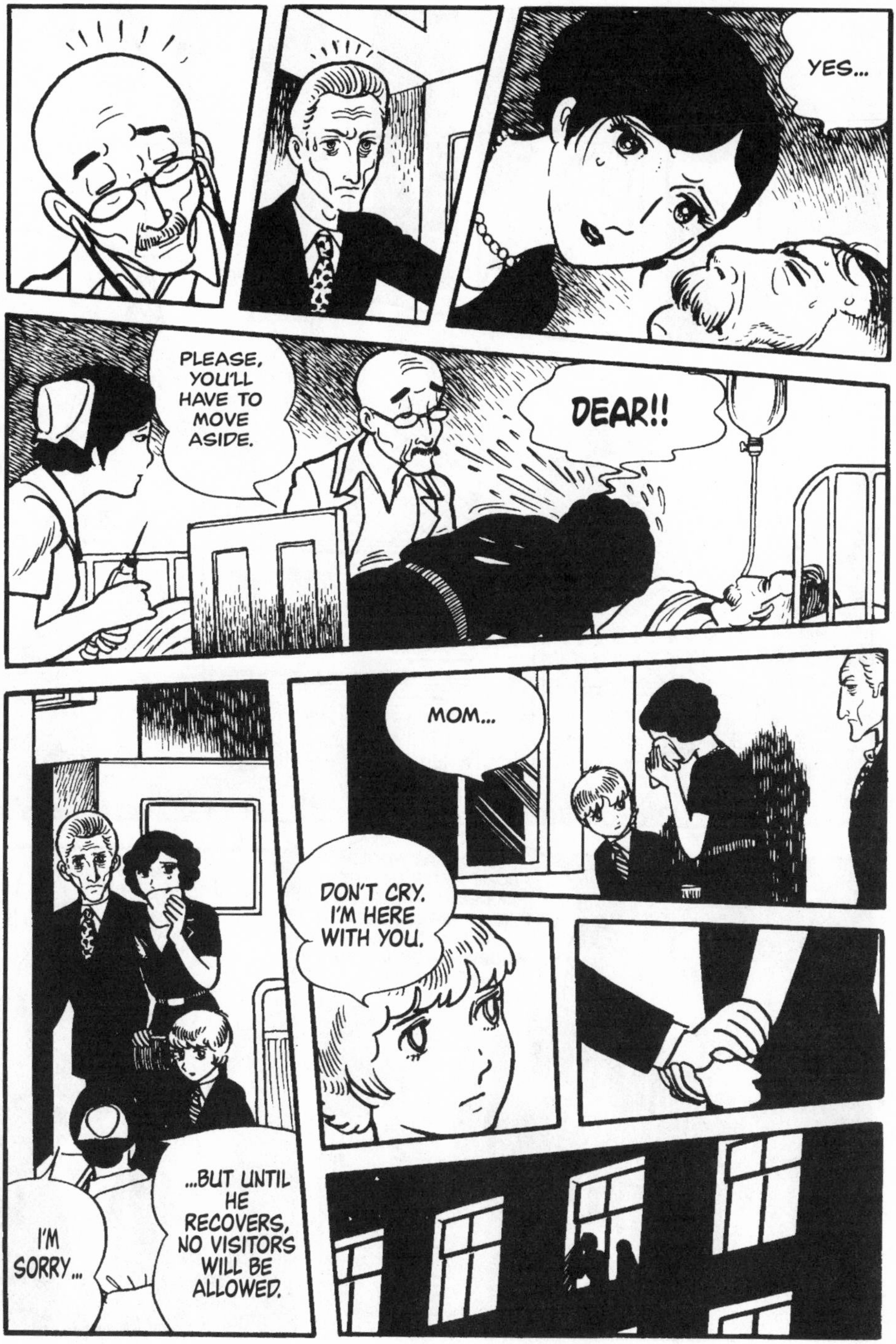
YES...
PLEASE, YOU'LL HAVE TO MOVE ASIDE.
DEAR!!
MOM...
DON'T CRY. I'M HERE WITH YOU.
I'M SORRY...
...BUT UNTIL HE RECOVERS, NO VISITORS WILL BE ALLOWED.

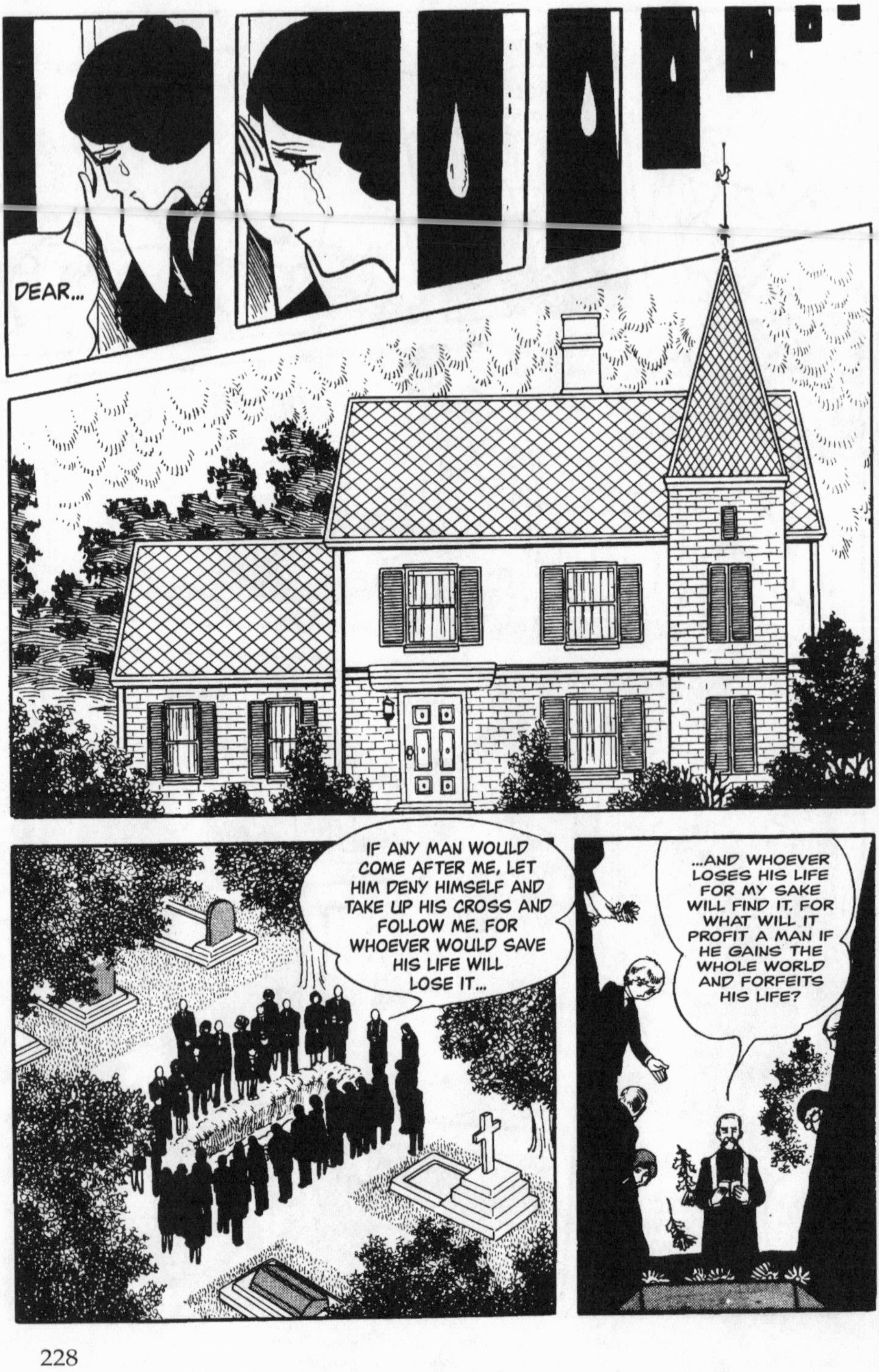
DEAR...
IF ANY MAN WOULD COME AFTER ME, LET HIM DENY HIMSELF AND TAKE UP HIS CROSS AND FOLLOW ME. FOR WHOEVER WOULD SAVE HIS LIFE WILL LOSE IT...
...AND WHOEVER LOSES HIS LIFE FOR MY SAKE WILL FIND IT. FOR WHAT WILL IT PROFIT A MAN IF HE GAINS THE WHOLE WORLD AND FORFEITS HIS LIFE?

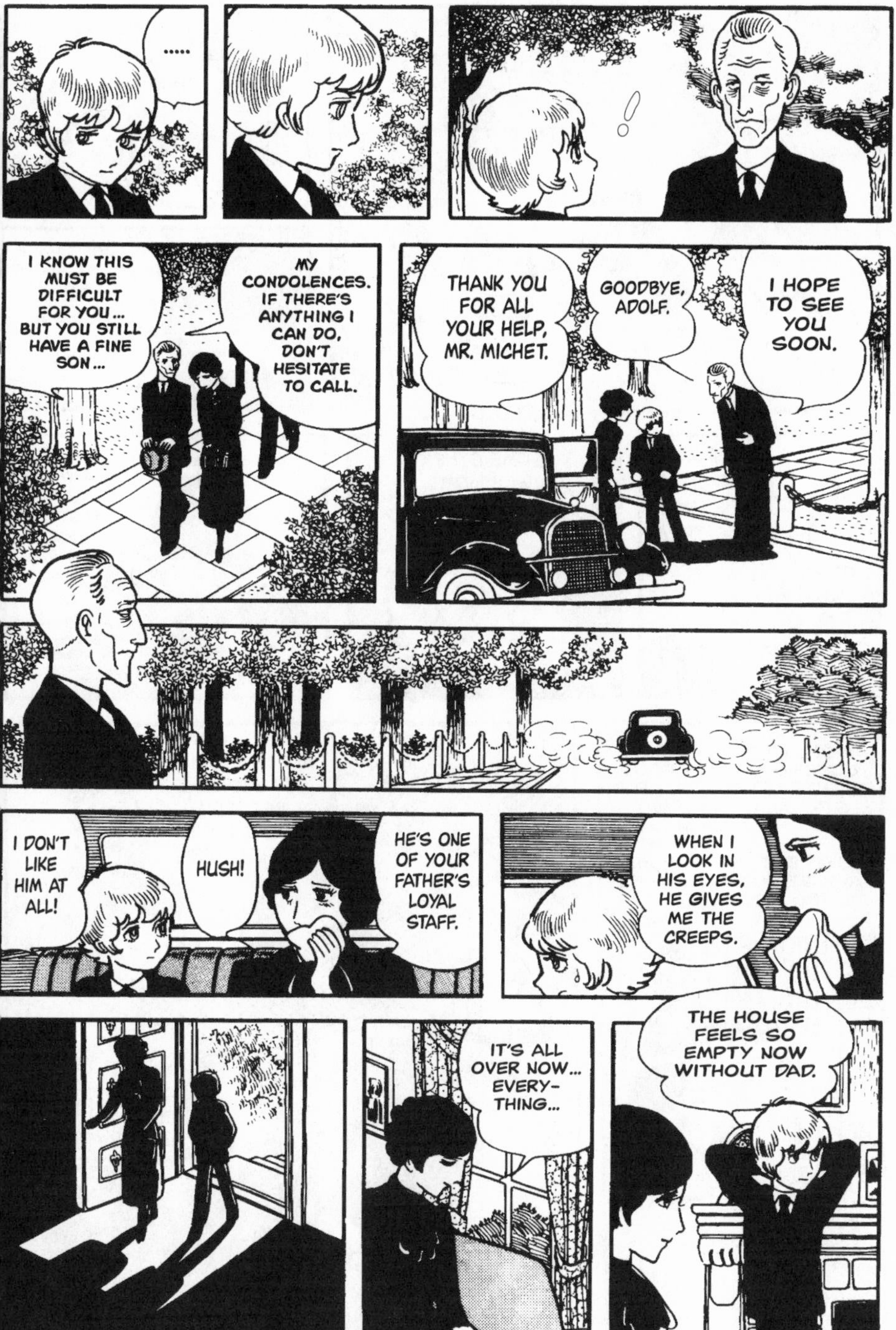
......
!
I KNOW THIS MUST BE DIFFICULT FOR YOU... BUT YOU STILL HAVE A FINE SON...
MY CONDOLENCES. IF THERE'S ANYTHING I CAN DO, DON'T HESITATE TO CALL.
THANK YOU FOR ALL YOUR HELP, MR. MICHET.
GOODBYE, ADOLF.
I HOPE TO SEE YOU SOON.
I DON'T LIKE HIM AT ALL!
HUSH!
HE'S ONE OF YOUR FATHER'S LOYAL STAFF.
WHEN I LOOK IN HIS EYES, HE GIVES ME THE CREEPS.
IT'S ALL OVER NOW... EVERY-THING...
THE HOUSE FEELS SO EMPTY NOW WITHOUT DAD.

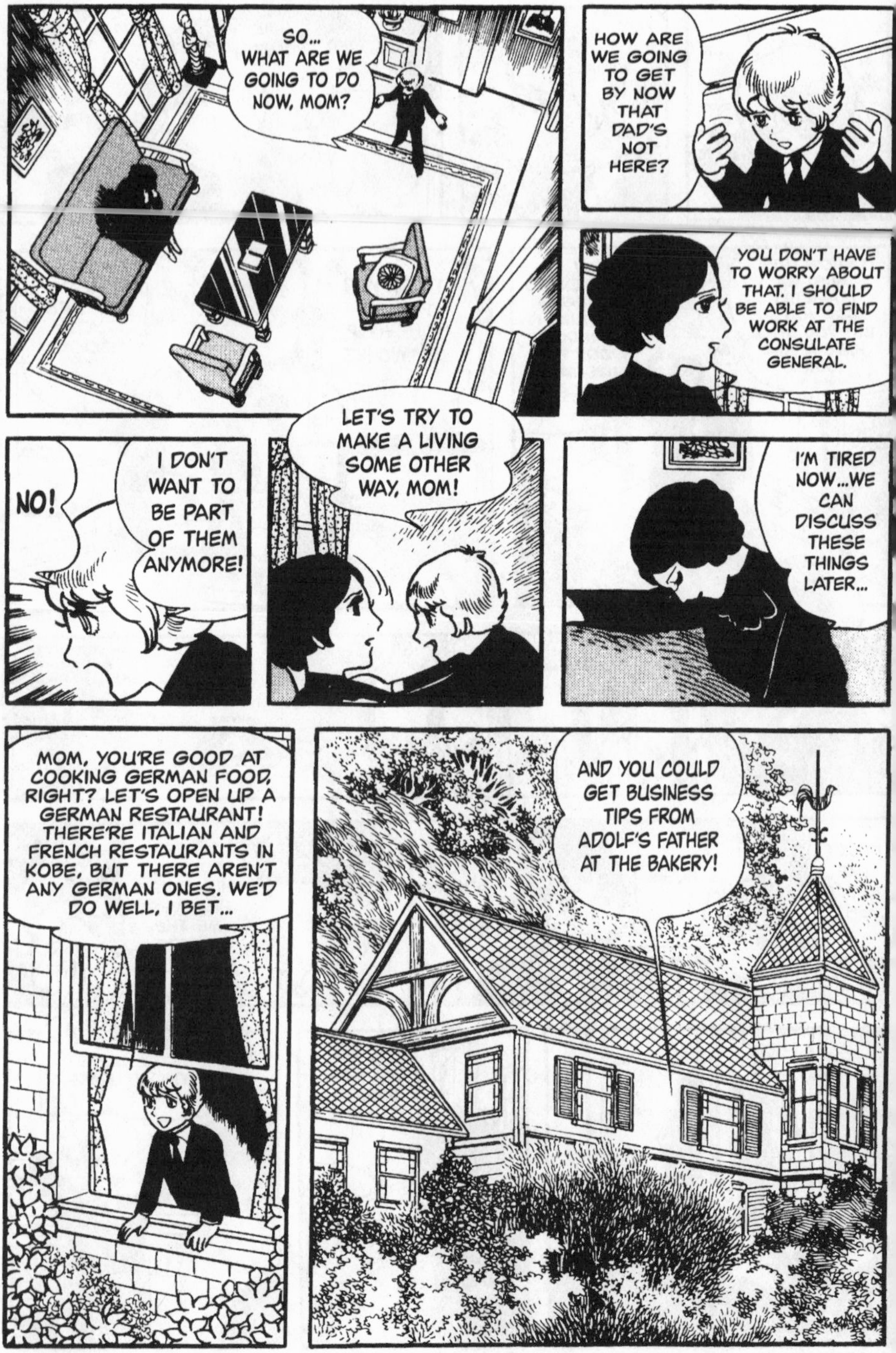
SO... WHAT ARE WE GOING TO DO NOW, MOM?
HOW ARE WE GOING TO GET BY NOW THAT DAD'S NOT HERE?
YOU DON'T HAVE TO WORRY ABOUT THAT. I SHOULD BE ABLE TO FIND WORK AT THE CONSULATE GENERAL.
NO!
I DON'T WANT TO BE PART OF THEM ANYMORE!
LET'S TRY TO MAKE A LIVING SOME OTHER WAY, MOM!
I'M TIRED NOW...WE CAN DISCUSS THESE THINGS LATER...
MOM, YOU'RE GOOD AT COOKING GERMAN FOOD, RIGHT? LET'S OPEN UP A GERMAN RESTAURANT! THERE'RE ITALIAN AND FRENCH RESTAURANTS IN KOBE, BUT THERE AREN'T ANY GERMAN ONES. WE'D DO WELL, I BET...
AND YOU COULD GET BUSINESS TIPS FROM ADOLF'S FATHER AT THE BAKERY!

CHAPTER
SIX

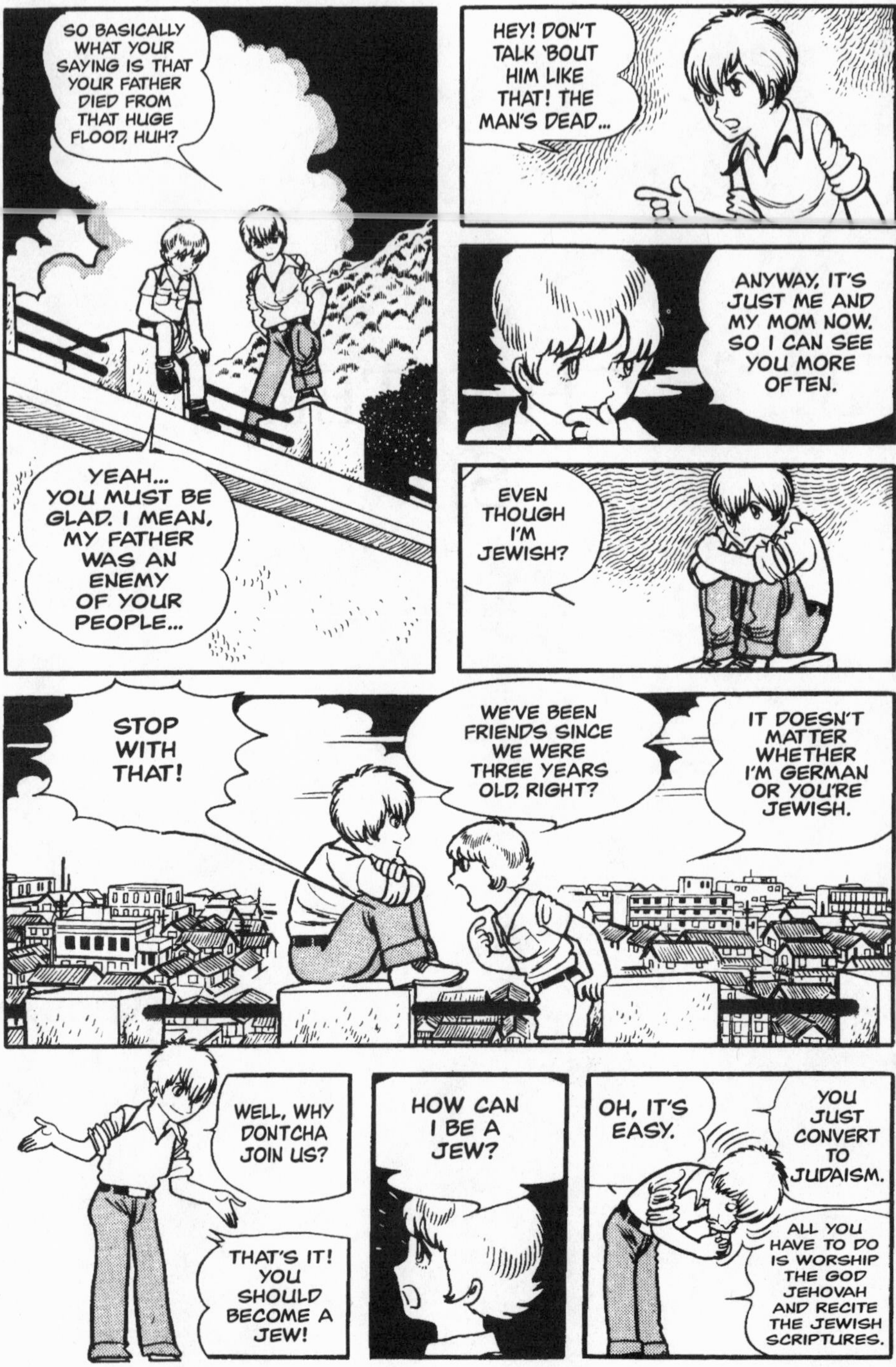
SO BASICALLY WHAT YOUR SAYING IS THAT YOUR FATHER DIED FROM THAT HUGE FLOOD, HUH?
YEAH... YOU MUST BE GLAD. I MEAN, MY FATHER WAS AN ENEMY OF YOUR PEOPLE...
HEY! DON'T TALK 'BOUT HIM LIKE THAT! THE MAN'S DEAD...
ANYWAY, IT'S JUST ME AND MY MOM NOW. SO I CAN SEE YOU MORE OFTEN.
EVEN THOUGH I'M JEWISH?
STOP WITH THAT!
WE'VE BEEN FRIENDS SINCE WE WERE THREE YEARS OLD, RIGHT?
IT DOESN'T MATTER WHETHER I'M GERMAN OR YOU'RE JEWISH.
WELL, WHY DONTCHA JOIN US?
THAT'S IT! YOU SHOULD BECOME A JEW!
HOW CAN I BE A JEW?
OH, IT'S EASY.
YOU JUST CONVERT TO JUDAISM.
ALL YOU HAVE TO DO IS WORSHIP THE GOD JEHOVAH AND RECITE THE JEWISH SCRIPTURES.

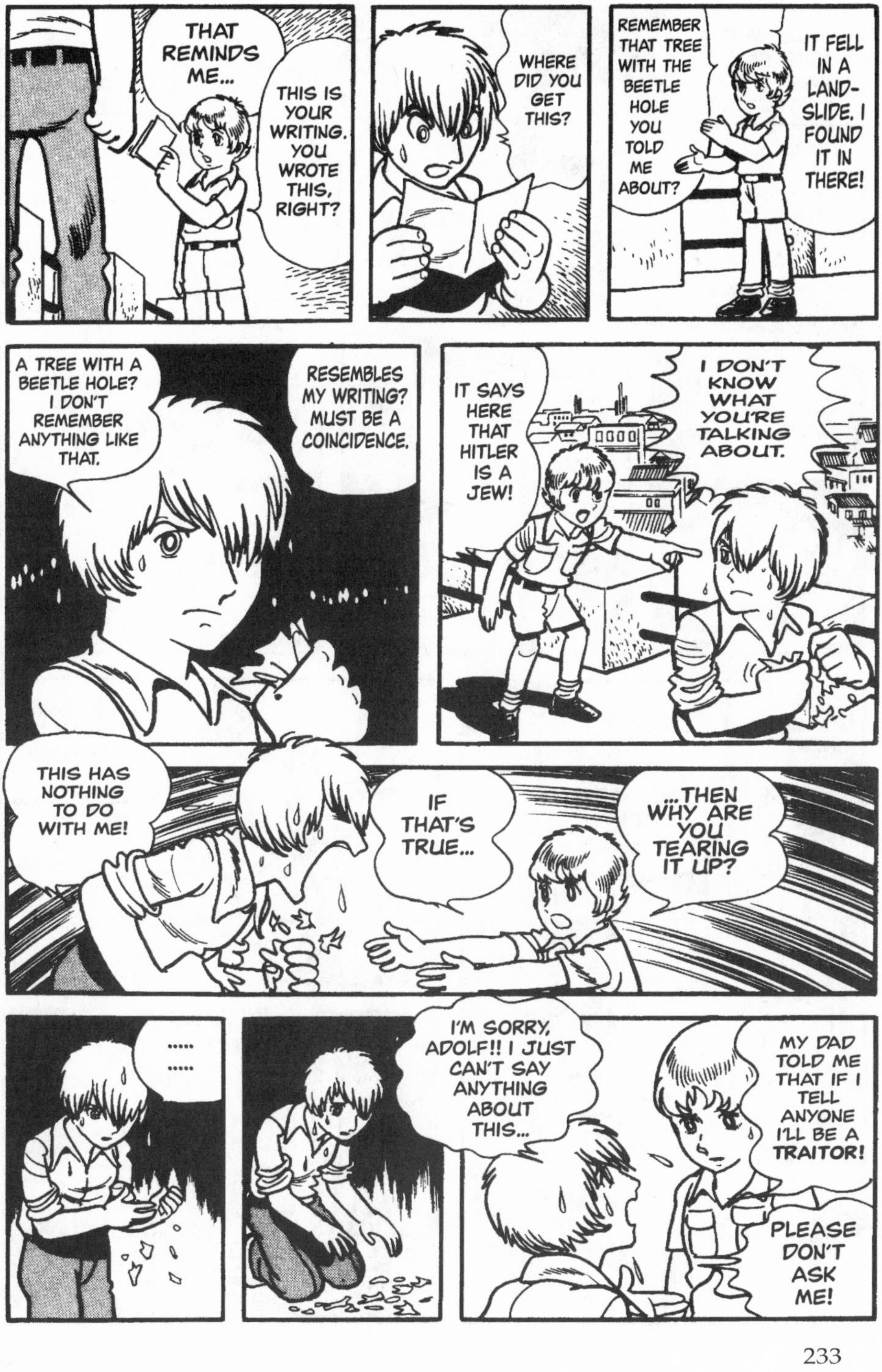
THAT REMINDS ME...
THIS IS YOUR WRITING. YOU WROTE THIS, RIGHT?
WHERE DID YOU GET THIS?
REMEMBER THAT TREE WITH THE BEETLE HOLE YOU TOLD ME ABOUT?
IT FELL IN A LAND-SLIDE. I FOUND IT IN THERE!
A TREE WITH A BEETLE HOLE? I DON'T REMEMBER ANYTHING LIKE THAT.
RESEMBLES MY WRITING? MUST BE A COINCIDENCE.
IT SAYS HERE THAT HITLER IS A JEW!
I DON'T KNOW WHAT YOU'RE TALKING ABOUT.
THIS HAS NOTHING TO DO WITH ME!
IF THAT'S TRUE...
...THEN WHY ARE YOU TEARING IT UP?
......
......
I'M SORRY, ADOLF!! I JUST CAN'T SAY ANYTHING ABOUT THIS...
MY DAD TOLD ME THAT IF I TELL ANYONE I'LL BE A TRAITOR!
PLEASE DON'T ASK ME!

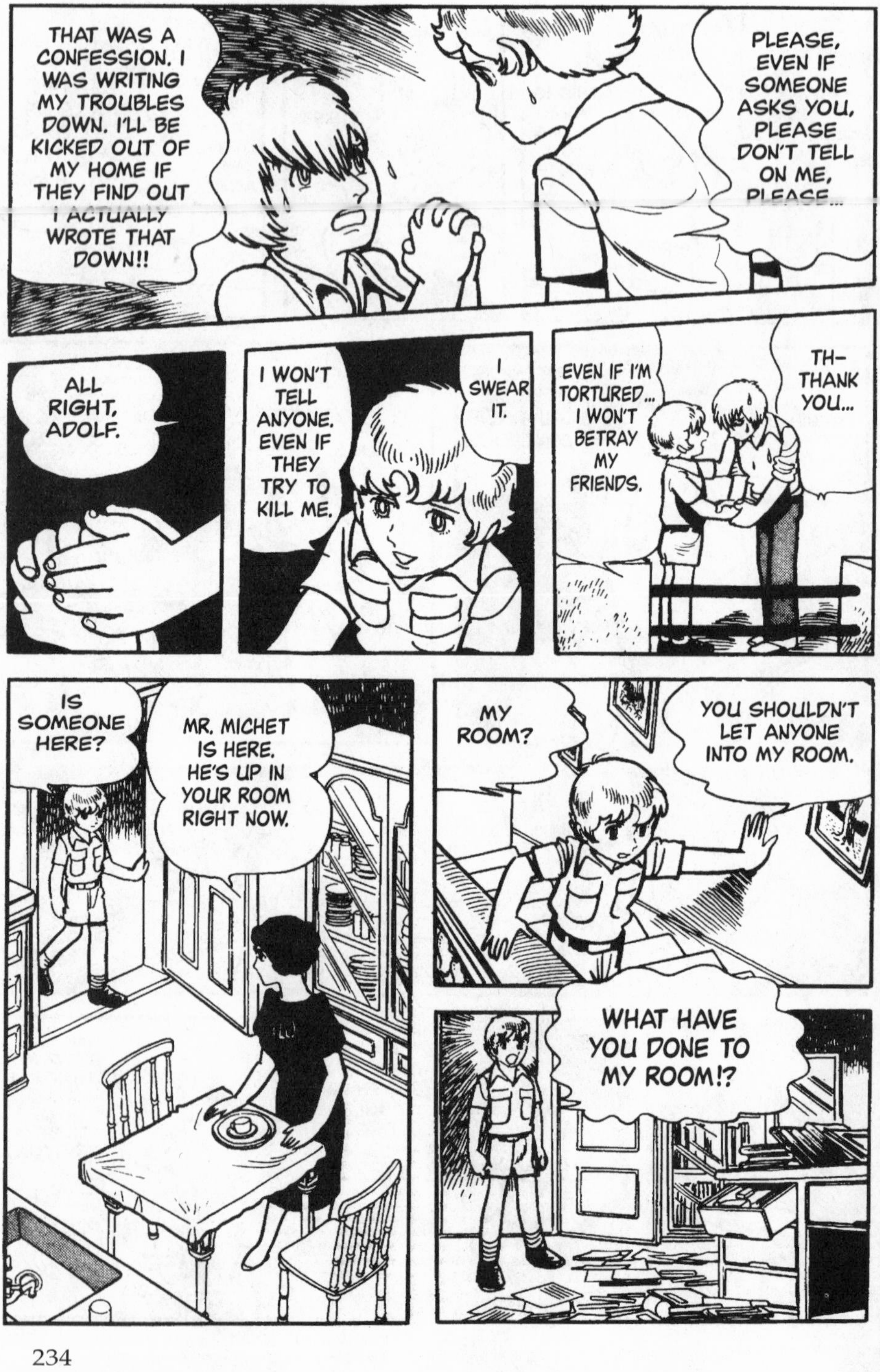
THAT WAS A CONFESSION. I WAS WRITING MY TROUBLES DOWN. I'LL BE KICKED OUT OF MY HOME IF THEY FIND OUT I ACTUALLY WROTE THAT DOWN!!
PLEASE, EVEN IF SOMEONE ASKS YOU, PLEASE DON'T TELL ON ME, PLEASE...
ALL RIGHT, ADOLF.
I WON'T TELL ANYONE. EVEN IF THEY TRY TO KILL ME.
I SWEAR IT.
EVEN IF I'M TORTURED... I WON'T BETRAY MY FRIENDS.
TH-THANK YOU...
IS SOMEONE HERE?
MR. MICHET IS HERE. HE'S UP IN YOUR ROOM RIGHT NOW.
MY ROOM?
YOU SHOULDN'T LET ANYONE INTO MY ROOM.
WHAT HAVE YOU DONE TO MY ROOM!?

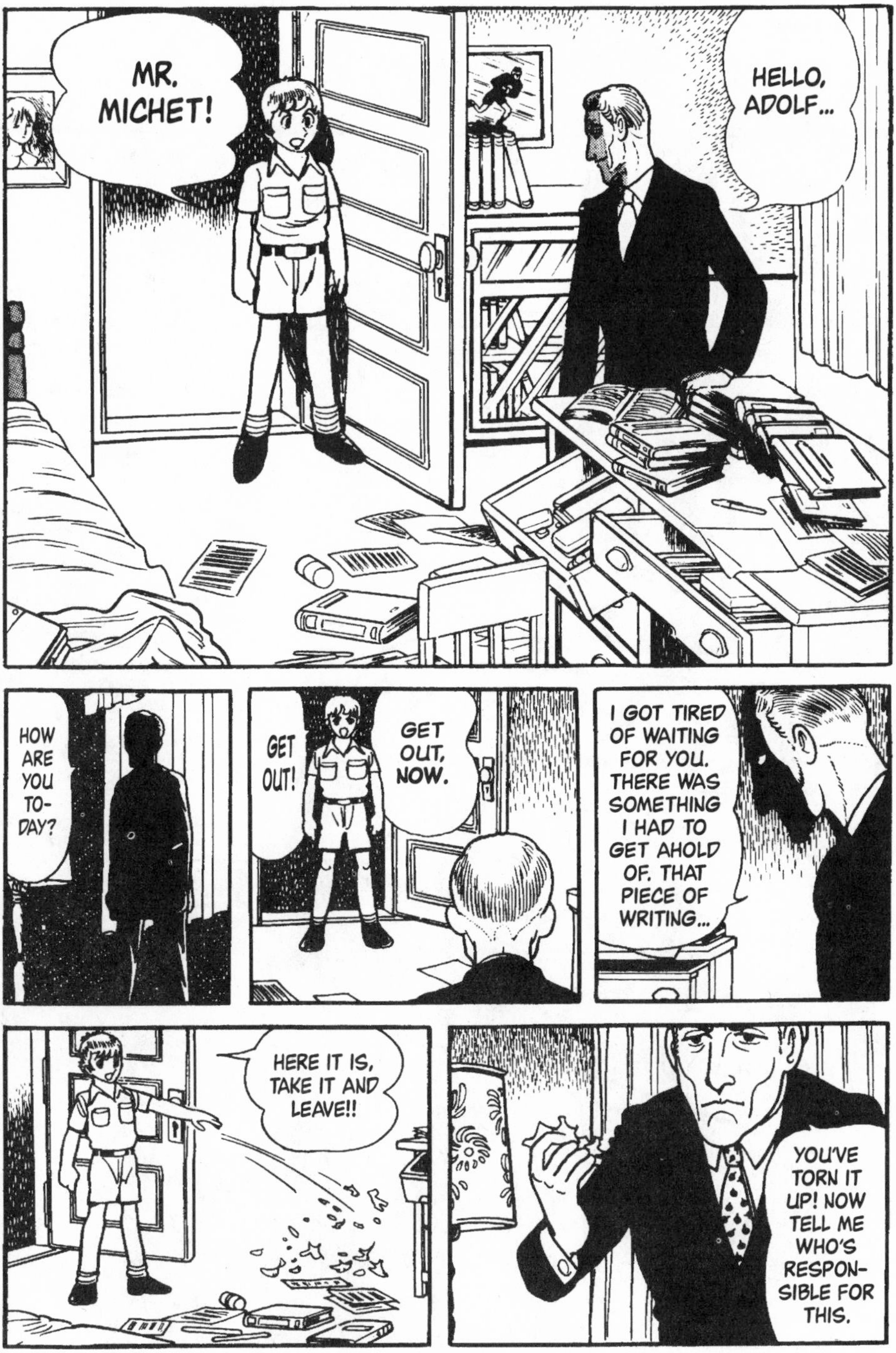
MR. MICHET!
HELLO, ADOLF...
HOW ARE YOU TO-DAY?
GET OUT!
GET OUT, NOW.
I GOT TIRED OF WAITING FOR YOU. THERE WAS SOMETHING I HAD TO GET AHOLD OF. THAT PIECE OF WRITING...
HERE IT IS, TAKE IT AND LEAVE!!
YOU'VE TORN IT UP! NOW TELL ME WHO'S RESPONSIBLE FOR THIS.

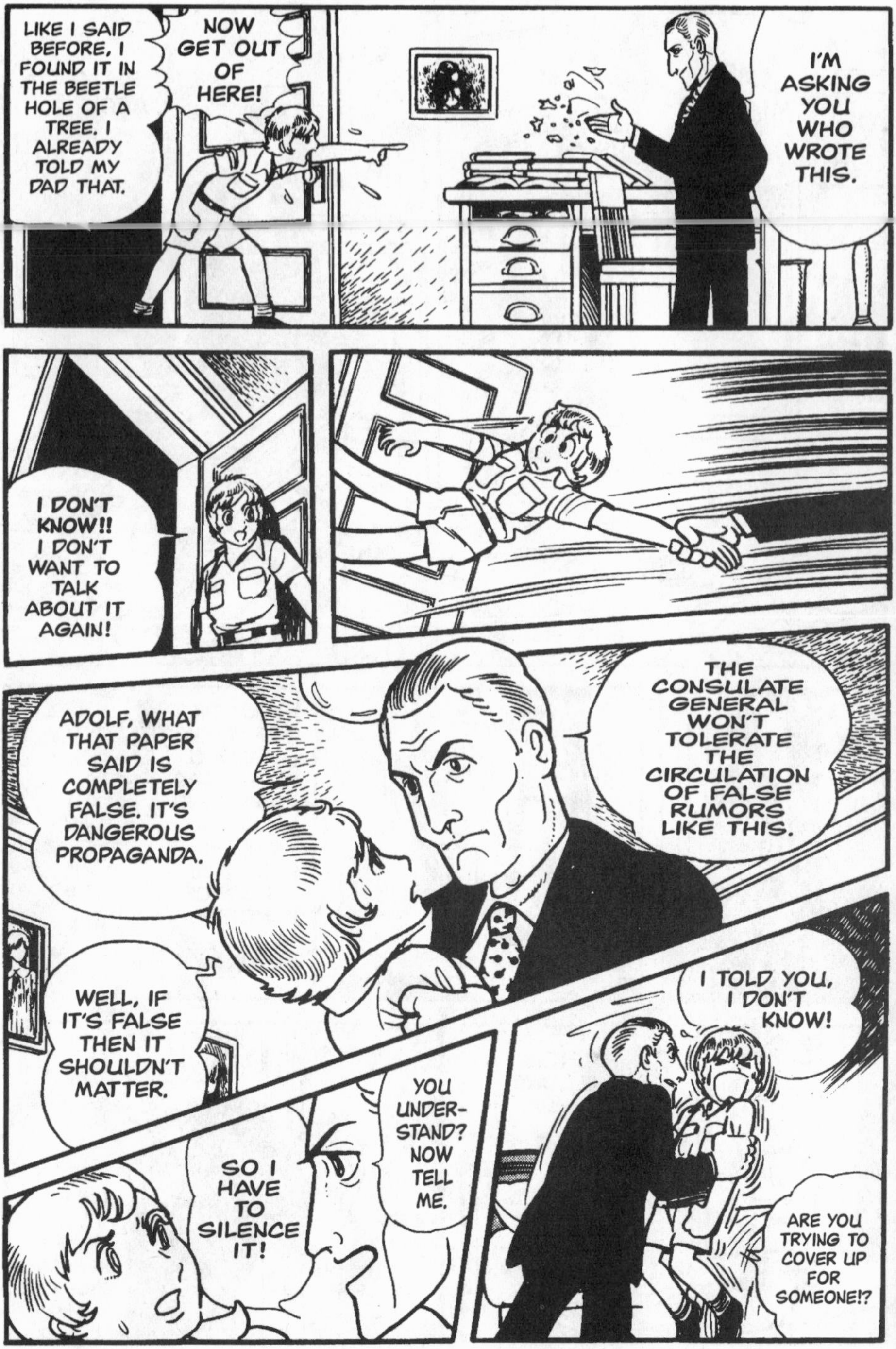
LIKE I SAID BEFORE, I FOUND IT IN THE BEETLE HOLE OF A TREE. I ALREADY TOLD MY DAD THAT.
NOW GET OUT OF HERE!
I'M ASKING YOU WHO WROTE THIS.
I DON'T KNOW!! I DON'T WANT TO TALK ABOUT IT AGAIN!
ADOLF, WHAT THAT PAPER SAID IS COMPLETELY FALSE. IT'S DANGEROUS PROPAGANDA.
THE CONSULATE GENERAL WON'T TOLERATE THE CIRCULATION OF FALSE RUMORS LIKE THIS.
WELL, IF IT'S FALSE THEN IT SHOULDN'T MATTER.
SO I HAVE TO SILENCE IT!
YOU UNDERSTAND? NOW TELL ME.
I TOLD YOU, I DON'T KNOW!
ARE YOU TRYING TO COVER UP FOR SOMEONE!?

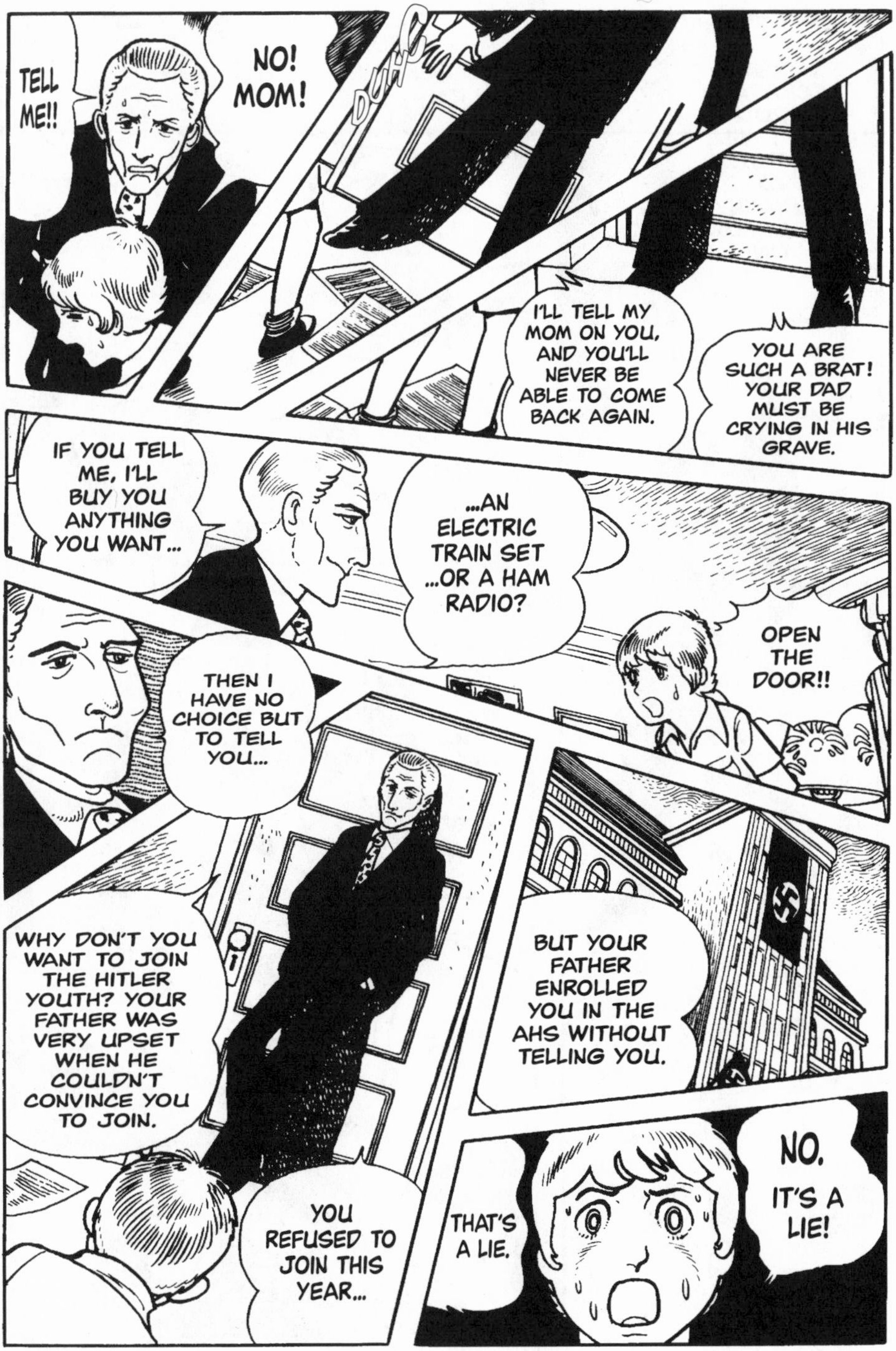
TELL ME!!
NO! MOM!
I'LL TELL MY MOM ON YOU, AND YOU'LL NEVER BE ABLE TO COME BACK AGAIN.
YOU ARE SUCH A BRAT! YOUR DAD MUST BE CRYING IN HIS GRAVE.
IF YOU TELL ME, I'LL BUY YOU ANYTHING YOU WANT...
...AN ELECTRIC TRAIN SET ...OR A HAM RADIO?
OPEN THE DOOR!!
THEN I HAVE NO CHOICE BUT TO TELL YOU...
WHY DON'T YOU WANT TO JOIN THE HITLER YOUTH? YOUR FATHER WAS VERY UPSET WHEN HE COULDN'T CONVINCE YOU TO JOIN.
YOU REFUSED TO JOIN THIS YEAR...
BUT YOUR FATHER ENROLLED YOU IN THE AHS WITHOUT TELLING YOU.
THAT'S A LIE.
NO.
IT'S A LIE!

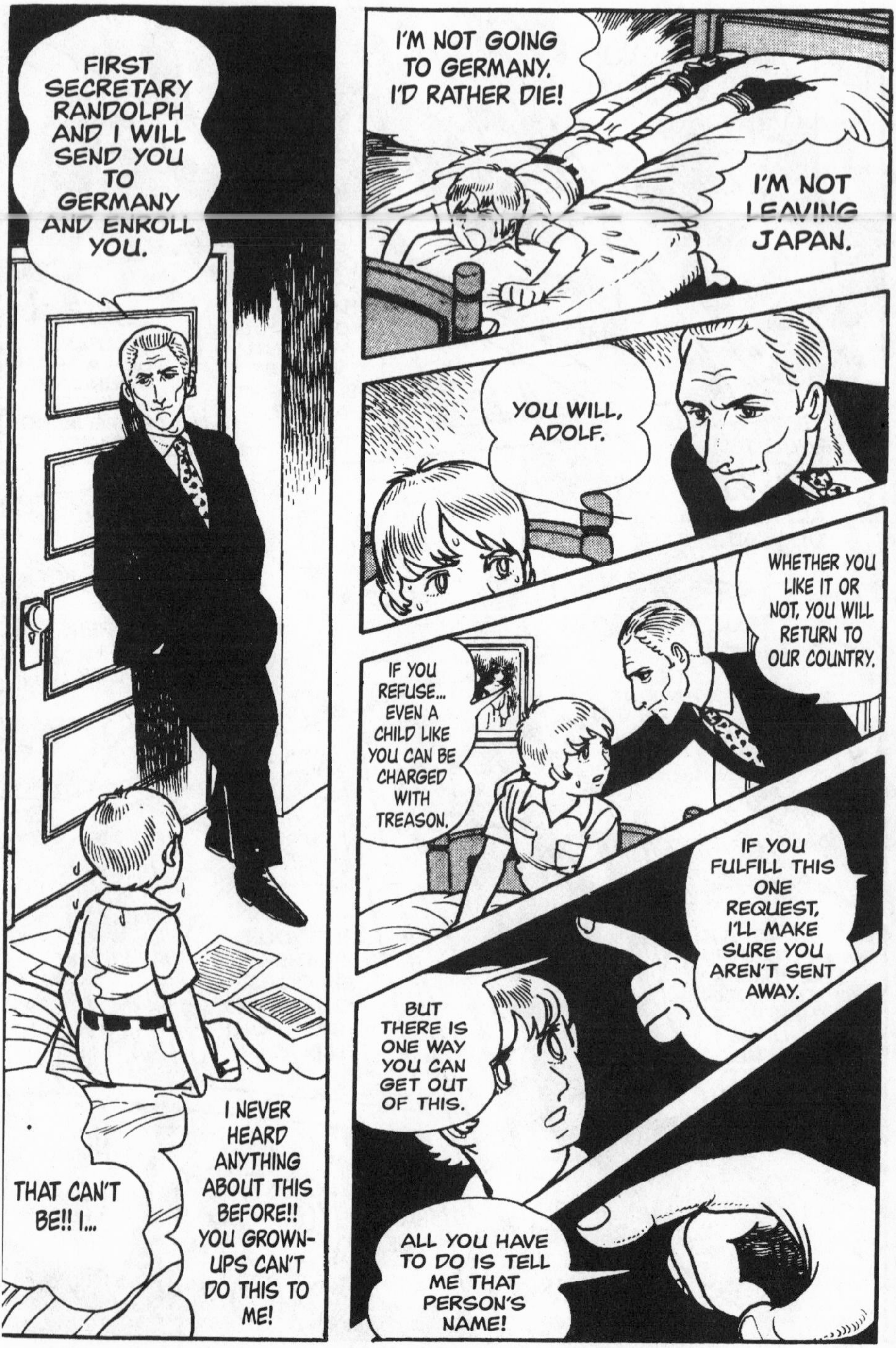
FIRST SECRETARY RANDOLPH AND I WILL SEND YOU TO GERMANY AND ENROLL YOU.
THAT CAN'T BE!! I...
I NEVER HEARD ANYTHING ABOUT THIS BEFORE!! YOU GROWN-UPS CAN'T DO THIS TO ME!
I'M NOT GOING TO GERMANY. I'D RATHER DIE!
I'M NOT LEAVING JAPAN.
YOU WILL, ADOLF.
WHETHER YOU LIKE IT OR NOT, YOU WILL RETURN TO OUR COUNTRY.
IF YOU REFUSE... EVEN A CHILD LIKE YOU CAN BE CHARGED WITH TREASON.
BUT THERE IS ONE WAY YOU CAN GET OUT OF THIS.
IF YOU FULFILL THIS ONE REQUEST, I'LL MAKE SURE YOU AREN'T SENT AWAY.
ALL YOU HAVE TO DO IS TELL ME THAT PERSON'S NAME!

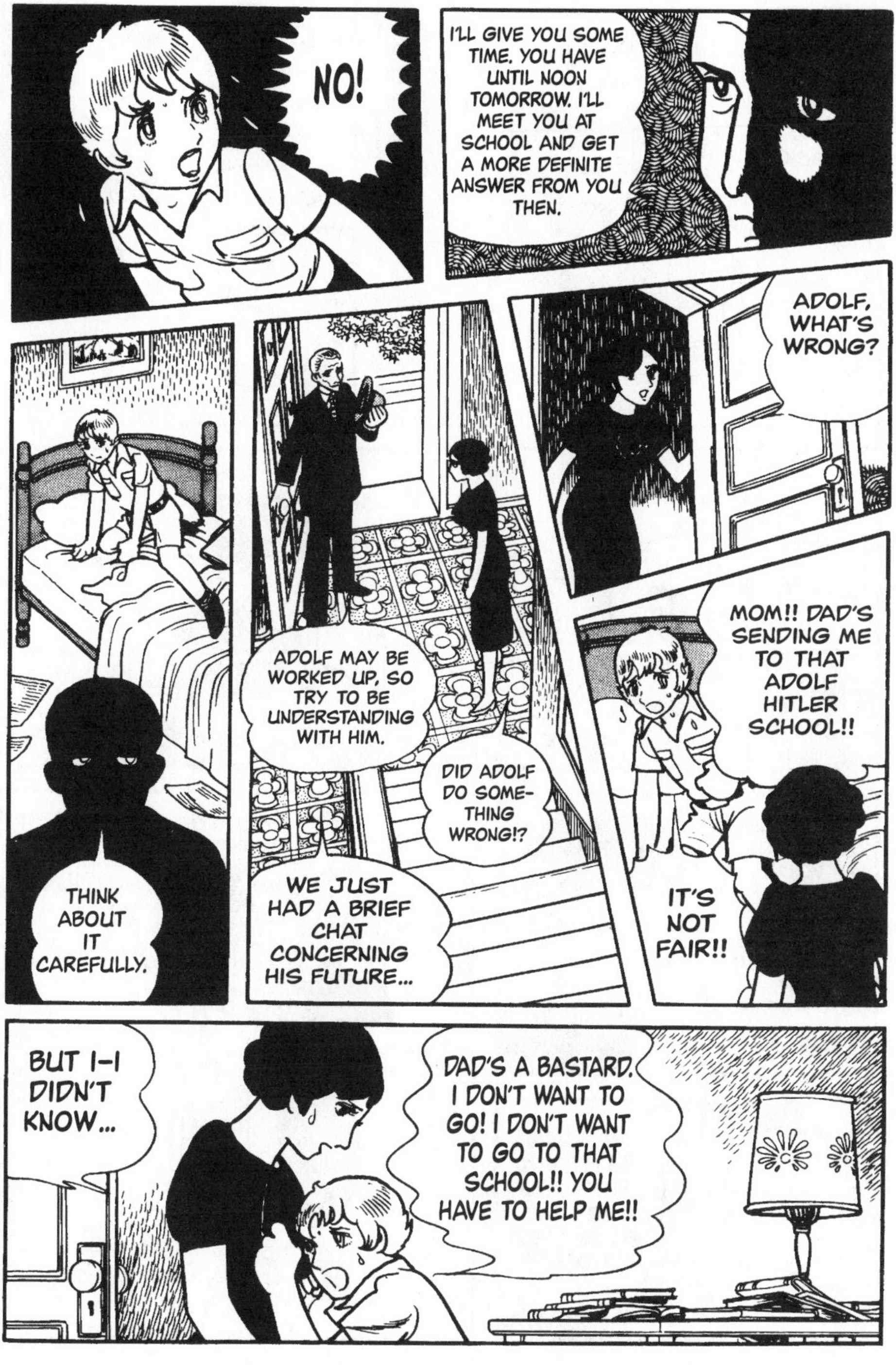
NO!
I'LL GIVE YOU SOME TIME. YOU HAVE UNTIL NOON TOMORROW. I'LL MEET YOU AT SCHOOL AND GET A MORE DEFINITE ANSWER FROM YOU THEN.
THINK ABOUT IT CAREFULLY.
ADOLF MAY BE WORKED UP, SO TRY TO BE UNDERSTANDING WITH HIM.
DID ADOLF DO SOME-THING WRONG!?
WE JUST HAD A BRIEF CHAT CONCERNING HIS FUTURE...
ADOLF, WHAT'S WRONG?
MOM!! DAD'S SENDING ME TO THAT ADOLF HITLER SCHOOL!!
IT'S NOT FAIR!!
BUT I-I DIDN'T KNOW...
DAD'S A BASTARD. I DON'T WANT TO GO! I DON'T WANT TO GO TO THAT SCHOOL!! YOU HAVE TO HELP ME!!

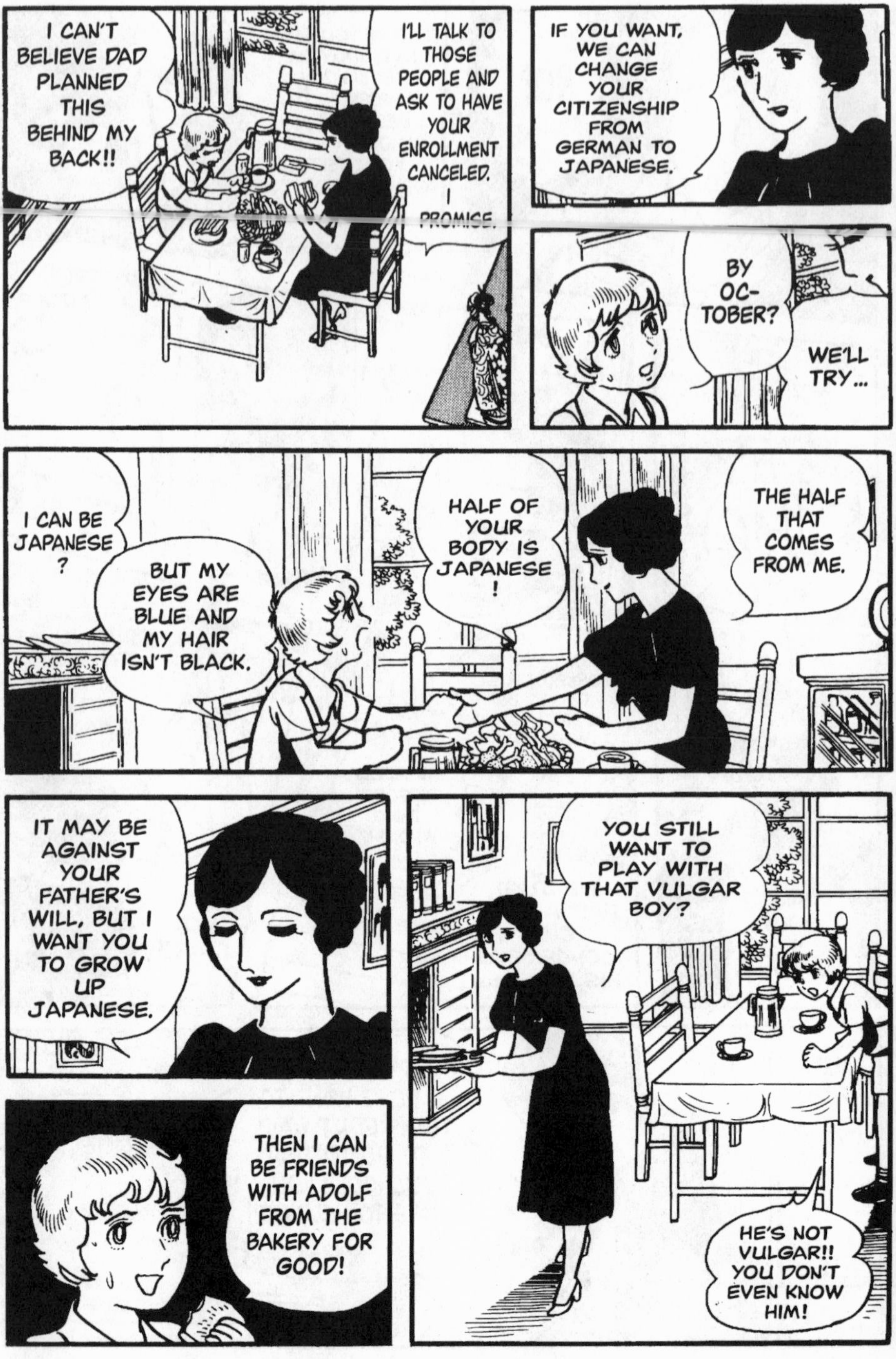

I CAN'T BELIEVE DAD PLANNED THIS BEHIND MY BACK!!
I'LL TALK TO THOSE PEOPLE AND ASK TO HAVE YOUR ENROLLMENT CANCELED. I PROMISE.
IF YOU WANT, WE CAN CHANGE YOUR CITIZENSHIP FROM GERMAN TO JAPANESE.
BY OC-TOBER?
WE'LL TRY...
I CAN BE JAPANESE?
BUT MY EYES ARE BLUE AND MY HAIR ISN'T BLACK.
HALF OF YOUR BODY IS JAPANESE!
THE HALF THAT COMES FROM ME.
IT MAY BE AGAINST YOUR FATHER'S WILL, BUT I WANT YOU TO GROW UP JAPANESE.
THEN I CAN BE FRIENDS WITH ADOLF FROM THE BAKERY FOR GOOD!
YOU STILL WANT TO PLAY WITH THAT VULGAR BOY?
HE'S NOT VULGAR!! YOU DON'T EVEN KNOW HIM!

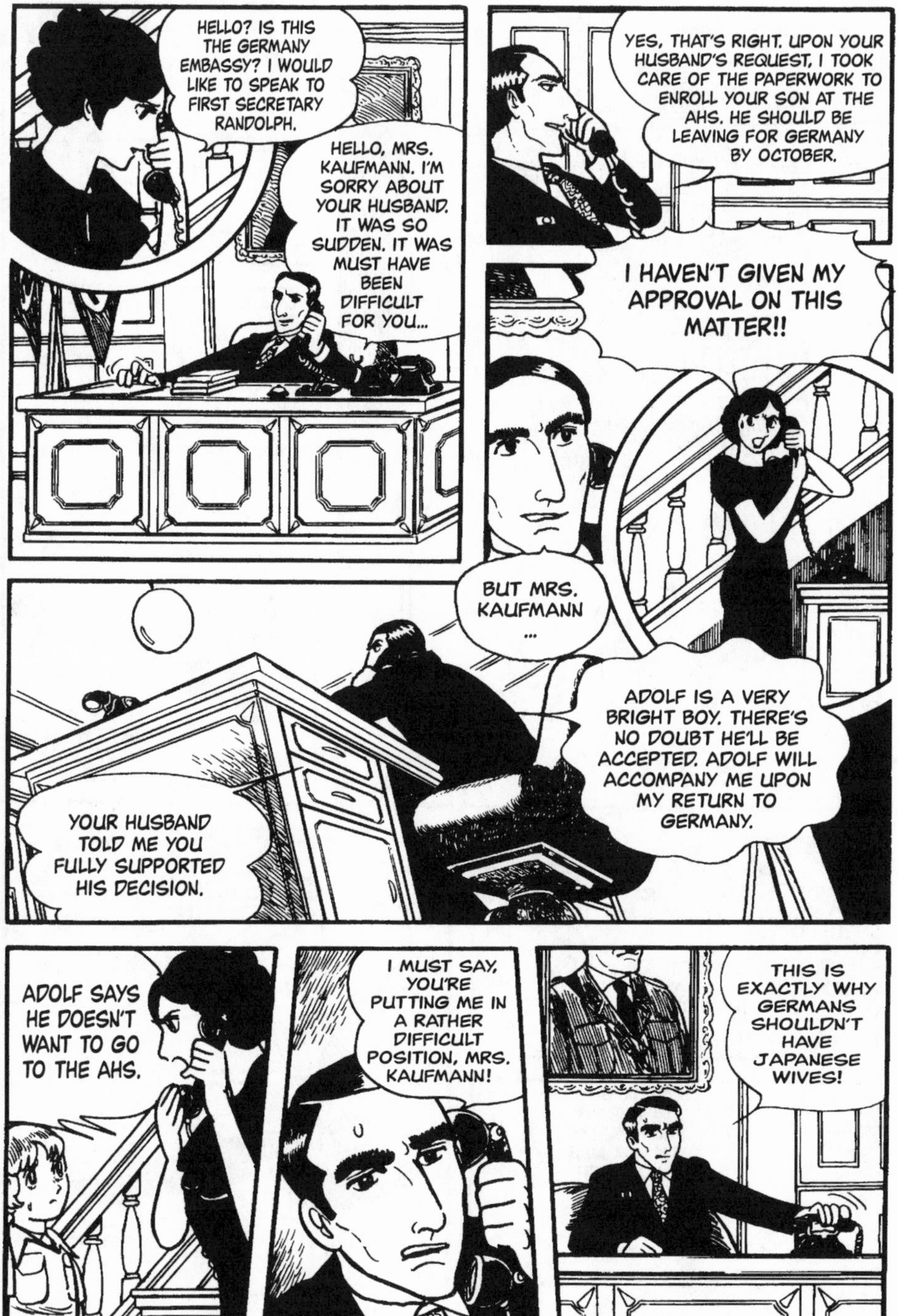
HELLO? IS THIS THE GERMANY EMBASSY? I WOULD LIKE TO SPEAK TO FIRST SECRETARY RANDOLPH.
HELLO, MRS. KAUFMANN. I'M SORRY ABOUT YOUR HUSBAND. IT WAS SO SUDDEN. IT WAS MUST HAVE BEEN DIFFICULT FOR YOU...
YES, THAT'S RIGHT. UPON YOUR HUSBAND'S REQUEST, I TOOK CARE OF THE PAPERWORK TO ENROLL YOUR SON AT THE AHS. HE SHOULD BE LEAVING FOR GERMANY BY OCTOBER.
I HAVEN'T GIVEN MY APPROVAL ON THIS MATTER!!
BUT MRS. KAUFMANN ...
YOUR HUSBAND TOLD ME YOU FULLY SUPPORTED HIS DECISION.
ADOLF IS A VERY BRIGHT BOY. THERE'S NO DOUBT HE'LL BE ACCEPTED. ADOLF WILL ACCOMPANY ME UPON MY RETURN TO GERMANY.
ADOLF SAYS HE DOESN'T WANT TO GO TO THE AHS.
I MUST SAY, YOU'RE PUTTING ME IN A RATHER DIFFICULT POSITION, MRS. KAUFMANN!
THIS IS EXACTLY WHY GERMANS SHOULDN'T HAVE JAPANESE WIVES!

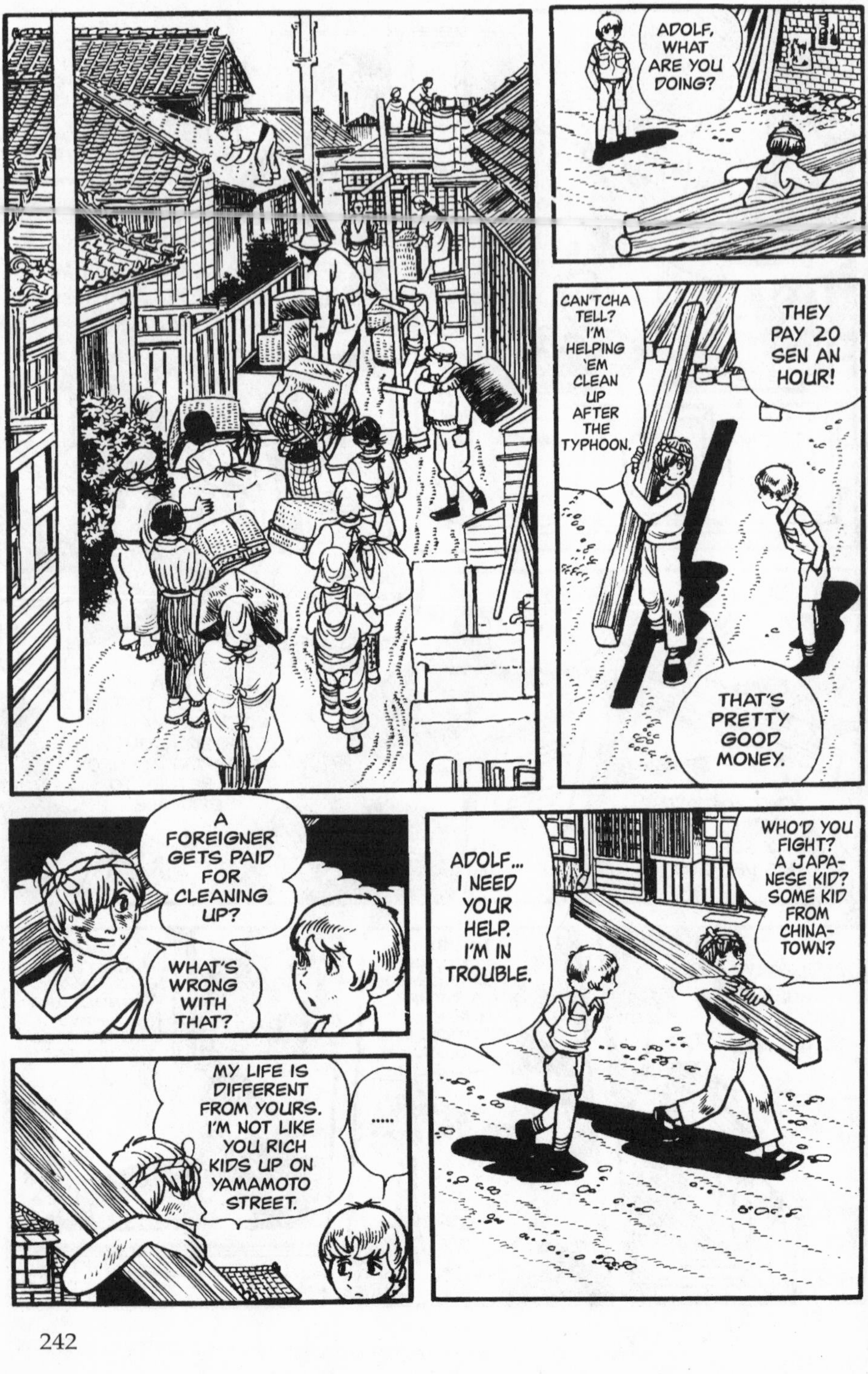
ADOLF, WHAT ARE YOU DOING?
CAN'TCHA TELL? I'M HELPING 'EM CLEAN UP AFTER THE TYPHOON.
THEY PAY 20 SEN AN HOUR!
THAT'S PRETTY GOOD MONEY.
A FOREIGNER GETS PAID FOR CLEANING UP?
WHAT'S WRONG WITH THAT?
MY LIFE IS DIFFERENT FROM YOURS. I'M NOT LIKE YOU RICH KIDS UP ON YAMAMOTO STREET.
.....
ADOLF... I NEED YOUR HELP. I'M IN TROUBLE.
WHO'D YOU FIGHT? A JAPANESE KID? SOME KID FROM CHINATOWN?

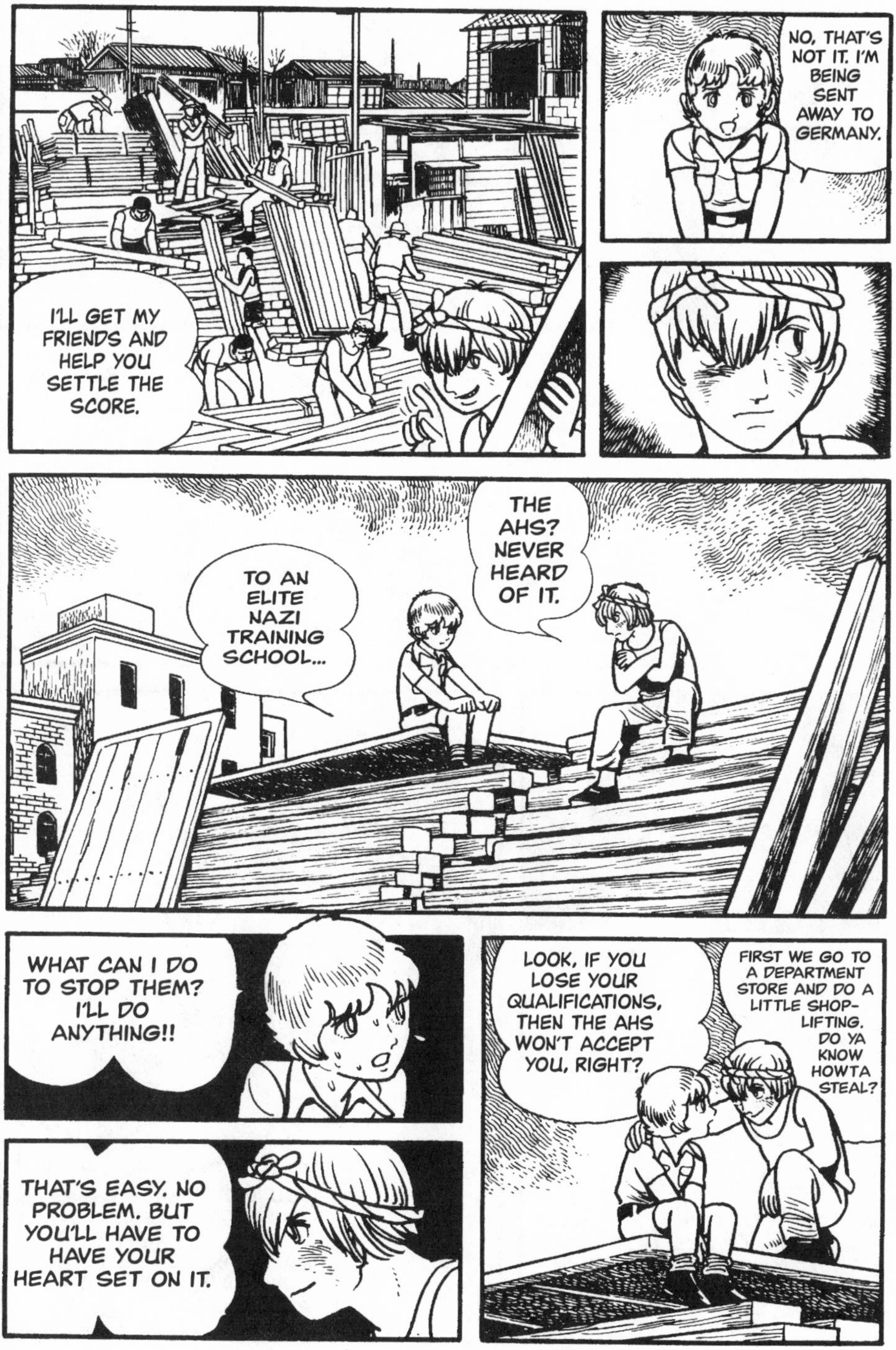
I'LL GET MY FRIENDS AND HELP YOU SETTLE THE SCORE.
NO, THAT'S NOT IT. I'M BEING SENT AWAY TO GERMANY.
TO AN ELITE NAZI TRAINING SCHOOL...
THE AHS? NEVER HEARD OF IT.
WHAT CAN I DO TO STOP THEM? I'LL DO ANYTHING!!
THAT'S EASY. NO PROBLEM. BUT YOU'LL HAVE TO HAVE YOUR HEART SET ON IT.
LOOK, IF YOU LOSE YOUR QUALIFICATIONS, THEN THE AHS WON'T ACCEPT YOU, RIGHT?
FIRST WE GO TO A DEPARTMENT STORE AND DO A LITTLE SHOP-LIFTING. DO YA KNOW HOWTA STEAL?

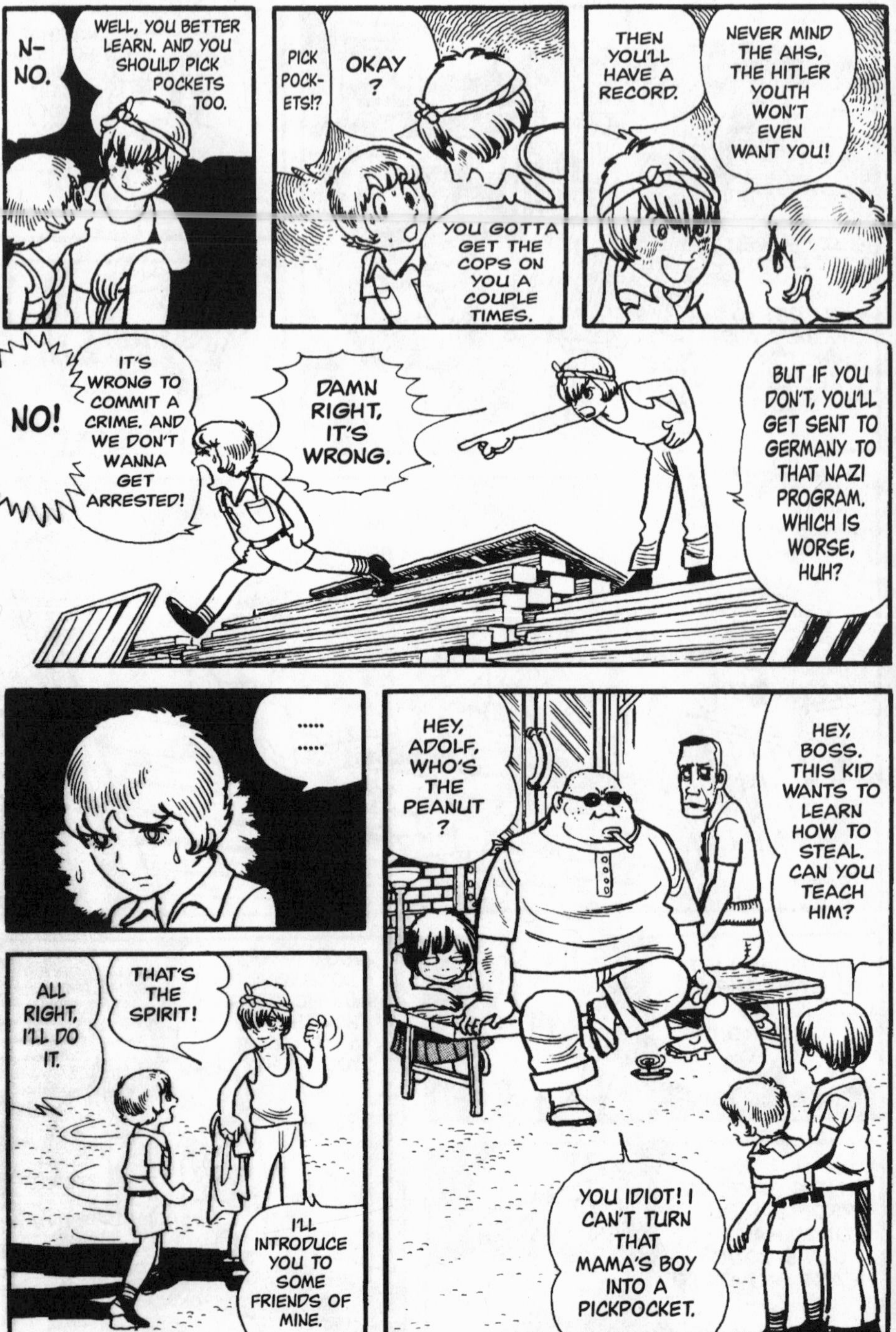
N-NO.
WELL, YOU BETTER LEARN. AND YOU SHOULD PICK POCKETS TOO.
PICK POCK-ETS!?
OKAY?
YOU GOTTA GET THE COPS ON YOU A COUPLE TIMES.
THEN YOU'LL HAVE A RECORD.
NEVER MIND THE AHS, THE HITLER YOUTH WON'T EVEN WANT YOU!
NO!
IT'S WRONG TO COMMIT A CRIME. AND WE DON'T WANNA GET ARRESTED!
DAMN RIGHT, IT'S WRONG.
BUT IF YOU DON'T, YOU'LL GET SENT TO GERMANY TO THAT NAZI PROGRAM. WHICH IS WORSE, HUH?
....
ALL RIGHT, I'LL DO IT.
THAT'S THE SPIRIT!
I'LL INTRODUCE YOU TO SOME FRIENDS OF MINE.
HEY, ADOLF, WHO'S THE PEANUT?
HEY, BOSS. THIS KID WANTS TO LEARN HOW TO STEAL. CAN YOU TEACH HIM?
YOU IDIOT! I CAN'T TURN THAT MAMA'S BOY INTO A PICKPOCKET.

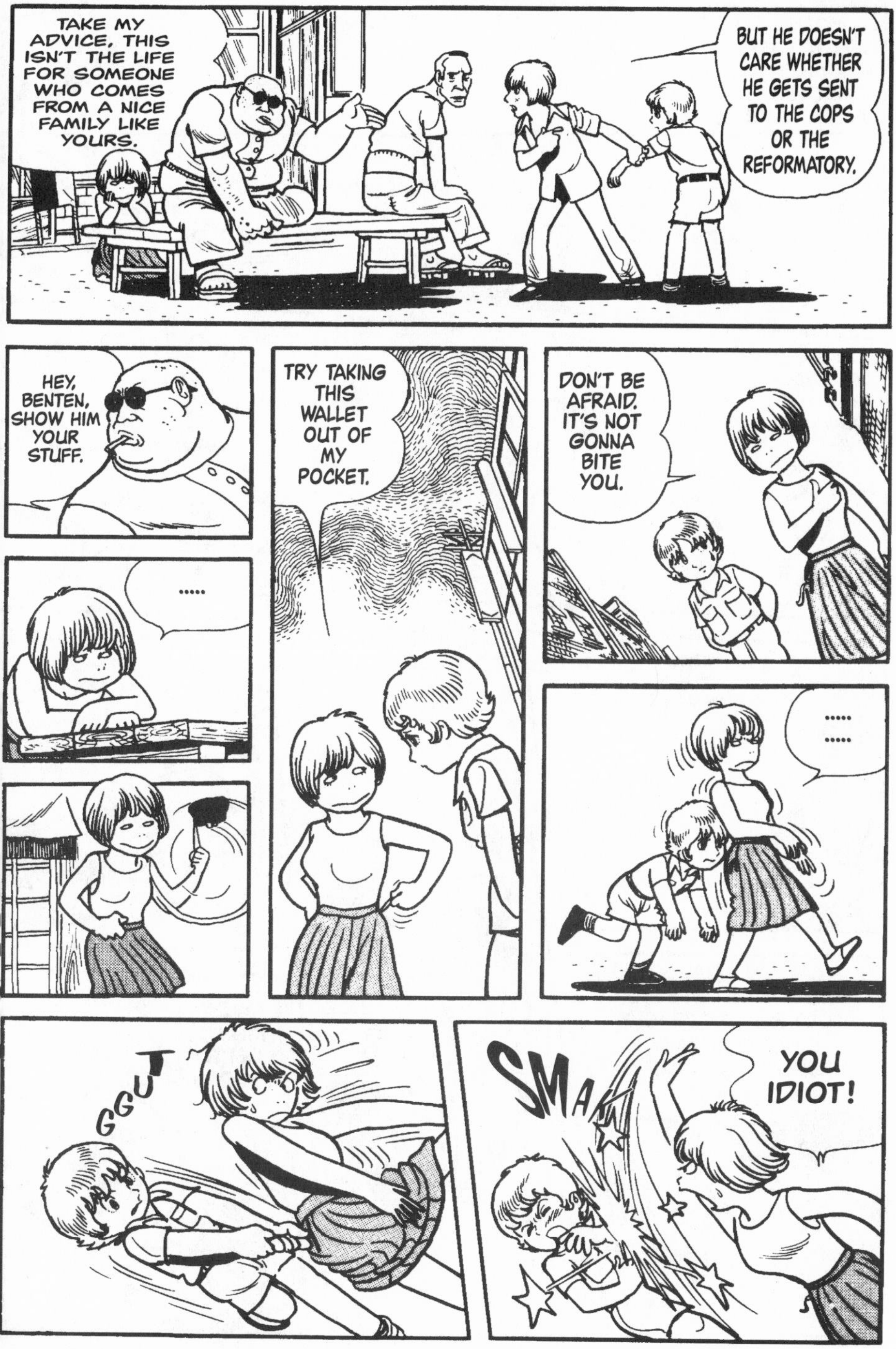
TAKE MY ADVICE, THIS ISN'T THE LIFE FOR SOMEONE WHO COMES FROM A NICE FAMILY LIKE YOURS.
BUT HE DOESN'T CARE WHETHER HE GETS SENT TO THE COPS OR THE REFORMATORY.
HEY, BENTEN, SHOW HIM YOUR STUFF.
......
TRY TAKING THIS WALLET OUT OF MY POCKET.
DON'T BE AFRAID. IT'S NOT GONNA BITE YOU.
......
......
GGUT
SMAK
YOU IDIOT!

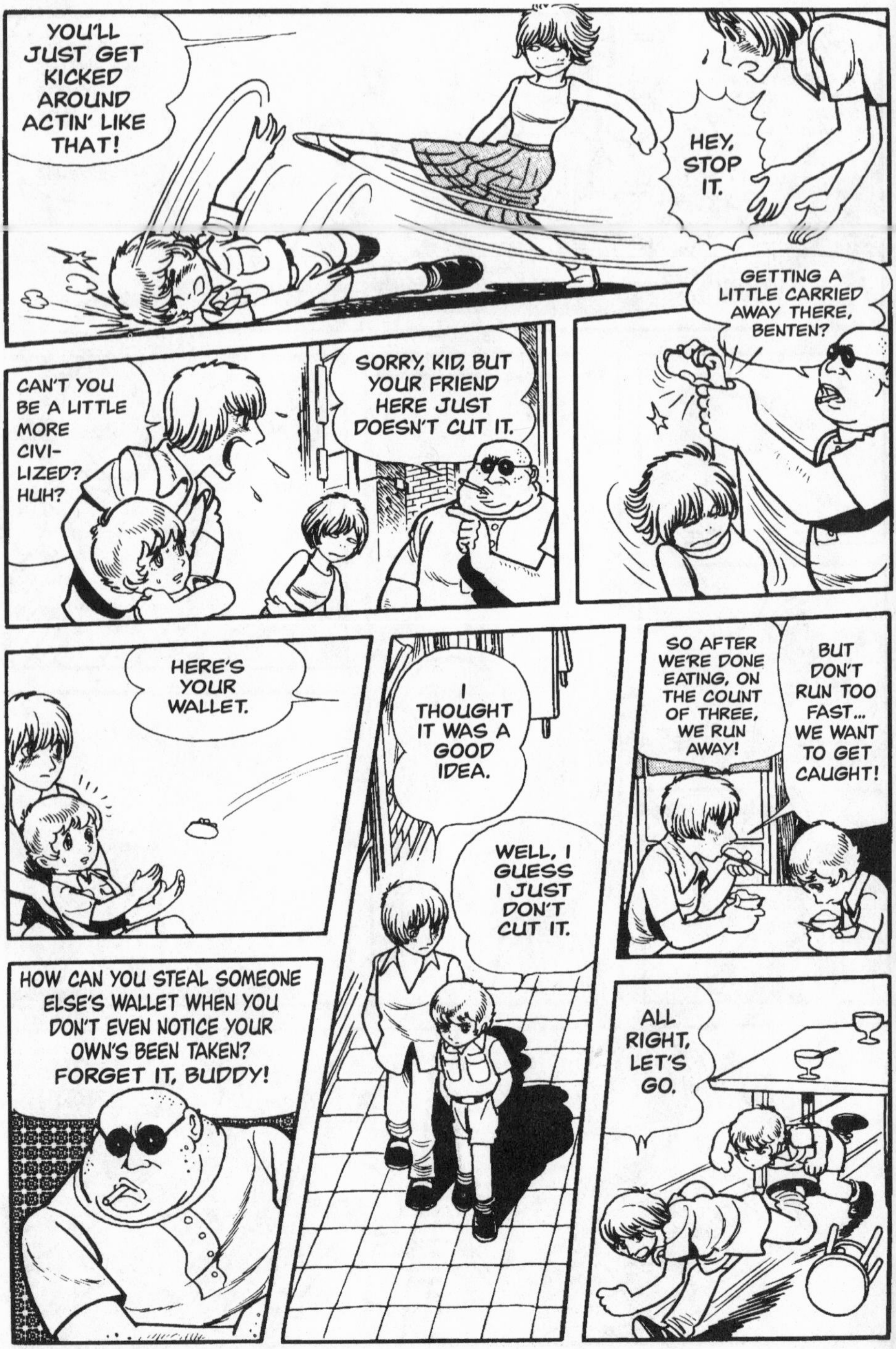
YOU'LL JUST GET KICKED AROUND ACTIN' LIKE THAT!
HEY, STOP IT.
CAN'T YOU BE A LITTLE MORE CIVI-LIZED? HUH?
SORRY, KID, BUT YOUR FRIEND HERE JUST DOESN'T CUT IT.
GETTING A LITTLE CARRIED AWAY THERE, BENTEN?
HERE'S YOUR WALLET.
HOW CAN YOU STEAL SOMEONE ELSE'S WALLET WHEN YOU DON'T EVEN NOTICE YOUR OWN'S BEEN TAKEN? FORGET IT, BUDDY!
I THOUGHT IT WAS A GOOD IDEA.
WELL, I GUESS I JUST DON'T CUT IT.
SO AFTER WE'RE DONE EATING, ON THE COUNT OF THREE, WE RUN AWAY!
BUT DON'T RUN TOO FAST... WE WANT TO GET CAUGHT!
ALL RIGHT, LET'S GO.

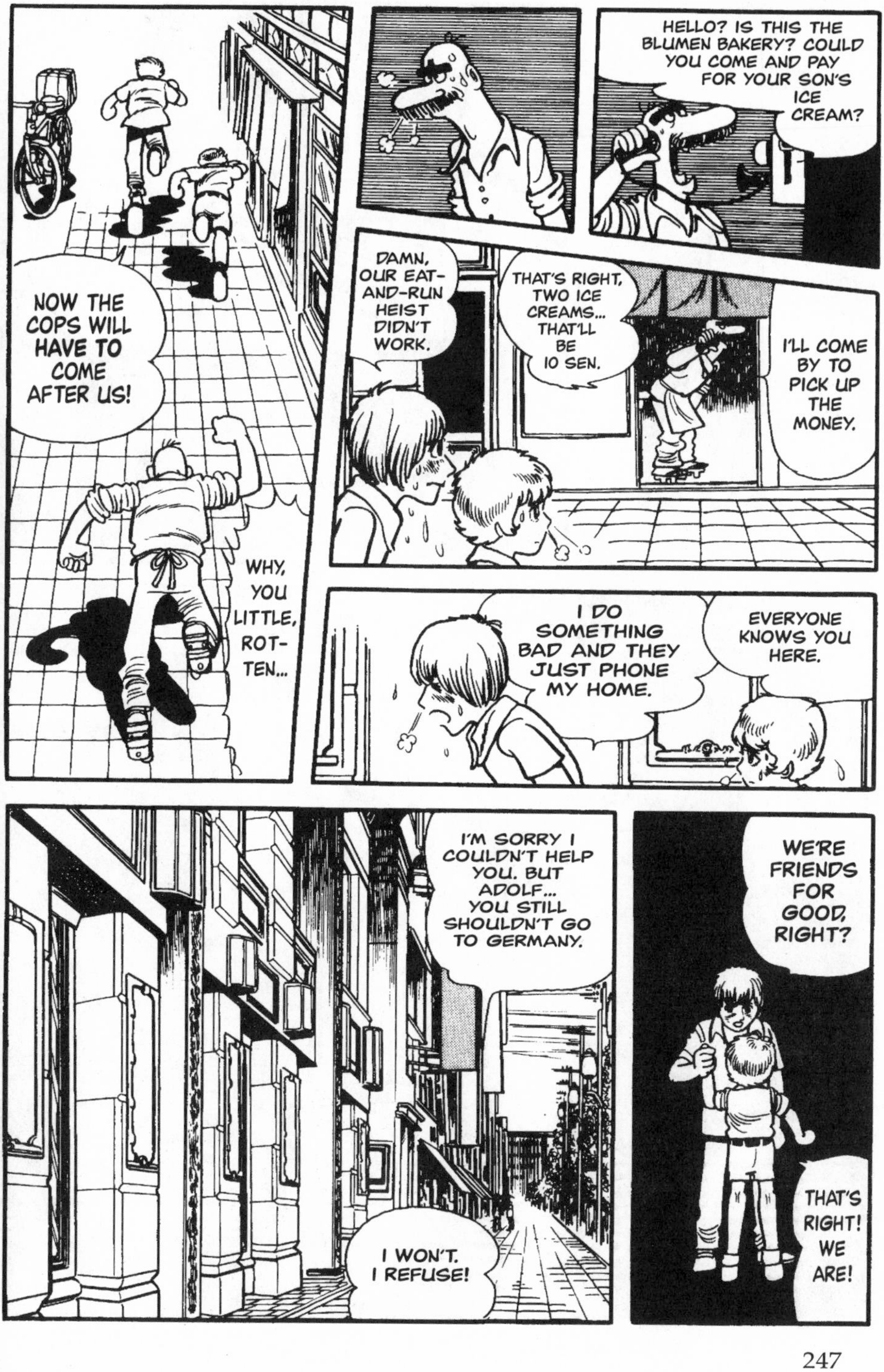
NOW THE COPS WILL HAVE TO COME AFTER US!
WHY, YOU LITTLE, ROT-TEN...
HELLO? IS THIS THE BLUMEN BAKERY? COULD YOU COME AND PAY FOR YOUR SON'S ICE CREAM?
DAMN, OUR EAT-AND-RUN HEIST DIDN'T WORK.
THAT'S RIGHT, TWO ICE CREAMS... THAT'LL BE 10 SEN.
I'LL COME BY TO PICK UP THE MONEY.
I DO SOMETHING BAD AND THEY JUST PHONE MY HOME.
EVERYONE KNOWS YOU HERE.
I'M SORRY I COULDN'T HELP YOU. BUT ADOLF... YOU STILL SHOULDN'T GO TO GERMANY.
I WON'T. I REFUSE!
WE'RE FRIENDS FOR GOOD, RIGHT?
THAT'S RIGHT! WE ARE!

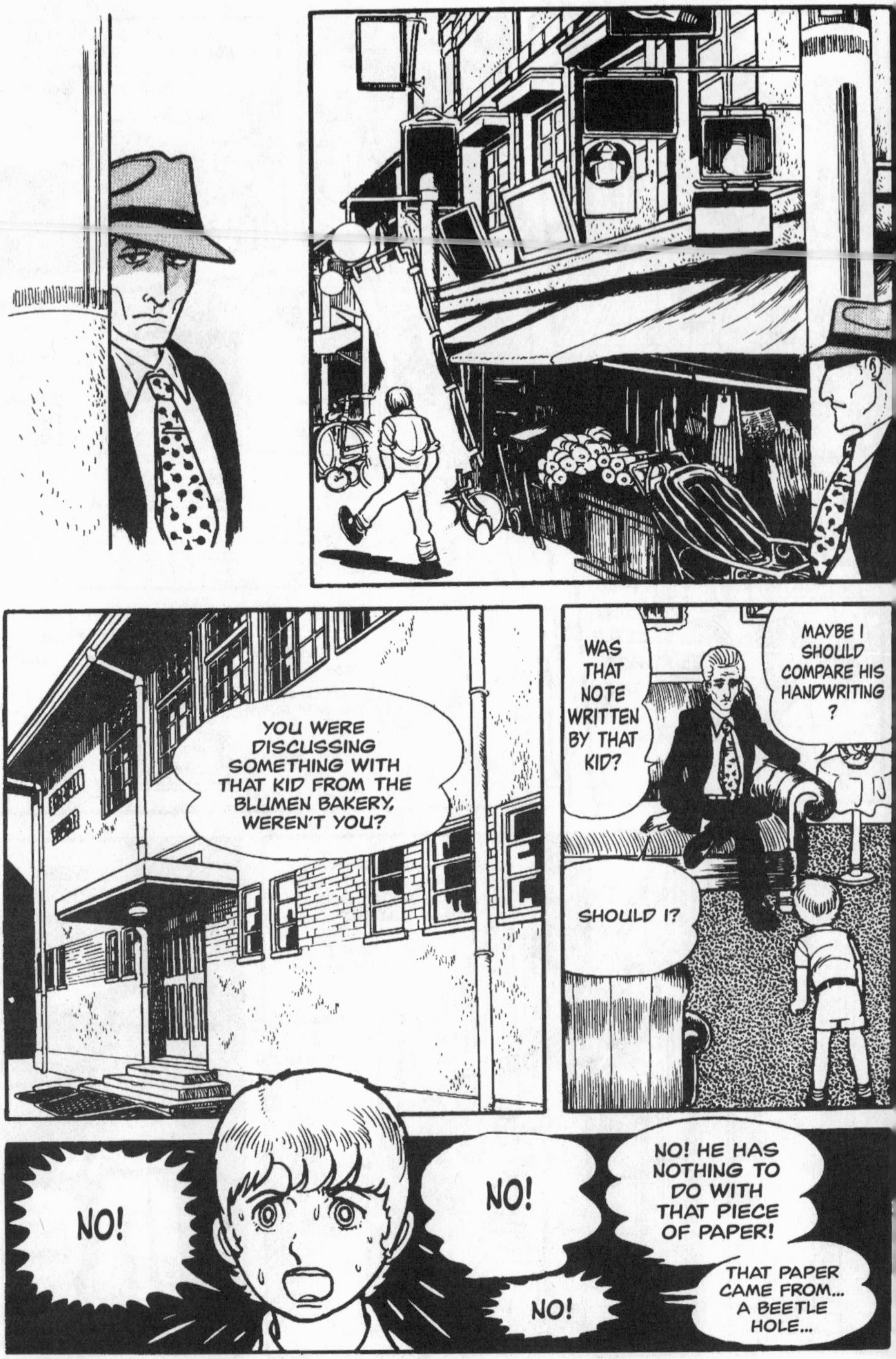
YOU WERE DISCUSSING SOMETHING WITH THAT KID FROM THE BLUMEN BAKERY, WEREN'T YOU?
WAS THAT NOTE WRITTEN BY THAT KID?
MAYBE I SHOULD COMPARE HIS HANDWRITING ?
SHOULD I?
NO!
NO!
NO! HE HAS NOTHING TO DO WITH THAT PIECE OF PAPER!
NO!
THAT PAPER CAME FROM... A BEETLE HOLE...

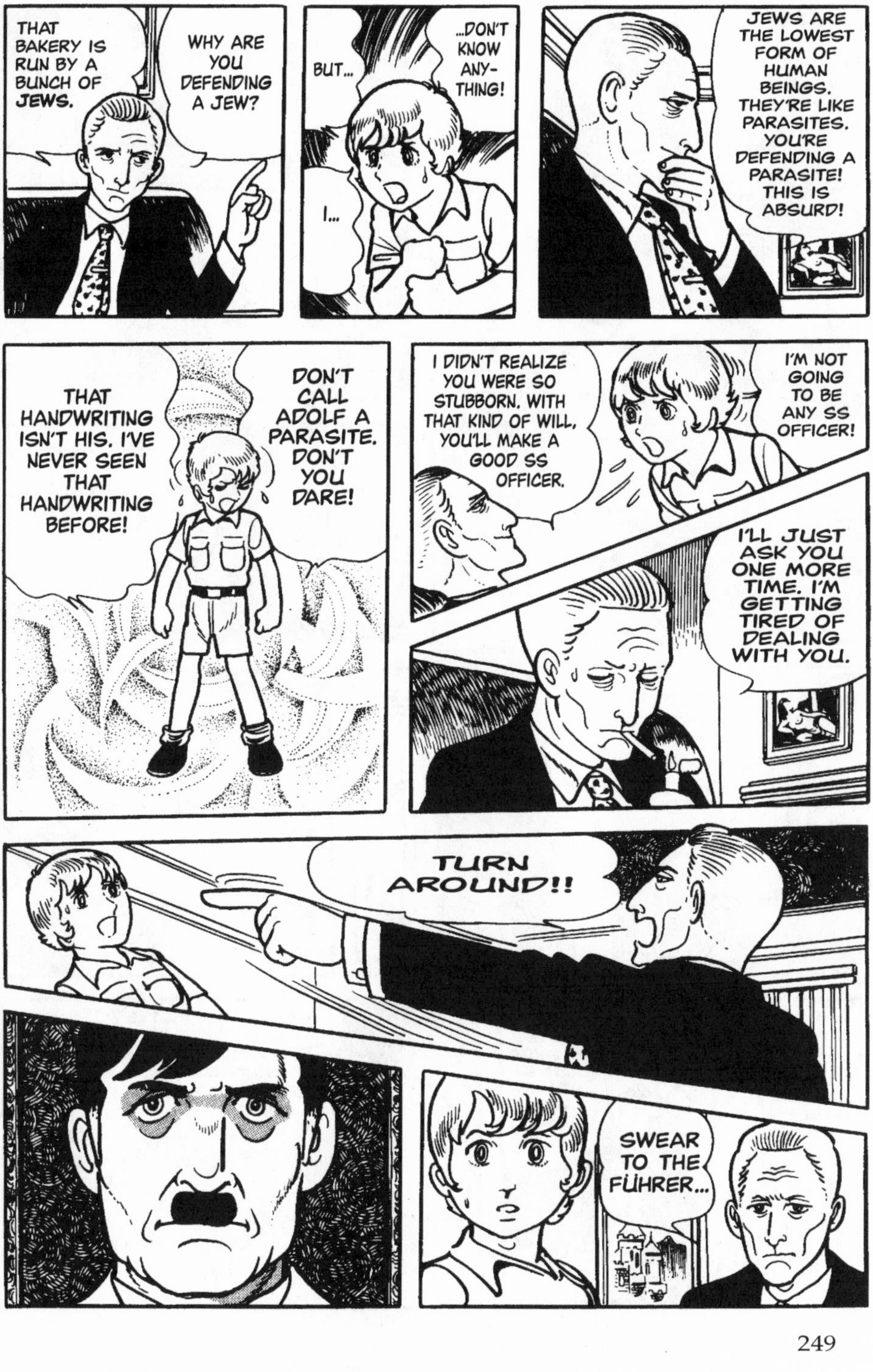
THAT BAKERY IS RUN BY A BUNCH OF JEWS.
WHY ARE YOU DEFENDING A JEW?
BUT...
...DON'T KNOW ANY-THING!
I...
JEWS ARE THE LOWEST FORM OF HUMAN BEINGS. THEY'RE LIKE PARASITES. YOU'RE DEFENDING A PARASITE! THIS IS ABSURD!
THAT HANDWRITING ISN'T HIS. I'VE NEVER SEEN THAT HANDWRITING BEFORE!
DON'T CALL ADOLF A PARASITE. DON'T YOU DARE!
I DIDN'T REALIZE YOU WERE SO STUBBORN. WITH THAT KIND OF WILL, YOU'LL MAKE A GOOD SS OFFICER.
I'M NOT GOING TO BE ANY SS OFFICER!
I'LL JUST ASK YOU ONE MORE TIME. I'M GETTING TIRED OF DEALING WITH YOU.
TURN AROUND!!
SWEAR TO THE FÜHRER...

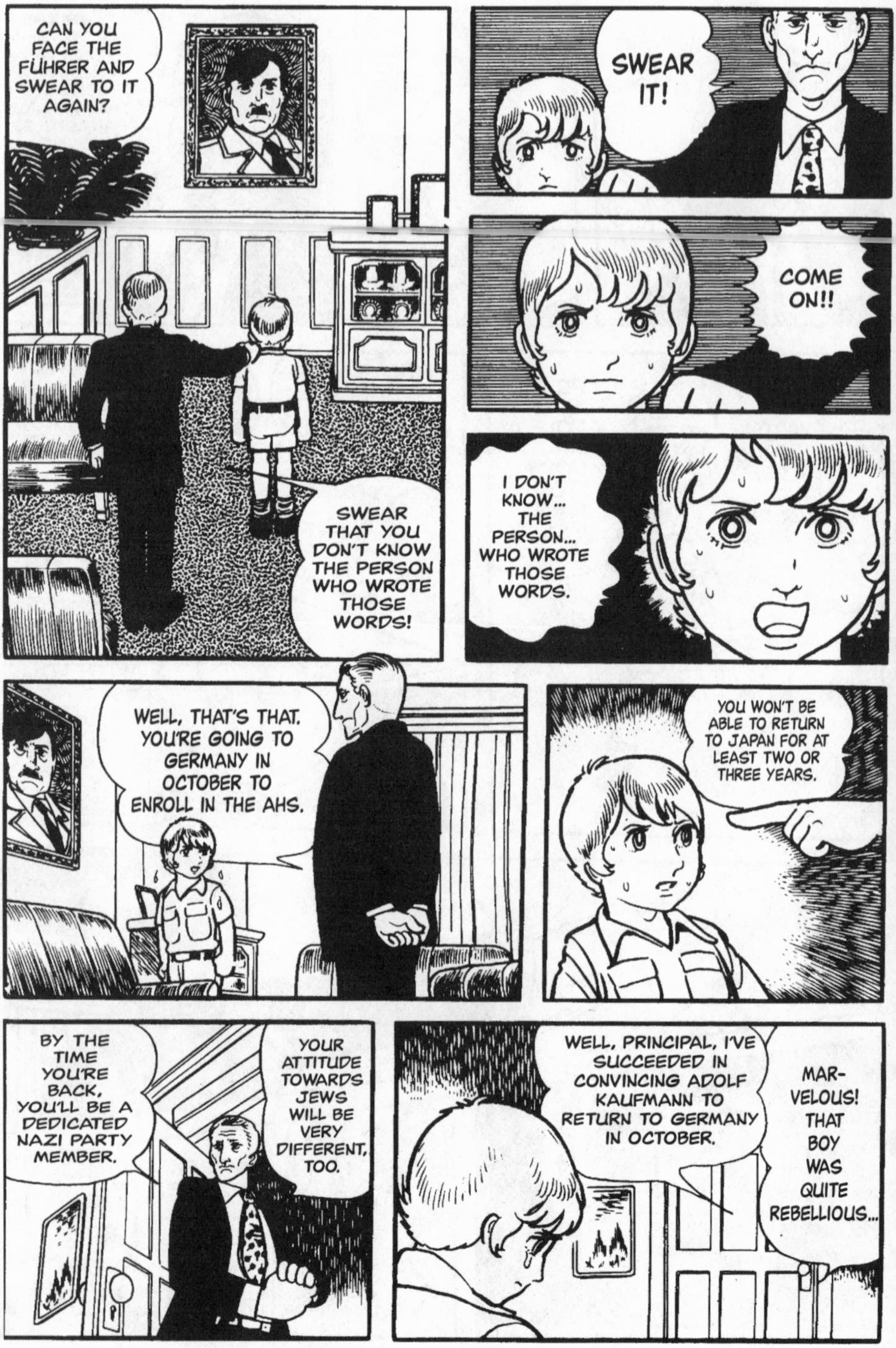
CAN YOU FACE THE FÜHRER AND SWEAR TO IT AGAIN?
SWEAR THAT YOU DON'T KNOW THE PERSON WHO WROTE THOSE WORDS!
SWEAR IT!
COME ON!!
I DON'T KNOW... THE PERSON... WHO WROTE THOSE WORDS.
WELL, THAT'S THAT. YOU'RE GOING TO GERMANY IN OCTOBER TO ENROLL IN THE AHS.
YOU WON'T BE ABLE TO RETURN TO JAPAN FOR AT LEAST TWO OR THREE YEARS.
BY THE TIME YOU'RE BACK, YOU'LL BE A DEDICATED NAZI PARTY MEMBER.
YOUR ATTITUDE TOWARDS JEWS WILL BE VERY DIFFERENT, TOO.
WELL, PRINCIPAL, I'VE SUCCEEDED IN CONVINCING ADOLF KAUFMANN TO RETURN TO GERMANY IN OCTOBER.
MAR-VELOUS! THAT BOY WAS QUITE REBELLIOUS...

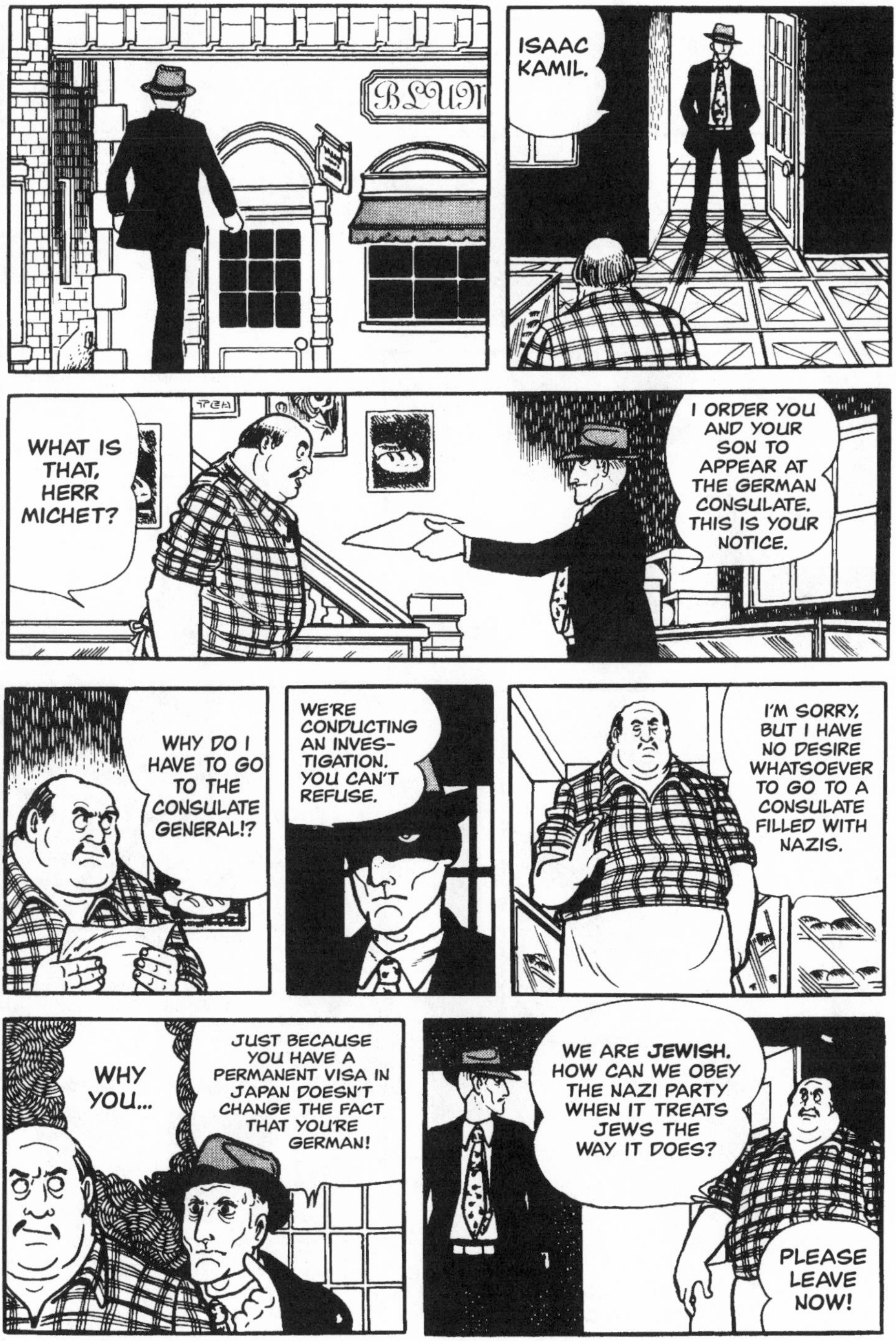
BLUM
ISAAC KAMIL.
WHAT IS THAT, HERR MICHET?
I ORDER YOU AND YOUR SON TO APPEAR AT THE GERMAN CONSULATE. THIS IS YOUR NOTICE.
WHY DO I HAVE TO GO TO THE CONSULATE GENERAL!?
WE'RE CONDUCTING AN INVESTIGATION. YOU CAN'T REFUSE.
I'M SORRY, BUT I HAVE NO DESIRE WHATSOEVER TO GO TO A CONSULATE FILLED WITH NAZIS.
WHY YOU...
JUST BECAUSE YOU HAVE A PERMANENT VISA IN JAPAN DOESN'T CHANGE THE FACT THAT YOU'RE GERMAN!
WE ARE **JEWISH.** HOW CAN WE OBEY THE NAZI PARTY WHEN IT TREATS JEWS THE WAY IT DOES?
PLEASE LEAVE NOW!

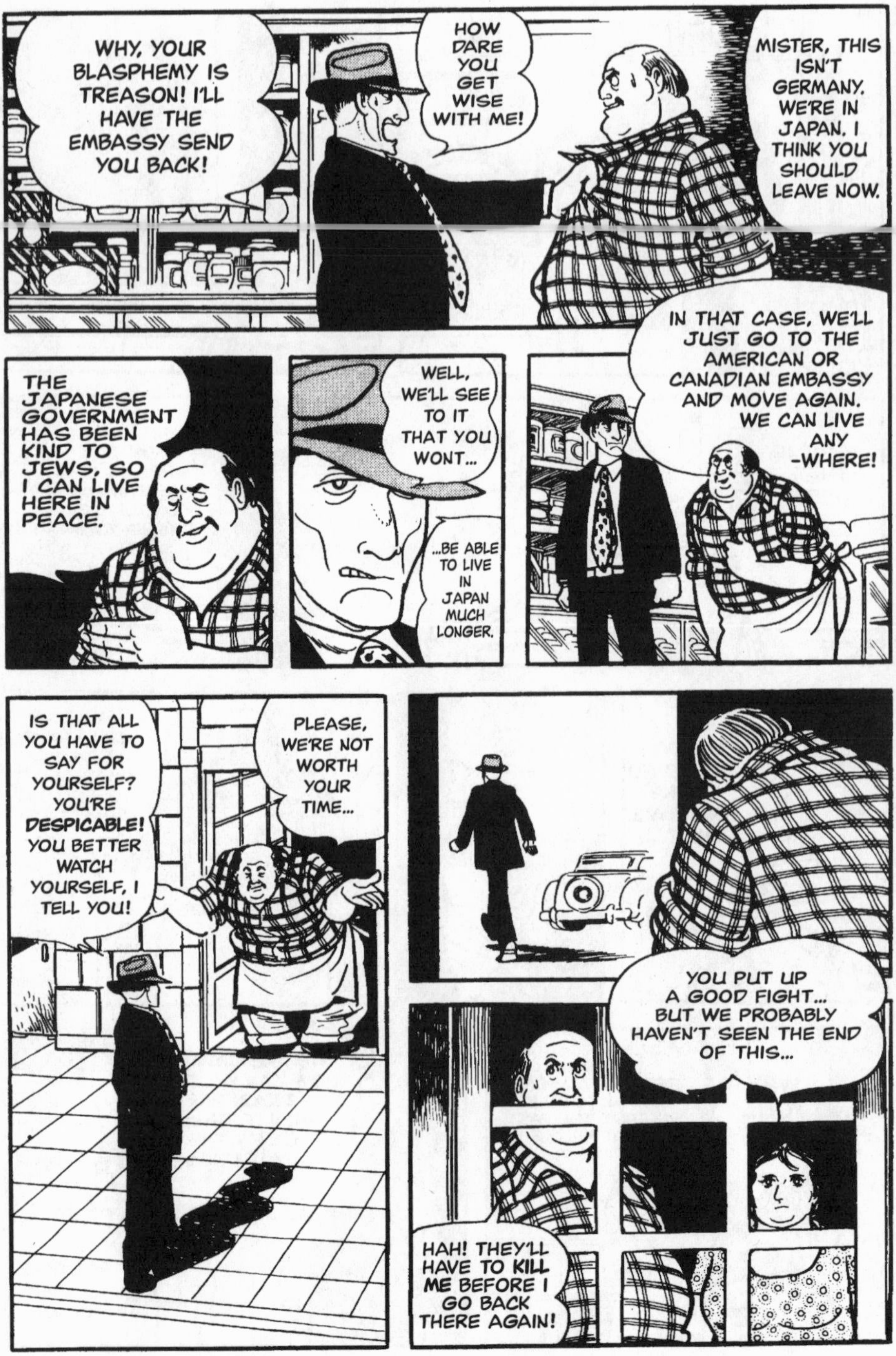
WHY, YOUR BLASPHEMY IS TREASON! I'LL HAVE THE EMBASSY SEND YOU BACK!
HOW DARE YOU GET WISE WITH ME!
MISTER, THIS ISN'T GERMANY. WE'RE IN JAPAN. I THINK YOU SHOULD LEAVE NOW.
THE JAPANESE GOVERNMENT HAS BEEN KIND TO JEWS, SO I CAN LIVE HERE IN PEACE.
WELL, WE'LL SEE TO IT THAT YOU WONT...
...BE ABLE TO LIVE IN JAPAN MUCH LONGER.
IN THAT CASE, WE'LL JUST GO TO THE AMERICAN OR CANADIAN EMBASSY AND MOVE AGAIN. WE CAN LIVE ANY -WHERE!
IS THAT ALL YOU HAVE TO SAY FOR YOURSELF? YOU'RE DESPICABLE! YOU BETTER WATCH YOURSELF, I TELL YOU!
PLEASE, WE'RE NOT WORTH YOUR TIME...
YOU PUT UP A GOOD FIGHT... BUT WE PROBABLY HAVEN'T SEEN THE END OF THIS...
HAH! THEY'LL HAVE TO KILL ME BEFORE I GO BACK THERE AGAIN!

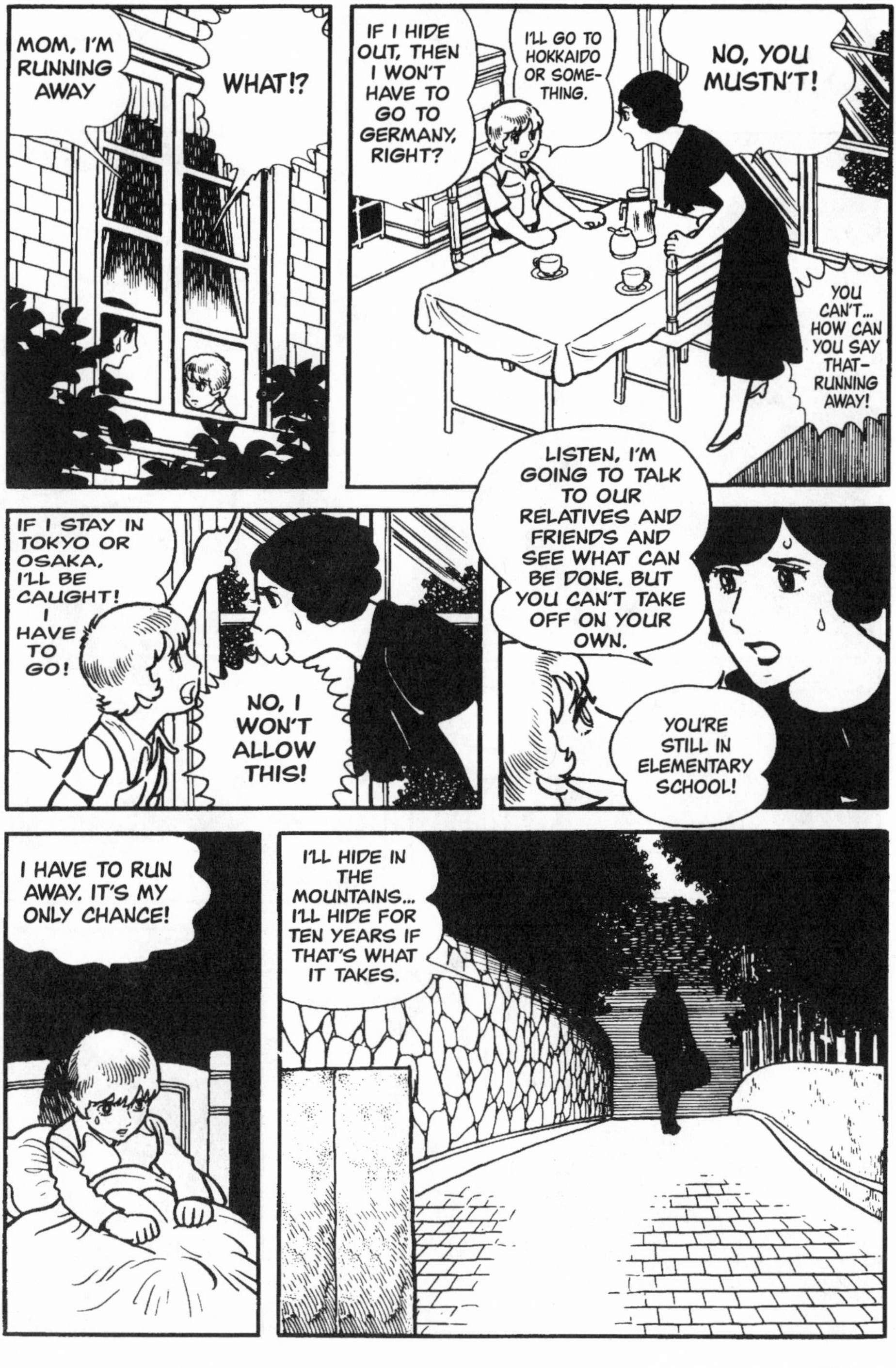
MOM, I'M RUNNING AWAY
WHAT!?
IF I HIDE OUT, THEN I WON'T HAVE TO GO TO GERMANY, RIGHT?
I'LL GO TO HOKKAIDO OR SOME-THING.
NO, YOU MUSTN'T!
YOU CAN'T... HOW CAN YOU SAY THAT-RUNNING AWAY!
IF I STAY IN TOKYO OR OSAKA, I'LL BE CAUGHT! I HAVE TO GO!
NO, I WON'T ALLOW THIS!
LISTEN, I'M GOING TO TALK TO OUR RELATIVES AND FRIENDS AND SEE WHAT CAN BE DONE. BUT YOU CAN'T TAKE OFF ON YOUR OWN.
YOU'RE STILL IN ELEMENTARY SCHOOL!
I HAVE TO RUN AWAY. IT'S MY ONLY CHANCE!
I'LL HIDE IN THE MOUNTAINS... I'LL HIDE FOR TEN YEARS IF THAT'S WHAT IT TAKES.

Adolf

HUF HUF

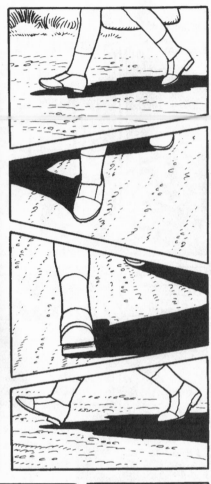

MY SON IS MISSING! HE'S BEEN GONE SINCE THIS MORNING.

HE'S NOT IN SCHOOL OR ANYWHERE ELSE I COULD THINK OF LOOKING. I NEED HELP!

AND WHERE DO YOU THINK HE WENT?

HE DOESN'T HAVE MUCH MONEY. HE COULDN'T HAVE GONE ANY FURTHER THAN...

...WHERE THE HANKYU TRAIN WOULD TAKE HIM...

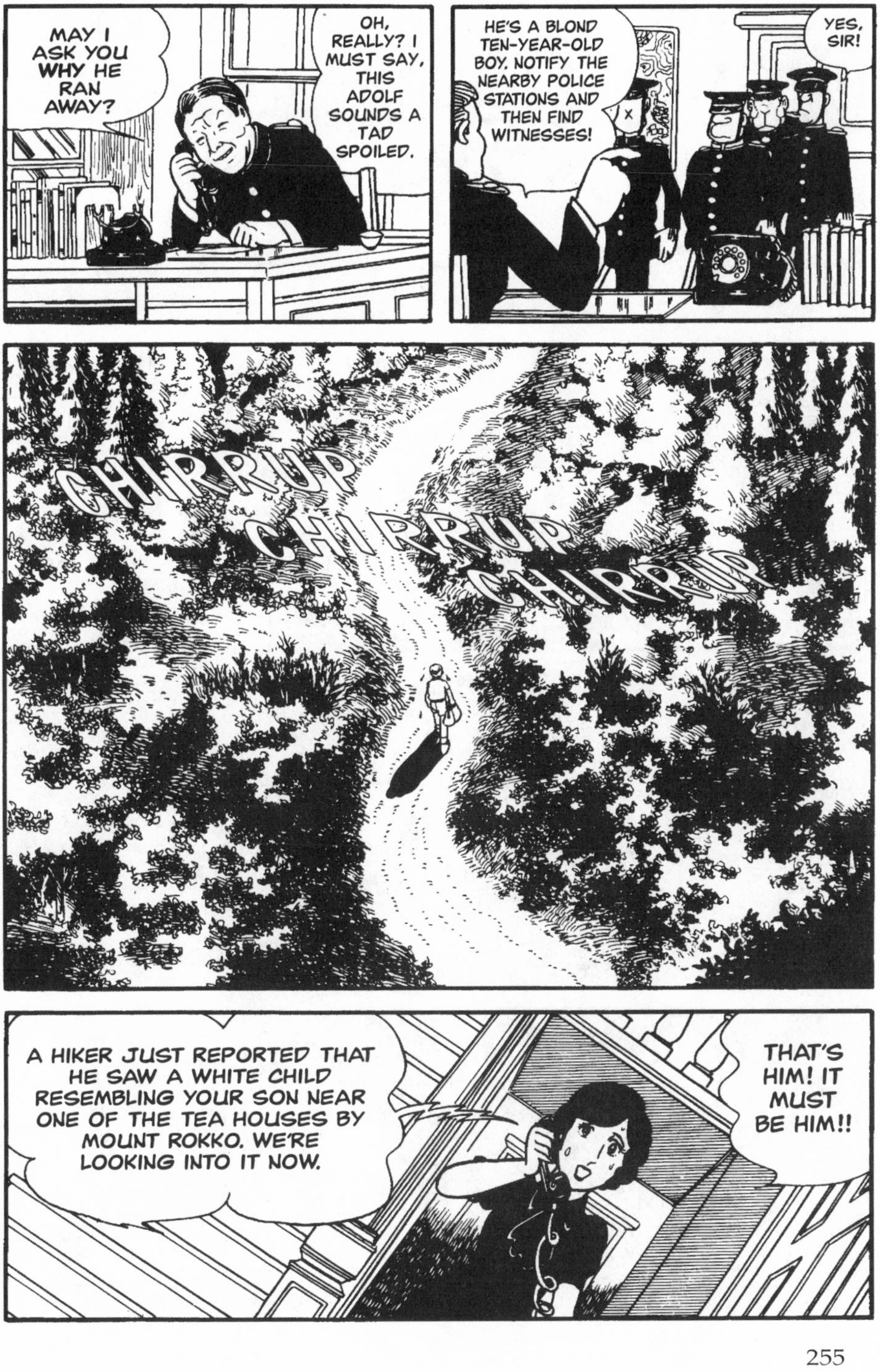
MAY I ASK YOU WHY HE RAN AWAY?
OH, REALLY? I MUST SAY, THIS ADOLF SOUNDS A TAD SPOILED.
HE'S A BLOND TEN-YEAR-OLD BOY. NOTIFY THE NEARBY POLICE STATIONS AND THEN FIND WITNESSES!
YES, SIR!
CHIRRUP CHIRRUP CHIRRUP
A HIKER JUST REPORTED THAT HE SAW A WHITE CHILD RESEMBLING YOUR SON NEAR ONE OF THE TEA HOUSES BY MOUNT ROKKO. WE'RE LOOKING INTO IT NOW.
THAT'S HIM! IT MUST BE HIM!!

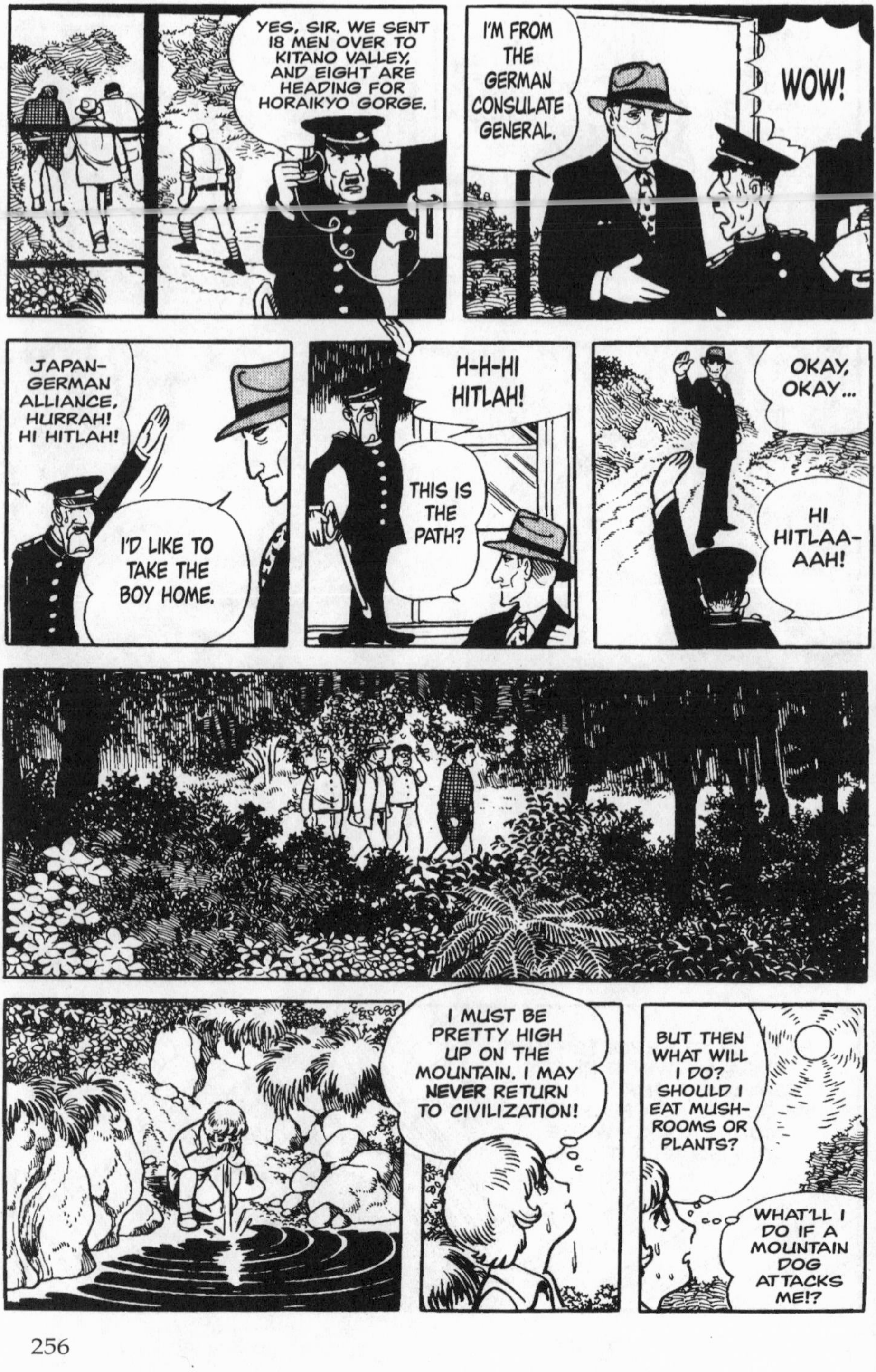

YES, SIR. WE SENT 18 MEN OVER TO KITANO VALLEY, AND EIGHT ARE HEADING FOR HORAIKYO GORGE.
I'M FROM THE GERMAN CONSULATE GENERAL.
WOW!
JAPAN-GERMAN ALLIANCE, HURRAH! HI HITLAH!
I'D LIKE TO TAKE THE BOY HOME.
H-H-HI HITLAH!
THIS IS THE PATH?
OKAY, OKAY...
HI HITLAA-AAH!
I MUST BE PRETTY HIGH UP ON THE MOUNTAIN. I MAY NEVER RETURN TO CIVILIZATION!
BUT THEN WHAT WILL I DO? SHOULD I EAT MUSH-ROOMS OR PLANTS?
WHAT'LL I DO IF A MOUNTAIN DOG ATTACKS ME!?

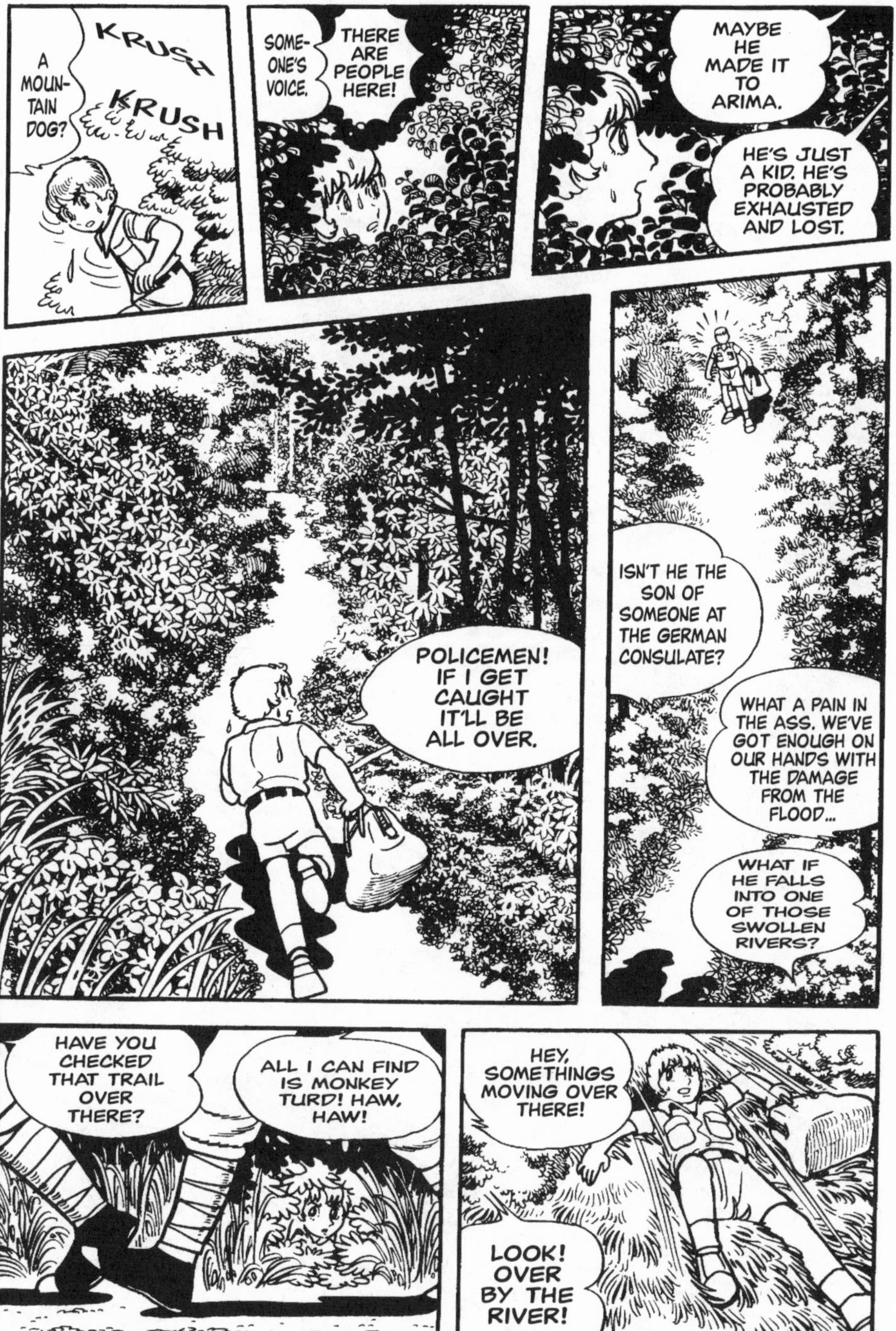
KRUSH
A MOUNTAIN DOG?
KRUSH
SOME-ONE'S VOICE.
THERE ARE PEOPLE HERE!
MAYBE HE MADE IT TO ARIMA.
HE'S JUST A KID. HE'S PROBABLY EXHAUSTED AND LOST.
POLICEMEN! IF I GET CAUGHT IT'LL BE ALL OVER.
ISN'T HE THE SON OF SOMEONE AT THE GERMAN CONSULATE?
WHAT A PAIN IN THE ASS. WE'VE GOT ENOUGH ON OUR HANDS WITH THE DAMAGE FROM THE FLOOD...
WHAT IF HE FALLS INTO ONE OF THOSE SWOLLEN RIVERS?
HAVE YOU CHECKED THAT TRAIL OVER THERE?
ALL I CAN FIND IS MONKEY TURD! HAW, HAW!
HEY, SOMETHINGS MOVING OVER THERE!
LOOK! OVER BY THE RIVER!

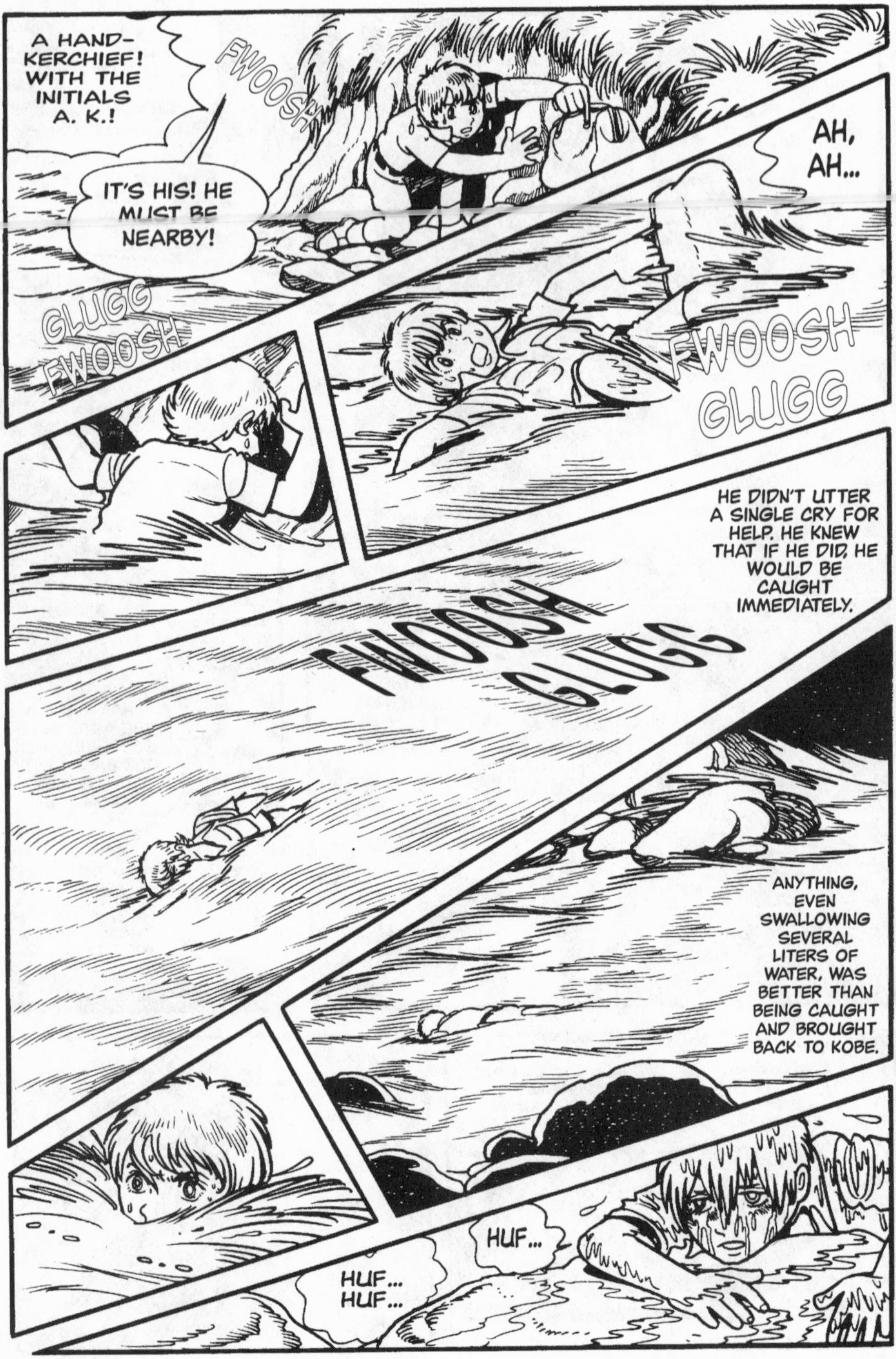

A HAND-KERCHIEF! WITH THE INITIALS A. K.!
FWOOSH
IT'S HIS! HE MUST BE NEARBY!
GLUGG FWOOSH
AH, AH...
FWOOSH GLUGG
HE DIDN'T UTTER A SINGLE CRY FOR HELP. HE KNEW THAT IF HE DID, HE WOULD BE CAUGHT IMMEDIATELY.
FWOOSH GLUGG
ANYTHING, EVEN SWALLOWING SEVERAL LITERS OF WATER, WAS BETTER THAN BEING CAUGHT AND BROUGHT BACK TO KOBE.
HUF...
HUF... HUF...

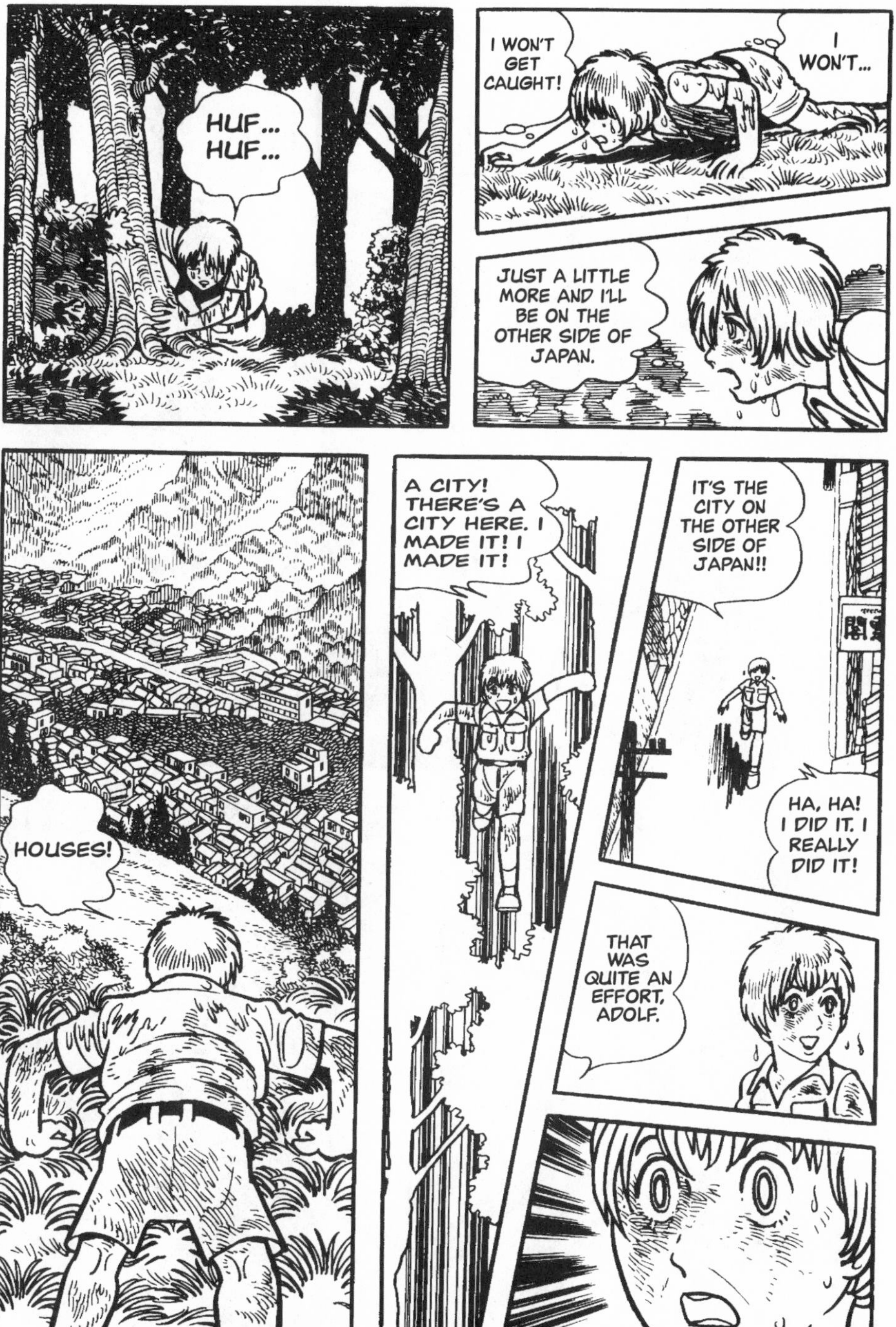
HUF... HUF...
I WON'T GET CAUGHT!
I WON'T...
JUST A LITTLE MORE AND I'LL BE ON THE OTHER SIDE OF JAPAN.
HOUSES!
A CITY! THERE'S A CITY HERE. I MADE IT! I MADE IT!
IT'S THE CITY ON THE OTHER SIDE OF JAPAN!!
HA, HA! I DID IT. I REALLY DID IT!
THAT WAS QUITE AN EFFORT, ADOLF.

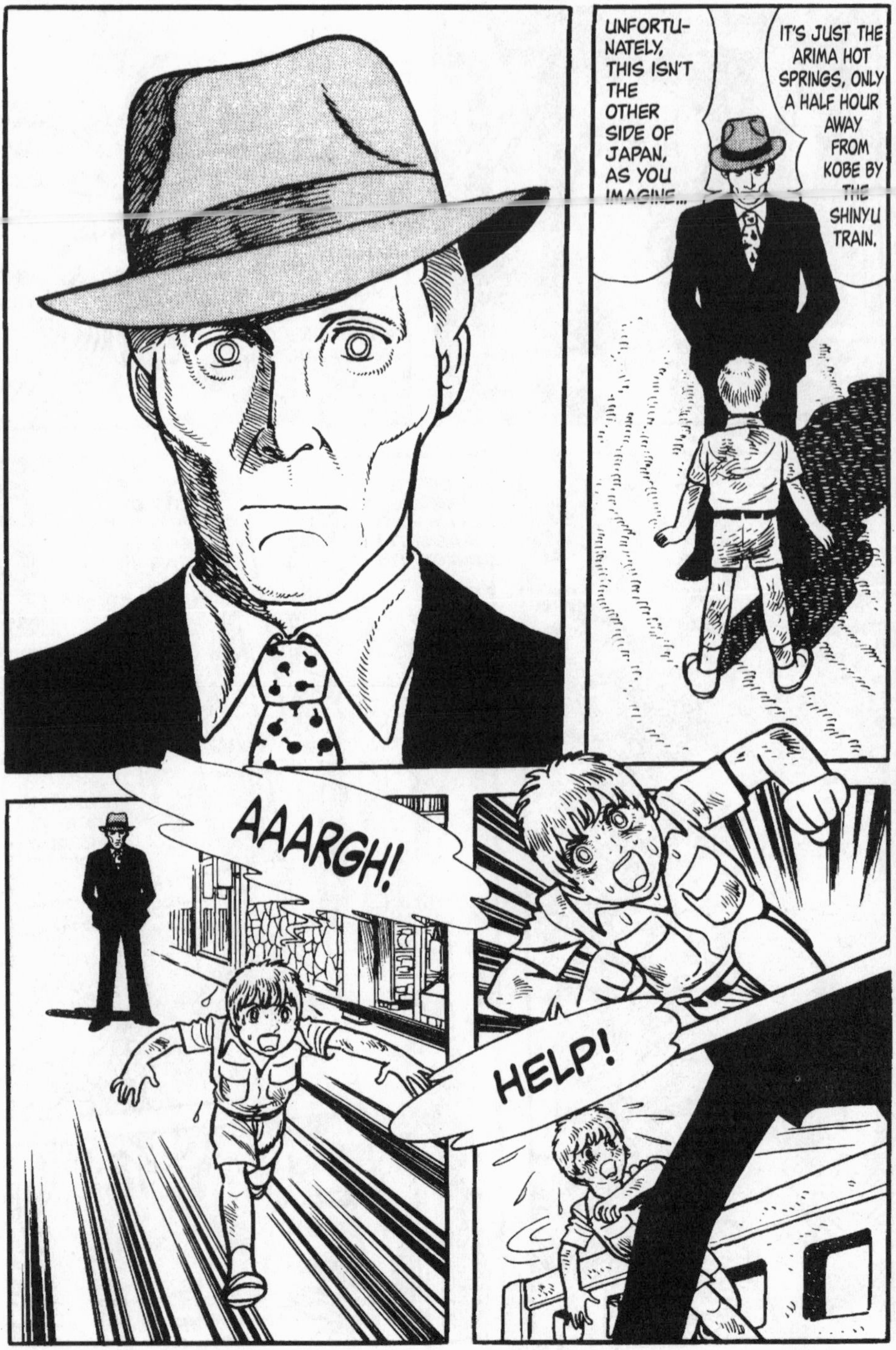
UNFORTUNATELY, THIS ISN'T THE OTHER SIDE OF JAPAN, AS YOU IMAGINE...
IT'S JUST THE ARIMA HOT SPRINGS, ONLY A HALF HOUR AWAY FROM KOBE BY THE SHINYU TRAIN.
AAARGH!
HELP!

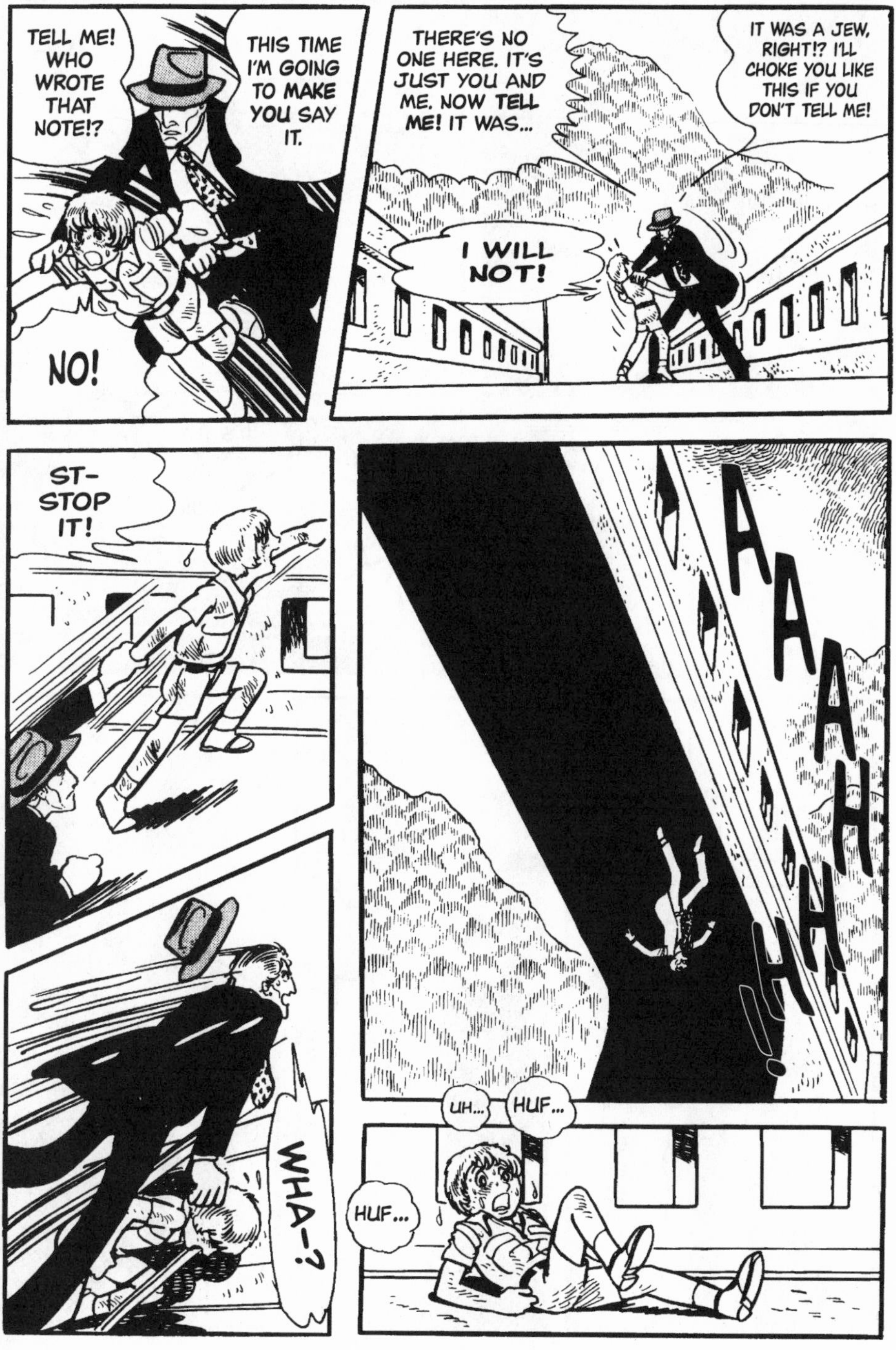
TELL ME! WHO WROTE THAT NOTE!?
THIS TIME I'M GOING TO MAKE YOU SAY IT.
NO!
THERE'S NO ONE HERE. IT'S JUST YOU AND ME. NOW TELL ME! IT WAS...
IT WAS A JEW, RIGHT!? I'LL CHOKE YOU LIKE THIS IF YOU DON'T TELL ME!
I WILL NOT!
ST- STOP IT!
WHA-!?
AAAAHHH!
UH...
HUF...
HUF...

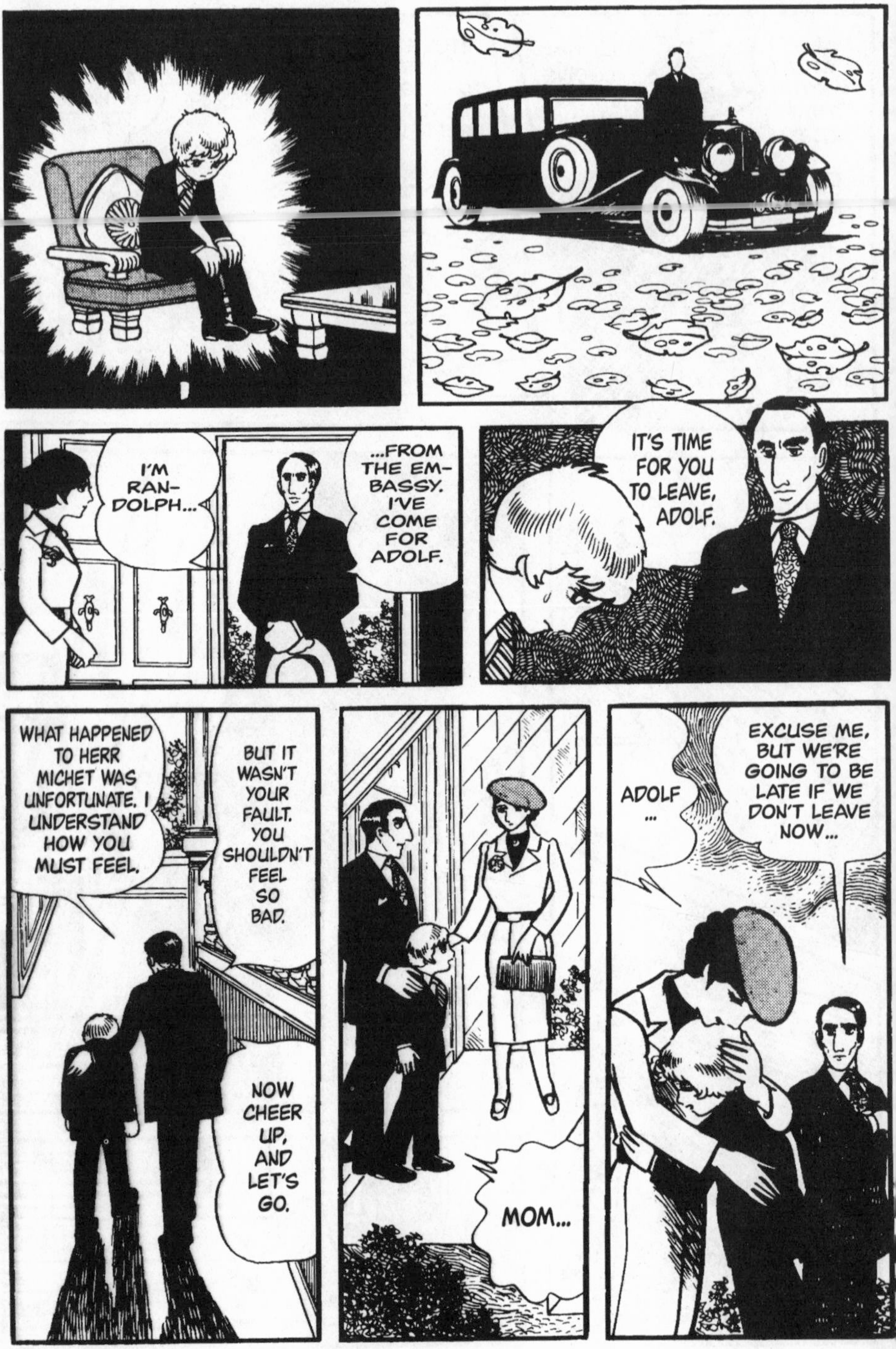
I'M RAN-DOLPH...
...FROM THE EM-BASSY. I'VE COME FOR ADOLF.
IT'S TIME FOR YOU TO LEAVE, ADOLF.
WHAT HAPPENED TO HERR MICHET WAS UNFORTUNATE. I UNDERSTAND HOW YOU MUST FEEL.
BUT IT WASN'T YOUR FAULT. YOU SHOULDN'T FEEL SO BAD.
NOW CHEER UP, AND LET'S GO.
MOM...
ADOLF ...
EXCUSE ME, BUT WE'RE GOING TO BE LATE IF WE DON'T LEAVE NOW...

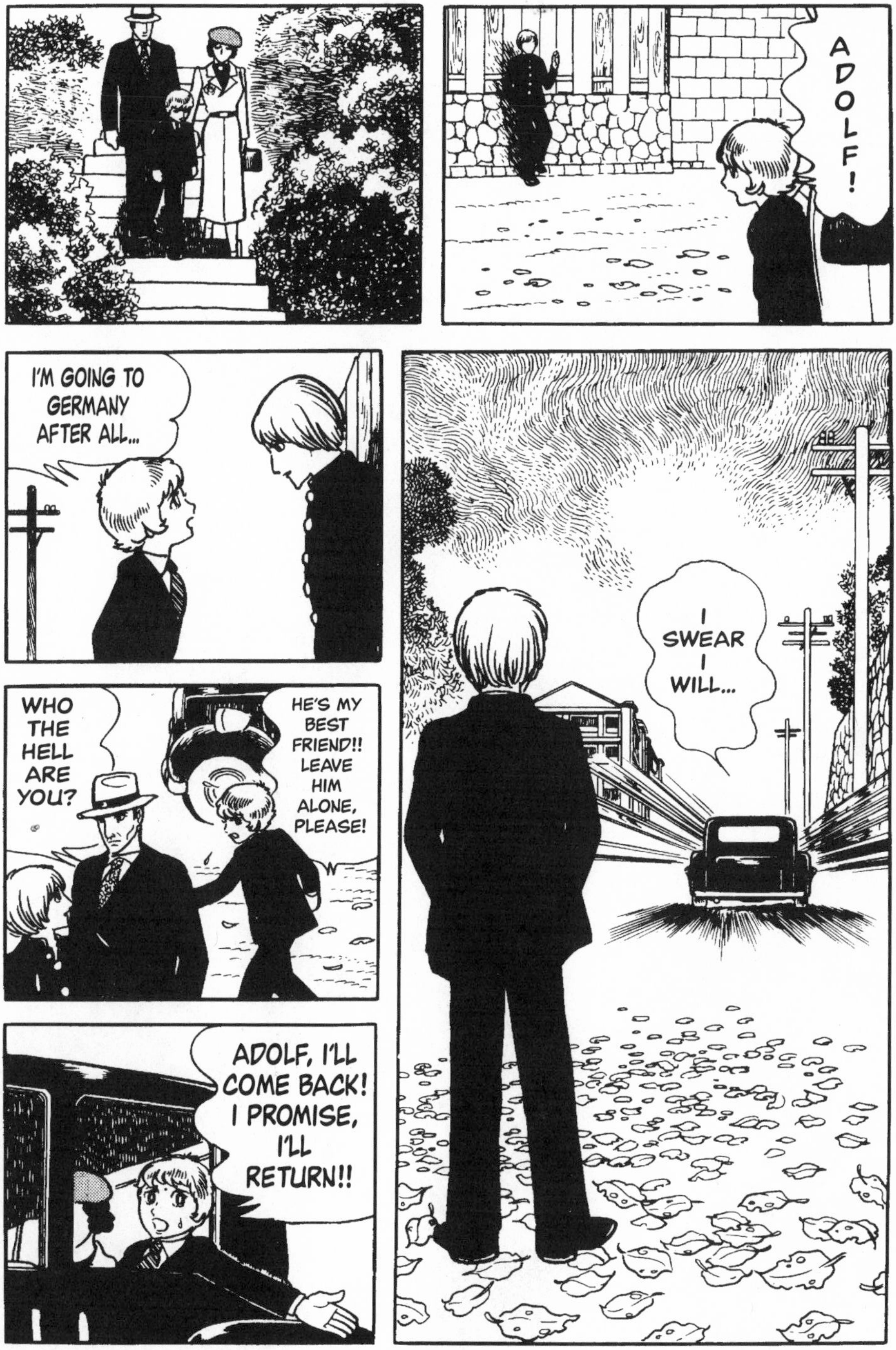
ADOLF!
I'M GOING TO GERMANY AFTER ALL...
WHO THE HELL ARE YOU?
HE'S MY BEST FRIEND!! LEAVE HIM ALONE, PLEASE!
ADOLF, I'LL COME BACK! I PROMISE, I'LL RETURN!!
I SWEAR I WILL...

O BE CONTINUED IN *ADOLF: AN EXILE IN JAPAN!*